CUSTOM MAID KNOWLEDGE
For New World Disorder

The Post-Global Interlocal Sino-American Century

Peter G. de Krassel

CAL Books

Hong Kong, Los Angeles

Published in Hong Kong by CAL Books

Library of Congress Cataloguing-in-Publication Data is available
ISBN 978.988.97666.7.2

THIS BOOK IS DEDICATED TO TEACHERS, WHO ARE OUR
SALVATION. "QIAN SHI BU WANG HOU SHI ZHI SHI" - PAST
EXPERIENCE, IF NOT FORGOTTEN, IS A
GUIDE FOR THE FUTURE.

Also by Peter G. de Krassel:

Custom Maid Spin for New World Disorder

Custom Maid War for New World Disorder

The principal factor promoting historically significant social change is contact with strangers. It was the major motor of historical change. No population can overtake and then surpass the rest of the world without using the most efficacious and powerful instruments known anywhere on earth; and by definition, such instruments are located at the world's centers of wealth and power – wherever they may be.

– William H. McNeill
The Rise of the West: A History of the Human Community

Contents

I never let my schooling interfere with my education.

– Mark Twain

Education is the key to national salvation.

– Jose Rizal

Education is what remains when one has forgotten all that he has learned.

– Albert Einstein

Acknowledgements

Knowing and not doing is yet not knowing.
– Confucius

I first want to acknowledge and thank the teachers I had starting in primary through high school who repeatedly tried to flunk me because of my "incorrigibility." My father was a correspondent for the BBC who had been assigned to Switzerland and Cyprus. My parents divorced in Cyprus and I moved with my mother to Israel to attend high school. After graduation, I went to America to attend university. My wandering Jewish-Viking heritage has kept me on the road and in the air most of my life. As a result, I am a perennial geopolitical social and political student observer.

I want to thank all my teachers – academic and social – whose teachings and observations helped me coalesce my thoughts about our future educational necessities. These teachers taught me academic survival in environments in which I was destined to fail. It started with primary school at an English school in Cyprus. I had arrived from Switzerland, fluent in Russian and German. Academic survival got worse when the teachers at the Army Childrens School in Famagusta, Cyprus, repeatedly abused me verbally because I lived off base among the locals and was not an Army brat. The teachers at the American Academy in Larnaca, Cyprus, who flunked me because I was Jewish, gave me my first wake-up call about religious hatred and persecution. The teachers in Israel – frustrated at my elementary knowledge of Hebrew, which I started to learn only when I enrolled in high school – deserve special mention. Their determination to teach me Hebrew while I was preoccupied with the very approachable coeds – who were unlike anything I experienced in Cyprus – was commendable, but futile. My knowledge of English and Greek helped me pick up the walking dictionaries – hot chicks – who were impressed with my knowledge of foreign languages.

Helping them with their English homework in exchange for Hebrew lessons – and not just the language – was quite an education.

Getting through university and law school in America and graduating with honors was largely attributable to the coeds impressed by the fact that I graduated high school in Israel and spoke Hebrew. Study groups were very helpful in picking up the smartest student – always of the opposite sex, especially in the mid-to-late '60s in "Flower Children" blooming Chicago, Los Angeles, New York City and San Francisco. I'm all for diversity these days, but I've always stuck to what I know best.

Teaching university students, as I have on occasion, is a reminder that many students still try to beat the system and just get by, so they can get that piece of paper known as a diploma. I am grateful to my friends who are teachers, and their colleagues, for sharing with me their experiences and frustrations with the U.S. education system. They are the real dedicated Maids determined to sweep in the changes necessary to ensure that our children are able to intelligently compete and tackle the global mess they will inherit. Dr. Kristin Berman, Laurie and Mark Tigan, Scott and Valerie Beall, Heather Hill and Brandon Royal are teachers who taught me that the "No Child Left Behind" campaign actually puts all children further behind. These teachers kept me focused on what ails the U.S. education system today and why America is in dire straits academically as it enters the 21st century, unprepared for the geopolitical realities it faces.

Unlike many of the teachers I have met who engage in and practice phenomenological qualitative research – I am an active participant-observer in the unqualitative political policies of America, domestic and foreign, that have adversely affected the quality of life of all Americans – especially students.

The people acknowledged in Volume I of this trilogy, *Custom Maid Spin for New World Disorder*, are again recognized and applauded for their ongoing contributions. David Weiner, Bill Corsa, Rose Carrano, David Farnsworth and Vivienne Wong deserve a special thank you for their patience and persistence in getting my books into bookstores.

My interlocal transglobal editors in North America and Hong Kong, Jim

Houston, Jim Hollander, Stuart Wolfendale, Ralph Herman and Brandon Royal, took on the awesome editorial commitment to improve the reading quality of the book and deserve special mention for their editorial guidance and caustic scalpels.

American idiot.
– Green Day

Preface

You can fool all the people some of the time, and
some of the people all the time, but you cannot
fool all the people all the time.
– Abraham Lincoln

New World Disorder

I finished writing this book in early 2006. I was getting ready to sign off on the editorial changes before it went to publication in July and was enjoying an early evening outing on the rooftop garden atop my three-story village house in Hong Kong's Sai Kung Peninsula. It was a welcome respite from the week's climatic and global political pollution – especially during the summer of 2005, when politics took an ominous turn in America's midterm elections, sectarian violence escalated in Iraq along with U.S. casualties, and war broke out in Lebanon.

President George W. Bush said it best at the Radio and Television Correspondents' Association dinner in March 2007. "A year ago my approval rating was in the 30s, my nominee for the Supreme Court had just withdrawn, and my vice-president had shot someone. Ah, those were the good ol' days."

The political mudslinging that spreads hatred and lies about candidates running for office was beginning – and reached an all-time destructive high on November 7 – Election Day. Americans can be forgiven if they are confused by the political expression, "The enemy of my enemy is my friend." America deposes and executes Saddam Hussein, a secular Sunni, and replaces his government with a democratically elected religious coalition supported by Iran. The anti-democratic and anti-American-coalition occupation Sunni insurgent Saddam loyalists backed by Syria and U.S. friend, ally and protectorate Saudi Arabia, contribute more than their fair share of support for the political and military confrontations that kill and maim U.S. and coalition military and civilian personnel, along with countless innocent Iraqi civilians.

Sunni-dominated Saudi Arabia raised and contributed to America and the world – Osama bin-Laden, 15 of the 19 9/11 hijackers, and Sunni insurgents combating Shiite militias backed by Iran, yet they are, according to the Bush-dominated dynasty political spin doctors, a friend of America. To add fuel to the fire of confusion, Syrians, Iranians, Saudis and all three factions of Iraqis hate Israelis and distrust Jews. Democratic Israel, where Arabs sit in parliament, is vitally dependent on U.S. military and economic support to live comfortably while being stressed out by their determined, fanatical, suicidal neighbors hell bent on annihilating Israel. As if that isn't enough, al-Qaeda, led by Osama is right there, leading the anti-U.S.-Israel alliance.

Al-Qaeda, a theocratic Sunni group hates Shiites and democracy, so it should befriend the majority Sunni dictatorship Syria and be an enemy of Shiite-dominated, semi-democratic Iran. Not so. Shiite Iran allegedly shelters al-Qaeda terrorists while Syria kills them. If whoever shelters al-Qaeda is a U.S. enemy, why is Pakistan considered a friend? Pakistan has agreed with its pro-al-Qaeda, pro-Taliban border tribes not to enter or permit U.S. forces to attack their territory. Great – what better shelter for America's enemies? The democratically elected Afghan government has even become hostile to the dictatorship in Pakistan for sheltering its enemies, the Taliban and al-Qaeda.

Iraqi Kurds are U.S. friends, but the Turks, who are allies, regard the Kurds as enemies, and vice versa. The Iranians are enemies of the Kurds, so the Turks regard Iranians, enemies of their enemies, as friends – so how can they be friends? But officially they are. Right back to the Border Rievers of Scotland and England culture and feuding family heritage that took root in the Appalachian mountains – the Hatfields and McCoys.

Foreigners visiting America can be forgiven if they believe only gays, pedophiles, peaceniks and bigots run for political office. The movie "Borat" was a refreshing reminder that what distinguishes intelligent man from politically correct man is the ability to laugh about anything – especially during a U.S. election. Trying to understand America's incoherent geopolitical quagmire requires a 21st-century abbreviated encyclopedia made relevant to the events of the day, which is so doable in our cyber age. I hope this book can shed an illuminating spotlight on our historic biblical silkroad to Armageddon – which can be avoided with a right turn, starting with education and knowledge.

America is busted – broke. The political leadership in Washington pursues shattered foreign policies and broken domestic policies. And it finances a bankrupt Treasury indebted to foreign bondholders. A mess We the People – *The Maids* – are repeatedly asked to clean up and pay for with our hard-earned tax dollars.

Sitting on the rooftop, I enjoy watching the constantly changing breezes and tides. My eyes feast on the low-flying herons wind-surfing the waves, following on the pounding heels of the local fishermen's net-casting techniques. Boats moored to buoys bob in the wake of speeding motorized zap cats. In the distances, low-lying summer clouds caress and embrace the mountains surrounding the bay, rinsed to a bright green by a light, cleansing drizzle that thankfully washes away the day's humidity and pollution. I couldn't shake loose the dark clouds building in my mind as the evening news replayed the ever "breaking" U.S. economic news and the growing global crisis and expanding wars.

Ignorance Is Bliss
Wars in Afghanistan, Darfur, East Timor, Iran, Iraq, Israel, Kashmir, Lebanon, Palestine, Somalia and Sri Lanka which have spiraled out of America's control, only benefit self-serving political opportunists. "The lunatics are definitely running asylum America and ripping the country and world asunder," I said out loud to my dog Spud, who was gazing up at me with his tail wagging. Ignorance is bliss.

I prefer being my own self-serving maid during these rare solitary moments in maid-overloaded Hong Kong. Sipping a rum and coke and enjoying a slow-burning Cuban panatela, digesting recent events and their potential ramifications in an already dysfunctional post-global interlocal geopolitical world disorder, is disheartening and downright depressing.

Watching America and China, the midwives of the 21st century, paralyzed by their disciples and global political constituencies being led over the precipice to Armageddon while *We the Apathetic Maids* remain clueless about the truth, and silent because of it, is sobering enough though to force me to snub out my cigar, stop the publication of the book and go back to my laptop. I realized I had to expand the interlocal concept and place greater emphasis on the futility of perpetuating the United Nations in light of the Lebanon, Palestinian, Iraq and Afghanistan wars and the nuclear standoffs in Iran and North Korea.

The vulgarity of the rhetoric and record amount of money spent on the mid-term U.S. elections adds fuel and material to support my thesis that the two-party system in America is a mess and in desperate need of diligent political maids to sweep in new ideas and ideals to replace globalism and nationalism.

New Political Landscape
The perfect political tsunami was brewing in America: disparity between growth in productivity and gross domestic product on the one hand and growth in wages for the average American worker on the other, with Sino-U.S. relations on the verge of rupturing and geopolitical realignments that crystalized with the swearing in of the new Democratic Party-controlled 110th Congress in January 2007.

I reflected on my 2005 U.S. book tour and the numerous radio interviews in which callers repeated their frustration with America's policies. I was emphatic that "America needs a change" and decided to see if *We the Maids* would clean house – and thankfully we have started.

The concerns I raised and anger I voiced in *Custom Maid Spin* and *Custom Maid War* about hypocrisy, sex, corruption, lobbyists and the wars in Iraq and Afghanistan, thankfully, resonated and registered with voters.

Americans are starting to wake up to the fact that international and national politics have an impact on their lives and they reject the popular notion that "all politics is local." It is interlocal. Americans are not fools. They are just slow to catch on. That allows political opportunists and their financial backers to exploit their lapses.

Now that Democrats control both houses of Congress, they can take back control of national policy, spending and the wars in Afghanistan and Iraq –

and get America back on track before the 2008 presidential elections, when the partisan mudslinging starts all over again. Congress must reassert its strong legislative oversight of the executive branch of government.

The Democrats' promise to "drain the swamp that is Washington" by intro-ducing stronger ethical guidelines is wishful thinking that hopefully will be achieved at the dawn of the 21st century. The Democrats' agenda of "six for '6" – the six promises on which they campaigned during the midterm elec-tions – has a greater chance of becoming law than any ethics legislation.

The six items, which are political and controversial but necessary for America to survive the 21st century, are: strengthen homeland security, raise the fed-eral minimum wage, reduce college fee interest charges for the middle class, reverse Republican tax breaks for oil companies, reduce prescription drug prices for seniors, and protect Social Security.

Interlocalism

Interlocalism is the proposed interaction between different local communi-ties promoting their collective well-being with minimum government participation. The concentric circles start with the local village, town or city and expand over the county, country, and compatible global communities. It is the fusion of local strengths spread widely over similar minded and com-patible people. From the San Fernando Valley, Los Angeles, California, Mexico, the Americas, Quebec, Hawaii, Scotland, Wales, Ireland, Italy, Indonesia, Cyprus, Germany, Korea and China.

Globalism died in the last decade of the 20th century. It was a 19th-century model of economics based on scarcity, but the whole world was in surplus. The debates on globalization, secession or separatism must therefore be re-placed with an all-encompassing discussion on inter-localism. Interlocalism will accelerate as the economic benefits and natural growth become evident in the 21st century.

Interlocalism is adaptation and expansion of the industrial concept of "clusters." Compatible communities competing and collaborating in a net-work of mutually supportive, global-wired urban hubs that recognize and accept that economics – fueled by the natural resources that empires, countries, communities, tribes and villages have gone to war over – are, and always have been, the underlying driving engine of the locomotive of politics and senseless wars that get innocent, uneducated children killed because of their parents' ignorance.

China has rejected the globalization economic model just as it did with rural communism, and is forming Confucian humanist city clusters as the essential national cornerstone and integral part of its future inter-local cluster economic model. Most of the megacities such as Beijing, Shanghai and Wuhan – already home to millions of people – have room to grow. Smaller cities around the megacities – especially those with populations of around 1 million – will become an integral part of a city cluster.

City clusters have already formed on the Yangtze River Delta and the Pearl River Delta, with Hong Kong, Shanghai and Guangzhou as their respective cores. The key to succesful growth is good management. Hong Kong is the best-managed city in China, probably the world. It's got the population density of most cities in China, yet is the most efficient and functional. A great place to raise and enjoy pets – not by eating them – but loving, bonding, teaching and learning.

Crash and Burn
While political bureacrats continue to mouth off at an impotent U.N., the war in Afghanistan and Iraq has expanded to Israel, Palestine and Lebanon, with North Korea, Syria and Iran itching to further inflame the world with their smash-mouth political rhetoric. The result: Oil prices hit record highs of $100 a barrel and threaten to climb even further, while America and China compete – and scramble – to figure out how they can corner the world's dwindling supplies.

Meanwhile, motorists across America search for cheaper gasoline prices, as their fellow Americans seek shelter from the sweltering heat waves that ravaged America under the smoke clouds that drift across the country from thousands of acres of California wildfires.

This while America's Latino backyard hemisphere, which Monroe and his doctrine so vigorously defended as America's "sphere of influence," made a radical left turn. Mexico's presidential election became an instant replay of its northern neighbor's 2000 and 2004 presidential elections. At the same time, America's 2006 midterm elections kicked into high gear with a congressional sex scandal and heretofore undisclosed intelligence reports that repeated what I had written in *Custom Maid War* in 2004. America has wasted billions of dollars in Iraq and the country is in the midst of a civil war.

America is simply not living up to its proud ideals and is in fact becoming just as impotent as the U.N.

Everybody is beating up on America, in basketball, baseball, the dollar, economics, political esteem, image and perception. This was best witnessed at the millennium basketball championships in Sydney 2000, Indianapolis in 2002, the Athens Olympics in 2004, and World Championship 2006, where America finished third.

Custom Maid Spin for New World Disorder – Volume I of the "Custom Maid" trilogy – addresses the hypocrisy that permeates the "American axis" and perverts America's domestic and foreign policies. The hypocrisy exists because *We the Maids* have been dumbed down – given a down-sized education – by our religious and political leaders who tell us to accept hypocrisy as human nature and the will of God.

Immigrant Nation
Americans' lack of knowledge about America, or the world in which it blindly offends all cultural and religious sensibilities, is inexcusable for a country of immigrants who applaud their favorite baseball and basketball team whose dominant players are immigrants who are the top of their leagues back home and get bought by America.

I am a perpetual immigrant. Born in England, I moved with my parents to Switzerland, Cyprus and Israel, and then, on my own volition, America and now to China. Immigration is constantly changing, the cultural and demographic makeup of all countries, but especially growing economic powerhouses that attract immigrants like bees to honey.

With the U.S. population passing the 300-million mark, confirming America's status as the world's third most-populated nation – behind China and India – it is a joke for America to pass a law to build fence to keep "Illegals" out.

There are more than 12 million undocumented immigrants in America that should be included in a comprehensive guest-worker program with earnable citizenship.

The 200th-millionth American, Bobby Woo, was born in 1967 to Chinese-American parents whose families had been in the U.S. since the 19th century. In less than four decades, America gained 100 million residents. In the 1960s, 5 percent of the population were immigrants. Today it is 12.7 percent. The main reason immigrants are attracted is America's enduring popularity as a destination. On average, a new immigrant arrives every 31 seconds.

America has always been a nation of immigrants, and today it has more than 33 million foreign-born residents, many of them illegal. About 600,000 people become naturalized U.S. citizens every year. I am one of them. When I took the citizenship exam back in 1970, it was easy and very welcoming. It was updated in 1986 and again in 2006. To many immigrant groups, the new exam is the "second wall," after the wall between Mexico and the U.S., a barrier to full participation by legal immigrants because of the level of difficulty and the breadth and scope of the new 96-question exam culled from 144 sample questions. Questions most Americans can't answer.

With an estimated 12 million illegal immigrants in America, the question is whether to ignore them, send them back home or legalize their status. Building a wall between America and Mexico will not make the problem go away. America has to accept its immigrant heritage and politically realign itself during this period of dramatic social change. For legislators in 42 American states to introduce 368 bills to restrict undocumented immigrants is a colossal waste of taxpayers' money.

Arrogant, Indebted Nation
The federal deficit and unemployment figures rose during the 2004 and 2006 elections, along with U.S. and coalition casualties in Afghanistan and Iraq. Iraq, like Vietnam, is a reminder of U.S. hubris and illusion. America is an unwelcome occupier losing geopolitical capital at U.S. taxpayer expense. U.S. officials predicted shortly after the invasion of Iraq in March 2003, that Iraq oil production would rise by the end of 2003 to 3 million barrels a day from the pre-invasion level of 2.4 million. Instead, it has sunk to 1.9 million. The cost of the Iraq war is more than four times greater than the value of the

oil America is securing for itself, according to Joseph Stiglitz, a Nobel Prize-winning economist, and Linda Bilmes, a Harvard University professor, who took a broad approach to accounting for the Iraq war, including valuations for lives lost and individuals injured, and attached a price tag of more than $2 trillion. The government accountants admit to the war costs being in the $300 billion to $500 billion range.

It costs $275,000 to deploy one soldier in Iraq for a year, according to the Congressional Research Service. The cost rises to $360,000 if additional investments in sorely lacking equipment and facilities are added. Taking a scenario in which U.S. troop levels fall to 73,000 in Iraq by 2010, the Congressional Budget Office estimates the cumulative cost of the global war on terror could reach $808 billion by 2016. The war on terror is now projected to last 30 years.

Since 2003, the Iraq war has annually fueled the largest U.S. emergency spending bills. In 2006, the Senate voted to allow the national debt to swell to nearly $9 trillion to prevent the first-ever default on Treasury notes. The increased debt level represents about $30,000 for every American taxpayer. The war on terror has now lasted longer than World War II and is portrayed by Washington's spin doctors more like a corporate marketing pitch than progress against the enemy. The political spin was best summarized by President George W. Bush in one of his infamous Bushisms in 2004. "Our enemies are innovative and resourceful, and so are we. They never stop thinking about new ways to harm our country and our people, and neither do we."

The Bush administration's piecemeal funding of the Iraq war was terminated by the new Democratic Congress. The Democrats promised to reassert more control over the billions of dollars spent on the war – and did. The congressional Out of Iraq Caucus is leading the charge to control the wars' pursestrings and set a definitive date to start bringing U.S. troops home. The congressional power of the purse must be reasserted by Congress to manage the wars America is fighting. Congressional control over money is imbedded in the Constitution and is one of the most powerful weapons Congress has. With Republicans in power, that right was ceded to the White House. Congress can and must impose restrictions on how money is spent and demand more detailed information from the White House on its recipients, beneficiaries and goals – with timelines. Is there any reason benchmarks and standards of progress are not included in the bills approving funding? The White House and Pentagon arguments that military demands are unpredictable and can change quickly are no longer acceptable to *We the Maids*.

When the costs of the Vietnam War were eventually absorbed into the normal budget, it brought about a quick peace that Americans and Vietnamese today mutually cherish and enjoy. The cost of future military operations through a series of emergency requests with limited congressional scrutiny is no longer acceptable. Americans have the right to know the true cost of the war.

Since the 9/11 attacks, military spending outside of the regular budget process, primarily for the wars in Iraq and Afghanistan, has totalled more than $400 billion.

The Iraq Study Group, the bipartisan committee headed by former Secretary of State James Baker and Congressman Lee Hamilton, made 79 recommendations. Recommendations 46, 72 and 78 deserve special mention. Under separate headings dealing with the military, the federal budget and the nation's intelligence agencies, they share one basic idea: Government officials should not lie to the public or each other, especially in matters of war.

Why do *We the Apathetic Maids* need an unelected panel of political career has-beens to tell us we deserve the truth? The report was a delicately worded indictment of America – and its humiliating defeat in Iraq and the Middle East. America's vision of a peaceful democratic transformation in the Middle East lies in tatters, with Iran coming up the big winner.

Loss of National Consciousness

We the Apathetic People have lost our collective memory and national consciousness. The result is we have created a national tragedy that must be remedied. Too many politicians now believe their purpose in Washington is keeping power for its own sake. The reform impulse has given way to incumbent protection. This is the root of the earmarking epidemic that now mars every spending bill and has become a vast new opportunity for corruption. Power for its own sake also explains why House Republicans decided to join Senate Democrats in killing serious reform of Fannie Mae and Freddie Mac, despite S16 billion in accounting mistakes or fraud.

The Iraq and Lebanon wars have proven that military strength doesn't bestow power. Strength, if not properly used, does not translate to power. Power is the ability to get others to do what you want. America has lost that ability. It's political muscle has been clipped like the wings of America's jumbo jets sitting in the airplane graveyards in the Arizona and California deserts. War is no longer an acceptable solution. Everyone loses in a war. There are no winners. The consequences of the 21st-century conflicts are that America is blamed for the global quagmire it has created – and America tries to shift the blame to China. During and after the 2004, 2006 and 2008 elections, China-bashing became a convenient vocal outlet for career politicians frustrated with their own failed economic and geopolitical policies.

China was accussed of being a "peer competitor" to the U.S. as the 2006 midterm congressional elections heated up. China's economic and military expansion may ultimately lead to it attaining superpower status on a par with America, John Negraponte, the former U.S. director of national intelligence warned in early 2006, during a congressional hearing. With 1.5 billion people and an awesome capacity for making a buck, you don't need much intelligence to see that coming.

China as Scapegoat

China is the scapegoat for everything that goes wrong for America. It is a convenient political football. It is blamed for the failed 2003 World Trade Organization meeting in Cancun, Mexico. It is the villain that keeps the value of the yuan artificially low to maintain a trade advantage over U.S.-based manufacturers, and it caused the higher prices for raw materials, including oil, increased exports of cheap manufactured goods that have condemned America's work force to redundancy because of outsourcing, global warming and bird flu. Economists who warned the Bush administration of the potential trade war that will destabilize China's economy and set off a global financial crisis if America insists on the revaluation of the yuan were shunned in favor of the political spinmeisters who wanted to appease the voters in the critical red states during a tight 2004 presidential election and the run-up to the 2006 congressional elections and 2008 presidential election.

Congress also wants to impose sanctions on China for its successive inclusion since 1999 on a U.S. blacklist of "severe" religious freedom violators.

U.S. politicians – like most interlocal ones – habitually make sure that whatever blame is directed their way for their "voodoo economics" is deflected and redirected at China. This was magnified during the 2004, 2006 and 2008 elections. The U.S. decision to impose quotas and tariffs on some Chinese textiles and televisions because of the trade imbalance between America and China was pure spin. The point is, Bush is the most protectionist American leader since Herbert Hoover, whose policies in the late 1920s bestowed America and the world with the Great Depression. The rise of protectionist sentiment in America over the trade deficit with China could have devastating consequences on the global economy. Quotas on textiles and televisions from China will not save U.S. jobs. The quotas will only increase imports from other low-cost manufacturing centers that have lost market share to China. This will raise the prices paid by U.S. consumers. The fact is, affordable Chinese textiles and goods are an integral piece of fabric of the American lifestyle. If the U.S. insists on messing with Chinese currency and quotas, Americans will end up wandering around like the Timorese – the poorest people on earth.

America seems to have forgotten a certain 1980s Japan trade history lesson. Japanese low-cost, fuel-efficient cars terrified Detroit so much in the '80s that the U.S. automakers persuaded Congress to impose quotas on them. The Japanese then started to make luxury cars that are far more profitable. The result is that Japan's Infinitis, Lexuses and other luxury makes – along with their low-cost, fuel-efficient cars – have almost bankrupted the Detroit automakers and their part suppliers who once dominated the luxury market.

The quota agreement reached between America and China on November 8, 2005, to limit the number of cheap Chinese bras, T-shirts and baby socks for three years in order to help U.S. manufacturers compete was an expensive political spin that only increased the cost for U.S. consumers. Chinese officials have already announced that they will use the quotas to force manufacturers to produce high-end garments. That is a replay of what happened to U.S. auto manufacturers. The U.S. textile and apparel manufacturers in the more profitable luxury end of the market have written their own obituary.

In 2004, China received more than $50 billion in foreign investment. Add the $13 billion Hong Kong received and the total is more than double the amount foreigners invested in America. Much of that investment is in high-end Italian knitwear and other luxury goods.

Strategic Economic Dialogue

The meeting of American and Chinese political heavyweights in mid-December, 2006, was a reminder of how China is misperceived by America. The American delegation to Beijing included seven cabinet secretaries, and the head of the U.S. Federal Reserve, to lobby and bully China. While America came to lecture China on currency revaluation and market theories that would benefit China, America and the world, China aired its call for America to reform its own economy and end its addiction to Chinese goods and loans that sustain massive U.S. trade and budget deficits. The Chinese prefer gradualism. After all, they are the biggest economic experiment in history. Transforming a highly centralized, state-controlled economy into a market economy, and transforming an export-driven economy into a consumer-driven economy that affects a quarter of the world's population, many of whom live on less than a dollar a day, is, to say the least, a challenge. China is not a threat to America. It is America's most important ally if it is to survive, thrive and continue to guide in the 21st century.

U.S. politicians received a Chinese Power Point history lesson on the country's 5,000-year history of poverty, colonial subjugation and civil wars – which I also discuss in Chapter 2. Americans don't know or understand China.

China must maintain an annual investment growth rate of around 20 percent if it is to avoid a crash landing and implode – with devasting global implications, especially in America. China's per capita GDP is only slightly higher than $1,000, while the per capita GDP in America is nearly $40,000. This while China's reliance on external demand is growing. The ratio between trade turnover and gross domestic product jumped 72 percent in the first three quarters of 2006, from 63.9 percent in 2005, 59.8 percent in 2004, 51.9 percent in 2003 and 42.7 percent in 2002.

The fact is that the Chinese government is beholden to China's vast export sector, which accounts for more than one-third of the country's economy.

Letting the yuan float upward could massively weaken the export-driven economy and create political instability. For example, the textile industry alone supports 90 million workers but makes miniscule profits. The consequence of millions of textile workers being unemployed or the government extending more subsidies to the textile industries while it is trying to reform its market economy would have a devastating political impact.

The first Sino-U.S. strategic economic dialogue addressed long-term concerns and agreed to:

- Establish New York Stock Exchange and NASDAQ offices in China.
- Enhance bilateral contacts to push for a successful resolution of the World Trade Organization Doha Round of international talks covering farm subsidies.
- Establish a working group to discuss opening the Chinese services sector to competition and investment.
- Launch talks to encourage protection of investor rights in each country.
- Reinvigorate discussions within a joint committee on commerce and trade to improve transparency and intellectual property protection.
- China will formally participate in the American FutureGen renewable energy project, which receives large subsidies from the U.S. government.
- The two sides also signed an agreement facilitating financing to support U.S. exports to China and agreed to relaunch bilateral air services negotiations.
- Both sides also agreed to take measures to address global imbalances. Both reaffirmed commitments to pursuing macro economic policies. China agreed to carry out exchange rate reform and the U.S. said it would increase savings rates to promote balanced and strong growth.
- The Chinese also agreed to help the Motion Picture Association of America and other groups do more to tackle copyright piracy on the Internet.

America also gave China the green light to join the Inter-American Development Bank. In return, China signed an $8-billion contract to buy four nuclear power plants from U.S.-based Westinghouse. The deal creates 5,500 U.S. jobs and is a concrete first step in reducing America's trade deficit with China. Westinghouse also agreed to transfer to China technology that could be used in the construction of more nuclear reactors in China during the next 15 to 20 years. It's a pity Westinghouse is owned by Japan's Toshiba Corporation. However, the two-day session failed to produce any short-term solutions to the schizoid Sino-U.S. relationship, other than an agreement to meet again in Washington in May 2007 – where the Democratic-controlled Congress, angry that China was not labeled a currency manipulator, was waiting with its flexed muscle.

Joint Vision

The Sino-U.S. road map toward achieving consensus on the lofty strategic goals within a mutually agreed timeframe is the millennium challenge. When the world's sole superpower and the biggest developing giant talk to each other to resolve a wide range of bilateral issues with global implications – there is hope. Especially when they agree that America needs to rein in its appetite for cheap foreign imports and avert a negative savings rate.

Both sides agreed that oil exporting countries had excessive surpluses that were a major source of global imbalance. That is a refreshing millennium awakening.

The joint vision to engage in ongoing intelligent dialogue to resolve complex economic, military and political issues is a major constructive adjustment for America.

Anything else is self-destructive and would create a global economic tsunami. Shock waves would rupture corporate America. A stronger yuan would make household-name brand companies like General Motors, Microsoft, Boeing or even Exxon-Mobil prime acquisition candidates for the acquisitive Chinese with their excess dollars.

The diplomatic significance of the high-level delegation to China was that it only went to China, not Japan, South Korea, or any other major U.S. trading partner in Asia. There is no doubt China is the foremost strategic global partner for America, especially after it surpassed Mexico in 2006 as the second-largest U.S. trading partner.

The weak yen has left Japan mired in its mercantilist strategies of the past. China knows this, and until the yen rises sharply, the yuan won't either. The fact is America is living unsustainably beyond its means. Consumer spending accounts for 70 percent of the U.S. economy. A stronger Chinese currency won't change the unbalanced nature of U.S. growth. Remember that the Plaza Accord of 1985, which sharply weakened the dollar versus the yen, did little to improve the U.S. balance of payments. Instead, it contributed to the asset bubble that led to Japan's lost decade of the '90s. Is it any wonder China is in no rush? To try and push China into an unjustified economic crisis with the threat of protectionism is not only shortsighted – it won't work and is a waste of time.

Protectionism
Protectionism never has and never will work. The protectionism Detroit sought failed to protect the auto manufacturers, and the same will happen to America's textile and apparel manufacturers. America should focus on educating and training Americans for new growth industries rather than keeping them in dying ones. The days when a man could work for life on an assembly line and keep a house, wife, two kids and two cars and loaf on the sofa from Friday to Monday are gone.

China is a convenient political scapegoat. Trade imbalance, revaluation of the yuan, quotas and U.S. sanctions if China failed to comply became the rallying call for American politicians fighting for votes in the 2004, 2006 and 2008 elections. So much so that the Department of Commerce set up a political team to "take care" of China in the 2004 election. Former Commerce Secretary Donald L. Evans led the charge in speeches across America and then resigned after Bush's reelection. China-bashing was then reassigned to Defense Secretary Donald Rumsfeld.

In preparation for the 2006 midterm elections, America established a China Enforcement Task Force, the first time the U.S. Trade Representative has set up a body to monitor a single country – this after U.S. exports to China rose by 20 percent in 2005. In early 2006, two bipartisan "anti-China" bills were introduced in Congress – one to revoke China's Permanent Normal Trade Relations status and the other to impose a 27.5 percent tariff on all Chinese products. New calls went out as the midterm elections heated up demanding that China revalue the yuan. The *2006 Economic Report of the President* blamed China's tightly managed, pegged exchange rate for America's record $725.8-billion global trade deficit. Nobel laureate economist Robert Mundell of Columbia University warned in early 2006 that a change in China's exchange rate could cut China's growth rate in half and cause a financial crisis. He did not think a major revaluation would help the U.S.

To make matters worse, the fact that China was opening its retail banking sector to U.S. and other foregn banks was totally ignored by the mainstream media. Starting in December 2006, foreign banks, including America's leading banks, began offering yuan services to individuals.

Analysts estimate that foreign banks could see their China bond business, which tripled in the first 10 months of 2006, more than double in 2007 – and continue growing at such rates in subsequent years. Forty-eight foreign banks traded 643 billion yuan of bond repurchase agreements on the interbank market in the first 10 months, four times the amount a year earlier. Their spot bond trading more than doubled to 620 billion yuan, and total bond and bill holdings hit 36.09 billion yuan, nearly triple the amount at the end of 2005.

How does America reciprocate? In July 2007, it approved import investigations by the Commerce Department that could lead to stiff duties on steel nails and pipes from China. American nail producers have asked for duties ranging from 55 to 118 percent on imports from China, which they claim are being dumped in the U.S. at less than fair value. Nail imports from China totaled $452 million in 2006 and had increased by 79 percent in volume since 2004.

U.S. producers of steel pipes demanded similar anti-dumping duties of 51 to 86 percent be imposed on Chinese pipes. With the 2008 elections looming on the horizon, it was clear that China bashing will reach an all-time high during the presidential campaign.

China Blamed For Global Slowdown

China's accession to the World Trade Organization in 2001 had a far greater global economic impact than 9/11. It was one of the most important events in modern history. A warning America detailed in a 100-page report submitted to Congress by the Bush administration to mark the end of China's five year accession to WTO on December 11, 2006. Bush and company identified "troubling indications that China's momentum toward reform has begun to slow," according to Susan Schwab, the U.S. trade representative, who went on to claim that China's "incomplete" reforms were "creating massive distortions that could leave the Chinese and global economies at risk."

In fact, China has changed more than 3,000 regulations to comply with WTO requirements. It also reduced tariffs on goods of great importance to U.S. industry from an average of 25 percent in 1997 to 7 percent today, with similarly significant reductions for agricultural products.

In addition, it has reduced or eliminated numerous non-tariff barriers, increased market access for international service providers and improved the transparency of its governmental procedures. These steps have expanded economic growth in both countries and contributed to a roughly 190 percent increase in U.S. goods exported to China over the past five years. Today, China is America's fourth-largest export market – up from 15th more than a decade ago. Wal-Mart operated 66 stores in China at the end of 2006. Home Depot paid $100 million for a majority stake in China's HomeWay to get a piece of China's vast consumer market as it goes head-to-head with U.K.'s B&Q. Home Depot, like many other U.S. companies, is counting on China to provide fresh growth as it runs out of room to expand in America.

When China joined the WTO in 2001, its account surplus (trade plus a few other cross-border payments) was a modest 1.3 percent of gross domestic product. But in 2006, China's surplus hit a breathtaking 9 percent of GDP. In absolute terms, it has overtaken Germany's surplus and even Japan's, despite the fact that Japan's GDP remains more than twice the size of China's.

America's repeated lectures to China and China's reaction remind me of the "Chinese Sick Day" joke. Hung Chow calls into work and says, "Hey, I no come work today. I sick, headache, stomach ache, legs hurt. I no come work. " His American boss says, "You know something, Hung Chow. I really need you today. When I feel like this, I go to my wife and tell her to give me sex. That makes everything better and I go to work. You try that."

Two hours later, Hung Chow calls again. "I do what you say. I feel great. I be work soon.... You got nice house."

Let's face it, America's problems were created by its career politicians, not the Chinese.

Subtle Racism

Career politicians are responding to complex issues with tired racist slogans as a substitute for sound policies. If China does what U.S. politicians are demanding while threatening tougher tariffs, that would slash the profits of Standard & Poor's 500 Index companies by 8 percent, or $50 billion.

To blame China for manipulating its currency and saying that is the cause for the $200-plus-billion annual trade imbalance with America is just more political and economic fiction. China s trade surplus with the U.S. doesn't mean that the yuan is overvalued. A more meaningful statistic is China's global trade balance with all nations. China's global surplus is smaller than that of Germany, the Netherlands, Thailand, Argentina, Malaysia and Singapore.

Before China revalued its currency in 2005, it had kept the yuan pegged to the U.S. dollar since January 1, 1994. U.S. services exports to China grew 20 percent in 2005, nearly double the rate of increase for the world as a whole. China has also taken the billions it has earned in U.S. trade and purchased U.S. federal bonds – which help U.S. career politicians underwrite their rapidly growing budget deficits. China is the second-largest purchaser of U.S. bonds.

America owes China more than $350 billion. That is the value of U.S. Treasury notes that China owns. It was fitting that the 2006 midterm elections coincided with estimates that China's currency reserves reached $1 trillion. Standing between a stable U.S. economy and one mired in crisis is China's vast dollar holdings. It keeps interest rates low so that America can manage its massive current-account and budget deficits.

"Never in the history of our republic have we ever financed a military conflict by borrowing money from somewhere else," former President Bill Clinton said in a television interview after Hurricane Katrina. Beijing, he noted, keeps lending us money "for Iraq, Afghanistan and Katrina."

Instead of blaming China for America's economic woes which, are actually caused by self-serving career politicians, America should lift many of the export restrictions imposed on goods and services to China. That would certainly help balance trade. America had a trade surplus with China for 21 straight years from 1972 until 1993. China only started having a trade surplus with the U.S. in 1993. More importantly, more than half of the Chinese exports to the United States are produced by foreign-funded enterprises in China, many of them U.S. companies. And lower-priced Chinese-made goods save money for American families – lots of money.

China is the fastest-growing economy in the world today. It is the world's fourth-largest economy after America, Japan and Germany. It will become the world's largest economy before 2041 and will join the ranks of fully developed countries by 2080. By 2100, China will be in the top 10 of the world's most developed economies, according to the *2005 Report on China's Modernization*. Chinese companies are buying up U.S. and European name brands the way America did in the last century. IBM's personal computer division, France's Thomson and Britain's Rover are now in the hands of Chinese companies. Maytag and Unocal would have been too, were it not for the U.S. government again not practicing what it preaches – free trade.

Blame Game

It happened again when Dubai Ports World proposed buying London's Peninsular & Oriental Steam Navigation Co., which happened to run six American ports. Although the deal was blessed by the Bush administration after an official vetting process, many congressmen became furious because they hadn't been briefed beforehand. Congress scuttled the deal and consequently has been mulling even tighter controls on direct foreign investment in America. Blocking transactions that do not credibly threaten national security discourages job-creating investments, encourages other countries to restrict investments in their home markets, and takes the focus away from more serious efforts to counter threats to national security. In 1996, U.S. officials tried to block Hong Kong's Hutchison Whampoa Limited from being awarded 50-year concessions at both ends of the Panama Canal, which it viewed as vital to American trade and security interests. In 2003, the Bush administration blocked Hutchison's bid to acquire the remnants of the bankrupt U.S. telecom firm Global Crossing, again on security grounds.

When Hutchison Port Holdings was being awarded a contract to electronically scan U.S. bound containers in the Bahamas, U.S. politicians opposed the transaction because of company Chairman Li Ka Shing's links to China. In the Country Reports on Terrorism 2005, issued by the State Department, Hong Kong is praised as a "model" for Container Security Initiative implementation for its transparent and cooperative performance. This is no ordinary achievement in the post-9/11 world – especially when compared to the shortcomings of ports in America.

Why is it OK for U.S. companies to go global and not Chinese firms? Chinese corporations are merely giving U.S. companies a taste of their own medicine. When China Ocean Shipping Company tried to build a cargo container terminal at the former Long Beach Naval station in the late 1990s, it was killed by Congress because of fears of espionage and smuggling. But COSCO didn't go away. It quietly became one of the biggest terminal operators in a port and an industry where nearly all the players are foreign. Today, COSCO has risen from suspected spy to model tenant in the Long Beach and Los Angeles ports.

By 2100, Chinese expatriates working in the States may live in gated neighborhoods away from the American poor and run country clubs which locals can join on a quota.

Practice What We Preach
Isn't it time for America to stop using dated Cold War slogans against China and start practicing what it preaches? Isn't it time America stopped imposing quotas, tariffs and sanctions that protect campaign donors for their unprecedented campaign contributions? Isn't it time America got up front and joined in free trade opportunities with China in what could be a harmonious Sino-American century? America must accept, accommodate and embrace the emerging Chinese powerhouse before it is too late and it is discarded as an unreliable partner. America's conservative pro-Taiwan lobby must be ignored and relegated to a historical footnote as the economic and geopolitical interdependency of America and China fuse.

China has opted for peaceful integration and benign global competition. It is preoccupied with national economic development, national unity and party legitimacy and is not concerned with world domination.

The political abuse and attacks China was subjected to during the 2004 and 2008 presidential campaign and the run-up to the 2006 congressional campaigns was reminiscent of the ingrained hatred that Boston Red Sox fans had for the New York Yankees. Just as the "Curse of the Bambino" has been vanquished, the political license to blame China for what ails America must also be revoked. The vitriolic smash-talk between President Bush and challenger John Kerry climaxed at the height of a raw autumn weekend when 3.2 million people – roughly half the population of Massachusetts – packed the parade route to celebrate the defeat of the dreaded Yankees. The Red Sox triumph dawned on a passionate global audience mesmerized by the U.S. election and the choice of 120 million voters whose decision had global ramifications.

The "Curse of the Bambino" went the way of "the house that Ruth built," and everything it symbolized. The new Yankee Stadium built to replace the old ballpark is arguably a metaphor for the decline of America's power and the end of the American Century – but not Yankee fans' pride. Yankee Stadium was a landmark of New York's emergence in the 1920s. It opened in 1923, during the Roaring '20s, after America emerged victorious from World War I and New York's office towers started scraping the skies. The stadium became the showplace for America's national pastime – and America's decline as a global military and baseball power.

Divided We Fall
The 2004 U.S. election confirmed that there are two Americas and a divided world that have to be reunited before they drift irreparably apart – like Chicago and New York baseball fans are over the White Sox and Cubs, Yankees and Mets respectively. When the White Sox won the 2005 World Series, ending their 88-year drought and the Black Sox curse of 1919, they highlighted the cold windy divide in Chicago – America's Second City – when they goaded and partied in the South Side as they goated and taunted the more celebrated Cubs fans of Wrigley Field on the North Side. The emotional depth of the schism in America was highlighted when Republican lawmakers injected themselves in baseball's sale of the Washington Nationals. Republicans were upset when financier George Soros, a vocal critic of Bush

and major donor to liberal causes, joined the ownership bid. Is it any wonder more Americans tune in and vote for "American Idol" than for politicians? Polls confirm that 35 percent of the 34 million viewers who tune in to "Idol" think their votes court more than their votes in the presidential election. Voters prefer "Idol" because there is no confusing Electoral College.

The red and blue camps in America decided to move on after the election and pitched their tents near the president's ranch under the sizzling Texas sun in Crawford – over the Iraq war – in the summer of 2005. Several thousand people converged on Crawford to voice their views on the war and the president who launched it. The war opponents gathered at Camp Casey, an outpost near the Bush ranch named for the late son of anti-war activist Cindy Sheehan. Across town, at the high school football stadium, Bush supportetrs listened to like-minded speakers say that the U.S. must prevail in Iraq, lest the country fall to terrorist insurgents.

America is becoming more like Iraq than the other way around. Like Iraq, which is divided between Shiites, Kurds and Sunnis – and the fractious Sunnis further split between radical jihadists and the other mostly Baathist Party insurgents – the conservatives in America are deeply divided over Supreme Court nominees, immigration, eavesdropping, economic and fiscal policy while liberals are split over the Iraq war, environment and energy policies. America's founding ideals have been betrayed by the political elites in both major parties.

The bipartisan Iraq Study Group report exposed the deep fissures in both parties – especially among Republicans. Conservatives labeled it "strategic muddle," "absurd," and "stupid." Moderates accepted the report, fearing a repeat of their defeat in the next midterm elections in 2008.

It's downright shameful the way political elites are constantly pandered to by the ever-increasing number of lobbyists who represent embattled clients with conflicting policies. Since 2000, the number of registered lobbyists in Washington has more than doubled, from 16,342 to 34,785. Their divisive and scandalous behavior was brought to light with the indictments of lobbyist Jack Abramoff and former House Majority Leader Tom DeLay, and the FBI raid on Congressman William Jefferson's Capitol Hill office as part of a federal bribery investigation in which the Louisiana Democrat was videotaped accepting a leather briefcase containing $100,000 in cash from a government witness. About $90,000 of the money was found hidden in a freezer at his home. Former San Diego Republican Randy Cunningham is in prison after admitting he accepted $2.4 million in bribes. Several other congressmen are under investigation for accepting bribes from lobbyists.

The divided nation of America was exposed for what it is to the world by the terrorist acts of 9/11. The Freedom Tower that will rise from the dusty 6.4-hectare cavernous concrete void at Ground Zero will be the symbol of the divisive acrimony and fear that permeates American society today. Seven in 10 of the 40,000 people who worked at ground zero and Fresh Kills on Staten Island have felt their lungs deteriorate and many have died as a result, while left to suffer on their own without any government support. The ugly infighting over the design, money and safety of the tower is a symbolic aftertaste of a bitterly divided country living in resentment and fear. Mired in delays, lawsuits and controversy, the memorial's costs, like the national deficit, soared out of control while the victims of 9/11 and the war on terror are exploited by career politicians. It also illustrates a dearth of political and design talent in the face of a monumental challenge.

The deepening divide in America and across the globe must be bridged if America and humanity are to survive the 21st century. The world's free-trade world economies retreated from openness between 1914 and 1950. They are doing so again because globalization has created bigger gaps between the average incomes of the rich and poor nations than ever before. By the end of 2005, 1 billion people were on the Internet and the number of mobile phone users was at least 1.4 billion. Our age of instant communication has made the world aware of the widening cavernous gap between hopeless poverty and abundant wealth. Knowledge has become a threat to global economic and political stability and to established career politicians and their entrenched financial backers. Understanding each other as Americans and working together to foster a balance of culture while developing a closer relationship with China will only protect and enhance all of humanity.

The clarion warning of Abraham Lincoln, "A house divided against itself cannot stand," applies not only to America today, but the world. To stop the ongoing divides from increasing and start to bridge the gap, we have to rationalize local and interlocal aspirations – not imperial fiats by career politicians, bureaucrats and managers. None of them have ever created the capitalist wealth they know how to talk about and do nothing about.

Imperial Theocratic Presidency

Even the president was conflicted and schizoid – living in fear of impeachment after Michigan Rep. John Conyers published a 370-page report, *The Constitution in Crisis: The Downing Street Minutes and Deception, Manipulation, Torture, Retribution and Coverup in the Iraq War, and Illegal Domestic Surveillance,* in 2005 before the midterm elections. That fear became more real after Conyers ascended to the chairmanship of the House Judiciary Committee and vowed to launch an impeachment probe against Bush – over the protestations of House Speaker Nancy Pelosi.

This is the same president who expanded his party's majority in 2002's off-year elections, the first president to do so in his first term since Franklin D. Roosevelt in 1934. He added seats again in 2004, the first to do so while winning reelection since Roosevelt in 1936. He then lost it all in the 2006 congressional elections – as has happened to every two-term president in his sixth year in office since the American Civil War, with the sole exception of Bill Clinton in 1998.

A theocratic president loathe to concede mistakes, Bush reluctantly did so after the thrashing Republicans were subjected to in 2006. A leader usually dismissive of his critics, embraced their right to differ – and even fired his Defense Secretary Donald Rumsfeld, whom he had repeatedly said he would let stand by his side until the end of his term. A man whose patience is easily stretched seemed to ask for empathy for decisions gone wrong. This from the ultimate Big Brother, who authorized eavesdropping and the bugging of 200 million U.S. phone subscribers rather than seek approval of the special federal court set up for that purpose. Fifty to 60 percent of Republicans believe in Armageddon and are influenced by the argument that the "destruction of the new Babylon" in Iraq will hasten the coming of the Messiah.

The political messages from the White House are "double-coded," meaning one thing to secular America but something else to people with the "biblical worldview." Hence the use of the phrase "I believe" 12 times in Bush's 2004 Republican Convention speech.

The Patriot Act, and its interpretations and implementation by the Bush administration, has eroded the great pillars of American liberty, justice and basic civil rights in the name of security. It was Nazi propaganda chief Joseph Goebbels who noted how readily people would surrender their liberties if persuaded that their security was at risk. The authoritarian legacy of 9/11 has also eroded America's democratic values and fundamental rights, which are gradually and only grudgingly being restored.

President Bush was forced to agree to legislation banning cruel, inhumane and degrading treatment of prisoners in U.S. custody. His U-turn was the latest example of how divided and rudderless the U.S. is. Americans have turned against each other as only ugly Americans can on issues of free speech, religion and war. The nation's soul, its moral authority and integrity have been tarnished. Its credibility as the champion of democracy has been severly damaged and challenged. The ideological divide between a Republican imperial presidency and the country's constitutional cornerstone of "separation of powers," which gives Congress the power to protect the rights of *We the Apathetic Maids*, has created a constitutional crisis and backlash that threatens the very survival of the republic. On another level, America is forgetting how to be a benign imperial power, not demanding tribute, or forever sending in the legions. Now it has panicked itself into enforcement, tearing at the throats of disobedient satraps.

The New Divide

Washington continues to be a city of divided government despite having recaptured the checks and balances so sorely lacking in America since 2000. The 2006 elections elevated and reinforced the partisan confrontational gridlock and warfare. The election of the first African-American Muslim to the House got Republican congressmen warning that the nation's traditional values are threatened. The Democrats slim majority in the Senate was imperiled when Senator Tim Johnson of South Dakota underwent emergency brain surgery. The diversity and tender hooks of the Democratic majority in the new Congress is representative of the new divide in American politics. The old school liberal leadership is reluctantly trying to embrace the moderate and conservative "Scoop" Jackson Democrats, who are in many ways more aligned politically with the moderate wing of the Republican Party, while trying to minimize the inevitable clashes on foreign policy, especially toward China.

The congressional investigation into the political intervention by the White House and political machinations in the Justice Department to fire eight federal prosecutors to force the attorney general to resign is just one of a number of ongoing investigations.

The use of Congress and subpoena powers to investigate the president's conduct of the war, the exposure of former CIA rush agent Valerie Plame to avenge her diplomat husband's criticism of the rush to war, Vice President Dick Cheney's secret energy policy deliberations and White House links to Republican corruption scandals further widened the expanding fissure.

California Rep. Henry Waxman – whose formidable and combative Waxman-Berman political machine I had the memorable experience of having been on the team that handed the machine its first electoral defeat in the Yaroslavsky-Savitch Los Angeles City Council race in the early 70s – lost no time as head of the House Government Reform Committee in giving Bush's team the real thumping it deserved. Impeachment investigations. Payback time for the wasteful Republican-led Clinton impeachment effort.

The political debates about increasing everything that is long overdue for an increase, starting with higher taxes on oil and pharmaceutical company profits, the minimum wage, Medicare benefits, immigration quotas, and simultaneously reducing the costs of fundamental human necessities such as education, health care, drugs for seniors and other entitlement programs, such as the mentally and physically impaired – as well as the budget deficit – are a welcome respite from the dysfunctional and divisive political rhetoric of denial in the interest of political self-preservation and perpetuation of unnecessary wars.

Political posturing in preparation for the 2008 presidential election – by both parties and their candidates – exposes the lack of new ideas or sweeping policy reforms so desperately needed for America to survive as a superpower.

The political debris left in the wake of the destructive political blue tidal wave that crashed on the shores of the Potomac in early 2007 is drowning America's democratic form of government. A major political cleaning is needed and long overdue by *We the Maids*.

Poor Drowning America

Hurricane Katrina's ferocious onslaught drowned New Orleans, but far worse, it exposed the ongoing divide between black and white, rich and poor Americans afraid of each other, who do not know or communicate with each other – much like the communication among emergency personnel after Katrina hit. Nothing has changed since 9/11. The Homeland Security Department was expected to remedy the communication failures among emergency personnel, but just like 9/11, communications among emergency personnel failed in the aftermath of Katrina.

The bloated infant corpses were a grisly reminder that the infant mortality rate in Washington, D.C., is twice as high as in Beijing. The number of babies who died before their first birthday was 11.5 per thousand in 2002 in D.C., compared with 4.6 in Beijing.

America's worsening poverty is creating a schism that has the potential to rupture America the way Katrina did the levees in New Orleans. Watching hospital workers in New Orleans relocate patients to upper floors, because like hospitals in Baghdad, the lower floors had been lost to looters, confirmed how divided America is. Yet, New Orleans, Banda Aceh, Darfur and Kashmir generated the largest donations from Americans for stricken people in history. This all happened in 2005.

The kind of abuses and failures seen in Iraq are alive and well in America – and were further exposed by Katrina. Overpriced, no-bid contracts for well-connected companies – neglect and indifference to the nation's poor. A bifarcated and continually dissected, further divided nation.

When Hurricane Rita hit a few weeks later, evacuation routes reached gridlock, with many vehicles running out of fuel. Once again, the poor and disenfranchised were abandoned and left to languish and face the storm's fury. American citizens deserve better from their government.

The rapid collapse of command and control, and the lumbering indifference from the nation's capital had a banana republic odor to it that alarmed the world.

The Washington-based Pew Research Center released the results of a global attitudes survey in November 2005 that found that 76 percent of mainland Chinese living in urban areas expected their lives to improve over the next five years. In the United States, it was 48 percent, much closer to Russia's 45 percent. When asked if they were 'satisfied with the way things are going at home," 72 percent in China responded "satisfied" and 19 percent "not satisfied." In America the survey elicited only 39 percent "satisfied" and 57 percent "not satisfied." Is it any wonder that 100,000-plus Americans are now living in China – myself included? We eat real Chinese takeout and not those coagulates in paper cartons cooked especially for gringos.

Bilateral Strategic Dialogue

With anti-Beijing politicians taking control of both the House and Senate, Sino-U.S. relations appear to be heading into choppy seas. House Speaker Nancy Pelosi, who opposed normal trading relations, was against Beijing being awarded the 2008 Olympics. She has also criticized China's human rights record, and supports Taiwan. U S. policy toward China will undoubtedly get more hostile as the 2008 presidential campaign heats up. There are already, as of the publication of this book, more than 50 anti-China pieces of legislation in the congressional pipeline. Human rights, appreciation of the yuan, new tariffs, labor, expansion in Africa, and support for Taiwan independence dominate the agenda.

Drawing a line in the political sand and pulling the trigger on sanctions may seem like smart economic policy, but it is not.

America's harsher rhetoric toward China and its preoccupation with short-sighted domestic issues will only benefit China, which has been boosting its own diplomatic profile globally – especially in Asia and the developing world – at America's expense.

Africa and Latin America's left turn away from America in favor of China is not surprising. America's neighbors that were exploited by U.S. corporations are no longer apathetic. They are rising up through the ballot box. Isn't it time *We the Apathetic Maids* in America did the same?

The strategic dialogue started by President Bush with Jiang Zemin at the president's Texas ranch in 2003 must continue with Hu Jintao. Though how the wit of a recovering alcoholic bar top hick goes down with that of a square of a karaokeing, drinking city slicker, we may never know. It is essential that both countries' future leaders find ways to develop closer ties and propel the momentum of the symbiotic bilateral Pacific and global partnership. America and China are Siamese twins – linked by a geopolitical umbilical cord across the Pacific.

China Rising

China was the world's leader between 500 and 1500, although without global reach. Only in the last half of the last millennium was it overtaken by Europe and America. The Asian Development Bank has calculated that in 1820, at the beginning of the Industrial Age, Asia generated an estimated three-fifths of world product. By 1940, this had fallen to one fifth. China is reemerging as a global power, leading an Asia that America cannot afford to alienate or build a future relationship based on fear. America must always keep in mind Thucydides' warning more than two millennia ago that belief in the inevitability of conflict can become one of its main causes. Each side, believing it will end up at war with the other, makes reasonable military preparations that are then read by the other side as confirmation of its worst fears.

America and China must initiate an end to the balance of economic and political terrorism that permeates Sino-U.S. relations today. America's paranoia of economic encirclement by China, like China's fear of American military encirclement, must be abandoned by both if they are to lead a harmonious inter-local world in the 21st century and beyond. Dialogue between American and Chinese leaders is essential to avoid a military or economic confrontation. A constructive first step is for America to sign a "fourth communique" with China to confirm China's sovereignty over Taiwan. The U.S. has signed three communiques with China pledging its support of a one-China policy and opposing Taiwanese independence. But America has still pledged to come to Taiwan's defense if China were to attack. The fourth communique must dispose of that policy once and for all.

America has to acknowledge that China is reemerging in the 21st century as a global superpower for the third time. The first was with the Jesuit missions of the 16th century; the second with Britain during the Opium Wars of the 19th century. In the 19th century, the imperialist West, led by Britain, famously carried out a three-way trade: Opium was sold to China for silver currency, which was used to buy tea in India, which was then shipped to the home country for consumption. When China tried to stop the sale and importation of opium, war erupted. The current third encounter will be longer lasting than the first two.

"China's Peaceful Rise" is its non-ideological long-term foreign policy that contrasts dramatically from America's short-term "containment" policy. It can prevent the current inevitable conflict if Chinese values are acknowledged and accepted. The current mistrust and hostility that permeates the Sino-U.S. relationship must be replaced with a bedrock policy of bilateral and global partnership. *We the Apathetic Maids* must acknowledge that the political establishment in Washington D.C., is more of a threat to America than China.

America and China must take a realistic and pragmatic approach to forging their strategic alliance. There has to be a fusion of military thought and might – a meaningful engagement with the goal of achieving pan-Pacific integration. A union of peaceful and prosperous ideas with regional as well as global appeal, which will benefit all humanity.

Arnold J. Toynbee concluded in his definitive *A Study of History* that the ultimate cause of imperial collapse was "suicidal statecraft." The phrase applies to the policies pursued by America domestically and toward China in particular. America's efforts to contain China and dissuade it from seeking to become a regional power have had the opposite effect. In December 2005, China launched the first East Asian Summit, which excluded America. China follows the advice of its ancient strategic guru Sun Tze, who taught that the best way to win is to let your rival defeat himself.

America should heed the words of its 2005 Nobel laureate, Thomas C. Schelling, a political economist who said it was in the best long-term interest of parties to foster cooperation rather than conflict. His 1960 book, *The Strategy of Conflict*, pointed out that a party could have long-term success by giving up some short-term advantages, even if that meant worsening its own options. By making concessions, the stronger party could build trust with the other party and that long-term relationship could be more beneficial to both. In the Oval Office, you can hear a reedy voice asking, "Could you run that by me one more time?"

America Left Behind

The No Child Left Behind Act is leaving America's children in the slow schooling lane – while China and the rest of the world accelerate their educational systems and move them into the fast lanes of knowledge. America will become a second-rate power unless it can match the educational performance of China in math, reading and science.

Teaching at Risk, a report released in 2006 by the U.S. Teaching Commission, found an urgent need to upgrade the quality and pay of America's K-12 teachers. Education has to become the key pillar of U.S. power, on a par with the military. America must start tending to education in militaristic and strategic ways. Otherwise, America will become a third-rate nation. An extraordinary nation can remain so only if it has a critical mass of extraordinary teachers and educated people.

The failure of the education system in America to instill a fundamental knowledge of American history, or the history of the civilizations that helped create America – including China – has contributed directly to the geopolitical quagmire America finds itself in. The 21st century dawned on the twilight of U.S. supremacy because China is destined to eclipse an overextended, misguided America living beyond its means.

To extricate itself with honor and dignity, America must make education and knowledge the No. 1 priority. *We the Apathetic People* have to re-allocate and redirect our hard-earned tax dollars away from the corporate and military failures of the last century. There can be no more dollars wasted on negativism. They must be diverted to fund our children's education and spark a desire to explore and learn about other cultures and countries to ensure a peaceful civilization in the 21st century.

The violence of the 20th century and early 21st century can and must be stopped. The age of instant communication has brought the global community closer together. It enables exchanges, dialogue, understanding and tolerance to replace violent confrontations. Negativity – negative teachings, negative thinking – about people because of their religion, race, sex, social status, migration status, sexual orientation, age, color or culture must be replaced with positive, honest knowledge.

The cornerstone and underlying essential ingredient of the recipe of the *Custom Maid* post 9/11 trilogy – hypocrisy, ignorance and apathy – is knowledge. Knowledge is power.

The tragic consequences of globalisation are best exemplitied by the death of Princess Diana. An English princess with an Egyptian boyfriend crashes in a French tunnel, driving a German car with a Dutch engine, driven by a Belgian who was drunk on Scottish Whisky, followed closely by italian paparazzi, on Japanese, motorcycles, treated by an American doctor, using Brazilian medicines.

Put Your Lights On.
–Santana Band with Everlast

KNOWLEDGELESS
The Post-Global Interlocal Sino-American Century.
Living Right Next Door to Hell.
– Guns & Roses

The walls of ignorance that confine America have to be brought down, and the career politicians and professional bureaucrats who perpetuate deliberate multicultural animosity, hatred and wars must be swept out. The people have to be educated about the real needs of the country. Volume II of the trilogy is a historical analysis of global events that have led America to where it is today, with a few recommendations on what needs to be done to survive in the 21st century. Knowledge will lead to intelligent political decisions by We the People.

*When I want to understand what is happening today
or try to decide what will happen tomorrow, I look back.*

– Oliver Wendell Holmes Jr.

Chapter One

Learn Baby Learn – Back To Basics

War is God's way of teaching Americans geography.
– Ambrose Bierce

Loaded To Kill

The wars in Afghanistan and Iraq are a 21st-century confirmation of Bierce's observation. Atlases are cheaper. Three American teenagers won the 2005 National Geographic World Championship in Budapest, Hungary, the fourth consecutive U.S. victory in the test of geographic knowledge. Unfortunately, it is the only subject Americans excel in. When it comes to science, China, India, Japan and Europe all do better. Even worse – and downright humiliating – is that American 12th-graders rank only in the 10th percentile in math – that's 10th percentile – not 10th. But America's students rank first in their assessment of their own performance. America is not only poorly prepared academically, it has delusions of grandeur.

Looking at Hong Kong youngsters in their uniforms and heavy knapsacks full of books traveling to and from school – on subways and buses, reading books instead of comics – contrasts dramatically with their counterparts in America who hang out in malls listening to their ipods and then go to school with loaded weapons to kill schoolmates. In Hong Kong, schoolbags, not guns, are killers. Nine-year-old Lee Ka-kit was carrying a backpack full of books on his first day back at school after the Christmas holidays when he stood on a ledge to look over the railings of his 20th-floor lift lobby. His school bag apparently slipped over his head and pulled him to his death.

Yeung Sau-ying, the family life education officer of the Boys' and Girls' Clubs Association of Hong Kong, says that while parents attached primary importance to the health of their children, most also "felt a great deal of pressure from expectations over the academic performance of their children and choice of schools." More than 52 percent said they suffered from at least three stress-related symptoms, including migraines, mood swings and insomnia. That's when their children are alive. American parents suffer identically over their fears of their children's drug consumption.

Hong Kong children are overly susceptible to school pressure, and their suicide rate is one of the highest in the world. The same holds true in China, where the pressure to succeed through education has become intense. The high suicide rates have been linked to failed exams, inability to meet parents' high expectations and pressure for tuition fees.

More than half of Hong Kong teenagers have suicidal thoughts, double the rate in North America, two independent reports found. One survey concluded there is a particularly "robust" relationship between anxiety about tests and depression. School pressure is also pushing Hong Kong teachers over the edge. Five teachers killed themselves in 2005 and early 2006 after complaining about work pressure. Education policymakers were urged to rethink the school workloads after the deaths of two teachers in January 2006. The teachers' suicides were a wake-up call that brought out more than 8,000 teachers, parents and their supporters on January 22, 2006, in the largest demonstration of teachers held in Hong Kong to demand a rethinking on education. Their demands included a reduction of class sizes, an end to the closure of schools and a reduction in the number of classes, more permanent teaching staff, and sabbatical leave – with full pay – for professional development. The Hong Kong education minister named an independent commission to investigate teachers' workload and pressure as a result of the march.

The Hong Kong education system has a novel problem. As a legacy of colonial rule, it cannot decide whether to teach in English or Chinese. For years, children have been learning science and geography in English, when they could barely order a Big Mac in that language.

The noontime crowds of anxious mothers and Filipino nannies congregating on the sidewalks outside every preschool or grammar school in Hong Kong to pick up their darlings is a daily reminder of how important education is. You have to elbow your way through the waiting crowd. "Can you believe how early and consistent through college Hong Kongers are about education?" I asked Dr. Kristin Berman, an American educator who was visiting Hong Kong, "Why are American parents and teachers failing as educators?"

Berman has taught grades 1-9 in eight states and teaches aspiring teachers. We are longtime friends and inevitably get into heated discussions on the shortcomings of the American educational system whenever we get together. There is a gulping contrast. "Schools have become factories," Berman lectured. "Teachers have become very frustrated because of the whole pressure of accountability movement measured primarily by high-stakes test scores. Basically, no one wants, or can take the time for, effective learning because the results are not measurable by standardized tests. Rules governing educators are even dictated by politicians and bureaucrats." That is something we have to change in the New World Order.

Kris went to meet her husband Jake and their children, daughter Lielle and son Alex. I decided to go to the Foreign Correspondents' Club for lunch. I went to the Main Bar and took a stool at the bar, next to Brandon Royal. I don't know too many people with Brandon's background. He was one of the few Westerners to work for Ernst & Young's China Division in the early '90s, where he audited joint venture companies such as Coca-Cola and Holiday Inn Hotels in China. He subsequently obtained his MBA from the University of Chicago and, afterward, worked in the education field while launching his writing career. Among his books: *The Little Red Writing Book*. He served as director of business development for Kaplan Educational Centers (Hong Kong) – a *Washington Post* subsidiary and the oldest and largest test preparatory organization in the world.

Through his work as a Graduate Management Admissions Test test-prep instructor, the test required in order to go to business school throughout the world, and MBA admissions coach, he has helped hundreds of applicants get accepted to some of the world's leading business programs. He is one of Asia's most well-known university admission specialists.

Brandon and I have debated what is wrong with America's system of education, politics and Americans in general for a couple of years. Canadians can't wait to let Americans know how wrong they are going about just about everything – especially knowledge, history, current affairs and their northern neighbor. Oddly enough, we usually agree. Brandon is passionate about everything, especially teaching and Filipinas. "The problem with America," Brandon says, "is that the country is caught in a giant group think. Americans have lost their ability to analyze and think as individuals. They lack the real passion to discover new viewpoints. And I don't mean Republicans and Democrats debating issues on American television and thinking they are 180 degrees apart."

Brandon's not afraid to take on any topic in true Foreign Correspondent Club tradition. As a writer and internationalist, he is zealously committed to saying what he means without worrying whether everything's politically correct. Like many foreigners living abroad, he has grown weary of hearing the words freedom and democracy used so cavalierly. "Having access to information is probably a sine qua non for good thinking," he says. "But it's only a necessary condition, not a sufficient condition. Americans confuse having access to information with knowledge. These are not the same thing. Having a free society does not mean that knowledge and true understanding come automatically.

"Let me share the contents of an e-mail I received from Amina, a bright 20-something I worked with in Beijing at Ernst and Young, who is now in corporate finance with a major U.S. investment banking firm in Shanghai. 'I have to say that I have been quite disappointed by the U.S. and, particularly, the American people after being here in New York for a month. Never have I seen a people so CNN-watched, overconfrontational and ignorant. It's depressing! I can't wait to be back in Shanghai in two days.' Sums it up for me," Brandon said as we ordered lunch.

Why do Americans allow politicians to continuously dumb down the country and make it a knowledgeless society? Whether the subject is education, Iraq, Afghanistan, gun control, death penalty, gay rights, religion, foreign affairs – and I don't mean the political kind. Sex and sex education of all North Americans is one topic Brandon and I have yet to have a disagreement about.

We also agree that American schools don't educate. They school. Schooling is for the young. Education comes later, usually much later in life. The best thing schools can do is prepare and ground students for continued learning later in life by giving them the tools and skills of learning and the desire to do so. The worst thing bad schools can do is be a child-minding facility for working parents.

Schools are the preparatory institutions for the education life has to offer. The ancient proverb "Awareness of ignorance is the beginning of wisdom," is worth keeping in mind at all times. Most adults are under the illusion that they have completed their education when they have only finished their schooling. An op-ed piece in 2001 in *The New York Times* by Mortimer J. Adler, the former chairman of the board of the Encyclopedia Brittanica, sums up the dismal state of education best. Adler wrote: "When young adults realize how little they learned in school they usually assume there was something wrong with the school they attended or with the way they spent their time there. But the fact is that the best possible graduate of the best possible school needs to continue learning every bit as much as the worst. How should they go about doing this? The brief and simple answer: Read and discuss."

Never just read, for reading without discussion with others who have read the same book is not nearly as profitable. And as reading without discussion can fail to yield the full measure of understanding that should be sought, so discussion without the substance that good and great books afford is likely to degenerate into little more than an exchange of opinions or personal prejudices.

Illiteracy Blues
Cleveland, Mississippi, is where the blues were born and raised. Bolivar County is to blues what Philadelphia is to democracy. The founding fathers of blues – W.C. Handy, Robert Johnson, Charley Patton – drank and caroused all over the county, and not 10 minutes from the Depot library sits a hallowed farm, Dockery Plantation, where musicians from throughout the South came to blend moans and chants and spirituals, all the disparate sounds of an enslaved culture, into one hautingly American plaint. Then they hopped a fast train out. Like Ronnie Wise in 2006 – an extraordinary librarian who spent 30 years at the Depot library helping people learn how to read – until he took off. People have been writing songs for over 100 years about how hard it is to escape this poor and illiterate part of America. Even today, Bolivar County is one of America's least literate places, where 41 percent of

40,000 residents can't read.

Reading is life, Wise once told an interviewer. Illiteracy, therefore, is death. He witnessed its stranglehold every day for 30 years. The same holds true for the rest of America.

One in five American adults 16 and older – 40 million Americans – can read and calculate at no better than the lowest of five levels of literacy, called Level One. Literacy experts say that 20 percent of the population of America cannot read or write English proficiently. Hiding illiteracy from a boss is common. Why does America have so many functional illiterates? And not just in Appalachia, the Mississippi Delta and Kentucky, but in New York and California?

A quarter of a million students from 32 countries participate in a competition administered by the Organization for Economic Cooperation and Development. Fifteen-year-old students from America rank near the bottom of industrialized countries in math skills, ahead of only Portugal, Mexico and three other nations. In 2006, the U.S. ranked 24th among 29 countries. The study also showed that huge numbers of U.S. students can barely do math. Among 15-year-olds, one-quarter scored at either the bottom rung or, worse, scored so low that they didn't even make that level. The students performed at an average level in the other subjects. Former U.S. Education Secretary Ron Paige said he was disappointed that American students had not stood out. "In the global economy, these countries are our competitors," he said. With nine-year old Hong Kong math prodigy Maradi Boedihardo starting university in September 2007 – America can bet its bottomed out dollar.

Is this a case of imperial slouch? America has calculators and computers to do the simplest math and then there is the call of the mall. Who needs the hassle to study math? Mexicans were brought in to pick fruit. Soon Chinese and Indians will be there to do the difficult sums.

America came in 20th in a U.N. survey of child welfare in 21 countries that assessed everything from infant mortality to whether children ate dinner with their parents or were bullied at school. The conclusion, America does not invest in its children. Widespread divorce and parents' long working hours leave kids at home alone, starved of healthy activity and supportive relationships and gorging on high-sugar junk food. The U.S. topped the list of countries with teens reported overweight. American child well-being expert Richard Barth said that the U.S. had "lost its way." What is clear is that there is no consistent relationship between wealth in the form of per-capita GDP and a child's well-being.

The failure of families and teachers in America to appreciate the support children need at an early age has to be brought to the forefront of all educational and political agendas, regardless of party affiliation. Do we really want to continue mass-producing children with degrees who are barely literate and who fight or support any war without knowing or understanding why?   Unfortunately, the evening news death tolls from Afghanistan and Iraq also have a high percentage of well educated bright NCOs and officers, who patriotically trusted their commanders – especially the commander in chief. Is this any way for America to use its bright graduates? Are schools America's new cannon fodder and assembly lines, her new Detroit?

Isn't it time America got smartened up instead of dumbed down? Americans must correct their ignorance of the global community they live in. Many have compared 9/11 to the attack on Pearl Harbor as a wake-up call for Americans to learn more about their global neighbors. American indifference to other people and other nations' foreign affairs is construed as arrogance and breeds resentment.

Most Americans don't know the difference between Austria and Australia, and many think New Mexico is a foreign country. Although with the number of foreigners and illegal immigrants living there, they may not be altogether wrong. Some 25 percent of American high school students did not know that the Pacific Ocean separates North America from Asia. Eighty percent of adults did not know India is the world's largest democracy – a lot of Indians don't know that either. More depressing, half of all adults and two-thirds of students incorrectly identified Vietnam as an island country, even though 58,000 U.S. lives were lost in the Vietnam War.

The same holds true for Iraq, according to a Roper poll conducted for National Geographic in 2006. Even though America has been at war in Iraq for four years, 60 percent of 10-year-old Americans are unable to locate that country on a map. As if that's not bad enough, their older siblings did worse. One-third of Americans between the ages of 18 and 24 could not locate the states of Louisiana or Mississippi, notwithstanding the wall-to-wall coverage of the havoc Hurricane Katrina inflicted.

"Geographic illiteracy impacts our economic well-being, our relationships with other nations and the environment, and isolates us from the world," National Geographic President and CEO John M. Fahey, Jr., said in announcing a program to help remedy the problem. The goal is to motivate parents and educators to expand geographic offerings in their children's schools. No wonder. Fewer than three in 10 Americans think it important to know the locations of countries in the news, and just 14 percent believe speaking another language is a necessary skill.

For American students, the Israeli-Palestinian conflict has been in the news their entire lives, yet 75 percent were unable to locate Israel on a map of the Middle East.

Although thousands of jobs have been outsourced to India, and the sale of nuclear technology to India has been in the headlines for some time, 47 percent could not find the Indian subcontinent on a map of Asia.

Six in 10 did not know the border between North and South Korea is the most heavily fortified in the world. Thirty percent thought the most heavily fortified border was between the United States and Mexico.

Visiting the States during the suicide bombings and intifada against Israel in the opening year of the 21st century, professors I spoke to shared their disbelief that graduate students were referring to Palestinians as "Palestillians." Sounds like something President Bush started. People in Hong Kong are called "Honkarians" by U.S. students who aren't sure of the proper terminology.

President Bush has said he wants to be the education president. Whether that means he wants to educate himself, the country or both remains to be seen.

Our graduates should feel they are worthy of that diploma. Kids who are graduated out of high school through social promotion and dumbed-down curricula know it. The scroll of paper they get is about as valuable as that slip of paper from a fortune cookie and only marginally more useful.

Why Johnny Can't Speak or Read

A sad commentary of the U.S. education system was an e-mail of actual test questions and answers from schools in the Huntsville, Alabama, metropolitan area in 2004.

Q. Name the four seasons.
A. Salt, pepper, mustard and vineager.

Q. Explain one of the processes by which water can be made safe to drink.
A. Flirtation makes water safe to drink because it removes large pollutants like grit, sand, dead sheep and canoeists.

Q. How is dew formed?
A. The sun shines down on the leaves and makes them perspire.

Q. What is a planet?
A. A body of earth surrounded by sky.

Q. What guarantees may a mortgage company insist on?
A. If you are buying a house, they will insist you are well endowed.

Q. What are steroids?
A. Things for keeping carpets still on the stairs.

Q. What happens to your body as you age?
A. When you get old, so do your bowels and you get intercontinental.

Q. What happens to a boy when he reaches puberty?
A. He says goodbye to his boyhood and looks forward to his adultery.

Q. Name a major disease associated with cigarettes.
A. Premature death.

Q. How are the main parts of the body categorized?
(e.g., abdomen).

A. The body is consisted into three parts – branium, the borax and the abdominal cavity. The brainium contains the brain, the borax contains the heart and lungs, and the abdominal cavity contains the five bowels, A, E, I, O, and U.

Q. What is a fibula?
A. A small lie.

Q. What does "varicose" mean?
A. Very close.

Q. Give the meaning of the term "Caesarian Section."
A. The caesarian section is a district in Rome.

Q. What is a seizure?
A. A Roman emporer.

Q. What is a terminal illness?
A. When you are sick at the airport.

Q. What is a turbine?
A. Something an Arab wears on his head.

Q. What is a Hindu?
A. It lays eggs.

Any wonder U.S. students repeatedly rank at the bottom of international competitions and tests?

Language Studies

America must impose strict guidelines that are in the best interests of the children. America, like Hong Kong, is multilingual. Both speak English because of their colonial parent. One also widely speaks Spanish and the other Chinese because of the makeup of their populations. The standard of English spoken in Hong Kong, like America, has declined since the handover in 1997 when Chinese replaced English in many schools. It is interesting to note that China's attempt to force on Hong Kong a "Mother Tongue" policy after the handover did nothing to raise the standard of education. It is now hastily being disassembled.

California's Proposition 227, approved by voters in 1998, banned bilingual education in the state's schools. Educators widely opposed it; so did President Clinton. Prophecies of doom were widespread. Clinton said it would condemn immigrant children to "intellectual purgatory." What happened? Test scores of children from Spanish-speaking families didn't drop. They rose. Among second-graders, average reading scores of students with limited English ability jumped from the 19th percentile nationally to the 28th percentile. In math, the same students went from the 27th to the 41st percentile, according to *The New York Times*.

English is the national language of America. However, it is important to be bilingual or even trilingual in the New World Order. Learning a second and third language is more important for American children than any other subject. Especially if America wants to continue to be a global leader in the 21st century. All high school and university graduates should be required to speak, read and write either Spanish or Chinese fluently, preferably both. Admittedly, once students have had a brief look at what is involved in each, there may be an overwhelming choice for one option, amigo. Only then will Americans be true global citizens able to survive in the 21st century.

The example set by the kindergarten class at Woodstock Elementary School in Portland, Oregon, should be emulated by all schools in America. Students there are on the front lines of a U.S. government-backed effort to get more students to learn Chinese. The Oregon program is the first in the country to track students from kindergarden to college. The school district and the University of Oregon won a $700,000 grant from the Defense Department for the program. The idea is for students to move from the Portland school system to the university, where scholarships will be offered to students who take a standard college curriculum taught primarily in Chinese. Students can also opt to spend their junior year abroad studying at Nanjing University.

The Pentagon is including Chinese studies in its long-overdue 21st–century linguistic arsenal – the National Security Language Initiative – which also includes Arabic, Farsi, Korean and Swahili. Students who take the

Chinese course are paid a $1,000 stipend and competition for admission is fierce. More than 1,000 students apply for 69 places.

The languages involved skew heavily toward current or potential global conflict spots. The initiative aims to direct U.S. foreign language education away from European languages towards languages that are perceived to be more useful in the 21st century. At the U.S. Military Academy, where future Army officers are educated, the number of students taking introductory Chinese has steadily risen, from 65 in 2000 to 94 in 2007. The Pentagon has identified about 5,000 service members who speak Chinese in 2007, up from just 1,400 in 2000.

The White House and Congress have finally agreed to spend more than $100 million on the National Security Language Initiative. The Pentagon also plans to spend $750 million over five years to increase foreign language proficiency in the armed forces.

The dual immersion programs at the Glenwood Elementary School in Chapel Hill, North Carolina has its pupils – half native Chinese, half native English speakers – do their lessons in both languages. The program is indicative of one of the fastest-growing curriculum trends in U.S. schools. Chinese language, in addition to Chinese food.

Why isn't every school district and state university system doing the same? Today there are more than 800 American colleges that have Chinese language programs.

The number of students nationwide who are learning Chinese is still relatively small, about 24,000, most of them in elementary and high schools. That compares with 3 million or so who study Spanish, the most popular language in America's schools. Number two is French, with about 1 million students. A number of urban school districts have launched Chinese language programs, including Chicago, Philadelphia, Houston and Boston. The most ambitious program is in Chicago. It was started in 1999, and there are more than 5,000 students, virtually all of them native English speakers, studying Chinese in 17 elementary and 10 high schools.

The biggest obstacle to expanding Chinese instruction in U.S. schools is finding qualified teachers. The problem is complicated by the federal No

Child Left Behind legislation, which requires all teachers to be certified. Most states don't have a language certification program and need to get one started.

The number of students in two and four-year college courses studying Chinese rose by 20 percent between 1998 and 2002, to slightly more than 33,000. "Now that the pipeline is active at the high school level, we expect many more students to be enrolling in advanced courses," said Rosemary Feal, executive director of the Modern Language Association. More American families also are employing Chinese nannies so their children grow up speaking Chinese.

The Senate Foreign Relations Committee is considering a proposal to allocate $1.3 billion to boost Chinese language and culture classes in secondary schools. Whats to consider? China is assisting by establishing Chinese cultural centers under a program called Confucius Institute, to teach Americans, and foreigners worldwide. By year-end 2006, there were 11 such institutes in America – the latest at the University of Oklahoma – and 80 worldwide in 36 countries. China started to push Mandarin as a second language worldwide in 1987, but the scheme did not really take off until 2004. Confucius Institutes take the form of a joint venture, with venues and basic hardware provided by local partners.

The institute teams up with local partners, taking space in their buildings or getting the host government to pay for their housing. Instead of sending teachers who will instruct foreigners directly, the institute sends teacher-trainers who can upgrade the skills of local Chinese teachers.

The Chinese strategy is smart. Beijing has figured that promoting education and language as tools for understanding is the most effective way to spread its influence far and wide. It learned the hard way that gunboats frighten people into temporary submission, but a shared language can make them friends.

China's Ministry of Education hopes to teach 100 million foreigners to speak Mandarin by 2010. Some estimates say that number has already been achieved.

Confucius was an educator, but also represents peace and harmony, values that China insistently proclaims, hoping to disarm fears about its rapid rise. Confucius also taught principles of filial piety and social obligation, which tend to turn Americans white.

Confucius revolutionized education in China 2,500 years ago by making it accessible to commoners. There are more than 30 million commoners learning Chinese worldwide at his namesake institutions, according to the Ministry of Education.

More than 90,000 foreign students go to China each year to study Chinese, and another 30 million people around the world study the language as well. The Chinese government has sent language teachers to nearly 300 schools in 70 countries.

Chinese language or culture-related classes are taught in more than 2,500 colleges and universities in 100 countries.

Classes in American schools should be taught in English, with Chinese or Spanish as a required second language. It would then be up to each family and community to decide how to teach their children their mother tongue. Speaking it regularly at home and at family functions is helpful and should be encouraged. It would help if the bilingual families in America were also biliterate.

Learning a second language should also be mandatory in all U.S. high schools. If the rest of the world is mandated to learn American, shouldn't U.S. high schools require Mandarin, Spanish or Arabic as a mandatory second language required for graduation? The hard part is that classroom teaching of languages to ambivalent children does not have a high success rate and never did. Better off having them practice in Chinatown or the barrio.

Cities should have schools that specialize in all the different major cultures. New York has schools specializing in Asian Culture, Chinese language and is opening one that centers on Latin American culture and an Arabic themed school. The Khalil Gibran International Academy is named after the Lebanese-American Christian poet who promoted peace. It would be one of a few schools in the U.S. that incorporate the Arabic culture and language.

The shortage of qualified bilingual Arab speakers who can interpret in Iraq for the coalition forces, not just the language, but the cultural, religious and political subtleties, brought home how unprepared America is to deal in non-English-speaking countries. During World War II, America had crash language programs in Japanese and German that were noted for their efficiency and high rate of success. Qualified speakers were heavily recruited so that America was ready when the occupation of Japan started. Why didn't this happen before America went to war in Iraq? U.S. military language specialists should have been canvassing colleges and companies looking for young Americans with qualified backgrounds and language skills. Children of missionaries, oil company executives and Arab majors would have been an obvious initial pool.

After the Soviets launched Sputnik in October 1957, America went on a crash course in Russian in all universities. The National Defense Education Act focused on harnessing brain power rather than weaponry for the Cold War. As a result, federal money stimulated the study of mathematics, science and Russian. The result was that 30,000 or more American university students took Russian courses each year. Shouldn't America be doing the same with Arabic after 9/11? Why is it that four years after 9/11, Congress and the Bush administration have failed to support and endow courses in the languages of the Muslim world?

Of the more than 1.8 million graduates of American colleges and universities in 2003, only 22 took degrees in Arabic, according to Department of Education statistics. Chances are they won't know or appreciate their value or know how to charge a proper fee for their services. "Compared to the Cold War, we're not even at the level of zero," said Dan E. Davidson, the president of the American Councils for International Education in Washington and a professor of Russian at Bryn Mawr College in Pennsylvania. "We're at minus one." Why? Isn't it time *We the Maids* sweep in the legislation necessary to understand our Arab and Muslim adversaries? The ruling class of Iran, potentially the most powerful country in the Middle and Near East – with an influence that can reach from the Black Sea to the Chinese border – speaks Farsi. They get really upset when Americans call them Arabs. Why isn't Farsi taught in more universities in America?

One of the many major problems that led to 9/11 was that the FBI had a backlog of thousands of hours of audiotape and thousands of pages of written material in Arabic and Central Asian languages waiting for translation. The State Department had to call back from retirement a diplomat fluent in Arabic to appear on the Al Jazeera cable network. A report in early 2002 by the General Accounting Office confirmed that shortages of linguists had "hindered U.S. military, law enforcement, intelligence, counterterrorism and diplomatic efforts."

The British, the U.S. lapdog in the invasion of "rubble" states, have clearly been infected by this insularity. The once highly prestigious departments of Middle Eastern and Chinese studies at the University of Durham have been closed.

Why aren't taxpayer dollars earmarked for education being applied to what is best for our children and global community in the 21st century?

The ideals of the French Revolution, ideals that brought France to America's side in its war of independence against Britain, and not the French language, should be both America's and France's focus in the 21st century. Otherwise America and France will see the fundamental ideals on which each republic was built erode while they remain hopelessly devoted to a beautiful language imbedded in literature and the arts. Both countries have to confront racist rightists by teaching their children the dominant languages, cultures and religions of the 21st century so that they can better communicate and understand each other. The alternative is that America and France will follow in the footsteps of Rome. God forbid. They'll both get Popes.

Healthy Body and Mind

"We must get back to building our children the way we know how rather than building jails across America," former Secretary of State Colin Powell told delegates at the 2000 Republican Convention. "Our children are not the problem. It is us that is the problem."

The quality of education our children receive also depends on the safety of their learning environment. Safety from guns. Safety from unhealthy diets. Safety from abusive parents. Children die and suffer unnecessarily. Those who survive are traumatized forever.

Lisa Sullivan, a community activist and founder and president of Listen, says: "It's about education. A lot of our children are not getting fed. They are not being nurtured. The character, the talent, it's not being developed. And where are they supposed to get it? I compare young people in poor communities to computers with no software. They don't have anything in them that is going to help them make effective decisions or figure out who and what they want to be and aspire to. They've got junk thrown at them." Not just junk food but junk TV.

Eight million students in 12,000 classrooms watch Channel One, an in-school news and advertising program every day – and we were talking earlier about literacy and math skills? You do not get to read and add up through moving pictures. We are no challenge to the Chinese if it's the Cookie Monster taking our children from 1 to 10. Michael Moore in his book, *Stupid White Men*, points out that "kids are spending the equivalent of six full school days a year watching Channel One in almost 40 percent of U.S. middle and high schools. Instructional time lost to the ads alone? One entire day per year. That translates into an annual cost to taxpayers of more than $1.8 billion."

A meaningful education starts on full stomachs filled with nutritious food. The resources allocated to school meal programs have to be wisely and nutritiously invested in our students. They are our future human capital.

The U.S. Department of Agriculture's school lunch programs were established after World War II to stave off health and learning problems caused by inadequate nutrition. Through these and other government-funded programs, school districts are reimbursed for providing low-income children with free or reduced-price meals, which also are supposed to help children stay healthy. Why aren't all schools providing these meals?

Unfortunately, legislators and school officials are not focused on the eating-learning link. Far too many children are either arriving at school hungry, or are not eating healthy meals. For some children, especially low-income children, both problems exist. Jesus and Muhammad both spoke of feeding the bodily man before handling the spiritual.

Despite the continuing need to improve children's health through school meals, a decline in state education funding has forced many school district food services officials to put revenue generation above child nutrition. Cash-strapped administrators have turned to corporations such as Pizza Hut, Coca-Cola and McDonald's to generate revenue. Shortage of money is not an excuse for everything, especially an unhealthful education.

When children are not offered healthy choices, it's not surprising that both learning and health suffer. Preliminary findings from a 2000 UCLA School of Public health survey of students at 14 low-income schools in the Los Angeles Unified School District indicate that more than 50 percent of the children were obese or overweight. These findings reflect both the wrong kind of food as well as a lack of physical activity.

All legislatures and governing school bodies should study a number of inno-vative programs in America, many initiated by parents and school officials, for clues on how to improve things.

At McKinley Elementary School in Santa Monica, California, where about 50 percent of the students are from low-income families, children can choose a salad bar lunch of seasonal fruits and vegetables, low-fat legumes, meats, cheeses, breads, pastas and milk. The school district buys the salad-bar food from regional farmers in partnership with local farmers markets.

The Occidental College Community Food Security Project, which co-spon-sors the program, found that a farmers market salad-bar meal was actually less expensive than a typical hot meal composed of a hamburger, pizza, hot dog or other processed item. The project does require more labor at the school sites to prepare the fresh fruits and vegetables. And that has brought parents back into the cafeterias, as volunteers or paid staff. Parents and students help decide what items are offered at the salad bar and how they are pre-pared so that meals will be appealing to the children. Heeding their sugges-tions has led to a significant increase in the number of children choosing to eat a salad-bar meal. Thus through a cost-effective program in which com-munity involvement is central, child nutrition is improved.

One fourth-grader from 59th Street Elementary School in Los Angeles said after tasting food from the farmers market: "If we had this food in our school, I'd eat vegetables every day. And that would be good." Out of the mouths of babes ...

Most soft drinks will be banished from almost every U.S. primary and secondary school by 2009-10.

Speaking of food, ever wonder why the meat of cattle is called beef, and that of pigs called pork, while chicken is just plain chicken? It is believed the differentiation between beef and cow, and between pork and pig resulted from the Norman conquest of England in 1066. The conquerors came from the Normandy region of what is modern-day France and hence spoke Norman French – largely descended from Latin – as their native tongue. Under the rule of William the Conqueror and his successors, the language of the English court and the aristocracy became Norman French. The country's new elite would refer to the meat of cattle using the word *buef*, meaning ox or cow. Similarly, the gentry would refer to pig flesh using the Norman French word *porc*, meaning pig and *moton* for sheep. The English word chicken has continued to be used to refer to the flesh of the bird because chickens have always been available as food to the lower classes because they are less costly to raise and keep than cattle, pigs or sheep.

Texas is also reaching beyond the vending machines, demanding that cafeterias switch to lower-fat ways of cooking, dramatically cut back transfats and prohibit teachers from handing out candy for good behavior. Cafeterias also must offer more fruits and vegetables – fresh, whenever possible.

Nutrition is important, not only for learning, but living. Discussing the subject with Alex Berman, whom I've known since he was born to Kris and Jake, really puts the importance of nutrition into 21st-century perspective. Alex is really into fresh vegetables, like, real fresh – alive. Live food is as fresh and healthy as it gets. I was introduced to it by Alex after he was diagnosed with Hodgkin's disease, a lymphoma, at the age of 21. He went through every experimental, latest of the best Western cancer treatments at Memorial Sloan-Kettering Cancer Center in New York, only to be told that his form of the disease, having resisted all efforts, was not curable at this point in time.

Alex, a bright geopolitical musician, grew up in New York and Connecticut, then went to Sarah Lawrence to study politics, theatre, music and women. "I can't believe the crap people eat and what corporate America sells," Alex said as we ordered an Indian vegetarian meal in the East Village. "The only thing that has kept me alive the last five years is getting rid of all the crap I've been fed, food, school – education, what a laugh – politics, values. It's all bullshit. It almost killed me." It's not just killing him. It's killing off his generation, because they have bought into the program. It's up to him and his peers to wake up the world and its self-destructive ways before it is too late. "Yeah, lets drink to it," Alex said as we hoisted our lassis – a healthy, non-alcoholic Indian drink.

Physical activities, like live food, have to be increased in the New World Order to counterbalance the number of hours children now spend at their computers. Physical education classes should start early. Maybe that will also do away with teenagers being embarrassed to take showers in high school, a topic I addressed at length in *Custom Maid Spin*.

Wise Investment

Elementary teacher training programs could pay great dividends for students if the teachers actually learn how to teach reading and math fundamentals. They need research-based training that is tied to rigorous academic standards linked to new textbooks and aligned with new standardized tests. Anything less would be a colossal waste of public money. Commitment to public education will not come cheaply. But if it's done wisely, it won't be as expensive as the neglect of decades. The cost will pale next to the better lives that will result.

The proposed combined budgets for the Pentagon over the first five years of the new millennium, not taking into account the budget for the war being waged in Iraq, is $1.6 trillion. The amount the General Accounting Office says is needed to renovate and upgrade every school in America is $112 billion. Today, the percentage of all school budgets coming from the federal government is five to six percent, the rest is from state and local governments. Isn't it time the federal government spent more on education?

If we decided not to build the rest of the F-22 fighter jets the Air Force asked for back during the Cold War, that money – $45 billion – would fully fund the Head Start preschool program for every child in America who needed it for the next six years and we wouldn't waste more money on planes zapping rock formations in the hunt for Osama bin Laden. The F-22s can be deferred. Head Start is the more than 40-year-old federal program for preschool children whose parents have below-poverty incomes. The landmark Perry Preschool Study tracked a group of poverty-level African-American children from when they attended pre-kindergarden in Ypsilant, Michigan, in the early 1960s until they were well into middle age. The findings are astonishing: a $17 return to the individual and society for every dollar spent on their early education. Those who went to Perry were considerably more likely than children who didn't attend preschool to have graduated from high school and married and they were significantly less likely to have gone to prison multiple times or to have been on welfare. They're earning an average of $30,800 a year. That's 25 percent more than similar children who lacked the preschool experience – enough of a difference to lift them above the poverty line.

All children are ready and eager to learn. America has to start spending more on education – starting with preschool. The spending of tax dollars to educate 3-and 4-year old preschoolers is a wise investment. A study released in December 2005 by the National Institute for Early Education Research, the leading think tank in the field, found that children who attended state-sponsored preschools in five states scored 31 percent higher on vocabulary tests than a similar group of youngsters who didn't participate – the equivalent of three months of learning. On tests of early math skills, the state preschoolers outscored their peers by 41 percent. A similar study of state pre-kindergarten classes in Tulsa, Oklahoma, showed essentially the same result.

A similar evaluation of Head Start differed from state preschools in two critical ways. The state initiatives place greater emphasis on preparing children for a kindergarten experience that stresses reading and arithmetic. And though most state preschool teachers have bachelor's degrees, many with an emphasis on early childhood education, fewer than a third of Head Start teachers have graduated from college.

New Fuel Race

America is backpeddling on the secondary and university educational and scientific front. The generation of scientists, engineers and mathematicians who were spurred to get advanced degrees by the 1957 Soviet launch of

Sputnik and the challenge by President John F. Kennedy to put a man on the moon is retiring – with no replacements in sight to lead America into the global frontiers of the 21st century. America must galvanize its students around a vision of educational excellence – a beacon of educational leadership to meet our most pressing global challenge – a cost-effective substitute for oil.

When did the Soviet Union collapse? When did reform take off in Iran? When did the Israeli-Palestinian Oslo peace process begin? When did economic reform become a hot topic in the Arab world? In the late 1980s and early 1990s. And what was also happening then? Oil prices were collapsing. In November 1985, oil was $30 a barrel. By July 1986, oil had fallen to $10 a barrel, and it did not climb back to $20 until April 1989. "Everyone thinks Ronald Reagan brought down the Soviets," said noted oil economist Philip Verleger. "That is wrong. It was the collapse of their oil rents." It's no accident that the 1990s was the decade of falling oil prices and falling walls.

Energy independence should be America's moon shot to dry up revenues for terrorism and force Iran, Saudi Arabia and other oil producers to take the path of reform – which they will never do as long as a barrel of oil costs more than $45. This can be the magnet to inspire students of all ages to contribute to the war on terrorism and global warming by becoming scientists, engineers and mathematicians. To paraphrase New York Times columnist Thomas L. Friedman, who first made this suggestion in one of his 2005 columns, "Summoning all our energies and skills to produce a 21st-century fuel is America's opportunity to be both Nixon to China and JFK to the moon – in one move."

Universal Education
There are more than 700 million illiterate people in the world – one- fifth of humanity – and of the other 6.6 billion, nobody's writing much that's worth reading anyway. A better and healthier world starts with education. Let's look at an $82 billion emergency supplemental bill approved by Congress in the summer of 2005 to finance military operations in Iraq and Afghanistan. Joel Cohen, a professor of populations at Rockefeller University and Columbia University in New York, and David Bloom, a professor of economics and demography at the Harvard School of Public Health, were outraged. They co-wrote an editorial opinion *Peace through education for all*, in

July 2005, published in the *South China Morning Post* that said: "That is more money than is needed on a yearly basis to permit every child in the world to receive, within one decade, both primary and secondary education. Clearly, the question is not whether universal education is affordable, but whether America and the world can afford to neglect the political, economic, social and health benefits of educating the roughly 380 million children around the globe who currently do not attend school. Education, no less than military might, is a security imperative. It helps the world – both individuals and societies – to escape the consequences of widespread poverty, rapid population growth, environmental problems and social injustices."

UNESCO's International Institute for Educational Planning (IIEP) is a think tank that provides training to national governments' education bureaucrats and research to achieve the U.N. goal set at the 2000 World Education Forum in Dakar, Senegal, to provide every child in the world with access to quality primary education by 2015. It is headed by Mark Bray, the former University of Hong Kong dean of education who was heavily involved in education policy-making as an advisor to the governments of Azerbaijan, Cambodia and others.

The primary goal of IIEP is to abolish primary school fees in developing countries around the world.

Free education has resulted in millions of impoverished African and Asian children being enrolled in schools. The huge influx of children has overwhelmed understaffed and ill-equipped facilities. Teacher-student ratios have been wildly upset and prospects for student advancement remain uncertain at best and dim at worst. Sub-Saharan Africa faces the greatest challenge. It will need to raise its current stock of teachers by 68 percent – from 2.4 million to 4 million – by 2015 in order to provide universal primary education. Some schools with 3,000 children only have four teachers.

In the Philippines, teachers routinely struggle to house the students, cramming them into every available space, including corridors, bathrooms and garages. The once-proud Philippine education system in the former U.S. colony is failing students badly. Public schools lack teachers, textbooks and schools. Many teachers leave to work overseas as maids because they can make more money than teaching in the Philippines. The dropout rate in secondary schools rose to 15.8 percent in 2005-06 from 8.5 percent in 2000-01. Armando Ducat, the day-care center owner who took hostage a busload of his 5-to 7-year-old students in Manila in March 2007, had a 10-hour stand-off with police while he protested the horrible condition of education, corruption and child poverty in the Philippines. He demanded politicians honor their promises to provide free education and housing for the poor. Jose Rizal, the founding father of the Philippines, said: "Education is the key to national salvation." He started his drive for Philippine independence from Spain in Hong Kong.

The world's "youngest children have been neglected" by a global lack of investment in early-childhood education, according to U.N. studies. Ten percent of the world's children, some 77 million, are still not attending school.

While developed countries now record nearly a 70 percent enrollment rate in early-childhood education, which includes day care and preschool, rates in Sub-Saharan Africa and Arab countries are just over 10 percent.

John Wood, a former Microsoft executive who quit a promising career in 1999 at the ripe old age of 35, decided to dedicate his time, money and business contacts to building schools and libraries for underprivileged children in the developing world. His organization, Room to Read, has opened 2,300 libraries and 140 schools throughout Asia. It is constructing another 60 schools and has donated 1.2 million books and given scholarships to 1,750 girls who otherwise would have received no schooling. I met John at the Foreign Correspondents' Club in Hong Kong in January 2006, where he came to drum up interest and cash for Room to Read. The Hong Kong chapter is the number one fund-raising support group, having raised more than $1 million. "People don't necessarily want to give money to a beggar. They realize that education is also long-term and they know that if you cannot give a kid an education, they cannot become self-sufficient," said Wood.

He realized that education is the vital component in pulling people out of the poverty cycle, and cites how his own education was key to his success. His grandfather didn't go to university and his father was the first in his family to do so, followed by John and his sister. "So in my own family, over the generations we could see that we were rising up and using education as a lever," he said. His hometown has one of the 3,000 public libraries opened by industrialist and philanthropist Andrew Carnegie in the late 1800s and early 1900s throughout the U.S. and Europe.

Today, more than ever, education and formal skills dictate how our local and global communities will fare in the new economy. Schooling is more than ever the key to ending racism, religious misunderstanding – and the key to a livelihood. Children who lack schooling are marginalized to the detriment of all. All our children's education must come first in the 21st-century – for all humanity to survive.

Wake Up Kamikaze

Students at New York's Stuyvesant High School in the shadow of the World Trade Center – like students across America – learned overnight the horror of terrorism and war. Hopefully they will appreciate what their fellow students in war zones and impoverished developing countries have been experiencing for decades, or in some cases, centuries – especially in Africa, where children to this very day are forced to take up arms and kill. Fireballs roaring, people leaping to their deaths, the smell of death and destruction.

The students reflected the millions of their fellow Americans. They expressed disbelief at the rapid evaporation of their world, and were shocked not by a morning radio jock, but a 21st-century kamikaze reality tune-in call. One *We the Apathetic Parents* had not prepared them for.

For almost 100 years, Stuyvesant has drawn from among New York's smartest students. Background, influence and income do not matter. The only criterion for admission is one grinding, two-and-a-half-hour entrance exam, and the result has long been a student body that ranks tops in the nation. Year after year, Stuyvesant has produced about 70 National Merit scholars out of a senior class of 700. Nevertheless, these brightest Americans, like the rest of their countrymen, were unprepared. Can we allow this to continue in the 21st century?

Shouldn't the lessons of 9/11 be taught in all schools? Isn't it time *We the Apathetic Maids* swept in a curriculum that teaches our children the truth about America, its heritage, culture and empire? Isn't it time we end the ignorance perpetuated by religious leaders as knowledge? Isn't it time teachers explained to bright Stuyvesant classes that people their president calls terrorists are immensely popular with millions of people thousands of miles away – and have them wonder why?

The 1,776-foot Freedom Tower that will rise at the northwest corner of the World Trade Center complex – the tallest building in America – will be a "beacon of light" for all students worldwide.

Stuyvesant High is a few blocks from where the slave auction blocks operated in Lower Manhattan when the republic was founded and near to Federal Hall, where George Washington was inaugurated president in 1789, a caustic reminder that America has to reinvent itself.

The Federal Republic
George Washington, like most wealthy people of his time, owned slaves. During British rule, about 40 percent of New York City's residents owned at least one slave. Thousands of slaves throughout the 13 American colonies rallied to the Britiish lines during the revolutionary war because they believed that is where freedom lay. Not only slaves, but freed men too. They were hunted down by the Revolutionary victors.

The Continental Congress was ambiguous about blacks, even though many African-Americans had died for the cause. In 1776, Washington was in dire need of soldiers. Congress told him he could keep the freed blacks he already had, but he could not recruit any more. Slaves were to be excluded completely. Whites in the North and South had issues with blacks fighting on their side. New Hampshire, for instance, excluded "lunatics, idiots and Negroes" from its militias. On the other hand, the British offered unambiguous freedom. Any wonder so many blacks fought to keep America British?

After the British lost the war, Americans demanded their slaves back. To their credit, the British honored their commitment and evacuated the black men, women and children who had supported Britain, together with the white loyalists, to Canada. Not that they found the promised land in Canada – a conclusion many Canadians agree with to this day. The British went even further and resettled many of them back on the African continent in Sierra Leone, where their descendants live today.

America's Founding Fathers knew full well the double standard embedded in the liberty they preached. Patrick ' give-me-liberty-or-give-me-death" Henry admitted that he might be against holding slaves in principle, but "I'm drawn along by the general inconvenience of living without them."

Slavery was no more benign in New York than the South. Slaves helped build the wall on Wall Street, and were sold there. Slaves also built the first City Hall and Trinity Church. Slavery was the lifeline for hundreds of city businesses. At one time, 20 percent of New Yorkers were slaves. That's one in five people. Slavery lasted in New York until 1827, longer than in any other Northern state, except New Jersey. Clearly, schools in America are failing to teach students about the history of slavery and its contribution to the birth and growth of the republic – and the fact it still exists today in America and many other countries. There are as many as 27 million slaves worldwide today. Sex slaves, domestic-servitude slaves and bonded-labor slaves are the three dominant categories.

Education, not litigation for compensation by descendants of slaves is the smart way to redress the wrongs of the past. The Chicago-based 7th U.S. Circuit Court of Appeal rejected a lawsuit that consolidated 10 suits filed around the U.S. by slave descendants against JP Morgan Chase, Aetna, Bank of America and other U.S. household names, which allegedly profited from slavery by making loans to slaveholders to buy slaves while others were paid to insure and transport them. The court ruled that statutes of limitation could be extended in some cases but not for acts committed a century ago. Slavery was abolished in America in 1855. But the court kept alive a slender portion of the lawsuit, claiming that major U.S. corporations may be guilty of consumer fraud if they hid past ties to slavery from their customers. Isn't the U.S. Department of Education guilty of education fraud for not teaching the history of slavery in U.S. schools?

When Bill Cosby took to the podium in Washington in 2004 and criticized inner-city parents for doing too little to educate their children, I applauded. He was right when he said those parents were spending too much on expensive sneakers and not enough on books. My only issue was that his comments were limited to African-Americans. They should apply to all Americans. If parents and children spent as much time talking about history, civics or geography as they do about sneakers, jeans and music, America would be kicking sweet geopolitical butt.

America and its model of government is a fusion of the Native American form of confederacy and the ideas of the European Enlightenment. A home-grown hybrid of native democracy fused with the best that European history had to offer to prevent tyranny. I wonder if anyone has bothered to point this out to Native Americans. It would be one of the very few things that has been done for their self-esteem in a long time.

There is widespread misperception in America, and the world for that matter, that democracy is a peculiarly Western European system that is not in tune with the foundational values of Asia, Africa or the Arab world. The ancestry of democracy goes back much further than the narrowly defined European practice. Tribute must, of course, be paid to the powerful role that modern Western thinking linked with European enlightenment played in the devel-opment of liberal and democratic ideas. But the roots of these ideas can be found in Asia and Africa.

The belief that democracy is a quintessentially "Western" practice probably is rooted in the practice of voting in ancient Greece, especially in Athens. But such thinking is surely a leap into confusion. The problem here is the partitioning of the world into largely racial categories in which ancient Greece is seen as an integral and exclusive part of an identifiable "European" tradition. From this classificatory perspective, no great difference is per-ceived in considering the descendants of, say, Goths and Visigoths as proper inheritors of the Greek tradition.

To Europeans, "they are all Europeans," while there is a reluctance to admit to the Greek intellectual links with ancient Egyptians, Iranians and Indians, despite the fact that the ancient Greeks showed a preference to talking and interacting with them rather than the ancient Visigoths. The "An-cient World," as its pocket description would have it, had a great deal more to do with the hot and grubby Middle and Near East than it had to do with what we perceive as cool, neat Europe. Pure political and religious spin.

While public reasoning flourished in ancient Greece, it did so in several other ancient civilizations as well. For example, some of the earliest open general meetings aimed specifically at settling disputes took place in India, in the sixth century BC onward, in the so-called Buddhist "councils," where adherents of different points of view gathered to argue their differences.

Emperor Ashoka, who hosted the largest of these councils in the capital city of Pataliputra – now Patna – in the third century BC also tried to codify and promote what must have been among the earliest formulations of rules for public discussion – a primitive version of the 19th-century Robert's Rules of Order. Similarly, the so-called "constitution of 17 Articles," produced by the Buddhist Prince Shotoku in Japan in 604, insisted, much in the spirit of the Magna Carta six centuries later: "Decisions on important matters should not be made by one person alone. They should be discussed with many." This doesn't mean the largest number of people that can be squeezed under secrecy oaths into the West Wing.

There is a considerable history of the cultivation of public reasoning, with good use of tolerance of heterodoxy, also in the Muslim countries, including in the Arab world. When Maimonides, the Jewish philosopher, was forced to emigrate from an intolerant Europe in the 12th century, he found refuge in the Arab world and was given an influential position in the court of Emperor Saladin in Cairo. To take another example, when at the turn of the 16th century, the heretic Giordano Bruno was burned at the stake in Rome during the Inquisition, Akbar the great Moghul emperor of India – who was born a Muslim and died a Muslim – had just finished his project of legally codifying minority rights, including religious freedom for all.

Akbar also set up in Agra perhaps the earliest multi-religious discussion groups, and there were regular meetings in the 1590s of Hindus, Muslims, Christians, Jains, Jews, Parsees and even atheists, to discuss where and why they differed, and how they could live together – a practice Native Americans brought with them from Asia to America.

Democracy is the opportunity of participatory reasoning and public decision making – a "government by discussion."

In 1744, Benjamin Franklin was printing texts of Indian treaties, including the words of Canassatego, the chief of the Iroquois nation. Canassatego recommended the federal system practiced by the Iroquois as a model the British colonists should adopt. In the early 1750s, Franklin observed the Iroquois Grand Council at Onondaga. The system worked as a federal republic governed by local and national councils, which selected leaders by clan-based consensus. The Grand Council operated as a one-house legislature. In 1754,

Franklin presented his Albany Plan for a colonial union, advocating a federal system and a one-chamber legislature. Iroquois leaders were invited to Philadelphia to observe debates over the Declaration of Independence in 1775.

Native Americans, like other clan-based societies from Asia, had forms of government based on representation, peaceful negotiation and consensus. The same was true for 18th-century Europe, which had evolved from countries with warring clans and tribes. In Philadelphia, the Founding Fathers debated ideas about governance, freedom and liberty derived from ancient societies, native clans and modern Europe. They emerged with the U.S. Constitution, a written constitution unlike the unwritten Ancient Constitution of England.

American schools should teach Native American history, as it is an integral part of America. Only a handful of states – Montana, New Mexico, Washington and Wisconsin – mandate the teaching of Native American history. America's knowledge of its Native American history would help heal many of the wounds and misunderstandings between Native Americans and others. Students would learn that Native Americans' rights to hunt, fish and establish casinos on their sovereign reservations were legally negotiated in exchange for the land they had to give up, land that now makes up America. Tracing how native Americans ended up with casinos, the ultimate in hunter-gathering, would be a sparkling education in how the Indian has fared under the white man.

The U.S. Constitution, like America itself, was influenced by the intellectual and multi-civilizational ideas and definitions of liberty. It makes no reference to Christianity or God. America's roots are as diverse as its branches, making America the unique multiracial and multicultural country it is.

Dollar Value

One of America's finest creations is the dollar. Yet most Americans don't know anything about their dollar bill. Take out a one-dollar bill. The bill you are looking at first came off the presses in 1957 in its present design. This so-called "paper money" is in fact a cotton and linen blend, with red and blue minute silk fibers running through it. It is actually material. We've all washed it without it falling apart. A special blend of ink is used; the formula we will never know.

It is overprinted with symbols and then it is starched to make it water resistant and pressed to give it that nice crisp look. Maybe it is time for America to look at the plastic money used by some other governments who have seen counterfeit currency cases decline by more than 60 percent as a result.

If you look on the front of the one-dollar bill, you will see the seal of the United States Treasury. In the upper part of the seal, you will see the scales for a balanced budget. In the center you have a carpenter's square, a tool used for an even cut. Underneath is the key to the U.S. Treasury. That is all pretty easy to figure out. But the back of the dollar bill is a little more interesting.

First, notice the two circles. Both circles, together, comprise the Great Seal of the United States. The first Continental Congress, meeting in Philadelphia in 1774, requested that Benjamin Franklin and a group of men, including Thomas Jefferson and John Adams, come up with a seal. It took them six years to accomplish this task and another two to get it approved.

Now look at the pyramid. Notice that the face is lighted, and the Pyramid casts a shadow that represents undiscovered lands to the west. The pyramid is uncapped, signifying that the country was not close to being finished. Inside the capstone is an all-seeing eye, an ancient symbol of divinity. It was Franklin's belief that one man couldn't do it alone, but a group of men, with the help of God, could do anything.

The motto "IN GOD WE TRUST" was placed on the currency during the Cold War by President Eisenhower, to show the godless communist Russians and Chinese that America was a God-fearing country. The Latin above the pyramid, ANNUIT COEPTIS, means "God has favored our undertaking." The Latin below the pyramid, NOVUS ORDO SECLORUM means, "A new order has begun." At the base of the pyramid is the Roman numeral for 1776. The seal in the right-hand circle appears in all U.S. paper currency. It is also on the National Cemetery at Arlington and on the Parade of Flags Walkway at the National Cemetery in Bushnell, Florida, and is the centerpiece of most heroes' monuments.

Slightly modified, it is also the seal of the president of the United States, and it is always visible whenever he speaks, yet very few People know what the symbol means. The bald eagle was selected as a symbol for victory for two reasons: First, it is not afraid of a storm; it is strong and smart enough to soar above it. Secondly, it wears no material crown. America had just broken from the king of England. Also note that the shield is unsupported. This country can now stand on its own. At the top of the shield there is a white bar signifying Congress, a unifying factor. We were coming together as one nation.

In the eagle's beak are the words, "E PLURIBUS UNUM," meaning "one nation from many people." Above the eagle, there are 13 stars, representing the 13 original colonies, and any clouds of misunderstanding rolling away. Again, we were coming together as one. Notice that the eagle holds an olive branch and arrows in its talons. This country wants peace, but will never be afraid to fight to preserve peace. The eagle always wants to face the olive branch, but in time of war, his gaze turns toward the arrows.

They say that the number 13 is unlucky. This is almost a universal belief. You rarely see a room numbered 13, or public buildings with a 13th floor. But think about this:

13 original colonies.
13 signers of the Declaration of Independence.
13 stripes on our flag.
13 steps on the pyramid.
13 letters in the Latin above.
13 letters in "E Pluribus Unum."
13 stars above the eagle.
13 bars on the shield.
13 leaves on the olive branch.
13 fruits.
13 arrows.

And, for minorities, there is the 13th Amendment. How come so few people are ignorant of these basic historic facts?

Minds are like parachutes. They only function when open. From 1940 until the dawn of the 21st century, the U.S. dollar has been the primary universal currency. In 1940, much of the gold in the world was deposited in Fort Knox by governments terrified that Adolf Hitler would win the Second World War. When it became clear in 1944 that the Allies would prevail, U.S. leaders launched a number of conferences on postwar planning. One of them was the Bretton Woods Conference. Seven hundred and thirty delegates attended from 44 countries.

The two main protagonists were the Allied leaders America and Britain. America made the U.S. dollar the dominant currency that decided the value of other countries' currencies because the trove of gold in Fort Knox gave America immense power to bend the recalcitrant countries to Uncle Sam's will.

A global currency must have three strengths to be accepted all over the world. Most important is that it always delivers the economic values expressed on coin, paper and now electronic numbers. Second, a global super-currency must be prevalent enough to finance capital anywhere and anytime. And third, it must be a safe haven. The fourth unofficial rule is that all notes of all denominations must be the same color so they won't be confused with anybody else's. Just kidding.

The unraveling of the American super-dollar began during the Vietnam War. In March 1968, then-President Lyndon Johnson announced that he was not going to run for reelection. The bulk of his speech was not about the war, but about the gold crisis. And in 1971, President Richard Nixon announced he would cut the link between the U.S. dollar and gold. Nixon made the right decision and in the same year accepted an invitation to visit China and embrace it as a geopolitical partner to contain the U.S.S.R.

The Afghanistan and Iraq wars have accelerated the decline of the dollar. Hurricane Katrina sealed its fate when the government announced it would rebuild New Orleans without taxing Americans. The only way that could be done was to become more dependent on foreign governments buying U.S. treasury bonds. While the dollar has been declining in value, the Chinese yuan, like China itself, has been quietly growing as a global currency that America must embrace and learn to live with in the 21st century.

Moral Values

"I believe that God wants everybody to be free. That's what I believe. And that's been part of my foreign policy," President Bush said in the last debate of the 2004 presidential election. Religion and "moral values" were the dominant themes of the 2004 presidential campaign. Not terrorism, not Iraq and not the economy. A country founded by Christians that made a conscious effort to separate church and state, forbidding the word "God" in any of the nation's founding documents, is today a country politically dominated by religion.

Nearly 85 percent of Americans say they consider religion important. Even among Democrats, 60 percent tell pollsters they pray each day. What they don't tell pollsters and what might be truly alarming is what they pray for. By no coincidence, the last two Democrats to win the presidency – Jimmy Carter and Bill Clinton – were from the religious South and comfortable with Christian spirituality.

What is significant about the religious conservative shift in America is that the traditionally more politically tolerant Protestants, who are the foundation stone of the republic, are now being eclipsed by less-tolerant conservative believers and are no longer the majority religion in America. The University of Chicago's National Opinion Research Center has reported that the proportion of adult Americans calling themselves Protestants, a steady 63 percent for decades, dropped to 52 percent from 1993 to 2002. The study's authors also projected that "perhaps as early as this year [2004] the country will for the first time no longer have a Protestant majority." John Jay wrote in the "Federalist Papers" that America was "united by a common religion." America no longer is.

The self-appointed guardians of America's moral values want to control all aspects of morality, including the movies we see on television. Even Academy Award winner "Saving Private Ryan" couldn't be saved from the Moral Squad because of its use of vulgar language by soldiers under fire. The actions of these self-appointed guardians of morality mimic those of the Taliban and the religious police in Saudi Arabia. Their actions are not only un-American, but probably unconstitutional. There is no question they violate the principals of the Founding Fathers.

A study of 44 nations released in 2003 by the Pew Research Center showed that on attachment to religious values, Americans were markedly different from people in other developed countries. Rather than being on a par with Western Europeans, they were ranked with Saudi Arabians and Nigerians. Is it any wonder America's children are also joining the bottom rungs of the undeveloped world in international math and science subjects? Isn't it time *We the Maids* sweep in the reforms needed to get America back into the leading ranks of the developed world?

Religious Education

Part of the education curriculum must be religious. We should teach our children the history of all religions, not just Christianity. An objective comparative education without prejudice or agenda. How else can we better understand people from other cultures and civilizations, or America for that matter, in the 21st century? Conversely, schools in Saudi Arabia, Nigeria, Indonesia, Pakistan, Iran and all Muslim countries should teach their children about the diversity of religious life in America. The fact that Islam is the fastest-growing religion in America – and there will soon be more American Muslims than American Jews – makes it all the more important.

American Jews, educated, skeptical and secularizing, show no signs of re-entering the immigrant breeding states.

Archaeologists have traced the historical development of religion back 7,000 years to the Oaxaca Valley of southern Mexico.

Religion is a series of structures, beliefs and practices that evolved over the centuries. At the first stage, the hunter-gatherer stage of human development, ceremonies took place on a plain dance floor, its sides marked by stones. To judge by the behavior of modern hunter-gatherers, ritual dancing took place at times of the year when many foraging groups came together for initiations and courtship. The practices were not limited to dancing. Other rituals to reinforce beliefs also took place, including human sacrifices.

When people settled in permanent villages, their rituals became more formalized at fixed times determined by the position of the sun or stars. With time, these permanent societies saw the emergence of elites, whose houses had metamorphosed into temples. At the next stage of human development, the temples grew more complex, with special rooms for the new caste of religious officers – the priests.

As humans developed, religion became both more elaborate and more exclusionary. The hunter-gatherers' ritual dances were open to all, but the men's houses were open only to the initiated members, and by the state stage, religion had come under the control of a special priestly caste. Religion evolved because of the cohesive role it played in structuring society.

Rituals were especially important in hunter-gatherer societies, which were egalitarian and had no chiefs or hierarchy. Religion served as the principal source of cohesion in the first settled societies until they developed systems of political authority. But when elites and kings emerged, they did not dispense with the religious systems. Instead, they employed religion as another mechanism of social control and as a means of maintaining their privileged position. "Ritual becomes part of the justification for being politically elite," Joyce Marcus, professor of anthropology at the University of Michigan, said in describing her extensive studies and archaeological digs on the subject in the 2004 *Proceedings of the National Academy of Sciences*. Alternatively, religion could have developed simply because an almighty God wanted it to, which would put Marcus and other anthropologists and archaeologists out of business.

Religion, because of its universality, has played a salient role in human evolution in all cultures and societies. Historically, politics dictated religion and religion dictated politics. No different than today, especially in America.

America is a nation of faith founded by religious people subjected to religious persecution. Precisely the reason they wanted to ensure and enshrine and build a republic not constrained in its evolution by any one religion or belief. On the contrary, they believed all religions and beliefs should be tolerated and respected. In the 1963 case, *Abington v. Schempp*, which dealt with prayer in public schools, Supreme Court Justice Tom Clarke, writing for the majority, stated: "It might be said that one's education is not complete without a study of comparative religion ... and its relationship to the advance of civilization."

Sir Sigmund Sternberg is perhaps the most prominent campaigner for multifaith peace. He is coordinator of the religious component of the World Economic Forum, patron of the International Council of Christians and Jews and founder of the Three Faiths Forum, a Christian-Jewish-Muslim dialogue group in Britain. "It's rather difficult to have an agreement between Christian, Jews and Muslims," he said. Where do we start to make it easier? How about teaching world religions in all American schools, and putting the Koran and Torah next to the Bible in every hotel and hospital room in the country.

History and the basic knowledge and understanding of other religions is the foundation stone of peace. Religion must be taught in all schools if we are to achieve lasting peace in the 21st century.

Is it any wonder the education of nearly every student in America is woefully inadequate and rapidly declining in the 21st century? The First Amendment does not ban the teaching of religion; it only bans the preference for a particular religion. There is a constitutional difference between teaching religion, which is unconstitutional, and teaching about religions, which is not only constitutional, but essential for America to survive in the 21st century. There is, of course, a streamlined way of teaching people about religions and the background to them. It is called "history." If history was taught comprehensively in U.S. schools, there would be less chance of entire school districts believing that the Earth is 6,000 years old.

Harvard University was founded in 1637 to train Puritan ministers. In 2006, a faculty committee recommended that all Harvard undergraduate students study religion, along with U.S. history and ethics. Comparative religions and history should be made mandatory, starting in high school, probably sooner.

It is possible to inculcate in our children a real sense of wonder at the universe, at history and culture, without having to resort to third-rate religious fiction, props and harmful superstition. The ongoing lawsuits in America today about teaching creationism, more than 80 years after the 1925 Scopes monkey trial, make a mockery of America and its retarded Dark Ages approach to education.

Evolution
The battle between scientists and religious fundamentalists over human evolution started in Dayton, Tennessee, when John Scopes, a 24-year old high

school football coach and science teacher, agreed to become the defendant in a trial testing Tennessee's recently enacted law that made it illegal to teach "any theory that denies the story of the divine creation as taught by the Bible, and to teach instead that man has descended from a lower order of animals." Darwinism did not ignite a culture war until the 1920s, when high school education became common in the rural South, where Christian fundamentalism was strong and school seemed to threaten children's souls. The idea of being descended from an ape was repugnant to many God-fearing Christians.

If exchange visits could be arranged between these people and the Taliban and Hezbollah, the war on terror would end in no time.

America was not the only country passionate about the issue at the time. The young Soviet Union, in its effort to stamp out religion, was determined to prove that men were descended from apes. In 1926, a Soviet scientist named Ilya Ivanov decided the most compelling way to do this would be to breed a humanzee – a human-chimpanzee hybrid. He set off for a French research station in West Africa. There he inseminated three female chimpanzees with human sperm. Not his own, for he shared the Colonial-era belief that the locals were more closely related to apes than he was. He stayed long enough to learn that his experiment failed.

Next Ivanov wrote to Cuban heiress Rosalia Abreu, who was the first person to breed chimps in captivity. She had a large menagerie outside Havana. Ivanov asked if any of her male chimpanzees might be available to inseminate a Russian volunteer known only as "G." At first Abreu was agreeable. But Ivanov made the mistake of approaching Charles Smith of the American Association for the Advancement of Atheism for fundraising support. Smith promptly went to the newspapers with Ivanov's proposal. *The New York Times* headline read, "Soviet Backs Plan to Test Evolution." The resulting publicity brought the case to the attention of the Klu Klux Klan, which threatened Abreu with retaliation if she went ahead with Ivanov's experiment, calling it "abominable to the creator." Abreu withdrew her consent. Before Ivanov could find another chimpanzee breeder, he fell out of favor in one of Stalin's purges and was exiled to Kazakhstan in 1931. He died a year later in conditions that would have made him wish he'd been born a monkey.

Twelve months later, the first "King Kong" movie opened in New York, in the darkest days of the Depression – and was a hit – as have been the many King Kong remakes. Cynthia Erb, in her book, "Tracking King Kong," suggests one of the factors behind the success of the first "King Kong" movie in 1933 was racist fear of miscegenation. It is this inherent racist fear that makes it hard for many people to accept the scientific argument that supports evolution.

Science has proved that evolution, although difficult for many to understand or believe, is a fact, notwithstanding that it undercuts the very basis of Christianity. Charles Darwin was a religious, God-fearing man who carried a Bible with him wherever he went, a reminder that he had been studying for the ministry before he went on his revolutionary voyage to the remote archipelago of the Galapagos. The God versus Science debate has been reignited in the 21st century under the guise of "intelligent design."

And it is making waves in state legislatures across America and in the U.S Congress. In California, neoconservatives introduced a bill called "An Academic Bill Of Rights," which in fact is an assault on universities and professors to teach religiously and politically correct dogma. Under the language of the bill, students are to be graded on the basis of their "reasoned answers, " and reading lists must "respect the uncertainty and unsettled character of all human knowledge." The real purpose of the bill is not to provide students with "rights" but to institute state monitoring of universities to impose specific points of view that have been intellectually discredited – and ultimately to silence dissenting voices by punishing universities that protect them.

Students should be encouraged and motivated to study – paid if necessary – not forced to read "crap" and paid to spy on professors, as was the case at UCLA. Students there were encouraged in 2005 to report professors who criticized President Bush, the war in Iraq, or the Republican Party. They were offered $100 and a free tape recorder by an alumni group of Republicans. In Colorado, students walked out of a high school class after they tape-recorded geography teacher Jay Bennishe criticizing Bush's Iraq policy and played it at a press conference demanding the teacher's dismissal. Is this any way to develop or encourage leadership?

Scientific Study

Life is about evolution, not revolution. To survive as a global leader in the 21st century, America must encourage scientific study and discussion in all schools. What distinguishes humans from all other species is the capacity to formulate questions – and to find answers that lead to more questions. We the *Apathetic Hominids* can't afford to be bored of politics. The more we know and learn, the more chance we have to stay alive. There is "no eternal truth – only provisional truth," said Charles Darwin.

"Children ask the most natural and the most difficult questions because they really do want explanations in which they understand relationships between cause and effect," said Donald Kennedy, executive editor-in-chief of *Science*. One can't help noting that when miscreants in the Old Testament caused God's wrath, they certainly got an effect.

Science is about questions, while research is about answers. The ancient Greeks were masters at asking questions and coming up with philosophical answers that were intellectually satisfying but usually not testable. It wasn't until the Age of Enlightenment began in the 1600s that the scientific method – observe, form a hypothesis, test it – took hold. A good example is the battle on the scientific front to prevent an H5N1 bird flu pandemic. Scientists researching for ways of preventing bird flu have won approval to exhume the body of British politician and diplomat Sir Mark Sykes, co-author of the Sykes-Picot agreement that dismantled the Ottoman Empire.

He was a victim of the Spanish flu epidemic, which claimed at least 30 million lives, and is buried in England. The epidemic was caused by an avian virus, H1N1, which is similar to the present virus, H5N1, and came from a bird in France. Sykes was buried in a sealed lead coffin, which researchers hope will produce well-preserved tissue samples. These could provide unparalleled insight into the mechanism by which bird flu kills and, with luck, contribute to finding a treatment for the virus. A legal scientific first where a court had given consent for a body to be exhumed for medical research.

The rock star reception that science guru Stephen Hawking received in Hong Kong in the summer of 2006, when the British theoretical physicist came to deliver the inaugural lecture at Hong Kong University of Science and

Technology's Institute for Advanced Studies, was beyond belief. Crowds of adoring and admiring fans greeted him at the airport and everywhere he went.

His book, *A Brief History of Time*, published in 1988, sold 9 million copies by 2002 and has been dubbed by some the "unread best-seller." The book has popularized some of the more arcane notions of theoretical physics. Black holes and big bang are almost household phrases because of it.

Hawking is famous for combining quantum mechanics with general relativity. These two fields of science are considered by many scientists to be the most important in 20th-century physics but seem to have two separate sets of laws that don't have anything in common. His studies on general relativity and new mathematical techniques he developed were applied to black holes, revealing that they could emit radiation, known as Hawking radiation. He also proposed his "no boundary" theory in 1983, in which time and space are finite but have no edges. What sounds like a dull discovery is such popular reading that it led to Hawking making a guest appearance on The Simpsons.

Hawking is a vocal advocate for the study of science for its own sake. He has dedicated his life to answering the big questions: "Where do we come from? Why are we here?" He has contrasted various ideas on man's beginnings with scientific reasoning, saying 17th-century bishop James Usher had calculated the date of "creation" as October 27, 4004 BC. Greek philosophers, by contrast, thought the universe had existed forever. Scientists believed in absolute time until Albert Einstein came up with a new geometric model of space-time in his general theory of relativity in 1915.

Hawking's visit to Hong Kong and the Chinese mainland created a scientific renaissance. Why isn't there one in America?

In Britain, creationist teaching aids are banned. John Sulston, a Nobel Prize winner in physiology and prime mover in the Human Genome Project, said about schools that teach creationism and science: "Students are somehow being told these agendas are alternative ways of looking at things. They are not at all. One is science – a rational thought process which will carry us forward into the indefinite future.

The other is a cop-out, and they should not be juxtaposed in science lessons."

Sulston is supported by Richard Dawkins, the Oxford geneticist, best selling author and atheist who has set up his own foundation to counter the religious indoctrination of young people. He is challenging religious education as "pseudo science" and "irrational."

"The Enlightenment is under threat. So is reason. So is truth. So is science, especially in the schools in America," Dawkins said. "I am one of those scientists who feels it is no longer enough just to get on and do science. We have to devote a significant proportion of our time and resources to defending it from deliberate attack from organized ignorance. We even have to go out on the attack ourselves, for the sake of reason and sanity."

Scientists agree that dinosaurs became extinct 65 million years ago. So why do creationists insist that the world is only 6,000 years old and started with Adam and Eve in the Garden of Eden?

The U.S. educational wars can be traced back to the founding of the republic. In Anti-intellectualism in *American Life*, written in 1966 by Richard Hofstadter, a historian at Columbia University, the author argues that America's problems lie in the fact that it had much more of a fundamentalist foundation for religious beliefs than Europe, where there is a much longer history of an intellectual approach to religion. America was colonized by largely uneducated people living on the frontiers, resulting in much less access to education and enabling a more emotional approach to religion. Is this emotional approach something America wants to perpetuate in the 21st century?

The fact is the Earth is but a small grain of sand on the beach when compared with the size of the known scientific universe. *We the Maids* are insignificant, more so because we choose to remain passive and uninvolved while the religious garbage piles up around us. The stench only retards our children – best exemplified by the child scavengers sifting and searching for anything to eat, wear or sell in staunchly religiously indoctrinated countries like the Philippines and ...

Stem Cell Research

The stem cell research debate across America is dominated and controlled by the same religious extremists that advocate Intelligent Design and want to ban all research using stem cells. There are more than 128 million Americans who could benefit from the research and live healthier and longer lives. It is "an important obligation to foster and encourage respect for life," as President Bush said. The question is, whose life? A genuine concern for life should focus on living human beings, as no embryo is capable of suffering, or have hopes and desires for the future that are abruptly cut off by their death. Bush is doing a good imitation of a Counter-Reformation Pope – assuming he knows what one is.

President Bush made 141 veto threats during his time in office while the Republicans controlled Congress, and typically Congress responded by changing bills to his liking. He exercised his first veto to block legislation to expand federal funding of embryonic stem cell research – a victory for the pro-life lobby led by the religious right – and a setback for medical science.

Scientists should be allowed to better understand and harness the power of stem cells, the basic building blocks of the body. From these microscopic wonders, all our other cells are formed – the ones that create our organs, nerves, muscles, blood, bones and brain. If we can control the incredible morphing power of these progenitor cells, they can be used to replace damaged cells with new ones, possibly opening the door to cures for diabetes, Alzheimer's, Parkinson's and genetic blood diseases. Failing organs could be restored through drug therapies that reinvigorate stem cells. Paralyzing injuries might be reversed through stem cell injections.

China supports many stem cell initiatives and encourages partnerships with private industry. The country is "at, or approaching, the forefront of international stem cell research," British scientists concluded in 2004. China engages in "significant recruitment" of U.S. and other Western scientists, luring them with promises of greater freedom and well-funded centers. Why isn't America doing the same?

Advanced Cell Technology in Worcester, Massachusetts, has developed a technique comparable to the procedure already performed at in vitro fertilization clinics to diagnose genetic defects. An embryo is allowed to grow eight cells, then one is plucked and the remaining seven allowed to go on and develop. The eighth cell used to determine genetic defects is instead used to derive stem cells. Another technique developed at the Massachusetts Institute of Technology, a variant of the method known as "therapeutic cloning," can produce exact genetic matches but is anathema to religious conservatives because it involves first creating and then destroying a human embryo. The Bush administration's stand on stem cell research is no different than the 17th-century church stand opposing autopsies.

The M.I.T. research demonstrates the feasibility of the approach recommended by William Hurlbut, a Stanford professor and member of the President's Council on Bioethics, to avoid ethical objections. Instead of creating a full-fledged embryo, the scientists manipulated genes to create embryo-like entities that were incapable of being implanted in the uterus.

Scientists in Switzerland have grown the first human heart valves from stem cells in amniotic fluid – offering a revolutionary approach that may be used to repair defective hearts in the future. People may one day be able to grow their own replacement heart parts – even before they are born. One percent of all newborns, or more than 1 million babies born worldwide each year, have heart problems. These kill more babies in America in the first year of life than any other birth defect, according to statistics from the National Institutes of Health.

The president's decision to veto legislation supporting medical research using embryonic stem cells was made on moral grounds rather than scientific grounds. The decision has the potential to keep America's science locked in the past. This is nothing new. Medical progress has historically generated religious and moral objections – objections that were overcome as the benefits of medical advances became overwhelmingly obvious. In the 11th century, European church leaders warned monks that treating illness with medicine showed such a lack of faith in God that it violated holy orders.

America's future educational and scientific health must be determined by science, not religious, ethical, moral or political dogma. There are more than 400,000 frozen embryos in America that can be used for medical research. They will be destroyed and disposed as hazardous waste if they are not used in research to extract stem cells. How does this benefit America? Those embryos will be destroyed either way. Are *We the Apathetic Maids* not better off using them in research instead of disposing of them as hazmat? If America wants to survive and be part of the fittest in the 21st century, it must take the lead and be in the forefront of stem cell research – and science. The 100 Greatest Discoveries and the 20th-Century Greatest Scientific Discoveries on the Science Channel must be made mandatory viewing at every school in America – and the world.

American Character

America is a borderless and seamless hybrid created from popular philosophies of liberty and freedom known to the Founding Fathers. America's founders created a country based on their conscience, not their religion. Shouldn't all Americans today be doing the same to ensure America stops slipping down the developed world's educational, religious and political survival rankings and gets back to the top ranks of the leading capitalists in the 21st century?

To create the American character and ideals, America evolved into a mythical empire founded on character assassination that consciously and deliberately expanded militarily to become a terrestrial and global giant.

U.S. mythology converted the natives to savage and heathen Indians. Their nonwhite Christian spirituality and beliefs became the essential ingredients in the development of America's expanding "frontier." The Indian Wars were the initial justification for expanding America's frontier to Mexico through the Mexican War, and the oil-rich Middle East through the Iraq War.

The propaganda tool that developed the American character and ethos was the Western. Violence became a tool of survival. The solitary cowboy with his gun, alone, independent, creative, conquering the wilderness and fighting heathen savages to teach them the ways of American civilization. The reality is that cowboys were a brief phenomenon in the West. Many were herders quietly rendered obsolete by the railways, mostly found in shacks or ranches. They were uneducated workers dependent on low wages, who rarely carried side arms and couldn't hit a barn door when sober. It's a bit like being told that Japanese samurais were mostly drunken homosexuals.

The U.S. government and various Native-American groups signed 800 treaties, of which 430 were never ratified by the U.S. Senate, yet the natives were expected to abide by their provisions. As Sen. Daniel K. Inouye, a member of the Senate Select Committee on Indian Affairs, observed: "Even more tragically, of the 370 treaties that were ratified, the United States proceeded to violate the provisions of every one." Sound familiar?

Throughout history, immigrants of all faiths have brought new ideas, ambition and labor to America in the good-old American cowboy tradition. A faith and belief in America's founding principals.

Arthur Miller, in his autobiography, *Timebends*, quoted the great physicist Hans Betha as saying, "Well, I come down in the morning and I take up a pencil and I try to think." It is a notion *We the Apathetic Maids* have to sweep into the forefront of America – thinking for ourselves and our nation. Thinking is out today and ignorance is in, something we have to sweep out. The essence of America, as Archibald MacLeish had written – its greatness – is in its promises.

The individual, in Miller's view, has an abiding moral responsibility for his or her own behavior, and for the behavior of society as a whole. He said that while writing *The Crucible*, "The longer I worked, the more certain I felt that as improbable as it might seem, there were moments when an individual conscience was all that could keep a world from falling." Miller was one of America's great thinkers, and it is time for all Americans to wake up and think about what can be done to stop America and the world from falling any further.

In *Timebends*, Miller wrote about the Depression-wracked 1930s and the prosperous postwar 1950s: "It was not that people were more altruistic, but that a point arrived – perhaps around 1936 – when for the first time unpolitical people began thinking of common action as a way out of their impossible conditions. Out of dire necessity came the surge of mass trade unionism and the federal government's first systematic relief programs, the resurgent farm cooperative movement and the Tennessee Valley Authority and other public projects that put people to work and brought electricity to vast new areas, repaired and built new bridges and aqueducts, carried out vast reforestation projects, funded student loans and research into the country's folk history – its songs and tales collected and published for the first time –

and this burst of imaginative action created the sense of a government that for all its blunders and waste was on the side of the people."

People in America today, like during the Depression-wracked '30s, know "little or nothing" about the forces manipulating their lives. It is time for *We the Apathetic People* to take time out and think about our lives, the way Miller did to stop the republic from running any further amok.

Bio Americanism

The American character and ideals are infectious. I know first hand. I and many I know caught the American bug. Australian cultural critic and science writer Margaret Wertheim, who lives in Los Angeles, suggests that to much of the world, "American culture seems like a virus, a particularly pathological one at that. We might, not without some justification, compare American culture to the AIDS virus, HIV. Like that brilliantly adapted organism, U.S. culture is endlessly self-replicating and alarmingly adept at co-opting the production machinery of its hosts. The reason HIV is so hard to stop is precisely because it harnesses the host's cellular functions, turning the body's power against itself to produce ever more copies of the viral invader. So too, American fast food culture, pop music, films and television infect the cultural body of other nations, co-opting local production machinery to focus their efforts on mimicry. This pattern of viral replication repeats itself the world over, with American pop culture norms chocking out and stifling native flora and fauna."

Wertheim describes culture in terms of a virus and I can understand why she thinks the way she does. She lives in Los Angeles, a brilliantly adaptive organism – pathological and unstoppable – which has replicated itself to half the size of Belgium, turning all the bodies that live within it against each other.

The "virus" of American culture and lifestyle replicates like AIDS, SARS and bird influenza so readily because it is founded on a promise of abundance, the lure of affluence, sex, drugs and cultural revolution. Materialism and abundance of sex and drugs is universally appealing. So are U.S. universities that educate the world's elite.

University

America's 4,200 universities, with a combined annual budget of $200 billion, are the backbone of the country's progress and the magnet that brings the world's brightest students, scholars, researchers, academics and children of the world's leaders and elite to America. I was one, although I know I don't qualify for any of the aforementioned categories. America's universities are the most accessible and democratic in the world. That is the only reason I was accepted.

America has believed in investing in the future since 1862, when Congress enacted the Land-Grant College Act, which offered the opportunity of higher education to all Americans, including women and minorities. Since their founding, land-grant colleges have awarded more than 20 million degrees. Today they award more than 500,000 degrees each year, including a third of the nation's bachelor's and master's degrees and 60 percent of the doctorates. The National Academy of Sciences, created by President Abraham Lincoln during the Civil War to advise Congress on "any subject of science or art," is the cornerstone of America's leading research capability today. The academy convinced President Franklin D. Roosevelt that it was the federal government's responsibility to provide funds for basic research that was to be conducted by universities because they were the best suited. That is what distinguishes America from the rest of the world. Other countries centralize their research in government laboratories. China is now adopting the U.S. model.

The federal Family Education Loan Program founded in 1965 has funded more than 74 million student loans worth more than $180 billion. I was one of those beneficiaries. Since 1973, when the Pell Grant student loan program for low-income students was created, more than $100 billion has been awarded to an estimated 30 million students, effectively shifting control of the largest share of financial-aid dollars from institutions to students.

When the U.S. Congress was getting ready to cut back the program, Vartan Gregorian, president of the Carnegie Corporation of New York, wrote an editorial opinion opposing the cutback: "Enrollment in higher education grew from just 4 percent of the college-age population in 1900 to more than 65 percent by the end of the century. As we enter the 21st century, it is no exaggeration to say that the United States has made it possible for Americans to participate in higher education on a scale unprecedented in world history. Let the learning begin."

The House of Representatives voted at the end of 2005 to slash funding for the student loan program by $14.3 billion, reversing decades of expansion that helped open America's most expensive universities to poor and middle-class students. The cuts would add about $5,800 to the average $17,500 student loan debt, according to the Congressional Budget Office. Talk about short-sighted career politicians and their total disregard for their constituents. According to the nonprofit College Board, average tuition and fees to public universities rose 40 percent over the first five years of the 21st century. The median family income over the same period rose only 16 percent. Yet the U.S. Department of Education tweaked its eligibility requirements for Pell Grants, eliminating aid to more than 80,000 students, and reduced awards to about 1.5 million others.

Part of a larger budget package to rein in federal spending by $55 billion, the House's plan tacked higher fees and interest rates onto student loans. It also restricted students' ability to refinance their loans to take advantage of lower interest rates while appropriating billions more dollars toward the war effort in Iraq. America's career politicians have priced middle-and low-income families out of college at the expense of funding their children to go to war. Education has moved from being an obligation on the public treasury to becoming a business, and in the Princeton of profit, there is no space for the poor.

As a result, those who need student loans are relying on high-interest private loans and then have to pay them off over many years. "For hundreds of thousands of citizens, the worst mistake they ever made was to go back to school," says Alan Collinge, founder of the advocacy group Student Loan Justice. Is this any way for America to compete in the 21st century?

At the same time student loans were being cut back by Congress, unknown millions of dollars were being spent at the state level on tutors for needy children in primary and secondary schools, even though no one knows the effect of the tutoring program since it went into effect in 2002.

The broad overhaul of student aid that became law in 2007 slashed $19 billion in federal subsidies to student lenders, increased grants for needy students and halved interest rates on federally backed loans with the savings.

To make student loans a partisan football, as Bush and Kerry did in the 2004 presidential election, which Congress replayed in the leadup to the 2008 presidential election, benefits nobody – especially U.S. students trying to get an education with a student loan. The all-American objective should be how to maximize the number of students who can participate in the program at the lowest cost to taxpayers – not the maximum profit for participating banks – or political contributors to candidates.

Close to 600,000 international students come to the U.S. each year to attend university. In 2004, 565,039 foreign students contributed about $13.3 billion to the U.S. economy. The majority come from India and China. For every 100 foreign students who received an American Ph.D in engineering or the physical sciences, the U.S. got 62 patent applications. As for the students who returned home, many took with them warm feelings toward America, democracy and free enterprise.

Do the math. Yet, since the Patriot Act was enacted, all foreign student applications have to be screened by the Office of Homeland Security, which gets bogged down, forcing students to defer their studies for a year. University presidents are justifiably outraged. "We don't want our students saying we might as well go to Britain rather than the U.S.," Yale University President Richard Levin said during a student recruitment visit to China. Well, they are. Is it any wonder they'll grab those cash cow foreign boys and girls right out of America's hands – even American students? More than 200,000 U.S. students studied abroad in 2004-05, the most ever reported by the Institute of International Education, which conducts the annual surveys involving more than 3,000 colleges. There was a 35 percent rise in the number of students studying in China.

While the enrollment of foreign students is on the decline in America, it is increasing dramatically since 9/11 at universities in Britain, Germany, Australia, New Zealand and Singapore. The European Union is even considering offering citizenship to foreign students who complete their doctorates at European universities. U.S. universities are suffering from the visa constraints imposed by an insecure America. The nation is suffering from Rajiv Ghandi's famed formulation: "Better brain drain than brain in the drain."

Unfortunately, America is suffering from both. Technological leadership is the key to prosperity and security, and America remains the world's technology leader – for now. But, as highlighted by a 2005 report from the National Academies, the U.S. lead in science and technology is not guaranteed; America must now "prepare with great urgency to preserve its strategic and economic security." Asian universities now produce 47 percent of engineering graduates worldwide and foreign-born inventors account for nearly half of all U.S. patents.

China has moved up to third place in the world after Japan and the U.S. in the number of patent applications filed. According to the World Intellectual Property Organization, China inventors submitted 173, 327 patent applications in 2005, a 33 percent increase over the previous year and the biggest leap in submissions of any country that year. Japan had the most filings followed by the U.S.

Joseph Stiglitz, a Nobel laureate in economics, questions the validity of the patent system in the 21st century. He argues that drug companies spend far more money on advertising and marketing than they do on research. The research is for lifestyle drugs rather than for lifesaving drugs, and almost no money on diseases that afflict hundreds of millions of poor people such as malaria, because the poor can't pay for the drugs. There is little research on their diseases. The solution: a medical prize fund that would reward those who discover cures and vaccines. Since governments already pay the cost of much drug research directly or indirectly, through prescription benefits, they could finance the prize fund, which would award the biggest prizes to developers of treatments or preventions for costly diseases affecting hundreds of millions of people.

Foreign students historically contributed $13 billion to the U.S. economy annually. That figure has been cut in half since passage of the Patriot Act. Enrollments of all foreign students, in undergraduate, graduate and postdoctoral programs, fell for the first time in three decades in 2002, according to an annual census released in 2004. Not surprising when one reads about

U.S. university newspapers parodying Asian-American students in broken English and playing "hunt the immigrant" in which students search the campus for the student wearing a name tag saying "illegal immigrant." The winner receives a reward.

There were 62,523 students from China studying in the U.S. in 2004-2005, making it the second-largest source of foreign students in the U.S. after India. China has the most scholars visiting the U.S. The number could be much higher if not for the delays in processing visas. A pity, as more Chinese students exchanging ideas with their U.S. counterparts could help bridge the Sino-American understanding gap.

Another side effect of the 9/11 attacks is the cutback of H-1B visas, the three-year work visa that allows foreign students to stay in the U.S. and work. The number was cut back from 195,000 per year to 65,000. The cut in the quota caused many U.S. companies to freeze hiring of foreign IT professionals, again adversely affecting U.S.companies in the competitive global market.

Americans have been especially wary of Chinese scientists. The National Aeronautics and Space Administration turned its back on Hong Kong's Ng Tse-chuen, a dentist and designer of planetary sampling tools. He was in contact with Nasa pre-9/11. Since 9/11 he has been cut-off. He is now doing work for the European, Russian and Chinese space agencies. He is part of the team working on the Russian spacecraft scheduled for liftoff in 2009, and the mission to Venus scheduled for 2017.

More than half of the high-technology startups launched between 1995 and 2005 had at least one founder of overseas origin, a 2007 study by Duke University in Northern Carolina found. It revealed that in the Silicon Valley, 52.4 percent of startups in the past decade had at least one founder of for-eign origin, significantly higher than the California average of 38.8 percent and the national average of 25.3 percent. Sergey Brin, from Russia, co-founded Google, while a German, Andy Bechtolsheim, and Vinod Khosla from India founded Sun Microsystems. Jerry Yang, a Chinese, co-founded Yahoo.

The end result is that the U.S. is losing its dominance in critical areas of science and innovation, as evidenced by the rise of foreign patents. "The rest of the world is catching up," said John E. Jankowski, a senior analyst at the National Science Foundation, the federal agency that tracks science trends. "Science excellence is no longer the domain of just the U.S." This is best exemplified by the number of patents registered today. Asians, most notably Chinese and Indians, have become more active and in some fields have taken the innovation lead.

The U.S. share of its own industrial patents has fallen steadily over the decades and now stands at 52 percent.

Close to 800,000 Chinese students have gone abroad since the government first started sponsoring them for overseas study in 1978. Drawn by job opportunities overseas, fewer than a third have come back, though the rate at which they are returning is accelerating. In 2005, about 35,000 students returned, three times the number in 2000, according to official statistics that are significantly conservative. Many of the returnees, armed with cutting-edge technical and managerial skills have helped kick-start new technology businesses. At the same time, foreign venture capitalists are flooding the country with unprecedented amounts of money. Combined with the mind-boggling opportunities from an economy expanding 10 percent annually, the result has been the creation of private wealth on an unprecedented scale.

Educational Hub
America's loss is Hong Kong's gain. As a result, Hong Kong's government has shifted into high gear to develop the Special Administrative Region as a regional education hub. Immigration controls are relaxed, and universities are allowed to accept more nonlocal students – who can take part-time jobs to support themselves.

The government increased the number of foreign students from 2 percent of the undergraduate population in 1995 to 10 percent in 2005. The universities need dormitories to house the foreign students. The problem is that the official government policy is that every student should have at least one year of dormitory experience, which is not happening because of the shortage of dorm rooms.

With the universities demanding an increase in the quota for nonlocal students from 10 percent to 20 percent, for Hong Kong to become a regional hub, the traditional New Year fireworks started on the human side in the summer – antipodean winter.

Chinese students in the mainland have made both the Central government and the prestigious Chinese universities conscious of the fact that Hong Kong is a preferable educational option. That is why Hong Kong universities have stepped up their recruitment drives. With offers of self-financing degree programs by the 20 colleges in Hong Kong, it is understandable why the pace of the "educational hub" concept is picking up speed. The concept could be speeded up even more if the eight universities and 12 colleges would cooperate. Especially since the government provides 82 percent of educational fees and the students pay only 18 percent. Talk about going to Golden Mountain. I know – I went to the real one in California.

But like California, guess what the problem is? Political protests by Hong Kong University students against "hasty internationalization." Why? Because of the impact of dorm living. How can local students live in the dorms and benefit if they can't stay in the dorms and embark on cultural exchanges because their dorms are taken by foreign students? Valid point. Nevertheless, mainland students continue to aggressively pursue the Hong Kong universities for the internationalization experience. Kind of ironic considering China, with its rapidly growing economy, is becoming one of the world's major educational destinations. The year 2005 saw the largest number of overseas students going to China since 1949 – about 141,000, up 27.28 percent from the previous year, according to the Ministry of Education. South Korea and Japan are the top two student exporters to China.

The protests and shortages are understandable. Since 2001, the proportion of Hongkongers between 17 and 20 years old going to university has doubled from 33 to 66 percent – easily beating the government's target of 60 percent by 2010.

China Burden

Another reason Chinese students flock to Hong Kong is the high cost of a university education in China. The proportion of government spending on education in China is about 3.2 percent of GDP – much lower than the average developed economy, and even lags behind several developing Asian nations, including the Philippines and Thailand.

The government met almost all educational expenses until the mid-'80s when the economy opened. Until then, the economy was centrally planned. China's market forces have also had a revolutionary impact on the education system.

The rigorous examination system takes its tolls on both the students and parents. In 2006, 4.1 million university graduates fought for more than 1.4 million jobs requiring a university degree. Is it any wonder outsourcing to China is so cheap. U.S. companies can employ scientists and engineers for the cost of a good expensive *dim san* meal.

A college education for Chinese villagers, much like their U.S. and global country bumpkins, is a pipe dream. First they have to compete in an examination system against their better funded and educated city slicker counterparts. Then, should they succeed, their parents have to be able to afford to send them to university. Just another dream for many. Consequently, it is not unusual for parents whose children have successfully passed the university entrance exams to commit suicide out of shame because they cannot afford to send them to university. The ultimate loss of face. The additional burden the successful students are saddled with on top of their already heavy educational burden remains to be seen. The same holds true for the mainland students who go overseas for their university education and come home to face unemployment.

Night School
I taught a night class in International Business Law to about 30 graduate students at California State University in Los Angeles in 1973. Most of the students had jobs and attended night classes to get their graduate degree in business. The rest were full-time students who picked my class because all the day classes were filled. I had a very simple philosophy. I would teach them what I knew and it was up to them to read the assignments, because in the end they were competing with each other and not me.

I was invited to be a luncheon speaker at one of the International Business Student Union monthly meetings. One of the people in the audience was the dean of the Business School. "How would you like to teach a graduate Business Law class with an emphasis on international business?" he asked me as he walked me to my car. I accepted the challenge.

I told my students before the midterm exam that I would first read all the answers to each question and pick the best answer for the top grade and grade the rest of the answers against the best answer. "Remember, you are competing with each other. Not me or some arbitrary standard," I told them. "This is your first test in the real business world. It isn't going to be pretty. But it is real." I followed this procedure for every answer and then totaled up the scores to each answer for the final grade. More than 70 percent of the students failed the midterm exam. As I was handing back the exam books to students with their scores, I was shocked at some of the students audible comments. "Hey man, what did you get? An F? Me too. What the fuck does this honky think we are. Stupid?" That was one of the nicer comments. I was threatened with the review board because it was clear to the majority of the class that I was a racist out to screw them out of their degrees.

After letting them vent their anger, I calmly read the names of the students who had received the best score for each answer and asked them to read out loud to the class their answers. As the last answer was being read, I could feel the deafening silence that had overcome the room. I sensed they knew they deserved the scores they received. I told them, "If there was a lower grade than F, I would have given it out, as some of your answers deserved an absolute zero. You know who you are. If you feel taking me up before the review board is going to improve your chances of survival in the real world, you are wrong. Take me up. I'm not worried. I have a nice day job to get back to and you have a life of failure to look forward to if you think your solution to problems is blaming teachers just because they are trying to do their best to give you survival tools."

The best answers were written by female African-American students. After class I was surrounded by apologetic students who had failed asking me what "special assignments" they could do to pass the class. "Just do the homework," I told them, "listen to what I say and if you have any problems or questions see me after class or during my office hours or call me at home." I had given them all my phone numbers and came to the university two hours before class to beat the rush hour traffic and prepare. What a difference an honest confrontation can make. Over 80 percent of the students passed the class. Much to my surprise, those that failed did not file a complaint with the review board.

What was really appalling was the atrociously poor writing and spelling skills of many of these "graduate" students. They truly represented all the bad jokes about how students know the three R's: Reading, Riting and Rithmetic. Not that much has changed in the more than 30 years since I taught. The average U.S. college graduate's literacy in English has declined dramatically. A nationwide test conducted by the National Assessment of Adult Literacy in 2005 found steep declines in the English literacy of Hispanics in America, and significant increases among blacks and Asians. Three percent of college graduates demonstrated "below basic" literacy, meaning that they could not perform more than the simplest of literary skills.

Yet they are college graduates because of their bullshit and ass kissing. A sign to be posted in every classroom that can confirm this mathematically reads as follows:

What makes 100 percent? What does it mean to give MORE than 100 percent? Ever wonder about those people who say they are giving more than 100 percent. Here's a little mathematical formula that might help you answer these questions.

If A B C D E F G H I J K L M N O P Q R S T U V W X Y Z is represented as 1 2 3 4 5 6 7 8 9 10 11 12 13 14 15 16 17 18 19 20 21 22 23 24 25 26 then

H-A-R-D-W-O-R-K
8+1+18+4+23+15+18+11 =98%

and

K-N-O-W-L-E-D-G-E
11+14+15+23+12+5+4+7+5 = 96%

but,
A-T-T-I-T-U-D-E
1+20+20+9+20+21+4+5=100%

and

B-U-L-L-S-H-I-T
2+21+12+12+19+8+9+20=103%

and look how far ass kissing will take you

A-S-S-K-I-S-S-I-N-G
1+19+19+11+9+19=19+9+14+7=118%

I cannot shake the sense of sheer relief that I put my children in private schools. At least they learned the fundamentals without the bullshit and ass kissing that so many of their contemporaries had to subject themselves to in public schools. Why can't all children attending public schools just learn the fundamentals?

"Hold on there," said Stuart Wolfendale, the Los Angeles-based correspondent for a Hong Kong newspaper. "You have to take into account the time needed for 'social subjects' with no academic basis, for youths to sulk, intimidate other youths, beat up teachers, take drugs, clean their guns and be persuaded to simply stay on the premises. After that, if anybody is left alive and conscious, they'll learn, just you wait and see," Stuart added as we both burst into hysterics. Funny, sad, but true.

Not as bad as India when students rioted and demanded authorities reset the exams and let them continue cheating "the way they had for years." Cheating in exams is common place in Bihar province in India. More than 11,000 students boycotted their secondary school graduation exams because they were not allowed to cheat and then damaged police and education department vehicles and set fire to one of the examination halls..

Shaquille O'Neal, the Miami Heat center, went back to college to get his bachelor's degree at the age of 28 in the last year of the millennium. He was excused from a game against the Memphis Grizzlies so that he could attend graduation. Martin Sheen who played President Josiah Bartlett in "The West Wing," decided to go back to college at 65 as a student of philosophy and English literature. Nola Ochs, a 95-year-old grandmother, is the oldest college graduate. She graduated with her 21-year-old granddaughter. If Ochs,

Shaq and Sheen take the time, shouldn't everyone who wants an education try harder in the 21st century?

In Hong Kong, elderly learning centers are being set up for seniors who are being invited to go back to school to "discover the fun of learning." Their teachers will include primary and secondary school students who will teach them computing, Chinese literature, interpersonal communication and health tips on how to stay fit and healthy. Shouldn't America be doing the same?

Every Child Left Behind

Schools in America are underfunded. Each election year, candidates make promises and "commitments" to education that are never fulfilled. The 2004 and 2008 presidential elections are no different. Bush's No Child Left Behind campaign hid the fact that every child in America is in fact being left behind. The law requires 100 percent of the nation's students to reach "proficiency" – as each state defines it – by 2014. No Child Left Behind was a reauthorization of the 40-year-old Elementary and Secondary Education Act, which called for increased testing, particularly in grades 3-8, with the aim of getting all students to a "proficient" level, with severe consequences for schools that failed to meet the academic standards. More than 1 million students drop out of high school each year. That's 1 million students who aren't being left behind. They are simply getting off the bus of their own free will and going home to make a living. Campaign slogans alone will not educate children. We cannot fast-forward children's knowledge the way we do video games and smart bombs. Children are not that wired.

The first tests to measure the success of No Child Left Behind revealed that students were able to ace state tests because standards had lowered to meet the federal requirements and ensure future funding. They failed the first federal test under No Child Left behind in 2005. Department of Education officials administered the test to 660,000 students in the 50 states and the District of Columbia, and on military bases around the world from January to March 2005. A comparison of state test results against the National Assessment of Educational Progress, a federal test mandated by No Child Left Behind law, showed wide discrepancies between the state and federal results. Many cities and states are abandoning the program. Even Houston, President Bush's birthplace of No Child Left Behind, is dropping standardized testing because of teacher and parent objections that students are learning less under the program and are in fact being left behind.

Jack Jennings, president of the nonprofit Center on Education Policy, said that from 2000 to 2003, before the federal law took effect in classrooms, the percentage of fourth graders scoring proficient in math rose eight percentage points, compared with four points in 2005. Jennings also said that eighth graders proficient in math rose three points before the law, compared with the one-point rise in 2005. "The rate of improvement was faster before the law," Jennings said. "There's a question as to whether No Child is slowing down our progress nationwide."

To allow school administrators to compromise our children's education because of their need to get in on the latest political fad for funding does not benefit our children's education. "Public education is about politics, politics is about power, and if parents want control over what happens to their kids, they have to go out there and steal power from someone else" said Joe Williams, author of *Cheating Our Children: How Politics and Greed Ruin Education*. "I'm not suggesting that parents be out there running schools, but if they were more demanding, we wouldn't be in this mess."

Campaign slogans have to be backed by legislative action that will ensure every child is given the best educational opportunity to develop according to their individual ability. To do so will require deep systematic change, especially in the realm of teacher quality, pay and funding to support learning at all academic and preschool levels. Piecemeal funding programs that are exemptions and violations of the No Child Left Behind law, such as federally funded tutorial programs for students at schools failing to meet academic goals, is a shortsighted quick-fix solution that is doomed to fail.

Hard and determined work is what is required of our politicians, bureaucrats – and, most importantly, parents – to bring about the tumultuous changes needed to propel America into the competitive, global 21st century.

Teaching is not for the timid and unimaginative. One needs the wisdom, dedication, patience, courage and intuitive ability to adapt to new and sudden changes. Teachers have had to learn and unlearn many things over the last few decades to keep up with political policy changes.

Laurie D'Amico taught sixth graders language, arts and reading in Rhode Island for 25 years. When she retired she became the director of literacy volunteers of Greater Worcester, Massachusetts. There are more than 1,000 literacy volunteers affiliates worldwide. Most of the students attending D'Amico's literacy classes come from single-parent homes where parental neglect is prevalent. More than 50 foreign languages are spoken by children in the Worcester public school system. Approximately 6,000 children out of 28,000 public school attendees speak a language other than English as their first language. I went to visit Laurie and her husband Mark in the fall of 2005, and was invited to join them for dinner with members of her board of directors at the home of board member Nancy Walsh, a local businesswoman, and her husband Jonathon Walsh. Michael Mills, the chairman of the board, and his wife Marsha, peppered me with questions about the education system in Hong Kong. They wanted to know why Chinese and Asian students do so much better than others in America. Marsha was a second-grade teacher.

Trying to be as diplomatic as possible so as not to embarrass Laurie and Mark, I answered the questions whenever I could with another question in the hope of learning more about why No Child Left Behind was such a failure. "The expectations were so much higher because of the tests that were supposed to be given, but that never materialized," Laurie said. "Prior to No Child Left Behind, schools worked for five years on personal assessments of children that were performance based," Marsha said. "Overnight, with No Child Left Behind, the performance-based tests were thrown out and schools went to multiple-choice bubble tests."

It became clear to me that students had to be taught overnight how to take new tests and a new education system because states bought into the program to tap into federal funds without any consideration for students' individual needs.

The education system in America today is based solely on test scores. As a result, the side effects are profound. Instead of devoting their time and attention to teaching, teachers focus on instructing children how to pass tests. Tests used to measure a student's knowledge. They solely determine if the student should be left behind or moved up the educational assembly line. Teachers focus more of their attention on test preparation – to ensure a higher passing rate – than teaching. "Teachers are doing the greatest good for the greatest number, rather than individual attention, and try to get the most out of the individual," Laurie said in exasperation. What can be done about it? I asked her."It is all about the individual and not the pack," Laurie said. "If we want students to take ownership and responsibility for themselves, we have to give them the right environment and individual attention they crave. They don't get it at home and they don't get it at school either."

"How did Steven Spielberg become a great director?" Laurie asked, "His dad gave him a movie camera when he was 10. Every child today in America should have a computer. Kids today should be using modern technology and the new tools of the Information Age, not just books. They should be doing Power Points instead of homemade posters, diagrams and mobiles that are so dated. I just can't believe that this is how we are preparing our future," Laurie said in disgust. "Many kids have better state-of-the art equipment at home than they do in school." "What about electronic pen pals, like the old letter-writing days?" I asked.

"Imagine if American kids communicated by e-mail with their contemporaries all over the world," I asked. "You know, that is a good idea that has not been adopted in any significant way by any school district that I know. Of course, a lot of kids do have electronic, as well as traditional, letter-writing pen pals." What better way for American students to get to know and understand the world they live in than developing a personal direct relationship that is removed several steps from a chat room or blog? After all, they are not mutually exclusive.

Parental Responsibility

Academic disengagement is a reality that must be confronted before it is too late. Children are tuning out because they get spoiled at home by guilty parents who are too busy to devote the time necessary to engage their children academically – or teach them to respect their teachers or school. To many students, teachers are no different than a computer screen – an inanimate object that gives them answers. Many students use technology and parental guilt and lack of discipline and respect for teachers to abuse and punish their teachers by getting unwitting parents to complain to the teachers' superiors.

To make matters worse, most children are technologically more savvy than their teachers and parents, and as a result, have taken over the communication process. Children today are more likely to show their parents and grandparents how to keep up with the latest developments in gadgets, hardware, toys, computer games, software, communicating shortcuts and piracy. More children communicate with each other on computers than ever before. Kids used to just talk on the phone and tie up the phone line. Now they communicate for hours on a computer while their parents talk on the phone. Chances are that as soon as a teacher reprimands or punishes a student, the child will have text-messaged their parent to complain and the parent will call the principal to discipline the teacher – all within minutes of the occurrence.

"Kids want to be challenged," Laurie continued in disgusted frustration. "Most don't know how to find a book in a library. They are lost. They don't know how to research and in fact learn a lot more from each other than they do from their parents and teachers." That is the fundamental problem with America's education system. Most of what children learn comes from outside the classroom. Schools have become degree factories instead of teaching institutions. They're hugely expensive child-minding centers. Schools for the ordinary population were a creation of the 19th century. It's up to *We the Maids* to come up with something better in the 21st century.

Valerie Beall, a sixth-grade teacher in Beacon. New York, confirmed and validated what Laurie told me when I went to vist her and her husband Scott, who is also a teacher. "There is a total disrespect and lack of constructive interaction between teachers and students," Valerie said when I asked her to share her observations about school and teaching today. "They'd much rather interact with themselves on their cell phones. Most of my students are ingrate brats who have no time for critical thinking. They are on a straight line to get through school, get their degrees and profession because that is how their parents are bringing them up," Valerie said.

Students and their parents are materialistic, myopic and unbelievably permissive and destructive in their nonexistent discipline. Schools have become a circus tent, a show in which teachers are outflanked by kids who use guilty parents to lobby on their behalf. Parents have become overindulgent and obsessive in blaming teachers for their children's personal and academic shortcomings. The kids are in control today. They manipulate their parents and make them take on the teachers. Not only that, many of them have become hackers and they get into school administration sites with wi/fi mouses and change teacher's screens in the middle of class. Kids are preoccupied with computers and computer games and the school systems have just not caught up to today's reality. Hackers and delinquents in the same class as students who really want to learn but can't because of the disruption and chaos caused by brats? "Absolutely. There is no separation in public schools of dysfunctional, destructive, spoiled morons who slow the class down for the real achievers who want to learn," Valerie said before Scott announced that dinner was ready.

Schools are clumsy and outdated. Besides, given the amount of time spent in cyberspace, why do the little morons have to travel to an inadequate building miles away to move around from room to room listening to a sequence of individuals trying to tell them something they already know or don't care to know? There is a lot to suggest that children in these group situations don't socialize so much as terrorize each other.

Laurie and Valerie echoed what I had heard in Hong Kong from Heather Hill, a New Zealand teacher who taught there for 12 years before coming to Hong Kong. She had been in Hong Kong teaching four-and five-year-olds for six years at the Hong Kong International School before becoming the principal at a kindergarten. More than 50 percent of her students at the Hong Kong International School were Americans. 'Parental neglect is unbelievable," Heather told me one night over dinner. "The level of parental neglect is high. Many children are raised by maids, and spend too much time by television and with electronis games. Time is often filled by formal afterschool classes, and little emphasis placed on down time and being with friends. Parents busy schedules mean that both Mom and Dad can be absent for days at a time leaving children to feel unimportant and sometimes unloved."

" Teaching is emotionally and physically exhausting. It is really important to balance math, reading and other academics with socialization. That impacts on a child's development and their ability to function successfully in life. Many children today don't know how to socialize. Parents often don't realise that success in life is not just about the academic component, but a balance between this and social and emtional learning."

A worrisome trend in the U.S. are the studies coming out saying that the programs of 20 years ago could be behind trends in how young Americans see themselves. The me-first generation of college students are more narcissistic than their Generation X predecessors. A San Diego State University study showed that narcissism scores of college students in 2006 were 30 percent higher than a similar 1982 study. More and more students have their own cell phone and iPod with which they do their own thing in their own world. It seems like students today are very bottom line-oriented. They just want to get through school, get the diploma and go make a fortune.

If parents would use the amount of time they spend protesting against teachers, teaching mediums, exam systems and syllabuses with their children, educating them, America and the world would be a much better place. Education starts with parents at home.

Parents have to teach motivation, self-discipline and work ethic, basic Confucian ideals ingrained in Chinese and many Asian societies. Until parents instill these basic values, students will never master their subjects and will continue to blame their teachers. A study released in December 2005 by the University of Pennsylvania suggested that the reason so many U.S. students are "falling short of their intellectual potential" is not "inadequate teachers, boring textbooks and large classe sizes" but "their failure to exercise self-discipline."

It is easy for parents who feel guilty for the lack of time they spend with their children to subscribe to any theory that shifts the blame from them onto teachers and the system.

Napoleon famously declared that a child's education should begin 20 years before it is born with its mother's education. His pronouncement is just as true today. A child does not exist in the innocent isolation of the nursery. It is caught in the web of adult cross-currents and tensions, including racism and discrimination.

Education has to be all-encompassing and holistic for children to acquire knowledge and social skills. Education, like life, is all about balance – ying and yang.

Yank Department of Education

Conservative columnist George Will illustrates the problem graphically: "About 50 percent of urban area public school teachers with school-age children send their children to private schools. What do they know that we ought to know? If public schools are not good enough for the children of those who teach them, why should other children have no choice but to attend them?" Will asks in his 1992 book *Restoration*.

The U.S. Department of Education must be abolished. The education of America's future has to be restored to the states. Education has to be managed and controlled on a local level. Nevertheless, there still has to be a national coordination official to make sure curriculums are similar enough so that children moving from state to state could do so seamlessly.

The other big issue that has to be tackled head-on is class size. Classes have to be reduced to 15 to 25 students. "Children are smarter today and they need more individual attention because they don't get it at home because so many come from single-parent homes," Laurie D'Amico said during my fall 2005 visit when we explored what needs to be done to make America competitive again.

The National Education Association, which represents 2.7 million teachers, and 10 of its affiliates filed a lawsuit in 2005 against the U.S. government for the hypocrisy and shortcomings of the No Child Left Behind law. It is to be applauded. Resistance to the law is growing and should be encouraged. The suit asked a U.S. District Court in Detroit to free schools from having to comply with any part of the No Child Left Behind law. The suit charged that the law is being implemented illegally because billions of dollars worth of federal underfunding has forced states to use their own money to carry out its mandates.

The NEA suit correctly alleges that the financial burden is contrary to a provision in the law that states: "Nothing in this act shall be construed to ... incur any costs not paid for under this act." The basis of the suit, according to Reg Weaver, the NEA president was: "If you regulate, you must pay."

Smarter Digital Kids

Kids are getting smarter and cleverer. Blaming better grades on grade inflation, curve grading and falling exam standards is not entirely valid. As much as mass-media culture dumbs down most people, children who demand speed and immediacy are the great imperatives, meaning that complex ideas are reduced to sound bites and text messages. The Internet gives students access to more information than they ever had on how to prepare for exams. The fact is, human beings are becoming more intelligent. From the printing press to artificial intelligence, people have become smarter collectively as a species, more creative. Creativity and originality is what separates smart people from students subjected to rote-learning in backward societies.

Embracing technology is second nature for today's children. Yet Many parents and educators don't get it. Computer games allow children to make decisions and solve problems. Schools that allow and encourage students to travel the mystical interactive world engage their students and teach them a lot more effectively than those that don't. Computer games improve mental spatial processing abilities. Still, parents worry that their children spend too much time in front of a screen – be it the television, computer, or video game console – and not enough time on their studies or outdoors playing with friends. In the U.S., more than 80 percent of eight to 19-year-olds have at least one game console at home. In America, half of all children under six have used a computer and 30 percent have played a video game. Today's children will spend their entire lives surrounded by and using computers, mobile phones, video games, digital music players, video cameras and all the other tools of the digital age.

By the time an average student gets to college in America, he or she will have spent 5,000 hours reading but 10,000 hours playing video games and 20,000 hours watching TV. The ongoing debate about the positive and negative effects of computers on children raises the same issues that have been raised with all new technologies in the past. For example, the consequences of exposing children to violent, sexual and age-inappropriate content have been deliberated since films were first introduced in the early 1900s, radio in the 1920s and television in the 1940s.

Even books were viewed with suspicion when the printing press was invented. The fact is, humans fear what they do not understand.

Students must be encouraged and allowed to satisfy their hunger for knowledge and enjoyment of intellectual discovery. Students must be their own masters, while teachers are the facilitators in a system that creates the right conditions for learning. Educational systems must allow students to make the choices of what they want to learn so that they can not only enjoy their education, but their careers. The tools of modern technology make creative learning, and learning in general, an enjoyable educational journey.

The rapid development of information and communications technology in schools has happened in partnership with the major purveyors of the machines and software. The education market is massive business for companies such as Microsoft, IBM, Cisco, Adobe and Oracle and there is intense competition between them to collaborate with the education sector.

In Hong Kong, there are theater companies that stage interactive musical dramas to further stimulate creativity. It was founded by merchant bankers bored with "yawn city," who wanted to make kids laugh, while they learn literature and participate in enjoyable educational theatrical productions, rather than boring lectures.

Creativity

Traditional schools and traditional parents do not foster creativity. On the contrary, they encourage rote learning and cheating. Data shows that most children start with their creativity intact and in full gear, but by the time they get to fourth grade, they have become more conforming, less playful, less spontaneous, less likely to take risks and therefore less creative. Traditional school and traditional parenting do not foster creativity.

Creativity is the ability to generate something new and original. It means having the power to express oneself in one's own way – not to be confused with intelligence or talent.

Untapped Brain Power

Brains are responsible for our behavior, good and bad. The rapidly expanding discipline known as neuroethics – the brain science of morality – is another science that defies and proves false religious dogmas. "What the late 20th century was for molecular genetics," said professor Martha Farah, a leading researcher at the University of Pennsylvania, "the early 21st century is proving to be for neuroscience."

We already have the drugs to enhance mood (lithium and Prozac), concentration (Ritalin) and memory (Aricept). Is a drug that regulates morality far away? "It brings closer the untowardly potential consequences of biologically engineered morality," said Dr. Laurence Tancredi, a psychiatrist who practices law in New York. He predicts a "new society" in which "moral" aberrations will be predicted and corrected by drugs.

Weird behavior caused by crude connections between the brain and our behavior have long been familiar. Take railroad worker Phineas P. Gage, a polite, quiet, decent individual who in 1348 suffered a prefrontal-lobe injury when an iron rod shot through his skull while he was dynamiting a tunnel in Vermont. He survived but became a loud-mouthed, vulgar, annoying jerk.

My favorite example, especially when wearing my lawyers hat, is the 1979 "Twinkie defense" trial in which Dan White, who had shot dead San Francisco Mayor George Moscone and Supervisor Harvey Milk a year earlier, was found guilty of manslaughter rather than murder because, as the public saw it, the jury accepted that White had eaten too many of the sugary cakes that day, and the sugar in his brain turned him into a killer.

The cases are mounting by the year. In 1992, a man surnamed Weinstein was charged with strangling his wife during an argument and throwing her body out of the 12th-floor window of their apartment to fake a suicide. A positron emission tomography (PET scan), showed an arachnoid cyst. His psychiatrist claimed the tumor had caused metabolic imbalances leading to loss of impulse control, a claim that led to a lesser charge of manslaughter.

Three years later, a charity manager, William Aramony, was charged with embezzling hundreds of thousands of dollars to fund a lavish lifestyle. His defense lawyers argued it was his brain, not him, that stole the money. He could not form the requisite criminal intent for embezzlement, argued the defense, because his brain had been shrinking during the late 1980s and early '90s, a fact that could be substaniated by a magnetic resonance imaging scan. It worked. The prosecution agreed to a plea bargain.

It is universally accepted that alcohol and drugs can be detrimental to moral behavior. Evidence that our diet can also alter our actions was demonstrated in a research trial at a maximum-security British prison. A zinc supplement was added to prisoners' food culminating in a significant reduction, it was claimed, in the rate of reoffending. It is now seriously being considered that zinc, like flouride, be introduced into drinking water, to combat criminality.

I haven't quite figured out how Twinkies, or zinc, make good people bad and bad people good. But scientists continue to learn more about the complex action of brain chemicals, known as neurotransmitters, on our emotions and behavior, including learning, memory, decision-making and anger. At the same time, brain scans taken while people perform a variety of cognitive and emotional processes, including lying and fantasizing about sex, have located specific areas in the brain crucial to the decision-making process.

Most importantly, what neuroscience is telling *We the Maids* is that while brains are broadly similar, they are also highly individual.

The religious doctrines of original sin – meaning we are prone to prefer wrong by nature – conscience and free will have been eroded by rationalism, science and secularism over the past two centuries. Yet a powerful belief in responsibility for our actions remains – in family, friends, the criminal justice system. The tendency to find excuses for bad behavior was inherent in Sigmund Freud. But it was neuroscience, which took off in the mid-'80s, that accelerated the process. The '90s came to be known as the Decade of the Brain.

The collapse of communism resulted in a large piece of the American national science funding pie being diverted into researching the biology of the brain, as part of the post-Cold War peace dividend. The anticipated payoff was the promise, lobbied and spun by the pharmaceutical industry, that the U.S. economy could save $350 billion a year by reducing brain-related problems, including Alzeimer's disease, workplace stress, and, above all, violence. "Your sense of personal identity and free will are in fact no more than the behavior of a vast assembly of nerve cells and their associated molecules," said the late Nobel laureate Francis Crick, a co-discoverer of DNA.

Most of what we know about how our brain works was discovered in the closing years of the last millennium and must be utilized and capitalized on in the 21st century. Here are some of the recently discovered facts on the human brain. Speed is about 150 gigabytes per minute. Weight is some 2.5 percent of our bodyweight, but it uses 25 percent of the calories we consume and 30 percent of the oxygen we breathe. So aerobic exercise assists its efficiency. The brain is a physical organ with 100,000,000 cells, and we all have the same basic model.

One way to tell which model a child has is to look at the length of a child's index and ring fingers. Kids with longer ring fingers compared to index fingers are likely to have higher math scores than literacy or verbal scores in the entrance exam for primary school, while children with the reverse finger-length ratio are likely to have higher reading and writing, or verbal, scores versus math scores. The different levels of the hormones testosterone and estrogen in the womb account for the difference. Exposure to testosterone promotes the area of the brain associated with spatial and mathematical skills. Estrogen exposure does the same for areas of the brain associated with verbal ability.

The mind, on the other hand, is the connectivity between our brain cells, and here every human is totally unique. Of our 80,000 thoughts per day, researchers say in excess of 70 percent are negative. Memory capability can increase as we grow older, as long as we exercise the mind with new challenges. Call this the mind gym. Present research tells us that we use less than 1 percent of our brain's capability. Surprised? Is it any wonder We are apathetic?

The brain has two sides. The brain skills on the left side are numbers, words, logic, lists, details and order. On the right side are pictures, imagination, color, rhythm, spatial and global thought. Some people argue that President George W. Bush occupies a previously neurologically unnoticed vacuum between the two halves. It does not take much to realize that our education system – schools, universities and business training – are strongly left-brain dominated. However, the full integration of all brain skills is required for business creativity (going from an initial idea to a practical product or process).

What is amazing is that those who learn the fastest – babies, from birth to three years, and geniuses – are continuously using both sides of the brain in conjunction with each other. For the vast majority, this process ends when we attend school. Child psychiatrist Buckminster Fuller said it best: "All people are born geniuses, we spend the rest of their lives degeniusing them." I can relate. The very moment my mother delivered me, screaming in protest, at age five into the hands of a teacher at the Army-Childrens School, I actually felt the two halves of my brain disconnect.

Our learning preferences are visual, auditory and kinesthetic. Albert Einstein and Thomas Edison, who had strong kinesthetic preferences, were considered dunces and both were expelled from school. They preferred to learn by experimenting, rather than listening to the teacher. How many other great minds have been flunked or dropped out of school in the old-world order because of our outmoded and outdated education system?

Steve Jobs, CEO of Apple Computer, is one such example. He was the commencement speaker at Stanford University on June 12, 2005, and delighted in letting his audience know he never graduated from college. "Truth be told," he said, "this is the closest I've ever gotten to a college graduation." How many more brilliant minds have to be lost to a mindless academic system that sacrifices them for athletes who cannot graduate high school, but are able to receive $399 correspondence diplomas that entitle them to go on to college where they can play on a university sport team just because of the television money college sports generate?

What about offering hope to students with great minds who are incapacitated and whose school is a hospital? Those suffering from cerebral palsy, muscular dystrophy or victims of accidents with spinal cord injuries or traumatic brain injuries.

School Vouchers

The school voucher system was first advocated by renowned Nobel Prize-winning economist Milton Friedman in 1956. When Richard Nixon became president, he advocated the school voucher system Friedman advocated a system that would "force schools to compete for funds by competing for students. Teachers' unions have waged all-out war against school choice, especially those plans that allow parents, as they should, to choose private as well as public schools," he said. In 1993, California teachers' unions spent

$18 million confiscated from teachers' paychecks to defeat a ballot initiative on school choice with television ads that were so distorted and cynical that they made the dirtiest congressional campaign seem like High Mass at St. Patrick's Cathedral. But the unions' self-interest was blatant. School choice proposals will become policy when enough parents insist on it. All it requires is parents' active participation.

Former New Mexico Gov. Gary Johnson was the first governor in America to declare that every pupil in the state must have a school voucher.

The Florida Legislature passed into law America's first plan that allows children in the state's lowest-rated schools to attend private schools with state-paid vouchers. A great beginning for the New World Order of the 21st century. Education should be the issue of primary concern to all parents and politicians in the New World Order. But it should be a secular education, not a religious one.

The city of Milwaukee has the oldest and largest school voucher program in America. Launched in 1990, the program is still controversial because about 70 percent of the voucher schools are religious, and not all of them good – at either education or religion.

The first two voucher plans to gain approval in Milwaukee and Cleveland were limited to low-income families and passed with the allied support of white Republicans and black Democrats concerned about education in poor neighborhoods. All parents want to give their children a good education close to home regardless of party affiliation – or religion – but not a religious education at public expense.

A federal appeals court in 2000 upheld a lower court ruling declaring the Cleveland school program unconstitutional. It ruled that public funds cannot be used for parochial schools because it breaches the First Amendment on separation of church and state. Public funds should not be used for parochial schools. However, they should be used for private non-denominational secular schools with classes on comparative religions. Churches and taxpayers who want their children to go to religious schools should fund and pay for vouchers to be used in parochial schools. All it would require is a tax credit allocating a portion of all religious tax dollars to a voucher fund.

Honky Voucher Program

Hong Kongers and their dollars are affectionately referred to by expats, especially Americans, as Honky. Hong Kong has adopted a school voucher plan that gives all Hong Kong parents 10,000 Honky dollars a year that can be applied toward kindergarten fees. Up to $3,000 Honky per child will go to support teacher training. The government approved a $2 billion Honky fund for the program.

About 90 percent of children aged three to six are expected to benefit from the scheme, and more than 80 percent of kindergarten children are eligible. The annual subsidy per child will rise to $16,000 Honky by 2011-2, and from then on, parents will receive the whole amount to set off their kindergarten fees.

To Hong Kongers, education is one of the top priorities, and an issue they demand government constantly address and increase funding for. Education accounted for 22.5 percent – the biggest share – of recurrent public spending in 2006. One of the proposals was that each newborn be entitled to a $1 million Honky voucher for education as each student receives about that amount in government subsidies during their 16 years of primary to university education. "Providing quality education for our next generation is an integral part of government support for the family," said Hong Kong Chief Executive Donald Tsang, the head of the city state in 2006.

Hong Kong is one of the few jurisdictions in the world to embrace an education voucher scheme that forces the Catholic Church to comply just like every other school with the requirement that at least 40 percent of its management committee members need to be independent and elected representatives of parents, teachers and alumni – something it objects to vehemently. In America, evangelical Christians who object to government decisions separating church from state and their scientific approach to education are taking their children out of school and teaching them at home. Home schooling, in many cases, is based on the Bible.

Jailhouse Schools

One-third of American public school high school students drop out – 25,000 a day, every day and the numbers are growing rapidly. Many of them wind up in jail – 68 percent of prison inmates are high school dropouts.

More black men than ever languish in American prisons. Black academic achievement still lags behind that of whites. And suicides among young black men have risen sharply, reflecting a deep "sense of hopelessness," said Jewelle Taylor Gibbs, a psychologist and University of California, Berkeley professor.

While the number of blacks languishing in jail rises, so do the fortunes of their black brothers who do have an education. The reversal of black fortunes is a signal event, one that "must be acknowledged and celebrated," said Joe Hicks, executive director of the Los Angeles Human Relations Commission. Yet, for the most part, blacks are not celebrating, which raises a question: "If the news in black America is so good these days, why are people not dancing in the streets instead of staying off them and barring their windows?" asks Hicks.

I met Dave Layman, a teacher, on an Amtrak train from Santa Fe, New Mexico, to Los Angeles in 2005. He taught at the Los Lunas Correctional Facility in central New Mexico. We struck up a conversation in the observaton car as we admired the New Mexico landscape. He was adamant that what is needed in jails across America is vocational training. He said he enjoyed prison teaching because there were no parents to contend with.

Extensive education programs should be offered in every jail, regardless of whether it is a self-imposed sentence at home or at the invitation of the government. With a proper education, cons can re-enter the community with confidence, knowledge and a degree that can keep them from returning to the jailhouse. Isn't this a more effective use of tax dollars than making license plates? Instead of giving convicts a license to steal, why not give them one to join our community as productive citizens?

The U.S. is not alone in having to make a decision on what jails are for. Do they simply keep criminals off the streets? Are they meant to give criminals a thoroughly awful time so that they won't go back, or are they supposed to make criminals better? They only do the first with any conviction. It is now possible to also make criminals better because of the numerous school principals, administrators, auditors and other white-collar professionals across America who have been indicted and convicted of misappropriating school funds who are now also in jail. The teaching pool in jailhouses is increasing. Why not put the teachers who are in jail to work?

The debate about whether gang member Stanley "Tookie" Williams should be executed highlighted that criminals can change and get an education. He made amends by writing children's books about the dangers of gangs and violence – and he was executed anyway.

Crisis

America's reading crisis must be solved in the early grades with competent, well-trained and well-paid teachers who are equipped with the proper tools. Chief among those tools are the right reading texts and language arts framework that recognize this, focusing on the importance of systematic and explicitly phonics-based reading.

The first step to solve the educational crisis is to attract qualified people to the teaching professions by paying them better salaries. They deserve to be paid more than government and educational bureaucrats. Definitely more than career politicians. They educate and train our future. Future butchers, bakers, candlestick makers, doctors, lawyers and policy makers. Butchers and bakers have been subsumed by supermarkets but, boy, with all those dinner parties being held in cookie-cutter McMansion-style gated homes, we certainly need those candlestick makers.

Pulitzer Prize-winning and retired teacher Frank McCourt, who taught at Stuyvesant High School, wrote in *Teacher Man* his book about being a teacher: "Teaching is harder than working on docks and warehouses." He is right. Yet the average teacher today only makes $30,000 a year. Their hours of work are endless. Early mornings are for students who need extra help, evenings are for test corrections and lesson plans, and weekends and summers are for second and third jobs to make ends meet. According to the U.S. Department of Education, one in every five teachers leaves after the first year, and almost twice as many leave within three. As *Newsweek* columnist Anna Quindlen wrote in 2005: "If any business had that rate of turnover, someone would do something smart and strategic to fix it. This isn't any business. It's the most important business around, the gardeners of the landscape of the human race." The Bush missionary plan for teachers is not working. It has failed.

There is a shortage of about 50,000 teachers in America each year, according to the National Education Association. That gap is being filled by foreign educators who are outsourced to America, where they earn more than they would back home. For example, Filipino teachers earn $9,000 to $12,000 a year in the Philippines and are lining up to come teach in America, where they can earn as much as $45,000 a year.

The downside to learning from foreign teachers is that many have difficult accents for American students to understand, or worse, American students learn to speak English with a foreign accent. Joel Weingarten, a friend of mine in Los Angeles who immigrated to America, learned English from a Japanese teacher. "For years, I went around saying 'mudah' and 'fada,' for mother and father, and 'jumpin japs' for jumping jacks," Joel told me during one of our many discussions on the sad state of the U.S. education system.

Many schools have resorted to e-tutors and mentors from India. If schools are going to e-teaching, why bother having schools? With today's new technology, the world is at the fingertips of every student. All they need is a keyboard at home – no classroom or teacher. There has to be a balance between what one learns in a disciplined social setting at school and alone at home interactively in the 21st century.

The education system in America is a mess. "You want to know why we have fallen so far behind and what the solution is?" Laurie D'Amico asked me as I was discussing the subject with her and her husband Mark, who is a professor at Clark University, the oldest graduate school in America. "Better pay for teachers. Teaching is not for slackers. It is hard work to see 125 students a day, five classes a day, plus meetings with administration officials, parents and their problem children," Laurie said. "Teaching is not for the faint of heart either. There is no place to hide anymore. No foxholes. Teachers need planning time, which they don't have today. It's very hard to do five shows a day a la Letterman or Leno. Teachers have to be entertaining, provocative and educational. It's hard educating children who are media savvy today."

Starting salaries for teachers are woefully low and have to be increased dramatically to attract and keep high-caliber instructors. Teachers deserve better pay than politicians and school administrators. It is up to *We the Apathetic Maids* – parents and former students – who owe our schooling knowledge to them, to get them the pay they deserve. That is the only way talented long-term teachers will be recruited to educate and prepare America's future generations to compete effectively in the 21st century.

Why not start teachers out at $60,000 and let them earn up to $175,000? Why should inexperienced career politicians start out at more than what teachers get at retirement? Who is more valuabe to our future?

In 1984, Ross Perot was appointed by Texas Gov. Mark White to head a commission on how to reform that state's public education. The Perot Commission proposed a package of dramatic reforms, including small class sizes, expanded kindergarten programs and testing to make schools accountable. The Perot reforms encountered resistance from all quarters. From the left by African-Americans and Latino activists who complained that nonwhite students would disproportionately fail tougher tests. But the greatest opposition came from small-town white Texans, who were shocked by the commission's proposed "no-pass, no play" rule, which applied to high school football players. There is no clearer indication of the anti-intellectualism of mainstream U.S. society than jock-pandering in the education system.

Perot's report was enacted into law. Studies by a RAND Corp. team and other scholars showed dramatic improvement in the academic performance of students in Texas by 1996. Shouldn't *We the Maids* be sweeping in similar academic reforms in every school district in America?

All Americans must be re-inspired to have the same hunger for knowledge that the Chinese and Asian-Americans do. Granted not all Chinese and Asians are smart. I know some who are seriously lazy, dumb, uninterested and uninteresting. The Chinese Confucian sponge for knowledge is a commodity that every household in America must strive to acquire and instill in our children. Research and development at American universities relies heavily on foreign students in the crucial fields of science, technology, engineering and mathematics (the STEM fields). Scott A. Bass wrote a compelling piece in *The Boston Globe* about the perils America faces in the future because of the shortcomings of the country's education system: "While foreign students are attracted to STEM fields at U.S. research universities, our own domestic students are not. Many have not been sufficiently encouraged, and others may have found the academic rigors of the STEM fields too challenging. Between 1986 and 1996, foreign students earning STEM field Ph.D.'s increased at a rate nearly four times faster than domestic students. In 2000, 43 percent of physical science PhD's went to non-U.S. citizens." Is this any way for America to remain competitive at the dawn of the 21st century?

Radical Surgery

Not a year goes by without stories about a corrupt school system or administration in some state in America. State and federal investigations into kickbacks, payments to former employees, nonexisting employees repeatedly trump the improved progress of the education system. Reading First, the federal annual $1 billion reading program to states – five years into the program and $5 billion later – turns out to be corrupt, riddled with conflicts of interest, with contracts going to cronies and based primarily on politics and not merit.

From New York to California, the story is the same. "When checks are regularly sent to dead people, and they're cashed, you know you have a problem," said New Orleans school board member Jimmy Farenholtz.

One of Hurricane Katrina's saddest legacies is the abandoned students left to fend for themselves because they were separated from their parents who lived hundreds of miles away. Angry children raising themselves, being educated in schools with no books, a shortage of teachers and food, in battered buildings. America at its third world worst performance.

Alan Bonsteel and Carlos A. Bonilla co-wrote an article in the *Los Angeles Times* in 1998 that pointed out that the California Department of Education, which took over the Compton Unified School District in 1993 because of mismanagement and bankruptcy, had turned the district into a "kleptocracy" with policies characterized as "genocide." The authors raised some profound questions. The most obvious: "If the state schools superintendent and her department couldn't manage even a moderate-sized school district, why were they being permitted to dictate to the other 998 school districts in California?" An equally crucial question is why, when not just Compton but all of America's big-city school districts have failed at educating inner-city kids, are public educational establishments opposed to "opportunity schol-arship" school vouchers for the most disadvantaged kids?

A more pressing question is why do the parents of the more than 1 million students in the nation's largest urban poor-performing schools keep their children there when they have a chance to move them to better performing schools?

New York City ended the millennium by letting a private company run some schools in an effort to turn the entire public school system over to the private sector. Under the plan, parents in a school could vote to convert the school to a charter school and a private sector firm would manage the school. In addition, Mayor Michael Bloomberg fought the state to gain direct control of its schools. He won and achieved what every mayor should be doing. New York City is a model to be followed by all cities in the New World Order. The Los Angeles Unified School District, like most school districts in America, is in desperate need of radical reform.

How about the Bovis Lend Lease program to spend several hundred million dollars on a capital-improvement program for more than 70 schools in and around Charlotte, North Carolina? Company employees also spend time tutoring, counseling and taking students on field trips because it is in the interest of the community, which benefits the company.

Financier Theodore J. Forstmann has proven the need and demand for chil-dren to get a better education in private schools. He turned his business acumen to help thousands of children escape failing public schools and go to private and religious schools. He raised $170 million in scholarships.

Forstmann said the number of applicants – 1,237,360, was even more com-pelling given that the scholarships will amount to only $600 to $1,600 a year for four years, not enough to cover the $2,500 tuition at most parochial schools. The winners will be required to make a matching contribution from their own pockets averaging $1,000 a year. Why aren't the religious schools paying the difference?

The applicants were, in effect, turning down a free education from the government. "So they're quite impoverished, they get their product for nothing and they're lining up around the corner to pay $1,000," Forstmann concluded. Is this any way to educate our children? Dramatic, radical changes need to be made to the free public education system if America is to survive the 21st century. There was a time when private, religious, charitable, subsidized, cooperative schools, a whole hodgepodge of types of schools, was the hit and miss way children were educated. Then came the magic wand. The state would lay on a comprehensive system of free compulsory education so that everybody got a fair shot at getting one. That has been gospel for too long. Now we are looking at ways of actually returning to a form of the original situation and many are shocked. It seems like deconstruction and a return to academic anarchy.

Bill Gates, the founder and CEO of Microsoft, pledged $1 billion to pay for full scholarships for the first 20 years of the new millennium for minority students in the fields of education, math, science and engineering. Gates' Millennium Scholarships will be open to all racial minorities. However, it is aimed primarily at black, Hispanic and Native American students. It's a great example of improving the knowledge of our inquisitive windows of the future. In addition to his generous financial contribution to scholarship and knowledge, Gates also dispenses words of wisdom. Love him or hate him, he knows how to hit the nail on the head when it comes to advice to our children. At speeches he gives at high schools, he talks about the 11 things children will not learn at school. He talks about how feel-good, politically correct teachings created a generation of kids with no concept of reality and how this concept set them up for failure in the real world.

Rule 1: Life is not fair – get used to it!

Rule 2: The world won't care about your self-esteem. The world will expect you to accomplish something BEFORE you feel good about yourself.

Rule 3: You will NOT make $60,000 a year right out of high school. You won't be a vice president with a car phone until you earn both.

Rule 4: If you think your teacher is tough, wait until you get a boss.

Rule 5: Flipping burgers is not beneath your dignity. Your grandparents had a different word for burger flipping: they called it opportunity.

Rule 6:   If you mess up, it's not your parents' fault, so don't whine about your mistakes, learn from them.

Rule 7:   Before you were born, your parents weren't as boring as they are now. They got that way from paying your bills, cleaning your clothes and listening to you talk about how cool you thought you were. So before you save the rain forest from the parasites of your parent's generation, try delousing the closet in your own room.

Rule 8:   Your school may have done away with winners and losers, but life HAS NOT. In some schools, they have abolished failing grades and they'll give you as MANY TIMES as you want to get the right answer. This doesn't bear the slightest resemblance to ANYTHING in real life.

Rule 9:   Life is not divided into semesters. You don't get summers off and very few employers are interested in helping you FIND YOURSELF. Do that on your own time.

Rule 10:   Television is NOT real life. In real life people actually have to leave the coffee shop and go to jobs.

Rule 11:   Be nice to nerds. Chances are you'll end up working for one.

Tiger Woods and his $25 million Tiger Woods Learning Center, in the neighborhood where he grew up in Anaheim, California, is another such example. The center is next to the H.G. "Dad" Miller Golf Course, where Woods played when he was in high school. Kids come to the center after school for interactive programs in science, mathematics and technology. Tiger donated the first $5 million and relied on the Deutsche Bank Championship, which he started, net proceeds and 25 founding partners, including Target, Nike and Augusta National.

Celebrity philanthropy does not a system make. By the way, if technuts like Woods and Gates get to give out the goodies and dictate the academic rules, we won't have an historian, musician, artist or French speaker left in America.

If America's 200 richest people each donated 1 percent of their wealth per year, and the funds were properly managed and utilized, every child in

America could have access to a quality primary education.

Veteran adventurer Simon Murray trekked 1,300 kilometers in 2003 across the Antarctic continent to the South Pole to raise funds for education. It was a death-defying mission involving sub-zero temperatures, ice, winds and hidden crevasses. "We are raising money to help unlock the archives of the Royal Geographical Society and open up that vast reservoir of knowledge and maps and manuscripts to our youth " he said. "Unlocking and digitalizing this material for the general public and the Internet will bring huge benefits to education throughout the world "

When Hong Kong-born Ravi Gidumal and Shalini Mahtani, your average noncelebrity couple, decided to get married, they asked their friends and family to make donations to a trust fund for children's education in India in lieu of wedding gifts. The fund educates 107 children – mostly first-generation learners. Christians. Hindus and Muslims study side by side. The school employs community members who would otherwise be cast aside, such as survivors of domestic violence and the physically disabled.

The private trust is administered for free by friends. The school's director in India, Vijaya Murthy, formerly with the Singapore Ministry of Education, works without remuneration. Their friends and the community contribute to the fund to educate needy children. A model millennium wedding gift to the needy. What if all well-off couples getting married, which seems to be a diminishing number these days, followed Ravi and Shalini's lead and allocated all or part of their wedding gifts to a trust to finance education?

Christian Havrehed, who is Danish, and Sun Haibin, who is Chinese, both living in Hong Kong, decided to row across the Atlantic and take part in the Ward Evans Cross Atlantic Rowing Race to pay for eight scholarships for mainland Chinese students to attend the United World College of the Atlantic in Wales. The school has 350 students from 70 countries and promotes international understanding. Havrehed enrolled for two years when he was 16. "The difference between life before Atlantic College and after is you really believe everything is possible," he said. "You can go and fulfill your dreams. It gives you a lot of self-confidence." Shouldn't those of us who can afford to do so try and sponsor a high school student so that as many of them as possible who graduate feel the same way in the 21st century?

I am a graduate of the California State University system and know first-hand how affordable it was to go to school in the '60s. All one had to do was have the desire to study, do so and graduate. University costs today are out of reach for most people. Community colleges, on the other hand, are accessible to all. Governments have to revisit the issue of providing an affordable quality education to our children. Only a well-educated humanity can feed, survive and improve civilization.

A debate at all levels over teacher training, teacher salaries and licensing practices is long overdue. Education has to be provided by local communities and local governments. The federal government has no business being in the education business. It is time for real long-term educational reform. Not just a quick-fix short-term solution.

All ideas, no matter how extreme, must be considered. That is the only way to come up with real solutions for the 21st century. Michael Lind, in *The Next American Nation*, suggests a radical idea on how higher education should be restructured in the New World Order: "For generations, Americans have perceived the link between universal public education and social mobility. That link needs to be restored....

"We should give some thought to turning higher education from a largely private luxury into a universal entitlement and a regulated public utility. The rationing of access to higher education by parental income and wealth – the chief means by which inherited money is converted into managerial-professional credentials – should be brought to an end. One way to achieve this goal might be the adoption, from some health care schemes, of a universal, single-payer system for higher education.

Here is how it might work: Colleges and universities would be banned from accepting any payments from students or their parents except for government higher education vouchers, on pain of losing their federal tax-exempt status. All young adults would be entitled to a voucher, though the amounts would vary based on academic achievement, measured by achievement tests. Most might receive two or four-year vouchers; the top 10 or 20 percent, in terms of academic achievement, would get six or eight- year vouchers. The vouchers would not be loans. They would be free of any obligation, except the obligation to adequately finish a course of study." Cuba is a good example.

Lind adds, "In order to prevent the costs of this new middle-class entitlement from spiraling out of control, the government would have to impose tuition caps on all colleges and universities, private or state, that accept the vouchers (and the tax-exempt status that comes with it). The tuition at Yale and Harvard would be exactly the same as the tuition at, say, the University of Nebraska – say, a few thousand a year. Would this tend to erase the difference between the expensive Ivy League schools and other colleges and universities? Naturally – and about time, too. The abolition of private financing of higher education, along with the outlawing of alumni preference, would force the Ivy League to abandon its historic role as a credentialing institution for a social oligarchy. The prestige of a college in the new system would depend on its attracting the brightest students, of all backgrounds, not on coaxing funds from rich alumni parents in return for warehousing their mediocre children for four years."

George Bush exemplifies this point. At a Yale graduation he said: "And to the C students, I say, you too can be president of the United States."

Sure a warehoused C student can become president. It helps if his father was president first and his grandfather was a senator, and he was born into a family that straddles the Northeast WASP aristocracy and the Sunbelt business establishment. A C student at a prep school can get into Yale and other Ivy League schools by "adopting a similar plan of strategic birth control. That is controlling whom you're born to," Michael Kinsley wrote in an editorial in 2001. C students born to the right gene pool make up "the happy bottom quarter" of classes at Ivy League schools. To qualify, all they need is a C, alumni parents, be athletes, or have rich parent donors.

A billboard ad for the launch of *Radar Magazine*, in the summer of 2005 in the East Village, summed it up best. A picture of Paris Hilton and President Bush with the tag line: "NO TALENT? NO PROBLEM! HOW TO BE FAMOUS FOR DOING NOTHING AT ALL."

In most Ivy League universities, "legacies" make up between 10 percent and 15 percent of every freshman class. At Notre Dame, they make up 23 percent. Benjamin Franklin said that "a man who makes boast of his ancestors doth but advertise his own insignificance." George Bush is a classic 21st-century example.

History has taught us that those who ignore history are condemned to repeat it, a lesson Bush clearly missed while he was busy partying. Is it any wonder he has led America into quagmires in Afganistan and Iraq, two countries with a rich history of defeating foreign armies?

The quality of "the happy bottom quarter" graduates is another matter. This was best exemplified again by the C president during his summit with Russian President Vladimir Putin in Crawford, Texas. Bush's fuzzy math left many wondering what he meant about the new era of U.S.-Russia relations when he said: "And so one of the areas where I think the average Russian will realize that the stereotypes of America have changed is that it's a spirit of cooperation, not one-upmanship; that we now understand one plus one can equal three, as opposed to us, and Russia we hope to be zero." If he'd been stopped by a highway patrol officer and said that, he'd have been breathalized. This is the same guy who proclaimed that he wanted to be the education president.

Is it any wonder he couldn't add up the casualties in Iraq and reach the conclusion that his policies there were a failure? Or how about his fellow Yalie, Senator John Kerry, whose botched joke before a college crowd during the 2006 congressional elections drew fire from Bush for insulting U.S. troops in Iraq: "You know, education, if you make the most of it, you study hard, you do your homework and you make an effort to be smart, you can do well. If you don't, you get stuck in Iraq." He meant to say, "You end up getting us stuck in a war in Iraq."

Michael Lind's proposal merits consideration. However, there is a middle ground that will allow bright underprivileged students to benefit from the same higher education as their bright rich contemporaries. They can even become president, like their correct gene pool contemporaries, if the political process reverts back to what the Founding Fathers envisioned. What about also adding and requiring students to take a few practical experience courses in their field of study?

Instead of universities investing their billions of dollars of endowment funds in the stock market to get higher yields on their capital, why don't they spend a third of their capital on improving the country's return on human capital? That would result in billions of dollars being invested in our future by funding scholarships and student loans that benefit the entire community and not just the universities. More college and university doors must be opened to the poor, needy and working-class citizens in the 21st century.

Trade Schools

Before I went to college I attended an agricultural high school in Israel. It was an agricultural trade school. Many of my friends went to nonagricultural trade schools and studied mechanics, woodworking, auto repair and aircraft repair. We all learned trades. Many of us went on to college. It didn't mean one stayed in the trade they started at high school. Everyone has the right to change their mind. Many still do. I went from farmer, to lawyer, to writer, with a lot of career changes in between. The point is, with a good education, trade, or profession, one can do anything, even harvesting.

In China, the Vocational Education Law requires that 20 percent of the annual education budget go to vocational education. Shouldn't America be doing the same?

Kevin Parker is an Englishman from Devon living in Edinburgh, Scotland, with his Scottish wife Katy and their two children Beth and Iain. His wife was a University of Edinburgh classmate of my partner Pauline. He has a PhD in chemistry and an MBA in teaching management accounting. He teaches applied mathematics to graduate students and has had in his classes Syrian, Israeli, Serb, Croat, Greek, Turkish, Indian and Pakistani students. "Makes for very interesting political exchanges," he said. He started his business career as a British Petroleum researcher in the 1980s and then got into sales – selling oil to Arabs. He had a sales catalogue of 18,000 lubricating oils – and was responsible for corporate planning as well. I learned a few things about how one goes about selling lubricants to Arabs. Interestingly, Iranian crude is the best for lubricants.

Kevin, is also a scoutmaster. What really amazed him, was how "really blown away" his cub scouts are when they go hiking, camping or other outdoor activities without cell phones, iPods, or any other electronic device. Life is an exploration that has become a journey cluttered and disrupted by

electronics, disabling people from learning how to make their own decisions and taking control of their life. Life is about finding a recipe for sanity,
even if it involves an element of irrationality as one follows their instincts.
There is no set formula for success in life. Each person has to find their own.
Life is not linear.

Schools in America have cut out classes that teach vocational skills, such as
woodshop, auto repair, electrical repairs, computers and other trades, for
budgetary reasons. When I lived in America, I never once needed an MBA.
I was always in need of a mechanic or a plumber. Not much business went
on in my front yard with neighbors, but the car or toilet were forever bursting.
Isn't it time we considered funding trade schools again in the 21st century?

Trade schools should be funded and supervised by local governments. Many
students want to learn one of the trades on which we all rely. Not everyone
has to go to college. Not everyone wants to. As far as earning power goes,
drug dealers earn less than plumbers. More than one friend tells me that they
have to use social intermediaries – otherwise known as lobbyists – to persuade plumbers to fit them into their schedule. Why push kids through high
school and college to create a society of illiterate degree holders? If students
cannot read, cannot write and cannot speak English, why should they
graduate?

Some of my classmates in high school came from underprivileged neighborhoods and the underclasses. Some were even convicted juvenile delinquents doing their time working the fields while they got an education. The
school gave them a social education as well and allowed them to integrate
into society. Isn't this a model America can adopt to prepare students from
the underclasses?

These boarding schools can be modeled after the turn-of-the-century settlement houses for European immigrants of Jane Addams or the Israeli
kibbutzim, where I spent my senior year of high school, and immigrant re-
settlement schools that managed to absorb and educate millions of immigrants from all over the world and integrate them into society. "It is difficult
to imagine a successful program for dispersing the ghetto poor that would
not have an intermediate stage of education and acculturation and, if
necessary, rehabilitation. That stage would have to involve a period of sepa-

ration from the ghetto environment and incentives for learning standard
English, mainstream manners, and useful skills," Lind wrote in his 1995
book *The Next American Nation.*

Such schools do not have to be limited to children from the ghetto. They can
also be beneficial to children of migrants who work America's fields, or-
chards and farms. In 2004, one in every 10 U.S. farm laborers was a migrant,
the Department of Agriculture estimated. Instead of subsidizing agro-
business, the department should consider subsidizing these migrant children's
education. The Bracero program was started during World War II to fill the
jobs left empty by men at war. Today, too many children of migrant workers
are also working the fields like slaves rather than studying. It is time to get
them into classrooms.

Wake-up Call

Is there any valid reason why all schools, public and private, are not open
until 7 in the evening – or later if necessay – with day-care centers for young
children to make life easier for working parents? How about night school
for high school students who have to work during the day to support their
family? Studies show that high school students do better at night than they
do in the early morning when most have to be in school. I did and still do
like it best in the morning. Most high school students sleep through their
early morning classes because their brains, according to sleep researchers,
are wired to stay up later and require more sleep than children of other age
groups.

High schools in America should consider starting classes later than the 7:30
a.m. norm to allow students to get the sleep they need. School leaders in
Edina, Minnesota, flipped their bus schedules for teenagers by having high
school classes there start at 8:30 a.m. – with better attendance and academic
results. A later starting schedule would also have the added benefit of teenagers not leaving school in the early afternoon and being unsupervised until
the evenings when their working parents get home.

There are a lot of ways to improve America's high schools. "The single most
important way to improve high schools is to improve elementary and junior
high schools," said education historian Diane Ravitch of New York
University. "If a student arrived in ninth grade ready for instruction in math,

science, history, literature and foreign language, then no further reform is needed."

Under laws now being passed, organizations or individuals – often parents and teachers – can petition an officially designated body for a charter to operate a school that is free from some or all of the union and civil-service rules and budgetary restrictions that govern ordinary public schools. The charter functions as a contract in which the prospective school spells out how it plans to operate as well as what it vows to accomplish; the sponsoring agency monitors the school, and chooses whether to renew the charter at the end of a specified period, typically five years.

The premise of the charter school movement is that the difference between good and bad schools lies not in any particular classroom practice, but in the way the school itself is administered. Ideologically, the charter proposal occupies a position midway between "choice" – the idea that children can attend any school in their district – and vouchers, which allow children to attend private or parochial schools with public money. Liberals prefer choice; free-market conservatives favor vouchers – and both have found they can live with charters.

Born Again GI Bill

The Hong Kong government spends 21 percent of its budget on education. Shouldn't America be doing the same? The annual cost of a private college education in America is more than $22,000, not counting room and board. The average for state colleges is around $10,000. What does the education president want to do? He wants to spend $300,000,000 a year on his educational campaign to promote marriage, particularly in low income-communities. Schools promoting abstinence over other forms of sexual education would receive $135,000,000 annually under his proposal. Now really, is this the best use of *We The Apathetic People's* tax dollars. Why can't the money just be spent on education, period? Why does it have to be directed to religious right schools preaching what nobody practices?

The Servicemen's Readjustment Act of 1944, enacted into law after World War II, better known as the GI Bill, transformed America in more ways than its proponents anticipated. It not only promoted educational opportunities for families who never had access to a higher education, but created a better informed electorate, albeit an apathetic one. America's decision to reward

WWII returning GIs with the opportunity to upgrade themselves from the blue-collar working class into the white-collar educated elite transformed America from a completely uninformed active working class to educated informed apathetic couch vegetables.

Subsequent GIs who took advantage of the educational opportunities offered by the GI Bill also transformed their families and upgraded themselves in the process. The GI Bill still offers U.S. veterans the opportunity to get a higher education, but things have changed. Service members now find a policy that is much less generous, inclusive and fair.

For GIs returning from Afghanistan and Iraq, education benefits have fallen way behind college costs, even for the active-duty forces. That is because, in recent decades, GIs have been returning from fighting unpopular or at least suspect wars. Congress and cynical civilians are just not feeling the same sort of gratitude – but they should. Reserve and National Guard units, though they make up fully half of the U.S. troops deployed in Iraq, receive substantially less. The word from Washington is that there is simply no money – even for the 1 percent of Americans who make up our all-volunteer military.

The landmark GI Bill of 1944 epitomized the granting of widespread opportunity for those who did their civic duty. More than half of all returning veterans – 7.8 million – made use of the bill's provisions. The benefits gave veterans from less-advantaged backgrounds chances they never dreamed possible and a route to the middle class. Since World War II, as the military became less representative of the citizenry, the scope of the GI Bill narrowed as well. Today's GI Bill, created in 1984, means much to its beneficiaries but it pales compared to the original. Benefits today – despite recent increases – have not kept up with the rising cost of higher education.

The World War II version gave veterans a full ride, covering tuition at any college, public or private, as well as vocational training programs. Today's veterans face bills of $1,712 per month for full-time tuition, room and board at the average four-year public university or college, but the GI Bill offers them, at most, $1,034 monthly. And though most are married, they receive none of the "subsistence allowances" that helped World War II veterans and their families cover living expenses. If the GI Bill is to be fair again, it needs to reach the broader parameters of today's total force. Of the 152,000 troops serving in Iraq, 75,000 are in the Guard or Reserve, with tours of duty lasting at least one year. They suffer casualty rates that exceed those of the active-duty troops. Yet when they come home, their benefits are only one-third as much. And if they leave the service, they get nothing. Suzanne Mettler, the author of *Soldiers to Citizens: The GI Bill and the Making of the Greatest Generation*, wrote that when the nation united against Nazis and facism, those on the home front were called on to contribute to the war effort. They saved scrap metal and rubber, planted victory gardens and worked in defense plants. Today, we've been asked to do nothing, unless you count President Bush's request after 9/11 that we go shopping. Sacrifice? Heck no. We've got tax cuts, the lion's share of which go to the wealthiest 1 percent of Americans. Mettler added, "Surely we owe those few Americans who volunteer on our behalf a GI Bill equal to that which benefited the 'greatest generation.' That's the least the other 99 percent of us can do."

What the GI Bill did for returning GIs is what America needs for its ghettos and underprivileged children. A "Ghetto Instruction" bill that would allow all children from all pockets of poverty in America to have affordable access to higher education. A born-again GI Bill that substitutes minorities, the underprivileged and impoverished for veterans. Only then can America effectively combat ignorance. An educated and informed public is much better prepared to confront the rapidly changing cyber world of the 21st century.

The existing educational bias towards students in poor communities has to be ended in the 21st century if America is to become competitive again. A study conducted by the Chinese University and City University that drew data from a U.N. study that tested 193,076 15-year-olds in 41 countries and regions in various subjects found that scores in countries with high equality, including Hong Kong and Finland, were higher than those with an unequal system, such as the United States and Argentina. The study concluded that since poor students benefited more from additional resources from the government, a skewed distribution of resources that favored schools attended by richer students led to lower scores.

Historically, every generation in America has gotten a better education than their parents. That does not translate to a job guarantee upon graduation. No one owes any American a living. There are no job guarantees upon graduation in America. All one has to do is look at all the unemployed university graduates. I get disgusted and annoyed listening to all the complaints voiced by career politicians about outsourcing and how unfair it is to the American worker. What's better for the U.S. worker, higher hourly wages while being unemployed, or a lower salary and employment? High U.S. wages have priced the American worker into the unemployment lines.

A Chinese furniture worker earns $100 a month; a U.S. worker earns $20 an hour. Is it any wonder there is outsourcing?

Inevitably, online high schools and universities that have been around for years are another alternative to be properly funded and implemented in the cyber New World Order.

Child Labor
In our cyber world, the education of children should not be limited to working children in America. Children everywhere affect us if they are not properly educated. This was brought home by 9/11 and the stories that explained why Muslim fundamentalists were angry at the West, and by Hurricane Katrina. The squalor, deprivation and lack of education most poor children receive while subjected to oppressive working conditions, especially in many Muslim countries, was registered loud and clear in the post-9/11 stories analyzing the reasons people are willing to become suicide bombers. Children are the best investment

Research has shown that for every dollar invested in early childhood programs, countries enjoy cost savings of seven dollars. Young children who receive good early care are less likely to die, get sick, fail in their school education or require remedial services. They will be able to support themselves and their families, push their societies forward and help break the cycle of illness and deprivation. Investing in early childhood plays a direct role in sustainable poverty reduction. China is living proof.

China has invested heavily in human capital that promises to sustain growth and create greater prosperity. Parents in China spend $90 billion a year on their childrens' education. This is over and above what the governemnt spends. Government and families constantly increase their investment in primary and secondary education. Elite English private schools are setting up campuses in China to capitalize on the educational opportunities. Given the excellent core curriculum available across China to its 230 million students, the country is well positioned to continue to upgrade its human capital over the next decade. Shouldn't America be doing the same? Shouldn't every country invest wisely in a secular education and rid itself of the fundamentalists who teach hatred and violence? Numerous articles were written after 9/11 pointing out the squalor and abuse children in Muslim countries are subjected to and the reasons why they become suicide bombers. Such practices are not limited to Muslim countries.

Fahkromron Watdirany, a 12-year-old boxer in Bangkok, is an example of abusive child labor practices in a Buddhist country. He has had 40 professional bouts since he was eight. His thoughts on a proposed law that would bar kids under 15 from entering the ring? "If the law stops me from boxing, I don't know where I would get the money for my school and family." This is a form of child abuse that we must stop in the New World Order.

The International Labor Organization reports that 250,000,000 children between the ages of five and 14 worked, mostly in Asia and Africa. Some 50 million to 60 million children aged five to 11 are working in dangerous jobs. We must ban abusive child labor practices, especially the use of children in pornography and prostitution.

One in 12 of the world's children is involved in the worst forms of forced labor, sexual exploitation or forced military conscription, according to the U.N.'s children's agency UNICEF. It concluded in a report released in 2005 that 180 million people under 18 are involved in slavery, bonded labor, commercial sexual exploitation and military activity. One of the ways Al-Qaeda funds its activities is through the kidnapping of Christian children in Pakistan who are sold into slavery.

In some developing countries, up to two-thirds of children under 18 hold down full-time jobs, while an estimated 114 million children of primary-school age are not enrolled in school. That is why we have to applaud U.S. Winter Olympic gold medalist Joey Cheek, who donated his Olympic winnings to the children's organization Right To Play, which gives children who have been exploited in wars and other forms of exploitation the opportunity to play and be a child.

The study found that in some countries, children as young as 11 were being forced into prostitution to support younger siblings because both parents had been killed by AIDS. The AIDS epidemic in Africa has meant that children as young as 13 or 14 are heading the households and need to work.

Hong Kong is the first Asian city to outlaw the possession of child pornography. The problem has deteriorated globally. Children are a symbol of our promising future and should be protected from being porn material.

Every day tens of millions of children work in conditions that "shock the conscience." These are not some archaic practices out of a Charles Dickens novel. These are things that happen in too many places today. The International Labor Organization unanimously adopted a convention that would outlaw work dealing with toxic substances and labor that is deemed harmful to children's health, safety and morals.

Life Sciences

Schools teach algebra and many other subjects that most of us never use or benefit from in our everyday lives once we have taken the final exam. Why aren't schools teaching real life sciences that have application and bearing in our everyday lives? Reality survival classes that are useful in day-to-day living. Why is reality limited to shows on TV?

Children need preparation for the real tough world. They cannot be educated like flowers in a greenhouse, unable to stand the brute forces of nature.

Travel to foreign countries, including student exchange programs, should be part of every school curriculum. Actress Angelina Jolie said it best after she visited Africa as a U.N. goodwill ambassador. "I became more aware of the world when I started to travel," she said. "And that's given me a social conscience. I think travel has that effect on most people."

Why aren't schools offering courses in life, marriage, relationships, responsibility, parenting, having a baby, raising a child, balancing checkbooks like they did in the 1950s? President Bush asked Congress to set aside $360,000,000 in the welfare reform law to promote "healthy, stable marriages." To proponents of the func, that means programs urging marriage and counseling to keep couples together. A *Los Angeles Times* editorial correctly pointed out that "the money should be spent on something more than promoting marriage; it should be spent on one obvious element that helps encourage a strong marriage: financial stability. That means much of it should go to vocational training and jobs."

Why should men have to wait until they have gone through several decades of relationships to understand women – or conversely – women to understand men? The thought occurred to me during a discussion on the subject in the Philippines, a staunchly Catholic country, with my good friends Jun and Isa Valenton, who each have two children from a previous marriage. Jun also has three grandchildren. They had just found out Isa was pregnant. Jun was lamenting the fact he was going to be a father again just as he found out his daughter Angela, who was not married at the time, was going to make him a grandfather again. "I just don't understand women and how we misread their desires and intentions," Jun told me as we adjourned to the adjoining room. I was somewhat taken aback by his comment as Jun is considered the dean of womanology in Manila and the one many forlorn lovers – male and female – and couples go to for advice about their relationships.

It just so happened I had a printout of a recent e-mail someone sent me about "The Answers We Men Have All Been Waiting For About Women," so I decided to read them aloud to Jun as he refilled our wine glasses.

Q: What are the small bumps around a woman's nipples for?
A: Its Braille for lick here.

Q: What is an Australian kiss?
A: It is the same as a French kiss, but only down under.

Q. What do you do with 365 used condoms?
A: Melt them down, make a tire, and call it a Goodyear.

Q. Why are hurricanes normally named after women?
A: When they come they're wild and wet, but when they go, they take your house and car with them.

Q: Why do girls rub their eyes when they get up in the morning?
A: Because they don't have any balls to scratch.

The Bush administration's insistence on education programs that teach abstinence is a short-sighted deferred tax bill *We the Apathetic Maids* will pass on to our children. Abstinence does not preclude masturbation – in fact it encourages it – which is the only benefit of the program. Research by Australia's Cancer Council in Victoria state found that the more often men ejaculate between the ages of 20 and 50, the less likely they are to suffer prostate cancer. The survey of 1,079 prostate cancer patients and 1,259 healthy men found that those who masturbated or had sex at least once a day in their 20s were a third less likely to develop the disease. Costs a small fortune in Kleenex and hand towel laundry, but its not bad for you. "Masturbation isn't bad for you. I don't believe in the blindness and hairy palms theory. Prohibitions against ejaculations are not based on science," Graham Giles, who led the research team, said in July 2003 when the results were released.

Premarital sex is nothing new in America. More than nine out of 10 American men and women have had premarital sex, according to a 2006 study released by the Guttmacher Institute, a private New York-based think-tank. The high rates extend even to women born in the 1940s, challenging perceptions that people were more chaste in the past. "This is reality-check research," said the study's author, Lawrence Finer.

Sex education is vital to minimize AIDS and other sexually transmitted diseases – and pregnancies. Religious groups that are opposed to classes on premarital sex, homosexuality, artificial contraception, abortion, artificial insemination and same-sex marriages are not preparing their students for the real grown-up world. The height of hypocrisy of religious leaders opposed to sex education and same-sex marriages is the high profile resignation of Reverend Ted Haggard, the leader of the 30 million-member National Association of Evangelicals, after admitting he paid for sex with a man for three years.

It's bad enough and shortsighted for America to advocate abstinence at home, but globally? It makes the country sound like an "irresponsible nitwit," in the words of columnist Stuart Wolfendale, when countries at a 2005 U.N. meeting of the Commission on the Status of Women adopted a resolution for female economic advancement over the objections of the U.S. The resolution capped a contentious two-week meeting with the U.S. at odds with the rest of the world over issues of reproductive health and abortion. The U.S. was opposed to sexual rights and abortion and said that abstinence was "the healthiest" and "most responsible choice" for adolescents and parents had the primary responsibility for sex education. Washington rushes in where even Rome is uneasy treading.

The government's advocacy of abstinence echoes a Ugandan member of parliament who in 2005 pledged to reward girls for chastity by paying their university fees if they were virgins when they graduated. Worldwide studies show that a majority of the teenagers who took the abstinence pledge did not live up to their promise and developed sexually transmitted diseases at about the same rate as adolescents who had not made such a pledge. The authors of the latest study, published in March 2005 in *The Journal of Adolescence Health* by Dr. Peter Bearman, the chairman of the sociology department at Columbia University, and Hannah Bruckner of Yale University, wrote that all the promises did was "to delay the start of intercourse by 18 months."

Some of the letters to editors written by teenagers in America in response to abstinence articles are the most telling about how teenagers feel and act. My favorite was the one written by Abby Forsythe, from Fort Bragg, California to *U.S. News & World Report*. "Regarding the article 'Just Don't Do It!'" [October 17, 2005]: I am 14, and in my opinion, sex education should be taught with a comprehensive approach. A comprehensive approach actually teaches about sex and protection as well as about abstinence. It allows teen-agers to make informed, mature decisions about sex and teaches us how to protect ourselves against unwanted pregnancies and sexually transmitted diseases. If teens have information about sex, then we can make informed decisions. But if we are told that we cannot 'do it,' then we probably will because we're teens. We like to do forbidden things to break the rules."

In the UK, sex education classes teach oral sex in an attempt to stop inter-course and bring down the high rate of teenage pregnancies. In England, it gives a whole new meaning to the term "headmaster." In China, where AIDS is an epidemic because of the lack of sex education in the rural provinces until the 21st century, children start their sex education classes in kindergar-ten to protect the society from HIV/AIDS and teenage pregnancies. Shouldn't America be doing the same instead of wasting money on abstinence courses?

Schools should teach our children about the art of deception and the hypoc-risy of our civilizations. Teach them Allah, not algebra. Honest, factual comparative religious classes without advocating or proselytizing on behalf of any particular religion is educational and can only benefit our children and enhance tolerance and mutual respect in the 21st century.

Propaganda, terrorism, managed misperception and their benefits, delusions and pitfalls should also be taught, not as an elective but as a requirement to graduate. Schools should also teach disarmament – especially in school cor-ridors – and nonproliferation, capitalize on new communication technolo-gies and simulation. Just like history, sexuality, racism, math and chemistry.

There is no reason for any child in the world to be afraid to go to school because of random acts of violence. Whether they are Catholic children in Northern Ireland, Muslim or Asian children in America, or Chinese students out in the rural provinces.

Former Gov. Jessie Ventura of Minnesota has "advocated spending increases for schools. We need to get more teachers into our public classrooms, and we need to be able to pay good teachers well enough that they will want to stick around." He added "We need to strengthen and retool civics classes to help kids develop a working understanding of our system of government and their role in it. They need to be taught, and have the lesson reinforced at every grade level, the principles of the Constitution and the structure of our government. They need to be taught specifically about those duties that are their responsibility: voting...."

A California State Bar publication, *When You Become 18: A Survival Guide for Teenagers*, is a 16-page newspaper-style document written in easy-to-understand language and broken into sections that deal with alcohol, money, jobs, crime and other relevant subjects. Teachers in California schools find the guide to be a useful classroom tool because it provides context and rel-evance for academic themes relating to law, sociology, democracy and government. It helps make better citizens by making high school civics classes relevant. A survey conducted in 2005 by Mills College for the California Campaign for the Civic Mission of Schools found that "in classes where students frequently talked about current events, 61 percent reported they were interested in politics compared to 32 percent in classes with no discussion of current events."

Credit & Money Management

Classes on credit and money management must be introduced early on to our children. The number of teenagers and young adults filing bankruptcy and moving back home with their parents because of financial mismanagement is staggering. Children do need financial guidance in our increasingly cashless society. Parents and teachers have to instill in our children a sense of how to manage money on paper to cope with the cashless future. Credit cards are misleading to many who believe they can live beyond their means because credit is a bottomless pit. "Stay away from credit cards and invest in yourself," investment guru Warren Buffet said. It is not hard to remind and educate children that "money does not grow on trees," as my mother used to tell me constantly.

America's Generation Debt was never taught money management. Financial planning is an essential part of life and survival. Is it any wonder one in five young American adults are boomerang kids – children who return home to live with their parents, sometimes with their own family in tow? James Joyce summed it up best: "Mistakes are the portals of discovery."

Survey after survey shows that teenagers are signing on for more debt than they can repay. Why can't classes be taught that show students how to monitor their income and expenses, develop personal and family budgets, establish savings goals, research into global economic indices and exchange rates, explore investment options and define life strategies?

Money management training should start at an early age so children can build up good habits and cultivate a greater sense of financial responsibility for themselves and their community.

Educational Pork

Funds earmarked for our children's education are repeatedly ripped off by career politicians for themselves. Congress "went hog wild" bestowing such benefits, said Scott Fleming, the U.S. Department of Education liaison to Capitol Hill back in 1999. It is a congressional practice that is alive and well in the 21st century – just another example of career politicians elected to represent us taking care of themselves and stroking their egos first – and their constituents and our children's education be damned.

The new 2007 House ethics rules that restrict lobbyist-funded travel exempt colleges and universities, a powerful lobbying force in Washington. Colleges, universities and other higher-education groups spent at least $75 million on federal lobbying efforts in 2005, and have paid more than S900,000 worth of travel for lawmakers since 2000, according to a *USA Today* analysis of travel and lobbying reports compiled by nonpartisan data-tracking firms.

The special federal grants known as earmarks are often anonymously inserted into spending bills by lawmakers. *The Chronicle of Higher Education* tallied more than $2 billion in earmarks to universities in 2003, the most recent count by early 2007.

Lawmakers repeatedly dispense tens of millions of dollars in education grants that are quietly slipped into the budget process without hearings. This below-the-radar spending receives less scrutiny because it is usually lumped into the federal budget by politicians who have their spin doctors, the front line troops of this legislative abuse, down play it and make it sound and look like they are actually doing something for education.

Many of the desperately needed educational dollars are diverted to university programs named after retired senators. Most of the abuses happened in 1998 during "Monicagate," when education grants were slipped into the budget process while the media was busy with the salacious details of Bill Clinton's sexual scandal involving a former White House intern. Among some of the programs that were inappropriately funded with tax dollars are the Robert J. Dole Institute for Public Service and Public Policy at the University of Kansas; the Paul Simon Public Policy Institute at Southern Illinois University, which previously had hired the former senator at $120,000 a year; and Portland State University's Oregon Institute of Public Service and Constitutional Studies at the Mark Hatfield School of Government. "Don't forget the Peter de Krassel Institute for Recreation in the Horizontal University of California at Anywhere along the Pacific Coast Highway," columnist Stuart Wolfendale added after a delicious lunch at Neptune's Net on the Pacific Coast Highway at the Los Angeles/Ventura County line where we stopped to review his editorial comments for this book. It was such a ludicrous suggestion, but appropriate to the ludicrous pork doled out by politicians, I decided to mention it. Profiteering private diploma mills that bilk both the government and students must be better regulated.

Democratic Senator Tom Harkin, the senior Democrat on the Senate Appropriations Committee, inserted language in legislation that resulted in California, the nation's largest state, receiving less than 10 percent of the money Harkin snagged for Iowa, his home state. Iowa's funding for special projects nearly equals the amount currently devoted to professional training for teachers nationwide. A *Los Angeles Times* editorial accurately concluded: "Bringing home the bacon is a Washington tradition, but funding pet pork at the expense of education projects is a new level of shortsighted greed, even for Washington."

My favorite is Taiwan government funds linked to college endowments and a museum at the Jesse Helms Center in North Carolina, named after the formidable former head of the Senate Foreign Relations Committee and probably, at the time, the most powerful foreign policy figure in Congress. Sen. Helms referred to "Red China" until the day he retired.

With such shortsighted greed, is it any wonder America's children are uneducated, lost, confused and leading the retarded education retreat?

"We're all entitled to grow up. George W. Bush had his problems with alcohol. I was a Republican. We both got over it," said North Carolina Superior Court Judge Ray Warren, a conservative Republican until he became a Democrat in 2001.

Why are *We The Apathetic People* allowing politicians to take our tax money and our time to work for themselves or foreign governments? We know that dishonesty and insincerity are rampant in our political system. We know that many of our political leaders have made their careers out of yanking our uneducated, apathetic chains. I truly believe that the best way for us to combat all of these scams is to become experts at thinking for ourselves. Every citizen needs to understand the basics of sound thinking, and needs to apply them by staying informed. The more you're armed with good information, the less any of these tricks are going to work on you. These are words of wisdom from former Gov. Ventura, which I wholeheartedly endorse.

The sad news is that it's not just politicians ripping off our tax dollars for their own benefit. It is also universities and university hospitals that actually do get billions of dollars in grants not siphoned off by politicians, which then get siphoned off by university and hospital administrators. There is something incongruous and yet oddly familiar about universities and university hospitals stashing away money. They are the modern equivalent of the rich and privileged medieval monasteries.

Billions of dollars in grant monies are going to phantom studies at such prestigious universities as Cornell, Harvard, Johns Hopkins, Northwestern and the University of Alabama, all of which have settled civil lawsuits for their misdeeds since 2003. In a 2005 survey of 3,300 research scientists, researchers at the Minesota-based HealthPartners Research Foundation and the University of Minnesota found that more than 50 percent of established grant-getting scientists used grant money designated for one project on some other project – often for undisclosed research that might lead to future grants.

Benjamin Ladner, president of American University, agreed to resign in 2005, as part of a multimillion-dollar settlement after he was accused of lavish spending of university funds on himself and his wife, in the form of overseas trips, private parties and gifts. Marilee Jones, MIT's beloved former dean of admissions, had to resign after nearly three decades because she admitted she fabricated her own educational credentials. She did not even have an undergraduate degree.

In 1670, Anne Bradstreet, in her *Meditations Divine and Moral*, noted that "authority without wisdom is like a heavy ax without an edge-fitter to bruise than polish." In any country, the authority to rule runs in inverse proportion to its intellectual development. Our highest duty is to respect legitimate authority. But our future depends on how those who we have vested with authority respond to the corresponding responsibility that comes with their authority to educate and inform.

Some elected officials grow when they are given authority. Career politicians seem to just swell. In all parts of their body. Too many career politicians are dodging their responsibilities. We all have a tendency to blame the plight of the poor on the rich. This is as logical as blaming sickness and death on the healthy. What we really have to do is fight poverty. This is the true enemy, and the best way to fight poverty is to fight ignorance. *We the Apathetic People* must give our children an opportunity to develop their talents. The focus should be not on what they are, but what they can be. A good education is the best training for a job – any job or career. Job skills and desires change constantly. I know this from personal experience. I tried out as a bee keeper, builder, gardner, lawyer, teacher, entrepreneur, media executive and writer; today I am a combination of all those. The ability to adapt is provided by the basic knowledge acquired at school.

Honky Education

Honk Kong schools follow the English and Christian parochial school systems. Unlike their American counterparts, Hong Kong students seldom have academic difficulties when they transfer to schools in other countries. In fact, when they transfer to schools in the States, they usually wind up at the top of the class.

Teachers in Hong Kong are well paid. Their salaries are commensurate with that of well-paid government bureaucrats and professionals. Salaries are increased based on experience. Isn't it time America does the same?

Hong Kong has adopted the Scottish self-evaluation approach of school and teacher reviews that determine the funding a school receives from the government. The concept is based on three simple questions: How good is our school? How do we know? Now what are we going to do about it? The key is the gathering of evidence from within the school and the classroom in the assessment process.

Historically, all schools in Hong Kong are taught in English. Today the government promotes mother-tongue teaching. Chinese is the medium of instruction in many schools while English continues to be used in the rest. The goal is to enable students to be biliterate, to master written Chinese and English, and trilingual, to speak fluent Cantonese, Putonghua and English. In September, 1998, most secondary schools in Hong Kong were forced to switch to Chinese teaching. One hundred and fourteen schools were granted exemptions to teach in English. Victor Fung Kwok-king, University of Hong Kong council chairman who repeatedly calls on the private sector to support the development of local talent and a global outlook, said it best in 2005 in his Digby Memorial lecture at the university. "A crucial factor in our future success is the ability to communicate effectively with the rest of the world. This means that we must ensure that our graduates are fluent in English." The rationale was that it is the only way Hong Kong can maintain its edge as an international city. "Give a man a fish and you feed him for a day; teach him how to fish and you feed him for a lifetime," is an old Chinese saying.

That includes teaching children, as young as four, their fundamental human rights under the U.N. Convention on the Rights of the Child, as Hong Kong does. Schooling is all about education.

The Hong Kong Board of Education is advocating that mother-tongue language teaching be expanded and that teachers be periodically tested. About 14,000 English and 4,300 Mandarin teachers were required to pass the language benchmark test by 2005. It mirrors the debate in the U.S. over whether to teach first-generation immigrant kids in Spanish.

Under the existing system, the Primary Six level test makes it easier for students to be sent to a school that suits their ability and the language in which they should be taught. The Education Commission is considering scrapping the system. "Parents in Hong Kong are still very choosy about English schools. I am sure parents will create long queues outside some elite schools," an Education Commission spokesman said. This is a future concern. Shouldn't this be a current concern in America – where many parents are too busy to bother about schools, yet alone queue up?

Professor Cheng Kai-ming, a senior member of the Education Commission, believes each school in Hong Kong should be allowed to independently decide its medium of instruction with the only rule being no mixing of languages. In his opinion, the Education Department cannot police and regulate everything. "Many of us are still bound by some old and conservative concept. They think a horse would not know how to run if you don't teach it every step. They don't know the horse will just fly if you loosen the belt around his neck." Shouldn't education departments across America be loosening the noose they have tied on our children's education? Isn't it time parents everywhere made sure all schools in America are giving children the tools and skills needed to fly?

Civics

California students get a "D" in civics knowledge. Only half of those surveyed could identify the function of the Supreme Court, and 33 percent could not correctly identify even one of California's two U.S. senators. California students, the survey added, "also show limited commitment or capacity to become politically involved." Only 47 percent of high school seniors felt that it was their responsibility to be involved in state or local politics. However, the survey found there may be an antidote to political apathy. "A curriculum emphasis on the importance of civic engagement and relevant content regarding civic and political structures and functions helps students develop the skills and knowledge they need for effective citizenship. In addition, as students develop knowledge and interest in issues, their commitment to participate grows." I can't really blame students for being horrified by the antagonistic stupidity of the adult world that makes them want to run away.

Why don't civics classes teach how the community can be continuously improved through the political process? How the lack of participation by *We the Apathetic Maids* in the *United States of Apathy* is only benefiting self-serving career politicians – at the expense of our children.

The mind-walls built by a dysfunctional education system have to be brought down. None of the great national or global challenges can be tackled unless they are. Why can't education be made something all children can't get enough of? When I needed to threaten my children with punishment when they misbehaved, I would tell them, "You won't go to school if you don't...." It worked. School became something to look forward to. Why can't civics, political science and all classes for that matter, be made as exciting as a baseball, basketball, hockey, or football games?

Traveling in America, especially during a World Series or Super Bowl, I never cease to be amazed by how absorbed America gets, with a total disregard and disrespect for what is happening around them, even though it adversely affects their pocketbook. This was brought home during the 2004 election and the World Series. There is no question in my mind what America is passionate about. Sports. Politics, even during a critical presidential election, plays second fiddle. If America spent 10 percent less time devoted to sports and 10 percent more time on politics – wow! What a difference that would make. Kinky Friedman would be governor of Texas and Dennis Rodman could be speaker of the House.

Why can't Americans learn fundamental civics lessons, history and political science in order to understand and participate in their own democracy the way they do in sports? 'Cos its boring, dude. Watching the Patriots-Steelers football game the Sunday of the Red Sox victory parade, two days before the 2004 presidential election, I couldn't get over how seamlessly Americans go from sport to sport, season by season, even during a critical election season. The presidential election and the war in Iraq be damned. The fact that it was also the weekend with the highest one-day death toll in Iraq since the fighting had been declared over, eight Marines killed in Faloujah – made no difference. In a way, Caesar had things neatly arranged. The war on terror – Afghanistan and Iraq – is not wildly popular, but it's not bothersome either. The numbers of dead and wounded are incremental. It's a volunteer army. At home the circus is still rolling. It's what the neo-cons are really after: an acceptance of the U.S. promoting its interests somewhere around the globe – all the time.

America's Caesars have definitely gotten the masses to come out to support their teams and devour the Christian gladiators. The distraction allows Caesar to perpetuate his misdeeds at the expense of the tuned-out masses. Is it any wonder America has become a nation of checkers, baggers and servers?

Democracy should be a required course in all high schools, not just in America, but every country, especially those seeking financial aid and assistance from global institutions or America. "A high-quality democracy, with broad participation and legitimacy, depends on an informed citizenry that values and understands democracy," the second international nongovernmental forum of more than 100 countries held in conjunction with the Community of Democracies ministerial conference concluded in Seoul in 2002. Let us not forget that most of the world's Muslims already live under democratically elected non-Arab governments as well. Let's hope they remember to appreciate that.

Confucius Says
The headline Adulthood? Later, Dude! caught my attention as I leafed through the newspaper sipping my cafe latte on Main Street in Santa Monica one picture-perfect L.A. morning. "Why are so many people refusing to grow

up? Could it be the cost of living, the need for more education....

Or is it the fact that apathetic American parents have failed to instill the value of a good education. Coupled with their failure to spend enough time with their children to give them the emotional support and security to leave home, is it any wonder they are afraid to face the New World Disorder?

"What do you think?" I asked Mary Catherine who joined me for coffee. Mary Catherine Harold was the line producer of "Knotts Landing" and was now producing the "American Film Market, the biggest American movie and television sales convention of American movies and TV shows sold to foreign markets. It is held in Santa Monica once a year. Mary Catherine and I get together whenever we can when I'm in town and philosophize about life, our children and the cultural differences between Americans, Chinese and every other color of the human rainbow.

"Think about what?" I pointed to the article I had just read. "Oh, that! I read it this morning. Pretty depressing, uh?"

"Do you realize American kids don't even know American history," Mary Catherine asked me. Then she showed me an article under the headline Its History in the Unmaking, U.S. Students Oblivious to Past, Study Finds. The study was about how more than half of American high school seniors lack a basic knowledge of American history. Only 18 percent of fourth-graders achieved "proficiency" in a national standardized history test. For 12th-graders, the figure was 11 percent. In other words, they get dumber as they get older. A survey commissioned by the Colonial Williamsburg Foundation found a lack of knowledge about U.S. history among a large segment of American youth. More than 20 percent of U.S. teenagers do not know that the U.S. declared independence from Britain in 1776. Many think the colonial ruler was France. Wishful thinking. They'd have had a happier time with sex, fewer Southern Baptists and better take-away food.

By contrast, in Hong Kong, elementary school children repeatedly rank Sun Yat-sen, the father of modern China, ahead of local movie star Jackie Chan and other pop idols in popularity surveys conducted by the Hong Kong Children and Youth Services.

Jay Leno periodically shows on "The Tonight Show" scenes of interviews he conducts with college students and young adults. He asked basic questions about American history. Questions like what the 4th of July celebrated? Who is George Washington? ("A bridge in New York?") They didn't know the answers. One woman told Leno that it was Washington who defeated Hitler. Call it the Sam Cooke generation that don't know much about history. Maybe the Hollywood wave of historic epics released at the dawn of the new millennium will enable people to relive, experience and learn history.

George Washington was the greatest American, and for nearly two centuries Americans knew it. His portrait hung in every classroom. His birthday was a national celebration, marked by parades, speeches and feasts – like Mao Zedong's is in China to this day. Among his contemporaries, Washington lacked the incendiary brilliance of Thomas Jefferson, the sophistication of James Madison or Alexander Hamilton, the folksy charm of Ben Franklin. His greatness rested instead on the more prosaic but firmer ground of character. At a time of great peril, Washington became the rock on which America was built. He embodied the largely forgotten virtue of disinterestedness. People could rely on him to resolve disputes and chart a principled course because they knew his devotion was to a cause larger and more enduring than his own advancement. American history shapes Americans and makes them who they are. America should delve into its past to cure its current and future ills.

"I just wish we did as good a job teaching Americans born here about our nation's principles as we do with immigrants to our country. It's ironic that we require more knowledge of new citizens than of natives. It ought to be standard for everybody," Jesse the Body Ventura suggested in his book *Do I Stand Alone?* "Thinking is largely a learned behavior, it's a skill. It can be taught. There are specific, teachable principles to follow in constructing a valid argument and a sound opinion. I think we ought to start kids off at an early age learning the basic skills required in thinking for themselves, and we need to reinforce that training in all 12 grades. When you consider how much of our society today is working against free thought, when you realize how much media of all kinds contribute to the dumbing-down of our kids, you begin to see how vital this kind of training is." He's right. To see dumbing down in action, watch how patronizing, dismissively joking U.S. television presenters, hosts and celebrities are when they are on the subject of foreigners, or interviewing them directly. There is a cold snideness that always makes me shake my head in utter disbelief whenever I turn on a television in America and see one.

A great thinking tool is the book *Why Didn't I Think of That?* written by Judge Charles W. McCoy based on his experience of watching and listening to lawyers and witnesses being caught off guard and missing the obvious. An educated America can recapture its government from career politicians and not be terrorized by bankrupt religious zealots. It can understand the real power We The People have. All it requires is thoughtful action.

The 858-page report issued by a blue-ribbon Presidential Task Force on Education Quality in 2001 concluded that schools in America are producing students who are "stupid." Is this something *We The Apathetic People* want to perpetuate in the 21st century?

It is interesting to think about our predecessors. The "Magnificent Seven," as Joseph Ellis describes George Washington, John Adams, Thomas Jefferson, James Madison, Alexander Hamilton, Benjamin Franklin and Aaron Burr in his book *Founding Brothers*. The Founding Fathers were afraid the masses would hijack the political process. The Founding Fathers did not know then what we know today. We the People just assume they did. The fact is they didn't. They gave us democratic institutions for an 18th-century America that have more relevance in the 21st century than they did when adopted. Modern-day communications make it inexcusable for high school and college graduates not to even know American history, let alone who the "Magnificent Seven Founding Fathers" are. Is it any wonder America's *Apathetic Maids* are treated like irresponsible citizens whose opinion and vote don't count?

The Declaration of Independence, the nation's founding document, is a work of genius for its vision of what America is, something most of *We the Apathetic People* have forgotten – and need to keep in mind at all times if America is to regain its glory in the 21st century. The enduring vitality of America's mission statement is to be admired and recited in every school and home throughout the nation, at least once a year – on the 4th of July. In the interest of encouraging all Americans to do so without any excuse, it is reprinted below.

In Congress, July 4, 1776

The unanimous Declaration of the thirteen united States of America.

When in the Course of human events, it becomes necessary for one people to dissolve the political bands which have connected them with another and to assume among the powers of the earth, the separate and equal station to which the Laws of Nature and of Nature's God entitle them, a decent respect to the opinions of mankind requires that they should declare the causes which impel them to the separation.

We hold these truths to be self-evident, that all men are created equal, that they are endowed by their Creator with certain unalienable Rights, that among these are Life, Liberty and the pursuit of Happiness.

• That to secure these rights, Governments are instituted among men, deriving their just powers from the consent of the governed.

• That whenever any Form of Government becomes destructive of these ends, it is the Right of the People to alter or to abolish it, and to institute new Government, laying its foundation on such principles and organizing its powers in such form, as to them shall seem most likely to effect their Safety and Happiness. Prudence, indeed, will dictate that Governments long established should not be changed for light and transient causes; and accordingly all experience hath shewn that mankind are more disposed to suffer, while evils are sufferable than to right themselves by abolishing the forms to which they are accustomed. **But when a long train of abuses and usurpations, pursuing invariably the same Object evinces a design to reduce them under absolute Despotism, it is their right, it is their duty, to throw off such government, and to provide new Guards for their future security.** *(Emphasis added).*

• Such has been the patient sufferance of these Colonies; and such is now the necessity which constrains them to alter their former Systems of Government. The history of the present King of Great Britain is a history of repeated injuries and usurpations, all having in direct object the establishment of an absolute Tyranny over these States. To prove this, let Facts be submitted to a candid world.

• He has refuted his Assent to Laws, the most wholesome and necessary for the public good.

• *He has forbidden his Governors to pass Laws of immediate and pressing importance, unless suspended in their operation till his Assent should be obtained; and when so suspended, he has utterly neglected to attend to them.*

• *He has refused to pass other Laws for the accommodation of large districts of people, unless those people would relinquish the right of Representation in the Legislature, a right inestimable to them and formidable to tyrants only.*

• *He has called together legislative bodies at places unusual, uncomfortable, and distant from the depository of their Public Records, for the sole purpose of fatiguing them into compliance with his measures.*

• *He has dissolved Representative Houses repeatedly, for opposing with manly firmness his invasions on the rights of the people.*

• *He has refused for a long time, after such dissolutions, to cause others to be elected, whereby the Legislative Powers, incapable of annihilation, have returned to the People at large for their exercise; the state remaining in the mean time exposed to all the dangers of invasion from without, and convulsions within.*

• *He has endeavoured to prevent the population of these States; for that purpose obstructing the Laws for Naturalization of Foreigners; refusing to pass others to encourage their migrations hither, and raising the conditions of new Appropriations of Lands.*

• *He has obstructed the administration of Justice by refusing his Assent to Laws for establishing Judiciary Powers.*

• *He has made Judges dependent on his will alone for the tenure of their offices, and the amount and payment of their salaries.*

• *He has erected a multitude of New Offices and sent hither swarms of Officers to harass our people and eat out their substance.*

• *He has kept among us, in times of peace, Standing Armies without the Consent of our legislatures.*

• *He has affected to render the Military independent of and superior to the Civil Power.*

> • *He has combined with others to subject us to a jurisdiction foreign to our constitution, and unacknowledged by our laws; giving his Assent to their Acts of pretended legislation:*
>> • *For quartering large bodies of armed troops among us:*
>> • *For protecting them, by a mock Trial from punishment for any Murders which they should commit on the inhabitants of these States:*
>> • *For cutting off our Trade with all parts of the world:*
>> • *For imposing Taxes on us without our Consent:*
>> • *For depriving us in many cases, of the benefit of Trial by Jury:*
>> • *For transporting us beyond Seas to be tried for pretended offenses:*
>> • *For abolishing the free System of English Laws in a neighboring Province, establishing therein an Arbitrary government, and enlarging its Boundaries so as to render it at once an example and fit instrument for introducing the same absolute rule into these Colonies:*
>> • *For taking away our Charters, abolishing our most valuable Laws and altering fundamentally the Forms of our Governments:*
>> • *For suspending our own Legislatures, and declaring themselves invested with power to legislate for us in all cases whatsoever. He has abdicated Government here, by declaring us out of his Protection and waging War against us.*
>> *He has plundered our seas, ravaged our coasts, burnt our towns, and destroyed the lives of our people.*
>> *He is at this time transporting large Armies of foreign Mercenaries to compleat the works of death, desolation, and tyranny, already begun with circumstances of Cruelty & Perfidy scarcely paralleled in the most barbarous ages, and totally unworthy the Head of the civilized nation.*
>> *He has constrained our fellow Citizens taken Captive on the high Seas to bear Arms against their Country, to become the executioners of their friends and Bretheren, or to fall themselves by their Hands.*
>> *He has excited domestic insurrections amongst us, and has endeavored to bring on the inhabitants of our frontiers, the merciless Indian Savages whose known rule of warfare, is anundistinguishable destruction of all ages, sexes and conditions. In every stage of these Oppressions We have petitioned for Redress in the most humble terms: Our repeated Petitions have*

been answered only by repeated injury. A Prince whose character is thus marked by every act which may define a Tyrant, is unfit to be the ruler of a free people.

Nor have We been wanting in attention to our British brethren. We have warned them from time to time of attempts by their legislature to extend an unwarrantable jurisdiction over us. We have reminded them of the circumstances of our emigration and settlement here. We have appealed to their native justice and magnanimity, and we have conjured them by the ties of our common kindred to disavow these usurpations, which would inevitably interrupt our connections and correspondence. They too have been deaf to the voice of justice and of consanguinity. We must, therefore, acquiesce in the necessity, which denounces our Separation, and hold them, as we hold the rest of mankind, Enemies in War, in Peace Friends.

We, therefore, the Representatives of the united States of America, in General Congress, assembled, appealing to the Supreme Judge of the world for the rectitude of our intentions, do, in the Name, and by the authority of the good People of these Colonies, solemnly publish and declare, That these united Colonies are, and of Right ought to be Free and Independent States, that they are Absolved from all allegiance to the British crown, and that all political connection between them and the State of Great Britain, is and ought to be totally dissolved; and that as Free and Independent States, they have full Power to levy War, conclude Peace, contract Alliances, establish Commerce, and do all other Acts and Things which Independent States may of right do. And for the support of this Declaration, with a firm reliance on the protection of Divine Providence, we mutually pledge to each other our Lives, our Fortunes and our sacred Honor.

Much of the Declaration of Independence is a highly political and partisan catalogue of objections, some of which are, according to modern historical interpretation, highly arguable. From paragraph five onward, it is a blistering end-of-term report on King George III. It is the first four paragraphs in which the Founding Fathers issued a timeless, lucid gentlemanly call to revolution which has a clarion appeal to all manner of men and women beyond any particular dispute. What I added emphasis to gives license to liberty through revolt, from which no system of rule can claim exemption.

America must relearn its roots and restart and repeatedly continue to ring the liberty bell of freedom in the 21st century. It must stop firing and selling the muskets of oppression that sustain the totalitarian monarchies and dictatorships our Founding Fathers rebelled against. Those great men would blow their tops if this reality were brought to their attention in their afterlife. Not a pretty sight. Our children should learn the bedrock principles of the Declaration of Independence and the U.S. Constitution, ideas like equality, freedom and justice under law.

Former Education Secretary and drug czar William Bennett, in an editorial, implored all parents that our children "should know about the honor and courage of the independence movement of 1776, and how so many laid down their lives to defend freedom in the world during the world wars. Nowhere else has freedom flourished like it has in America; never before in the history of the world have so many benefited because there is a Land of the Free and a Home of the Brave." Something all children must be taught.

They also have to be taught the historical facts that led to American independence. It was not the Boston Tea Party, after the British government imposed a tax on the tea it shipped to its American colonies in 1773, that led to the Revolutionary War in 1775. The drink in question was rum, not tea.

The dispute started decades earlier in 1733, when the British government passed the Molasses Act. This imposed a tax on all molasses imported into the colonies from French sugar-producing islands in the West Indies. Molasses is the leftovers from the sugar-making process. New England distillers used molasses to make rum, which was consumed locally and exported to West Africa, where it was used as a currency to purchase slaves. The resulting Atlantic traffic in rum, sugar and slaves is sometimes called the "triangular trade." The imposition of a heavy tax on French molasses was intended to encourage the American colonists to buy their molasses from the British sugar islands instead. But British molasses was considered inferior and was not available in sufficient quantities. At the time, rum accounted for 80 percent of New England's exports and was the preferred drink of the colonists, who each consumed an average of four gallons a year. So the Molasses Act struck directly at the prosperity – economic and alcoholic – of the colonists. In other words, British molasses produced inferior rum which procured fewer slaves and left New Englanders with bad hangovers. An honorable start.

Despite the tax, the colonists continued to rely on French molasses as before. This undermined respect for British law and set a dangerous precedent. Henceforth, the colonists felt entitled to defy other laws that seemed unreasonable. The British government, for its part, did almost nothing to enforce the law. This changed in 1764, when the government passed a new Sugar Act – which lowered the 1733 tax but made it enforceable – and began collecting duty on molasses to pay off the debts incurred during the French and Indian War.

New England rum distillers led the opposition to the new law by organizing a boycott of imports from Britain. The cry of "no taxation without representation" became a popular slogan. Advocates of independence, known as the Sons of Liberty, began to mobilize public opinion in favor of a break with Britain. They often met in taverns and distilleries. John Adams, the revolutionary leader and future president, noted in his diary that he attended a meeting of the Sons of Liberty in 1766 in a distillery where the participants drank rum punch, smoked pipes and ate cheese and biscuits. So much for tea!

The Sugar Act was followed by other unpopular laws that imposed duties, including the Stamp Act in 1765 and the Townshend Acts of 1767. Finally, the British government staked its authority on the taxation of a single commodity, tea, which led to the Boston Tea Party. "Although this meant that tea remains the drink associated with the origins of independence, rum had played a more important role in the decades leading to the Revolutionary War," Tom Standage, technology editor at the *Economist*, and author of *A History of the World in 6 Glasses*, wrote.

Wine historian Alexis Lichine, among others, recounts a story about Paul Revere. On the eve of the outbreak of hostilities, when Revere made his famous ride from Boston to Lexington to warn of the approach of British troops, he stopped off for a rum toddy – rum, sugar and water, heated by plunging a red-hot poker into the mixture. Once the fighting started, rum was the preferred drink of American soldiers. The taxation of molasses, which began the estrangement of Britain from its American colonies, had given rum a distinctly revolutionary flavor. Many years after the British surrender in 1781 and the establishment of the United States of America, Adams, by then one of the country's Founding Fathers, wrote to a friend: "I know not why we should blush to confess that molasses was an essential ingredient in

American independence. Many great events have proceeded from much smaller causes."

A real quality society requires "a continuing churning of the social classes, abetted by a radical (and race-neutral) restructuring of the political, educational, and economic orders that will accelerate the upward mobility of middle-class and working-class talent – as well as hasten the downward mobility of upper-class mediocrity," Michael Lind wrote in *The Next American Nation*. A bottle of rum a day certainly did get things churning.

For a democratic society to be functional, with authentic power, its people need a well-grounded education. "No Taxation Without a Good Education" should be every parent's battle cry in the 21st century. Starting in kindergarten through college. How else can people properly exercise their democratic rights when they go into the voting booth? Confucius reminds us that education starts in the womb – prenatal education using devices strapped to the belly are common in Hong Kong and China – and is a seamless web through infancy, adulthood and death.

Why can't Americans be more conscious and active about their children's education? The state of education is another state of emergency. Just as important as the war against terrorism. America must go to war against illiteracy, and for better, affordable education for all our children if we are to realistically survive the 21st century.

Americans should go to Hong Kong to learn about a functional alternative. Hong Kong is the fulcrum of The Renaissance. It is a global multicultural bridge for all Americans to study and cross. The former colony, with its cross-cultural pollination of all major empires, is the New World Order model for America and China. The rest will follow.

Chapter 2

Empires and Leftovers – Hong Kong Melting Pot

*I bring you the stately nation named Christendom,
returning bedraggled, besmirched, and dishonored,
from pirate raids in Kiao-Chou, Manchuria, South
Africa, and the Philippines, with her soul full of
meanness, her pocket full of boodle, and her mouth
full of pious hypocrycies. Give her soap and towel,
but hide the looking-glass.*
– Mark Twain

Empires

America and Hong Kong are both products of empire. A brief review of the Chinese, Arab-Ottoman, British, Dutch and Spanish empires is helpful to better understand the harmonious Anglo-Sino-Latino blend that are America and Hong Kong, and why America must rebuild its political and economic institutions to reflect the Hong Kong model. Americans, like Hong Kongers, are the hybrid offspring of these five empires. One has to examine the characteristics of the people who created empires, together with the subject peoples in their colonies, to understand how they converged in America and Hong Kong The word "colony" dates back to the ancient world. It mean a place of distant settlement. The Phoenician colony of Carthage, Greek colonies in Italy, Roman colonies.... America is still grappling with its colonial and imperial heritage. Hong Kong has come to terms with its colonial heritage. In the words of German sinologist Wolfgang Kubin: Hong Kong "is both the East and the West. It offers an openness for someone who is not Chinese. People would never tell me, 'You cannot understand us because you are not Chinese.'" A cursory look at the American empire and its appendage in the Philippines is enlightening because Filipinos are the largest expatriate group living in Hong Kong and one of the largest Asian-American communities in America.

Hong Kong, like America, is the product of a colonial British parent with Chinese, Dutch, Arab-Turkish and Latino influences. America and Hong Kong are today populated by British, Chinese, Arab-Turkish, Dutch and Spanish descendants of imperialists and their slaves. The use of slaves and indentured servants was a common practice in all empires. The Jews were slaves in Egypt during the Roman Empire. The sweat, blood and lives of slaves and indentured servants built the Chinese, Roman, Arab, Ottoman, Spanish, Dutch, Japanese, British and American empires.

The rebellious American colonies came of age during a time when the fastest mode of transport and communication was the horse. Hong Kong, the older subservient territory, power-surged at the sunset of the Second Millennium when the quickest mode of communication was the Internet and the preferred mode of transport, jet planes.

Both America and Hong Kong are melting pots of people, cultures and civilizations. America's melting pot is a slow simmering stew with new ingredients being constantly added. Hong Kong's, on the other hand, is a fast-burning hot pot, or a barbequed chicken leg. Hongkies haven't got the patience to build a slow-burning fire, so the leg comes off burnt on the outside and pink on the inside. America can learn from Hong Kong how to fast cook, fuse, blend and harmonize its multicultural and institutional differences.

Hong Kong's best-known poet, Leung Ping-kwan, said at the dawn of the 21st century about living cultural contradictions: "I think this kind of position helps you see things from more than one perspective. One is less extreme. One encounters, all the time, different layers of history, enough to remind you that your presence is not the only reality, your view is not the only truth. One undergoes self-negation, self-congratulation, and at the end still is looking for self-identities."

The ancient Europeans saw themselves as the center of the world, and called the countries near the eastern Mediterrannean sea Near East, the Asian countries west of India were called Middle East, the Asian countries east of India Far East, and America the New World. The initial trade between Europe and China was in merchandise such as porcelain and china – hence the country name, China.

The Chinese Empire

To understand 21st-century China, one has to have a cursory understanding of Chinese history. Many of today's Chinese practices, fears, prejudices and behavior are directly attributed and linked to its history.

Hong Kong has played a key role in mainstream Chinese history for several thousand years. Archeological digs in Sai Kung have yielded a substantial number of artifacts from the late Neolithic Period (2500-1500 B.C.), the Bronze Period (1500-221 B.C.) and the Tang Dynasty (618-907 A.D.). Had we been walking down the streets of the more populous parts of Hong Kong in the year 1000, for example, Tuen Mun, Kowloon City, Tai Po, Chuck Ko Wan (where Disneyland is), we would have had mixed feelings of anxiety and hopefulness similar to what we sense in Hong Kong a millennium later – minus the freelance journalists, living and drinking on the cheap from the late 20th century.

In 1000, Hong Kong was a key salt production and pearl harvesting center, as well as a major duty collection post for international trade.

Present day Tai O, Kowloon Tong and Lam Tin have been imperial salt production centers since the first century. Salt "boring," or drilling, was developed in China, with wells going down as deep as 3,000 feet. Around 1830, the Chinese method was imported into Europe and copied and later used to drill for oil.

The elaborate tomb of a Han Dynasty official, still standing at Li Cheng Uk today, bears witness to the existence of a sizable imperial administration in Hong Kong some two millennia ago – nearly one- tenth the size of the present-day government.

Also since Han times, Tai Po has been one of the two best pearl harvesting centers of the empire. In the 10th century, the industry was so lucrative that a garrison of 2,000 soldiers was stationed to protect the divers. Since the fourth century, Tuen Mun, under the direct administration of the provincial capital Guangzhou, has been a major maritime customs post. The import and export duties, together with income from salt and pearls, made many a governor of Guangzhou the richest man in China.

The first emperor of China was known as the Yellow Emperor, the "Great Yu." He is a largely legendary figure and is thought to have reigned somewhere between 2852-3322 B.C., which is approximately the time of the beginning of the Assyrian Monarchy in the Middle East and 3,000 years before Julius Caesar invaded Britain. A bronze rectangular round-cornered vessel recently found in a Hong Kong antique market is the first solid evidence to confirm the existence of China's first legendary emperor.

The inscriptions on the vessel, according to experts, belonged to the Duke of Sui, the head of the Sui State, who lived about 2,900 years ago. The inscriptions go on to describe in great detail how Yu conquered the floods and established a series of codes of virtue for his administration. "Yeah, right, and democracy was promised 'when the time is right'," Stuart Wolfendale said as we wrapped up our working editorial lunch at Neptunes Net and got ready to leave. "And from one of the last inscriptions, was it clear that a goods and services tax should be considered?" he asked as I pushed him out the restaurant door onto the balcony to ascend the stairs to our waiting car.

Excavations around Hangzhou in Zhejiang province have built a picture of a hitherto unknown urban civilization that point to a sophisticated state existing between 3,300 B.C. and 2,000 B.C., predating earlier semi-legendary dynasties. China was unified by armed force under the Qin and Han empires at the end of the 3rd century B.C. Qinshihuang united seven warring states and founded the Qin Dynasty in 221 B.C. This was about the time the armies of Alexander the Great defeated the Persians and reached India's borders. During the peak of the Han empire, it was matched by that of the Romans in the West.

After the fall of the Han empire, divisions within China threatened its civilization. Warlords ran their own mini-empires within the country, fighting with the northern tribes trying to take over the country. For 280 years, until 1279, most of northern China was in the hands of nomadic tribes.

For nearly 300 years, all of China was ruled by the Mongol Yuan Dynasty (1279-1368) and the Manchu Qing (1644-1911). Only under the Song Dynasty (860-1279) and the Ming Dynasty (1368-1644) were the emperors

Han Chinese.

Monarchs have a habit of being foreigners. The kings of England from, 1714 to 1951, were effectively Germans. Since the public they rule rarely gets to speak to them, this presents no problems.

The British, Dutch and Spanish were mainly maritime empires, whereas the Chinese empire, like the Arab-Ottoman empires, was a continental expansion of territory. In the 16th and 17th centuries, Spain was akin to America, huge, rich, powerful and respectable. The Brits and the Dutch were a bit like Iran and Syria today; sponsors of state terrorism and lying through their teeth about it.

China created the world's first organized state, and is the largest surviving political entity in history. It reached its zenith during the Qing Dynasty 1644-1911, when it had expanded to include territories outside the borders of today's China, such as Outer Mongolia and parts of the former Soviet Union, Korea, Vietnam and Myanmar.

China isn't emerging so much as it is reemerging. The Chinese economy outperformed Western Europe's for more than 1,000 years, until the 16th century. After that, China stagnated, and its economic output stayed virtually flat for three centuries. But even as recently as 1820, China was responsible for 33 percent of world GDP. By comparison, America's share of world output peaked in 1950 at 27 percent.

India began to build its civilization at the same time that China built its state. India exported its culture and religion to China, while both countries for centuries carried on the biggest bilateral trade in the world. Now they are on the verge of repeating this feat in the 21st century.

To the Chinese, China has always been the center of the world, and the emperor, who was known as the Son of Heaven, was regarded as sacred. When things went wrong, the emperor was believed to have lost the Mandate of Heaven.

Chinese navies went as far as Africa and the Americas. The unveiling in South Africa's parliament of a replica of an ancient Chinese map that includes a recognizable outline of Africa has raised interesting questions about which foreigners first explored Africa. The "Da Ming Hun Yi Tu," the Amalgamated Map of the Great Ming Empire, dates back to 1389, decades before the first European voyages to Africa. Records dating as far back as the first century A.D. have been found in China mentioning places in Africa.

At the time, the Chinese were seeking tribute for their emperor rather than trade. Consequently, they would not have set up bases or left signs of their presence, as was the case with Europeans. The same happened in the Americas. America's cultures were fertilized by Chinese explorers before Christopher Columbus made his four trips to the Caribbean and South America between 1492 and 1504.

There appears to be a trans-Pacific connection between Mayans and China in what is now Mexico from 2,000 B.C. until the Roman Catholic Spanish conquistadors arrived. There are some very compelling similarities between early Chinese and Native American cultures. Ancient Mayan jade tablets, dating back 3,000 years, have inscriptions that are early Chinese characters from a well-known poem from a Chinese classic, the Book of Odes from the First Millennium B.C. Song Baozhong, author of Chinese Ancestors Opened Up America said: "After 20 years of research, I've come to the conclusion that it was the Chinese who discovered the Americas, and that subsequently there were frequent contacts."

The Chinese explorer Admiral Zheng He is believed to have visited 11 countries and traveled a distance equivalent to three circumnavigations of the globe over a period of 28 years between 1405 and 1433. His travels took him to America, France, Holland, Italy, Africa, Arabia, throughout Aisa and New Zealand during the Ming Dynasty. Zheng was born into the Semur minority in Yunnan province, under the name Ma Sanbao. He was a Muslim who went by the alias Haji Mahmud. He became a eunuch through forced castration when the Ming army conquered Yunnan. He became a houseboy to prince Zhu Di and helped him overthrow his nephew, the Chinese emperor. This singular service marked a turning point in Ma's career. The new Ming emperor, Zhu Di, bestowed on him the name Zheng He and rewarded him with the command of a great fleet that allowed him to assert China's preeminence in the world.

As early as 1761, French sinologist Joseph de Guignes claimed that Chinese sailors had been traveling up and down the American West Coast in the fifth century A.D. China's rich historical literature has also helped spawn the belief in ancient Sino-American links. According to one record, a Chinese monk traveled to a country called Fusang, located somewhere east of the Asian continent, in the late 490s A.D. Fusang derived its name from a tree that provided the inhabitants with food and clothing and paper to write on, and has been identified by researchers as the maguey tree, indigenous to the Americas.

Records also show that in 219 B.C., a grand fleet carrying thousands set out from China towards the eastern seas, in search of an elixir that would bring immortality to the emperor. It never returned, leading some to speculate it probably wound up in Central America, imprinting the Western Hemisphere with Chinese culture. They landed south of the Rio Grande. Not a mistake their descendants would make today.

To some researchers, encounters like these are the only explanation for the near-identical nature of many cultural features on both sides of the Pacific. One of the most striking is the funeral practice in both China and Mexico of putting pieces of jade, colored with red cinnabar, in the mouths of the deceased. This may also explain why Central Casting's Apache Indians always had a striking resemblance to Chinese.

The first Europeans to reach North and South America found colonies of Chinese people in California, Mexico, Venezuela and Peru. They found wrecks of Chinese junks in the Mississippi, off the Florida coast, and on the tributaries of the Amazon. Descendants of those people remain to this day. "There is also the theory that these were Hong Kong expatriate weekend 'junk-trips' gone seriously astray," Wolfendale said as we pulled out of the parking lot and headed back to Los Angeles. "It is ironic that it is only people from the West who sail around in craft resembling junks," Wolfendale continued as we both admired a beautiful double-masted sailboat.

Gavin Menzies, in his book *1421: The Year China Discovered the World*, claimed the Chinese fleet was bigger and better equipped than any European vessels of that era. The Ming exploration vessels symbolized China's advanced technological achievement. Menzies, a retired Royal Navy submarine commander, claimed that the Chinese reached the Strait of Magellan 60 years before the Portuguese explorer Ferdinand Magellan was born and cracked the secrets of longitude 300 years before the Europeans. The information the Chinese exchanged in Italy allowed Columbus, Magellan, Captain James Cook and all the other great European explorers to sail for the New World with charts showing them the way. The Chinese also, according to Menzies, transported and transplanted principal economic crops, including rice, maize, potatoes, bananas, coconuts and cotton across the world.

Menzies said an armada of junks circumnavigated the globe a century before Magellan, reaching America 70 years before Christopher Columbus and Australasia 350 years before Cook.

Closer to home, nearer countries were considered vassal states from which the Chinese expected tribute. The inhabitants of nations outside the empire were referred to as barbarians, or outer barbarians in the case of the British and Americans. When Lord Macartney attempted to establish diplomatic relations between Great Britain and the Chinese Empire in 1793, he was escorted up the Grand Canal in a junk that carried a banner reading "Tribute Embassy from Red Barbarians." Contrary to popular belief, the term barbarian is not Chinese but originated in ancient Greece. Lord Macartney's mission was a failure. He refused to kow-tow. The concept of any other nation being equal to China was considered a heresy amounting to treason by the Chinese.

Lord Macartney presented the Qing Dynasty Emperor Qianlong a planetarium and a globe as the most important gifts to the imperial court from the crown. The instruments were then the most sophisticated mechanical models of both the earth and universe, summarizing a century of astronomical and geographical knowledge based on Isaac Newton's theory of universal gravitation. Qianlong took almost no interest in them. They were left to rot in storage in his summer palace until it was sacked by European troops in 1860.

Many of the dynasties of the Chinese empire were alien. For 248 years before the Republic of China was founded on the 1st of January, 1912, the empire was ruled by the Manchus or Tartars, called the Qing Dynasty, and was regarded by the Han (native) Chinese as foreign, in some ways similar to the response of the Anglo-Saxons to the Normans after the conquest of 1066.

The Manchus were a small nomadic people of around 1 million who managed to seize and control a nation of hundreds of millions for 250 years!

The Manchus humiliated the Chinese by forcing them to shave their foreheads and wear their hair plaited in a long queue hanging down their back. This was regarded by the Chinese as a token of subjugation. Pigtail-cutting parties were held throughout China, including Hong Kong, when the Qing Dynasty collapsed and China became a republic.

In Peking, the Manchus lived in the Tartar City, and similar Manchu enclaves were established in every major city and town throughout China. Initially, all Chinese officials were required to learn the Manchu language. This policy failed and the Manchu language went into decline. Intermarriage between Manchus and Chinese was forbidden and it was illegal for a Manchu to keep a Chinese concubine. The emperor's policy was to keep the Manchus racially pure.

In the 19th century, foreign countries again dominated China and divided it into spheres of influence. America played a key peacekeeping role in China on and off starting in the 1840s to the end of World War II. The U.S. Navy, like the British Navy in earlier years, protected American businessmen and missionaries. The Boxer Rebellion of 1900 was suppressed by a multinational force from America and Europe, similar to the multinational force put together in modern times to fight Saddam Hussein, the Taliban and al-Qaeda. U.S. Navy gunboats patrolled the Yangze River to preserve the peace the entire time with minimal casualties. The only patrol boat lost before World War II was the Panay, sunk by Japanese airplanes in 1937. The period is known to the Chinese to this day as the "era of humiliation."

Confucianism, a political philosophy dating back to the sixth century B.C., was designed to create a stable society based on filial piety. It also created a feudal bureaucracy where everybody was expected to conform. Nevertheless, the Chinese are individually very flexible in religious matters and a staunch Confucian might seek help from Taoist deities when ill and insist on having a Buddhist funeral after his death. Not far removed in policy from the current Chinese regime, the Manchus did not interfere with religion, provided it did not cause political problems. Christianity had been banned in China since 1724 and was not tolerated until after the Opium War, a century later, in the middle of the 19th century. There was the 1796-1804 insurrection by the White Lotus Society, a quasi-religious secret society, which had many offshoots: the Boxers, the Eight Diagrams, the Big Sword Society, the Small Sword Society and the Triads. Its objective was to destroy the Qing Dynasty and restore the Han Chinese Ming Dynasty (1368-1644). The insurrection only destabilized the Manchus and exposed the weakness of their army.

China has always followed an isolationist policy. The Manchus claimed that their empire was self-sufficient and it had no need to trade with "outer barbarians," whom it regarded – with a certain amount of justification – as dangerous pirates, particularly the British. Silver, which was the currency of China, was cheap in the West and was traded principally for tea, silk and porcelain. In 1685, a small trading area, a tiny ghetto known as the Foreign Factories, was opened in Canton. At first, trade was mainly conducted between the great national monopolies, the East India Companies – principally the English, Dutch, French and Swedish, and a Chinese monopoly known as the Co Hong merchants.

A basic question often asked by historians is why Japan adapted quickly and effectively to the threat presented by the demonstrable superiority of the West, while China responded slowly, reluctantly and unwillingly. The conventional answer has to do with Japan's tradition of cultural borrowing – mostly from China. It was a tradition of a country that always assumed it had something to learn, and it did.

China, on the other hand, possessed so deep and abiding a sense of cultural superiority, so strong a tradition of needing to learn nothing from the outside, that it was unable to adjust. It was so slow to see that it needed more than to learn a few material techniques to survive in the new globalized world that, in the end, its traditional system collapsed entirely.

After decades of turmoil, China has lost its conviction of cultural superiority, and, for only the second time in its history, has made a foreign import its own. The first time was the adoption of Buddhism from India starting about 2,000 years ago. The second time came when the Chinese Communist Party founded in Shanghai came to power in 1949 and made the writings of Karl Marx, a German-Jewish intellectual, the official policy of the state.

Shanghai was also one of the only places Jewish refugees could escape from Nazi Germany's Holocaust in the 1930s and '40s. As the person who organized the first Passover Jewish Reunion in 1989 of Holocaust survivors who made it through Shanghai – in Shanghai – it was a real eye opener into the role Chinese, Japanese, Germans and the U.S. played in the role of human rights. Shanghai was an open free port at the time that accepted more than 25,000 Jewish refugees fleeing the Holocaust.

A series of trade routes collectively known as the Silk Road was China's land link with Central Asia and Europe. Merchants and their goods flowed freely between East and West, from China's ancient capital of Xian to Rome. Marco Polo, Genghis Khan and Alexander the Great all traversed its diverse branches. The Silk Road was started over 7,000 years ago, but the establishment of the trade routes as we know them today occurred about 2,000 years ago in Roman times when the Indo-Greek Gandhara Empire was at its zenith and merchants from around the world traversed its many snaking routes and traded glass, paper products, ivory, jade, spices and silk. Between the 7th and 10th centuries, the road helped the Tang Dynasty to establish China as the world's greatest civilization. The different cultures and religions along its route lived alongside one another and absorbed each other's influences. The Silk Road didn't get its name until the 19th century when German geographer Baron von Richthofen dubbed it so – American geographers were rooting for Route 66, but they were overruled. Just kidding.

The question today, now that the challenge comes from China, is whether the West will continue to openly traverse China's modern Silk Road – in the skies – and learn and embrace the best China has to offer, or stick to its traditional political railroad.

The early China trading partners from the Silk Road era were mainly Arabs and Turks and the various people of the Arab-Ottoman empires. The goods and volume of trade carried by the camel caravans on the ancient Silk Road – from Rome through Central Asia to Hong Kong – were once unsurpassed in the trade and cultures transported.

The hybrid seed that is modern Hong Kong was sown.

Today in the rural heart of Zhejang province, the city of Yiwu has become the epicenter of China's trade with the Muslim world. It is the mecca of trade. Arabic script has replaced Chinese, Arabic music fills the air and baskets of hummus, falafel and pita bread have replaced *dim sum* in the restaurants near the Great Mosque.

Women Muslim imams in China's Ningxia region are also among the few Muslim women allowed to keep a centuries-old tradition that gives women a leading role in a largely male-dominated faith. Female imams are known as *ahong*, from the Persian word *akhund* for the "learned." The central government's push for gender equality helped broaden Muslim women's roles. Chinese Muslims are carrying on a tradition that fell away in many Muslim societies after national governments centralized religious institutions, making men the leaders.

Women's equal status in work and religion is evident across Ningxia, a swath of desert traversed by the Yellow River which was settled by Muslim traders from the Middle East a millennium ago. Women work beside men in government offices, banks, shops and schools. Religious schools for girls are common. These are women who also drive and cannot believe that women in many parts of the Arab world are not allowed to even drive.

The Arab-Ottoman Empire
Many Americans believe Islam poses the greatest threat to them in the 21st century. Therefore it is important that Arab and Turkish history and traditions that create today's challenge, fears and threats are better understood. A brief review of Islam's rich heritage is helpful. The Arab-Turk customs, traditions and religions came to China via the Silk Road from Baghdad, across Central Asia. They also took root in Hong Kong – most deeply in the Chungking Mansions.

The Arab system of *khalifa*, or the caliphate, is as grounded in religious tradition as in governmental structure. The term caliph means the rightful successor to the Arab state and grew out of the teachings of Muhammad. The caliph, like Caesar, became absolute king. There is nothing democratic about him. He was just like any other absolute monarch of his day. In theory he continued to be the religious head, also the commander of the faithful. There is no separation of church and state in Islam. But some of these rulers actually insulted Islam, of which they were supposed to be the chief protectors. The principal offenders of this Islamic tradition seem to be embodied within the Abbasid caliphate, based in Baghdad, which came to power in 747 with a violent, bloody overthrow of the Ommayyad caliphate based in Damascus. Both of them are direct descendents of Muhammad either by blood or marriage. For centuries the Arab nation exhibited little or no contact with the great civilizations of the world. Arabia is desert country, and deserts and mountains breed hard people who love their freedom and are not easily subdued. Little different from Americans, except for the beer and baby back ribs. These were not rich lands and there was little to attract foreign conquerors. That is, until oil was discovered and became the fuel of the industrialized world.

The people of the country were largely Bedouins or *Baddeus* – the "dwellers of the desert." They were proud and sensitive – and quarrelsome. But once a year, they patched up their quarrels with other clans and families and journeyed to Mecca on pilgrimages to their many gods, whose images were kept there. How then, did this race of desert dwelling nomadic tribes band together to create a powerful nation? The answer lies within the religion of Islam and its prophet, Muhammad.

Muhammad was born in Mecca in A.D. 570. For almost 10 years, he struggled to preach God's message and gathered a small band of faithful followers. However, after the deaths of certain key and powerful protectors, opposition to his teachings in Mecca escalated from derision and verbal attacks to active persecution. The situation changed significantly in 620. Muhammad was invited by a delegation from Yathrib, later called Medina, to serve as chief arbitrator, or judge, in a bitter feud between tribes.

Islam took on a political form with the establishment of an Islamic community-state at Medina. Muhammad's phenomenal success in attracting followers and creating a community-state that dominated Arabia could be attributed not only to the fact that he was a shrewd military strategist who knew how to swing a very sharp sword, but also to the fact that he was an unusual man who elicited steadfast loyalty despite persecution and oppression.

This charismatic persona, combined with the religious fervor of Amos and Jeremiah before him, gave Muhammad the status of a "warner" from God who admonished his listeners to repent and obey God, for the final judgment was near. He returned to Mecca as its master within seven years of his departure. The Prophet Muhammad, Peace be upon him, succeeded in forging a nation from the many warring tribes of Arabia and infusing them with enthusiasm for a cause.

Islam is a religion without an institutionalized church, without a Vatican, without a formal priesthood; its animating principle is a direct relationship between believers and God, a personal relationship that transcends race, class and gender. It's a good thing they don't need a Vatican because, given Islam's attitude to painted imagery, they'd have been stumped to know what to do with the Sistine Chapel and the Raphael rooms.

The Arabs marched from conquest to conquest. Often enough, they won without fighting. Within 25 years of their prophet's death, the Arabs had conquered the whole of Persia and Syria and parts of north-west Africa. Baghdad became the capital of the Islamic world in 762 A.D. During a renaissance that preceded Europe's by more than 500 years, Baghdad's mathematicians discovered theories in algebra and calculus, while its literary salons translated Plato and Aristotle into Arabic and produced *Sinbad the Sailor* and tales from the *Thousand and One Nights*.

Egypt fell with the greatest of ease. It is said that the Arab general Okba marched right across northern Africa to reach the Atlantic Ocean in what is now Morocco. From there, the Arabs crossed the narrow sea into Spain and Europe. Spain was conquered rapidly, and the Arabs then poured into southern France. Within about 100 years of Muhammad's death, the Arab Empire ranged from the south of France, across northern Africa to Suez, and across Arabia and Persia and Central Asia to the borders of Mongolia.

Their further conquest of Europe was finally checked by Charles Martel during the Battle of Tours in France in A.D. 732. This king had no connection with the French brandy or the outcome may have been rather different. "On the plains of Tours," a historian has said, "the Arabs lost the empire of the world when almost in their grasp." There can be no doubt that if the Arabs had won at Tours, European history would have been tremendously changed. It was also the foundation stone of the Medieval Christian Europe uniting to fight the nonbeliever infidels.

When the Europeans discovered the Indian Ocean in 1498, they found that Islam was entrenched in parts of India, China, the Philippines, the East Coast of Africa, in southeastern Europe, in the Danube basin and along the Silk Road of Central Asia.

The difference between the Muslim and European conquests lay in belief. Muslim warriors fought mounted on fast-moving horses and were convinced God and history were on their side. They were doing God's work. European beliefs were based on modern firepower and profit: the three Gs: God, Gold, and Glory. Gold paid the bills and was more important than God.

In spite of their triumphs in distant countries, the Arabs could not rid themselves of their old habit of quarreling among themselves. Of course, there was something worth quarreling about now. The Arab tendency to quarrel is highlighted and brought to the world's attention today in Iraq and Palestine. It was previewed and showcased during the 2002 Arab Summit in Lebanon. One would think that 9/11 and the Israeli-Palestinian conflict would create a united front. Instead, more than half the heads of state did not attend the summit, including the two most moderate heads from Egypt and Jordan. The Palestinian and Saudi Arabian delegations walked out. Sheik Abdullah bin Zaid al Nahayan, the information minister of the United Arab Emirates, summed it up best: "The summit is heading toward total chaos." These quarrels resulted in a major division in Islam over the dispute about the line of succession from Muhammad after his death in 632 and religious orthodoxy. One faction believed that the prophet's son-in-law, Ali, should inherit his religious authority; the descendants of those Muslims are today's Shiites. The other faction thought the mantle should pass to four caliphs who were chosen by Mohammed's disciples; they became the Sunnis. The division still exists.

The bitterness between the two groups reached its zenith when Ali was murdered while praying. He was entombed in Najaf, which became the holiest Shiite city. Ali's son Hussein and his family were then killed in Karbala when he was abandoned by most of his followers. Hence the pilgrimage, guilt and self-flagellation at Karbala during the festival of Arbaeen, commemorating the 40th day after Hussein's death, witnessed after the city was liberated by coalition forces. The Iraqi cities of Najaf and Karbala contain the holiest and most revered Shiite shrines and are the centers of Shiite learning.

Among the world's 800 million Muslims, Sunnis outnumber Shiites by 10 to 1 and they dominate every Arab country from Morocco to Egypt and Iraq before the fall of Saddam. The Shiite minority is concentrated in the Gulf states atop all the petroleum fields and reserves. This includes southern Iraq and Saudi Arabia.

Former *Newsweek* editor Kenneth L. Woodward wrote: "The Shiites, for example, dominate Iran, where they have developed a hierarchy of clerical authority – the ayatollahs – roughly similar to Roman Catholics. By contrast, the majority of Sunni Muslims are rather like Protestants in their stress on individual interpretations of the faith.

And then there are the great Sufi saints and poets like Rumi, who give Islam its mystical dimension."

The caliphate deserves recognition and restoration for what it was and what it can do for peace. This is one point on which I do agree with Osama bin Laden. I'm sure we disagree on the reasons for the caliphate and its geographic limitations. The 21st century is a lot different than what Osama and his followers want to reinstate – or the caliphate was.

The Mongols

The 500-year-old Abbaside caliphate was brought to an end in 1258 when the Mongol hordes led by Genghis Khan's grandson, Hulegu Khan, sacked and destroyed Baghdad, the City of Peace. Like the 21st-century Iraq War when coalition forces bombed and "liberated" Baghdad, the Mongols had allies from throughout the Mongol Empire when they entered Baghdad. Uzbeks, Kazakhs, Georgians and many other ethnic groups were in their coalition. The Mongol coalition was put together by Kubla Khan, who was the first person to chart the whole world. His charts allowed Chinese Admiral Zheng He to be the first person to circumnavigate the globe.

The Mongol Empire was the largest contiguous land empire in history, covering modern Mongolia, China, Korea, Russia, Iran, Iraq, Afghanistan and Syria in the 13th century.

The Egyptian Mamluks halted the Mongol advances in 1260 at the Battle of Ayn Jalut in Palestine. This was 14 years before Marco Polo completed his 3.5 year journey from Venice to China. In less than a century, the Mongol conquerors converted to Islam, and Islamic power resurged in Turkey and India after being dislodged from the Arabian heartland. This history lesson has not been forgotten by Muslim fundamentalists.

Mongolian historian Shagdaryn Bira explains that similar ideological differences led to conflict in both 1258 and 2003. "Mongolia's nomadic and shamanistic culture came into conflict with the values of the sedentary and Islamic peoples of Persia. The U.S. is a product of Christian and European values that also find conflict in Iraq. I am not saying that the Mongols or the U.S. purposely pursued a holy war, but the lack of common values led to war rather than a compromise."

The Turks

The final death knell for the great Arabian caliphate came in the form of internal unrest and outside conquerors. The infiltration of Arab society by Turkish dynasties further helped to weaken the already debilitated Arabian caliphates. The Gokturk Empire, which lasted from 552 to 744, was little more than a confederation of nomadic tribes with a level of civilization mainly reflecting less than the sum of its components.

Their assimilation into the Arabian state occurred under the Abbasid caliphate, as the Seljuk tribe, where they were employed as defenders against attacks from their uncivilized brethren. The Turkish Fatamid caliphate rose to power in Egypt and North Africa, and the Seljuk Turks enjoyed a period of ascendancy. They installed one of their number, Tughri Beg, as the ruler in the caliph's capital in the year 1037. As fresh Turkish tribesmen swelled their armies, the Seljuks extended their conquests in all directions until once more Western Asia was united into one Muslim kingdom and the fading glory of Muslims arms was revived.

Seljuk Turks were the predecessors of the Ottoman Empire. The Seljuks were a group of Oguz warriors that apparently entered the Middle East in the 10th century. They arose originally as mercenary guards. Moreover, the Turks, from the ninth century onward, began to renounce their pagan beliefs and to embrace Islam. The Arabs were quick to discern the martial qualities of the Turkish people. Apart from such moral virtues as endurance, self-discipline and foresight, the nomadic way of life had bred in them a combat-ive spirit, the habit of mobility, equestrian skill and an unusual dexterity as archers on horseback.

The armies of the Abbasid caliphate thus began to recruit Turks into their ranks. They were Muslim converts with the status of superior slaves, free to rise through promotion. By the end of the ninth century, most of the military commands and many political offices in the Arab Empire were held by Muslim Turks. As the empire waned in the 11th century, the Seljuk Dynasty filled the vacuum with an empire of its own. In 1055, the real founder of the Seljuk Dynasty, Tughrul Beg, forced the Abbasid caliph to make him pro-tector of orthodox Islam and to recognize him as sultan, or temporal ruler.

For approximately 200 years, the Seljuk Turks were the dominant force on the Arabian plain. However, the invasion of the Mongols from Asia in 1243 delivered a crushing defeat and forced them into servitude, but not for long. The rise of the first Ottoman Empire began in 1280. It was founded in 1299 and lasted until 1413. The contributions of its first leader, Osman I, had been limited to establishing the dynasty and beginning the policy of devel-oping it primarily at Byzantine expense while avoiding conflict with the more powerful Turkoman neighbors until the state was strong enough to deal with them.

Under Osman, the Turks were able to make some valuable conquests and squeeze Byzantium. Osman's successor, Orhan, succeeded in further isolat-ing Byzantium by seizing the remaining territory under Byzantine control. He doubled the size of the state that he had inherited and placed it in a position where it could and did become an empire under his successor.

In 1453, Constantinople, the eastern capital of the Holy Roman Empire, was captured by the Ottoman Turks. The Turks use of artillery in the siege would prove to be a turning point in the history of warfare. It also ended any hope of reconciliation between Roman Catholicism and the Greek Orthodox "schismatics." Ironically and coincidentally, the last Christian emperor of the east was named Constantine and was killed by Mohammad II, who founded the modern Ottoman Empire that lasted into the 20th century. At its zenith, the Ottoman Empire covered all the Muslim Middle East countries around the Black Sea, all of North Africa and a good piece of southeast Europe.

Gallipoli

Gallipoli became the first permanent Ottoman base in Europe, from which the initial Ottoman raids into and conquests of the Balkans were made in subsequent years. The savagery of these wars was unprecedented. So much so that on the 600th anniversary of the Ottoman's June 15, 1389 victory at Kosovo, Slobodan Milosevic celebrated by launching his nationalist Serbian Orthodox campaign against Albanian Muslims, whom Serbs regard as the descendants of the Ottoman conquerors. Milosovec's 1989 speech ignited the four Balkan wars of the 1990s and the first at the dawn of the 21st century.

World War I brought an end to the Ottoman Empire. European democracy was introduced to Turkey. Turkey and the Ottoman Empire were beaten by the European military technology they imitated but couldn't match.

Ironically, in spite of the Vatican's prohibition on arms sales to Muslims, in defiance of clerical anathemas and excommunications, much of Turkey's armaments came from Europe. No different than today's violations of U.N. sanctions and embargoes.

Meanwhile, in Saudi Arabia, Muhammad Ibn Saud was born in 1710 and grew up to become a local ruler in Ad-Dar'ia. He forged a long-lasting political and family alliance in 1744 with the Muslim scholar and reformer Muhammad ibn Abd al-Wahhab. The two men took an oath in 1744 that they would work together to revive and purify Islam and restore it to its original form. Muhammad Ibn Saud's son, Abdul Aziz, married the daughter of Iman Muhammad. The pact sealed between the two families has been the basis of the Saudi royal-religious pact that is now funded by the oil discovered in 1938.

The pact in the Saudi desert between Ibr Saud and ibn Abd al-Wahhab came to the attention of the Ottoman rulers, who decided to quash what was clearly emerging as a new nation based in the heartland of the religious

Ottoman Empire. Many cities fell under the fighting sword of Abdul Aziz within 15 years of the pact. Riyadh fell to Abdul Aziz in 1773. His son Saud ibn Abdul Aziz captured the holy city of Mecca in 1803. Before Saud ibn Abdul Aziz died in 1814, the Ottomans had retaken several of the cities they lost to him. They also captured his son and removed him to Istanbul, where he was executed. In 1818, Turki, a cousin of Saud bin Abdul Aziz, became amir of the territory and recaptured Riyadh and retained control until 1824. The see-saw battles between the House of Saud and the Ottomans continued until 1901, when 21-year-old Abdul Aziz, known as ibn Saud, the son of Abdul Rahman bin Faisal, the future king of Saudi Arabia, recaptured Riyadh. He ruled until his death in 1953.

Saudi Arabia is ruled by a tribal monarchy and governed by Sharia law. The kingdom's religious and legal practices were brought to Hong Kong when Saudi Arabia funded the building of the Kowloon Mosque on Nathan Road in Kowloon. But since the mostly Pakistani and Indian worshippers there are regarded with deep suspicion by the majority Chinese population, the practices have not been spread very far from Nathan Road. If Sharia law was to be applied to all manner of theft, there would not be a merchant or a street vendor down that busy tourist thoroughfare whose limbs were intact. The hybrid seed that is Hong Kong was fertilized.

The Spanish Roman Catholic Empire

The Roman emperors chose the Trojans as their ancestors and Troy the mother city of Rome because Aeneas, a Trojan prince, fled to Italy and married the daughter of a powerful king and founded their city. Because the twin brothers Romulus and Remus, the actual founders of Rome, were born in the city founded by Aeneas and were his descendants, Aeneas was always held to be the real founder of Rome.

Troy was in modern day Turkey and new DNA studies suggest the Etruscans, whose civilization dominated northwestern Italy for centuries until the rise of the Roman republic, originally migrated from Turkey. Greek historian Herodotus wrote that the Etruscans emigrated from Lydia, a region on the eastern coast of Turkey. While archaeologists have long been skeptical of Herodotus' account, three new DNA studies on Tuscans and their cattle confirm they came from Turkey 6,400 to 1,600 years ago. The Etruscan culture permeated Roman art, architecture and religion. They were master metallurgists and skilled mariners who dominated much of the Mediterranean. Social relations were freer than other ancient cultures, with the women famed for their beauty and "expert" drinking.

The Roman Imperial period which began in the late first century B.C. became the Roman Catholic Empire in A.D 325 under the Emperor Constantine after he convened the First Council of Nicaea. Rome was attacked by the hordes of Attila the Hun in 452, by the Vandals in 455, and by the Burgundians and Suevi in 472. The end of Rome's 1,000 year-old empire came on the morning of September 4, 476, when Ocoaker, a barbarian partly Goth and partly Hun, deposed Rome's last emperor, Romulus Augustus.

For more than 2000 years, a legend has persisted about a group of Roman legionnaires who settled in the village of Liqian, China. Many people in the village to this day have cerulean eyes set in a squarish, ruddy face and look more European than Hun. In the words of Cai Junnian, a local farmer, "I believe I am a Roman." There are various historical theories as to how they got there. One is that they came there before the birth of Christ and more than two centuries before the first officially recorded contact between Rome and China, in A.D. 166, when a delegation sent by Emperor Marcus Aurelius arrived in the then-capital of Luoyang.

There have been tantalizing references in official and unofficial histories of 145 Roman soldiers, possibly captured in 36 B.C. by a Han Dynasty (206BC-AD220) army during battle with the fierce Huns, the ancestors of today's Mongolians. Another theory is that the legionnaires were the remnants of a group who survived the defeat of Roman general Crassus by the Parthians – warriors based in what is now Iran – at the Battle of Carrhae, in 56 B.C. Carrhae, now a site of archaelogical interest in southeastern Turkey, marked the end of Rome's eastern expansion. Rattled and scared by the animal-skin wearing, silk-banner waving Parthians, who howled like animals when attacking, the Romans crumbled. Tens of thousands of soldiers were killed and several thousand were taken prisoner.

According to Roman author Pliny the Elder, "People have been researching these people since the Han Dynasty." Parthians posted their prisoners on frontier duty in the east of their empire, on the central Asian border with the Huns and the Chinese. Pliny writes that the Parthians and the Han had commercial and diplomatic contact. From there, a group could have escaped. Oxford professor Homer Dubs agrees and believes they joined the Huns as mercenaries. After Hun leader Jzh-Jzh's defeat in 365 B.C. by Han general Chen Tang, Chen was magnanimous towards the foreign soldiers and offered them sanctuary in the parched, sandy plain around Liqian. The Han shu, or official history book, states that "Liqian was established by prisoners captured by Chen Tang." Proponents of the Roman legend say the event is referenced in at least seven history books, including the Han and the Jin shu, both written about 2,000 years ago. Skeletons in the local museum along with numerous other artifacts appear to confirm that China welcomed foreigners as far back as Rome. Romans, like the lost tribe of Israel, were accepted by China then – as they are today.

There is other research that confirms that Caucasians lived in the west of present-day China long before the Han arrived. Tests on mummies found in Xinjiang's Taklamakan desert prove they were Caucasian, most likely a branch of Europe's own ancestors who wandered east. They were buried in tartan, raising the intriguing possibility that China's far west was populated by Celts 3,000 years ago and that Romans may just be part of a larger story.

With Rome's demise, Visigoth and Franks expanded throughout western Europe. Both nations formed mighty empires. In the final outcome, King Theodoric's heirs were the winners. The battle of Chalons was one of the decisive battles of history. A victory by Attila would have brought about the collapse of Western civilization, the end of Christianity, and possible domination of Europe by Asian masters. It brought about the end of Rome. In its stead, a new world power emerged, the Catholic Church. Its spiritual leader, the pope, replaced Imperial Rome as the only valid authority throughout the Middle Ages. It was then gradually and subtly succeeded by the Spanish Roman Catholic Empire of the Iberian Peninsula.

For seven centuries, much of the Iberian Peninsula had been under Moorish Muslim rule. It consisted of five main sovereign states: Castile, Aragon, Navarre, Portugal and Muslim Granada. The Crusades were not only foreign military expeditions from Europe to the Middle East. They were also directed at Moorish Muslim Spain and Portugal. The border between Christian Europe and the Muslim world was the Spanish-French border where Charles Martel stopped the invading Moors. One of the reasons al-Qaeda and Muslim fundamentalists target Spain currently is that they want it back. They say it is theirs.

The marriage of Isabella of Castile and Ferdinand of Aragon in 1469 led to the unity of Spain a decade later. The Spanish monarchs drove the Moors out of Granada in 1492. This was the year that Christopher Columbus, under the patronage of Isabella, accidentally discovered America. His voyage was a continuation of the Crusades against the infidels to find a way around the lands and trading routes controlled by Islam to the Indies and the spices, silks and teas so popular in Europe. The quest to end the chokehold Muslim traders had on Europe and recapture Jerusalem created the Age of Discovery, a well-spun updated version of the Crusades. Columbus' novel approach was to sail westward across the Atlantic to get to the Spice Islands of the East, and as mentioned in his own writings, make possible the reconquest of Jerusalem.

Columbus has been credited with finding the New World even though he believed he had actually landed in Asia – and the Chinese, Vikings and others had already reached the shores of the Americas before him. He had set sail with the latest European maps and books by the ancient Greek astronomer Ptolemy, which had under-calculated the circumference of the earth. On returning from his first voyage, Columbus was convinced that he had found a quick route to the fabled Spice Islands of the East Indies. In fact, he had only reached the Dominican Republic. If he rediscovered that country today, he would be in no doubt of his failure.

Columbus in death, as in life, remains a mystery. The ongoing debate over whether his remains are in the tomb in Spain or the Dominican Republic will hopefully be finally resolved in the 21st century by matching DNA samples from his brother and son.

The more complex questions of who he was and where he came from are more difficult to answer. Across southern Europe, Columbus is variously hailed as Italian, Catalan, Basque, Corsican or Greek. It has even been proposed that the Catholic Church's most ruthless colonizer, evangelist and enslaver of native peoples was a convert Jew. What is interesting is that Columbus was never known to speak Italian and wrote only in Castillian Spanish and gave many of his discoveries in the New World Catalan names. Most of the places in the Caribbean and Central America named by Columbus can be linked directly to the Balearic island of Ibiza. The preponderance of evidence indicates that he was from somewhere in the central region of Catalonia, near Barcelona.

Why was Columus so secretive about his background? There are a couple of theories. One is that he deliberately tried to conceal his past because he was a pirate and conspirator against the king. Historians have speculated that he may have been a Catalan nobleman who joined a failed uprising against King John II of Aragon, father of King Ferdinand, and took orders from the French in various acts of piracy, including the sinking of Portuguese galleons. Columbus expunged his former identity and Hispanicized his name to avoid reprisals and maintain the support of the new monarch for his planned voyage to America. Another theory based on Old Testament references in some of his writings is that he was Jewish. The targets of the Spanish Inquisition at the time were Jewish converts to Catholicism, whose faith was apt to be tested by lengthy internments and interrogations. It would have given a Jewish Columbus every reason to be discreet. I have even heard one story suggesting he was a closet homosexual. But I don't think that would have any meaning to anyone beyond his cabin boy.

Columbus Day in America is not really about Columbus. Nor is it about 1492; in fact it is about 1892, the year President Benjamin Harrison issued the proclamation establishing a day to honor the "400th anniversary of the discovery of America." Up until then, Columbus wasn't at the forefront of America's mythology. Before 1892, his landing in the New World had been barely noticed. The proclamation was handed down at the beginning of the Progressive era, at a time of intense immigration. Political spin at its finest, to deal with the political realities at the polls. It's an example of how a changing nation and politicians use and continuously reinvent the past to address their present needs. No different than today.

At the beginning of the 1880s, there were about 300,000 Italians in the U.S.; 10 years later, that number had doubled. And by 1910 there were 2 million Italians in the U.S., more than 10 percent of the nation's foreign-born population. The Italians – along with Poles and Portuguese among others – joined the swelling Irish (Celtic) community to form a new political bloc: the urban Catholic who worshipped God differently from the Protestant majority.

Catholics needed a hero. And what better symbol to mobilize and Americanize these immigrants than one of their own?

From 1492, when Columbus landed on Hispaniola, to 1526, when Ferdinand Magellan completed the first European circumnavigation of the earth, Europe experienced a quantum leap in knowledge about the world. Europe was finally catching up with the Chinese and Muslims.

The Portuguese Empire was rapidly expanding to the East and Ferdinand and Isabella persuaded the pro-Spanish Borgia Pope Alexander VI to divide the New World between Spain and Portugal. The demarcation line was originally 100 leagues west of the Azores and Cape Verde Islands. It was moved another 270 leagues west at the Treaty of Tordesillas in 1494, thus giving Portugal as yet undiscovered Brazil. As the existence of the Pacific Ocean was still unknown in Europe when the treaty was signed, what happened when the empires met on the unexplored side of the world had yet to be resolved. It was no different than the U.S. and Russia – carving up deep space.

Magellan had been on Diogo Lopes de Sequeira's Portuguese expedition to Malacca in 1509. Magellan was Portuguese. He returned to Portugal and was accused of dishonesty. Although he was acquitted, he became embittered against the Portuguese monarchy. By studying Portuguese charts and ship logs, Magellan worked out that the Spice Islands must be in Spanish territory as opposed to Portuguese territory. Actually he was wrong, but he managed to convince King Charles I of Spain, who was only 18 at the time, that his theory was correct.

Charles provided him with five ships and in 1519 he set sail. He crossed the Atlantic, passed through the Straits of Magellan and sailed across the Pacific. He arrived in Guam on March 6, 1521, and the Philippines 10 days later, which he claimed for Spain and where he met his death in a skirmish.

New research and maps claim that a Portuguese fleet searching for Marco Polo's fabled island of gold discovered Australia and New Zealand 250 years before Captain James Cook. The four ships, captained by Christopher de

Mendonca, left the Portuguese base of Malacca on a secret mission in 1522, sailing down the east coast of Australia, bumping along the bottom of the continent and returning home by way of New Zealand's North Island. The maps, dated 1522, accurately marks geographical sites along Australia's east coast in Portuguese.

The Portugese failed to settle either of the newly discovered lands because of an acute shortage of manpower and resources, according to Australian author Peter Trickett in his book *Beyond Capricorn*. The Portugese kept Mendonca's discovery secret to prevent other European powers from reaching the new land, said Trickett, who believes his theory is supported by discoveries of a lead fishing sinker, cannonball and helmet on the Australian and New Zealand coasts made of materials mined in France in the 16th century. Imagine Portuguese spoken with an Aussie accent.

Spain began its overseas empire in the 15th century with the colonization of the Atlantic Canaries and Madeiras Islands. There were two Spanish empires, the European empire and the South American Empire, which included Guam and the Philippines. For seven centuries, much of the Iberian Peninsula had been under Moorish Muslim rule. The marriage of Isabella of Castile and Ferdinand of Aragon united Spain and marked the beginning of Spain's European Empire.

European expansion was a conscious religious undertaking. "It had a rationale and a justification shaped by the history, ideas and identity of Western Christendom. These are set out explicitly in the series of Papal bulls and charters that licensed the 'Voyages of Discovery'... the basic premise of Western expansionism," Ziauddin Sardar and Merryl Wyn Davies wrote in *Why Do People Hate America?* The religious bulls justified Europe's right to attack, appropriate and possess lands and people who, from their own perspective, had every right to believe they were the owners of their own land, property, persons and destiny.

Dum Diversas is the earliest in the series of Papal bulls, granted to the Portuguese monarch in 1453. Its language and ideas were used by all European nations that sponsored imperialism. Dum Diversas authorized the king of Portugal to attack, conquer, and subdue "Saracens," pagans and other non-believers who were inimical to Christ; to capture their goods and their territories; to reduce their persons to perpetual slavery; and to transfer their lands and properties to the king of Portugal and his successors. Similar bulls were granted to the Spanish monarchs Ferdinand and Isabella before Columbus set sail. The same terms appear in the charter granted by Henry VII of England to John Cabot in 1482 before his voyages exploring North America, the basis for all subsequent English claims to what became America.

The South American Empire started in 1531 with the invasion of Peru and expanded through the 16th century and lasted until the end of the Spanish-American War at the end of the 19th century.

The Spanish European Empire was acquired through inheritance. Ferdinand and Isabella's youngest daughter, Joanna, married Philip of Austria, the son of Maximillian, the Holy Roman Emperor. Their son, Charles V (1500-1558), became Holy Roman Emperor in 1519. When he abdicated, he split the empire between his brother Ferdinand, who succeeded him as Holy Roman Emperor in 1558, and his son Philip II. Charles V was the last emperor crowned by a pope. Nevertheless, the designation Holy Roman Emperor continued into the 19th century. Charles V abdicated in 1556 and took refuge in a monastery. He was succeeded by his son Philip II, who in 1556 inherited his possessions in Spain, the Netherlands, Italy, Franche-Comte, America and the Philippines. Through the brief reign of his brother, Ferdinand, to his son, the austere autocrat Philip II, Charles V and his family managed to consolidate their empire when Philip also became king of Portugal and thus acquired the lucrative Portuguese Empire.

Christendom was destined for another breakup – the Reformation. The English Lollards and Protestants in several European countries had translated the Bible from Latin to the local vernacular. People started reading and thinking for themselves instead of listening to church leaders. The spiritual anarchy that had been uprooted in Spain flourished in Europe and was led by the Calvinists. The result was the introduction of the Holy Office of the Inquisition in 1522-23. Exemplary executions only enraged the public and mobilized resistance. The Spanish destroyed the prosperity of their northern provinces. Flourishing commercial centers like Antwerp were destroyed.

Ferdinand and Isabella, and their Catholic Monarch successors, also created a certain amount of commercial chaos by expelling the Jews from Spain.

What is not as well known is that Ferdinand and Isabella also later banished the Muslims, who were the backbone of the farming community, and agriculture suffered. Philip II's strict religious policies drove his Protestant subjects in the Netherlands to rebellion. He attempted to invade England, which supported the Dutch. In order to prevent a Protestant from becoming king of France, Philip II claimed the throne for his eldest daughter Isabella through his wife Elizabeth de Valois, and attacked France. The vast wealth Spain received from the gold and silver mines of South America was squandered by Philip and his successors on religious and dynastic wars that they usually lost.

Six centuries ago, Malacca on the Malay Peninsula hosted 2,000 ships each day, as many as crowd into modern-day Hong Kong, which boasts of being one of the world's busiest ports. Malacca was a place where Gujratis, Tamils and Bengalis from India lived and traded in secure harmony with Malays, Chinese and Arabs. It was a city of 100,000 where 84 languages could be heard in the markets. The Malay sultans who ruled Malacca ensured that the strait was free of pirates. Goods could be stored safely in hundreds of well-guarded godowns, and in case of dispute, the city's laws were administered fairly to both Malaccans and foreigners. The Portuguese brought that to an end when they tried to convert everyone to Christianity in the 16th century. If one looks at the Portuguese Empire from then right up to their withdrawal from Timor, Mozambique and Angola, institutionally all they left was wreckage.

The biggest boost to trading with Asia came with Spain's discovery of silver in newly conquered Mexico, Bolivia and Peru in the early 16th century. When galleon trade across the Pacific between Acapulco and Manila started in 1572, Spanish silver began flowing into Asia in huge quantities. By the time the trade ended in 1811, Manila had become the busiest commercial hub in Asia.

The conquistadors were motivated by gold and God – in that order. They never found El Dorado, the legendary city of gold, but they did discover a massive amount of silver in Mexico and Potosi, Peru. Hernan Cortes conquered Mexico in 1821; Francisco Pizarro invaded Peru in 1531; Argentina came under Spanish rule in 1836; and Pedro de Valdiva attempted to subdue Chile in 1541, but was killed by the Araucanians in 1553, and the country south of Concepcion was not finally subdued until 1883. At the height of Spanish power, their American Empire stretched from Chile to California.

Miguel Lopez de Legazpi crossed the Pacific from Mexico with 400 men and established the first Spanish colony in the Philippines at Cebu City in 1565. The islands were named after Philip II. The Malay people of the archipelago spoke 77 separate languages and had not yet developed into a nation. With the conquistadors came the friars: the Dominicans, Franciscans and the Jesuits and established a friarocracy. They found no gold and almost no spices apart from cinnamon. The friars introduced Catholicism and more efficient agricultural methods. They became the most powerful force in the colony, but the Spanish were never able to colonize the Muslims in the south.

Let's not forget that Spain was once occupied by the Moors. Spain finally drove them out and when they conquered the Philippines, they were surprised to learn that there were also Muslims there. So they called them Moros – after the Moors in Spain. Filipino Moros are Muslim, but they are not Arab Moors. The fighting now between Philippines government troops and Moros identified as Abu Sayyaf terrorists in league with the Misuari Breakaway Group, is simply a continuation of the Crusades. The Moros were first regarded as infidels, like the Moors in Spain, then as outlaws, then as pirates, then as fanatics, then accepted as a backward minority. Sound familiar?

The Philippines had an economy based on selling spices, silks, tea and Chinese goods to South America, mainly Mexico. Unlike Portugal, the Spaniards had no entrepot like Macau on Chinese territory, so the Chinese merchants brought their goods directly to Manila by junk. It was paid for in silver, which was transported once a year from Acapulco, Mexico, in a treasure ship known as the Manila Galleon The goods were then sent to Acapulco in the returning galleon. It was very much a question of putting all your eggs in one basket, and if a galleon was lost, it would take the economy a few years to recover. Some ships were sunk in storms, but British pirates and the Royal Navy seized four Manila Galleons. The Covadonga was captured by Lord Anson in 1743. The galleon yielded the greatest amount of treasure ever looted from a single ship, more than $1.5 million, which would be worth a few billion dollars today.

The current ongoing litigation in Florida and Spanish courts over the undersea rights to the bullion in the long-lost galleon Notre Dame de Deliverance gives us a glimpse at what one galleon contained. The Deliverance was carrying an estimated $3.2 billion worth of treasure for the Spanish King Charles III from his New World empire. The galleon was hit by a fierce hurricane as it passed near the Florida Keys on November 1, 1755, a day after setting sail from Havana with treasures extracted from mines in Mexico, Peru and Columbia. Many of its crew of 500 Frenchmen and Spaniards who survived the wreck were reportedly eaten by Florida's cannibalistic Calusa tribe.

Thousands of Chinese settled in Manila and became quasi-colonials who took advantage of the security provided by the Spanish to trade. They intermarried with the indios and created the Chinese *"mestizo,"* a merchant class of landowners and businessmen whose descendants, together with the Spanish *"mestizo,"* dominate the Philippines today. The security was destroyed when the British captured Manila in 1762 during the Seven Year's War.

The same year the British frigates Argo and Panther seized the outward-bound galleon en route to Acapulco. The inward-bound galleon slipped into Palapag harbor and landed her cargo. The war cut off the vital trade lifeline with Mexico for two years, and when peace returned, only a few galleons made the direct route to Mexico. The revolutions against Spanish rule in South America devastated commerce and by 1825 the Philippines total trade with the New World was 2 percent of the 1810 level. Manila's historic walled district of Intramuros is home to the country's oldest church, San Agustin, a fine example of 17th century Asian baroque architecture. In nearby Plaza San Luis, the government has re-created a colonial-era Manila neighborhood.

The loss of the Spanish American Empire not only ruined the Philippines' economy but added to the silver crisis in China. Most of the silver from Mexico had ended up in China, where silver was the unit of currency. The Mexican dollar was still favored as a trade dollar in China up to World War II. The silver Mexican dollar can still be found in many antique and pawn shops in China today.

There was also an influx of *penisulares*, Spanish refugees from South America who looked down on the *creoles*. Their arrogant attitude had been one of the causes of the revolutions in South America. By the time of the Opium War, Spain had lost all its major colonies except Cuba, Puerto Rico and the

Philippines. The loss of the Spanish Empire was largely due to its foreign policy and religious fervor, which caused so many wars. Spain simply ran out of money and men. The people of its former colonies seem to have inherited three things from their former masters: a self-destructive pride that creates a machismo attitude; the *mañana* syndrome (never do today what you can put off until tomorrow) and extreme Catholicism.

During these years, thousands of Filipinos settled in Mexico, as did thousands of Mexicans in the Philippines. Many of their descendants moved to America and Hong Kong with their Spanish and Portuguese relatives or business associates. In fact, until the 1950s the Portuguese were the largest non-British, non-Chinese community permanently domiciled in Hong Kong.

The Chinese handled most of the business in Manila, and cornered much of the retail trade and provided the craftsmen. Most of the Spanish grandees thought that trade was beneath them, and came to rely on the Chinese for just about everything except food. The countryside remained under the strict control of the friars. As in post-war British Hong Kong, it was the Chinese who made most of the money.

The hybrid Hong Kong seed sown by the Chinese, Arabs and Turks was further fertilized by the Spanish and Filipino-Latinos.

The 1,000-year-old Holy Roman Empire started by Charlemagne in 800 was abolished by Napoleon in 1806 at the Battle of Ulm at Austerlitz. The "Sun of Austerlitz" shines forever through the triumphant arch on the Champs-Elysees that Napoleon had built to honor his army's glory. An interesting and not so glorious recent discovery about Napoleon is that his defeat in Russia, after reaching Moscow in 1812, was not because he was laid low by the Russian winter and then finished off by hunger, but by the less poetic *Pediculus humanus* – the human louse.

A team led by Didier Raoult of France's National Center for Scientific research examined the remains of Napoleon's soldiers who had been buried in a mass grave. The samples of earth, cloth and teeth recovered from the site suggested that more than 30 percent of these troops were killed by bacterial fever transmitted by lice. The unusual research was published in the January 2006 issue of the *Journal of Infectious Diseases*.

Another interesting Napoleon sidebar closer to America took place in Mexico. Emperor Maximilian I of Mexico was an Austrian archduke – a member of the Hapsburg family installed by Napoleon III of France. Napoleon was trying to recover unpaid debts from Mexico and keep a European presence there. In 1864, a French expeditionary force expelled Benito Juarez – Mexico's first indigenous elected president – and put Maximilian in power. Juarez launched a guerrilla war that gradually gained strength. Napoleon decided he'd made a mistake and withdrew his troops, leaving Maximilian stranded. Maximilian and his Mexican allies were defeated and executed by firing squad.

The Dutch Empire

Adrian VI (1522-1523), a Dutchman, was the last non-Italian pope until Karol Jozef Wojtyla became John Paul II in 1978. He was a reformer. He tried to reign in corruption and sensed that the church had to be reformed, but he failed to appreciate the strength of the Reformation.

The seafaring Dutch played an active role in the northern European Protestant movement known as the Reformation. It was not just a religious difference. It was a struggle between the established aristocratic landowners and their Catholic Church and the emerging class of merchants and artists in the cities. The "old money" based on land ownership versus the "new money" earned through trade and manufacturing.

The form of Protestantism practiced in the Netherlands was Calvinism. Calvinism was an essential component in the struggle for independence from the fanatically Catholic Philip II of Spain, who had acquired the Netherlands through inheritance, as mentioned earlier. In 1566, a coalition of Calvinist and Catholic nobles petitioned Philip II not to introduce the Spanish Inquisition in the northern European low countries. Philip refused and the low countries fought an 80-year war of independence.

The Calvinist merchants also objected to the heavy taxes imposed by the Spanish. In 1578, they captured Amsterdam. The seven northern provinces of Europe led by Holland and Zeeland then formed the Union of Utrecht the following year and declared themselves an independent republic. William the Silent of the House of Orange, who was the chief magistrate at the time, became the leader of the new republic. The House of Orange is the forefather of today's Dutch royal family.

William the III of Orange, like his grandfather, repelled the Catholic French attack in the 1670s, when Louis XIV capitalized on the British-Dutch naval battles and marched into the low countries to occupy three of the seven Dutch republican provinces. William III then supported the Protestant factions in England against the Catholic King James II, who was supporting Louis the XIV. In 1688, William of Orange, Stadtholder of the United Provinces, invaded England at the invitation of parliament and proclaimed himself king. His wife, Mary Stuart, James II's Protestant daughter, became queen. The overthrow of James II was intended to take over the English crown to prevent it from joining with France against the Netherlands. This was the last successful invasion of England, and the first since William of Normandy invaded England in 1066. After the English placed William of Orange on the English throne, they became partners. They combined resources in war, commerce and to prevent French territorial ambitions.

Carrots are naturally purple on the outside and orange on the inside. It was their natural color until the Dutch decided in the 1720s to change the outside to blend with the inside to match their national color, orange, in honor of the Williams of Orange.

Calvinism embraced economic enterprise as a work of religion. It was the ideological cornerstone for capitalism as we know it today. Consequently, merchants, artists and Jews were welcomed. Amsterdam welcomed merchants and artists from all over Europe. Persecuted Jews from Spain, Portugal and from central and eastern Europe flocked to Amsterdam, where they were warmly received. Persecuted Calvinists from France and other Catholic countries were also welcomed with open arms. The Jewish refugees taught Dutch mariners about distant trade routes, which the Dutch pursued and explored by sea.

The Dutch became premier traders and founded the world's first stock exchange in 1602 in Amsterdam to trade in East India Company shares. Amsterdam attracted global funds and remained the financial center of Europe until the Napoleonic wars, when London took over.

Cash was king and Amsterdam was not averse to trading with the enemy.

Spanish armies were paid with money borrowed from Amsterdam, fed on grain imported through Amsterdam and their wrecked ships were rebuilt with timber supplied by Amsterdam merchants. The Dutch preferred being the middlemen. However, when Spain annexed Portugal and closed the ports of Seville and Lisbon to Dutch vessels in 1585, it forced the Dutch to become fighting marines. In 1619, Dutch traders expelled the Portuguese from Malacca and established the Dutch East Indies.

In 1624, they founded a trading post on Manhattan Island and called it New Amsterdam, which became New York. They also established trading posts on the west coast of Africa and plantations in South America and the Caribbean. Like the Spanish, they were active in the slave trade to work their plantations and colonies.

In 1641 they established a trading post in Taiwan. In 1652, they captured the Cape of Good Hope from the Portuguese. The future South Africa was one of the few Dutch colonies that attracted a large number of Dutch settlers. The Dutch also took Ceylon from the Portuguese, which today is known as Sri Lanka. The Dutch explored the coastlines of New Zealand and Australia as well. They also transplanted Brazilian rubber in 1883 to their colonies and discovered oil in Borneo and Sumatra in the late 1880s and founded the Royal Dutch Petroleum Company in 1890. Is it any wonder the Koreans are feverishly studying Dutch history after they placed fourth in the first World Cup of the 21st century because of a Dutch coach?

The Dutch, unlike their Spanish, French and British co-colonizers, didn't have the population necessary to establish settler-type colonies. They were interested in trade only. Consequently, they were welcomed by the local rulers who had suffered the missionary zeal of the colonizers the Dutch replaced. To maintain and retain their trading colonies, the Dutch used bribery, gunship diplomacy and, where necessary, local mercenary forces.

In 1650, the Dutch had more seagoing merchant vessels than England and France combined, and half of all ships sailing between Europe and Asia were Dutch. Hong Kong was a frequent port of call for the Dutch armada. The Dutch started bringing Chinese to the ports of Amsterdam and Rotterdam in the late 1880s as stokers, sailors and cooks. They lived together in dormitories which became the precursors to today's Chinatowns.

The hybrid Hong Kong seed sown by the Chinese, fertilized by the Arabs, Turks, Spanish and Filipino-Latinos, was spiced and toughened by the Dutch.

The British Empire

The British, like the Romans, think they are the descendants of Troy. According to an English legend, one of the followers of Aeneas was called Brutus. They left Troy together but had an argument and went their separate ways. Aeneas to Italy and Brutus to Great Britain. Because of his military prowess, the island was named Britain.

The Tudor monarchs, from Henry VII to Elizabeth, turned their kingdom away from the old territorial preoccupation with the European continent toward the Atlantic. Henry VIII rejected Catholicism and the pope as God's intermediary and established the Church of England in 1533. Puritanism and the English and Scottish Reformations propelled the growth of the British Empire.

Earlier, England had been inhibited by a pre-Reformation acceptance of the pope's division of the New World between Spain and Portugal, by the constraints of massive church land ownership, and the church strictures on economic practices. Protestantism, probably more out of greed than credo, led England to develop a more active domestic and global economy that resulted in the British Empire. The seizure and distribution of the Catholic monastic lands under Henry VIII put new capital to work in agriculture, industry and on the high seas.

The English Civil War started after King Charles I, who Cromwellians refer to as Charles Stuart, dissolved parliament. He was determined with the Orthodox Anglican Church to do away away with a parliamentary system of government and stop the evolution of a constitutional government. The bloody Puritan revolution of the English Civil War, which resulted in the execution of King Charles Stuart in 1649 by the victorious Parliamentarians, became the model for the U.S. war of independence. The English Civil War sent countless waves of Puritans fleeing the conflict to the American colonies.

The British Atlantic empire included the American colonies, Canada, Nova Scotia, Newfoundland, Bermuda, Bahamas, Jamaica and the Sugar Islands – Barbados. The empire, before the loss of the American colonies, is often referred to as the First British Empire. After that loss, the British are sup-posed to have said, "Oh Shite! We'll have to start all over again." The focus and strategy changed from settlement to the Second British Empire, which was much more India-centric. Having been called a "colonial" on more than one occasion by Brits in Hong Kong who know their history, especially at Scottish country dances when I made a misstep and upset the square dancers around me, I would merely retort with a smile and "Sore grudge holder, huh?"

In the middle of the 19th century, at the time of the Opium War, the Chinese and Dutch empires were in decline and the Spanish Empire was close to collapse. On the other hand, the British Empire was on a high. It was at a stage in its history when anything seemed possible. This surge of invincible arrogance lasted until World War I and fizzled out after the second. The British, like the Spanish, ran out of people. The wars had taken their toll. Numerically, physically and emotionally. In the United Nations, the moral-ity of imperialism was being seriously questioned. All great empires eventu-ally break up or collapse.

While the Spanish Empire was destroyed because of its foreign policy of aggressive evangelism, the British simply lost faith in the ideology of imperialism, as the Russians later lost faith in communism. It must be stressed that the British imperialism of the later Victorian era became more than opportunism – it was for many a faith, often a blind faith. The high point of faith and power is probably well marked by Queen Victoria's 1897 Golden Jubilee celebrations. The Boer War in South Africa, which Britain lost, much like it did in America, to the Dutch and British settlers and their local native supporters, was a terrible shock to confidence and rectitude came immedi-ately after. Once an empire loses faith in its mission, its very existence is threatened. A lesson America is learning the hard way.

For the purpose of this trilogy, the word "British" includes the Irish and the peoples of the colonies of British descent who played an enormous part in the building of the British Empire. Although the Anglo-Norman English kings at one time ruled most of France, and Sir Walter Raleigh started a colony in Virginia during the Elizabethan era, the British nation really be-gan when James VI of Scotland was crowned James I of England in 1603 and the two countries were united under a single monarch. The main driving force behind the British Empire was commerce. British trading posts, often little more than fortified warehouses, sprang up all over the world. These godowns developed into fortresses, then towns and eventually grew into full-fledged colonies, dominions – and in the case of India – an empire.

As well as the trading posts, true colonies with settlers developed in North America, and later Australia, New Zealand, South Africa and Kenya. The colonies were founded by people who left Britain for a variety of reasons: In the case of the Pilgrims, it was religious intolerance; often it was simply an individual unable to fulfill their potential because they were Scot or Irish, but more often because of belonging to the wrong social class or just plain poverty.

There were also adventurers, opportunists, traders, missionaries, carpetbaggers, remission men and the younger sons of the aristocracy and the middle class. There were sailors, soldiers and administrators who simply liked the place where they were stationed and decided to settle there. There were also those unfortunates who were transported against their will, the rebels and the criminals. In Hong Kong, most of the early colonialists were traders who intended to return to Britain after they had made their fortune. They were very different from the settlers in other colonies whose ambition was often to build some sort of new Jerusalem – in Hong Kong, that's Discovery Bay.

No two colonies were the same: There were the Pilgrims in America, the splendor of the British Raj in India, the aristocratic farmers in Kenya, the Protestant missionaries in the South Sea islands, the pirate communities in the West Indies and the penal colonies in Australia.

The great British trading company in Asia was the Honorable East India Company, known as the John Company. It was founded in 1600, when Queen Elizabeth I granted a 15-year charter. The first fleet did not sail until 1601 and returned in 1603, the year the Scottish King James became King of England. It had a Royal Charter, a monopoly to trade, and at the height of its power it had its own army and navy and often waged war without the consent of London. The company concentrated on trade with India, where it established three bases: at Madras in 1640, Bombay in 1661 and Calcutta in 1696. The survival of these early fortified settlements depended on the protection of the local Indian ruler. The merchants were extremely vulnerable until the defeat of the French in India during the Seven Years War in 1764, when the John Company, by circumstance rather than design, became ruler of Bengal and consequently the strongest power in the subcontinent. After that it systematically annexed large chunks of India, parts of Burma and colonized Penang and Aden.

The John Company's monopoly did not cover the "country trade," which was the term used for British commerce conducted between India and other Asian nations, and China, with the goods being carried on British ships. The country traders were called "interlopers." They were mainly hardy, unprincipled Scots like William Jardine and James Matheson.

The Scottish traders and merchants played a pivotal role in Britain's global trade. The opium trade and establishment of permanent trading stations in China were given to the Scots. The Scots eagerly accepted the challenges and opportunities because of the poverty the English created in Scotland.

The Act of Union that united Scotland and England in 1707 was the result of brilliant English political strategy. It forced Scotland to embark on disastrous speculation in colonial trade in America, which virtually bankrupted Scotland. The Scots resisted the union with England with disastrous consequences. The rebellions of 1715 and 1745 in opposition to the union were so brutally suppressed that more Scotsmen preferred to leave for America and Hong Kong. We also have to bear in mind the Scottish climate, which is abysmal.

Communications were so bad during the 19th century that it generally took more than a year for a government to know what was happening on the other side of the world. Wars that had ceased frequently continued to be waged by the overseas colonial forces. The Battle of New Orleans is an example. It took place in 1815, although the war of 1812 between Great Britain and the United States officially ended in 1814. Sometimes the man on the spot, like Henry Morgan, who was more a pirate than a privateer, made up his own rules and got away with it. Morgan sacked Panama in 1671 even though Spain and Britain were no longer at war. Jameson's Raid, a fait accompli engineered by the arch-colonialist Cecil Rhodes in 1899, led to the Second Boer War which ended in 1902. That resulted in the creation of the Union of

South Africa in 1910. Although parliament was often angered and horrified by random wars started by colonial adventurers, it felt obliged to support them once British blood had been spilt. Ruthless colonial powers sometimes exploited the cynical tactic of sending a couple of fanatical missionaries into a territory they fancied, wait for them to be killed – thus providing a valid reason to send in an avenging army – which often resulted in the seizure of a new territory. Often an imperialist power would simply wait for an excuse for a war and agent provocateurs were sometimes deliberately used; these were the suicide bombers of the age.

The self-confidence of the British colonialists during the 19th and 20th centuries was on a par with that of the Spanish conquistadors in their heyday, men like Hernan Cortes who attacked the Aztec Empire with only 600 men, 16 horses, 14 cannons and 13 muskets. Cortes, like Robert Clive, who used mainly Indian troops to capture India, allied himself with the Tlaxcalans whom he had defeated, and other enemies of the Aztecs to destroy Montezuma's empire in Mexico. There was Gov. de Sande of Manila, who tried to persuade Philip II to let him invade China with a force of between 4,000 and 6,000 men. This proposal was not as ridiculous as it sounds, when one considers that two and a half centuries later, Irish Gen. Sir Hugh Gough forced the emperor of China to cede Hong Kong to Britain with an army of around 7,000 troops. China had a population of 400 million at the time. The Who Dares Wins approach often worked. Look at what the U.S. and Brits can't do today in Iraq with 150,000 men.

The British realized that with the advent of 20th-century communications it would no longer be possible for a small country of people to rule a quarter of the world. Even a diehard imperialist like Sir Winston Churchill reluctantly conceded this. The British Empire had been held together by a masterly piece of managed perception that could not possibly be maintained any longer, and the British in the 1950s simply did not have the human resources or the dedicated enthusiasm of the empire's pioneers. Britain was close to bankruptcy and colonialism was not a popular political philosophy with the post-war socialist generation, even if the self-determination of a former colony might lead to poverty or tyranny. Some ex-colonies, like Australia, Canada or Hong Kong, have been enormously successful, but for others like Kenya and Nigeria, independence has been a disaster.

In fact, independence for all African countries has been a disaster. Colonization in Africa was most recent, most cynical, most shallow – almost flippant.
One of the big "ifs" of modern history is how Africans would have fared if
colonization had been put off – as upsetting as that sounds. Africans seem
the least comfortable in the management of the European model of a nation
state. That is why they like the Chinese model. East Asians, by contrast,
bluff that one very well.

There were many ingredients that transformed Tudor England into the leading world empire. Of the numerous reasons, from commerce and individualism to sea power and parliamentary government, the political and historical experts agree that the most important initially was Protestantism. Kevin
Phillips in his novel *The Cousins' Wars* painstakingly details the triumph of
the Anglo-America empires through religion and politics. "The talk about
God being an Englishman only began when He – with some political assistance from Henry VIII in 1533 – established the Church of England, eliminating the pope in Rome as an intermediary. Protestantism quickly became
one of England's strongest self identifications. Religion and English nationalism began what would be a memorable convergence," Phillips wrote. Not
only in Britain, but in America.

The American Empire

The Protestant Reformation was the foundation stone of America. The Reformation allowed people to come in touch with their conscience and develop the ideas of individual liberties suppressed by the Catholic Church. To
do so they had to get away from Britain and Europe. "The Reformation
began as a movement to overcome the corruption, abuses and inaccuracies
of the received religion of the Universal Roman Catholic Church. A new
world, a promised land of faithful observance of a proper relationship to
God, opened before those who made the spiritual and intellectual journey
into reformed theology. Armed with their new approach to the Bible, within
the fold of a reformed Body of Christ, adherents of the new denominations
would build a new Jerusalem in their civic society on earth. The Pilgrims
who ventured to the New World truly saw themselves as new Israelites seeking the land of Canaan," Ziauddin Sardar and Merryl Wyn Davies wrote in
Why Do People Hate America? The Pilgrims set out to establish a new
society – and did.

As he sailed for America in 1630, John Winthrop, the future first governor of Massachusetts, wrote: "We must consider that we shall be a city upon a hill, the eyes of all people shall be upon us."

The charter granted by Henry VII of England to John Cabot in 1482 to settle Asia and America, licensed Cabot to occupy and set the king's banners and ensigns "in any town, city, castle, island or mainland whatsoever, newly found by them," anywhere in the "eastern, western or northern sea," belonging to "heathens and infidels, in whatsoever part of the world placed, which before this time were unknown to all Christians." The charter empowered him "to conquer, occupy and possess" all such places, on condition of paying the king "the fifth part of the whole capital gained" in every voyage.

America was founded by Europeans seeking to create a New World Order. People who wanted to break the cycle of religious hypocrisy, violence and persecution the Old World Order in Europe was living and experiencing. Although America was created by imperialism, the people who founded the country were seeking to create a new "City on the Hill."

Before 1776, Catholics were not allowed to vote or hold office in most of the American colonies. England barred them from voting or holding office in the years between the Glorious Revolution of 1688 and the enactment of Catholic Emancipation in 1829. One must keep in mind that through most of the 18th century, Catholic France and Spain enforced the Inquisition and remained autocracies hostile to the basic notions of parliamentary government and political liberty practiced in England, Holland and America.

We must also remember that Protestant lands were in a state of rebellion against something so great, eternal and ubiquitous that it was simply "The Church" – and Protestants felt this keenly. They were aware that what they were doing was so heretically outrageous to conventional Catholics that any one of them might happily be an agent of Rome or a Catholic prince ready to subvert or assassinate within Protestant realms.

English settlers first arrived in Jamestown, Virginia, in 1607. By 1774, disputes over taxation sparked the war for independence. America became a country when the 13 colonies made their Declaration of Independence in 1776. Britain was defeated in the War of Independence and surrendered at

Yorktown in 1783. The American Revolution officially ended with the Treaty of Paris signed on Sept. 3, 1783. The Constitution of the United States of America was enacted in 1788, and George Washington was elected the first president in 1789.

Many Native-Americans adopted the religion of the Puritans and fought alongside them against the British. Presbyterian and Congregationalist Church Indians of eastern New York and southern New England – the Mohegans, Stockbridge, Oneidas, and so-called Praying Indians along the Long Island Sound – also fought alongside their white neighbors. They suffered even higher casualties than white New Englanders.

The country expanded across the continent by Manifest Destiny. The idea was first enunciated by John L. O'Sullivan in his political magazine, *Democratic Review*, in 1845. "America had the right of our manifest destiny to overspread and to possess the whole of the continent, which Providence has given us for the development of the great experiment of liberty and federative development of self-government entrusted to us. It is the right such as that of the tree to the space of air and the earth suitable for the full expansion of its principle and destiny of growth."

Once the continent was conquered courtesy of America's Manifest Destiny, Hispaniola became the next logical target. President James Monroe created the conquest vehicle in 1823 when he established the Monroe Doctrine.

The Monroe Doctrine established the "American hemisphere," which became off-limits to all foreign countries and influences because America would view such influence or interference as "dangerous to our peace and safety." As a result, there is not one Latin American country that has not felt the wrath of America when domestic politics were perceived as being dangerous to America's "peace and safety."

Theodore Roosevelt, the 26th president, published a four-volume history, *The Making of the West (1894-96)* and numerous other books based on his experience establishing a cattle ranch in the Dakota Territory in 1883. When he became president, his personal experience as a frontiersman convinced him to expand the idea of Manifest Destiny across the Pacific and around the world. Speaking of the U.S. acquisition of the Philippines, which took place in 1898, Roosevelt declared: "Every argument that can be made for the Filipinos could be made of the Apaches. And every word that can be said for Aguinaldo could be said for Sitting Bull. As peace, order and prosperity followed our expansion over the land of the Indians, so they'll follow us in the Philippines."

True to the mythology of the Western, in the operation of foreign policy Roosevelt also famously observed: "No triumph of peace can equal the armed triumph of war."

The disintegration of the Spanish Empire at the end of the 19th century added Puerto Rico, Cuba, Guam and the Philippines to the American Empire.

When the battleship U S.S. Maine blew up in Havana harbor on Feb. 15, 1898, America and Spain went to war. In May, Commodore George Dewey attacked and sank the Spanish fleet in Manila. He sent the U.S.S. McCulloch back to Hong Kong to pick up Emilio Aguinaldo, the Filipino revolutionary hero bribed by the Spanish to leave the Philippines. He had already declared the Philippines a republic. The first national flag of the Philippines was made in Hong Kong at the house of Felipe Agoncilla on Morrison Street, Sheung Wan, in March 1898. Dewey used Aguinaldo's partisan Filipino army to bottle up the Spanish forces in Manila until reinforcements arrived from America. When the Spanish surrendered, Aguinaldo expected, quite reasonably, that his allies would support the cause of Filipino independence and acknowledge him as the president of the Philippines.

Never a great decision-maker, President William McKinley had no idea what to do. He said: "I went down on my knees and prayed to Almighty God for light and guidance." He claimed to have experienced some sort of revelation and he concluded: "There is nothing left for us to do but to take them all [the Philippine Islands] and to educate the Filipinos, and uplift and civilize and Christianize them." As the majority of the Filipinos were already devout Christians, it was an extraordinary reason to give for a piece of blatant empire-building. However the Filipinos, led by Aguinaldo, wanted independence and were prepared to fight for it

The result was a particularly bloody colonial war in which about 225,000 Filipinos and about 5,000 Americans lost their lives. An editorial reflecting

America's racist imperial policy proclaimed: "It would be absurd to think of ever making a state of them. No more can they be made a territory, with the Mongrel Malay-Asiatic population. True the Western Territories were originally wild wastes, peopled by savage Indians. But the territory was quickly transformed with the advent of white settlers." The British poet Rudyard Kipling wrote a poem about the colonization of the Philippines where he suggested that America should "Take up the white man's burden."

Americans have never admitted that they had an empire. In fact it existed, and still exists in everything but name. It was expansionist just like the Chinese, Arab, Ottoman, Spanish, Dutch and British empires. They gradually annexed the land of their neighbors, the Native-Americans, or seized territory from the Mexicans. In the words of Thomas Jefferson, it was "an empire of liberty stretching from sea to shining sea." Sometimes they simply bought it from the French, the Spanish or the Russians, but McKinley was the first American president who actually annexed overseas territories: Cuba, Puerto Rico, Guam and the Philippines. The colonies he created he tactfully called "commonwealths" so as not to upset anti-imperialist America.

Mark Twain wrote against American intervention in the Philippines at the turn of the century. So upset was Twain about his country's conduct in the Philippines that in one essay he suggested a change in the flag – its white stripes be painted black and the stars replaced by skulls and crossbones.

The Filipinos have largely forgiven the Americans for the slaughter of almost a quarter of a million of their countrymen during the occupation of the Philippines, which was a far greater number of deaths than the Chinese suffered during the Opium War, the Arrow War and the Boxer Rebellion put together.

Japan's imperial loss of the Pacific Islands after World War II and the collapse of the Soviet Union at the end of the 20th century enhanced America's presence in Asia and global reach. The U.S. intervention in Taiwan, Korea and Vietnam enhanced the U.S. presence in the Pacific from the U.S. military bases in Guam, the Philippines and Japan. "American belief in its own national myth as a model for all nations became a major factor on the world stage in the aftermath of World War II," Sardar and Davies wrote in *Why Do People Hate America?*

"This single-minded, monolithic outlook was received as something other than simple altruism. America's stance toward the rest of the world appeared as a new imperialism, different but not distinct from the varieties of imperialism that have been distorting the aspirations of three-fifths of humanity for centuries. Indeed, as an accumulation of all previous imperialisms, the pursuit of the American dream as a global dispensation laid the basis for hyper-imperialism, in which America subsumed the rest of the world as its own backyard, to be known and engaged with in purely American terms." Is it any wonder globalization to many is Americanization?

Historically, whenever an empire starts to fall apart and collapse, the vacuum left in its wake is filled by a successor. Both predecessor and successor have historically used propaganda and spin doctors to camouflage the truth. Not withstanding the Founding Fathers' aversion to and prohibition of imperial designs, America has always harbored imperial ambitions. However, America's motivation, much like the British and Dutch, is not religious, rather it is economic benevolence. America was and continues to be an empire. Puerto Rico remains a colony at the dawn of the 21st century. A constitutional empire, political, cultural and economic.

Like the Roman Empire, America has become a modern holy empire subtly run by a military dictatorship at the Pentagon spreading Christian fundamental values under the guise of democracy. Every war fought by America during the last two millennia has enabled it to enlarge its global base structure. The Gulf War added bases in Qatar, United Arab Emirates, Saudi Arabia, Kuwait and Oman. In the wake of the Afghan war, America has established new bases in Bahrain, Tajikistan and Kyrzstan. The Iraq war has created a 21st-century military base housing 150 000 U.S. troops around the second-largest oil reserves in the world. These bases nicely compliment the bases America established in Japan and Germany after World War II, and in Korea and the Balkans after the Korean and the Kosovo wars. Let's also keep in mind that America established bases in Cuba, Puerto Rico and the Philippines after the Spanish-American War. The only bases America had to give up to date were the two in the Philippines because America allowed its foot-soldier president Ferdinand Marcos to be dragged down by the weight of the gold he stuffed in his military boots.

Empire-building under the guise of nation-building has repeatedly failed.

The last nine attempts at the sunset of the 20th century and the dawn of the 21st are a vivid reminder. Somalia, Haiti, Bosnia, Kosovo, Sierra Leone, East Timor, Liberia, Afghanistan and Iraq. With the possible exception of Iraq, because of its oil, these are all territories which, in their present conditions, no prudent empire builder would want to set foot in. In Iraq, he would have had a "client regime" rather than a direct occupation. Oddly enough, that is more or less what was there until the imperial power started to send the volatile client mixed messages.

U.S. client puppets still cannot function on their own and continue to pose threats to their own citizens as well as U.S. national interests.

The great Victorian prime minister Lord Salisbury once famously described what could happen to a great empire that relied too much on unilateral action. "Splendid isolation" was the phrase he used, and he meant to imply that there was nothing splendid about it at all.

For nation-building to be a success, as it was in Germany, Japan, South Korea and Italy, America has to make a long-term military and financial commitment. U.S. troops are still in all four countries that are an example of successful nation-building today. All short-term commitments have been followed by failure.

As the world's sole superpower, America today can be likened to the Chinese Empire, Arab-Ottoman Empires, Roman Empire, Spanish Roman Catholic Empire, or the British Empire in their heyday. Is it any wonder revolutionary terrorists want to secede from America and cut it down to size?

Border Rievers
When President Richard Nixon took his oath of office in 1969 flanked by Lyndon Johnson and Billy Graham, and Neil Armstrong landed on the moon the same year, it was a momentous reminder of the deep-rooted role Border Reivers have had in the political and religious development of America. All four names hail from the clans of the Border Reivers of England and Scotland. Many of the politicians, companies, streets, communities and towns in America are common Scottish Border Reiver clan names and the towns and communities they populated. Armstrong, Nixon, Johnstone, Anderson, Haliburton, Melrose, and Cheviot Hills, to name but a few.

The 16th-century English and Scottish Border Rievers were the terrorists of their day. They terrorized the border area dividing England and Scotland and played a critical yet unheralded role in the development of both the British and American empires. The Border Rievers were cattle rustlers, robbers, arsonists, extortionists, murderers, kidnapers, blackmailers, and rapists that roamed freely between the border of England and Scotland for more than three centuries until England and Scotland united under James VI of Scotland, who became James I of England. His determination to rid the borders of the Rievers resulted in their expulsion to Ireland and America.

The lawless English-Scottish borders were a precursor to the Wild West frontier that propelled Manifest Destiny to the Pacific Ocean. The Reivers "deadly feud," the conflict between the different clans that was the root of many of the border problems, was shipped to America, where it is best known as the feud between the Hatfields and McCoys, as well known in America as the feud between the Maxwells and the Johnstones in Scotland. Revenge was so much a part of the Border Riever's way of life, that even the church was forced to recognize it. At a baptism, the right hand of a male child was left unchristened so that "it might deal the more deadly, in fact the more hallowed, blow to the enemy." A practice enforced with religious fervor against the Native-Americans, Mexicans and African-Americans.

The English-Scottish frontier is and was the dividing line "between two of the most energetic, aggressive, talented and altogether formidable nations in human history," George MacDonald Fraser wrote in *The Steel Bonnets*. Any number of factors, including geography, weather, race movement, and Hadrian's Wall decided where the border line should be and the endless conflicts that ensued.

Countless battles and wars were fought that created a hard and crusted people that could endure and survive the greatest of hardships known to mankind. To survive, the Border Reiver was a nomadic farmer, professional cattle rustler, fighting man who, on the evidence handled his weapon with superb skill on horseback, and a guerrilla soldier of great resource to whom the arts of theft, raid, tracking and ambush were second nature.

In 1066, when William of Normandy conquered England, he, like his Roman predecessors, dealt ruthlessly with its northern areas, making a scorched desert from York to Durham, which resulted in floods of refugees fleeing to Scotland. Refugees who had left relatives behind in England and who collectively became part of the Border Reiver clans that never recognized the border line.

The Anglo-Scottish Wars lasted for nearly 300 years without anyone winning a long-lasting peace. Even during so-called peaceful periods, the cross-border destructive raids by the Border Reivers continued unabated, preventing borderers from living a settled existence. While both the English and Scottish governments deplored the Reiver economy, both encouraged it and cynically exploited it for their own political goals. No different than modern-day career politicians. The Border Reivers were a political necessity. They were an ever-ready source of fighting men, a permanent mobile task force to be used whenever war broke out. A tradition that endured well into the 21st century. A tradition that helped create both the British and American empires.

The border people were small in number. What they lacked in numbers they made up for in ferocity. It is estimated that the 16th-century population of the borders was 120,000 English and 50,000 Scots. They intermarried and lived by their own laws with a total disregard for the dictates from London or Edinburgh. They were the original outlaws. They wrote the book on gang warfare and organized crime. The term blackmail was coined on the borders. Its literal meaning is "black rent" – in other words, illegal rent – the modern equivalent of the protection rackets. Blackmail was so widespread in the borders that it became punishable by death in Scotland in 1567 and became a capital offense on the English side of the border in 1601.

King Henry VIII's desire for divorce and new wives, which triggered England's break from the Catholic Church, had strong repercussions in Catholic Scotland, especially in the borders where the Reivers were the paid mercenaries on both sides of the conflict, depending who was paying the most at any given time.

Catholic France sided with Scotland in the religious conflict, which only made matters more difficult for England because it was already at war with France. In 1549, England withdrew from Scotland and the Border Reivers were again able to continue their unabated raids.

Border reiving flourished more than ever when women took to the thrones of both England and Scotland. The middle of the 16th century saw the powers of both the thrones of England and Scotland in the hands of women. Marie of Scotland, widow of James V. and her daughter Mary Queen of Scots, and "Bloody" Mary of England and her sister Elizabeth I.

France decided to take over Scotland. Marie, James V's widow, became regent, and French influence peaked. Many in Scotland viewed this development with alarm, particularly the new adherents to Protestantism. In England, the reformers faced an even greater menace, for with the death of Edward VI in 1533, the throne passed to the rigidly Catholic Mary, who in 1554 married the arch-enemy of Protestantism, Philip of Spain. This resulted in England being drawn to the Spanish side of the struggle against France for dominance in the Roman Catholic Empire. So while England and Scotland were on opposite sides of the Catholic conflict, the Protestants and Reformists in England and Scotland proceeded with the Reformation, since neither the English or the Scots wanted to fight on behalf of France or Spain. Meanwhile the Border Reivers, who were more interested in loot than conquest, continued to be of service to all sides and factions under government license.

The death of Elizabeth I without an heir, and her desire to make James VI of Scotland the King of England, brought an unceremonious deadly and violent end to the Border Reivers. James VI and I decided to end the Borders. What used to be the extremes of England and Scotland were to become the the Middle Shires of the United Kingdom. The Reivers, with no border to fight over any more, were forced to settle down or face "Jeddart Justice," which meant the gallows first and trial later, or exile in Ireland or America.

The Ulster Scottish-Irish, who were settled on the 17th century frontier of Northern Ireland to drive back the native Irish Catholics, which they did, made the politicians in London believe that their border-taming skills could be used against America's Indians, which was also true. By the 1760s, the Scottish-Irish borderers were expansionist almost by nature. "Religion was a related spur, because to the covenanting Presbyterianism that many shared, Ulster had been the first new Israel – and now America would play a grander role," Kevin Phillips wrote in *The Cousins' Wars.*

Now here's a thought. Forget putting the French, who haven't won a war since 1815, into Southern Lebanon. Ask Britain to send elements of their regiments traditionally recruited from the Borders and Ulster.

These are the same Protestant Scottish forefathers of the Anglo-Celts who settled and dominated the Ozarks, Appalachians and Texas political and economic landscapes. Texas was originally named the New Philippines by the Spanish conquistadors. At the time the Dutch were fighting Spain for independence while Native-Americans were being tortured in the New Philippines.

The Border Reivers were at home on the Indian frontier, killing, robbing and cattle rustling.

Capitalists and their capital traditionally gravitated and prospered in countries where they and their business are secure and not subject to arbitrary confiscation by the church or government.

Risk Takers

Capitalists are risk takers, calculated risk takers, but risk takers non-the-less. Risk takers founded and built America. Risk taking gamblers from all over the world – legal and illegal gamblers – staking it all for their beliefs and desire to provide a better life for themselves and their families, many also have the desire to escape oppression and wars. I know first hand. I am such a risk taker who came to America and made my way to California – the ultimate risk takers destination and paradise. Earthquakes, fires, floods, landslides, not just once, but over and over and like, isn't this enough, even for a risk taker? I for one who has lived through it all, sometimes wonder. That is what triggered me to sit down and question our conventional beliefs. My son Jonas, who grew up experiencing both the drama and trauma on our family as I fought fires, floods, mother nature – and his mother and the havoc she created – opted to start his professional career as a firefighter and licensed building contractor.

The California Gold Rush started attracting ultimate risk takers. The 49ers had to cross the unchartered territory of the Sierra Nevada, Death Valley – Badwater – at its heart, was the ultimate risk before getting to the gold fields. Risking it all for the American Dream. Some loose it all, others make fortunes.

Gold, railroads, oil, agriculture, real estate development, entertainment, garments, defense – all industries requiring various degrees of risk. As if the risks taken in pursuing a dream is not enough, California risk takers also face the additional risks of earthquakes floods, fires, mudslides and actors who become governors. Religious extremists need to become the same kind of constructive risk takers to ignite knowledge – not suicide bombers. Why continue to ignore the lessons of history? Aren't knowledge and progress the keys to survival for all people's, cultures, tribes and religions?

The Opium Traders

Opium is usually credited with causing the war with China that led to the cession of Hong Kong Island to Britain. However, the fact is that it was the phenomenal European demand for tea that was the ultimate cause of the conflict. Tea drinking became the rage in 18th century Europe and America, and for decades supply could not keep up with demand. Tea could only be paid for in silver, which led to a serious balance-of-trade deficit in favor of China. It was largely to redress this imbalance and stem the outflow of British silver that the opium trade developed.

The second governor of Hong Kong, Sir John Davis (1844-1848), inherited a colony that was desperately short of funds because it was a free port and could not collect custom duties, which were the government's major revenue source of the day. He despised the opium traders. Because his administration was short of cash, he created a government opium monopoly that allowed him to tax the opium traders. This caused the colonial treasurer, Robert Montgomery Martin, to resign as a matter of principal, saying: "Private vice should not be made a source of public revenue."

The British forced Indian farmers to switch from wheat and rice to opium, thereby causing a famine in India. The opium was then forced on the Chinese. America did the same to Native Americans with whisky in order to get their land.

In the late 1830s, the principal nations trading with China were the British and the Americans, who were free traders. The Americans were led by the Massachusetts firm of Russell and Co., the closest commercial rival to Jardine, Matheson and Co., the leading Scottish trading company in Hong Kong that was the leading importer of opium to China. They jointly decided to replace silver as the currency of trade with opium, which became the preferred currency.

Demand for opium grew as more Chinese became dependent. However, the import of opium had been banned in 1796 by the Emperor Kia King. Although the East India Company observed this edict and its ships did not import the drug, this did not stop it from manufacturing opium in India, which it sold to the interlopers, who smuggled it into China. The Americans bought their opium in Turkey and brought it to China on Yankee Clippers. The Opium War was the result of the Chinese trying to ban the importation of a lucrative commodity that allowed Great Britain and America to access a vast market and commodities needed back home.

Theodore Joset, a prolific letter-writing Swiss priest, graphically illustrates the havoc the drug caused in China. In January 1840, six months before the British fired the opening bombardment of the Opium War, he wrote: "I would like to write a few words about the situation here. We are close to a fight between the Chinese and the British, caused by the trade of opium which is transported from India to China: Chinese smoke it like tobacco; but it enslaves them, stupefies them; renders them incapable of any work. Once hooked, they can't drop it without risking their lives. China did not spare anything to try to stop the commerce of such poison: seeing that all other means were useless, the Emperor sent to Canton a plenipotentiary to try to stamp it out. But he thought he could treat the British like the locals: assaulted the warehouse of some of them, others were arrested, condemned to suffer hunger and thirst; some were put to death. At the end the Mandarin told the British Consul that if he did not get rid of it (opium) within a certain time he will put them all to death. ..."

He went on to describe the events that ended with the occupation of the island of Hong Kong, which was anything but a "barren rock," the description given the island by it's first governor. It was a highly coveted harbor which was already being used by the British fleet as an anchorage without China's permission. Joset was quick to grasp the implications of the Opium War and he even forecast the British seizure of Hong Kong before it actually happened.

The American opium traders were just as active as their British counterparts in setting up the "coolie trade" – Chinese indentured servants traded for opium. Coolies were taken as a form of payment for the opium, as China was unable to make up its trade deficit otherwise. These Chinese coolies were shipped to America, Australia and South Africa. This trade was no better than that of the enslaved blacks imported from Africa to work the plantations of America's South. The Chinese coolies were brought to "Gold Mountain" – The Chinese term for California, to work the gold mines and build the transcontinental railroad – an important development in America's westward expansion. What is amazing is that Chinese peasants today pay vasts amounts of money to unscrupulous smugglers to get them into America.

Like the African-American slaves on the East Coast, the coolies were denied citizenship, could not vote, and could not testify in court. However, they were taxpayers. They had to pay a personal tax, hospital tax, school tax, and property tax. They had such severe restrictions imposed on their movement that if they dared venture into new areas, whites could beat, rob and kill them. Hence the expression, "Not a Chinaman's chance."

Their abuse and exploitation continued long after the emancipation of African-American slaves.

The 1872 Chinese Exclusion Act severely restricted the immigration of Chinese to America. Only those who could prove their father or grandfather was a naturalized citizen were allowed admission. The law was abolished only when China allied itself with the U.S. during World War II. But even then the abolition was in name only – only 100 Chinese immigrants were allowed in legally each year. The notorious Angel Island immigration station in San Francisco Bay, through which about 175,000 Chinese – mostly men – were detained and mistreated between 1910 and 1940, is being restored as a museum.

The San Francisco 1906 earthquake that destroyed the city brought out blatant racism against the Chinese. Chinese immigrants were shot and beaten in an attempt to stop them from rebuilding Chinatown. City officials tried unsuccessfully to move Chinatown from its valuable central location to a remote outpost.

Opium had been imported into China from the West since the early 18th century, but at first only in small quantities. In 1729, only 200 chests were imported, but by 1836 the figure had risen to more than 20,000 chests. This caused a massive flow of silver out of China, which played havoc with the economy and created thousands of Chinese addicts. In 1839, the emperor sent Lin Tse-hsu to Canton to straighten things out. Commissioner Lin suspended trade with Britain and refused to let any of the British merchants leave the Canton factory until they had surrendered all the opium in their ships. The British merchants did give up their opium and were allowed to leave Canton. The Opium War started because the British and American opium traders wanted to resume their lucrative business.

After the Opium Wars and the series of one-sided post-war 19th-century treaties, the opium trade to China operated on a firm legal footing. With annual quota systems and customs inspections, the opium business in Hong Kong was as legitimate as any other. And it wasn't only Europeans and Americans that were involved. Many Chinese, Parsee, Jewish and Eurasian business leaders took part.

Growing international moral repugnance led to the Hague Convention of 1912. The treaty banned the direct sale of opium from India to China and came into full effect in 1919, but the drug remained openly available in Hong Kong, Malacca, Singapore and Penang until 1941. Opium purchases were limited to registered users for consumption in their homes. Illegal opium dens were regularly raided by the police. Until the 1950s, when U.N. pressure finally put a stop to the trade. In the '50s and '60s, the Hong Kong plastics production provided a useful cover as both plastic production and heroin refining are smelly industries.

The important role opium played in many economies at the turn-of-the-century was the equivalent of the tobacco industry today. Many of the arguments put forward by the opium syndicates were the same as the tobacco lobby in the 21st century. Many economies, like Afghanistan today, were dependent on poppy growing and customs revenue. Smuggling and corruption of officials increased with prohibition.

During the negotiations on the handover of Hong Kong in the 1980s and '90s, Chinese politicians were forever blaming the Opium Wars on the Tory government of Margaret Thatcher and John Major. Thatcher and Major were surprised because Sir Robert Peel's Tories had opposed the Opium War, and in 1857 Lord Derby's Tories actually brought down Palmerston's Liberal government over the opium trade and the Arrow War with China to preserve it. They even forced an election in Britain. Under today's rules of international law, a government policy to sell opium would be prosecuted as a crime against humanity – the Afghan U.S. puppet government being the exception. The seizure of the opium was the event that sparked the war, but according to the Western view, it was China's refusal to accept any other foreign country as its equal or to enter into diplomatic relations with the West that was the real cause of the war.

I very much doubt that many early 19th-century Britons and Americans would have regarded Chinamen as their equals at heart. On the other hand, the Manchu cannot be blamed for keeping their distance from these very smelly men.

Slavery

Slavery was started in ancient Greece, globalized by the Roman Empire and became an accepted way of life in Medieval Europe and the New World of Hispaniola and America. The word "slave" derives from "Slav," referring to the white Slavic people of Eastern Europe.

Spain, the first imperial power in the New World authorized by the Papal Bulls to enslave native inhabitants, debated whether Native-Americans were what Aristotle termed "natural slaves," the segment of mankind set aside by nature to be slaves in the service of those born into a life of manual-free labor, the biblical warrant in the sons of Ham who were destined to be "hewers of wood and drawers of water," or as the rebellious Spanish priest Antonio de Montesinos preached in a sermon in 1511 in Hispaniola, "Are these Indians not men? Do they not have rational souls? Are you not obliged to love them as you love yourselves?" These contradictory opinions led to decades of debates in Spain finally resulting in the Requimiento, a set of instructions concerning the treatment of natives.

The Requimiento was the legal justification for the Roman Spanish Empire to appropriate and possess the land and the people in its empire. The Requimiento was a requirement to read out, in a language the natives could not understand, a formal declaration offering the Indians a choice. They could submit to Spanish rule and allow the preaching of the faith. If they refused, the Spaniards were empowered to undertake punitive measures and enter their land with fire and sword. "We shall take you and your wives and your children, and shall make slaves of them, and as such shall sell and dispose of them as his Highness may command; and we shall take away your goods, and shall do all the harm and damage that we can, as to vassals that do not obey."

The first record of African slaves in America, then a British colony, was in 1609 in a letter written by John Rolfe, the future husband of Pocahontas, about "servants" bought from a Dutch ship in Jamestown.

African slaves were sold to the Americas and all the islands of the Caribbean to work the plantations by the Dutch, French, Spanish and British slave traders. According to *The Slave Trade* by Hugh Thomas, an estimated 11 million Africans were sold as slaves. Other historians estimate the number as much as 25 million to 40 million.

The enormous profits of the slave trade paid for Britain's industrial revolution, created Western financial systems and endowed European cultural institutions. The processing and distribution of tobacco, sugar and cotton produced on plantations resulted in massive investments in European and American ports, quays, warehouses, factories and banks. Cities grew on the back of this trade. Europeans living in the centers of the slave trade – London and Amsterdam – salted away their profits in banks which financed slavery.

The British Museum was started with a collection of 71,000 artifacts collected by Sir Hans Sloane with money made on his wife's Jamaican plantation. Britain's great liberal prime minister, William Gladstone, came from a family whose fortune was made from slavery.

Africans who sold fellow Africans were equally complicit. Britain seized the high ground with the 1807 Abolition Act, withdrawing from the trade in spite of self-interest and the mores of the time. The act imposed a £100 fine for every slave found aboard a British ship. The 1833 Slavery Abolition Act outlawed slavery itself throughout the British Empire. However slaves did not gain their final freedom in the empire until 1838.

New York City had more slaves in 18th-century America than any other city except Charleston, South Carolina. African-Americans made up as much as one-fifth of the population of colonial New York City. The 18th-century African Burial Ground unearthed at Broadway and Duane Streets during excavation at the end of the 20th century contained the remains of more than 20,000 people. "There are people who try to put slavery into a neat package as something that only happened south of the Mason-Dixon line," Dr. Sherrill D. Wilson remarked during the reburial at the dawn of the 21st century. The reburial was a "return to the past in order to build the future."

Two of the 2008 presidential candidates, Arizona Senator John McCain and former Democratic senator John Edwards of North Carolina, are descendants of slave owners. In 1860, McCain's great-great-grandfathers in Mississippi owned slaves and two ancestors of Edwards owned slaves in Georgia. Senator Barack Obama's great-great-great-great-grandfathers on his mother's side were also slave owners. A descendant of a slave owner marries a student from Kenya and produces a son who becomes a U.S. senator and candidate for president of America.

The modern anti-slavery movement began with the Enlightenment and French Revolution at the end of the 18th century. The transoceanic slave trade was abolished in South Africa in 1807. When Britain outlawed slavery in the Empire in 1833, it led the effort to suppress it elsewhere. France ended slavery in 1848. Abolition progressed rapidly in Latin America as the continent liberated itself from Spain. Slavery was prohibited in Argentina in 1813, in Colombia in 1821 and Mexico in 1829. The Spanish and Arab slave traders continued to pursue their trade. Slavery remained legal in Brazil and the Roman Catholic Spanish Empire, most notably Cuba, until the late 19th century. It remains legal today in Saudi Arabia, Pakistan, and many countries in Africa and other parts of the world.

Today the slave trade involves men, women and children tricked, coerced or intimidated into prostitution or forced labor. Slavery today is the third-largest illicit trade in the world after narcotics and weapons, with an annual estimated value of $32 billion. More than 20 million people are trafficked annually.

In America, the issue of extension of slavery into the new states of the border and West, where Chinese coolies were in great supply, became the most important political issue from 1830 until the American Civil War, when Lincoln's Emancipation Proclamation in 1863 declared the slaves free.

Meanwhile, collaboration had developed between Cubans who wanted to break with Spain and retain slavery, and America's Southern states, which wanted to either finance and sponsor Cuba as an independent slave state, or annex the island to strengthen the South against Yankee abolitionists.

South Carolina's secession from the union that led to the Civil War was initiated by Charleston editor Robert Barnwell Rhett, a longtime and ardent secessionist who was considered an extremist who was ultimately ineffectual. He predicted that a historian in A.D. 2000 would write of the Confederate States of America: "And extending their empire across this continent to the Pacific, and down through Mexico to the other side of the great gulf, and over the isles of the sea, they established an empire and wrought out a civilization that had never been equaled or surpassed."

Just goes to show, yet again, that you shouldn't believe everything you read in the papers – or on the Internet.

America and Cuba's slave heritage is affecting their political relationship today. Cuba was a slave society 100 years before the first shipload of African slaves arrived in Virginia in 1619. Cuba remained a slave society until 1886.

When Cuba achieved independence because of U.S. intervention in the Cuban uprising in 1898, leading to Spain's defeat – it proved less than total. The United States continued to occupy Cuba until 1902 and imposed on the Cuban constitution a "right" of U.S. intervention, which was maintained until 1934. America exercised this right when Cubans revolted against Yankee commercial imperialism in 1906, reoccupying the country until 1909, and intervened again in 1912 to put down a protest movement against discrimination against blacks.

From 1933 until Castro's revolution in 1954, the country was dominated by Fulgencio Batista, a corrupt former sergeant in the U.S. Marine-trained Cuban militia. He was the subject of FDR.'s well-known remark, – "He's an SOB, but he's our SOB."

The U.S. military base on Guantanamo, where hundreds of the Taliban and al-Qaeda fighters are detained, is a political trophy retained by the U.S. to this day in Communist Cuba.

The Clash of 20th-Century Empires

Japan was a feudal, insular, closed society before the Meiji reforms of 1868 that imported Western business practices, philosophy and ideas that transformed Japan into the modern society it is today. Christianity first arrived in Japan in 1549 in the form of a Basque Jesuit, Francis Xavier and his two Jesuit companions and a Japanese interpreter. By the 1580s, there was a flourishing congregation of more than 200,000 and the senior Jesuits were on intimate terms with the warriors who controlled the country and wanted to trade with the outside world, a counterweight to the powerful Buddhist clergy. Then on July 24, 1587, the shogun Hideyoshi Toyotomi ordered all missionaries to leave within 20 days. He saw them as the advance guard of the country's colonization after the pilot of a stranded Spanish ship had boasted that the greatness of the Spanish Empire was partly due to the missionaries who preceded them and prepared the way for the Spanish army.

Richard Cocks, a 17th-century English visitor to Japan, described the country as "the most puissant tyranny the world has ever known." Referring to the treatment of Japanese Christians, who were seen as a fifth column for Europeans: "I saw 55 of them martyrized at one time in Miyako. Among them were children of five or six years, burned alive in the arms of their mothers." This was not really about religion. Indeed, Toyotomi, the Japanese ruler who first banned Christianity, had earlier toyed with the idea of becoming a Christian himself, deciding not to when he learned that he would then be limited to one wife. Rather, then, like today, it was about social conservatives trying to protect their way of life from Western onslaught.

In 1873, under pressure from the West, the new Meiji government lifted the ban on Christianity. Foreign priests were astonished to find practicing Christians who had clung to their faith through hundreds of years of brutal persecution. When it occupied Japan in 1945, the U.S. made it easy for foreign missionaries to come, believing that the spread of Christianity would prevent a return to militarism.

Widespread modernization propelled Japan into the role of a regional empire. Starting in the early 20th century, oil-starved Japan embarked on an aggressive imperial march to secure natural resources to fuel its expanding modern economy. Japan's desire to secure oil led to World War II in the Pacific. Japan conquered Korea, China, Philippines and many parts of Asia. Why it never occurred to Japan to just buy the oil is something I have never quite come to grips with.

The Japanese invaded Hong Kong in 1941, the same day they bombed Pearl Harbor. Japan, like America, also had a Pacific empire on that infamous day. Japan had colonized Korea, Taiwan, parts of mainland China, Pacific islands and other countries in Asia before its sneak attack on America.

In Hong Kong, British, Canadian, Indian forces and the Hong Kong Volunteers, which included members of almost every community in the colony, put up a brave fight, but on Christmas Day in 1941, they surrendered. The British and their allies were interned by the Japanese and the Chinese were encouraged to leave Hong Kong. Many Eurasian civilians chose to be interred as enemy aliens.

British and Canadian internees were subjected to the same inhumane abuses their American and Filipino counterparts were in the Philippines. Decapitation and the mass slaughter of POWs was the norm.

Missionary Launch Pad

The arrest of Hong Kong Bible smuggler Lai Kwong-keung in 2002 for attempting to spirit 16,000 Bibles across the border to the Christian "Shouters" in China was just the latest act of the continuing drama of missionaries doing God's work in China from Hong Kong. Christian missionaries used Hong Kong as a springboard to all corners of China for centuries. I am reminded of an amusing story Charles Weatherill, a longtime Hong Kong resident and journalist, told me one day at the Foreign Correspondents Club. He was born in China in 1924 to missionary parents. "The Chinese, to this day, don't understand why my parents went to China to give birth. The Chinese, especially Hong Kong Chinese, try to go overseas preferably, the U.S. and Canada to give birth." The Chinese preoccupation is conversion to foreign passports, not religion.

The FCC religious law-and-order constituency received its fair share of ridicule at the Main Bar when veteran Russian spy and FBI counterintelligence agent Robert Hanssen was arrested. The fact that he belonged to the secretive group of conservative Catholics known as Opus Dei – a movement ideologically opposed to a staunchly atheist communist ideal – while he brought Priscilla Sue Galey, a Washington stripper, to Hong Kong in his effort to convert her to Christianity, highlighted both America's religious sexual hypocrisy and Hong Kong's traditional religious role.

Before Hong Kong became a British colony in 1841, Christian missionaries were active in China. St. Francis Xavier, after his success in Japan, went to China, where he died in 1552. He was followed by other Jesuits, notably Matteo Ricci, the first Catholic priest to reach Beijing. He stayed in China for nearly 30 years and is credited with initiating the interaction between China and the West. He died in 1640. His mission was to convert the Emperor Wan Li to Christianity. The emperor was interested in science and Ricci asked the Jesuits to send him an astronomer. They sent Adam Schall, who became the emperor's director of the Bureau of Astronomy.

During the Qing Dynasty, another Jesuit, Ferdinand Verbiest, refitted the Beijing Observatory. The Jesuits' aim was to become scientific tutors to the emperor. This they hoped would put them in a position to convert the Son of Heaven to Christianity. Everything seemed to be going according to plan until the Emperor Kang Hsi asked the pope to give him one of his nieces as a concubine. The pope refused and as a result the Jesuits lost their influence over the Son of Heaven.

There are 50 Western missionaries – including Matteo Ricci, the first Jesuit missionary to succeed in securing a foothold for Christianity during the late Ming Dynasty (1368-1644) – buried in the historical Zhalan Cemetery, a protected cultural relic, located at the Beijing Administrative College. Generally, foreigners who died in China had to be buried in Macau, according to the code of the Ming Dynasty. There are 49 tombstones remaining memorializing missionaries from eight European countries buried there during the Qing Dynasty (1644-1911).

America, like Rome, also sent missionaries. It still does. In 1854, President Bush's, alma mater, Yale, bestowed a bachelor's degree on Yung Wing, who became the first Chinese native to graduate from an American college. The following decades saw many Yale men travel to China to spread the word about Christianity, including the father of Henry Luce, the founder of *Time* magazine, who had a life-long interest in China. In 1901, a missionary project called Yale-in-China was founded that would later build a teaching hospital and a secondary school in Hunan province. The project is still active today.

One of the problems that the missionaries faced was that the Chinese emperor, like the Roman emperor, had the status of a god. To convince a man who thinks that he is a god that there is a god greater than himself was not easy. To set any other god above him was tantamount to treason.

It was the same problem Jesus faced when addressing Caesar. Even in a protected society like Macau, a Portuguese outpost for more than 400 years, there were very few converts, and of those, most of them were Rice Christians, converts who did so solely for the rice they received for converting. Nor were the Protestants any more successful. The great Robert Morrison of the London Missionary Society, who was the first person to translate the Bible into Chinese, converted only four Chinese to Christianity during his 27 years on the China coast.

On the face of it, Christianity is a difficult religion to pitch to the Chinese. Its text is huge, implausible and all about Jews. Its central theme is about a God who came down to earth disguised as a carpenter, did magic tricks assisted by 12 very thick fishermen, failed miserably, got executed and went back to himself saying he had forgiven everybody and was living forever. His followers now perform an ongoing magic trick and eat bits of his body once a week. To a people with a very wide range of mythological hocus pocus at their disposal already, Christianity just doesn't really cut it.

The other major problem the early missionaries faced was that China was closed to foreigners except for a small area in Canton, where European and American traders were allowed to stay for a few months of the year to do business. Karl Gutzlaff, the first Lutheran missionary in China, solved the problem by signing on as an interpreter aboard a Jardine, Matheson & Co. armed opium clipper, the Sylph. It was a smuggling ship and Gutzlaff preached Christianity to the Chinese and sold them opium at the same time. Back in Macau, he printed religious tracts, which he gave to his converts to distribute. They sold them back to the printer, who resold them to Gutzlaff. This frustrated his ambition "to evangelize en masse a great nation." Mary Gutzlaff, his wife, ran a school for blird girls. American Southern Baptists Rev. S. Lewis and Henrietta Shuck also had a school in Macau before moving to Hong Kong, where they built the first church in the new colony. While the local merchants applauded the fact that the Shucks built a mission school and attempted to convert the Chinese to Christianity, they objected strongly to Henrietta Shuck's militant efforts to save the souls of British merchants, whom she described as vile sinners.

Despite the militant nature of missionaries like the Shucks, there seems to have been remarkably little friction in Hong Kong between Protestants and Catholics. The more extreme evangelists tended to head straight for China. There was a very small permanent European and American population in Hong Kong in the first decade of its colonial days, around 500 people, not counting the British forces. The Chinese attitude on religion is rather refreshing. A staunch Confucian would consult a Taoist monk if he was ill and have a Buddhist funeral on his death. This is true today, with the added attraction of Christian weddings. Devotion exclusively to a single religion is alien to many Chinese and even Chinese Muslims who employ feng shui experts. The Hong Kong Census and Statistics Department is driven to despair by some of the answers on religion they get in their multiple-choice surveys.

It is said that the road to hell is paved with good intentions. The Rev. Issachar Roberts, an American Baptist minister, converted failed scholar Hung Hsiu-chuan to Christianity. Hung had his own nonconformist theories. He founded the religious Taiping cult. He called himself the Heavenly King, claimed to be the brother of Jesus Christ and announced that it was his sacred duty to liberate China from Manchu rule. He started the Taiping Rebellion that raged for 13 years and cost 25 million lives. His armies conquered about a third of China. When it was discovered that the Heavenly King kept a harem of 88 wives and 1,000 concubines, the missionaries began to question his motives. His teacher, Roberts, visited his former disciple in Nanking in 1861, when he was at the height of his power. On his return, he wrote: "I believe he is crazy, especially on religious matters." Hung almost became the Chinese

Constantine. All the major rebellions in China during the later years of the Qing Dynasty, the White Lotus Rebellion, the Taiping Rebellion, the Boxer Rebellion and the numerous Muslim rebellions, were either religious or quasi-religious in origin. Thus it is not surprising that the present Chinese government looks upon religion with suspicion.

The Christian missionaries sent to Japan from Hong Kong encountered a different fate from 1597, after a Spanish galleon fully loaded with a valuable cargo ran aground. The captain appealed to the taiko Hideyoshi, the top warlord, and tried to intimidate him with the power and might of Spain's King Philip by pointing out on a globe the worldwide Spanish Empire. When the taiko inquired how such a small country acquired such a vast empire, the incautious seaman said, "His very Catholic majesty would first send out priests to Christianize the population, and these converts would then help the Spanish forces in their conquest."

With that kind of evidence, Hideyoshi refused to return the cargo and ordered the crucifixion of 26 Christians, 17 of them Japanese, the rest Jesuits and Franciscans from Europe. The Japanese then went about eradicating Christianity with characteristic ferocity. In 1616, all foreign merchant vessels – except Chinese – were barred from ports other than Nagasaki and Hirado. Foreigners were limited to Edo, later named Tokyo, Kyoto, and Sakai. In 1624, the Spanish were barred completely; in 1639, the Portuguese. The British just stopped coming. That left the Dutch and the Yankee Clippers.

Religious Persecution and Paranoia

China is very much aware of the part religion played in the collapse of the Soviet Union. With three new nation states peopled by Muslims – Tajikistan, Kyrgyzstan and Kazakhstan – ranged along its western borders, it fears the spread of Muslim nationalism spreading into its territory. The claim by the Xinjiang regional Communist Party secretary, Wang Lequan, that 19 terrorist bases staffed by Taliban instructors from Afghanistan had been discovered in the province fanned those concerns and encouraged China to join America in the war on terrorism.

Most Muslims in China, like their brothers and sisters in America, believe in the true preaching of the religion and live in peace. However, just as al-Qaeda cells exist in the U.S., Beijing estimates there are some 1,000 Chinese Muslims trained by Osama bin Laden grouped into activist cells. America and China have a common enemy and must join forces in the 21st century. The political rhetoric of career politicians in America indicating otherwise, especially those vocal about China being the enemy, have to be swept out by *We the Maids* if we are to honestly deal with political paranoia – which is unfounded and unsupported by history or reality.

The Roman Catholic community is closely watched in China, particularly those who recognize the pope as the head of their church rather than the director of the Religious Bureau of the People's Republic of China. The difficulty for Roman Catholics in the eyes of the Chinese government is that they have a loyalty to another head of state. The pope is the monarch of the Holy See – a state with one of the most extensive diplomatic and political influences in the world, punching well above its weight. The Holy See is a focus of understandable political suspicion.

Open worship is allowed in around 12,000 "registered" Protestant and Catholic churches in China, and there are thousands of unofficial meeting places, with and without walls. This became obvious to the world when Bill and Hillary Clinton went to church in Beijing during his 1998 summit meeting. During a speech from the pulpit of Chongwenmen Church, more than 2,000 worshippers turned up, far too many to actually get inside. However, most worship takes place in unofficial "house churches."

Traditional religious practices are also on the rise in rural China. More than 70 million city dwellers and farmers in China are reasserting their interest in ancient beliefs such as *qigong*, a martial arts-related discipline that teaches that human energy can be cultivated by yoga-like disciplines and directed to improve and heal oneself.

Falun Gong, which advocates a mix of *qigong*, Buddhism and Taoism and a sprinkle of other thoughts, opposes consumerism, rock music, television, extramarital sex and the use of alcohol. It is a version of Christian Science or Scientology with Chinese characteristics. L. Ron Hubbard and Falun Gong's leader, Li Hongzhi, both blended traditional religious beliefs with medical and scientific beliefs and wrote science fiction. Li Hongzhi was pressured to leave China and now lives in New York.

Of special concern to Beijing was the surprisingly large number of party cadres and military officers who embraced Falun Gong. By the government's own admission, there were 30,000 in the capital alone. For the party hierarchy, of course, it is intolerable that any cadre might have divided loyalties.

The Chinese government decided to ban Falun Gong on the ground that "it is an evil cult that tried to develop political power." However, followers continue to openly practice their beliefs in Hong Kong and protest Beijing's crackdown. A typical joke that circulates in Hong Kong has a Falun Gong woman selling a copy of Li Hongzhi's book to a passer-by at the convention centre for HK$20. He hands her a HK$100 bill, which she pockets. "Don't I get any change?" he asks. "Change must come from within," she replies.

Mainland leaders are fully aware and wary of the power of fervent religious movements, which have shaken the corridors of power before. Few though managed to organize a surprise mass demonstration right outside the leadership compound. Very close to the corridors, indeed.

All of China's mystic masters worry Beijing. Historically they've played a role in toppling weakened governments. Sinologist Charles Freeman, a former U.S. diplomat in China, said that both the Taiping and Boxer rebellions were about "overcoming [government's] impotence with magic." The history of mass uprisings in China is linked to the loss of the mandate of heaven – a signal that a leader's time has come. In Britain, it's when ministers start sleeping with their secretaries. In the U.S. it's when the president starts spending half his time planning his library.

It is no secret that behind China's strong economic growth lies a deeply troubled country lacking the anchor of traditional morals. In the 50-plus years of Communist rule, nearly every basic Chinese value has been savagely trampled on. In the past, family members often had to denounce each other simply to survive. These days, nobody knows what to believe anymore – except Mammon, the god of greed and money. Hong Kong is becoming the model for China. A model America should also study closer.

Sino-America Millennium

The third millennium dawns on an Asia run by Asians. The Spanish and Portuguese religious fanaticism left different colonial legacies in Asia and the Pacific than the capitalist mercantile British and Dutch. America and Hong Kong were settled by Dutch and British colonists who brought with them the property-rights structure. Because the British did not regard the colonies as critical to their own development, they were allowed a large measure of self-government. With relative political and economic freedom, the former colonies evolved into prosperous open societies after their independence.

The Spanish and Portugese established colonies to exploit the resources and extract the treasures of the land. The resulting institutional structure was one of monopoly and control from Madrid and Lisbon. With no heritage of political or economic freedom, the result was a half-century of civil wars in an attempt to fill the vacuum left by Iberian rule.

Portuguese Macau and Brazil, Spanish Philippines, South and Central America struggle economically and are poor, while Britain's Hong Kong, North America and other former colories, most notably those shared with the Dutch, prosper and are rich. The two extreme colonial heritages are best showcased in the New World by the large religious statues in the struggling former Spanish-Portuguese colonies contrasted with the large modern contemporary statues in the prosperous former British-Dutch colonies.

On top of the Corcovado Mountain in Rio de Janeiro in Brazil stands Cristo Redentor (Christ the Redeemer) – a statue of Christ with arms spread wide. The arms have the span of a Boeing 737's wings, and since its completion in 1931, the statue has become one of Brazil's most famous landmarks. It stands approximately 30 meters tall on a six-meter pedestal, and is visible day and night.

The Statue of Liberty in New York Harbor is in stark contrast because it represents the secular government America's Founding Fathers created. Built in France in 1886 to commemorate the centennial of America's independence from Britain, the statue is a symbol of freedom, democracy and international friendship. It stands approximately 93 meters from the ground to the tip of the torch.

Another vivid contrast that is a reminder whenever I walk down Ice House Street in central Hong Kong, is the modern multimillion-dollar high-rise

Portugese Club Lusitano built on prime commercial real estate. The club is one of the richest clubs in the world with the finest facilities, desperately seeking members who have any trace of Portuguese blood – 1/16th Portuguese are warmly embraced. Members must prove their Portuguese heritage to be admitted. By contrast, the very British Hong Kong Club further down the road, which is also very rich and owns a high-rise office building on prime central real estate, is open to all people regardless of their heritage, and it has an eight-year waiting list.

The same holds true for British private schools – known as public schools in Britain. An "empire of the mind" is being created throughout Asia from Kazakhstan through China to Thailand. British education, style, snobbishness and stiff-upper-lips are in high demand and they are gladly going after their fair share of the education pie. Replicas of London's Dulwich College in Beijing, Shanghai and Suzhou indicate that even Mao's Cultural Revolution cadres have developed a taste for British class. Dulwich College boasts an older connection with China through P.G. Wodehouse, the witty English novelist. The son of a Hong Kong judge, "Plum," as Wodehouse was known, was sent home to England because local missionary schools – filled with "natives" and the children of Britons who could not afford to send them home – were not good enough.

China spends nearly a trillion dollars a year on education, costing the average mainland family 10 percent of its income. Is it any wonder the Brits are mining the Asia education fields with such fervor? Shouldn't America be doing the same? As multicultural America and Britain have no room for starchy snobby education, the last repository of this life form might well be an Asian private-school boy in blazer and tie in Shanghai or Almatay. The empire is striking back.

The real damage of the last millennium was in the corruption of political dialogue – of the confusion between what was real and what had been mandated as real by religious leaders, career politicians, their lawyers, lobbyists, and spin doctors. The Communist threat and "domino theory" that resulted in the war in Vietnam is a contemporary example that has not been fully digested to be properly regurgitated in the Old World Disorder. There is no room for geopolitical ignorance or denial in the New World Order. The 21st century is one China and America can and must embrace to lead humanity.

Hong Kong is the bridge on which they must meet to plan the future. Hong Kong is home to the Tsing Ma Bridge, the world's largest suspension bridge, and there are plans to build an even larger bridge to Macau and Zhuhai, China.

Hong Kong is very accessible. It is a free port and its airport can easily accomodate all forward thinkers. It is the world's largest, most expensive facility of its kind and voted the world's best year after year. It is the largest enclosed indoor space in the world. It seamlessly moves an average of 95, 000 passengers every day.

Today America is the world's sole superpower – a Pacific-based empire. To constructively sustain itself and fulfill the will and desire of Americans in the 21st century, it has to learn from the mistakes and shortcomings of its predecessor empires. It is possible for a troubled civilization to rediscover itself by integrating change. To do so, it must adopt and fuse the best every empire to date has to offer our civilization. We The People must honestly extract and utilize the positive contribution of each empire's culture to further benefit the constructive development of our civilization's frontiers in the 21st century.

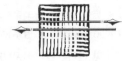

Chapter 3

Good Riddance to Religious Crusades
We will have peace with the Arabs when they love their children more than they hate us.
– Golda Meir

Political Brainwashing

Golda Meir, the former prime minister of Israel, was a mother and grandmother of two families – her own and Israel's. Both my mother and I, on separate occasions, had the privilege of meeting "Golda" as she was affectionately called. My mother idolized Golda and would bring up the above quote whenever the subject of peace between Israel and its Arab neighbors came up. What a pity Arabs haven't started this lovefest in the last century. Isn't it time all parents love their children more than they hate others?

The first U.N. Arab Human Development Report on Arabs by Arabs, completed in 2002, and the final one completed in 2005 by scholars and experts from the 22 Arab League countries, concluded that Arab nations are providing both too little education and the wrong kind. The report accused many countries from northwest Africa to the Persian Gulf of remaining in the Dark Ages, allowing scant political freedom, keeping women under subjugation and letting education standards drop sharply. Among those studied, 65 million adults, mostly women, were illiterate, 10 million children were not enrolled in schools and unemployment was three times the world average. "Given the political commitment, Arab countries have the resources to eradicate absolute poverty in less than a generation. Commitment, not resources, is the binding restraint," the report concluded.

The Israeli-Palestinian conflict has stunted Palestinian development and the Israeli occupation continues to provide most Arab states with "both a cause and an excuse for distorting the development agenda, disrupting national priorities and retarding political development," the report stated.

The report went on to say that growth in per-capita income in the region in the last two decades of the 20th century, at an average of just 0.5 percent, was the lowest in the world except for sub-Saharan Africa. Added together, the gross domestic product of the 22 nations was less than a medium-sized European country, such as Spain.

Walid Shoebat – a former Fatah terrorist – who converted from Islam to Christianity, said in Toronto, Canada, "The only illegal occupation in the Middle East is the illegal occupation of Palestinian minds by hatred." My friend, columnist Stuart Wolfendale, added: "We will have peace from al-Qaeda when Muslim societies learn how to create proper secular states – which is probably never."

Islam has become synonymous in the minds of many Americans with the biggest post-Cold War threat, even though most Muslims do not support fundamental extremism. We have to think outside the prism of the war on terrorism. "Even as it wages a resolute campaign against international terrorism, America should not believe that it is engaged in a fight to the finish with radical Islam," National Intelligence Council Chairman Robert Hutchings wrote in *Foreign Policy* magazine. "This conflict is not a clash of civilizations, but rather a defense of our shared humanity and a search for common ground, however implausible that may seem now."

An extreme example of how people are being brainwashed to their own detriment and suffering is in Nigeria, where people believe that the polio vaccine is part of an American plot to depopulate poor countries. Some local imams preach that it is laced with anti-fertility drugs, can cause AIDS and is even linked to mad cow disease. Given what the CIA has come up with in the recent past, could they be entirely wrong?

The speech former Malaysian Prime Minister Mahathir Mohamad gave at the Islamic Summit Conference in 2003 was widely quoted as being anti-Semitic. Many of his criticisms of Islam and its leaders were ignored or downplayed by the media. He actually also articulated why ignorance has been perpetuated in the Muslim world. He reminded his audience that Muslims aid and abet their detractors by attacking and weakening each other, and sometimes by doing their bidding, acting as their proxies to attack fellow Muslims. "We try to bring down our governments through violence, succeeding in weakening and impoverishing our own countries. Islam is not wrong, but the interpretations by our scholars, who are not prophets even though they may be very learned, can be wrong. We have a need to go back to fundamental teachings of Islam to find out whether we are indeed believing in and practicing the Islam that the prophet preached."

To end ignorance and instill knowledge, the teachers who spread hatred in our children have to be removed from the school systems. *We the Maids* have to draw a line in every school district that bars teachers who promote hatred and future conflicts from ever crossing to teach again. The lesson of the Altalena Affair must be taught in every school and madras.

When the modern state of Israel was being founded, there were several political and militant factions with opposing philosophies and goals on achieving statehood. Holding the fragile socialist democracy together was David Ben-Gurion, the first prime minister of Israel, who was steadfast in his views and policies for the Jewish state.

When Menachem Begin, the leader of the extremist group Irgun, which advocated violence against the British, challenged Ben-Gurion's vision of a single military force by trying to import weapons and fighters aboard the ship Altalena in June 1948, Ben-Gurion called the effort "an attempt to destroy the army, an attempt to murder the state." He ordered the Altalena shelled in sight of Tel Aviv with Begin aboard. Begin barely escaped and reluctantly integrated his forces with the Israeli army. Isn't this something every leader should do to corral the extremist organizations in Afghanistan, Iraq, Lebanon, Palestine, Pakistan, India, Indonesia and America?

There is a delicate balance between violence and diplomacy that enables fighting factions to use both without unnecessary deaths – locally as well. At the local level ethnic, cultural and religious gangs can and must defend their people against racist or religious fundamentalist thugs without guns or weapons of mass destruction. How about just going back to the good 'ol American cowboy ways?

During the rise of American Nazism in the 1930s, Jewish gangsters were staunch defenders of the Jewish people. The 1930s were a period of anti-Semitism in America, particularly in the Midwest. Father Charles Coughlin, the Radio Priest in Detroit, and William Pelley of Minneapolis, among others, openly called for Jews to be driven from positions of responsibility, and even out of America. Brown Shirts in New York and Silver Shirts in Minneapolis terrorized American Jews. While the older and more respectable Jewish organizations pondered a response that would not alienate non-Jewish supporters, others – including a few rabbis – asked the Jewish gangsters to break up American Nazi rallies.

German-American Bund rallies in the New York City area posed a dilemma for mainstream Jewish leaders. They wanted the rallies stopped, but had no legal grounds on which to do so. New York State Judge Nathan Perlman personally contacted Meyer Lansky to ask him to disrupt the Bund rallies with the proviso that Lansky's henchmen stop short of killing any bundists. Disappointed by the restraint imposed, Lansky accepted all Perlman's conditions except one. He refused to be paid for the assignment. "I was a Jew and felt for those Jews in Europe who were suffering. They were my brothers," Lansky said years later. For months Lansky's boys effectively broke up one Nazi rally after another. They broke arms, legs, ribs and cracked sculls, but no one died.

Lansky recalled breaking up a Brown Shirt rally in the Yorkville section of Manhattan: "The stage was decorated with a swatstika and a picture of Hitler. The speakers starting ranting. There were only 15 of us, but we went into action. We threw some of them out the windows. ... Most of the Nazis panicked and ran out. We chased them and beat them up. ...We wanted to show them that Jews would not always sit back and accept insults." In Minneapolis, William Dudley Pelley organized a Silver Shirt Legion to "rescue" America from an imaginary Jewish-Communist conspiracy. Just as "Mussolini and his Black Shirts saved Italy and as Hitler and his Brown Shirts saved Germany," Palley promised to save America from Jewish communists.

Minneapolis gambling czar David Berman confronted Palley's Silver Shirts on behalf of the Minneapolis Jewish community. When he heard of a rally at a nearby Elk's Lodge, he attended. When the Nazi leader called for all the "Jewish bastards" in the city to be expelled, or worse, Berman and his brothers burst into the room and started cracking heads. After 10 minutes, they had emptied the hall. His suit covered in blood, Berman took the microphone and announced, "This is a warning. Anybody who says anything against Jews gets the same treatment. Only next time it will be worse." After a few more punch ups, there were no more Silver Shirt rallies in Minneapolis. Historian Robert Rockaway, in his book *But They Were Good to Their Mothers* details how they were also good to Israel.

Knowledge

In 1597, Sir Francis Bacon coined the now-famous phrase: "For also knowledge itself is power." The prophet Muhammad had acknowledged the same almost 1,000 years earlier.

For too long we have lived next to each other without knowing or understanding each other. In order for dialogue to begin on an even footing, we must first dispense of some of our own misapprehensions. The prophet Muhammad said: "Whosoever wants success in this world, he must have knowledge. Whosoever wants success in the hereafter, he must have knowledge. And whosoever wants success in both worlds, he must have knowledge." Malaysian Shaikh Mohd Saifudden Mohd Salleh, a local imam, said in an editorial opinion he wrote in a local paper in 2002: "The prophet's words are simple and easy to understand. For anyone or any organization to succeed, the key is possessing knowledge. And this knowledge must be managed well in order for it to be beneficial to all."

We are an interglobal, interconnected network of societies based on the Internet and collaboration in research and other areas that were until now, impossible. They greatly increase creativity and the possibilities of exchange and sharing. These societies create an environment particularly favorable to knowledge, innovation, training and research.

Databases today have every kind of information imaginable stored in their vast archives. Databases, however, have limited power to create anything new or to innovate. That takes knowledge. Possession of knowledge enables people to further create new knowledge. This is what distinguishes knowledge from information. Karl Wigg, a practitioner of "knowledge management," sums up the difference concisely. "Information describes circumstances, situations and problems, whereas knowledge enables people to handle problems and to solve them."

Sharing knowledge is the most effective tool to fight ignorance and poverty. Knowledge is also the key to wealth production. On all continents, countries – even some with conflicting religions – are inventing new styles of development based on knowledge and intelligence. Future societies, much like Hong Kong today, will measure their development potential less on natural resources and more on their capacity to create, spread and use knowledge. The sharing of knowledge cannot, however, be confined to the creation of new knowledge or the promotion of knowledge belonging to the public domain. It implies not only universal access to knowledge, but also the participation of everyone, said Koichiro Matsuura, director-general of UNESCO.

Many obstacles stand in the way of knowledge-sharing. "Chiefly, these are social polarization and the 'digital divide' between those with – and without – access to the new networks," Matsuura said. "They also include the fracture of knowledge into various specializations, and gender inequality. To overcome these obstacles, societies will have to invest massively in lifelong education for all."

Societies must cultivate greater respect for the diversity of approaches to knowledge, and for local, traditional and indigenous knowledge. Sharing causes knowledge to grow and multiply. It does not divide. It allows for better understanding.

Hatred and Ignorance
The biggest problem We the People have to solve in the 21st century is how to love our children more by teaching them not to hate. Trouble is, most of them go to public schools. All children, including street children and orphans of war, rebellions, natural disasters and radical religious practices must be properly housed, fed and educated. Shouldn't that be a God-given right?

America has to lead the "education war" to teach, advocate and promote democracy and the ideals of the Founding Fathers globally. Especially in Saudi Arabia and the rest of the Arab and Muslim world. America must teach the benefits of a constitutional secular democracy as practiced in Turkey, Indonesia and India. Although secularism is losing ground in Indonesia's new democracy to mobs manipulated by Islamic fundamentalists.

These are countries that have avoided, for the most part, extreme Muslim terrorists because of their secular democratic institutions. India, with the world's second-largest Muslim population, is also the world's largest democracy – a thriving secular democracy at that. When compared to neighboring Pakistan, with a smaller Muslim population that educates its children in religious madrasses, the contrast in economic and political development between a secular democratic education and a religious totalitarian education becomes self-evident.

Madrassas are a hotbed of extremism in Pakistan and Indonesia.

Indonesia is a case study of mosques or schools built and paid for by Saudi Arabia. All the terrorists involved in the Bali nightclub bombings that killed more than 200 people in 2003 and the 2005 Marriot hotel bombing in Jakarta, were graduates of *pesantrens*, private Islamic boarding schools. The Al-Mukmin, a *pesantren* in the sleepy village of Ngruki on the outskirts of Solo city, is a no frills spartan institution that installs a sense of rigid austerity in 10-16 year olds, seven days a week for most of the year.

The students at the *Ngruki*, as it is commonly referred to, listen to Arabic music and are instilled with the ominous maxim posted on a board next to the main school gate that reads: "No prestige without jihad." Teachers at the school include known terrorists and radical clerics. The best known is the notorious radical cleric Abu Bakar Bashir, co-founder of the *Ngruki pesantren*, and the alleged ideological leader of Jemaah Islamiah, the regional terrorist organization fighting to unite most of Southeast Asia into a caliphate. He is now considering a run at the presidency in 2009. He will campaign to turn Indonesia into an Islamic state and impose sharia law. Recent studies estimate that 85 percent of Indonesia's 240 million people are Muslim. Currently, sharia law is practiced only in Aceh province.

Like many Indonesian clerics, Bashir is of Yemini descent and was born in East Java – well known for its Islamic extremism and rebellion. Rebels founded the extremist Darul Islam, which campaigned for an Islamic Indonesia and then gave birth to Jemaah Islamiah. He founded the *Ngruki* in 1972, spent time in jail for his rebellious firebrand sermons, and 13 years in exile in Malaysia. The chaos that followed Suharto's downfall allowed Bashir to slip back into Indonesia at a time when radicals thought their opportunity to overthrow the state and impose sharia law had arrived.

"At the *Ngruki*, there is only one truth," said former student Noor Huda Ismail, who attended the *pesantren* from 1985 to 1991 and is now studying for his doctorate in international politics at St. Andrews University in Scotland. "Teachers read the Koran and interpret it their own way. You don't even realize your forced into believing in something. That's the way it is, and that is all there is to it; there are no alternatives. All discussions are centered in this radical interpretation of Islam," he said.

Their days start at 4.30 a.m. and end at 10 p.m. They meet in the mosque for the subuh, the first of the five compulsory daily prayers.

Aceh, a fundamentalist Muslim oil-rich province in Indonesia, has adopted a harsh Islamic law – Taliban-style – that is enforced brutally by local sharia police. Radical Islam in Indonesia is opposed by most Indonesians who prefer to see pluralism prevail over Muslim radicalism. With the world's largest Muslim population, Indonesia is officially neither secular nor Islamic. After proclaiming independence in 1945, the many attempts to forge an Islamic state were thwarted when nationalists removed from the constitution the famous "seven words" – "with obligation for Muslims to practice sharia."

In Pakistan, there are more than 10,000 madrassas and they educate an estimated 1.7 million students, while public school enrollment is some 25 million. Most madrassas are still unregistered, their finances unregulated and the government has yet to remove the holy warrior and sectarian content from their curriculum. The standoff and commando raid in the late spring of 2007 in Islamabad at the Red Mosque, the city's oldest mosque, between clerics who want to topple the government and the army reflects just how widely religious extremism has become. The army will remain in control. President General Pervez Musharraf won't the minute the army abandons him for its own political survival. Pakistan's three previous military rulers exited from power under unhappy circumstances, which does not bode well for Musharraf. His political demise was hastened in July 2007, when the Supreme Court ordered Musharraf to reinstate the chief justice he suspended in March of the same year.

Musharraf came to power in a bloodless coup in 1999. He promised to quit as army chief by the end of 2004 as part of a deal with Islamists, but never did. Islamist groups have historically fared poorly in Pakistani elections. But they made big gains in 2002 partly by exploiting intense anti-American sentiment over U.S. military intervention in Afghanistan. The Islamists were also able to occupy part of the space left open by Musharraf's ban on popular politicians like former prime ministers Benazir Bhutto and Nawaz Sharif from returning to Pakistan to run for office. To survive politically, Musharraf, will need to ally himself with a powerful secular party to defeat the Islamists at the polls.

Pakistan did deport 1,400 foreign madrassa students and vowed to add science, math and other academic subjects to the schools' almost wholly religious curriculum, which Gen. Pervez Musharraf, the country's military dictator, said contributed to a "jihadi culture" in Pakistan. Sounds like the only people who can add up in Pakistan are the military and they learn that at Sandhurst, the elite British college.

Serving for centuries as a main source of learning in Islamic countries, madrassas mushroomed in Pakistan during the Soviet invasion of Afghanistan in the 1980s. Funded by Saudi money and backed by the CIA and Pakistan's intelligence agencies, many of these madrassas were turned into recruitment centers for producing thousands of foot soldiers to fight the Russians in Afghanistan and, later, the Indian security forces in Kashmir, and now in India itself as the bombings in New Delhi and Mumbai demonstrated, and the U.S. troops in Afghanistan and Iraq.

The teachers at the madrassas reject democracy because it subjects the will of God to popular opinion. Yet for terrorism to be eradicated, its supply of fanatically trained religious extremist foot soldiers has to be stopped and the existing ones have to be able to participate in fair and open democratic elections, so that their anger and frustration can be vented through peaceful means.

Hindu children should not just be quizzed on the ravages of Muslim emperors. Muslim children should not be quizzed on how much one plus one dead Jew or American equals. The same applies to the Christians in Iraq caught in the Muslim sectarian crossfire. Iraq's Assyrian Christians are among the world's most ancient practicing their faith in Mesopotamia almost since the time of Christ. The Assyrian Apostolic Church traces its foundation to A.D.34 and St. Peter. Likewise, the Assyrian Church of the East dates to A.D.33 and St. Thomas. The Aramaic that many of Iraq's Christians still speak is the language of Christ and his apostles. It should therefore be no surprise that the world's Christian leaders used their 2006 Christmas sermons to urge an end to bloodshed in the Middle East.

In the Armenian genocide of 1914-18, 750,000 Armenians – roughly two-thirds of their number at the time – were massacred by the Ottoman Turks with the help of the Kurds. In 1987, the Iraqi census listed 1.4 million Christians. In 2006, there were only 600,000 to 800,000 remaining. More than 60,000 have fled since the insurgency that followed the U.S.-led invasion in 2003. Some Christian women have been killed for wearing jeans or not wearing a veil. Since 2004, 27 Assyrian churches have been attacked.

The dysfunctional curriculums of hatred taught in many religious schools around the world must be exorcized and replaced with love and knowledge-based classes in the 21st century if we want a better New World Order for our children and grandchildren.

The example of Bulgaria's Orthodox Christian Metropolit Bishop Kiril, who shook his staff in 1943 and led the citizens of Sofia in widespread protests against the police and German authorities after they had rounded up the city's 50,000 Jews to ship out in cattle cars, should be taught in every school throughout the world. The protests convinced the authorities to withdraw the order and release the Jews. This story was a well-kept secret before 1989 because it credited the enemies of the communist regime – the Bulgarian Orthodox Church, Czar Boris III and the average Bulgarian on the street who loudly voiced opposition to his government policy, while communist partisans did little to help.

The resurgence of nationalism in Japan since 1999 is also a worry. Schools are now being forced by a government directive to display the Rising Sun and sing the national anthem at major ceremonies, the same dirge that rang in the ears of millions of imperial troops who went off to kill in the name of the emperor in the 1930s and '40s. "It's as though Germany brought back the Nazi swastika and forced teachers to stand for it," said Kazuhisa Suzuki, who teaches at a high school in Kanagawa prefecture. Actually it's not. Japan's equivalent of the swastika was never properly removed in the first place.

Every year, Suzuki demonstrates at his school's graduation ceremonies by wearing a white rose and raising his clenched fist in the air – a protest that has almost cost him his job. "In my view, Japan is drifting back toward fascism," said Eishun Nagai, another teacher who also objects to Japan's refusal to acknowledge or come to terms with its history.

"I'm personally against the directive," said Nagai, "but more important, I'm against forcing children to sing the anthem and stand for the flag. That's called brainwashing. Schools change first, then society. So our responsibility as educators is clear if we see something bad happening. And in my heart, I believe this is bad."

History cannot be changed. Only textbooks that teach the truth can. The Japanese textbook controversy about the country glorifying it's militaristic past is merely generating another generation of Japanese children who will be ignorant about an important part of their history and a generation of Chinese students who will hate them for it. How does this serve to improve relations and understanding between China and Japan's future generations? The Chinese will not forget what Japan did, and the Japanese will remain in denial. Another generation of angry, misunderstood people.

The sad fact is that there is no one to blame except America. Why? Gen. Douglas McArthur's occupation wanted an unresistant and cooperative Japan to "reform." To do so, it left much of the old Japan in place. With the retention of the emperor, the social hierarchy moved seamlessly from the pre-to post-war Japan. The country did nothing wrong. How could it? It is still there. There is no serious sense of war guilt in the older generation, and it is too late to create it in the new.

Japan can no longer fabricate historical facts to justify its wars of aggression. No one is buying into the fabrication. The only losers are the Japanese students. It is no surprise therefore that some of the fiercest critics have been teachers.

The World Bank has urged the world's richest countries to spend $3 billion a year over the next 10 years on the education of the 125 million children who are being taught to hate. That is what it will cost to reach the millennium goal of putting every child in the world in school by 2015.

Theocratic Failures

The shortcomings of extreme Islamist ideology have been on display in Afghanistan, Egypt, Iran, Saudi Arabia and Somalia since the establishment of the state of Israel in 1948. All *We the Maids* have to do is sweep in the benefits of the alternatives, and graphically show and educate all students of the disastrous failures Islamic republics have been – as have all theocratic societies, regardless of religion – Nepal and Thailand being two recent examples.

The vocal minority in the Muslim world who believe the only source of legislation is God, and that his will is set in the sharia, has to be challenged with the facts and educated about basic democratic institutions. And their religious leaders must see that the concept of individual freedom is not in conflict with their teachings on the will of God.

The fact is, once in power Muslims have no clue how to run a government. Salaries go unpaid, corruption replaces taxation, garbage isn't collected and the infrastructure and education systems are nonexistent. Islamist ideology is powerless when confronted with the basic duties of governance. Look at the Palestinian territories, where Hamas' unpopularity is derived from its inability to pay salaries and deliver basic services.

The Islamic states, actually all Arab states, though famous for their cafes and bazaars, have not been able to define national glory economically. They are still stuck in the old world, when nations were measured by whom they conquered, rather than today's emphasis on competition for economic success. This is a major shift in economics and culture that has evolved with various national and regional characteristics.

Failed Theocracies, Islamic & Otherwise

Theocracies, Islamic or otherwise, are not divine. They are man-made. Some are just better spun than others. Thailand is one of the best. At the other extreme are the Dear Leaders of North Korea. No matter how they are packaged, the end result is the same. Instability, violence and unnecessary human uncertainty and suffering – especially by innocent children.

In North Korea, hundreds of thousands if not millions of people have died from famines and floods during the '90s and first decade of the 21st century. More than a third of all children are reported to be malnourished. According to Amnesty International, 400,000 people have perished from political persecution; 150,000 are still held in underground concentration camps. Since the much-condemned July 4, 2006, missile tests, humanitarian aid has been cut drastically by the Dear Leader, concerned that aid workers are U.S. spies.

In 1945, Korea was divided along the 38th parallel; its industrial north was occupied by the Russians and the agricultural south by the Americans. The problem of reunification was referred to the United Nations. After efforts to hold a national election failed, the U.N. recognized the government set up in the south as the lawful government of the Republic of Korea. By then, the Soviet-controlled north also had a government claiming sovereignty over the entire country. After American and Russian forces withdrew from Korea, North Korean forces invaded the south in June 1950, with Stalin's knowledge and approval.

Within two days, U.S. President Harry Truman sent American forces to defend the south – the Security Council voted to resist aggression, because the Russians were stupid enough to boycott the session and not veto the U.N. resolution that sent the U.S. to fight them and the northerners.

Much like today in Iraq, America provided the bulk of the "coalition forces." Also like in Iraq today, other countries eventually, reluctantly, joined in. Within a few months the coalition was operating well north of the 38th parallel. The North Koreans looked sure to lose. But when the fighting drew near to the Manchurian border, the Chinese intervened and drove back the U.S.-led coalition.

Then, as now, there was a danger of a much bigger conflict – one with nuclear weapons. China was the second-largest communist state in the world, and the largest in terms of population. The U.S.S.R. was right there, with full backing. President Truman, in his wisdom, decided that the U.S. not get involved in a greater war.

But the Chinese could not overrun South Korea and drive out the Americans. Armistice talks started. A new American administration was sworn in 1953. Gen. Dwight Eisenhower's Republicans were fervent anti-communists. They thought the real communist Cold War threat was the Russians, not the Chinese. The armistice was signed in July 1953. A final peace agreement was never negotiated and the two sides remain in a state of conflict to this day.

North Koreans are taught to worship Kim Jong-il as a God. The government exerts extraordinary control through deification – a cult ideology of complete subservience – that goes beyond the Stalinist label often used to describe the new member of the nuclear club.

In a time of poverty and famine, government spending on Kim family deification – now 40 percent of the visible budget – is the only category in the country's budget to increase. The increase pays for ideology schools, about 30,000 Kim monuments, gymnastic festivals, films and books, billboards and murals, 40,000 "research institutes," historical sites, rock carvings, circus theatres, training programs and worship events. The government is increasing its ideological cult worship annually. The magnitude and scope of cult development even outdoes the cult of personality during Mao's Cultural Revolution.

The penetration of foreign ideas or information about the outside world is banned for fear that knowledge could undermine the rules of government.

Kim's media call him variously the Guardian Deity of the Planet and Lodestar of the 21st Century. Many loyal North Koreans bow twice daily to Kim's pictures, which often sit alone on the most prominent wall of their homes. Since the 1990s, the Dear Leader has claimed lineage to the first ancient rulers of Korea, a move intended to place him in a position of historical, if not divine, destiny as leader of the peninsula.

The Kim family represents the epitome of historical monarchies in which people believed they had a divine right to rule – just like the extreme Islamic fundamentalists. North Korea assists Iran in its nuclear program. Iran supports Syria and aggressively supports Hezbollah.

The 38th parallel is still there, and the off-on "six party" peace talks are going nowhere. The solution is the "five-party" talks that I propose in the next chapter.

Thailand is an example of a Buddhist theocratic failure – or success, depending on one's point of view. Its constitutional monarch rules with a divine mandate that carries the weight of god. A Swiss man was sentenced to prison for 10 years for defacing the king's portrait during a drunken spree. He was deported after the king gave him a royal pardon. The result of having a Buddhist theocracy: 18 military coups in the past 74 years, the most recent one in December 2006. Many people believe that the coup was payback for the prime minister's gun-blazing policies in the nation's 80 percent ethnic Malay Muslim south, where insurgents have sought a separate Islamic state. The three southern provinces of Narathiwat, Pattani and Yala – the only region with a Muslim majority in the predominantly Buddhist nation – were once an Islamic kingdom and were annexed by Thailand at the turn of the 20th century. Over the years, the separatist movement has waxed and waned but never completely ceased.

In January 2004, it suddenly surged, and when the government failed to ensure people's safety, more Muslims and Buddhists turned to guns for self-protection. The government also provided villagers with arms training and gave weapons to village defense volunteers and public school teachers – actions that only escalated the violence. More than 2,000 people have been killed in almost daily bombings, drive-by shootings and beheadings since early 2004. More than 60 teachers and 10 students have been killed and more than 100 schools have been torched. Teachers in Thailand, like teachers in America and elsewhere, are on the front lines of violence. There have been 310 teachers murdered in Colombia since 2000, 280 academics killed in Iraq since the fall of Saddam Hussein, and 150 bombings, arson and missile attacks on educational targets in Afghanistan in 2005-6.

New Year celebrations to usher in 2007 were canceled in Bangkok, yet eight bombs still went off in the Thai capital.

Gen. Sondhi Boonyaratglin, the country's army chief of staff, headed the peaceful coup that wrested control from the elected prime minister with the blessing of the king. He is the country's first Muslim army chief and has advocated negotiation over force – a concept the Palestinians and all Islamic movements should embrace.

Boonyaratglin confirmed his determination to negotiate in April 2007 during a visit to the south when he told protestors, over the charred corpse of a Buddhist woman burned alive by Muslim insurgents that was deposited in his path, that he was working with local officials to find a peaceful solution to end the violence. He failed. Lets see what happens now that Thaksin is back.

Palestine

The word Palestine derives from *Peleshet*, a name that appears frequently in the Bible and has been rendered into English as Philistine. The name began to be used in the 13th century B.C. for a wave of migrant "sea peoples" who came from the Aegean Sea and the Greek Islands and settled on the southern coast of Canaan. There they established five independent city-states, including Gaza, on a narrow strip of land known as Philistia. The Greeks and Romans called it Palastina.

The Philistines were neither Arabs nor Semites. They had no connection, ethnic, linguistic or historical, with Arabia or Arabs. The name Falastin that Arabs use today for Palestine is not an Arabic name. It is the Arab pronunciation of the Greco-Roman Palastina derived from *Peleshet*.

This brings to mind the story of the Israeli ambassador to the U.N. who got up and said, "Ladies and gentlemen, before I commence with my speech I want to relay an old Passover story to all of you. When Moses was leading the Jews out of Egypt toward the Promised Land, he had to go through the nearly endless Sinai desert. When they reached the Promised Land, the people were very thirsty and needed water. So Moses struck the side of the mountain with his staff and a pond appeared with crystal clean, cool water. The people rejoiced and drank to their heart's content. Moses wanted to cleanse his whole body, so he went to the other side of the pond and took off all his clothes and dove into the water. When he came out of the water he discovered that all his clothes had been stolen. Outraged, he said 'I have reasons to believe that the Palestinians stole my clothes.'"

The Palestinian delegate to the U.N., hearing this accusation, jumps from his seat and screams out, "This is a travesty. It is widely known that there were no Palestinians there at the time!" And with that in mind, said the

Israeli ambassador, "Let me now begin my speech."

The land had been known as Canaan for thousands of years before the Romans changed it to Palastina. The Canaanites had many tiny city-states, each one at times independent and at times a vassal of an Egyptian or Hittite king. The Canaanites never united into a state. After the Jewish exodus from Egypt, the Children of Israel settled in the land of Canaan. There they formed a tribal confederation, and then the biblical kingdoms of Israel and Judah, and the post-biblical kingdom of Judea. From the beginning of history to this day, Israel-Judah-Judea was the only united, independent, sovereign nation-state that ever existed in Palestine west of the Jordan River. In biblical times, Ammon, Moab, and Edom, as well as Israel, had land east of the Jordan, but they disappeared, and no other nation took their place until the British invented Trans-Jordan in the 1920s.

The Romans crushed the independent kingdom of Judea after the failed rebellion of Bar Kokba in the second century B.C. The Roman Emperor Hadrian, determined to wipe out the identity of Israel-Judah-Judea, took the name Palastina and imposed it on all the land of Israel. He also changed the name of Jerusalem to Aelia Capitolina. The genocide of the Jewish people had began. Those who were not killed were sold into slavery. Those that survived either lived in small isolated communities or fled. There was never a time when there were not Jews and Arabs and Jewish and Arab communities in Israel. Their size and conditions fluctuated greatly over the years.

After Palastina became a province of the pagan Roman Empire, it became part of the Christian Byzantine Empire and very briefly of the Zoroastrian Persian Empire. In AD 638, an Arab-Muslim caliph took Palastina away from the Byzantine Empire and made it part of an Arab-Muslim Empire. The Arabs, who had no name of their own for this region, adopted the Greco-Roman name Palastina, which they pronounced Falastin. During this period, much of the mixed population of Falastin converted to Islam and adopted Arabic. They were subjects of a distant caliph who ruled first from Damascus and then Baghdad. They did not become a nation or an independent state, or develop a distinct society or culture.

In 1099, Christian crusaders from Europe conquered Palestina-Falastin. It never again fell under Arab rule. The Christian crusader kingdom was politically independent, but never developed a national entity. It remained a military outpost of Christian Europe for less than 100 years. It was then joined to Syria as a subject province of the Mamluks, ethnically mixed Muslim slave-warriors whose center was in Egypt, and then to the Ottoman Turks, whose capital was in Istanbul.

During the First World War, the British took Palestina-Falastin from the Ottoman Turks. At the end of the war, the Ottoman Empire collapsed and the province of Palestine was assigned to the British, to govern temporarily under a mandate from the League of Nations. Mandate Palestine originally included all of what is now Jordan, as well as all of what is now Israel, and the territories in between.

The Balfour Declaration of 1917, confirmed by the League of Nations Mandate, committed the British government to establish in Palestine a "Jewish National Home." However, in 1916, Hussein, the Sharif of Mecca in the Hashemite domain of Arabia, had led the uprising against the Turks with the help of the English, most notably T.E. Lawrence, because Hussein and his three sons were promised to be installed as rulers of the various Arab constituents of the Turkish empire. They defeated the Turks in 1918.

Faisal, the youngest son, was put on the throne of Syria, one of the new countries carved out of the Turkish Empire, but was promptly deposed when control of Syria passed from the British to the French under their post-war agreement. Faisal was then promptly installed by the British as king of Iraq in 1921, another new country created from three provinces of the Turkish Empire that included Kurds, Sunnis and Shiites. Faisal, understandably confused by being shifted around so much, lost the plot and got hacked to death with his wife by the Iraqis, who have a penchant for that sort of thing. Ironically, the largest single group in Baghdad, Faisal's royal capital, were Jews, followed by Arabs and then Turks.

Faisal's brother, Emir Abdullah, who was originally destined for the Iraqi throne, was left stateless and therefore installed as king "of the vacant lot" which the British christened the Amirate of Transjordan. The realm created by the British included all of the Mandate Palestine east of the Jordan River. There was no traditional or historical Arabic name for this land, so it was named after the river: Trans-Jordan and later Jordan. This political act violated the Balfour Declaration and the Mandate. The British effectively cut off more than 75 percent of the "Jewish National Homeland." No Jew has been permitted to reside there since.

When statehood was first offered to the Palestinians in the 1930s and '40s, their leader, Hajj Amin al-Husseini, the Grand Mufti of Jerusalem, rejected the offer and moved to Hitler's Berlin in the hope the Nazis would grant him a political prize.

It was the Palestinians who rejected the United Nations decision in 1947 to partition the land between Arabs and Jews, with Jerusalem as an international city. The subsequent war in 1948, launched by the Palestinians and five Arab armies with the intention of eliminating the newborn Jewish state, was won by Israel. The departure of 800,000 Palestinians, who fled at the urging of their leaders to avoid being killed, was supposed to be temporary. However, they continue to exist in suspended animation and have not been assimilated into other Arab countries. Unfortunately, they remain useful political pawns in the Middle East millennium chess game. They have been perpetually promised by their leaders that they will return. Their leaders, including the late Yasser Arafat, became victims of their own propaganda. "The reason for this fantastic attachment to Palestine is partly because the Arabs encouraged it," said Kamel Abu Jaber, a retired Jordanian foreign minister and a peace negotiator. "To say, let's settle them, let's absorb them, was considered treason and still is."

To Israelis, the Palestinian insistence on the right of return, now that the refugees number 3.5 million – after Israel took in the more than 1 million Jews forcibly evicted from Arab countries – means that Arabs have not truly accepted the existence of the Jewish state and seek its elimination, one way or another.

Whatever their antiquity, the Al Aqsa Mosque and the Dome of the Rock in Jerusalem do represent Islam's third most holy site. It therefore makes more sense for it to be part of Jordan, which in turn should become part of Arabia. The royal family of the Hashemite Kingdom of Jordan are the descendants of the Sharif of Mecca, and are distant relatives of the prophet Muhammad, and therefore have a close connection to Mecca and the third most holy site of Islam. Since Jordan and Israel are at peace, a mutual accommodation on the holy site would resolve this contentious issue and allow Israel and Palestine to address the serious issue of peace and reconciliation.

The death of Yassir Arafat was hailed as a new beginning for the Palestinians. His legacy of corruption and personal use of billions of dollars of tax revenues and donations from the international community is stunning. In the words of Hamas leaders now using their tactical skills at the ballot box as well as the mortar launchers, it is time for "strong and honest" politicians. The time has come for the *Palestinian Maids* to sweep in the changes needed to bring about a lasting peace. In the words of Palestinian billionaire Munib Masri, "Palestinians work very hard at rebuilding other nations, and I think it is time we build our own."

The victory of Hamas at the polls in January 2006 confirmed how disgusted Palestinians were at the corruption of Arafat's Fatah party. Hamas won 76 of the 132 seats in the election, compared to just 43 won by Fatah. The vote was an exemplary exercise in democracy and one that has to be honored and respected.

When Hamas was founded in 1987, it put the goals of the Islamic Resistance Movement into writing: "Allah is its goal, the Prophet its model, the Koran its constitution, jihad its path, and death for the cause of Allah its most sublime belief." The close to 9,000-word document is replete with Koranic references instructing Muslims to wage *jihad* against the Jews on every last hilltop of historical Palestine – not just the West Bank and the Gaza Strip, but also Israel proper as established in 1948.

Each of its 36 sections breathes an Islamic ideology that seems incompatible with the concept of Palestinian-Israeli reconciliation. The time for establishing a Palestinian Islamic state, the charter states, "will not come until Muslim will fight the Jews [and kill them]; until the Jews hide behind rocks and trees, which will cry: O Muslim! There is a Jew hiding behind me, come on and kill him!" Ahmad Abdel-Aziz Mubarek, a senior elected Hamas official, said that he believed it would take 15 years to see the realization of the Hamas vision for an Islamic state in the region. The ongoing conflict promises to get worse before it gets better.

With Hamas in charge of the border crossing from Egypt, Israel has no control over weapons and militants entering the Gaza Strip. Israel supplies the Gaza Strip with its electricity and most of its water. It's going to be an interesting, bloody, cold and dark 15 years unless Hamas changes its tune, which is unlikely. Armed resistance movements change and there are many examples of groups laying down their weapons and pursuing peace. The Palestinian Liberation Organization, African National Congress, Irish Republican Army and even Israel's own resistance movements, the Hagana and Irgun, at one time all believed they were implementing the will of God. Hopefully, Palestinian Prime Minister Ismail Haniyeh, a father of 13 children and former dean of the Islamic University, who was born in the Shati refugee camp in Gaza and lived there until his election, will be pragmatic and do what is best for his children and former students.

Under the circumstances, Israel's unilateral decision to draw permanent borders to separate itself from the Hamas-dominated Palestinian Authority is understandable, but unworkable.

The Muslim stand-up comedian Goffaq Yussef summarized the relationship between Israel and its Arab neighbors best: "Good evening, gentlemen, and get out ladies."

"On my flight to New York there must have been an Israeli in the bathroom the entire time. There was a sign on the door that said 'Occupied'."

"What do you say to a Muslim woman with two black eyes? Nothing! You told her twice already!!"

"How many Palestinians does it take to change a light bulb? None! They sit in the dark forever and blame the Jews for it!"

"Did you hear about the Broadway play, 'The Palestinians'? It bombed!"
"What do you call a first-time offender in Saudi Arabia? Lefty!"

"Did you hear about the Muslim strip club? It features full facial nudity!"

"Why do Palestinians find it convenient to live on the West Bank? Because it's just a stone's throw from Israel!"

"Why are Palestinian boys luckier than American boys? Because every Palestinian boy will get to join a rock group!"

"A Palestinian suspect was being grilled by Israeli police. 'Honest, I'm not a suicide bomber,' he said. 'I didn't say I wanted to blow myself up so I could sleep with 72 virgins. All I said was I am dying to get laid!'"

"Thank you, thank you!!! My name is Goffaq Yussef." (Say the name out loud.)

Comedy, satire and comic books do make it easier for people to learn and understand how ridiculous some religious beliefs and practices are. The Saudi satirical series *Tash Ma Tash*, a Ramadan staple for 14 years, in 2006 angered Saudi and Egyptian viewers because the lead female star did not wear a veil. To make matters worse, one episode set in Saudi Arabia had "the guardians of virtue" ponder how best to ensure that women riding donkeys should be kept protected from mingling with men on the roads. One guardian proposes digging tunnels for women only, while another suggests that females should sit in closed wooden boxes atop their animals and navigate their way using periscopes. Eventually a wall is built dividing the village into a section for men and another for women.

The 99 is the first comic-book series to feature Islamic superheroes in the hope they can defeat prejudice. The comic is published in Arabic and English and tells the story of 99 heroes scattered around the world, each of whom holds one of the 99 attributes Muslims assign to Allah. The problem with the bad guys, who are also Muslim, is not their faith but how they use it.

The Solution

The stated goal of Hamas and Hezbollah is the destruction of the state of Israel, hence their refusal to recognize Israel's right to exist, which leaves the Israelis no choice but to fight for their survival. Hamas and Hezbollah's sponsor, Iran, repeatedly calls for the elimination of Israel. This gives Israel more reason to fight for its survival. It doesn't want to snooze and lose again. For real peace, forget about the Road Map and its unrealistic dates, unachievable deadlines and benchmarks, and all other maps for that matter that have mapped the numerous failed roads to peace.

The solution has already been agreed to on more than one occasion. The Camp David accord that U.S. President Bill Clinton, Palestinian President Yassar Arafat and Israeli Prime Minister Yitzhak Rabin agreed to, outlined the borders of the future Palestinian state. The accord was followed by another Camp David agreement in 2000 that Clinton and Israeli Prime Minister Ehud Barak endorsed, which included east Jeruslam as its capital, which Arafat rejected. With a few tweaks and modifications, it could form the basis of a permanent peace. The Saudi 2007 proposal for the establishment of a Palestinian state and a permanent peace is modeled after the 2000 Camp David accord.

Israeli Prime Minister Ehud Olmert offered wide-ranging peace concessions and a Palestinian state to Hamas in exchange for peace and recognition. An exchange of all prisoners from both sides would be part of the deal. Israel has also expressed its readiness to sit down and discuss the Arab peace initiative to find ways to implement the plan. Jordan and Egypt, the two Arab countries who have signed peace treaties with Israel, are charged with promoting the Arab initiated peace deal to Israel. What is wrong with this picture?

Nothing – it is a mere long-overdue continuation of the Camp David accords reached in 1979 between Egypt and Israel. Egyptian President Anwar Sadat, who signed the accord with Israel's Menachem Begin, in the presence of the U.S. facilitator President Jimmy Carter, was assassinated on October 6, 1981, by Islamic extremists who opposed peace with Israel. The failure to continue on the Camp David peace path may lead to the unravelling of the existing peace agreements Israel has with Egypt and Jordan.

The alternative to peace is war, and Israel no longer owns the battlefields. Its military quagmires in Gaza and Lebanon are stark testimony.

Hamas has offered a ceasefire of sorts – a *hunda*. A *hunda* extends beyond the Western concept of a cease-fire and obliges the parties to use the period to seek a permanent, nonviolent resolution to their differences. A *hunda* affords the opportunity to humanize one's opponents and understand their position, with the goal of resolving the inter-tribal or international dispute. "Such a concept – a period of non-war but only partial resolution of a conflict – is foreign to the West and has been greeted with much suspicion. Many Westerners I speak to wonder how one can stop the violence without the conflict," said Ahmed Yousef, a senior advisor to the Palestinian prime minister, Ismail Haniya. "After all, the Irish Republican Army agreed to halt its military struggle to free Northern Ireland from British rule without recognizing British sovereignty. Irish Republicans continue to aspire to a united Ireland free of British rule, but rely on peaceful methods," Yousef added.

Hamas has agreed to peace talks. The only question is pre-conditions and a date which can only be agreed to when communicating face to face. Israel and the Palestinians, and other Arab cousins should again join forces and work together the way they used to during the caliphates.

The alternative is civil war in the Palestinian territories and cross-border conflicts with Israel and Egypt. With Egypt because of President Hosni Mubarek's repression of Hamas' sister organization, the Muslim Brotherhood, for which Hamas is seeking political concessions by threatening that if Egypt fails to open its border with Gaza, "there will be no border." Hamas officials getting busted at the border carrying $20 million in cash, as guns and munitions are smuggled from Egypt to Palestine through tunnels beneath the border only escalate the tension and violence.

Assassination attempts on the leaders of Hamas and Fatah in the potentially suicidal civil war unnecessarily kill or injure their innocent children – as was the case in the botched assassination attempts on senior Palestinian intelligence officer and Fatah loyalist Baha Balousheh, which killed his three sons, or that on Prime Minister Haniyeh, which wounded one of his sons. "The spilt blood of innocent children is a crime of all the factions," columnist Nasser al-Lahham wrote on the news website Maan. "This is criminal, not chaos." In Gaza City, some schools canceled classes after students stayed away in protest.

Children continue to die unnecesarily in Palestine either because they are caught in the factional crossfire, or because their innocent curiosity brings them to the scene of a bombing where they become victims of secondary bombings or missiles – not just in Palestine – but in Lebanon, as in the recent military clashes between the Lebanese Army and the Palestinian militant group Fatah-al-Islam. The pictures of anguished children caught in the crossfire as they flee their homes once again was a millennium reminder of Golda Meir's admonition: "We will have peace when they love their children more than they hate us."

Why aren't Palestinian parents educating their children in the dangers of going to the scene of a missile attack or bombing, especially after an Israeli aerial assault? The childrens' lack of basic survival knowledge that should be dispensed by parents and teachers leads to their unnecessary deaths – with the exception, of course, of suicide bombers who are trained to die.

Israel's seizure of Hamas ministers in retaliation for the capture of an Israeli soldier and the continued barrages of missiles being fired by Hamas military factions, only exacerbate the situation and causes the voices of revenge to echo even louder. An Israeli military court was right in ordering the release of Deputy Palestinian Premier Nasser al-Shaer on the grounds that there was not enough evidence that he was a terrorist to keep him in jail.

A period of peaceful coexistence during which both sides refrain from any form of military aggression or provocation, while negotiating the terms of long-term peace, can only benefit everyone subjected to the current horrors of war. Peace does not have to be a dream. It is achievable. The time has come for Israelis and Palestinians to come to their political senses and break loose from the chains of crippling paralysis that prevents, them from living the lives they deserve to live in peace.

The search for a peaceful solution to the Palestinian problem should not blind us to the real 21st century flashpoint that has not received the attention it should by the media – the Caucuses – Muslim states of the former Soviet Union east of Turkey that have oil. "The deterioration of the situation in Chechnya and the Caucuses has been under-assessed," said Jean-Louis Bruguiere, the French magistrate considered by many to be the world's foremost expert on terrorism. "It is very irresponsible to see the Chechnya problem as simply a Russian problem and not a worldwide problem. We know that, presently, the majority of the militants operating in the Caucuses are connected to al-Qaeda. In Chechnya, it is no longer a local independence movement; it is now a jihadi movement. In the future, the Caucuses could be the aircraft carrier from which Islamist groups launch operations. It could be the new Afghanistan, but nearer," Bruguiere said.

The Alternatives

The alternative band-aid solutions aren't working for Israel or its Arab neighbors, and are merely further isolating and demonizing Israel and the Middle East geopolitical swamp it is drowning in. Israel's admission that it is a nuclear power should be seen as a warning to Iran and the rest of the world that it is ready to defend itself at any cost. If the U.S. allies can't control Iran, Israel most likely will fill the void.

There has been a rise in Israel of far-right politicians like Avigdor Lieberman, who in 2006 took the new post of minister for Strategic Threats, arguably Israel's most sensitive security job. He advocates the execution of Arab members of Israel's Knesset, transfering Arab areas of Israel to the Palestinian Authority, annexing Israeli settlements in the occupied West Bank, and bombing Egypt's Aswan Dam. He also wants to strip parliament of its powers and place all power in the hands of the prime minister. A dictatorship to survive in perpetuity. It's a good thing he resigned.

The alliance of Lieberman's Yisrael Beiteinu (Israel Is Our Home) party to Olmert's coalition shored up the alliance majority from 67 to 78 of the 120 Knesset seats. Azmil Bishara, an Arab-Israeli who is head of the Balad Party and recently resigned his seat in parliament, is calling for an end to Israel being a Jewish state and that it grant citizenship to all people there and their relatives wishing to immigrate there. A sure way to destroy Israel from within. Not voices to ignore. But not viable alternatives either as neither proposal is the solution for peace. One country two factions.

Hezbollah

Sheikh Hassan Nasrallah is the eldest son of a poor grocer who had nine children. He moved from southern Lebanon to the Iraqi city of Najaf in his late teens to study in a madras. His mentor there, and when he moved back to Lebanon in 1978, was Abbas Musawi, with whom he later founded Hezbollah as a fundamentalist movement associated with the Shiite community. He is a man of God, gun and government, a cross between Ayatollah Khomeini and Che Guevara, an Islamic populist as well as a charismatic guerrilla tactician.

The black head wrap – signifying his descent from the Prophet Muhammad – is now his trademark, and he is Lebanon's best known politician.

Hezbollah runs hospitals, schools, a satellite TV station, discount pharmacies, groceries and an orphanage and has 14 ministers in parliament and two ministers in the Lebanese cabinet. Altogether it provides benefits to an estimated 250,000 Lebanese and is the country's second-largest employer. Hezbollah was formed by the Iranian Revolutionary Guards after Israel's 1982 invasion of Lebanon and has been part of the political mainstream for years. It functions not just as a state within a state, but as the state itself. Its military wing, the Islamic Resistance, is widely lauded in Lebanon for its role in forcing Israel in 2000 to end its 22-year occupation of the south of the country – and for defeating Israel in the summer of 2006.

Hezbollah redefined extremist tactics in the Middle East. It deployed the first suicide bombers in modern times It was the first to launch multiple attacks simultaneously. Al-Qaeda, Hamas and Iraq's insurgents – all Sunni movements – have copied these tactics.

Nasrallah has created a fighting force that has proven itself a formidable opponent to Israel and a far cry from the cowardly Arabs who fled as Israeli troops approached – not much different from the U.S.-trained Iraqi forces who run in the face of the Iraqi insurgents. Hezbollah fighters are Islamists with deep religious convictions who are not intimidated by Israel's armed forces. It is the best guerrilla fighting force in the world because, not only are they good fighters, but they have not been infiltrated by any network of foreign intelligence. Furthermore, their military and intelligence apparatus is totally separated from the political structure.

Hezbollah's staying power on the battlefield comes from a classic fish-in-the-sea advantage enjoyed by guerrillas on their home ground, hiding in their own villages and aided by their friends and relatives. Nazrallah summed up the Hezbollah strategy in a televised address during the conflict: "We are not a regular army and we will not fight like a regular army."

He first confirmed this on July 4, 2006, not in Lebanon but Iraq, where Nasrallah activated a three-year-old sleeper terror and sabotage network Iranian and Hezbollah intelligence had established across Iraq shortly after the U.S. invasion. America's Independence Day 2006 was selected for attacks on U.S. forces in Baghdad and British units in Basra under the name of the Abu al Fadal al Abas Brigades.

The mute U.S. response to the attacks led Iran and Hezbollah to believe they had got away with it in Iraq and decided to open a second front against Israel on July 12 when Hezbollah attacked Israel and kidnapped two Israeli soldiers and killed three others. Israel's Operation Just Reward started out as a rescue operation for its two abducted soldiers, but quickly became a campaign to push Hezbollah back from the southern border. In reality, the war was a showdown between America and Iran, fought through their local proxies over a whole range of issues – especially Iran's nuclear defiance. The unacknowledged object of Israel's aggressive campaign was none of the highly rational goals outlined publicly by Israeli officials. Its primary purpose was to satisfy Washington that Tehran has been given a bloody nose and force it to pull back from its deepening political, military and intelligence interference in Iraq.

The amount of Iranian funds reaching Hezbollah has been estimated at $25 million a month, and some reports suggest it is significantly more since Mahmoud Ahmadinejad took over as president in Tehran.

Iraqification-Failed Nation Building
The British tried to do in 1920 what America started in 2003. They marched into Iraq, brought about regime change and expected to be welcomed with open arms. It didn't work then and *We the Apathetic Maids* should have realized it wouldn't work today. Iraq was carved out of the Ottoman Empire at the end of World War I. When the British realized they could not govern Iraq, they set up a government of Iraqis and handed the country over to them. It was the first British possession after the American colonies to achieve independence.

It's a history lesson America forgot. Invading armies cannot in the 21st century control or dominate a people who do not welcome their presence.

The tribes of central Iraq are the key to ending the violence there. For hundreds of years, the people of the high desert north and west of Baghdad survived waves of conquerors by joining with their kin for defense. When the Ottomans arrived in the 16th century, Istanbul co-opted the tribes of Fallujah and the Sunni triangle rather than conquer them. The British did the same after World War I. Tribal territories function by tribal rules, not by Western or American rules.

America does not want to repeat its past failures of nation-building. This does mean a long-term commitment, but not necessarily one using the military in a combat role. The history of past American attempts at nation-building in developing countries shows that the most lethal threat to Washington's undertaking tends to occur about four to six years after the end of American military intervention.

According to Polity, a database on democracy in the world, most of the countries where the United States intervened militarily either failed to democratize or became more authoritarian within the decade of the end of the American intervention. Iraq looks like it will join the list unless the country is divided into three separate states. The sooner the better. There is nothing immemorial about Iraq. The British created it in 1920. So what's wrong with uncreating it? Of the 14 created-ration cases, the level of democracy remained high in only three – Japan and Germany after World War II, and Panama after 1989. The other success, South Korea, involved a U.N. coalition led by the U.S.

Democratization failed to emerge in four cases – Cuba in 1902 and in 1909, Panama in 1936, and the Dominican Republic in 1966. In half the cases, the political system actually grew more autocratic – Nicaragua in 1933, Cuba in 1922, Haiti in 1934 and 1994, the Dominican Republic in 1924, South Vietnam in 1973 and Cambodia in 1973.

These examples show that the long-term success of American democracy-building efforts depends on America's willingness to act as a strict enforcer of fair electoral rules over the medium term. Rule enforcement is especially important during the second election cycle, about four to six years into the democracy-building process. In consolidating democracy, the most crucial test is the so-called second turn-over principle, whereby a new democracy passes its survival test when power is transferred, via elections, from the incumbent to the opposition.

In the Arab world, the rulers of all 22 states, except for largely Christian Lebanon, have traditionally hailed from the Orthodox Sunni majority. Until today, that also included Iraq and Bahrain, where Shiites actually make up a majority. The Iraqi election, along with the recent Palestinian elections, demonstrate that in the Arab world, people have more democratic electoral opportunities if they are occupied rather than soveriegn – a real concern to the oppressive Sunni monarchies. This concern was made public at the meeting initiated by the Bush administration of Muslim nations in Bahrain, in November 2005, to push for democracy in the Arab world. The Arab world was not persuaded by America's portrayal of Iraq as a beacon of democracy. On the contrary, they said Iraq represented the perils of imposing democracy from outside. They weren't far wrong, were they? Violence in Iraq is widely seen as offering a cautionary tale rather than an inspiration. Egypt, which represents more than half the population of the Arab world and is often a leader of its political concerns, led the opposition.

Iraq has become the boot camp for foreign jihadists to hone their skills in guerrilla warfare. They then return to their countries and put them to use toppling oppressive leaders.

According to recent surveys of the Middle East by the Pew Research Center for the People and the Press, significant majorities of people from Morocco to Jordan to Pakistan are democrats; they say they want to live in societies where leaders are freely elected, where free speech is protected, and where the rule of law is respected. Yet equally large numbers in the same countries said that they do not like "American ideas about democracy." What that means in Iraq is that several extremist Shiite parties – including those of Muqtada al Sadr and Ahmed Chalabi, two Iraqis who have un-American ideas of democracy – were elected into the assembly, and America must accept it. Just as the Algerian, Palestinian and Iranian democracy movements are sometimes difficult to rally around, at times we must find ways to accommodate even fundamentalist extremists like Hamas and Hezbollah.

Democracy does have a long history in the Muslim world. At the turn of the 16th century, while the heretic Giordano Bruno, whose brand was doing badly, was burnt at the stake in Rome – as part of the ongoing inquisition – Akbar, the great mogul emperor of India, who was a Muslim, codified the rights of minorities, and decreed religious freedom for all. Akbar also set up Agra, a city well known for its learning centers, one of the earliest multi-religious discussion groups.

There were regular meetings in the 1590s of Hindus, Muslims, Christians, Jains, Jews, Parsees and even atheists to discuss where and why they differed, and how they could live together – something the protagonists can do in Iraq once it is divided into three separate states.

Iraq is in a state of anarchy. The Sunni and Shiite clerics' call in late 2006 for peace and an end to sectarian violence because the "spilling of Muslim blood is forbidden" was ignored. The influence of religious figures, particularly on the Sunni side, is limited. Saudi Arabia, which hosted the clerics' meeting, faces its own domestic problems with a disgruntled Shia minority that has long been treated by the Sunni Wahabi clerics as heretic. As a result, Saudi Arabia announced plans to build a 506-mile security fence along its border with Iraq to protect against a spread of violence.

Arab democracy does not coincide with America's brand of secular liberal democracy. Nevertheless, it should be embraced. The shift of the Arab world's mainstream fundamentalist movements to democratic politics is tantamount to a repudiation of the jihadist al-Qaeda apocalyptic strategy.

Iraqis are a proud and stubborn people who have resisted foreign domination for centuries. Iraqis want to be ruled by Iraqis, even if they are not democratic leaders. "I call on all Iraqis – Arabs and Kurds – to forgive, reconcile and make up," said Saddam Hussein after being sentenced to death by hanging for war crimes against the Kurds in the 1980s.

The taunting execution of Hussein still echoes throughout the Muslim world and haunts the Iraqification of Sunnis with Shiites and Kurds. The redoubled insurgency in the wake of Saddam's execution only reaffirms that the country must be separated. The alternative is chaos or oppressive dictatorship. American style democracy? It won't ever work there. America must accept this reality and work out a solution that embraces reality on the ground instead of challenging and fighting to force-feed liberal secular institutions. Engaging political Islam will need to be the centerpiece of any successful peace plan for the Middle East.

Oppressive leaders like Saddam are preferred by Iraqis over any foreign invading power. That is why the Iraqification of Iraq is inevitable, better sooner than later. It is up to *We the Maids* to keep U.S. troops in Iraq until democracy – Iraqi style, Shiite, Sunni and Kurdish – takes root and then bring them home as soon as possible. To cut and run with helicopter diplomacy will only bring the jihadist war to the shores of America because fundamentalists are dedicated to the destruction of America and what it symbolizes. Conquering armies, no matter how powerful, can no longer govern a people who resist and resent their presence.

History of War

To better understand the nature of war requires an understanding of history. The ancient Greeks accepted the realities of war and sought to learn its lessons. Shouldn't *We the Apathetic Maids* do the same today? The Greeks offer contemporary leaders valuable analytical tools for such basic questions as: What are the root causes of war? Why do wars break out? What factors determine the victor and vanquished? How do wars end? And why do affluent societies especially detest war?

Here's what Victor Davis Hanson, a professor of classics at California State University in Fresno had to say about the Greeks at a Middle East forum in Philadelphia on February 26, 2003.

The Greeks rejected many of our modern interpretations of the origins of war. First, the Greeks rejected the notion that war is rare. Heraclites once declared: "War is the father of us all." Echoing the Greeks, the Romans' notion of *bellum interruptus*, or period between clashes, demonstrates that they, like the Greeks, viewed war as a normal part of life, Hanson said. This view did not indicate any admiration of violence but recognized that war cannot be excised from the human condition, that it is a permanent dimension of our existence.

Secondly, the Greeks would strongly rebut the now-prevalent idea that war results from material grievances or socioeconomic disparity.

During the fifth century, Athens was at war three out of every four years, and 75 percent of those conflicts centered on border disputes. Upon closer inspection of these struggles, one finds that the actual territories fought over were strategically worthless. The true sources of the clashes were rooted in differences of honor, status, fear and prestige. Two modern examples of this concept are discernible in the motivations behind the 1982 Falkland War and the Israeli-Palestinian conflict. The Falkland Islands were not a major strategic asset for Great Britain, but allowing an aggressor a foothold on its sovereign territory was an affront to its sense of prestige and it required a forceful response. Similarly, the Palestinian campaign of terror against Israel does not result from the Israeli presence on the West Bank but is part of a larger struggle that concerns honor, status and fear.

Wars begin when the attacker accepts a certain cost in relation to the benefits, whether rational or irrational, perceived or actual Wars are not fought when the price of the battle is expected to be too high. A Greek episode demonstrating this principle is found in the Spartan assault of 431 B.C. The Spartans struck because 15 years earlier they had entered Attica and the Athenians, failing to vigorously respond, conveyed a clear message – effective retaliation would not follow aggression. Likewise, Saddam Hussein invaded and conquered Kuwait believing that the repercussions from the West would not be serious, and his assessment was accurate. The first Gulf War did not end with U.S. or other allied forces occupying Iraqi soil, nor were Saddam Hussein and the Iraqi people made to feel defeated after being expelled from Kuwait. After an eight-year war with Iran, they probably didn't feel anything at all.

In another part of the Arab world, Palestinians continue to kill Israeli civilians, believing exhaustive violence will force their capitulation. They base this on Israel's lack of military retaliation after 39 Scud missiles landed within its territory during the first Gulf War, the unilateral Israeli withdrawal from southern Lebanon, and the offer to withdraw from parts of Jerusalem made at Camp David by the government of Ehud Barak, and its unilateral withdrawal from Gaza.

These events have been perceived by many in the Arab world as signs of a weak national character.

To predict victor and vanquished in a war, traditional analysis considers personal leadership, tactics, logistics and weaponry. In addition to these factors, the West is in a unique position by virtue of some key cultural factors, which give it a military edge. Its steadfast commitment to a secular society and the disconnect of research from politics, philosophy and religion are a huge plus. Western methods of warfare and planning are subject to relentless civic critiques. Again, the Greeks provide historical similarities. Over a 300-year period, rarely was a Greek general not punished, exiled or executed for his failures. Indeed, Pericles was fined and even he, the brilliant commander who had subjugated the whole of the Peloponness, later stood trial for his very life. The Western marriage of capitalism and the scientific tradition results in superior military technology. These cultural factors, often overlooked, allowed the British to conquer the fierce Zulu lands in nine months, while Cortez likewise brought huge swaths of Latin America under Spanish influence.

Wars do not truly end until the reasons they were fought are extinguished. The Athenians and Spartans battled each other for more than 27 years and the end did not truly arrive until Spartan soldiers stood, as conquerors, on the Athenian Acropolis. World War I was, in many ways, an unresolved war. The German army was never truly defeated and German soil was never conquered. Worse was the Allied decision in 1918 to impose a harsh regime onto a German people who had not felt a firm sense of defeat. These factors fanned the flames of German nationalism, which the Nazis were easily able to exploit. A second global war was needed to completely eradicate the German quest for hegemony. The Second World War's resolution bore little resemblance to that of the earlier war. Allied armies conquered German soil and split the country in two. There is little doubt that the German people felt a firm sense of defeat.

Germany was gutted, and the population ravaged. The government had been killed, executed or imprisoned. Everything to do with it was banned. The state ceased to function. The only authority was the occupying military. The genocidal crimes of the Germans were dragged out and displayed in front of them.

The Japanese never felt a firm sense of defeat after 1945. Their armies continued to exist intact. They did not have to fight over the homeland. The emperor remained in power. America acted as though it had been invited. As a result, Hiroshima and Nagasaki – the two Japanese cities hit with American atomic bombs – have been turned into a moral tale for all mankind. The current challenge to U.S. national security was just a matter of time. One need only look back at the various acts of militant Islamic terrorism committed against the U.S. and judge the efficacy of the U.S. responses. Time and time again the deaths of Americans – in Somalia, the Khobar Tower bombing, the East African embassy bombings, the USS Cole bombing – was met with weak reprisals. America was not decisive in dealing with the menace of militant Islam. In short, war was declared on America but *We the Apathetic Maids* did not fight to win, while the enemy continued to strike – determined to win.

To better understand the concept of winning, let's take a brief look back to World War II. Nazi Germany had overrun most of Europe and hammered Great Britain to the verge of bankruptcy and defeat. It had sunk more than 400 British ships in their convoys between England and America. Japan had overrun most of Asia, starting in Korea in 1928, killing millions along the way, and impressing into physical and sexual slavery millions more. Meanwhile, the U.S. was in an isolationist, pacifist mood, and most Americans and Congress wanted nothing to do with either war in Asia or Europe. Pearl Harbor – 12/7 – like 9/11 changed all that as America rushed into war.

America in 1941, like in 2001, was not prepared for war. Army units were training with broomsticks over their shoulders, and cars with "tank" painted on the doors because they didn't have tanks. The U.S. Navy had lost a significant part of its fleet at Pearl Harbor.

Britain was bust, only to be saved by a donation of $600 million in gold bullion in the Bank of England that was the property of Belgium. It had been brutally expropriated from the Belgium Congo in the 19th century. Belgium gave it to Britain to carry on the war after Belgium was overrun by Hitler. The fact is Belgium was really upset because it had surrendered in one day knowing it was no match for the Nazi army. Yet Brussels was bombed to rubble just for the hell of it.

World War II cost America an amount equal to approximately a full year's GDP – adjusted for inflation, equal to about $12 trillion, a fraction of today's cost in Afghanistan and Iraq – and all other military conflicts the U.S. is engaged in.

The Cold War lasted from about 1947 to the demolition of the Berlin Wall in 1989. Europe spent the first half of the 19th century fighting Napoleon, and from 1870 to 1945 fighting Germany.

Why do affluent societies shy away from such notions as war? This question is of particular importance because it affects free and affluent nations across the West. The Greeks firmly believed that "license," or material wealth produced hubris, a type of arrogance that views force as archaic and incompatible with economic power. The Greeks often lamented that with intellectual progress came moral regress. They were right. The toy industry that produces toy guns and war games that are so brilliantly marketed that every child has to play. I know I did as a child. Cops and robbers. Cowboys and Indians, and today I see expatriate children in my quiet tranquil neighborhood playing soldiers and terrorists as they run around with realistic Rambo super guns. The Chinese neighborhood kids watch in amazement and accomodatingly join in when one side or the other needs more recruits.

Such ideas clearly still threaten the survival of free societies. To guard against and deter future attacks *We the Apathetic Maids* must see our culture as uniquely imbued with a sense of purpose. *We the Maids* must see our cause and civilization as something worth fighting for and sweeping in globally.

Love with Knowledge

History cannot be changed no matter who tries to rewrite it. Honest multicultural curriculums are essential for a multicultural society to survive in the 21st century. The White-Christian-dominated educational curriculums used in America today dumb down our children, instill ignorance and fear of other cultures and religions, while perpetuating unnecessary cycles of domestic and international conflicts that only benefit career politicians and their financial backers. Ignorance can easily be replaced with knowledge. It's up to *We the Apathetic Maids* to become active participants in the knowledge imparted to those we love most – our children.

Love and hate are the strongest forces on earth, exemplified in the extreme by peace and war. *We the Maids* must face up to the challenge needed to sweep out the ignorance that breeds poverty, despair, frustration, violence and war. Especially in the Muslim world. It was Arab scholars who perfected the modern numerical system, wrote the first treatise on algebra, and formalized the discipline of geometry. They made pioneering advances in astronomy and physics, inspired by Greek texts that had been banned as "pagan heresy" in the Catholic West. Arabs invented the paper mill; its inexpensive substitute for parchment helped launch the publishing industry. The contrast today with Islam's golden age is devastating. According to the

U.N., a scant 330 foreign books are translated into Arabic in an average year. In Spain alone, 16,750 foreign books were translated in the first year of the 21st century, more than the total for all Arab nations combined in the past 50 years.

There are no quick fixes. Continuing to be ignorant and apathetic as we abandon the ones we love most will not bring about any of the long overdue changes.

Understanding Others

The trauma of 9/11 and its aftershocks made many Americans reluctantly recognize how insular and ignorant they are about other religions, cultures and people. Americans started realizing the power of knowledge. Knowledge of others. Knowledge of distant places. Knowledge of foreign countries. Knowledge of international relations. Knowledge of foreign languages. Campus teach-ins on Afghanistan and U.S. foreign policy were a grim reminder of the teach-ins of the 1960s. Grim because Americans only seem to crave knowledge and understanding of others after America is at war. Just look at the Japanese attack on Pearl Harbor, Korean War, Vietnam War, Persian Gulf War. Reading about the "anti-America" teach-in at City College of New York, both former Secretary of State Colin Powell's alma mater and the university where I completed my freshman year, I was heartened that the bombers had failed to instill fear of expression.

The assassination of John F. Kennedy sent the baby-boomer generation to Vietnam and the streets to protest the war. The kamikaze bombings of the World Trade Center and the Pentagon sent the boomers' children and grandchildren into the shadows of terrorism and the war of the New World Disorder. A war that knows no borders. A war in which everyone is fair game.

Many students are shunning slogans and signs in favor of educational leaflets and teach-ins about nonviolence as a philosophy and about Islam and Afghanistan. American students are focusing on racial profiling – scores of non-Muslim women have donned head scarves in solidarity with those who have faced discrimination – rather than the more complex questions about United States foreign policy. I have often wondered how they would react to being roughed up by Saudi religious police for showing an ankle.

"Being American does not mean blindly supporting the American government," said Fadi Kiblawi, a Kuwaiti-born Palestinian who went to high school in Saint Louis. "It means using your civil rights to say what you think America should be."

Newspapers and television news departments are addressing this appetite for knowledge and understanding by filling the front pages and lead stories with information on the war on terrorism, its roots and current ramifications.

The Middle East and Southeast Asia, both on the continent of Asia, suddenly don't seem so distant or far away. They have been brought close to home by the events of 9/11.

Americans now aggressively search and reach out to understand others and their complex government policies. They are trying to understand how Americans are perceived by others. Rich, dumb and spoiled.

To better understand the impact U.S. policies have on other peoples' lives, "Analyze me. Why am I not blowing up people?" said Ansar Haroun, a Pakistani-born American, who is a Muslim and an armed forces reservist who fought in the Gulf War. Now he's a forensic psychiatrist living in San Diego. "Because psychologically I have something to live for. If I lived in a refugee camp and I knew life would never get better, that the only thing I will see for years is bombing and missiles, that would drive me to terrorism. Open an English school in Afghanistan. Let them read *The New York Times*. Let them hear what [Thomas] Jefferson says. Let them eat bread. Then they won't be terrorists."

Academics, diplomats and other political analysts compare the sudden, urgent interest in foreign affairs to the national drive for improved math and science education after the Soviet Union launched the Sputnik satellite in 1957. Hopefully, this won't be ephemeral, lasting only as long as U.S. forces are engaged overseas or Americans feel threatened at home. It is up to *We the Maids* to sweep away our deep-caked layer of ignorance of others and draw in knowledge throughout the 21st century.

The publication of the satirical cartoons lampooning the Prophet Muhammad by the right-leaning *Jyllands-Posten* Danish newspaper, and reprinted in newspapers in Austria, Bulgaria, France, Germany, Italy, New Zealand, Malaysia, Poland, Spain, Switzerland, and the U.S. on the basis of freedom of speech, was a millennium reminder of the lack of knowledge and respect of Islam. Just imagine if the cartoonists who contribute to *The New Yorker* or Britain's *The Spectator* had done such cartoons – there would have been a body of work worth re-running the Crusades.

On the other hand, it is now clear that the printed word and cartoons are new battlefields in the cultural conflict between Islam and the West. America and the West have learned that, simply as a matter of self-censorship, not legal fiat, newspapers and other media outlets will not disseminate critical comments about Islam. But these gestures of cooperation with Muslim sensibilities have not been met by reciprocal gestures. As a result, the traditional liberal position in support of giving wide scope to freedom of speech, even for extremists, is losing ground everywhere. When it comes to fighting terrorism and the prospect of genocide, the world is now becoming afraid of dangerous words. That is why in the words of country singer Ricky Van Shelton, We have to "Keep It Between the Lines."

The Koran does not specifically prohibit artistic depictions of Muhammad. But the Islamic tradition that developed in the centuries after Muhammad's death in A.D. 632 includes several bans against the depiction of any human figure on the grounds that it might lead to idolatry, the worship of the object. As a result, traditional Islamic art incorporates geometric patterns of Arabic script rather than living figures. As Islam spread beyond the Arab world, the ban on figures was relaxed – miniature Persian art from the 12th century depicts birds, animals and even Muhammad, though his face is almost always hidden or obscured. Most modern Muslims do not have problems with photos of humans or figure paintings.

With freedom of speech comes a moral obligation and responsibility – self-restraint – to not insult or belittle any religion. Genuine anger voiced to express outrage at a religious insult is understandable. Organized violence provoked by politically motivated groups or governments is not. For a Muslim government to organize violent protests and then compound the problem by calling for cartoons to insult another religion – as Iran did to find the best cartoon about the Holocaust – is inexcusable. Jews helped shape Iranian identity for more than 2,000 years.

In Persia, the land of Queen Esther, whose virtue overcame evil, one could –
even Jews – by wit or by wisdom and knowledge overcome every bigot.
Some major Persian literary texts survived the Arab invasion of the seventh
century because they had been transliterated into Hebrew. Traditional Persian music owes its continuity to the Jewish artists who kept it alive when
Muslims were forbidden to practice it. Yet Iranian Jews have had to hide
their identity and suppress their religious expression. Iran remains home to
the second-largest community of Jews in the Middle East – second only to
Israel.

For Ahmadinejad to deny that Jews have been in Israel since biblical times,
dismiss the Holocaust as a myth, claim it was the cause of Jews being shipped
from Europe to Palestine and the Middle East – including Iraq and Iran –
and host a two-day Tehran conference on the Jewish Holocaust in 2006,
with former Klu Klux Klan white supremist grand wizards known for lynching and arson attending alongside Orthodox rabbis from the anti-Zionist
Neturei Karta Jerusalem stone-throwers movement – Palestinians are not
the only ones throwing stones in Jerusalem – showed the world and knowledgable Iranians how ignorant, extremist and out of touch with his people
his views are. The Holocaust conference was a political spin exercise for
consumption in the Arab world. Maybe that is why he took the beating he
did in Iran's December 2006 parliamentary election.

Debating the Holocaust is like debating whether the world is flat; sex, like
the Internet, is bad; and extreme fundamentalist theocracies of any religion
do work. To limit a so-called conference to the views of deniers is no way to
spread Iran's influence beyond its borders as it did in the good ol' days of the
Persian Empire of Cyrus. Calling for the annihilation of Israel only stirs
flames and invites a preemptive Israeli strike. Israel's last resort is not the
only resort.

A visit to Israel by a senior Iranian delegation is another. Former Iranian
President Mohammad Khatami told an Israeli journalist at the World Eco-
nomic Forum in Davos in January 2007, that he would like to visit Israel.
Get him there. He represents the majority of Iranians.

Christian Europeans were not the only ones who saved Jews from the
Holocaust. From June 1940 to May 1943, the Nazis and their allies con-

trolled North Africa and exported across the Mediterranean many elements of the final solution, from slave labor camps to the Yellow Stars that Jews had to wear to be segregated.

Arabs responded no differently than Europeans. Most were indifferent, others collaborated and a small but symbollically important group of Arabs helped and even saved Jews, like their fellow brothers in Europe. The stories of Arab men risking their lives to save Jewish women from being raped by Germans have not only been overlooked by the Tehran conference on the Holocaust– but the Western media.

The imprisonment of Holocaust denier David Irving is just as inexcusable. It makes a mockery of the claim that in democratic countries, freedom of expression is a basic right. I do understand the sensitivities of victims of the Holocaust. It was a topic my mother, uncles, aunts, cousins and classmates in high school – all of whom lost relatives to the death camps in Poland – discussed and debated at length. I lost a couple aunts to Germany's concentration camps in Poland, and remember being told by my mother and other relatives not to drive a German car or buy any German products. Now does that make sense when the Germans have come clean? Why drive a Japanese car made by people who live in denial of their history and won't repent for their own historic crimes against humanity?

It should not have come as a surprise to any student of Iran that students at Tehran's Amirkabir University of Technology staged a loud and disruptive protest during Ahmadinejad's speech, burning his picture and calling him a lying religious dictator. Some shouted: "Forget America and start thinking about us!" "If the lantern is needed at home, donating it to the mosque is haram [forbidden]." Iran's vibrant student movement is being driven underground – just as it was before the revolution.

The 57-member Organization of the Islamic Conference was right to call for Iranian nuclear talks without the pre-conditions set by the U.N. Security Council calling for Iran to suspend uranium enrichment and reprocessing.

Iran's reformers and moderate alliance inflicted a decisive defeat to Ahmadinejad after the Holocaust conference in the first nationwide vote since he took office in 2005.

In his classic defense of freedom of speech, *On Liberty*, John Stuart Mill wrote that if a view is not "fully, frequently and fearlessly discussed," it will become "a dead dogma, not a living truth." The existence of the Holocaust should remain a living truth, and those who are skeptical about the enormity of the Nazi atrocities should be confronted with the evidence of it.

Freedom of speech is essential to democratic regimes, and it must include the freedom to say what everyone else believes to be false – and even offensive, so long as it does not result in senseless violence and death.

I agree with Peter Singer, professor of bioethics at Princeton University, who wrote an editorial column in 2006 after the riots that followed the publication of the Muhammad cartoons. He wrote: "We must be free to deny the existence of God, and to criticize the teachings of Jesus, Moses, Muhammad and Buddha, as reported in the texts that millions of people regard as sacred. Without that freedom, human progress will always run up against a basic roadblock." The Muslim world periodically reminds us of these roadblocks when they legally ban the conversion of Muslims to another religion. The case of Afghan Abdul Rahman, who was to be executed in 2006 because he converted to Christianity, is a case in point. Luckily, he was granted political asylum in Europe and survived.

The Veil

A good example of such a roadblock is the veil. The debate in government, academia, courts, media and the streets over the propriety of Muslim women wearing veils is anything but religious.

The Vatican, naturally, had to butt in and demand that Muslim women wearing veils as 'guests' must follow the laws of the host countries, including any bans on veils. The church lamented that some Muslim countries, like Saudi Arabia, don't allow Christians, Jews, or anyone else to practice their religion in their desert kingdom. These countries, like the Holy See, are side-blinded by their religious veils and headdresses. They are like blinders on horses to eliminate peripheral vision.

The *hejab*, or head scarf that proud Muslim women wear is representative of the same historic, sexual and political spin *We the Maids* have been subjected to. Who defines "norms of decency" anyway? Religious extremists, or We the People?

The Turkish historian Muazzez Ilmiye Cig, the 92-year-old academic and author of 13 books, who specializes in Sumerian culture and history, was cleared by a court in Istanbul in 2006 of inciting religious hatred and insulting Muslim women by claiming that the veil's roots are not religious but sexual. Her scientific paper linked the origin of head scarfs in the Middle East to prostitutes in Sumer, 5,000 years earlier – several millennia before the birth of Islam – and were worn by priestesses who initiated young men into sex to hide their faces.

The Turkish supreme court concluded that as a woman of science, her actions did not insult Islam and therefore did not constitute a crime.

Many women veil-wearers agree. The veil is not a religious symbol. It is an expression of individual cultural heritage, pride and style. In the defense of their desire to wear veils, many of these women aren't citing religion or custom, but the post-Enlightenment traditions of individual freedom and the right of self-expression. "What we are seeing now is Muslim women have a voice. Isn't that what government is about?" said Mona Siddiqui, director of University of Glasgow's Centre for the Study of Islam.

Glasgow's Dome of Mosque, proudly and openly built by the city's 25,000-member Muslim community – alongside the Scottish Museum of Religion, St. Mungo Museum of Religious Life and Art – is a testimonial to the Enlightenment, religious tolerance and understanding. A few blocks away, in the White Hart Inn, established in 1516 – Robert Burns. last hangout – I ordered a whisky and jotted down some notes about John Knox, the fiery Scottish preacher who challenged the Catholic Church and led the charge to the Enlightenment, after I walked around the pub and looked at the dated pictures and read press clippings on its walls going back to the turn of the 20th century, as I repeatedly ducked to avoid knocking myself out. Not hard to do in a Scottish pub. Damn, those early Scots were short for being Viking descendants.

Muslims, as Strangers in a Strange Land, especially veiled Muslim women, have managed to secure positions of political, media and communal leadership. By becoming more enlightened, veiled women are unveiling the truth.

Baroness Uddin, the sole Muslim woman in England's House of Lords, went to Prime Minister Tony Blair in 2006 to make a case for Muslim women to take a leading role in tackling extremism. Good idea. No one else seems to know what to do. Head scarves worn with jeans and pink and turquoise sneakers embossed in Western brand names work for me. A lot more is needed. More Muslim women like Somali-born Muslim feminist author Ayaan Hirsi Ali have to speak up. She has called the Prophet Muhammad a "tyrant," a "pervert," and a "paedophile," for counting a nine-year-old among his nine wives.

Hirsi Ali argues that Islam enforces an unyielding hierarchy – leading down from Allah, to the prophet, to religious leaders and then to the father – that leaves no space for individual freedom. "Religion is an expression of culture, and Islam is an expression of desert Arab male culture," she said. She was born in Somalia in 1969, forced into exile in Saudi Arabia when civil war broke out and the military coup of Siad Barre. In Saudi Arabia she was raised on myths of a global Jewish conspiracy. "When we opened the tap and no water came from it, our neighbours would say: 'The Jews have done it. They want to dehydrate us.' When it rained, we got that from God's blessing. But if there were fires, if there were floods, if there were diseases, it was always caused by the evil Jews."

She moved around from country to country as her Columbia University-educated father, who was a dissident politician, was regularly asked to leave his host country. She had been subjected to the tradition of ritualized female genital mutilation, and became a member of parliament in Holland.

Listening and watching veiled Muslim sexologists expose sex for what it is to the uninformed in the Muslim world is a millennium step in the right direction. Listening to how sex is an emotional and human condition, not a religious one, gives *We the Maids* hope that sexual and religious taboos will be swept out as more people get to enjoy the pleasures of knowledge – and sex. The combination of the two is a carnal delight.

The Bible
Abraham, Moses and many other prominent figures of the Old Testament

probably never existed as portrayed. Especially David. He was probably a provincial leader whose reputation was overblown by spin doctors. The story of the exodus of the Jews from Egypt didn't happen and the walls of Jericho never came tumbling down, according to archaeologists who have searched in Israel for decades. The theories have gained acceptance among non-Orthodox rabbis. *Etz Hayim (Tree of Life)*, a new Torah and commentary published at the dawn of the 21st century, represents the latest findings from archaeology, philology, anthropology and the study of ancient cultures. The idea is to deal with the reality that the Bible is a human document rather than a divine one.

The raising of pigs has traditionally been forbidden in Israel because of Jewish dietary laws. However, the reality of suicide bombers now allows Israeli security forces to use pigs to guard West Bank settlements to thwart the would-be Palestinian suicide bombers. Pigs have a more highly developed sense of smell than dogs, which allows them to sniff out terrorists and their weapons. A pig can identify weapons from a greater distance than a dog and will walk in the direction of the terrorist, thereby pointing him out. More importantly, the animal is considered dangerous by Muslims because, according to their faith, anyone who touches a pig is not eligible for the virgins in heaven.

The biblical book of Genesis, according to *Etz Hayim*, originated in Mesopotamia and not Palestine. The notion that the Bible is not literally true "is more or less settled and understood among most Conservative rabbis," said Rabbi David Wolpe of Sinai Temple in Los Angeles and a contributor to *Etz Hayim*.

The evolutionary knowledge and objective of the Old Testament has enabled Jews and the state of Israel to survive centuries of political, religious and military persecution. Israel is the 100th smallest country with less than 1/1,000th of the world's population. It has been engaged in several wars with an implacable enemy that seeks its destruction. Its economy is continuously strained by having to spend more per capita on its own protection than any country on earth. But it can lay claim to the following: the cell phone was developed by Israelis working in the Israeli branch of Motorola; most of the Windows NT and XP operating systems were developed by Microsoft-Israel; the Pentium MMX chip technology was designed in Israel at Intel;

both the Pentium-4 microprocessor and the Centrino processor were entirely designed, developed and produced in Israel; voice mail technology was developed in Israel; both Microsoft and Cisco systems built their only non-U.S. R&D facilities in Israel; the technology for the AOL Instant Messenger ICQ was developed in 1996 by four young Israelis.

Israel has the fourth-largest air force in the world – after the U.S., Russia and China. In addition to a large variety of other aircraft, Israel has an aerial arsenal of more than 250 F-16s. That is the largest fleet of F-16 aircraft outside the U.S.

U.S. officials now look to Israel for advice on how to handle airborne security threats; Israel's $10-billion economy is larger than all of its immediate neighbors combined. Israel has the world's highest percentage of home computers; It has the highest ratio of university degrees to the population in the world; Israel produces more scientific papers per capita than any other nation by a large margin – 109 per 10,000 people – and has one of the highest per capita rates of patents filed. Israel designed the airline industry's most impenetrable flight security. It is the only country in the world that entered the 21st century with a net gain in its number of trees, made more remarkable because this was achieved in an area considered mainly desert. Israel has more museums per capita than any other country. Relative to population, Israel is the largest immigrant-absorbing nation on earth. It has the highest average living standards in the Middle East. The per capita income in 2000 was over $17,500, exceeding that of the U.K. When it comes to the number of Nobel Peace Prizes won, Israel tops the Arab World like 80 to one.

On the medical front, an Israeli company developed a simple blood test that distinguishes between mild and severe cases of multiple sclerosis. An Israeli-made device helps restore the use of paralyzed hands. This device electrically stimulates the hand muscles, providing hope to millions of stroke sufferers and victims of spinal injuries. An Israeli researcher succeeded in creating human monoclonal antibodies which can neutralize the highly contagious smallpox virus without inducing the dangerous side effects of the existing vaccine. Two Israelis received the 2004 Nobel Prize in chemistry for their research and discovery of one of the human cells most important cyclical processes that will lead the way to DNA repair, control of newly produced proteins, and immune defense systems.

The Movement Disorder Surgery program at Israel's Hadassah Medical Center has successfully eliminated the physical manifestations of Parkinson's disease in a select group of patients with a deep brain stimulation technique. For women who undergo hysterectomies each year for the treatment of uterine fibroids, the development in Israel of the Ex Ablate 2000 System is a welcome breakthrough, offering a non-invasive alternative to surgery. Young children with breathing problems will soon be sleeping more soundly, thanks to a new Israeli device called the Child Hood. This innovation replaces the inhalation mask with an improved drug delivery system that provides relief for child and parent. In relation to population, Israel is making a greater contribution to humanity than any other nation on earth.

Isn't it time the Koran and New Testament were updated and treated as human, rather than divine, documents so that the lives and living standards of people who live by their dictates are improved as well? There are many dated pronouncements in the Koran, New Testament and other religious texts that misguide the ignorant. It is up to all of us to interpret God's law in a way that is relevant. There is nothing wrong in discarding outdated ideas. It is far better than what the Taliban and religious extremists in America are trying to dictate. How can they know the absolute truth? It is up to *We the Maids* to sweep it in.

Muhammad's youngest and favorite wife, Aisha, vigorously contested the chauvinism of early Muslim clerics. She was the first Islamic feminist. The Arab-Saudi, Wahabi and Sunni custodans of Islam and Mecca are creating as big a divide in the Middle East as their Texas protectors did in America.

They actually fore-wrote it. Muslim Reformation must do to Islam what the Scottish Reformation did to the Catholic Church: Break the theocratic monopolists. Improving knowledge is about understanding others and improving relations.

Some *Muslim Maids* are doing just that. These scholars are ignoring the word of God, who allegedly spoke through the Angel Gabriel to Muhammad and said of the Koran: "This book is not to be doubted." Gabriel was a major force behind the Bible, which claims the same status. He was the first literary agent – and a damned good one.

Speaking of good agents, a book agent sold a fragile 16th-or 17th-century hexagonal leather-bound Koran measuring just 7cm in diameter, with intricate gold markings, to the Sultan of Brunei Hassanal Bolkiah, that nobody seems to want any more, after it was litigiously tied up in a Sydney, Australia court. It was sought after by the likes of the Sultan and Muammar Kaddafi's son Al-Saadi.

Getting back to the scholars – these scholars are constantly at great personal risk to themselves and their families. Some have been the targets of death. Christopher Luxenberg (a pseudonym) is a scholar of ancient Semitic languages in Germany and author of *The Syro-Aramaic Reading of the Koran*. He argues that the Koran has been misread and misinterpreted for centuries. The earliest copies of the Koran were derived from preexisting Christian Aramaic texts that were misinterpreted by later Islamic scholars who prepared the Arab-language editions commonly read today.

"OK, so they've got a big book you can't discuss. They've got no music, no choirs, no processions, no dressing up, no liturgy, no hymns, no gay or female clergy. What on earth is the attraction?" Wolfendale asked as we ordered another beer in our ongoing editorial debate about the pros and cons of the different religions. "Oh, yes, heavenly virgins waiting to be shagged by martyrs. Not much of a pull for gay Muslims – but then I forgot – there are none of those either," he continued at the FCC Main Bar to the amusement of some nearby inbibers.

Scriptural studies and interpretations of the Jewish and Christian scriptures played a key role in loosening the church's domination of the intellectual and cultural life of Europe and America. The Muslim clerics knowing this are well aware that once the Koran is questioned, it will be subjected to the same scrutiny. And why not? In the 1970s, John Edward Wansbrough, an American historian who taught at London University's School of Oriental and African Studies, wrote that subjecting the Koran to "analysis by the instruments and techniques of biblical criticism is virtually unknown." Wansbrough wrote that the Koran is a composite of different voices compiled over hundreds of years. Scholars agree that there is no evidence of the Koran until 691 – 59 years after Muhammad's death – when the Dome of the Rock mosque in Jerusalem was built, carrying several Koranic inscriptions.

These inscriptions differed from the version of the Koran that had been handed down to date, suggesting that the text may have been evolving in the last decade of the seventh century. More significantly, much of what we know today as Islam – the lives and sayings of the prophet – is based on texts from between 130 and 300 years after Muhammad died. As a result, some scholars suggest that Muhammad, like Jesus before him, was not the founder of a new religion but a preacher hailing the coming of a messiah.

Wansbrough believed Muhammad was manufactured, a myth. and that Judeo-Christian scriptures were adapted for the Arab perspective

Many of the early Koranic texts refer to the followers of Muhammad as Hagarenes, and the "tribe of Ishmael," the descendants of Hagar, the servant girl whom the Jewish patriarch Abraham used to father his son Ishmael.

The undisputed fact is that Muhammad was an illiterate camel trader, and that he received his revelations in Mecca, a remote and sparsely populated part of Arabia far from any centers of monotheistic thought, in an environment of idol-worshipping bedouins. It will be interesting when historians finally explain how monotheistic stories and ideas found their way into the Koran. "There are only two possibilities," said Patricia Crone of the School for Oriental and African Studies. "Either there had to be substantial numbers of Jews and Christians in Mecca, or the Koran had to have been composed somewhere else."

Aramaic was the language group of most Middle Eastern Jews and Christians during Muhammad's life. For example, the famous passage in the Koran about the virgins is based on the word hur, which is an adjective in the feminine plural meaning simply ' white." Islamic tradition insists the word hur stands for "houri," which means virgin. But Luxenberg says this is a forced misreading of the text. In both ancient Aramaic and in at least one respected dictionary of early Arabic, *hur* means "white raisins."

Luxenberg, who has traced the passage dealing with paradise to a Christian text called *Hymns of Paradise* by a 4th-century author, said the word "paradise" was derived from the Aramaic word for "garden." All references to paradise described it as a "garden of flowing waters, with abundant fruits and white raisins," a prized delicacy in the ancient Middle East and still special, if not as rare, today. In this context, white raisins, mentioned often as *hur*, makes more sense than a reward of sexual favors from virgins. Can you just see all the suicide bombers who expected virgins surrounded by white raisins instead?

If we can get word to the boys that they'll be sitting by a waterfall picking through a pile of raisins, I have no doubt there will be a dramatic drop in suicide bombings. After all, we have to put ourselves in their shoes. Young men humming with testosterone and forbidden to shag until a marriage and dowry are arranged with a young version of Golda Meir. Is it any wonder they may be keen to reach paradise simply for sexual release? If they realize all it's going to be is a mouthful of white raisins, they may stick around with us in hope.

Jihad

Since 9/11, *"jihadism"* has become synonymous with "terrorism," and *"jihadists"* as "terrorists." The use of the term to justify terrorist acts against civilians demonizes Islam. The term *"jihad"* has been and continues to be grossly misused and deserves to be removed from the vocabulary of Muslim politics.

Jihad is an intensely political term from the early years of Islam, associated as it has been with the expansion of Muslim empires and justified by the argument that Muslims had an obligation to spread the word of God to humanity. Early Muslim empires were not particularly concerned about converting non-Muslim subjects to Islam and were, therefore, more tolerant of religious diversity than their medieval counterparts in Christendom. The term *"jihad"* was used to justify territorial expansion usually undertaken for economic or strategic gain. Muslim rulers did not kill infidels to save their souls. They preferred taxing them to raise revenues, one reason for their luke warm attitude toward conversion.

The term *"jihad"* regained currency in the 19th century when the tide turned and European powers began to subjugate Muslim lands; *jihad* then took on defensive connotations. The quintessential jihad of the 19th and first half of the 20th century was resistance to colonial domination and war of national liberation. As nationalism in the Muslim world became equated with Muslim identity vis-a-vis the Christian colorizer, the term came to be defined in context-specific terms. The boundaries of the colonizer, later to become the borders of the post-colonial states, defined the geographic scope of specific *jihads*.

Decolonization universalized the model of the nation state, confining the notion of *jihad* further within national boundaries. This paradigmatic change cried out for *jihad*, interpretation based on reasoning to suit changed circumstances. But, unfortunately, none was forthcoming from the scholars of Islam, at least as far as the notion of *jihad* was concerned. The term has now been used to justify interstate as well as intrastate conflicts. Kashmiri extremists have waged a *jihad* against India in the name of Islam to achieve national self-determination, ironic since national self-determination is a recent concept that belongs to the era of nationalist, not religious, wars.

The notion of *jihad* is to defend the dignity of the religion, nation and country. *Jihad* is justified when defending a country from attacks by foreigners, outsiders, like Afghanistan fighting against the Soviets and U.S. coalition forces, or the Iraqis fighting the U.S. coalition.

Sectarian strife has also taken on the nomenclature of *jihad*. The Sunni Arabs of Iraq wage *jihad* against Iraqi Shiite Arabs by blowing up their holy sites and causing carnage in crowded markets. The Shiites retaliate by waging their own *jihad*, blowing up Sunni mosques and sending death squads to kill Sunnis. Saddam Hussein said he was fighting the battle of Qaddasiya, the 7th-century battle in which the Arab Muslims defeated the Sassanid

Muslim fundamentalist extremists have no right to advocate a world caliphate and the sharia – and express violent hatred for the West and Jews.

Muslims killing Christians in the name of *jihad*, as they do in Egypt, England, Indonesia, Pakistan, Spain and other countries, has no place in the New World Order of the 21st century. No *jihad* justifies the killing of innocent civilians. Nasir Abbas, a former leader of the Jemaah Islamiah, who fought the Soviets in Afghanistan and fought alongside Moro rebel fighters in the southern Philippines, said the terrorist bombings in Indonesia – from the series of church blasts on New Year's Eve 2000 to the Bali bombings, were "wrong" and "deviant." "That is not right, that is not *jihad*. That is criminal, causing destruction on the face of this Earth. That is murder," said Nasir.

Sharia

Sharia in its simplest form means nothing more than *"haram"* (forbidden) and *"halal"* (permissible). It used to mean the moral and ethical underpinning of faith. The definition of *sharia* as law is based on 500 verses of the Koran – that's just 16 percent of the Koran. The debate is whose *sharia?* Iranian, Saudi, Turkish, Malaysian, Indonesian, Iraqi or God? To the extremists, it can only be God's – as interpreted by them. Fundamentalists have reduced the *sharia* to a set of laws. Hence *sharia's* association with beheadings, stonings and amputations. "Where is the emphasis on kindness, mercy and social justice that lie at the heart of Islam?" asks Mona Eltahawy, a New York-based commentator.

In many Muslim countries, the legal system has been completely modernized with the exception of one area that stubbornly remains caught in the web of edicts issued by Muslim scholars who lived centuries ago – family law. In other words, *sharia* is used only to govern the lives of women and children.

In a climate of growing right-wing anti-Muslim rhetoric, particularly in Europe, some in the Muslim community find it difficult to stand up to radical Islamist posturing on *sharia*. Such hesitation is often based on a reluctance to openly criticize fellow Muslims and ignorance as to what *sharia* means. *Fatwas*, legal opinions, are priced, charged and collected to accommodate the needs of the mullahs issuing them. *Fatwas* are bought and sold daily.

It is imperative that non-Muslims hear the vigorous debates that are taking place between Muslims over controversial issues like *sharia* – the best proof that Muslim thought is not monolithic.

Islam Hadhari

Malaysia is Asia's Turkey when it comes to balancing Islam, democracy,

China and directing the Muslim wor d. It is a liberal Muslim state that balances tribal tradition, Islam and the best of English colonialism and the resistance to imperialism – British and U.S.

Malaysia's political concept of *Islam Hadhari* translates to "civilizational Islam." It promotes good governance within societies and goodwill between peoples and cultures. "Islam preaches peace between nations and peoples as well as tolerance between different rel gions and cultures," said Malaysian Prime Minister Abdullah Badawi in an editorial opinion in *The Strait Times* in 2005. Fundamentalist terrorists, he added "must be singled out only by the acts of terror and nothing else."

Islam and Muslim states also have to be more open to other religions and practice what they preach. They can't demand the West tolerate and accept Muslim extremists and ignore the fact that the countries in which the Muslim extremists were born prohibit them from voicing their opinions at home and won't recognize secularism or allow followers of other religions to practice their faith.

Imams have to meet with their Christian and Jewish counterparts continuously if there is to be better knowledge, understanding and tolerance between the Christian, Jewish and Muslim communities in the 21st century. The joint communique issued by the imams and rabbis in Seville, Spain, in March 2006, denouncing the use of religion to justify violence and urging respect for all religious symbols has to be repeated throughout all Muslim communities around the world.

Arab Spinoza

Al-Afif al-Akhdar, who is in his 70s, has for decades been fighting to expose the dangers of Islamic fundamentalism. He has been waging his war from a sparse apartment in the Muslim immigrant section of Paris, where he lives alone with his 4,000 books. His first name, Al-Afif, means the "modest one." He travels to the center of Paris every day for free on public transport because he is a pensioner – and gets a free hot meal in a "restaurant for the poor."

He has been likened by Arab scholars to America's Thomas Paine, who fought for human rights and secularism in America's War of Independence and in the French Revolution. He has been ostracized and persecuted – and likened to Baruch Spinoza, the Dutch Jewish philosopher born in Amsterdam in 1632 – because he insisted on grounding his thought, including his critique of religion, on reason.

"Seven lines are enough to present me to readers in Israel," says Akhdar in response to journalists questions about *jihad* against Israel. "It is far more important to concentrate on explaining the dangers that inhere in *jihadist* Islam."

Akhdar is in the vanguard of Muslim liberal scholars. As a student, he secretly read evolutionist Darwin during religious classes. "Saudi Arabia is the same Saudi Arabia that, as part of its plan to turn Mecca into a modern city, decided to demolish the building in which Mohammad married Khadija – a historic site," he said as he criticized Saudi Arabia.

Saudi Arabia is where the two different extremes of Islam came from – from Muhammad's period – Meccan, referring to his period there, which was influenced more by the peace-seeking Christians and Jews that prohibited violence and which gave root to the mystical Sufi movement – and Medinist, when Muhammed had to move from Mecca to Medina, where the second more violent and fundamentalist Islam developed. This is the Islam the fundamentalists and terrorists have adopted.

To justify the passage from the "conciliatory" peace of Mecca to the militant peace of Medina, Muhammad told Muslims that *jihad* is permissible only for self-defense [Surah of The Pilgrimage – Surah 23:29]. To those against whom war is made, permission is given to fight, because they are wronged. Muhammad was wronged. He was expelled from Mecca, and the purpose of the defensive *jihad* is to enable his return. Medinist Islam is the extreme fundamentalist violent Islam. Meccan Islam must reemerge as the dominant Islam.

Mellow Bellow

Muslim extremism is the exception, not the rule, in Muslim countries. A July 2005 Pew Global Attitudes Project survey in Indonesia, Jordan, Lebanon, Morocco, Pakistan and Turkey found that backing for Osama bin Laden and violence against civilian targets in Iraq and elsewhere had declined markedly.

For too long the extremists have been the sole voice of Islam. The portrayal of al-Qaeda and other Islamic extremists as vicious and corrupt by Saudi television and other Muslim media outlets in 2005 was long overdue. The launch by the BBC of an Arabic TV news and information service in the Middle East in 2006 will go a long way to educate the next generation. Meanwhile, Al Jazeera's new-English language news channel offers a realistic alternative from the Middle East to Fox News and CNN.

In today's wifi information age, whose story wins is more important than whose arms prevail. The current resurgent clash within Islam – in Afghanistan, America, Egypt, Europe, Indonesia, Iran, Iraq, Lebanon, Malaysia, Nigeria, Pakistan, Palestine, Philippines, Saudi Arabia, Somalia, Syria, Turkey – is a Muslim civil war for the soul of Islam. The mainstream Muslims will not win if they continue to be a silent apathetic majority, no matter what arms and firepower their military machines have. It is all about winning hearts and minds, not body counts.

The U.S. spends about 500 times more on its military than on broadcasting and exchanges, with little discussion of trade-offs. Public diplomacy – broadcasting, exchange programs, development assistance, disaster relief, military-to-military contacts – is scattered around the government with no "overarching strategy or budget to integrate them," wrote Joseph Nye, a professor at Harvard and former assistant secretary of defense. A comprehensive national security policy to win hearts and minds is long overdue.

My family has lost many members and property in Russia to the pogroms and in Europe to the Holocaust because it was part of the silent majority. Many people I know have also lost loved ones because of apathy and allowing the vocal minority to impose its will. The vast majority of Muslims do want to live in peace. That is irrelevant when a fanatical few fundamentalists are allowed to rampage and terrorize the globe in the name of Islam. The fact is that the fundamentalist extremists rule Islam at this moment of history. One of the most graphic visuals was the display of the female suicide bomber whose bombs didn't go off in an attack on a wedding party in Jordan that killed dozens and wounded hundreds.

The killing of teachers in Afghanistan, Iraq and Thailand, the killing of innocents and destruction of mosques across Iraq, the killing of tourists in

Egypt. The destruction of each other's universities in Palestine by Fatah and Hamas – the alma maters of the leaders of each faction – their only hope and place to acquire knowledge, says it all. "We want to keep education separate from politics," said Gehad Hamad, a spokesman for Al Azhar University, the stronghold of Fatah. In Iraq, historians and educators are fleeing universities and museums to avoid assassination. The sectarian assassination of Saddam Hussein at the gallows of his execution further contributed to the dramatic rise of killings and suicide bombings between Sunni and Shiite extremists. The Saudis, vow to fight the Shiites in Iraq only added fuel to an already violent Muslim civil war.

"We live in a world where, when Christians kill Muslims, it's a crusade. When Jews kill Muslims, it's a massacre. When Muslims kill Muslims, it's the weather channel. Nobody cares," Israel's U.N. Ambassador Dan Gillerman said in New York in May 2007. How dumb can Muslims be? Their actions only make Muslims' lives worse. So what is the point?

The majority of Germans were not Nazis and many thought they were a bunch of fools. After World War I, most just wanted to live in peace. The reason given for the Nazis' political success and why they were tolerated and allowed to succeed, was they restored German pride. The same with the Russians who just wanted to live in peace when the Communist Party came to power. The average Japanese individual before World War II was not a warmonger. Yet Japan murdered and slaughtered its way across Asia. Let's not forget the silent majorities who just wanted to live in peace in Cambodia, Rwanda, Serbia, Darfur.

History lessons are readily available for all to learn. Peace loving Muslims will find out the hard way if they don't speak out, just as my family did in Russia and millions of other families have worldwide. Peace-loving Germans, Japanese, Chinese, Russians, Rwandans, Serbs, Afghans, Iraqis, Palestinians, Somalis, Nigerians, Algerians, and many others have died because the peaceful majority did not speak up until it was too late. Peace loving Muslims must wake up to the fundamentalists who are threatening our way of life.

In Italy, the Muslims of Cremona, because of their disgust at fundamentalist extremists, have spoken up and marched publicly against terrorism and violence. "Our mistake is that we were quiet," said Sadiq el-Hassan, a leader at the Cremona mosque. "After all that happened after September 11, we never came out and said, 'These things are bad.' But it's not too late." Muslims should begin aligning themselves more clearly against terrorism and for peaceful values of coexistence. After all, Islam does recognize and accept the prophets of other religions. In fact, the Koran says that all peoples on earth have had a messenger from God come to them at some stage. As laid down in the Koran, it is forbidden to compel someone to convert to Islam.

The practice of Islam is not only prescribed by the Koran. Principal among other texts are the Hadiths, the sayings and traditions of the Prophet Muhammad. The Koran gives believers the principles, and the Hadiths advise how to live them. There are four categories of Hadiths: authentic, good, weak and fabricated, and in all they number in the thousands.

It is time at the dawn of the 21st century to put the virus of Islamic militancy under a microscope. Islamic militancy is a global phenomenon propelled by a diverse collection of groups and individuals with different grievances and agendas. Just as diseases do not emerge in a vacuum but evolve as a result of complex interactions between pathogens, people and their environment, so it is with Islamic militancy. Too often, we focus on the individual parts of the problem and miss the evolving big picture.

An example of fabrication is the number of Palestinians killed by Israel. The fact is that Palestinians killed by gunfire were more likely to have died at the hands of their own people, a Palestinian human rights group concluded in 2005. More Arabs are killed by Arab suicide bombers than by Israelis or by the coalition forces in Afghanistan and Iraq.

To avoid the looming clash of religious beliefs, it is crucial to undertake remedial initiatives that address the key environmental conditions underlying the spread of Islamic militancy. ' Chief among these are the numerous conflicts involving Muslims and non-Muslims – notably in Iraq, Israel-Palestine, Kashmir, Chechnya and Afghanistan, China and India – that serve to validate *jihadist* ideology and act as recruiting magnets and training grounds," wrote Paul Stares, vice president for research and studies at the U.S. Institute of Peace, and Mona Yacoubian, a special adviser to the institute's Muslim World Initiative in *The Washington Post* in 2005.

India, with the world's second-largest Muslim population after Indonesia, with Hindus who are 80 percent of the population and Muslims who are 13 percent of the country's 1.1 billion people, is a Ghandian leading light. It is the most secular country in the world – not only in symbol but substance. The head of state, President A.P.J. Abdul Kalam, is Muslim. Prime Minister Manmohan Singh belongs to the minority Sikh community. India's most powerful politician, ruling Congress Party President Sonia Ghandi is an Italian-born Catholic. What is more significant is that no Indian-Muslim has been associated with al-Qaeda, or any other international terrorist group – yet. What a contrast to its former imperial parts – Bangladesh and Pakistan – two Islamic regimes that are fertile recruiting grounds for Osama bin Laden's lieutenants. Let's not even get into Kashmir and Nepal.

The secular government has won the hearts and minds of the people, even in Muslim communities where orthodox Muslims, insistence on separate personal laws for marriage, divorce, inheritance and women's rights prevents integration. The orthodox Muslims' aversion to the secular education provided by non-denominational schools highlights and showcases their lower literacy rate, economic disadvantages, especially in rural areas where villagers blindly obey clerical *fatwas* or edicts, and the lower status of Muslim women. Muslims complain of not benefiting from India's economic prosperity. They are not because they cannot compete on equal terms without taking full advantage of all the benefits the state provides. To do so, argue their imams, would lead to cultural emasculation. They sound like the Evangelicals in America.

The annual mellow pilgrimage to the holy city of Mecca by more than 2 million Muslims, who pray for mercy and forgiveness at Mount Arafat, traces the journey made by the Muhammad to the scene of his last sermon. It is also where some believe Adam and Eve reunited after they were banished by God from the Garden of Eden, a refreshing millennium reminder.

Cradle of Religion
Mesopotamia was the cradle of civilization and religion. The Tigris and Euphrates rivers in Iraq are the fountains of our civilization, according to archaeologists and religious scholars. Nebuchadnezzar's Mesopotamian Empire was brought to an end by the Persians in 539 B.C., led by King Cyrus and the Achaemenid Dynasty. King Cyrus first united Persia and then

conquered Babylon, Asia Minor to Syria and Egypt.

At the time, it was the largest empire the world had ever known. King Cyrus respected and tolerated all religious practices and was openly celebrated and toasted by the Jews who had been oppressed by Nebuchadnezzar. Like the Chinese emperors, all he required of his subjects was tribute and loyalty.

Persia united the diverse people of the Old World Order. Indians, Medes, Babylonians, Lydians, Greeks, Jews, Phoenicians and Egyptians. The Persian Empire began to decline after the Persian Wars with the Greek city states from 490-480 B.C. and went into temporary decline when Alexander the Great defeated Darius III and proclaimed himself successor to the Persian throne in 331 B.C.

Through Alexander and his successors, the Achaemenids passed to Rome the idea of divine kingship, whose roots lay in ancient Mesopotamia. From Rome they went to the Byzantine Christian Empire and Europe.

Persia was always defined by geography, its language and religion. Persia changed its name to Iran in 1935. The word "Iran" first appeared in A.D. 600 and means "land of the Aryan." It is believed that around 1000 B.C., Aryan tribes from the north came to the high plateaus of Persia, which had sparse communities since 5000 B.C.

Zoroastrianism

The Persians' most refined religious cult was Zoroastrianism, a dualist religion in terms of a good and an evil god. Little is known about the prophet Zoroaster. He taught his disciples in the 6th century B.C. in Persia to uphold the cause of the god of light with ritual and moral behavior; ahead lay a messianic deliverance, the resurrection of the dead and life everlasting after judgment. This creed spread rapidly through Western Asia even though it was probably never more than a cult of a minority. J.M. Roberts, in his carefully researched *History of the World*, wrote that Zoroastrianism influenced "Judaism and the Oriental cults which were to be part of the setting of Christianity; the angels of Christian tradition and the notion of the hellfire which awaited the wicked both came from Zoroaster."

The "eternal pillars of fire" worshipped by the Zoroastrians on the arid

Aesheron Peninsula, an outgrowth of the Caucasus mountains projecting into the landlocked Caspian Sea, were, more prosaically, the result of flammable gas associated with petroleum deposits escaping from the fissures in porous limestone, according to Daniel Yergin in his Pulitzer Prize-winning book *The Prize*. It was the first hint of the vast oil deposits that lie in the region.

Zoroastrianism gave important privileges to its priests, the *magi*. This led in due course to political power as well. Priests confirmed the divine nature of the kingship, had important judicial duties, and also supervised the collection of property taxes, which were the basis of Persian finance. Their doctrines seem to have varied considerably from the strict monotheism attributed to Zoroaster, but focused on a creator whose viceroy on earth was the king. The royal claim to divine authority. It is a concept that was adopted by many mainstream religions, and is still practiced today.

Jesus The Jew
Christians have been taught and conditioned by their churches, religious leaders and their lobbyists and spin doctors about Jesus, the church, Jews and Muslims. Christian misperceptions about themselves and their relationship to Jews and Muslims have been a major cause of the endless wars and bloodshed for the past two millennia and the current war against terrorists.

Jesus, Peter, Paul and the rest of Christ's disciples were Jews. In Jesus' time, Israel was a colony of the Roman Empire. The Romans ruthlessly imposed on their subjects the belief that the emperor was God. The Romans did not believe in the separation of church and state. To Jews, therefore, the Roman occupation was a religious affront as well as a political one. Crucifixion on a cross was the Roman means of execution. Lenny Bruce, the Beatnik-era Jewish stand-up comic, used to say in one of his routines that it was a good thing Jesus wasn't born in 20th-century America because pious Christians would have to wear electric chairs around their necks.

Christianity was an offshoot of Judaism for three and a half centuries, and the two religions were very close. So close in fact that modern archaeology cannot easily distinguish Jewish tombstones from Christian ones as late as the fourth century A.D. The Dead Sea Scrolls, dating from 250 B.C. to A.D. 70, make no mention of Jesus, John the Baptist, or anything resembling the religious movement described in the New Testament. Nevertheless, they did give religious scholars a much richer understanding of the Jewish world during the life of Jesus.

The Gospel of Judas, published for the first time in 2006, after being preserved for centuries in an Egyptian desert grave, says it all – like it was. Contrary to his infamous traitor spin, Judas was Jesus' most loyal disciple, the person Jesus trusted to hand him over to his death. The so-called greatest betrayal turned out to be an act of pious obedience.

The *Gospel of Judas* survived in a third or fourth-century papyrus codex and was written in Coptic, the ancient language of Egyptian Christianity. It confirmed that Jesus was first and foremost a teacher and revealer of wisdom and knowledge, not a savior who died for the sins of the world.

In the New Testament, Jesus' disciples, on more than one occasion, come across as a bunch of dumb shmucks who fall asleep in the Garden of Gethsemane and disown Jesus as he faces death. Nevertheless, the resurrected Jesus bestows authority on them and in the end they become faithful missionaries of his message. By the second century, the Apostolic Succession – the doctrine that religious authority has been passed on from the apostles through an unbroken succession of bishops – was well established, and bishops claimed to have inherited their authority from the disciples, excluding Judas, of course.

The negative depiction of the apostles, and hence the bishops who acquire their legitimacy through them, must therefore have been intended to criticize the bishops themselves. After all, if the bishops' authority was inherited from a group of people who had worshipped the wrong god and had never learned Jesus' secret teachings, it was surely bogus. If the 12 disciples do indeed stand for the bishops who claimed apostolic authority, what could the text mean by suggesting that they were leading the crowd astray like sacrificial animals upon an altar. No different than *We the Apathetic Maids* today.

It seems likely this is a criticism of the bishops' endorsement of martyrdom, and the consequent acceptance by early Christians of execution by the Roman authorities. The author of the *Gospel of Judas* views martyrdom as a

vain sacrifice, and blames church leaders for leading their sheep-like congregations to the slaughter. The editors miss this aspect of the *Gospel of
Judas*, translating the text as saying: "This is the crowd whom you are leading astray before that altar." However, the Coptic literally says "upon."

The imagery of martyrdom as sacrifice became a powerful way for Christians to identify with Christ. In their view, the martyrs were reenacting Jesus'
death, which they believed had been a sacrifice on behalf of all humanity.
According to the *Gospel of Judas*, the bishops are just like the Jewish priests
they criticize, erroneously worshipping an inferior god, rather than the tran-
scendent one who no longer required sacrifice of any kind.

Religious discussions fueled with alcohol inevitably become endless, heated
arguments anywhere in the world, and the FCC Main Bar in Hong Kong is
no different. "There came a point, however, when I could no longer accept
the Christian doctrine as absolute truth. It increasingly stretched my credibility and finally that credibility snapped. I am not an agnostic, someone
who says he does not know whether it is true or not. I am an apostate. I think
it is false," said *South China Morning Post* columnist Jake Van der Kamp
during one such argument. Van der Kamp was raised in the most conservative branch of the Dutch Reformed Church – two services every Sunday,
prayers before every meal, Christian private school and Bible readings every day. "But this I do understand about Christianity, and most people who
have not gone through the Christian experience misapprehend," Van der
Kamp continued. "It's core is a set of detailed and explicit propositions, and
you must either accept or reject them. There is no middle ground. These
propositions are that we humans are by nature sinful creatures who could
never on our own be united with God, except that God himself came down
to earth in the form of his son, Jesus, who through his death on the cross,
expiated our sins. Jesus was then resurrected and redeems us to God, who
will grant us eternal life if we submit to him," Van der Kamp concluded as
the intellectually feeble listeners started wandering away.

James Carroll, a former Catholic priest, in his brilliantly researched book
Constantine's Sword: The Church and the Jews: A History, describes viv-
idly how the Roman tool of execution and what Jesus preached as a Jew
became the symbol and religion of the Roman Empire. Carroll carefully
walks the reader through the religious mythological maze that became

Christianity. He crystallizes how Augustus Constantine came to embrace Christianity as a practical political and religious vehicle to defeat his challengers and enemies by adopting the cross as his rallying standard. Its use as a tool of execution was then terminated.

The cross evolved as a symbol of violence when it was adorned on the garments of the crusaders. The crusaders started where the Holocaust ended. In Germany, Hitler's Final Solution tried to finish what the first crusade started. The first crusade set off from Northern Europe in 1096. "The cross-marked army's first act of belligerence took place in the Rhineland, not Jerusalem, and its target was not the Muslim infidel but the Jewish one," Carroll wrote. Christians were promised rewards in the afterlife and eternal salvation if they died in the struggle against the infidel. Violence became a religious act. No different than the Muslim suicide bombers of today.

Jesus became God in the way Emperor Constantine and his successors ordained him to be. Church and empire became one. A totalitarian Roman Catholic Empire. Constantine became Moses. Roman emperors became totalitarian Christian rulers. Jews became "servants of sin." The Catholic Church's anti-Semitic positions were adopted by the First Council of Nicaea in A.D. 325. It declared Jews to be "abhorrent to the will of God."

Their dress became prescribed, they were isolated in ghettos, barred from holding public office, forbidden to go out during Holy Week and taxed. The taxes were paid to the local Christian clergy. "The intimacy Jesus claimed to have with God the Father was made to seem unique, entirely his. More than anything else, to us it set him apart from Jews," Carroll concluded.

Carroll carefully walks the reader through his Catholic upbringing and realization of how Roman Catholics deliberately shifted the blame for Jesus' death from themselves to the Jews, who were portrayed as the agents of the devil. This image resulted in the anti-Semitism the world has experienced. The Catholic Church's mortal enemies became the triad, "Freemasons, Protestants, and Jews."

The Inquisition was against heretics – non-Catholics – Spanish Jews and Moors were the original targets from 1479 through the 18th century. But during the 16th and 17th centuries, captured English Protestants also were burned at the stake.

Many Jews converted to Christianity to avoid being killed. They were given a simple choice: convert or die. The forced conversions of Jews over the last two millennia created many Christians like Karl Marx, who were Jewish descendants of rabbis. Hundreds of thousands, if not millions, converted to avoid religious persecution.

During the Inquisition, that was the only way to survive. Even for Chinese in the Philippines. Many Filipino-Chinese converted to Catholicism during the Inquisition to avoid deportation, torture and death. Non-Christian Chinese were not employed by the Catholic. No different than Madeline Albright's parents and countless other Jews who converted during the Nazi Holocaust and endless pogroms. Now that their children have survived and prospered as Christians, they are getting in touch with their heritage while searching for spirituality.

During the 2004 U.S. presidential election, it was revealed that two of Sen. John Kerry's relatives, perished in the Holocaust and that his grandparents were Jewish. Sen. Kerry's grandfather was Fritz Kohn, a German Jew, who was born in 1873 in northern Moravia. After changing the name to Kerry and converting to the Catholic faith, the senator's grandparents immigrated to the U.S. in 1905. How many other Christians out there are really descendants of Jews?

It never ceases to amaze me how many people don't know their roots. Not just their religious roots, but their cultural, civilizational and personal roots, too. Many people today are stunned to find out they are what they despise.

Ralph Herman, a longtime friend who thought he was a pure German-Swedish WASP, and proud of it, was shocked to find out that not only was he Jewish, but a descendant of a rabbi and a distant relative of the Bronfmans.

When I wished him a happy Hanukkah, he was taken aback and became defensive – some might even say offensive. "Since my distant cousin never confirmed that I am the grandson of a rabbi, I not only don't celebrate Hanukkah, I have no idea what it is all about," he said.

"About the only knowledge I have is when the Dead Sea – or was it the Red Sea – parted and the group took a hike across the sands, they apparently ran across some Mexicans doing the same thing, who showed them how to bake tortillas on rocks, which they then named *matzos*.

"Actually, I thought they baked this stuff on their backs so they could keep traveling." Can you imagine what Ralph could accomplish in a Sunday school in an hour? Sounds like he was schooled in a Saudi-funded madrass.

How many millions of other Herman WASPS are there among us? Jewish blood has been mixed with Christian blood for the last two millennia. Just as European-Americans, African-Americans, Latin-Americans and Asian-Americans intermarried and blended races, so did Christians, Jews and Muslims. Christians, Jews and Muslims are blood brothers and sisters. New World Order Americans of the 21st century are pure hybrids. Physically, spiritually and culturally. Remove religious political agendas and they can live together in peace and prosper, as their brothers and sisters do in Hong Kong.

Anti-Semitism

Anti-Semitism is on the rise. Louis Farrakhan and his disciples have joined ranks with neo-Nazis to stoke the fires of anti-Semitism. Fueled by the Mel Gibson-directed anti-Semitic movie *The Passion of the Christ*, and then Mel Gibson himself in his Lexus, with a bottle of tequila, Jews are again being blamed for the death of Jesus – and his arrest. "Jews, it is often said, are the canary in the coal mine of civilization. When they become the objects of savagery and hate, it means the air has been poisoned and an explosion is soon to come. If Americans don't rise up and turn against the Jew-haters, the Jew-haters will rise up and turn against them," Jeff Jacoby wrote in 2002 in a opinion piece in the *Boston Globe*.

That is why the speech of Malaysian Prime Minister Mahathir Mohamad to the 57-member Organization of the Islamic Conference echoing Hitler's anti-Semitic pronouncements was noteworthy. "The Europeans killed 6 million Jews out of 12 million, but today the Jews rule the world by proxy," the former prime minister said. "They get others to fight and die for them," he continued. Jews "invented socialism . . human rights and democracy so that persecuting them would appear to be wrong, so that they can enjoy equal rights with others." Guess what: Mahathir received a standing ovation. For a man who doesn't drink, Mahatir comes out with amazing observations. Makes me wonder what he smokes.

Iranian President Mahmoud Ahmadinejad's comparison of Zionism to fascism in early 2006 was typical of the new anti-Semitism sweeping across the world.

With a neo-Nazi TV channel airing in Germany – and in the wake of Hitler's 21 watercolor paintings selling at an auction in 2006 at twice the expected price – one does have to wonder.

Having said that, America does appear to support Israel to the point that the U.S. is perceived as too supportive, and its tolerance of Israeli repression in the occupied territories arguably handicaps the war on terrorism.

Ahmadinejad

Amadinejad is a lost puppy in that his victorious campaign promises have proven to be yet another career politician's failed promises that *We the Maids* in Iran and America apathetically, angrily, and pathetically clued out and tuned out have accepted.

Born outside Tehran in 1956, he is the son of a blacksmith. He trained as a civil engineer, and during the Iran-Iraq War, joined the Revolutionary Guards. His biography remains strangely elliptical. He is believed to have been involved in the 1979 takeover of the U.S. Embassy, but he denies it. What exactly did he do during the war? His presidential website says he was "on active service as a *Basiji* volunteer as a combat engineer up to the end of the holy war against Iraq." He has positioned himself as the leader of the "second revolution" to eradicate corruption and Western influences from Iranian society – all non-starters doomed to fail.

The *Basiji* was composed of volunteers of illiterate conservative country boys between 12 and 17 and men over 45. They received a few weeks of training – more in theology than weapons and tactics. Upon graduation they received a blood-red headband that designated them for martyrdom. They made up nearly one-third of the Iranian army – and the majority of its infantry.

The chief combat tactic employed by the *Basiji* was the human wave attack, in which newly arrived children and teenagers would move continuously toward the enemy in perfectly straight rows. It didn't matter whether they fell to enemy fire or detonated the mines with their bodies. The important thing was that the *Basij* continued to move forward over the torn and mutilated remains of their fallen comrades, going to their deaths in wave after wave. Once a path to the Iraqi forces had been opened up, Iranian commanders would send in their more valuable and skilled Revolutionary Guards.

At the beginning of the war, Iran's ruling mullahs did not send human beings into the minefields. Donkeys, horses and dogs were the front line warriors. "After a few donkeys had been blown up, the rest ran off in terror," Mostafa Arki reports in his book *Eight Years of War in the Middle East*. Sounds like the Democrats they symbolize. Hey, what's wrong with the donkeys reacting normally in the face of death. Who wouldn't? The *Basiji*.

They marched fearlessly and without complaint to their deaths. The curious slogans they chanted while entering the battlefields are mind-boggling. "Against the Yazid of our time!" "Hussein's caravan is moving on!" "A new Karbala awaits us!"

Yazid, Hussein, Karbala – these are all references to the founding myth of Shia Islam. In the late seventh century, Islam was split between those loyal to the Caliph Yazid – the predecessors of Sunni Islam – and the founders of Shia Islam, who thought that the Imam Hussein, grandson of the Prophet Muhammad, should govern Muslims. In 680 AD, Hussein led an uprising against the "illegitimate" caliph, but he was betrayed. No surprise. On the plains of Karbala, on the 10th day of the month of Muharram, Yazid's forces attacked Hussein and his entourage and killed them. Hussein's corpse bore the marks of lance punctures and sword cuts. His head was cut off and his body trampled by horses. Is it any wonder Hussein's martyrdom has formed the core of Shia theology – which Saddam Hussein tried to replicate at his hanging – as a Sunni.

According to the Ayatollah Khomeini, life is worthless and death is the beginning of genuine existence. Really? ' The natural world," he explained in 1980, "is the lowest element, the scum of creation. What is decisive is the beyond. The divine world that is eternal." His words echo the latter world, created by the Catholic Church, which are now coming back, haunting and biting it in the ass in the form of suicide bombers.

In the world of martyrs – their death is no death, but merely the transition from this world to the world beyond, where they will live eternally either as mundane or spiritual victors, and in splendor. Whether the *Basiji* survived was irrelevant, Khomeini said in September 1980. Not even the tactical utility of their sacrifice mattered. Military victories were secondary. "The *Basiji*," Khomeini said "must understand that he is a 'soldier of God' for whom it is not so much the outcome of the conflict as the mere participation in it that provides fulfillment and gratification." Right. Something Americans must keep in mind at all times in Afghanistan and Iraq, yet alone Iran. Could Khomeniei's antipathy for life have had as much effect in the war against Iraq without Karbala? No way, Jose, as America is finding out first hand, the hard way in Karbala – and the rest of Iraq. With the word "Karbala" on their lips, the *Basiji* went elatedly into battle and their death. Is this any way to raise our children? With knowledge, they will hopefully be wiser and smarter and enjoy life.

The *Basiji*, like the U.S. troops in Afghanistan and Iraq, were nothing more than sacrificial lambs at the almighty altar of *We the Apathetic People-Maids*.

Let's not forget the U.S. was once on the other side, supporting Saddam Hussein. The pictures of Saddam and U.S. special envoy Donald Rumsfeld at the time are more memorable than ever, given the recent hanging of one and the resignation of the other. Karma, coincidence or synchronicity?

Bottom line, Iran has the martyrs necessary to fight America's and Israel's geopolitical agendas – and will, unless treated with the respect it deserves. The *Basiji* ranks have grown dramatically since the Iran-Iraq War, from the more conservative religious and impoverished communities of the country. During Ahmadinejad's presidential run, millions of *Basiji* in every town, neighborhood and mosque became his unofficial grass-roots campaign workers – 12 percent of Iran's population are *Basijis*. More importantly, a younger generation of Iranians, like Ahmadinejad, whose world views were forged in the ugliness of the Iran-Iraq War, have come to power. The children of the revolution are now its leaders. How many Americans are as committed?

Compare Bush to his counterparts in the Middle East and one easily understands why America has the short end of the stick.

No wonder World Cup soccer overtook the nuclear agenda and discussions in the summer of 2006. Soccer is Iran's national game. Is it any wonder why Ahmadinejad made his proposal that women not only attend soccer games, but play.

Neo-Nazi Islamaphobia – "Eurabia"

Neo-Nazis are on the comeback trail, not just in Germany, but the rest of Europe, America and Israel. Ironically, it was America that helped many of Hitler's Nazi henchmen go free, regroup and reseed the new neo-Nazis. America suppressed the whereabouts of Nazi war criminals to protect high-ranking West German officials, who were themselves Nazis. The CIA recruited Nazi war criminals as agents during the Cold War with the Soviet Union. They are now active trying to figure the Final Solution for Muslims – how to keep the Muslims out of Europe and what to do with those in Eurabia.

Many of the Nazis saved by America found their way to Latin America, which became home to many Nazis. Paul Schaefer, an 84-year-old unrepentant Nazi, is a case in point. He ran a secretive German enclave behind barbed wire in Chile, where he abused German and Chilean children with impunity. He was sentenced to 20 years in jail in 2006 for the abuse of 25 children. He fled similar charges in his native Germany in 1961. Schaefer, a former corporal and medic in the Nazi SS and later a Lutheran pastor, faces further charges of torture, kidnap and murder by using his Colonia Dignidad, or Dignity Colony, to help his Nazi sympathiser friend General Augusto Pinochet get rid of opponents.

He purchased the 70 square miles of forest and farmland which reminded him of Bavaria for his colony with financial support from the underground network of escaped Nazis in South America.

Today's Nazis direct their venom and hatred not just at Jews, but at Muslims. Europe's Muslims face deep-seated discrimination in education, housing and jobs and on the streets, where they are attacked by skinheads.

The European Union has 15 million Muslims, making it the second-largest religious grouping in the 25-nation bloc. As they grow in numbers, so does the discrimination and anti-Muslim Islamaphobia. This was showcased on the global stage during the 2006 World Cup in Germany when Italian defender Marco Materazzi called France's Zinedine Zidane "the son of a terrorist whore," before adding some juicy F words for good measure, resulting in the head butt that led to Zidane being expelled from the final.

Germany demonstrated its resolve to reach out to the more than 3 million Muslims living there by having leaders of the Muslim community and German government join hands and go together to see Berlin's reinstated Mozart opera "Idomeneo." It had been cancelled after receiving an anonymous threat. The production features a scene with the severed head of the Prophet Muhammad.

Self-censorship is not the way to end fundamentalist extremism, Muslim or Christian. Sharing ideas and exchanging knowledge is.

Right Road

The road to understanding other religions and interpretations of history in the 21st century is being built by professors Dan Bar-On, a social psychology professor at Ben Gurion University in Israel, and Sami Adwan, an education professor at Bethlehem University in the West Bank. Together, with teams of Israeli and Palestinian historians, they devised a series of booklets that set the competing versions of history side-by-side on the same pages for Israeli and Palestinian students. The professors say the project is an effort to bridge the chasm between the two peoples. "The way a conflict or history is taught in the classroom can either support that conflict or support coexistence," Adwan said. "The project aims to break down the stereotypes and build nuanced understandings." Added Bar-On: "What we're talking about is the disarming of history, where the teaching of history no longer feeds the conflict."

One student's hero can no longer be the other's terrorist if true knowledge is to be imparted to our children.

Jews, Jesus and early Christians, like all true believers, preached love and tolerance. Religious teachings of loving each other, neighbor, friend and foe have to again become cornerstones of civilization in the 21st century if we are to survive.

Jesus the Muslim

Unlike early Christianity, which was highly critical and blasphemous of all other religions and sought to establish a single dogma, Islam and Judaism studied and were complimentary of Christ. Islam regards Isa as the last great prophet before Muhammad.

Twenty-four of the 25 Islamic prophets are also Christian figures. Tarif Khalidi, an Islamic scholar at King's College in Cambridge, wrote *The Muslim Jesus*, which presents more than 300 stories and sayings adopted or modified by Muslim clerics to suit their needs. They show the efforts that sages made to claim Jesus as a spiritual guide. The essential common theme is the attack on hypocrisy. They started appearing within 100 years of Muhammad's death in 632. Khalidi calls his collection "a Muslim gospel." Early Islam, like Judaism, was a lot more accommodating than Christianity.

The book presents a valid east-west parallel by chronicling a 14th-century collection by the lawmaker al-Subki, in which Jesus is still a cherished figure, instructing Muslims that "the rich shall not enter the kingdom of Heaven." At about the same time, Dante consigned Muhammad to cruel suffering in "Inferno." Such dramatically different treatments can be explained by the fact that Imperial Islam was flourishing while Western Christianity was in turmoil. "Amid the current tensions between Christianity and Islam," Khalidi wrote, "it is salutary to remind ourselves of an age and a tradition when Christianity and Islam were more open to each other, more aware of and reliant on each other's witness."

Jesus' mother Mary is the most honored woman in Islam, and the only one to have an entire chapter named after her in the Koran. Muslim beliefs about Mary seem to be quite close to those of the Roman Catholic Church. The Islamic tradition holds that Jesus and his mother are the only two human souls who were not touched by Satan at birth.

The Unchosen People

With all the persecution Jews have been subjected to, it is understandable if they occasionally wonder what the benefits of being the chosen people are. I have had this discussion on more than one occasion with fellow challengers of faith. An e-mail I received from one of my fellow doubters, who happens to be a Catholic, summed it up best. It was a proposed e-mail that Jews send to God.

"To: The Lord G-d Almighty
From: The Jews: a.k.a. The Chosen People
Subject: Termination of Contract/Special Status (Chosen People)

As you are aware, the contract made between you and Abraham is up for renewal, and this memorandum is to advise you that after, yea, those many millennia of consideration, we, the Jews (The Chosen People) have decided that we really do not wish to renew.

We should point out immediately that there is nothing in writing, and contrary to popular beliefs, we (The Jews) have not really benefited too much from this arrangement. If you go back to the early years of our arrangement, it definitely started off on the wrong footing. Not only was Israel and Judea invaded almost every year, but we also went to enormous expense to erect not one but two Temples, and they were both destroyed.

All we have is a pile of old stones called the Western Wall (of course ,you know all this, but we feel it's a good thing to account for all the reasons we wish to terminate the contract.)

After the Hittites, Assyrians, Goliaths, etc, not only were we beaten up almost daily, but then we were sold off as slaves to Egypt of all countries, and really lost a few hundred years of development.

Now we realize that you went to a great deal of trouble to send Moses to lead us out of Egypt, and those poor Egyptian buggers were smitten with all those plagues. But, reflecting on those years, we are at a loss to understand why it took almost forty years to make a trip that El Al now does in 75 minutes. Also, while not appearing to be ungrateful, for years a lot of people have asked why Moses led us left instead of right at Sinai? If we had gone right, we would have had the oil!

OK, so the oil was not part of the deal, but then the Romans came and we really were up to our necks in dreck. While it's true that the Romans did give us water fit to drink, aqueducts and baths, it was very disconcerting to walk down one of the streets, look up, and see one of your friends or family nailed to a three-by-four looking for all the world like a sign post. Even one of our princes, Judah Ben Hur, got caught up with Roman stuff and drove like a crazy man around the Coliseum. It's a funny thing but many people swore that Ben Hur had an uncanny resemblance to Moses ... go figure.

Then of all things, one of our rabbis (teachers) declared himself 'Son of You' (there was nothing said about this with Abe) and before we knew what was what, a whole new religion sprang up. To add insult to injury, we were dispersed all over the world two or three times while this new religion really caught on! We were truly sorry to hear that the Romans executed him like so many others, but, ... alas (and this will make you laugh), once again WE were blamed. Now here's something we really don't understand. That our rabbi really came into his own. Millions of people revered and worshipped his name and scriptures ... and still killed us by the millions.

They claimed we drank the blood of newborn infants, and controlled the world banks (if only that were so). We could have bought them all off, and operated the world's media and so on and so on. Are we beginning to make our point here?

OK, so let's fast-forward a few hundred years to the Crusades. Oh boy! Again we were caught in the middle! They, the lords and knights, came from all over Europe to smack the Arabs and open up the holy places, but before we knew what hit us, they were killing us right and left, and center along with everyone else. Every time a king or a pope was down in the opinion polls, they called a crusade or a holy war, and went on a killing rampage in our land.

Today it's called jihad. OK, so you tested us a little there, but then some bright cleric in Spain came up with the Inquisition. We all thought it was a new game show, but once again we and quite a few others were used as firewood for a whole new street lighting arrangement in major Spanish cities. All right, so that ended after about a hundred years or so – in the scheme of things not a long time. But every time we settled down in one country or another, they kicked us out! So we wandered around a few hundred years or so, but it never changed. Finally we settled in a few countries but they insisted we all live in ghettoes ... no Westchester's of Moscow for us. There we were in ghettoes, when what do you know?

The Russians come up with the pogroms. We all thought they made a spelling mistake and misspelled programs, but we were dead wrong (no pun intended). Apparently, when there was nothing else for them to do, killing the Jews (a.k.a. the chosen people, are you getting our drift?) was the in thing.

Now comes some really tough noogies. We were doing quite well, thank you, in a small European country called Germany, when some house painter wrote a book, said a few things that caught on and became their leader. Boy, what a bad day that was for us...you know... your chosen people.

We don't really know where you were in the earth years 1940 to 1945. We know everyone needs a break now and then...even Lord G-d Almighty needs some time off. But really...when we needed you most, you were never around.

You are probably aware of this, but if you have forgotten, over 6 million of your Chosen People, along with quite a few unchosen others were murdered. They even made lampshades out of our skins.

Look, we don't want to dwell on the past, but it gets worse!

Here we are, it's 1948, and millions of us are displaced yet again, when you really pull a fast one. We finally get our own land back! Yes!!! After all these years, you arrange for us to go back...then all the Arab countries immediately declare war on us.

We have to tell you that sometimes your sense of humor really eludes us. OK, so we win all the wars, but it's now 2006 and nothing's changed. We keep getting blown up, hijacked and kidnapped. We have no peace whatsoever. Enough is enough.

So, we hope that you understand that nothing's forever (except you, of course) and we respectfully would like to pull out of our verbal agreement vis-a-vis being your chosen people.

Look, sometimes things work out, sometimes they don't. Let's be friends over the next few eons and see what happens. How about this? We're sure you recall that Abraham had a whole other family from Ishmael (the ones who got the oil). How about making them your chosen people for a few thousand years?

Respectfully,
The Committee To Be Un-Chosen"

Harambee! Feliz Hanukkah

Mid-December has been the time for celebration and compassion since ancient times. From the Near and Middle East Mithra and Osiris cultures to the Roman Saturnalia to the Norse Yule. In the fourth century, the church decided to fix December 25 as Christ's birthday to take advantage of all those celebrations. After all, Jesus, teachings called for compassion to all. Marketing, consumerism and political spin doctoring at its finest.

The winter solstice, which means the shortest day of the year, falls in the last week of December, specifically during the period from December 22nd to the 25th. That means the days after begin to get longer and bring more light, life and laughter in their wake. Hanukkah, Christmas and Kwanzaa are celebrated during this time. Harambee is the call of African-Americans to commence Kwanzaa, a seven-day festival between Christmas and New Year's. Each day a candle is lighted atop the kinara, a candleholder representing the seven principles that serve as a compass for many black families. Hanukah, with the lighting of eight candles atop the menorah, is a remarkable model. Kwanzaa began in 1966 as a reaffirmation of the kinship of native Africans and African-Americans.

Racism – Historical & Current

The race to liberate Paris on August 24, 1944, was a deliberate whites-only racist force. General Philippe Leclerc's was hand-picked for the task five months earlier. It was chosen partly because it was French but, more specifically, because its soldiers were white. British and American generals insisted that brown and black French colonial troops should be excluded from the liberation of Paris. What an insult to the North African troops who fought in Italy and southern and eastern France in 1943-44 against the Nazi Germans and Fascist Italians.

There were 550,000 men in the French army in 1944. They were partly assembled from the Free French forces that had gathered around General Charles de Gaulle in Britain from 1940. Many others were recruited – not always voluntarily – in the French African colonies. There were 134,000 Algerians, 73,000 Moroccans, 26,000 Tunisians and 92,000 men from colonies in black Africa. Nevertheless, the only way the French could participate in the liberation of Paris was if they came up with an all-white liberation force. "I have made it clear to the French that we would accept only with great reluctance anything but troops from France proper. It is unfortunate that the only white French unit is an armoured division stationed in Morocco. The other French divisions are only 40 percent white. I told the French authorities that they would get a place in the invasion force far more easily if they could produce a division of white infantry," said British General Frederick Morgan, the officer who headed the D-Day planning team.

Not much has changed. Today the media is periodically inundated with contemporary racist incidents. Britain's Celebrity Big Brother participant's racist remark to India's Bollywood star Shilpa Shetty, created international diplomatic incidents. But she prevailed, got the votes, won and the last laugh. Is racism and prejudice part of human nature?

The Virgina Tech student killings by a South Korean triggered racist reprisals against South Koreans and all other Asians because of ignorance – the same ignorance that got Indian Sikhs killed in hate crimes after 9/11 by Americans who thought they were Muslim-Arabs because they "are towel heads."

A Chinese-American student, Allen Lee, was arrested because of what he wrote in a creative writing class. The racist and religious tensions rippling across America, especially between the Sunnis and Shiites in Michigan, New Jersey's Arab community, is swelling and threatens to become a religious tsunami. Shiite students in universities across America face repeated discrimation by the Sunni-dominated Muslim Student Association. They have formed their own association because they are barred from leading prayers in the Sunni associations because they are labelled heretics. They are not only fighting over America's invasion of Iraq, but who has the right to interpret the scriptures and teachings of Muhammad.

Saudi Terror Grouping

The history of Osama bin Laden and al-Qaeda is deeply rooted in Saudi religious and dynastic politics and in an effort by Iraq and Syria to shift the balance of power in the Middle East. Why has this not been more widely discussed in the mainstream media?

In June 1982, Saudi Crown Prince Fahd ascended to his country's throne and reinvigorated Wahhabism. He gave himself the title "Protector of the Two Holy Places" – or Khadim al Haramayn al Sharifain. Locals tweaked the title to Khadim al Hariymayn al Sharifain – "Guardian of the Two Holy Harems." In 1995, a succession struggle began in the House of Saud after the self-indulgent, 300-pound King Fahd suffered a debilitating stroke. The king had difficulty recognizing family members. Nevertheless, the octogenarian King Fahd bin Abdul-Aziz, and his full-blooded brothers in the Sudairi branch of the family, including the defense minister, Prince Sultan, himself in his mid-seventies, were pitted against their half-brother, Crown Prince Abdullah, also in his seventies. It was an antiquated, undemocratic family enterprise whose rules of succession changed at the whim of an incapacitated monarch. Prince Bandar – Prince Sultan's son, the former ambassador to Washington who was spirited out of the country with bin Laden family members, royals and Saudi family friends after 9/11 – admitted to PBS Frontline that the royal family "misused or got corrupted" to the tune of $50 billion over the years. "What I'm trying to tell you is, so what? We did not invent corruption," Prince Bandar said.

Since when does one have to invent what they enjoy and profit from? The question is whether it was right, and should it be perpetuated. Or should it be swept out by We the Maids?

Fahd, who died in 2005, favored close ties with the U.S. King Abdullah prefers closer ties with Syria, Iran and Iraq, three nations that lead the challenge to the U.S. and are generally more enamored of pan-Islamic and pan-Arab ideas. Abdullah is also closely allied with the puritanical Wahhabi religious establishment, which has underpinned the Saudi government for over a century.

The Wahhabis oppose the American presence in the Middle East. They made this explicit in 1990 in a pronouncement known as the Muzkara an-Nasiha, originated by bin Laden and signed by virtually every sheikh in the Wahhabi establishment. It condemned Saudi Arabia's decision to allow U.S. troops and the coalition forces into the kingdom to stage the first Gulf War.

King Abdullah's determination to secure his throne, which led to his strategic relationship with Syrian President Hafez Assad, and their joint willingness to cooperate with Iran is essential background to the major terrorist attacks of recent years. When Abdullah invited Syrian intelligence into Saudi Arabia in the early '90s, he created an opportunity for Syria to foster a terror network on Saudi soil. The Khobar Towers bombing in 1996, which killed 19 American servicemen, originated in Syrian-controlled Lebanon. Less than 60 days after 9/11, members of the Syrian-backed Hezbollah were indicted in a U.S. court for the attack.

Once Syria and Iran became bedfellows against America, the Palestinian Authority became sufficiently established, and Abdullah invited Syria into the kingdom, finally, all the ingredients for the bin Laden network converged inside this Wahhabi/Abdullah-Syria-Iran-Hamas strategic alliance that became al-Qaeda.

"While al-Qaeda from the start was rooted in the Wahhabi religious establishment, it sprouted and flourished parasitically wherever Syrian, Iraqi and Saudi intelligence felt secure; Sudan, then Yemen and Qatar," said David Wurmser, the director of Middle East Studies at the American Enterprise Institute. "Bin Laden himself left Saudi Arabia in 1991 for Sudan, where he lived until his removal, via Yemen and Qatar, to Afghanistan in 1996."

Bin Laden did this with the backing and financial support of the U.S. government, which had the opportunity to arrest him if it wanted to. That, however, would have offended the House of Saud and the oil industry. And they already were made to suffer the incarceration of Bader Al-Saud, a member of the Saudi royal family who was convicted of killing Orlando Ramos in 2005 while driving drunk outside Boston. The judge allowed Bader's request that he serve his one-year sentence at the jail on Martha's Vineyard.

At its core, al-Qaeda is a product of Saudi dynastic politics. Its purpose is to swing Saudi politics toward the Wahhabi establishment and King Abdullah. The most virulent of Saudi dissident groups, such as al-Masari's Committee for the Defense of Legal Rights, calls for violence, but they pointedly direct their wrath against the Sudairis, the only target they mention by name. Bin Laden seeks to destroy the Sudairis indirectly, by separating them from America.

Since Abdullah took over for the ailing Fahd in the mid-1990s, Saudi intelligence, in the opinion of many intelligence analysts, has become difficult to distinguish from al-Qaeda. Bin Laden went to school with Prince Turki ibn Faisal, a young royal who became chief of Istakhbarat, the Saudi intelligence services. Saudi intelligence had served as bin Laden's nexus to the Wahhabi network of charities, foundations and other funding sources. This should come as no surprise as the bin Laden and Faisal families have long-standing ties. Wurmser said that ' bin Laden emerged from a dangerous strategic shift underway since 1995 that was driven by dynastic rivalries. Now al-Qaeda must be dealt with not only in Afghanistan, but also at its source in the strategic triangle of Syria, Iraq and the Wahhabi/Abdullah alliance, whose interests it serves and whose structures and politics brought it to life. To fail to strike at the roots of al-Qaeda will only lengthen the war that makes it more deadly."

Is it any wonder the Saudis lectured the U.S. against an attack on Iraq when Vice President Dick Cheney toured Arab nations before the eventual attack and occupation. "It is a mistake to think that our people will not do what is necessary to survive," King Abdullah said in 2003 on the way to Crawford, Texas, to meet President Bush. "If that means we move to the right of bin Laden, so be it, or fly to Baghdad and embrace Saddam like a brother, so be it. It's damned lonely in our part of the world, and we can no longer defend our relationship to our people." The time to call his bluff is long overdue.

A letter released by a group of 126 Saudi scholars and writers in the week when Abdullah was visiting Crawford proclaimed: "We consider the United States and its current administration a first-class sponsor of international terrorism, and it along with Israel form an axis of terrorism and evil in the world." Talk about the pot calling the kettle black. Actually, the statement is partially true. The U.S. has sponsored terrorism, but not in Israel. In Saudi Arabia, Algeria, Egypt, Angola, Indonesia and numerous other places in Africa, Asia, the Middle East and South and Central America, and it's done with warlords who control the oil America and the developed world need.

Relations between Muslims and the West will continue to deteriorate unless the internal crisis of the Muslim world is addressed. The root is the government-sponsored propaganda that usually focuses on Muslim humiliation at the hands of others instead of acknowledging the self-inflicted flaws of Muslim leaders. The focus on external enemies causes Muslims to admire power rather than ideas. Warriors, and not scholars or inventors, are generally the heroes of the common people. That is why the warrior Osama bin Laden is worshipped by the Muslim masses – even though he is determined to destroy the Saudi royal family and the oil facilities that keep it in power.

In the Post-Colonial period, military leaders in the Muslim world have consistently taken advantage of the popular fascination with military power. The Muslim cult of the warrior explains also the relatively muted response in the Muslim world to atrocities committed by fellow Muslims. The genocide being committed in Sudan by Muslim militia is a 21st-century example. "Ironically, Western governments have consistently tried to deal with one manifestation of the cult of the warrior – terrorism – by building up Muslim strongmen who are just another manifestation of the same phenomenon," said Husain Haqqani, a visiting scholar at the Carnegie Endowment for International Peace who served as an adviser to Pakistani Prime Ministers Benazir Bhutto and Nawaz Sharif.

"Osama bin Laden and those like him didn't spring, fully formed, from the desert sand. They were made," Carmen bin Laden, Osama's siste-in-law wrote in her book *Inside The Kingdom*. "They were fashioned by the workings of an opaque and intolerant Medieval society that is closed to the outside world. It is a society where half the population have had their basic rights as people amputated, and obedience to the strictest rules of Islam must be absolute. Despite all the power of their oil revenue, the Saudis are structured by a hateful, backward-looking view of religion and an education that is a school for intolerance.... When Osama dies, I fear there will be a thousand men to take his place."

The Saudis grudgingly woke up to this reality when *jihad* started hitting home in Saudi Arabia. With an unemployment rate rising by 100,000 men a year and a growing impatience with the extravagant lives of the royal family, Saudis desperately want political reforms but fear the chaos that will follow. Nevertheless, many believe that strong government institutions could run the country more effectively than a few aging princes beholden to the Wahhabi religious doctrines. Most conservative Wahhabi clerics in the kingdom believe that if they took democracy to mean the rule of the people, that would go against the principle of Islam because in Islam that is God's right. Is it? Or is it time *Muslim Maids* sweep it out?

Modern Truths
One of the biggest mistakes in Islam's history was its refusal to accept the printing press. It was seen as a potential instrument of "sacrilege and heresy." The Muslims, like the Catholic Church, denied their believers and martyrs contemporary knowledge – the truth. The truth is the most important ingredient in the political philosophy *We the Maids* have to sweep in. New knowledge is not *bid'a* – heresy. It is the most empowering aphrodisiac.

The truth is that many of the Saudi princes, notably Bandahar and Alwaheed, are modernists who want to lead Saudi Arabia into the modern world. Unfortunately, they are in the minority in their own country.

The House of Saud depends on the most radical southern and eastern clans for their political base. The southern faction is the center of popular support for al-Qaeda and the Taliban because it is the home of the most extreme Muslim sect, the Wahabbis. Ninety percent of the Muslim world rejects the Wahabbi religious tenets as utterly repugnant to the teachings and examples of the prophet as written in the Hadith.

Since most Wahabbis are functionally illiterate, they cannot read about this conflict on their own. Typically they memorize a few passages of the Koran taken out of context, and are unaware of the explanations contained in the accompanying Hadith. The Wahabbis, for example, are taught that Jews are subhumans and should be killed as a religious duty. In contrast, the Hadith explains that the Prophet Muhammad honored Jews, married a Jewish woman and forbade forced conversions of Jews, or any religion. He always bowed in respect when a Jewish funeral passed, and promised that good and faithful Jews would go to paradise just as good Muslims and Christians would. He taught that the Jews had their holy place in the west, meaning Jerusalem, while Muslims had their holy place in the east – Mecca.

The austere teachings of Mohammad bin Abd al-Wahhab have been prevalent in Saudi Arabia for more than two centuries. The House of Saud owes its control of the fractious tribes of the Arabian Peninsula to the fact that ancestors championed his teachings. Bookshops in Mecca and Medina sell 1,265-page souvenir tomes of his "greatest hits" *fatwas* or religious edicts. Most are rulings mandating the shunning of non-Muslims: do not smile at them, don't wish them well on their holidays and don't call them "friend." Muslims living in foreign lands are ordered to "harbor enmity and hatred for infidels." If we didn't have to fill up our SUVs, would we have to bother with these people? And would these people have enough money to be a bother anyway?

The Saudi royal family and their Wahabbi protagonists have decreed that women cannot work or even sit in the front seat of a car – and that includes the Saudi Queen. In contrast, the Hadith records that the prophet worked for his wife, and that she drove her own caravans in international commerce. The prophet forbade racism, whereas the Wahabbis practice it, especially against their non-Arab Shiite minority. The Wahabbis discriminate viciously against women. The prophet, who lovingly raised three daughters, insisted that women should have essentially equal rights in contract, ownership and divorce.

The Muslim faith envisioned by the prophet in the Koran and recorded by his contemporaries in the Hadith practices tolerance toward all races and religions, stresses the extreme importance of literacy and education, and elevates the status of women to unprecedented levels. This is the gentle, peaceful Muslim faith practiced everywhere in the world, except in Saudi Arabia and the Taliban provinces in Afghanistan and Pakistan. Something Christian Europeans should keep in mind because a strong case can be made that most of Europe today is post-Christian and that by the end of the 21st century, Islam will be the dominant religion. The Crusades will be fought all over again before that happens – on European soil.

Muslim scholars speak derisively about the primitive Wahabbi apostasy, but rarely in public. The reason for this deafening silence is simple. Most mosques are impoverished and depend upon Saudi subsidies for their survival and operation. In return, the Saudis have gained a foothold for proselytizing and radicalizing the Muslim youth through religious education. Children hate because they are being taught to hate.

Discussing Islam and the destructiveness of Wahabbism and Muslim fundamentalists with Malaysian and Saudi beer-drinking Muslims in May 2007, at the pool bar at the Berjaya Langkawi Beach & Spa Resort on Langkawi Island, in Kedah, Malaysia, man, did I get a jolt from the Cuba Libre, or was it the wake-up call of how constructive and educational it is to talk to the people we read about. Interaction in our interlocal world is essential to break down the artificial political barriers erected by career politicians and religious teachers.

I was pleasantly surprised and taken aback by Abdul, an American- educated engineer, who suddenly changed the subject to the destructiveness of Christian fundamentalists when he said: "Look at what is going on in Washington with Paul Wolfowitz, a Jew, and Shaha Riza, his Arab girlfriend. Is he really being removed as the head of the World Bank for ethics violations and conflict of interest, or are the European Christians persecuting him for being a Jew who is dating an Arab he promoted – who was more than qualified for the salary she received – unlike so many other Bush Christian cronies who are untouchables?" Before I could respond, he added: "It is examples like this that give Muslim fundamentalists ammunition to support their argument, 'Why bother being secular like Shaha. You get punished by the infidels. Stay pure and fight the infidel to get our way is the only way to defeat the infidel crusaders.'"

For a guy whose wife, sitting poolside under an umbrella, dressed like a ninja warrior in black from top to bottom, except for the slit for her eyes to witness the free world and women around her in skimpy bikinis, especially the Chinese from Hong Kong and Macau, forever competing for male attention, while eyeing the Japanese geishas frolicking in the pool to see who is more anorexic and desirable, must have been amusing, as I suspect she was an educated Arab woman who has probably done the same somewhere in the West, to be with a guy like Abdul. What was going on in her head?

Muhammad, a Malaysian real estate developer, and I looked at each other before he responded. "That is nonsense. The law is the law and has to be applied equally to all. Jews, Muslims and Christians. For Muslim fundamentalists to say this is another Christian crusade only perpetuates hatred and ignorance."

"Hear, hear," I said as I raised my Cuba Libre, ordered a round for everyone, explained what the alcohol was – and Ernest Hemingway's favorite drink. Once the drinks arrived, we toasted Muhammad's retort and ordered another round. Since Arabs invented alcohol, for a fleeting moment I thought of making a toast to Saudi Libre.

It is time for Arabs to face reality. "Only by facing facts can the Arabs begin to cut their losses instead of letting them mount along with their problems. Only then will they be capable of joining the world in its war against 'terror,' instead of abdicating responsibility by asserting that there is no proof that the suicide hijackers were Arabs, or by claiming that the crime was the work of Israel," wrote Khairallah Khairallah, a Lebanese journalist in 2005. Arab refusal to face up to this is an act of pure denial. It is like refusing to acknowledge that the Arabs let the industrial revolution pass them by two centuries ago, just as they are currently failing to keep pace with the communications revolution that began in the 1980s – except for the foreign-educated fundamentalists and suicide bombers like bin-Laden and Muhammad Atta, who headed the 9/11 suicide mission.

We the Apathetic Maids, Arabs and Saudis in particular, have to accept the fact that if America is to re-assert its primary role in the 21st century, it can no longer be bought with oil money through its retired elected officials, especially former presidents and their key cabinet officials, state and defense leading the geopolitical charge, for the highest paying retainers, with their cadres of bureaucrats, lawyers and lobbyists, like former presidents George H.W. Bush and Jimmy Carter. American ex-presidents and their key entourages are for sale to the highest bidder. No different than the best gun-slinger in America's Wild West and their forebearers, the Border Reivers. Columbia has put former president Bill Clinton in its corner. Does that sound right? That's what is going on because We the Apathetic Maids are so dumbed down and tuned out. Obviously our choice. C'mon. Let's get real. When the extensive financial connections between Arab oil money, particularly from Saudi Arabia and former U.S. presidents has been so extensively written about in books, articles and aired on TV and countless digital portals, I can't figure out why We the Maids keep cleaning up the mess these cabals have created. Politicians with apparent integrity get repeatedly bought off by the highest bidders, Arabs, led by the Saudis, Israel, Japan and Taiwan.

Alan M. Dershowitz, the Felix Frankfurter professor of law at Harvard Law School, criticized former president Jimmy Carter for continuously accepting money from anti-Semitic Saudis hell-bent on killing Jews, while he accepts money from Jews. Dershowitz reminds us of the bad old Harvard of the 1930s, which continued to honor Nazi academics after the anti-Semitic policies of Hitler's government became clear. Harvard of the 1930s was complicit in evil.

So are former U.S. presidents and their courtiers at the expense of *We the Apathetic Maids.*

If Americans and Arabs really want to be able to deal with the post-9/11 world, they need to ask themselves some painfully candid questions. What are the reasons that prompted 19 young Arabs to blow themselves up in America? Who is to blame for that? What role did Arab societies play in spawning such people? Is there a problem with the Arab media, and with Arab cultural and religious discourse? Are the education systems at fault? Who is bearing the brunt of these faults? *The UN Arab Human Development Report*, prepared exclusively by Arabs, concluded that a prime cause for the backwardness in the Arab world is that Arabs are the world's least free people, with the lowest levels of popular participation in government. Few Arab opinion-makers dispute or doubt their society's desperate need for far-reaching reforms that usher in democracy, human rights and accountability. Christian fundamentalists in America aren' far behind.

When the Taliban were expelled from Afghanistan, smiles came to the faces of Afghan children, women and old men. Their beards and burkas were shed and their hidden radios blasted forbidden tunes. Modern times, technology and the truth cannot be suppressed indefinitely.

Islam has not undergone a renaissance or a reformation. In present conditions, it is not likely to, which is why it feels so threatened. The materialistic, highly technical and sub-Christian forces that dominate cause Muslims deep insecurity. "Mainstream Islam," as liberals hopefully describe it, is no such thing. It is a broad, muddy estuary with no direction. The forces of radical conservatism, the fundamentalists, have nothing to draw on culturally or spiritually but the desert. They want to return to the purity and simplicity and authority of the caliphate, the fusion of absolute secular and spiritual power, a power-down-ruled land area, exclusive of all non-Muslims and their influences.

It is a pipe dream. Against all the promises of wealth from liberal, pluralist capitalism, the ease and attraction of consumer goods, electronic gadgetry and accessories, entertainment and on-tap eroticism, the cyber world and Internet search engines, oceans of exported alcohol, and the massive international black market in narcotics, the caliphate does not stand a chance. Apart from a stern romanticism, it has nothing to offer the secular Muslim – the sort of Muslim who goes to pray on Friday when he or she can.

Fundamentalism can fire up a mob and bring out resentments. But even if the mob put the fundamentalists in power on a wave of populist issues, like reaction to Israel, or American high-handedness, or rich rulers, or Chinese merchants, when the masses begin to feel the caliphate bearing down, when they experiece the laws that forbid, they will resent their new rulers. In time the fundamentalists will be the oppressors. They will not keep the masses with them as prosperity wanes. The West will remain unmoved, abundant in the export of its delicious corruptions, lapping at the caliphate's borders, hovering over it in cyber space, trickling in through the drains.

Al-Qaeda's killings are futile. Religious reaction will not grip future generations. Liberalism, pluralism and drugs probably will.

Muslims are a diverse community of more than 850 million people and 190 ethnic groups living in 37 countries. These nations control most of the world's oil and possess many of its most powerful armies and fanatical suicide bombers. In the New World Order, it is therefore imperative that democracy sprout there like oil gushers if We the People are to survive the 21st century.

Religious Political Reform

The resurgence of Islam and the Protestant Reformation have a lot in common. Both were reactions to the stagnation and corruption of existing institutions. They advocate a return to a purer and more demanding form of their religion: preach work, order and discipline. Both appeal to an emerging, dynamic middle-class. They are complex movements, with diverse strands. Christian strands include Lutheranism and Calvinism. Islamic strands – Shiite and Sunni fundamentalism. Both John Calvin and the Ayatollah Khomeini advocated a monastic discipline. The central spirit of both the Reformation and the Resurgence is fundamental reform.

The echoes of voices preaching a neo-Puritan revival have not been lost or gone unheeded in the United States, as seen during calls for Clinton's impeachment. Kevin Phillips wrote of the Clinton impeachment proceedings in his 1999 book *The Cousin's War:* "Americans, in particular, face the possibility that the continuing upheaval in Washington could bring about a religious revival and a related neo-Puritanism. The first-ever impeachment trial of an elected U.S. president, amid what is already described as a cultural civil war, could be leading toward a moral and ideological Gettysburg."

Final decades of centuries are often psychologically convulsive. In the United States, the upheavals of the 1790s – which saw the radicalism of Thomas Paine and the scoffing at religion so prominent in the French Revolution – led in the early 1800s to a great religious counter tide called the Second Great Awakening. With the 1990s counting down, the fear in Manhattan, Martha's Vineyard and Malibu was that President Clinton might have been the inadvertent provocateur of another such reversal. This is not so far-fetched. Even non-religious China has drafted new laws to crack down on adultery. But in the English-speaking world, morality and religion have a long history of being intertwined.

Does human DNA predispose people toward religious faith? The notion of a genetic inclination toward religion is not new. Edward Wilson, the founder of the field of sociobiology, argued in the 1970s that a predisposition to religion may have had evolutionary advantages. The evidence is explored in *The God Gene*, a book by Dean Hamer, a prominent American geneticist. Hamer identifies the particular gene as VMAT2. He found people with one variant of the gene to be more spiritual and those with another less so. This would probably scare the religious right as much as stem-cell research.

One bit of evidence supporting Hamer's genetic influence on spirituality is that twins separated at birth tend to have similar levels of spirituality, despite their different upbringing. And identical twins, who have the same DNA, are about twice as likely to share similar levels of spirituality as fraternal twins. "But what the research does suggest," *The New York Times* columnist Nicholas D. Kristoff wrote in 2005, "is that postindustrial society will not easily leave religion behind. Faith may be quiescent in many circles these days, or directed toward meditation or yoga, but it is not something humans can easily cast off. A propensity to faith in some form appears to be embedded within us as a profound part of human existence, as inextricable and perhaps inexplicable as the way we love and laugh."

Neal Gabler, in a 1999 editorial in the *Los Angeles Times*, titled The Deconstruction of Clinton, pointed out: "On one side are the Republicans, most of whom seem to believe in an objective reality and an absolute morality. Though it may sound drastic to say, if they often seem to act like the mullahs of Iran, it is because they think like those mullahs. For them every issue seems to resolve itself into black and white, wrong and right. Homosexuality is a sin against nature. Abortion is murder because life begins at the moment of conception. Not telling the truth before a legal tribunal is a crime no matter what the circumstances.

"As we saw during the House debate on the articles of impeachment, there could be no argument because there was no give, no tolerance. Just ask former House Speaker-designate Bob Livingstone (R-La). One toe over the line was like the whole body over the line. Mullahs chop off hands for thievery, however petty. The GOP mullahs, invoking some form of constitutional fundamentalism, tried to chop off Clinton's presidency, however petty his offense.

"Meanwhile, across the battle lines are the Democrats, most of whom seem to believe in a subjective reality and a moral spectrum. If they seem to act like a bunch of aging hippies, it is because they think like a bunch of aging hippies. For them, every issue seems to resolve itself into greys, into provisional rights and provisional wrongs. Homosexuality isn't a sin but just another sexual preference or lifestyle. Abortion isn't murder but a decision that every woman should have the right to make for herself. And not telling the full truth in a court of law isn't necessarily perjury; it all depends on the circumstances. Theirs is no holy war. It is a gigantic therapy session in which everyone is allowed, in 1960s rhetoric, to do his or her own thing."

The battle between Republicans and Democrats, and between Clinton's attackers and his defenders, was really a battle of one truth versus many truths, of fanatics versus moral fuzziness, of an essentially religious view of politics versus a secular view of politics. On the one side of mainstream U.S. politics you have ex-hippies from the '60s and on the other you have guys in button-down suits who think Nixon should have been left alone. Surely the sins of the fathers are being visited on the children – repeatedly.

"Congress probably should spend more time obeying the Ten Commandments and less time trying to exploit them for crass political purposes," Barry Lynn, director of Americans United for Separation of Church and State, said. He was opposing a House bill that would permit posting the Ten Commandments in schools to deter juvenile crime. Why aren't more Americans echoing such sentiments? *We the Maids* have to sweep in dormant constitutional principles in the 21st century.

When John F. Kennedy, a Catholic, ran for president in 1960, he had to promise to keep his religious beliefs in check for four years, to overcome secular America's fears that the pope would be dictating America's political agenda. Yet today, secular America allows career politicians to invoke the name of God and declare America to be "a Christian nation," as if there was no Constitution separating church from state.

The Bush White House and cabinet are on an evangelical crusade. Bush appointed a devout Pentecostalist and member of the conservative Assemblies of the Church of God, John Ashcroft, to be his first attorney general. Michael Gerson, the president's former speech writer who coined the phrase "the Axis of Evil," has a degree in theology from Wheaton College in Illinois, a leading evangelical institution. Bush's electoral strategist, Karl Rove, whom many consider the most important member of the Bush entourage, received an honorary degree from the controversial evangelist, the Rev. Jerry Falwell, at his Liberty University, for his "commitment to conservative ideas."

Is it any wonder Bush repeatedly reminds his listeners that "freedom is the Almighty's gift to every man and woman in this world. And as the greatest power on the face of the earth, we have an obligation to help the spread of freedom?"

Tom DeLay, the former House majority leader, has said: "Only Christianity offers a way to live in response to the realities that we find in this world – only Christianity." By this, DeLay means "a biblical world view" that rejects the teachings of Darwin. DeLay believes the shootings at Columbine High School in Colorado took place "because our school systems teach our children that they are nothing but glorified apes who have evolutionized out of some primordial mud."

Is it any wonder the religious right isn't thrilled with any of the 2008 presidential candidates?

America has become a religious-fascist state. Robert Paxton's *The Anatomy of Fascism* is a must read to understand how fascism can take root in America the way it did in Mussolini's Italy and Hitler's Germany. Fascism will return not simply because of a rousing leader, but because of *We the Apathetic Maids*, his timid accomplices. Paxton's definition of fascism: "A form of political behavior marked by obsessive preoccupation with community decline, humiliation or victimhood and by compensatory cults of unity, energy and purity, in which a mass-based party of committed nationalist militants, working in uneasy but effective collaboration with traditional elites, abandons democratic liberties and pursues with redemptive violence and without ethical or legal restraints goals of internal cleansing and external expansion." Sound and look familiar to America today?

Today's Islamic revival shares the dogmatism, communitarianism and scripturalism of American evangelist movements: both reject culture, philosophy and even theology to favor a literalist reading of sacred texts and an understanding of truth through individual faith, says Olivier Roy, research director at the French National Centre for Scientific Research. "Their quest for mythic messianic, transnational movements of liberation remains the same, as does the enemy."

Moderate Muslim Maids are waking up to this reality and starting to sweep in the reforms needed for change. In Malaysia, after the repressive era of Mahathir Mohamad, an increasingly outspoken government is taking shape under a more liberal stewardship. The same holds true in Algeria. Muslim authors, like Irshad Manji, question Islam and defend Israel. *Muslim Maids* are beginning to sweep in reforms and question the status quo.

I was in Los Angeles Several years ago when the Supreme Court upheld the phrase "under God" in the Pledge of Allegiance. I was having lunch with

Los Angeles County Supervisor Zev Yaroslavsky. He was in the midst of his own political-religious fray to remove the Christian cross from the Los Angeles County seal. He initiated the action in the face of a threatened American Civil Liberties Union lawsuit, and in the name of religious freedom. Federal courts have repeatedly found the use of a cross in a government seal unconstitutional.

More than 700 people packed the Los Angeles County Board of Supervisors meeting to protest the removal of the cross. "My office received over 3,000 calls asking me to withdraw my motion. We were so swamped I was even answering the phones to help the staff out," Yaroslavsky said as he drove out of the Los Angeles County Hall of Administration. "I told my staff this was one issue I was not going to back down on, even if it meant I get voted out of office. I told them I understood if they started looking for other jobs." I was stunned. Here was a politician putting his career on the line for a constitutional principle.

How rare and refreshing, I thought to myself as he maneuvered the car into the busy lunch-hour traffic. "You know what was really depressing and surprising? I didn't get one call of support. Not one from any of all the community leaders you and I know that support the removal of the cross. That was disheartening and depressing " He pulled up to our favorite downtown deli. "Why are you surprised?" I asked. "We are living in the new born-again era of the Christian fundamentalist crusades led by our great leader, who can't probably even spell fundamentalist."

Zev showed leadership by honoring America's history and the principles enshrined in the Constitution by America's Founding Fathers for all faiths.

Hopefully the election of Keith Ellison. the first Muslim elected to Congress, will bring about greater tolerance and better understanding of the ideals of the Founding Fathers. Ellison was a Catholic who converted to Islam in college.

Hong Kong politics is void of religion. It is not an issue. Never brought up, never has been. A candidate's religion is also irrelevant. Isn't that what the Founding Fathers had in mind for America?

Us Against Them

The European victory at the Battle of Tours united Christian Europe and became the defining moment of the Christian "us" versus "them" mentality and mindset that is still with us today. The Reconquista of Muslim Spain by the church further molded the "us" against "them" enmity based on religion. It was the European opposition to Islamic civilization that formed the foundation of the hatred that still prevails at the dawn of the 21st century.

"Medieval Christianity defined the identity of Europe, and in so doing produced a clear definition of who and what was the other: the unbaptized, non-Christians," Ziauddin Sardar and Merryl Wyn Davies wrote in their book *Why Do People Hate America?* "But not all other people were the same."

St Thomas Aquinas defined two basic categories: the vincibly and invincibly ignorant. The vincibly ignorant were those others who had knowledge of Christianity but had consciously rejected inclusion. As set out in Canon Law, this group comprised Jews and Muslims. Jews were the other who existed within the boundaries of Christian society, discriminated against and persecuted for their otherness. Muslims were the other without, people not expected to exist within European society. The invincibly ignorant were those others who had never encountered the message of Christianity. They were the distant savages in Africa, Asia and the New World, people who lived beyond the encircling Muslim lands who could be converted or enslaved.

The Crusades began on Nov. 27, 1095, after Pope Urban II gave a sermon at Clermont, France. The pope described the enemy as "a despised and base race, which worship demons; an accursed race; and unclean nations." There are two surviving accounts of the sermon by Robert the Monk and Fulcher of Chartres. In Robert the Monk's version, the pope presents the Crusade as the special mission of the Franks, the French people, and also an opportunity for this special people to escape the confines of lands "too narrow for your large population." Europe, Urban argued, was riven by conflict within. It was right that Europeans should turn from this sinful rivalry to their proper mission by attacking the pagans and infidels. The Crusade would be a Holy War in two senses: it would be an armed undertaking that would earn the expiation of sins for all who took part. Those who took the cross, becoming crusaders, would be set on the road to paradise. Sound familiar? How different is that from what today's Muslim suicide bombers believe?

Continuing Crusades

The current conflict between liberal democracy and Marxist-Leninism is only the latest fleeting and superficial historical "them" versus "us" phenomenon compared to the continuing and deeply conflictual relation between Islam and Christianity, Samuel P. Huntington wrote in the *Clash of Civilizations*.

The Crusades raged sporadically but intensely for five centuries. "For almost a thousand years from the first Moorish landing in Spain to the second Turkish siege of Vienna, Europe was under constant threat from Islam," wrote Bernard Lewis, the Princeton professor and ideological guiding light of the neo-cons. "Islam is the only civilization which has put the survival of the West in doubt, and it has done so at least twice." It is doing so again in the 21st century. However, to do so, it will have to develop a command of microbiological and nuclear weaponry, which it could deliver on human bodies or from rapidly mobile launch positions. No physical attack could be launched from an identifiable country. The U.S. would obliterate it.

Ultimately, the ruling Caucasian elites in the West will turn ruthlessly on attempts to Islamicize the European heartland. It is difficult to express the degree to which Islam is inimical not just to European values, whatever they may be, but to their desires.

Jean Daniel, editor of *Le Nouvel Observateur*, disagrees with Huntington. "There has been a real revolution, launched first by Anwar Sadat and then by Mr. Arafat in Oslo. As the world looked on, the vertical divide that Huntington sees between civilizations turned into a horizontal divide separating advocates of pacific projects from fanatic militants.

"That is a revolution because, in this part of the world, when you don't succeed on earth in victory, you can try to succeed in heaven by salvation – which explains why Mr. Sadat was assassinated by an Egyptian, Mohammed Boudiaf by an Algerian and Mr. Rabin by an Israeli. Builders were on one side and terrorists on the other....

"The tragic truth right now is that the terrorists and fanatics may be disavowed but are not, in their very madness, radically and wholly unpopular." They are popular because of the dysfunctional education system their fans have been subjected to.

The 21st century started like its predecessors, with Christian Crusaders trying to convert humiliated and frustrated infidels. Christian proselytizing is illegal in strictly Islamic countries like Afghanistan, and missionaries risk arrest and violent recrimination. Nevertheless, U.S. Christian-based missions, financed and backed by the 50 million-plus evangelical community, such as the Missions and Outreach Ministry of the Southeast Christian Church, persist in sending missions to Afghanistan. The International Assistance Mission from America was one of two aid groups expelled from Afghanistan in 2001, because it was accused of preaching Christianity. Rehmatullah Hashmi, an Afghan Foreign Ministry official, displayed Bibles, videos and other materials in the local language at a press conference and said: "These books say Jesus Christ was the son of God. We don't believe this. We believe Jesus was a prophet but not the son of God."

The number of missionaries working among Muslims almost doubled between 1982 and 2001, from about 15,000 to 27,000 – a far cry from the 62,000 missionaries in 1900 and 420,000 at the turn of the 20th century, according to the Center for the Study of Global Christianity in Massachusetts.

About half of today's missionaries are North American and a third are evangelical with a post-September 11 awareness of the Islamic world. Their goal is to share the gospel with every person on earth, thereby completing the so-called Great Commission set out by Jesus in Matthew 28:19: "Go ye therefore, and teach all nations, baptizing them in the name of the Father, and of the Son, and of the Holy Ghost." Missionaries are exporting Christianty on an industrial scale. Is it any wonder why Muslium Fundamentalists respond the way they do? The Korean missionary hostage crisis of August 2007 in Afghanistun, that resulted in the execution of two missionaries by the Taliban is another millennium reminder why all missionary movements must end in the 21st-century. Only then will religous crusades end once and for all.

The U.S. evangelical group Kids in Ministry teaches children as young as five to deliver prophesies. The aim of Kids in Ministry is to promote a vision of "how God sees children as His partners in ministry worldwide." It has been acussed of brainwashing youngsters and creating Christian terrorists. It does sound like a Christian madrass.

The chief target of this evangelical onslaught is what is known as the "10/40 window." For missionaries, this is the final frontier: a vast area lying between the northern latitudes of 10 and 40 degrees. It includes Muslim North Africa and the Middle East, Pakistan, Afghanistan and the Islamic republics of Central Asia, Hindu-majority India, and the Buddhists and Taoists of Southeast Asia and communist China. These "unreached megapeoples," as they are called, make up most of humanity. Mission literature is strongly militaristic. Missionaries are "Christ warriors," non-Christian countries are "enemy-held territory," God is the "commander-in-chief" and Islam, inevitably, is a "weapon of mass destruction."

Early missionaries packed their possessions in the coffins in which they expected to return. Today, the missionaries are on "the frontlines of God's war against sin," armed with satellite phones and global-positioning systems. Their actions not only ignite resentment toward America, but also endanger the indigenous Christian communities.

Aid workers in Afghanistan with the German-based agency Shelter Now – two Americans, two Australians, and four Germans, along with 16 Afghan workers – were tried and jailed for Christian proselytizing. These Christian missionaries were lucky. They were freed as a result of the more passionate missionary zeal of those they sought to convert – the bombers who brought about the devastation of 9/11 and sparked America's war on terror against the Taliban and al-Qaeda.

Those bombers included Lt. Gen. William G. "Jerry" Boykin, the new deputy undersecretary of Defense for intelligence, who likened the war against the Islamic militants to a battle against Satan. He made the statements in full military regalia before evangelical Christian audiences at churches and prayer breakfasts around America. Gen. Boykin also told the evangelical gatherings that Muslims worship an "idol" and not "a real God." As if that wasn't bad enough, he went on to add that radical Islamists hated America "because we're a Christian nation, because our foundation and our roots are Judeo-Christian ... and that the enemy is a guy named Satan." Of President Bush, he said: "He's in the White House because God put him there." Since when is America a Christian nation with God anointing the president?

One of the general's soldiers, Army Cpl. Joe Johnson, went to Iraq as a Christian missionary on a crusade against Islam following the death of his son, who was killed by an Iraqi roadside bomb. "I don't really have love for Muslim people," Cpl. Johnson said. "I'm sure there are good Muslims. I try not to be racist." Although he has not read the Koran or spoken to Muslims, he has "heard" the Islamic holy book "teaches to kill Jews and infidels. And it's hard to love people who hate you."

How and why do We the People repeatedly allow religious fanatics and extremists to commandeer the political process? Not only in America, but every country where being American is a state of mind. Is America's Christian moral minority really a humiliated and frustrated people? Especially today when they have to deal with a Mormon presidential candidate who is the former governor of liberal Massachusetts? If so, so what? That was the intention of America's Founding Fathers. Former Gov. Jesse Ventura echoes this concern. "It does seem pretty clear that a major worry on the Founding Fathers' minds was that a corrupt government might start using religion to manipulate people. Religious belief can be a powerful tool in the hands of the corrupt. Just look at what the church was doing in Europe during the Middle Ages. At the very least, the Founding Fathers intended the First Amendment to keep the government from establishing a 'national church' that it could coerce people into doing what it wanted. That much is clear."

The only solution to religious extremism packaged as the solution to the terrorist problem is education. The freedom from ignorance is paramount for America and humanity to survive.

The Roman Emperor Constantine permitted Jews to live so that they could be persecuted and blamed for all the church's faults. James Carroll, in *Constantine's Sword: The Church and the Jews,* recounts how Jews were allowed to survive but not to thrive so their misery would be "proper punishment for their refusal to recognize the truth of the church's claims." The church's spin doctors assigned the villain's role in the crucifixion to the Jews rather than to the Romans who became believers.

Such twisted views have no place in the new millennium. "Hunt out and talk about the good that is in the other fellow's church, not the bad, and you will do away with all this religious hatred you hear so much of nowadays." I echo Will Rogers' call for religious tolerance and hope it becomes the first stepping-stone to a harmonious New World Order.

Pope John Paul II marked the end the millennium by asking for forgiveness for the many past sins of his church, including its treatment of Jews, heretics, women and native peoples. "We forgive and we ask for forgiveness," the pope said in his homily, held on the Catholic Church's "Day of Forgiveness" for the 2000 Holy Year. He also prayed for God's forgiveness in the opening year of the millennium for "the occasions past and present when sons and daughters of the Catholic Church have sinned by action or omission against their Orthodox brothers and sisters."

This does not justify Christian brutality against fellow Christians, such as the cases of Orthodox Christians in Georgia attacking and brutalizing "nonbelievers." Father Basil Mkalavishvili's attacks on Jehovah's Witnesses and evangelists prompted 15 members of Congress to write a letter in 2002 to former Georgian President Eduard Shevardnadze after a school friend of former Atty. Gen. John Ashcroft witnessed such an attack.

Pope John Paul II was the first leader of the Roman Catholic Church to enter a mosque – the ancient Omayyad Mosque in Damascus – as well as the first pope to enter a synagogue, which he did in Rome in 1986.

The Omayyad Mosque represents the many cross-cultural parallels of religious history and conflicts. It was initially a place of worship dedicated to the Semitic god Hadad and later became a temple of the Roman god Jupiter. Following the adoption of Christianity by the Roman Empire in the fourth century, the temple was converted to a Christian church dedicated to Saint John the Baptist. Christians continued to worship at the church for several decades after the capture of Damascus by the Arabs in 636. It became a mosque early in the eighth century. "Salam alechum," the pope said in Arabic.

"Peace be unto you all."
While the pope was pleading for reconciliation, his host, Syrian President Bashar al-Assad, was perpetuating religious hatred and the modern-day crusaders myth. "They [Israelis and Jews] try to kill all the principles of divine

faiths with the same mentality of betraying Jesus Christ and torturing Him, and in the same way that they tried to commit treachery against Prophet Muhammad. ..."

Assad was merely echoing the grotesque distortion of the Damascus Blood Libel and history voiced for centuries and repeated by newspapers in Egypt, Iran and Syria in the opening months of the 21st century. Assad echoes the anti-Semitic drumbeats of Louis Farrakhan and Osama bin Laden.

The Damascus Blood Libel of 1840 claims that Jews kill Christians to obtain their blood for Passover. The Damascus Blood Libel started with the disappearance of Father Thomas, a Franciscan superior. The French consul accused a group of rabbis and their Jewish congregations of ritual murder and extracted a "confession" from one of them who was tortured to death. Pogroms followed throughout the Middle East. The consul then requested permission from Mehmet Ali, the Ottoman ruler, to kill the rest of the suspects. Others, including 60 children, were arrested and starved to convince their parents to confess. The charges were dropped when French politicians Sir Moses Montefiore, Adolphe Cremieux and Salomon Munk, intervened.

While moderate Christian and Jewish religious leaders and media preach tolerance of all religions, Muslim religious and political leaders continue to perpetuate virulent anti-Semitism, even after 9/11. Television viewers watching the Abu Dhabi state-run television network saw former Israeli Prime Minister Ariel Sharon depicted as a vampire who craves the blood of Arab children and markets "Dracu-cola." He is also depicted overseeing the tossing of Arab babies into a bonfire.

Anti-Semitism is not limited to the Arab Muslim world. Not since Kristallnacht, the infamous night of smashed windows in Nazi Germany in 1938, has Europe seen more synagogues attacked and burned as in the opening years of the 21st century.

The pope's call for a "new attitude of understanding and respect" among Jews, Christians and Muslims at his Damascus homily is a mandatory precondition for the survival of the human race.

The Crusades, for which Pope John Paul II sought forgiveness, were a series of military expeditions launched by Christians in Western Europe to recover

Jerusalem and the biblical lands from infidel domination. The fact is the holy sites were never in danger because the Holy Land is also holy to Jews and Muslims. What is not widely discussed is the commercial motive behind the Crusades. The merchants of Venice and Genoa wanted to get access to the Silk Road and the riches of China. The road started in the Holy Land. As an extra incentive, Pope Urban II promised land and estates across the Middle East to the sons of nobility.

Pope Urban launched the Crusades in 1095. They created an antagonism between Christianity and Islam that still exists today. When the British returned to Jerusalem after capturing it from the Turks in 1917, British Gen. Sir Edmund Allenby declared, "Today the wars of the Crusaders are completed." The British press at the time glorified his victory with cartoons of Richard the Lionheart looking down at Jerusalem above a caption reading, "At last my dream comes true."

"Now, that would have been an Arab boy," said Stuart Wolfendale, who is a well-known gay historical analyst with a smirk. "The main thrust of the European presence in the Middle East over the centuries has come from devout Christian warriors and specialist homosexual Arabists. Pope Benedict XVI should bear this in mind," added Wolfendale.

President Bush's use of the word "crusade" to describe America's war on terrorism is a millennium reminder.

The brutality of the Crusades horrified the Jewish and Muslim world. The narrow streets of Jerusalem became rivers of blood when the Crusaders invaded, sacked and took over the city When Saladin – a Kurd warrior from Saddam Hussein's Tikrit – recaptured Jerusalem on October 2, 1187, unlike the Crusaders, he spared the Christians and forbade acts of vengeance.
The Crusades at first inspired immense enthusiasm among all classes. Against expectations, they captured Jerusalem in July 1099 and established several Crusader states that clung on until the end of the 13th century. Confused in their objectives and often bloody in execution, they had profound social, religious and political consequences. Ones *We the Maids* and our children are now experiencing and paying with ever increasing doses of daily fear. A

needless, senseless fear that must be eliminated.

Then, like now, there was considerable loss of life, but Europe profited, not least from the fact that it entered into sustained contact with the ideas and technology of a civilization more advanced than its own.

The Catholic Inquisition was a near 700-year campaign of persecution of heretics in which hundreds of thousands of people were tortured and killed, including Chinese. It was begun by Pope Gregory IX in 1231 to repress heresy, witchcraft, alchemy and deviations such as devil worship. The Peruvian author Mario Vargas Llosa wrote that "the Inquisition forbade the novel for 300 years in Latin America. I think they understood very well the seditious consequence that fiction can have on the human spirit." Hell, the church wrote and inspired the best.

"The Inquisition was simply a tough critic, that's all," Wolfendale said as we continued our review of his editorial comments and suggestions back at the Foreign Correspondents Club Main Bar in Hong Kong several months later. "Given the yards of garbage being published as novels with 'advice' and self-help in business, we could do with something more like the Inquisition now," he added. "The Inquisition would probably have got quite a chuckle out of this book before they burnt it – and the author." He is right.

A little-known historical fact is that long before there was a state of Israel, there was a state of the Jews. Its name was Gibraltar, and it was ceded to Conversos – Spanish Jews who had been forced to convert to Catholicism – in 1474 at the urging of Pedro de Herrera of Cordoba, himself a Converso. After two years, the Conversos were forced to return to Spain and the clutches of the Inquisition.

In 1478, Pope Sixtus IV authorized the Spanish Inquisition. It reached its height under the rule of Ferdinand of Aragon and Isabella of Castille, whose armies swept across the Iberian Peninsula in the 15th and 16th centuries, forcing Jews, Muslims and Protestants to convert to Catholicism. Jews and Muslims were the original targets of the Inquisition, but during the 16th and 17th centuries, hundreds of captured English Protestants were also burned at the stake.

Suspicions still linger. Mohamed Al-Fayed's lawsuits alleging his son Dodi and Princess Diana were assassinated by modern-day crusaders to prevent the heir to the British throne from having a Muslim stepfather rings true to millions of Muslims worldwide, not withstanding the Stevens report, which concludes the deaths were an accident. Especially after a Church of England minister confirmed that they intended to marry. Diana was pregnant, according to a senior police source in France. She wrote the following to her butler and confidant, Paul Burrell, 10 months before her death. "This particular phase in my life is the most dangerous," the letter said. "My husband is planning 'an accident' in my car."

By the time it officially ended in 1808, the Spanish Inquisition had killed more than 300,000 people. Ethnic cleansing in its purest form.

Renewed Crusade?
For Holy Peace to replace Holy Wars, all religions have to acknowledge and respect other religions. Pronouncements such as those made by Pope Benedict XVI, when he was known as Cardinal Joseph Ratzinger, only inflame religious confrontations. His dictum "Dominus Jesus," of August 6, 2000, that the Catholic Church is 'the only true church' are not only offensive and disrespectful but perpetuate religious hatred and unnecessary wars in the new millennium.

Fighting evil with violence cannot contribute to Holy Peace," I wrote in *Custom Maid Spin*. It should therefore not have come as a surprise that when the Cardinal succeeded Pope Paul and became Pope Benedict XVI, he'd make an even more inflammatory speech. On September 12, 2006, at the University of Regensburge, he not only offended Muslims by accusing Muhammad of being a violent jihadist, but secular Christians and Jews by saying that Western science and philosophy had divorced themselves from faith – leading to the secularization of European society.

Why he had to quote what 14th-century Byzantine Christian Emperor Manuel Paleologos II said to a Persian scholar on the truths of Christianity and Islam escapes me. He quoted the emperor, who said, "Show me just what Mohammad brought that was new, and there you will find things only evil and inhuman, such as his command to spread by the sword the faith he preached." Is this any way for the head of the Catholic Church to talk to students of his faith? Was he really surprised he offended people and had to apologize?

His profuse apologies and pilgrimage of reconciliation to Istanbul, a former Christian metropolis known as Constantinople until Ottoman Turks conquered it in 1453, was acknowledged and reciprocated by Turkish Prime Minister Recep Tayib Erdogan, who met him at the airport.

Christianity was also spread by the sword. But, unlike Saudi Arabia, which still displays Muhammad's sword on its flag, Christianity plays down its symbols of violence. Watching Pope Benedict pray alongside an Islamic cleric in Turkey's Blue Mosque was an outreach of brotherhood and forgiveness.

Forgivness

Everyone has a reason to be resentful and angry at another person, country, religion or ethnic group. Indiginous people against colonizers, Christians, Muslims and Jews against each other, and America against anyone who disagrees with it. Family feuds, vendettas, blood feuds, *fatwas*, religious scores, honor killings and plain-old personal grudges only perpetuate the daily hatred and violence that surrounds us. To stop this continuous cycle of violence, we have to learn to forgive. It is ironic that in most religions, no matter how violent and combative their practitioners are, there usually is a huge, simple and immediate antidote to all hatred – forgiveness.

In Hong Kong, and throughout Buddhist societies in Asia, forgiving is commonplace. Japan and Vietnam have embraced their wartime enemy and forgiven America for the destruction of their countries and the millions of their citizens who died in those wars. The same holds true for the Vietnamese and Indians who fought border skirmishes with China, Cambodians of the Khmer Rouge, Koreans of Japan, Thais of Burma and vice versa. The reason is simple. In Buddhism it is more important to reflect and look for oneself rather than the other person, because we are the shapers of our own destiny.

A story I have heard several times in various versions throughout Asia has Buddha walking in a park and coming across a group of angry picnickers who were upset at a woman who had stolen their earthly delights. "What is more important?" he asked them. "To look for the woman, or to look for yourself?"

The world will be a much safer and better place if *We the Maids* sweep in the words of understanding and forgiveness that Buddha, the prophets of the Torah, Jesus and Muhammad preached. One common denominator in all cultures and religions is love and affection.

Chapter 4

U.N. – Funded Failures
*The organizational chart looks like it was
designed by a crazed kitten in a string factory.*
– Madeline Albright

American Dinosaur

Whenever I walk past the United Nations, usually
hunched forward to prevent the icy wind blowing across Turtle Bay off the
East River from enveloping my face, I try to make out what groups or individuals are protesting. While fighting the elements as I make my way through
the crowd or barricade I can't help wonder when this unfunded dinosaur
will join the ranks of other beautiful relics in New York's museums and
become a peaceful, historical, geopolitical Jurassic Park. The Museum of
Natural History comes to mind. Prime East River real estate, wasted on an
outdated global failure. Just like the U.N. peace missions and countless
resolutions. Twentieth-century failures as Sierra Leone, Rwanda, Iraq and
Sudan remind us. Isn't it really time for the U.S. to get out of the U.N. and
the U.N. to get out of the U.S.?

Walter Lippmann once wrote: "A policy is bound to fail which deliberately
violates our pledges and our principles, our treaties and our laws. The American conscience is a reality." One of the first lessons I learned when I started
practicing law was that "what starts fucked up ends up fucked up." Barnie
Shapiro, a senior partner at the firm where I started my legal career, ingrained that quote in me after I questioned why a particular company we
were representing went bankrupt. I've modified the expression to: "An organization is like a building. It's as good as its foundation."

The U.N. headquarters was built on the site of a former abattoir – a
slaughterhouse. Erected in 1952, the retro-modernist building, with stained

glass by Marc Chagall, murals by Fernand Leger and a tapestry of Picasso's celebrated anti-war painting, Guernica, violates New York's safety and fire codes. The building is packed with toxic asbestos, has no sprinkler system and leaks about a quarter of the heat used to warm it in winter. The U.N. General Assembly in 2006 approved a $1.9-billion remodel of the building which will take seven years. It will have to build another temporary office facility next door, so that the headquarters building can be gutted. How appropriate. Why not just go for the kill?

Why waste $1.6 billion on a temporary conference hall for the General Assembly that would be used only until the renovations are completed in 2013? The $1.6-billion price tag is 55% higher than first anticipated. No surprise there.

The Hong Kong government demolishes buildings with weak foundations, even brand new ones if the pilings are not up to code. The U.N.'s pilings, not to mention homosexual employees, piles, that security videos reveal along with their sexual activities in the the most secretive confines of the building, do not serve or comply with any moral or political code of today's world and, like substandard buildings in Hong Kong, should be replaced – superceded by a new global organization that is up to a geopolitical code relevant to the 21st century.

The U.N. squanders $20 billion a year on various failed missions and operations around the world. It spends $7 billion a year on peacekeeping operations. Ironically, peacekeeping was not specified in the original charter. It was invented by the second secretary-general, Dag Hammarskjold, and former Canadian foreign minister Lester Pearson after Britain and France invaded Egypt in the Suez crisis of 1956. Since then, U.N. peacekeeping forces have been deployed more than 60 times. There are now roughly 100,000 troops from various countries wearing U.N. blue helmets around the world.

Walking past "the tallest and most spectacular building in the world" built by Donald Trump across the street from the U.N., its dagger-shaped shadow piercing through the U.N. General Assembly, reminded me of the shadow of terrorism and its dark pall cast over the security of this global institution. I couldn't help wonder why the United Nations can't be dumped and replaced with something that can surpass in stature and geopolitical statement the Trump World Tower at the corner of 1st Avenue and 47th Street. Today the U.N. is back on center stage – a huge 21st-century blunder.

A few days after 9/11, all access roads to the U.N. were blocked by New York Sanitation Department dumpsters filled with concrete instead of the deadbeat U.N. bureaucrats they were protecting. A symbolic metaphor of America defending its Cold War relic with sanitation trucks that *We the Maids* have to fill with the right geopolitical bureaucratic garbage.

U.N. headquarters surrounded by New York sanitation trucks is a millennium reminder of the kind of political garbage *We the Apathetic People* have become immersed in and conditioned to accept. The World Trade Center public address announcements that the buildings were safe and people could go back to their offices only magnified the political garbage in the dumpsters. The fact is that the U.N. had an Ad Hoc Committee on Measures to Eliminate Terrorism, which had been meeting since 1996 – and failed to come up with a definition of terrorism, let alone a plan to combat it. One committee faction was insisting on an exception for violence committed in the cause of "national liberation" – a plea for the right to terrorize.

Just as many Americans ignored the public-address announcements, *We the Apathetic People* must start tuning in and ignoring the repeated deadly and destructive committees and pronouncements of career politicians and their lethargic, tuned-out entourage of bureaucrats.

The U.N. is a World War II relic of the Cold War that it was created to combat. The only warm and outright hot spots the U.N. vigorously protects today are the brothels and massage parlors within a 10-block radius of the headquarters, where international beauties relieve bureaucratic stress with back rubs and a wide range of sexual services to satisfy all 192 tastes and perversions of the representatives of its member states.

Now that the Cold War and communism have died a symbiotic death, shouldn't the U.N. be buried as well? The high-profile public squabble between America and "Old Europe," France and Germany, on whether the U.N. should authorize an attack against Iraq or give the inspectors more time highlighted the U.N.'s dysfunctional irrelevance. The U.N. headquarters in Baghdad was destroyed and its mission chief killed by a bomb-laden truck because of inadequate security. The U.N. then withdrew its staff and has been engaged in Iraq from overseas offices. For Iraq's January 30, 2005, election that the U.N. was supposed to supervise, it had a team of only 35 workers, only eight of whom were from the organization's electoral assistance unit. The world is crying out for a new organization that is relevant to the 21st century.

The calls for Kofi Annan's resignation because of his corrupt management style of a failed institution, brought to light by the Volcker Commission investigating the scandal ridden Oil-for-Food program, did not go far enough. It is not just the head of the corruption-riddled body that has to be decapitated – the whole quagmired body must be buried. A poll by the Pew Organization in 20 countries in the summer of 2003 concluded that the U.N.'s standing had declined in all of them. The U.N.'s reputation suffered in America because it did not support the Bush administration on the war – and in the 19 other countries because it was unable to prevent the war. People were waking up to the irrelevance of the organization.

The U.N. is not relevant and must be rebuilt, renamed and relocated. It must revise its purpose if it is to be relevant in the New World Order. It is not a "United Nations" and its chief governing body is not a "Security Council." It is an expensive "General Assembly" of insecure, corrupt and wasteful bureaucrats. If America is to continue being a major player in the New World Order and not follow in the footsteps of earlier lost empires, it should take the lead with China to restructure and relocate what remains of the U.N.'s noble managed misperception to Hong Kong or some other mutually agreed Pacific site.

The U.N. died on March 17, 2003, when President Bush declared the end of diplomacy and gave Saddam & Company 48 hours to leave Iraq. America's decision to remove Saddam without an 18th U.N. resolution blessing the war on Iraq with the seal of international approval was the last nail in the U.N. coffin. A nail hammered by France with its announced veto "no matter what the evidence showed." Both governments chose to disregard the wisdom in Harry Truman's closing address to the U.N.'s founding conference more than 60 years ago: "We all have to recognize no matter how great our strength, that we must deny ourselves the license to do always as we please."

The U.N.'s reluctant resolution to recognize the 25-member Iraqi Governing Council selected by America and Britain and to adopt the mandate supporting the U.S.-led multinational force in Iraq in 2004 – which was renewed in 2005 – sealed its own fate. Especially after Saddams nerve gas was
found in a U.N. filing cabinet in New York in the Summer of 2007. All
America had to do is go to war with the U.N. – not Iraq. All that is now
necessary are the funeral arrangements. A Security Council comprised of
five permanent members with three from "old Europe" no longer makes
sense or is sustainable in the 21st century.

Futile Resusitation and Hypocrisy
The U.N.'s feeble attempt to become relevant was to propose to expand the
Security Council to more than 20 members from 15, to include India,
Germany, Japan and Brazil. None of the newcomers would have veto power,
while the current five permanent members would retain theirs.

The speeches given by ambassadors in the General Assembly managed only
to resurrect national rivalries, regional divisions and great power objections
that forced negotiators to shelve any and all expansion ideas. The U.N. Charter
is obsolete. The structure leaves large parts of the developing world unrepresented on the Security Council.

A two-year seat on the Security Council can generate a 59 percent increase
in U.S. financial aid, according to a Harvard University study that tracked
American economic and military assistance from 1946 to 2001. In time of
crisis, U.S. aid to some member countries has risen as much as 170 percent.
Those aid levels tend to recede after the country leaves the 15-nation council.

A snapshot of U.S. aid in the year leading up to the American invasion of
Iraq in March 2003, a period of intense diplomatic activity in the Security
Council, confirms the U.S. practice. U.S. economic aid to Angola nearly
doubled to $160.5 million in 2003 from $81.6 in 2001, before dropping
more than $40 million in 2004. Assistance to Cameroon more than tripled,
to $16 million in 2003 from $5 million in 2001, before falling by about
$3.5 million in 2004.

It is therefore no surprise that small, unrepresented nations periodically propose reforms to include representatives from the developing world on the

Security Council. In 2005, Switzerland, Singapore, Jordan, Costa Rica and Lichtenstein proposed that the nonbinding vote of the General Assembly be taken seriously by the Security Council and questioned its most sacred symbol of power – the veto.

America, China and Russia opposed the proposed expansion and most other reforms. They prefer to perpetuate the ongoing hypocrisy.

America's proposed reform, which is opposed by the General Assembly, is that the power currently vested in the assembly be transferred to the secretary general's office. The clash between the General Assembly and the Office of the Secretary General was so fractious that Mark Malloch Brown, Kofi Annan's chief of staff said, "I think in many ways it is setting the outcome of whether the United Nations matters or not in 10 years' time."

The U.N. has been in its death throes for decades. It survives because there is no global institution to replace it as it is battered from all sides by its own members engaged in local, cross-border and regional wars in complete defiance of the U.N. Charter, while it endures the abuses of its high-handed superpower host.

Franco-Syria

While the world debated whether to approve the 18th resolution on Iraq, France, a permament member of the Security Council, went ahead and invaded the Ivory Coast without permission from anyone at the U.N. Syria, a non-permanent member of the Security Council during the debate on the 18th Iraq resolution, had an occupation army in neighboring Lebanon without approval from the U.N. – and in defiance of U.N. Resolution 1559 to remove its troops from Lebanon – until after its complicity in the assassination of former Lebanese Prime Minister Rafik Hariri was voiced in street protests throughout Lebanon and confirmed by an independent U.N. investigation. The U.N. Security Council passed a resolution authorizing a mixed tribunal be established in Lebanon to be composed of two chambers, a trial court with three judges – one Lebanese alongside two foreigners – and an appeals court with five judges, two of whom would be Lebanese.

Syrian intelligence chiefs, according to the report, told Lebanese legislators to extend the term of the pro-Syrian president, Emile Lahoud, in 2004 and warned them that failure to do so would "put their personal security at risk." The Constitution was amended two months before Lahoud's term expired to allow him to remain in power another three years. Assassination and murder are the most potent political tools in Arab politics. The sectarian violence in Iraq, Lebanon and Palestine are millennium reminders.

Syria openly supports terrorism, smuggles arms into Lebanon and Iraq and continues to assassinate prominent Lebanese politicians who are anti-Syrian – while hosting and housing Khaled Meshaal, who controls the Hamas-run Palestinian government from Damascus. Hence his visit by Palestinian Authority President Abu Mazen. Syria has also been the base from which many anti-American insurgents, including Saddam Hussein's brother and former Saddam regime stalwarts, enter Iraq to inflict death and misery upon coalition forces. For America to entertain, even momentarily, the notion of reconciling with Syria at the expense of Lebanon is short-sighted regional stupidity that will only expedite the evangelical belief of Armaggedon.

There should be reconciliation with Syria, probably starting with Israel over the Golan Heights. Not a bad exchange for Syria's complete and verifiable withdrawal of support for Hamas and Hezbollah. That will also require Syria's withdrawal from its reluctant romance of convenience with Iran and logistical support for trained volunteer insurgents to Iraq.

So what is wrong with this picture? Why doesn't America fully enforce the Syria Accountability Act enacted in 2003 that imposes travel and economic sanctions on Syria with punitive measures? The alternative is more war.

So What's New?
The same thing, to a much more extreme degree, happened in Kosovo. The U.N. charter forbids violating the sovereignty and territorial integrity of a member state without an express Security Council mandate. Kosovo's ethnic Albanian majority, which comprises 90 percent of the 2 million population, has the right to decide to become a sovereign state and independent from Serbia after eight years of U N. administration, according to U.N. Resolution 1224. It is a rare example on how democracy can work. Russia is clear about its intentions to reject any resolution that is not acceptable to Serbia. The Serbs objected loud and clear all the way to Washington, D.C. The Serbs in Kosovo "resist as any occupied people would do," the

head of the Serbian Orthodox Church, Bishop Artemje, told a Washington audience. The Russians opposed revision of Resolution 1244 to grant Kosovo effective independence, and the U.S. and its allies ignored these concerns and endorsed the plan put forward by special U.N. envoy Martti Ahtisaari, and independance was declared on February 17, 2008 with reverberations being felt well beyond the Balkans.

The Russians, and many other nations, have been irritated by the tendency of NATO countries, and the U.S. in particular, to bypass the Security Council when they cannot obtain a desired resolution. After Kosovo and Iraq, any U.N. resolution is laughable. The language has always been ridiculously funny because of its irrelevance. The wars in Kosovo and Iraq only confirm the obvious.

Russia's invasion and occupation of Hungary and Czechoslovakia while it sat on the Security Council were the first clear signs that the U.N. was terminally ill.

The U.S.-manipulated intelligence that led to the invasion of Iraq in 2003 was coordinated by Undersecretary of Defense for Policy Douglas Feith. Gen. Tommy Franks, who led the invasion of Iraq and Afghanistan, has been much quoted as calling Feith "the fucking stupidist guy on the face of the earth," apparently for ideas he proposed to Franks and his planners.

If the U.N. were a business, it would have been placed in bankruptcy years ago. Either dissolved or disassembled. It is mismanaged, broke and was built on unrealistic pilings that crumbled years ago. What business, other than Enron, or any other global organization for that matter, would throw a lavish international 50th birthday bash for·itself while openly admitting it is bankrupt?

The U.N. was founded on a noble vision – to unite all nations and build a secure future in the wake of World War II. When it was established in 1945, delegations from 51 countries gathered in San Francisco to pronounce "an end to war for all time." The Golden Gate Soiree was dominated by the American-led West and Russia. Only four countries from Africa were present and three from Asia: China, India and the Philippines – all grateful former colonies of Britain and America. The rest were still colonies of the West.

The U.N.'s golden jubilee placed great focus on the organization's debilitating state. Even its managed misperception doesn't help minimize the fact that it is an American dinosaur. The U.S. ambassador to the U.N. at the time, Madeleine Albright, phrased the choice facing the U.N. rather bluntly, "Reform or die." This was a far cry from the naive pronouncement made by U.S. Secretary of State Cordell Hull at the founding of the U.N. He proclaimed, "There will no longer be need for spheres of influence, for alliances, balances of power or any other of the special arrangements through which, in the unhappy past, the nations strove to safeguard their security or to promote their interests."

The U.N. now flies the flags of 192 states. The Vatican has observer status and the Palestinians also participate in the General Assembly as observers. More than ever, the secretariat appears to be a paper-making machine, the General Assembly an unwieldy debating society, and the mishmash of agencies spread around the globe a swamp into which good intentions can sink with barely a trace. Above all, the paramount U.N. duty of maintaining peace, security and unity is in disgrace.

The Millennium Declaration issued by the largest gathering of global leaders at the Millennium Summit sponsored by the U.N. is also unrealistic and unachievable.

The failure of the United Nations to heed the warnings of its own officials of the impending genocides in Rwanda and in Sudan are glaring examples of the U.N.'s institutional failure and irrelevance in the New World Order. The same holds true for what happened in Afghanistan, Croatia, Kosovo, the Congo, Myanmar, Somalia, Sierra Leone, Sri Lanka and Iraq.

Overdue Reforms, Dues and Credibility

The U.S. is the largest donor to the U.N. It contributes 22 percent of the regular operating budget and nearly 27 percent of the peacekeeping budget. It contributed $438 million to the U.N.'s 2005 budget of more than $1.9 billion. Congress repeatedly threatens to withhold or cut U.S. contributions unless the U.N. reforms. In the 1990s, the U.S. piled up so much debt in delinquent dues that its voting rights in the General Assembly were jeopardized. A U.S. proposal to tie the 2006 and 2007 budget process to reforms was opposed. The U.S. proposed the U.N. set an interim budget for the first three or four months of 2006 pending the resolution of a stalemate over management reforms. No wonder the Chinese and Russians resist U.S.-Japan proposals to modify the criteria by which U.N. dues are assessed, so that what member states pay better reflects what they can afford. China and Russia contribute only 1.1 percent and 2.05 percent respectively. China could more than match the U.S by putting up the real estate and building in Hong Kong as part of its contribution, subject to the U.N.'s restructuring. The overhaul of the U.N. is something a lot of career politicians – part of the elitist establishment of religious leaders, lobbyists, lawyers, financiers, managers and consultants in many countries, talk about but do nothing.

The latest proposed reforms were recommended by a panel formed by Congress and led by Newt Gingrich, the former House speaker, and George Mitchell, a former Senate Democratic leader. The panel's report, released in June 2005, called for corporate-style oversight bodies, personnel standards and accounting reforms. It also recommended the creation of a rapid reaction capability from its member states' armed forces to prevent genocide, mass killing and sustained major human rights violations.

The Gingrich-Mitchell task force was one of six investigations of the U.N. initiated in Washington. Five congressional committees and the Justice Department conducted investigations into the U.N. Oil-for-Food program. Isn't it time the hearings, studies and money wasted by Congress on the U.N. be put to better use? How much more must be spend by elitist career politicians and their elitist posse before *We the Apathetic Maids* wake up and start sweeping?

Is it any wonder so many Americans are opposed to the U.S. paying its dues to the U.N. – including U.S. Ambassador to the U.N. John Bolton before he was appointed to the post? Bolton maintained that the U.S. had no legal obligation to pay its U.N dues – and expressed his opposition to the U.N. as an organization and its presence in the U.S.

The time wasted by the Senate on confirmation hearings of Bolton's nomination as U.S. ambassador to the U.N. was an epic and classic waste of U.S. taxpayer time and money. After countless hearings and debates, his nomination was rejected by the Senate, yet President Bush used a constitutional provision that allows presidents to make temporary appointments without

Senate approval during a congressional recess. It is doubtful the presidential power to bypass the Senate was intended to be used to escape opposition to such a sensitive appointment. It was the first time since the U.N.'s founding in 1945 that the U.S. made the appointment using that backdoor procedure.

Ambassador Bolton had served in the administrations of Presidents Ronald Reagan and George H.W. Bush and had been an assistant secretary of state in charge of relations with the U.N. "There is no such thing as the United Nations," Bolton is on record as saying. "There is an international community that can occasionally be led by the only real power left in the world – and that is the United States, when it suits our interests and when we can get others to go along." Bolton also said that the U.N. headquarters in New York has 38 stories and "if it lost 10 stories, it wouldn't make a bit of difference." Bolton was once a paid consultant to the Taiwanese government, favors Taiwan's independence and its full U.N. membership – a dangerous and self-defeating position in light of the cross-straits tensions and America's efforts to obtain Chinese pressure on North Korea and others.

When Bolton tried to open his first meeting as head of the U.N. Security Council at 10 a.m. sharp, after the U.S. took over the council's rotating presidency, he was irked because no one showed up on time. "I brought down the gavel at 10. I was the only one in the room," Bolton said. "I believe in discipline. I think daily briefings constitute a form of intellectual discipline. Starting on time is a form of discipline. I failed today."

When the U.S. proposal to transfer many of the General Assembly's oversight duties and responsibilities to the secretary general's office was opposed by the assembly, Mr. Bolton raised the stakes by saying that if thwarted, America would snub the U.N. and pursue its interests in other international forums.

This is America's diplomat at the U.N., an ambassador with no credibility at home or in the U.N. A man sent to represent America without Senate approval. Is this any way for a superpower to be represented in the U.N.? A good thing the Democrats won the 2006 midterm election so that Bolton could resign, because he could not be confirmed as the Bush administration wanted. His successor, Zalmay Khalilzad, is a real piece of work.

Khalilzad is a Pentagon staffer and author of the *Draft Defense Planning Guidance*, which set forth a bold, unprecedented blueprint for America to become the world's policeman after the Cold War. He is the most senior Muslim in the U.S. government. He is a former ambassador to Afghanistan, where he was born in 1951 and raised, and ambassador to Iraq. Like many in the Bush administration, he shares an indifference to the U.N. Before becoming U.S. ambassador to Afghanistan, he was a consultant to Unocal, which was trying to build a pipeline through Taliban-controlled Afghanistan. His contradictory pro-and-anti-Taliban comments, depending on the occasion, are well documented and equally applauded and criticized. As a Sunni, he did have a heavy cross to bear as the U.S. ambassador in Shiite – dominated Iraq. A Muslim bridge in the General Assembly where the Muslim world plays a dominant role.

U.S. ambassadors to global institutions should be modeled after the first woman U.S. ambassador to the U.N., Jeane Kirkpatrick a powerful democratic moral voice to the Reagan foreign policy that helped break up the Soviet Union and bring down the Berlin Wall. President Reagan appointed her in 1981.

Russian Defiance

Reagan and his foreign policy team brought the Soviet Union to its knees and splintered it into the numerous independent states now circling in Russia's orbit and dependent on its largess, oil and gas. The minute any state, or Russian oligarth with money, political opponent or critic questions or challenges Russia or its oil czar, President Vladimir Putin, Russia instinctively resorts to Cold War totalitarian bombastic rhetoric and tactics, which includes assassination and embargo-like cut-offs of oil and gas, desperately belonging to and needed by its European neighbors during the frigid European winters. Western Europe imports 30 percent of its oil and 40 percent of its gas from Russia.

The new cold war Russia has launched, unlike the first one, is not a fight for military supremacy, but rather for respect and gaining control of energy resources. Putin is transforming Russia into a new oil and gas superpower with vast bargaining power over the European community. Russia is the world's eighth largest producer of crude oil and the largest of natural gas. Moscow is using its energy clout for geopolitical gain. Especially in the regions that were once under Soviet control but are now independent countries.

Assassinations in London included the high-profile nuke killing of Alexander Litvinenko, a former KGB spy who had accused Putin of leading an autocratic, murderous and corrupt government. Litvinenko was a figure in the struggle between the Putin government and Russian oligarchs for the country's most prized possessions – the oil and gas fields controlled by the Russian oil companies, the state-controlled Gazprom and the privately held Yukos.

Putin's government also harassed the British ambassador in Moscow, silenced the BBC broadcasts in Russian, and cut off oil and gas to the Ukraine, Belarus and all air, sea, rail and road transport as well as postal deliveries and money transfers through the Russian postal system to Georgia. Russia has established and deepened Europe's dependence on Russian energy sources, and elbowed the European Union into near silence in the face of threatened boycotts and Russia's refusal to sign the charter of good conduct between energy suppliers and their clients. After all, Russia holds veto power and a gatekeeper's prerogatives in relation to the West's hopes to stop Iran's nuclear program. Russia's support of Iran is short-sighted. Russia backing of Iran's nuclearization is a short-sighted financial goal that takes the world into another dangerous potential nuclear conflict zone, and puts even Russia in harm's way.

A nuclear-armed Iran on Russia's border is not in its national interest, especially with Russia's own 20 million Muslim citizens becoming more and more radicalized. That Iran is seen as a principle backer of the Chechen separatists is also testimony to the truly short-sighted vision of Russian policy.

On the remote island of Sakhalin in Russia's Far East, Exxon Mobil and Royal Dutch Shell have run into political obstacles with Russian authorities over their separate drilling agreements due to cost overruns and excessive pollution, which has environmental groups siding with Russia. It's a way for Russia to renegotiate the 1990s contracts it signed with the oil companies when crude prices were one-sixth their current level and Moscow was strapped for cash. "This is what happens when Russian oil companies have their headquarters at the Kremlin," says Robert Amsterdam, attorney for

Mikhail Khodorkovsky, the jailed former head of Russian oil company Yukos, which authorities seized and broke up in late 2004. The Kremlin plays hardball. It wants control of all strategic assets and projects.

Russia highlighted its determination to do so in August 2007, when it faked television footage of it planting the Russian flag on the seabed 4 kilometres beneath the North Pole to stake a claim in the energy-rich territory. Russia claims a section ofseabed at the pole is an extension of Russia's landmass, bolstering claims to its mineral riches.

Meanwhile, China has contracted to buy the ExxonMobil natural gas from Sakhalin, but the deal is now dependent on ExxonMobil being able to negotiate a deal with Gazprom, Russia's state-controlled gas monopoly, to get the fuel to market. China reached a broad agreement with Gazprom to import Russian gas. The first shipments are to begin in 2011, with volumes reaching as much as 80 billion cubic meters a year. Japan was supposed to get the gas but missed out.

Russia's hardball pipeline politics made Belarus and Ukraine reluctantly sign new gas deals on Russia's terms. Russia is going through one radical political and economic transformation. Today, Russia, after the collapse of the Soviet Union, fits Winston Churchill's characterization of Stalin's USSR as "a riddle wrapped in a mystery inside an enigma."

Russia is the second-largest "transitional" economy, with a gross domestic product about one-fifth that of China, but double in per capita terms. America and the European Union have formally accepted Russia as a "market economy." But the fact that Russia has not yet qualified for membership in the World Trade Organization suggests that this status may have been accorded as much for political as economic reasons. After all, the windfall of higher oil and natural gas prices played a greater role in Russia's economic transformation than improved economic policies or reform.

Russia and Putin are angry and fuming at America for what they perceive as deliberate bad-faith dealings. It dismantles the Soviet Union and the Berlin Wall, folds up and abolishes the Warsaw Pact. And what does America do instead of being supportive and welcoming? It surrounds Russia with NATO and a missile defense system it places in the former Soviet puppet states of

Poland and the Czech Republic to allegedly defend against any missiles launched from Iran. Ten U.S. interceptor missiles get planted in Poland and a radar superstation in the Czech Republic to allegedly defend against any missiles launched from Iran. Sound right? That only invites Russia to target its missiles toward Warsaw and Prague not to mention all the other geopolitical miltaristic economic confrontations. Is it any wonder Russian helicopter gunships fire missiles at political targets in Georgia? Georgia lost a war with Abkhaz separatists in the early 1990s. Since then the area has been a self-declared republic that seeks independence. No nation has formally recognized it, but Russia has provided aid and political support. That upsets strategic stability, not only in the region, but in America and elsewhere.

Polls show that a majority of Czechs and Poles are against the plans to have any part of the missile-shield based in their countries. The governments of Poland and the Czech Republic are still negotiating with the U.S. over whether to host the shield.

The Cold War border effectively moved from Germany to Poland and the Czech Republic. Not bad for America. Another first down in the Cold War that supposedly thawed and ended could become an ugly interception and touchdown by the Russians. Moscow will not under any circumstances accept that America is the sole world superpower. Russia's actions are supported and backed by the Russian people. A poll conducted at the end of 2006 by the independent EU-Russia Center in Brussels that was headed by the former British Liberal Party leader Paddy Ashdown, released in February 2007, found that only 16 percent of the Russians consulted wanted to see Western democracy installed in Russia. Twenty-six percent think that the quasi-authoritarian system put in place by Putin is more suited to Russia than democracy, and 35 percent would like to return to the Soviet system. What do *We the Apathetic Maids* want? The majority of Russians, much like the Bush neo-cons, want a state authority that coordinates the institutions of national power, rather than a separation of executive and legislative powers. How many Americans feel the same way?

Russians scorn Mikhael Gorbachev's belief that Soviet Russian governmental and administrative law, although in principle democratic, was actually applied. The fact that Soviet era mental hospitals are once again in vogue as a political tool that wrongfully hospitalizes political critics and journalists is of minimal concern.

Russians are comfortable today, after the fall of the Soviet Union and 70 years of totalitarian government – the darkest days of the Yeltsin period of liberty – poverty, unemployment and inequalities. Whatever Russia is, Russians are comfortable with it and have lots of good company. Chinese, Iranians, Europeans, Asians and most U.N. member countries. None of them want to see the U.S. as the world's sole superpower. So why doesn't America come to terms with geopolitical reality and form a partnership with China and an alliance with Russia? Because it is payback time for their sales of air defense missiles to Iran and Syria, and as an attempt to bind NATO members Poland and the Czech Republic more tightly into the Western military alliance that Russia opposes. Does America really need another enemy in the Russians? Doesn't it have enough already?

The fact is, the missiles would not stop Russia's strategic missiles because of the limited speed and range of the interceptors. The missile sites are more of a concern to the Russians because future technological advancements could create such a threat.

Where is Secretary of State Condoleezza Rice when America needs her? As a Russia specialist who speaks Russian, why is she in the Middle East with people she doesn't undertand or have a clue how to communicate with? She should be playing the diplomatic Soviet piano she knows so well and giving Putin and the Russians the hug they are due and rightfully expect.

Europe's oil supply was disrupted when Russia cut off supplies when it could not reach agreement with Ukraine and Belarus over charging them market prices instead of the subsidized price they had been paying. Poland and Germany were hardest hit. No wonder the EU no longer assumes that Russia is a reliable partner or even a friend. Russia doesn't care. It can sell all of its exportable oil to China, India and Japan.

America and Russia should reach an accomodation. George W. Bush hosting Russian President Vladimir Putin at the Bush family beachfront retreat in Kennebunkport, Maine is a step in the right direction. Russia wants to redefine the relationship and create a new "pattern of equal relationship," while America is trying its best to "maintain a reciprocal relationship" with Russia.

Any wonder Putin raised the stakes in the missile shield showdown once he got home with the U.S.-Russia relationship only intensifying in the negative military-showdown sense, and pulled Russia out of the Conventional Forces in Europe treaty, citing "extraordinary circumstances ... which effect the security of the Russian Federation and requiring immediate measures."

Russian strategic bombers have resumed their Cold War practice of flying long-haul missions to areas patrolled by NATO and the U.S. In August 2007, a Russian bomber flew over a U.S. military base on the Pacific island of Guam and exchanged smiles with U.S pilots who had scrambled to track the bomber.

The turboprop Tu-95 bombers give Russia the capability of launching a devastating nuclear strike even if the nuclear arsenals on its own territory are destroyed. Code-named the "Bear" by NATO. it can stay in the air for 13 hours and may be in service until 2040

America's "potatoes of democracy" planted anywhere the U.S. wants in Russia's neighbor countries and even in Russia itself are political flash points. Russia's so-called "sovereign democracy is repelling U.S. style democracy. The Russia America wants is not what Russia has in mind, nor is it realistic. Russia could go ahead with its threats of retargeting its missiles towards Western Europe. Russia is saying it will halt the NATO inspections of its military sites and no longer limit the number of its tanks and other heavy conventional weapons.

America China and Russia need to cooperate in the 21st century civil New World Order.

Embargoes

The U.N. embargoes on Serbia and Iraq have failed. Tobacco companies R.J. Reynolds, Philip Morris and Japan Tobacco sold billions of cigarettes in violation of the embargoes. Russia, a Security Council member, sent electronic jamming equipment, antitark missiles and night vision goggles to Saddam's regime in Iraq on planes with Russian businessmen in defiance of the U.N. sanctions and without the U.N.'s approval. Russia's $40-billion economic pact with Iraq further highlighted the futility of U.N. sanctions. The combination of the lure of the dollar and sympathy for cultural kin also made a mockery of U.N. economic sanctions against Serbia, as they did to the U.N. arms embargo against all the former Yugoslav republics.

But the most absurd embargo of all was the arms embargo imposed on the Taliban in Afghanistan. Even a United Nations study on the feasibility of imposing an arms embargo on the Taliban concluded that more than 300 border crossings existed between Pakistan and Afghanistan and very few were staffed. The report concluded that if the U.N. wanted to stop every truck with a capacity of more than 10 tons, more than 10,000 border guards would be needed. Nevertheless, the U.N. imposed the arms embargo and left enforcement to the bordering countries rather than external monitors. In other words, nothing was done after the embargo was imposed.

The U.N. embargoes are just as meaningless as the U.S. embargos on China, Cuba, North Korea, Haiti, Myanmar and Vietnam. Remember, America had an embargo on China from 1949-1979 and labeled it a rogue state. Vietnam was considered the enemy from 1975 until the embargo was lifted in 1994. Today both China and Vietnam epitomize capitalism, not the communism Washington feared. The same will happen in North Korea and Cuba once the embargoes are lifted. The embargoes merely perpetuate the dictatorships they are intended to bring down because they restructure their societies in detrimental ways to survive the sanctions while they impoverish their populace.

The U.S. wants the U.N. to impose economic sanctions on Iran because of its refusal to stop its nuclear program. But Russia and China are economically tied to Iran and can veto any such resolution. There is no doubt that Iran is developing nuclear technology and is willing to share such technology with other Islamic nations. But economic sanctions are not the solution to ending Iran's nuclear program. The same holds true for any U.S. efforts to impose a U.N.-sanctioned embargo on North Korea.

What got North Korea to agree to disarm its nuclear facility was the financial sanctions imposed by the U.S. Treasury Department and China's Central Bank on Macao's Banco Delta Asia. America never froze the North Korean funds in the bank. That was done by the authorities in Macau. Once the bank was labeled a money launderer for the North's illicit activities, no reputable bank would do business with the bank.

America's arsenal of financial tools are the most powerful weapons America has when it comes to sanctions. The Treasury Department has more effective power than the Department of Defense and Department of Commerce put together.

The same happened when America, Israel and Europe stopped giving financial aid or access to their financial systems to Palestine's Hamas Government and Israel stopped remitting the tax dollars it collects for the Palestinian Authority. The financial chokehold led to civil war and the effective partition of Palestine between Hamas and Fatah.

America must accept the fact that the only way it will resolve anything with Iran is through direct negotiations or U.S. financial sanctions similar to what it did to North Korea. The April 2006 announcement that the U.S. and Iran were holding official talks on how to stabilize Iraq offered the ideal opportunity to do just that. Iran threatening America that matters will get worse in Iraq if America does not get down to serious negotiations does not help matters, especially after America arrests Iranians in Iraq who are suspected of training and supplying insurgents.

The leaders of the countries against whom sanctions are imposed merely create a lucrative underground black market that allows their supporters and backers to profit handsomely at the expense of the people. Sanctions also create havens for gunrunners, drug traffickers and money launderers. In Haiti, sanctions reinforced what Sen. John Kerry in 1993 called "a partnership made in hell, in cocaine, and in dollars between the Colombian cartels and the Haitian military," solidifying Haiti's role as a conduit for drugs to the U.S. and hobbling Haitian democracy which the embargoes were meant to restore.

Cuba

Cuba is the longest-running example of how and why embargoes don't work. Cuba's economy is unique. More than 90 percent of the entire Cuban economy is state-owned by a military dictatorship that today is run by Fidel Castro's brother Raul after Fidel, who is recovering from serious illness, handed him the reigns of power – much like the Bush family in America. Raul is trying to bring about in Cuba a China-style transformation. A more open Chinese economic model. He has travelled a number of times to China to study first-hand Beijing's economic policies, and in 2003 invited the leading economic advisor to China's then-premier, Zhu Rongji, who played a key role in opening China to foreign trade and investment, to Cuba to give a series of lectures. Raul Castro trimmed the military to 45,000 active personnel, down from 300,000 just a few years earlier. He has created a lean and mean military business machine modeled on China's PLA. The miltary owns and manages hotels, resorts, transportation and has its fingers in just about every industry opening up. Better that Cuba adopt the Chinese model rather than the Russian model, which it could have so easily succumbed to.

Raul Castro has sent senior military officers trained in Russia's most prestigious military academies to learn hotel management in Spain and accounting in Europe, Latin America, Asia and Canada. Cuba is opening up and has been since Fidel Castro came to power in 1959. State of the art Israeli farms and Chinese-made bright-blue buses are right up there with the numerous joint ventures Cuba has established globally, even in the face of the U.S. embargo.

Cuba's foreign exchange earnings have nearly doubled since an integration agreement with Venezuela was signed in 2004, due mainly to the export of medical and other services to Venezuela and record high nickel prices. Economic growth has been three times what it was at the start of the new millennium when Cuba began to recover from the post-Soviet slump. Everyone is benefiting at the expense of America. The U.S. has slammed the door in its own face.

The 40-plus year "el bloqueo," the U.S. embargo on Cuba, is such a failure that every kind of U.S. made product is available there. MasterCard, Visa and U.S. consumer items from soft drinks to diapers can be found by the more than 200,000 American citizens who travel there in defiance of the embargo. Western Union has an office there to facilitate the wire transfer of Yankee dollars. American business delegations, backed by U.S. congressmen, openly defy the embargo. "I challenge Mr. Bush to tear down this embargo," said Mississippi cotton farmer John Newcomb in May 2007, borrowing Ronald Reagan's 1987 line to Soviet leader Mikhail Gorbachev at the Berlin Wall. Newcomb was one of the U.S. executives of 114 companies from 25 states negotiating sales of agricultural products to Cuba. U.S.

exports to Cuba totalled $1.55 billion from 2001-2007 and could easily reach more than $1 billion a year.

"Sanctions are a blunt instrument which have a tendency to hurt a lot of people they are not aimed at, while providing opportunities for clever people to make money," said Edward Mortimer, a senior advisor to U.N. General-Secretary Kofi Annan.

Oil-for-Food Fiasco

On April 14, 1995, the U.N. Security Council approved the Oil-for-Food program, allowing Saddam's regime in Iraq to sell controlled amounts of oil in return for medicine, health supplies, foodstuffs, and materials and supplies for essential civilian needs. To ensure the program did not enrich the Baghdad regime, the program was placed under U.N. supervision. U.N. Resolution 986, which established the program, called for openness and for the "payment of the full amount of each purchase of Iraqi petroleum into the escrow account." The program operated from late 1996 to 2003.

Saddam and his facilitators – which included Koji Annan, son of the U.N. secretary general, and high-ranking U.N. officials – had other plans. Saddam exploited the program to avoid the U.N. sanctions from the start and pocketed $21 billion in kickbacks in the process to finance his regime, buy luxury goods, including limousines, and to build a stadium. The program was "the most extensive fraud in the history of the U.N.," according to Sen. Norm Coleman, who headed one of six U.S. congressional committees investigating the scandal. Former Secretary of State Colin Powell said the responsibility did not "rest entirely on Kofi Annan. It also rests on the membership. And especially on the Security Council, and we are a member of the Security Council."

The single largest oil consignment smuggled out of Iraq by Saddam during the Oil-for-Food program took place with U.S. government approval just weeks before the invasion. While U.S. Navy ships were patrolling the Gulf in February 2003, making a show of boarding and searching leaky *dhows* and other small ships, they turned a blind eye to tankers carrying $54 million worth of Iraq oil. The Volcker report showed shipping records from a tanker that carried the oil, including voyage instructions for the ship's captain saying the U.S. Navy was "already aware about your passage and itinerary." A total of 7.7 million barrels of oil was smuggled through the Khor al-Amaya terminal in at least seven shipments in February and March 2003. The shipments were arranged by a businessman in Jordan named "Mr. Shaheen," who told an Iraqi official he had "the Pentagon in one pocket and the CIA in the other."

The oil was bought at a heavily discounted price of around $7 a barrel, the report said. If it had been sold at fair market value within the Oil-for-Food program, it could have earned $200 million to buy humanitarian goods for the hard-pressed Iraqi people. "The illegal sales of oil from Khor al-Amaya came at a staggering cost to the program in terms of potential revenue foregone," the report said. The 18-month investigation by former U.S. Federal Reserve Chairman Paul Volcker and his team of investigators cost $35 million. The central criticism of the report was that the U.N. had "a pervasive culture resistant to accountability and prone to escaping responsibility."

The fact is that the abuse of the program was well known by member states of the Security Council as well as the staff of the U.N. Secretariat. But no one blew the whistle because whistle-blowers are afraid of retaliation, being fired and losing their pension benefits.

The U.S. State Department and the Treasury Department's Office of Foreign Assets Control did virtually nothing to ensure U.S. firms enforced sanctions against Iraq. Texas oil companies and oilmen were indicted and convicted after the independent investigations were completed.

Secretary General Kofi Annan had twice met with top executives of Cotecna, the Swiss company that paid his son more than $300,000, before the company was awarded the Oil-for-Food contract – a relationship he concealed after the contract was awarded. Despite his denials, Annan was told of efforts by his son's employer to win an Oil-for-Food contract, according to a company executive's memo. "We had brief discussions with the SG [Kofi Annan] and his entourage," the memo states. "Their collective advice was that we ... could count on their support."

Koji Annan also received more than $750,000 from several oil-trading firms investigated for their role in the Oil-for-Food program. The scandal left its indelible mark on Kofi Annan, just as he and the U.N. did with their stinging criticism of America by accusing their biggest donor of dismal failure in fighting poverty in America, with special criticism of the rebuilding of New Orleans after Hurricane Katrina.

Let's not forget that the U.N. received an estimated $1.4 billion from the 2.2 percent fee it received for administering the program. Benon V. Sevan, the head of the Oil-for-Food program, received an illegal oil allotment himself worth up to $3.5 million, according to documents discovered at the Iraqi Trade Ministry after the fall of Baghdad. He also steered oil contracts to a firm linked to relatives of former Secretary-General Boutros Boutros-Ghali. Portuguese U.N. oil inspector Armanco Carlos received more than $100, 000, according to letters discovered in the same ministry. How many other officials benefitted? It's no wonder the U.N. tried to stonewall the investigation, shredded relevant documents and refused to cooperate on the grounds of immunity.

To make matters worse, the U.N. agreed to pay Sevan $1 a year after he retired so that he could retain his diplomatic immunity. It also agreed to pay his legal bills until the independent inquiry committee headed by Paul Volcker accused Sevan of a grave conflict of interest.

Since the U.N. has no power to prosecute, it is up to individual countries to decide whether to prosecute any of their citizens or companies that were implicated by Volcker in the kickback scheme. Chances are most countries will whitewash the scandal and the victimized *We the Apathetic* taxpayers around the globe will again have been hoodwinked.

Weapons-for-Wheat

The only country besides America that took immediate action and exposed its criminals and the corruption and shortcomings of the U.N.'s Oil-for-Food scandal was Australia. The government didn't even blink. Within two weeks after the release of the Volcker report, the Cole commission was appointed to follow the scent left by Volcker's report. Volcker fingered the former Australian Wheat Board, which supplied around 16 percent of the world's wheat, and was Iraq's largest single supplier of wheat – and which was the largest single payer of kickbacks to Saddam Hussein of the 2,200 companies from 66 countries involved in corrupting the program. From 1999 to 2003, the company paid some $221.7 million in kickbacks to Saddam through "transportation" and "after-sales service" fees designed to evade U.N. sanctions.

The commission cross-examined AWB's management, its shipping and transportation partners, the foreign minister and prime minister of Australia, among others – all done in public.

Besides America and Australia, no other country accused by Volcker of violating the U.N. sanctions has launched a full-scale independent investigation into crimes committed in the name of Oil-for-Food. What made the situation so offensive is that the U.N. knew about the crimes, but took no steps to publicize or warn member states of the Iraqi practices of transportation and after-sales service contracts, and it took no steps to stop them. No surprise there, since so many U.N. bureaucrats and their relatives, family and friends benefitted on the side.

The Shmucks

The U.N. doesn't even stick to its own unwritten policies and traditions. By tradition, the secretary general's job rotates every 10 years by region, and at the dawn of the 21st century it was Asia's turn to propose a candidate. But because Africa's 10-year term was split after Boutros Boutros-Ghali of Egypt was denied a second term, the U.S. endorsed Kofi Annan for a second term, giving the continent the job of secretary general for 15 years to 2006. No wonder the international picture of conflict, corruption and total disrespect for international law is spiraling out of control while Kofi Annan receives standing ovations at the U.N. from the corrupt beneficiaries of his administration.

Annan tried a replay of former U.N. chief Kurt Waldheim, who served two five-year terms as secretary-general of the U.N. and tried for a third term that Beijing vetoed. Waldheim managed to get elected secretary-general even though as early as 1948, the U.N. War Crimes Commission listed him as a suspected war criminal subject to trial. Yet no government pressed to bring Waldheim to account or even to reveal his Nazi past until he decided to seek the presidency of Austria. At age 19 he joined the National Socialist German Students League – just a month after Anschluss. Then in November 1938 he enrolled in the SA, the paramilitary Nazi organization of storm troopers. He served as a lieutenant attached to brutal German military units that executed thousands of Yugoslav partisans and civilians and deported thousands of Greek Jews to death camps from 1942-1944.

Like current Secretary General Ban Ki-noon, Waldheim worked his way to the top of the Austrian Foreign Ministry and became foreign minister before taking the reins of the U.N. from 1972 to 1982.

As if that wasn't bad enough, the U.S. through its bruising ambassador John Bolton recommended indirectly that Asia again be denied its role in the defunct organization by proposing that the top U.N. job be open to all to ensure getting the best candidate. Some speculated that Britain's Prime Minister Tony Blair was eyeing the job, which pays more than the American president earns. Some said Bill Clinton was also eyeing the post. America and Britain pushed the "best candidate" mantra that failed.

There is no provision in the U.N. Charter for removal of a secretary-general, who is chosen by the General Assembly at the recommendation of the Security Council, even when the U.N. staff and union have lost faith in senior management. That's how Kofi Annan managed to survive.

To his credit, Annan did insist it was Asia's turn to provide a successor. Asia, the world's largest region, has not had a U.N. chief since U Thant of Myanmar (then Burma) finished his second term in 1971.

Hopefully, the sad experience of Kofi Annan and the lessons he learned will be taken to heart by his successor, South Korea's former foreign minister, Ban Ki-moon. They are lessons Annan learned based on the U.N. Charter, which the U.N. itself ignores. Lesson one: We are all responsible for each other's security, and that includes the people of Darfur. Second, we are responsible for each other's welfare. All people have the right to share in global prosperity. Third, security and prosperity depend on respect for human rights and the rule of law. Fourth, governments must be accountable both domestically and internationally.

The problem is that poor and weak nations are easily held to account, since they need foreign aid. But the large and powerful states, such as America and China, whose actions have the greatest impact on others, can be contained only by *We the Apathetic People*. And the fifth lesson: Developing countries should be given a greater say in a restructured United Nations that reflects the reality of today's world.

There is one major disconnect worth mentioning between what the outgoing Annan has said, and what his successor, Ban, said in his first policy opinion regarding the execution of Saddam Hussein, which contradicted not only Ban's swearing-in promises, but the U.N. Charter as well. Global human rights, as embodied by the U.N. Charter, make clear that all human life should be protected, no matter what the circumstances. Ban should have urged Iraqi leaders not to proceed with the hangings of Saddam and others, and after the fact, should have been the first to condemn the executions. But Ban, who comes from a country that executes criminals, like much of Asia, did the opposite.

The problem is, Ban no longer represents South Korea in any government capacity – he heads the U.N. Its charter and more than half of its member countries have abolished the death penalty. The Philippines in 2006 became the latest Asian nation to do so.

Not only is the U.N. out of sync with the 21st century, but so is its secretary general, who has no idea as to what he should be. Secretary, general or stick to his job description – chief administrative officer. No matter which role he chooses to play, he will upset members. Ban acknowledged as much in his acceptance speech, saying: "Modesty is about demeanour, not about vision and goals. It does not mean a lack of commitment or leadership." It does mean loss and defeat. Talk about being caught between a rock and a hard place. Security Council members that don't want to make the body fair and a General Assembly that doesn't want to make it efficient. The selfishness of one side encourages the irresponsibility of the other. Things are going to get a lot worse before they get better.

As if the politics of the organization aren't bad enough, the spending policies are even worse. This is one subject on which I do agree with every ambassador to the U.N. who has criticised its spending policies, including John Bolton of the U.S.

The U.N. secretary general's 14,000-square-foot neo-Georgian attached townhouse, with four floors and a basement official residence, is in

Manhattan's exclusive Sutton Place near the East River. It is a great area to take a walk through after a delightful dinner at any one of the eateries on 1st Avenue. Unfortunately, Ban Ki-moon won't be able to enjoy it for a while because he will have to rough it at the Waldorf-Astoria during the residence's $4.5-million renovation. Hopefully, he can relate and communicate with North Korea's Dear Leader who is living in similar surroundings and life style and will be the bridge that will not only benefit both Koreas – but the world. The chief nuclear envoys from the two Koreas meeting in New York, and with their American counterpart, was a step in the right direction. The alternative is that Ban is angry at Kim Jong-il for raining nuclear fallout on his parade and stealing his thunder, and wants to get even. After all, it was the U.N. that was also nuked by North Korea's nuclear test. Appointing a South Korean slippery eel was the wrong political compromise. Watching Ban Ki-moon duck behind a podium in Iraq as a rocket landed inside the heavily guarded Green Zone in central Baghdad said it all.

Unbalanced Assembly & Checkbook

The concept of one country, one vote in the General Assembly is absurd in the 21st century. To think that a country like China, with a quarter of the world's population, and the United States, with the world's largest economy, have equal clout to Antigua with a population of 66,000 and Equatorial Guinea with a gross national product of $218 million and oppressive bandit dictatorships, is ridiculous. Let's get real in the New World Order. Why aren't America and China leading the charge for change?

The time, money and effort being spent to administer and manage the U.N. could be better spent winding it down and starting a new organization with a solid foundation and sound fundamentals that are relevant to the 21st century. Why waste more time, money and human talent beating a dead bureaucratic horse?

U.N. resolutions, like traffic lights in developing countries, are optional, unenforceable and discarded. The 1991 U.N. cease-fire resolution that ended the Gulf War is a glaring example. Seventeen resolutions were passed over a 12-year period and ignored by Saddam Hussein. The ignored resolutions passed by the Security Council for Israel to end its siege of Yasser Arafat's Ramallah compound were just more millennium reminders. Is it any won-der North Korea and Iran will not recognize any resolutions adopted by the

U.N.?

The U.N.'s own study, conducted by Deloitte Consulting, concluded that while procedures for reporting and combatting corruption exist, most staff members are either unaware of how to use them or fear retaliation if they do. "Senior leaders caught in serious breaches of ethics should be punished, not promoted as usual," one staffer complained. "Get rid of the old-boy network," another added. "That network is wide, tenacious and powerful. It is the ruin of the U.N. officers. So long as you can wind your way into that network, you are OK. If not, you are doomed." Kofi Annan acknowledged that U.N. employees "generally perceive that breaches of integrity and ethical conduct are insufficiently and inequitably addressed by the disciplinary system."

The U.N.'s internal auditor has existed for only a few years, and Madeleine Albright called it a "junkyard puppy." Combative U.S. envoy John Bolton went even further. He described the U.N. as "a great, rusting hulk of a bureaucratic superstructure ... dealing with issues from the ridiculous to the sublime." Waste and mismanagement is not reported because the U.N. bureaucracy is not responsible to any elected official or taxpayer. They are in the reporting twilight zone. The waste, nepotism, employment and promotion of mistresses and girlfriends, double billing for expenses and failure to account for millions of dollars allocated for specific operations is well known and repeatedly echoed in the worldwide press. So why bother perpetuating a corrupt dysfunctional global body in the New World Order? The U.S. is justified in not paying its dues. Great first step. But what is next?

They are trying. Water is now no longer served at many General Assembly meetings and interpreters now rarely work after 6 in the evening. I don't think these steps quite cut it. Do you? Why shouldn't every bureaucrat working for an international organization be accountable for waste and mismanagement?

Chinese President Jiang Zemin's remarks at the Millennium Summit are relevant to the New World Order. "The Cold War is over.... But the unfair and irrational old international political and economic order has yet to be replaced." He added: "The Cold War mentality must be abandoned once and for all and a new security concept based on mutual trust, mutual benefit, equality and cooperation should be established." Shouldn't America's leaders be saying the same and together with China, abolish the U.N. and create a relevant replacement?

New Moral Order

A new global moral order is emerging. It is one in which morality takes precedence over the politics and diplomacy of war and peace. The former pariah Libya is a good example, and their daily reminder is in New York's East Side in the building where their mission is based. Now that it has renounced nuclear weapons, it is warmly embraced by America and the West. Its properties in America, including the mission, were there before they came clean. The class-action lawsuits filed by the Filipino, Spanish and Swiss victims of martial law under Marcos and Pinochet are establishing a new moral high ground. Similar action against the Japanese, Nazis and their Swiss bankers by the victims of Japanese atrocities and the Nazi Holocaust helped reach that high ground. The Japanese still have a longer row to hoe.

This moral new high ground requires us to closely reexamine the world scene today, starting in South Africa, the cradle of the moral high ground. South Africa is a model for the rest of the continent as to how a country can make a peaceful and democratic transition from the tyranny of a white minority to black majority rule. Nobel Laureate Bishop Desmond Tutu, who together with Nelson Mandela, was instrumental in seeing the transition peacefully through, was correct in lambasting his government for voting in support of and giving comfort to the oppressive military regime in Myanmar. Tutu rightly suggests that South Africa, because of its history, has a special responsibility to pursue a foreign policy that supports international action to help oppressed populations.

Author Conrado de Quiros points out that there is a subtle shift in the conduct of nations occurring today, and we should be elated about it. Noninterference and respect for differences in cultures remain vital principles, and should be upheld. But that should not mean the kind of conspiracy of silence – or tacit collusion, in the case of the Swiss banks – that has allowed tyrants to flourish in the past. The shift isn't really that subtle. It's been demanded for years. It just hasn't been acted upon. No more. Marcos, Estrada, Pinochet, Bhutto, Sharrif, Fujimori, Suharto, Wahid and Saddam Hussein confirmed our new 21st century morality. Similar actions against Robert

Mugabe, Kim Jong-il, Bashar al-Assad, Hosni Mubarak, the House of Saud and their princely sons are the next logical steps to confirm that the new morality is here to stay.

In the 1970s, world leaders began to talk of a "new international economic order" that would distribute wealth more evenly across the globe. That did not happen. But the idea remains valid. I do not know why we shouldn't start articulating a "new international moral order" today, one that is capable of introducing moral judgment in the conduct of nations, even while respecting different ways of life. Some things in life are universally right or wrong. Those that are wrong the U.N. can no longer stop. Those that are right it cannot enforce.

The arrest of Pinochet in 1998 is an example of right. It's appropriate that it was the British and not the American authorities who arrested him for crimes against humanity while he labored from a pain in the ass – hemorrhoids. Lest we forget, it was Richard Nixon and Henry Kissinger who helped Pinochet murder Salvador Allende and set him on a throne of blood like Macbeth, shortly after they helped Ferdinand Marcos build a "throne of bayonets" – Ninoy Acquino's phrase – in his own country. The House of Saud, the only family to have a country named after it, and its numerous oil-gushing dictatorial cousins who grease American palms while professing to be friendly, are sitting on thrones of nuclear suitcases and the dirty bombs they finance.

Many American leaders have been a pain to many Pacific Islanders in the name of "national security." The U.S. has tested nuclear weapons and missiles on various atolls and islands in the Pacific for years. It sought to dominate other islands such as Palau for future defense needs.

"There is no justice in this organization," Palau's High Chief Ibedul Gibbons bemoaned as he and I prepared to go to the United Nations Trusteeship Council on May 3, 1991, to again – for the 15th time – present Palau's case that the U.N. and the U.S. were both in breach of their trusteeship responsibilities. "We have been coming here for years and gotten nowhere. Each year we point out their failures and each year they promise they will look into it," Chief Gibbons said. We had arrived a couple days earlier from Washington, D.C., where we had filed our lawsuit against the U.S. government on April 29.

Palau is a nation of 300 islands, 20,000 people, 1,500 species of fish, 700 varieties of coral and America's ideal location for a naval base in the Pacific. Only nine of the islands are inhabited. It is the last country in the world to shed its colonial status. It became independent in 1994.

The Trusteeship Council's failure to condemn the U.S. for its clear violation of its trusteeship responsibility to the Palauans was my initial first-hand experience of the agency's U.S. dominance, inefficiency and incompetence. The U.N.'s incompetence was magnified by the $3-billion election and democratization plan for Cambodia that ended in a bloody coup, the unabated murder and genocide of hundreds of thousands in Rwanda and Bosnia and the starvation of millions in Somalia, the eventual death of U.S. Rangers under the U.N. flag and the continued genocide in Sudan. Lt. Gen. Maurice Baril, who was Boutros Boutros-Ghali s top military advisor, recalled that "there was a lot of enthusiasm that we could put some order into the world, and that the U.N. was the best tool to achieve that. Then came Somalia – the coldest bucket of water dropped on the international community." The film Black Hawk Down showed the world the stupidity of it all. Well-meaning soldiers who end up killing thousands of innocent civilians in the interest of saving a couple of U.S. Rangers who went there to save millions with food aid on behalf of the international community, led by the U.N.

They should have heeded Richard Nixon's warning: "The popular idea that the United Nations can play a larger role in resolving international conflicts is illusory."

Nowhere is this truer than in Colombia, America's cocaine-producing backyard, which has been exploited to the max by the various revolutionary forces challenging the U.S.-imposed government. More than 2 million of its 36 million official inhabitants are refugees – right behind the Congo and Sudan – making a mockery of the Monroe Doctrine, especially since the U.S. has a military presence there to this day. The cocaine drug war, "Plan Colombia," a program on which the U.S. government has already spent more than $3 billion – most of it on military – is a failure and a waste of taxpayers' money. Colombia has been the third-largest recipient of American aid after Israel and Egypt. Is it any wonder U.S. and U.N. concerns have no credibility?

Lewis MacKenzie, a Canadian major general who commanded the U.N.'s Sarajevo sector in 1992, recalls sitting in his bunker under fire, "reading a Security Council resolution and saying to myself, 'Are these people out of their minds? What the hell do they want me to do?' Then you finally figured out what they wanted you to do, but they didn't provide the resources." U.N. speak is worse than Washington-speak. We have to constantly remind ourselves that U.N. vernacular is gibberish.

Trying to unify the U.N. is a hopeless waste of time and money – a conclusion even a U.N. independent panel reached, joining the growing calls for reform or replacement. Kofi Annan appointed Shaukat Aziz, prime minister of Pakistan, Luisa Dias Diogo, prime minister of Mozambique, and Jens Stoltenberg, prime minister of Norway, to head a panel to investigate and prepare a report on how the U.N. could greatly improve its effectiveness in the field of development, humanitarian assistance and the environment.

International cooperation is critical. The U.N. needs to be radically overhauled if it is to survive. If not, it will find itself increasingly marginalized. And the ones that suffer most will be the world's poorest and most vulnerable. The report went on to say that the system is failing widely through the lack of institutional effectiveness, cost efficiency and focus, encouraged in many cases by poor governance and unpredictable funding. Inadaequate cooperation has been hindered also by internal competition for funding, mission creep and outdated practices. Furthermore, the U.N.'s presence in countries and regions is often fragmented and weak. Much of this is the result of policy incoherence, program duplication and vested interests in the status quo. This notwithstanding the fact that even a majority of the U.N.'s members demand that drastic reforms be adopted before it is too late.

Is it any wonder the U.N. General Assembly heard Syria bombard the U.S. and call its "war on terror" a failure. North Korea called the U.S. a "highhanded" superpower, while Myanmar also jumped in with veiled threats of how U.S. bullying singles out innocent victims. The pillars of the U.N. Charter have been made a mockery by the countries that, as bad as they are and have to be harshly dealt with – are right. *We the Apathetic People* better wake up before it is too late.

Growing inequality in the advanced industrial countries was a long predicted but seldom mentioned consequence of globalization. Full economic integration implies the equalization of unskilled wages everywhere in the world. Though we are nowhere near attaining this "goal," the downward pressure on the bottom is self-evident, Nobel laureate Joseph Stiglitz wrote in his book, *Making Globalization Work*.

"In the year 2015, they plan to send a spaceship to Jupiter to search for water, yet in Africa or India we can't get water to the people who need it," said Kevin Watkins, lead author of a U.N. report calling for an end to "water apartheid."

Is it any wonder China has jumped into Africa feet first? They'll get them water and whatever else they need, in exchange for Africa's oil and gas resources, much to the dismay of America.

Racism
The U.N. gibberish was perpetuated into the 21st century in the name of the Conference Against Racism, which generated as much controversy as its name did questions. "Conference Against Racism, Racial Discrimination, Xenophobia and Related Intolerance" is a name that reflects its design by a dysfunctional U.N. committee.

The U.N. World Conference Against Racism that took place in South Africa in the opening year of the millennium was just the latest and first 21st-century example of the United Nations' string of embarrassing failures. It was another attempt by Muslim and African developing nations, some of which still practice slavery, to extort money from America and the developed world for the slavery they practiced for centuries and then encouraged America and the European nations to adopt before they became developed civilized countries and ended the practice. It became an anti-American hate fest that resulted in America walking out of the conference. The Durban Conference ended 72 hours before the 9/11 kamikaze attack that took place a few miles from the U.N.

While the Durban conference was preaching its lofty ideals, President Robert Mugabe in nearby Zimbabwe was expelling white farmers and expropriating their farms – just because they are white. The devastating effect of

Mugabe's racist policy is that in 10 years the country has been transformed from Africa's breadbasket into another African basket case. The evicted white farmers were warmly welcomed by other African nations that have benefitted from their agricultural knowledge and expertise. Zambia led the move and has gone from suffering food shortages in the 1990s to exporting food – ironically, much of it back to Zimbabwe.

The main problem of racism in Africa is its tribalism. It is what allows monstrous megalomaniacs to persist against all the interests of "the country." It is probably the antipathies of tribalism that keep them there rather than the rationalistic interests of the unit called Zimbabwe, a creation of white boys at the Berlin Conference of 1884-1885.

While Africa's liberating lion Robert Gabriel Mugabe was celebrating his 83rd birthday on February 23, 2007, even though he was born on February 21, 1924, in Kutama Mission, the country's teachers from public primary and secondary schools went on strike. He received his education in Jesuit schools. Primarily a teacher, he joined the National Democratic Party and earned a 10-year jail term, during which time he earned bachelor's degrees in law and education. When Rhodesian President Ian Smith allowed Mugabe to attend a conference in Lusaka, Zambia, he took off to Mozambique where he recruited volunteer freedom fighters. He and political rival Joshua Nkomo fought a successful guerrilla war with soldiers trained in China.

On December 21, 1979, the Lancaster House Agreement ended Britain's rule over Rhodesia and paved the way for democratic elections the next year, which Mugabe won. He brought his Marxist communist ideals that formed his personal philosophy and social justice to bear on addressing the inequalities left by the white regime. Within a year, free junior school education was every Zimbabwean's right. Those who qualified were guaranteed a place in secondary schools. A new housing law gave ownership to people who had rented their homes for 30 years or more. And the poor had access to free medical care.

Yeltsinize Mugabe
In the late 1980s, Zimbabwe was the textbook example of a functioning African state. Yet today, after two decades of rule, Mugabe has become a caricature of the African despot – in the footsteps and tradition of Uganda's

brutal Idi Amin. With the devastated economy left after Mugabe's seizure of white-owned farms, he now plans to take control of the country's two biggest diamond mines.

To his credit, Zimbabwe boasts a very high literacy rate for Africa. But, paradoxically, this is working against Mugabe. The young electorate – called the "Born Free" because they did not grow up under white rule, have learned the ideals of democracy and socialism yet they have also witnessed their president's descent into dictatorship and they want change. Shouldn't *We the Apathetic Maids* be doing the same?

Mugabe is determined to annoint his successor so that he can escape the almost certain criminal prosecution he will face if an opposition candidate wins. The ghosts of the 20,000 Ndebe people slaughtered in the Gukurahundi crackdown in the 1980s by the North Korean-trained Fifth Brigade, the starvation and brutality brought upon opposition supporters and their supporters in the media, the use of torture and the abuse of human rights all build a solid case against him. He knows he needs an exit strategy. And while he figures it out, the brutality and ban on opposition parties and politicians within his own party is destined to bring him down. Anytime a country is hungry and broke, its leader gets busted. That is the time to sit down with that leader and grant him immunity from prosecution and let him and his family keep a portion of their plundered loot that belongs to the people. That is the deal Boris Yeltsin cut with Vladimir Putin and the Russian people when the Russian economy was in tatters. Isn't it time Zimbabwe cut the same deal with Mugabe?

By the end of 2007, Zimbabwe had been run into the ground by Mugabe, who has been running the country for 28 years. Exchange rates double weekly if not daily. Inflation reached 66,000 percent in January, 2008 – the highest in the world and is estimated to reach 1.5 million percent by the end of 2008. Doctors, nurses, teachers, electricity workers, civil servants and the military all threatened to strike or quit as they demanded pay raises of up to 1,000 percent.

Unemployment reached 80 percent by mid 2007. It is estimated that more than 3.5 million people – about one-quarter of the population – have left the country, in a massive drain of youth and ambition. Opposition leaders getting assaulted and seriously injured by the police for no reason is reminiscent of what happened in South Africa in the apartheid era. Calls for Mugabe to resign or retire when his term expires in March 2008 have increased, especially after he shocked his party stalwarts and the opposition by announcing that he was going to stand for another six-year term. His hard-core supporters are pushing him to stay in power until 2010. Mugabe has been told by his intelligence chiefs that he will lose the election. Is this any way to allow a country to be run? He should be granted immunity from prosecution and asked to retire quickly and quietly like Russia's Yeltsin, so more people do not need to needlessly suffer.

Australia's former Prime Minister John Howard is to be commended for ordering Australia's cricket team not to attend a world match because it would give legitimacy to a "grubby dictator." The silence of world leaders, especially African leaders – and African-Americans and Afro-Everybodies – to Zimbabwe's continued racism as it descends into chaos makes the contentious racist Conference Against Racism just another of the many ongoing examples of the U.N.'s irrelevancy and dysfunctionality in the New World Order.

To make matters worse, which only the U.N. can do, Zimbabwe's environment and tourism minister, Francis Nheme, was elected in 2007 to head the U.N. intergovernmental body on sustainable development and the environment. This is a guy who is from a bankrupt country, ruined his own farm in Zimbabwe which was seized from a white farmer and presided over the collapse of the country's wildlife sanctuaries. How an incompetent manager from a bankrupt country can promote global sustainable development remains to be seen.

WHO

The U.N.'s World Health Organization Africa Office has been accused by the medical journal *The Lancet* of being autocratic, inefficient and little more than "a retirement home" for African officials. The selection of senior staff is rarely based on competence or qualification. "In particular, appointments of country representatives, who should coordinate WHO efforts in their countries, are often paybacks for political or other favors," *The Lancet's* Pierre Virot said. He added, "The regional office thus has strong, some might say incestuous, relations with African governments at the ministry level, to the extent that senior health ministry officials see WHO/AFRO as their future retirement home. Unless WHO's African office is transformed from a political club to an effective health agency, its right to existence is questionable."

The new top dog at WHO is Hong Kong's former health chief Margaret Chan Fung Fu-chun. She is the seventh director-general and the first Chinese – the first Asian for that matter – in U.N. history. Hong Kong is recognized as the medical heartbeat of China. A city state where doctors in the public hospitals are known to work 80-hour weeks and which has already been on the front lines in the war on bird flu and SARS, front lines that Margaret fought valiantly, and is well equipped to deal with a major threat to human health, such as pandemic influenza or other deadly viruses.

Hong Kong is a place where top-quality state of the art public hospitals are easily available and accessible virtually free to permanent residents. Hong Kongers are world leaders in longevity and have among the lowest levels of infant and maternal mortality, basic standards by which healthcare systems are judged. Its innovative approach to healthcare is now being offered to WHO. Margaret has made a unique proposition to fight the bird flu pandemic. Big donor countries should pool their resources to take out private insurance to pay for bird flu vaccines to allow poor, developing nations to receive vaccines and prevent a pandemic that potentially could kill millions.

Genocide
The U.N.'s inability and failure to do anything about Darfur – Africa's holocaust – is a replay of the 1994 genocide in Rwanda and another example of how dysfunctional and irrelevant the U.N. is in the 21st century. "Call it a civil war. Call it ethnic cleansing. Call it genocide. Call it 'none of the above.'" Colin Powell said, "The reality is the same: There are people in Darfur who desperately need the help of the international community. We concluded – I concluded – that genocide has been committed in Darfur and that the government of Sudan and the *Janjaweed* bear responsibility," Powell said. Sounds like a great weed that should go up in smoke. Since September 2003, nearly 2 million black non-Arab Africans have been displaced and from 300,000 to 400,000 killed by the *Janjaweed*, which means "devils with a gun on horseback." The genocide in Darfur is nothing new. It is just the scale. The Arab nomadic tribes of the region have been at odds with the

black African farmer and cattle-breeders for centuries. At one time the black Africans in Darfur were slaves to the Arabs. The conflict between the two groups is no different than that of descendants of slaves elsewhere, except it is a lot more violent because it is not about freedom or equal rights, but power, land rich with natural resources, including oil, and revenge. Emotions that have been bubbling inside the collective memories of tribes for centuries have erupted in a lawless vacuum in which human rights are non-existent. More than 50 percent of the displaced people lack adequate food. The U.N. estimates that up to 4 million people are at risk of famine.

This is the reality of what happens if one believes in Darwin's theory of the survival of the fittest, or any religious prophesy. The end result is the same.

That is why Israel cannot take the threat of annihilation lightly. It sees a threat to its very existence. Iran is not alone in its threats, just the most vocal. Arab opinion leaders openly advocate genocide – though few around the world seem to notice or care. Meanwhile, the Israelis sit and watch. They have the power to do to the Arabs what the Arabs want to do to them, but the Israelis choose not to use it. Israel could wipe out the entire Arab population of the West Bank, Gaza and Southern Lebanon if it wanted to – and still have plenty of firepower left over, conventional as well as nuclear, to destroy every Arab capital, plus Tehran in Iran.

Instead, in Israel, where Arabs make up 20 percent of the country's 7 million citizens, Arabs have 13 members in Israel's 120-seat parliament, and one Muslim cabinet minister.

Israelis are adverse to killing innocent civilians en masse because that's what has been done to them for centuries, most recently the Holocaust. Most Israelis and Jews believe mass murder is morally wrong. It is also a war crime, and although international law makes room for self-defense, the Israelis don't dare apply the doctrine to all their potential enemies – there are too many, in too many places. Better to try and make peace with them and together isolate and restrain Iran, something Israel is quietly negotiating. Israel and its Arab neighbors recognize that Iran is a threat to the entire region. Its success with Hezbollah in Lebanon against Israel has emboldened Tehran and it is replicating that Hezbollah model in Iraq. Iran is building an enormous military force in Iraq to exert influence there after U.S. and other troops leave.

Why create adversaries and take a hostile stand with one side? Why not work together for regional peace instead of conflict? That is why many Israeli soldiers who fought in the war in Lebanon are engaged in some soul searching under the auspices of Breaking the Silence, a group of former soldiers shocked at their own misconduct and that of others. They gather regularly to look in the mirror, recount their stories and bear witness.

But those who strike at Israel will be repelled and pushed back. That is why the confrontations with Hezbollah will continue. As long as Arabs, especially those on Israel's borders, talk about annihilation while Israelis talk about preserving the status quo – there will be no lasting peace in the Middle East – much to American arm merchants' delight. They keep selling arms to an instable region to ensure the continued flow of oil. The Arabs, particularly the Hamas leadership in Syria and Palestine, have a seemingly permanent gripe in that Israel exists. And so the two opposing sides, ultimately, have little to talk about – and the U.N. can't think of a way to get them to – while they keep arming themselves to the teeth.

The advocacy of the destruction of Israel is a flat violation of the U.N. Charter, which all member states must sign, but once again *We the Apathetic Maids* are tuned out to this fact because we don't want to be confused by the facts. We keep burying our heads in the sand. "It is inconceivable that ... a member of the United Nations continues to be received throughout the world as a legitimate leader while he stands up and says that another U.N. member state should be wiped off the map," Israel's Prime Minsiter Ehud Olmert said. Jews won't repeat the mistakes of the Holocaust by burying their heads in the sand.

The fact is that Iran's President Mahmoud Ahmadinejad should be tried for incitement to genocide. The other fact is that neither Iran nor Syria wants to be indicted by the U.N., and that is precisely why they want to talk but don't like U.S. pre-conditions. The U.S. doesn't like theirs either. None of the parties like the resolutions the U.N. passed relating to the regional conflicts and sovereign rights.

There is room for dialogue, but unfortunately the U.N. is unable to foster or create the right environment for it to flourish. None of the parties to the conflicts want the U.N. there since they have all experienced its track record of failure. Meanwhile, the deep underground tunnels keep being built by Hezbollah and Hamas, much like the Viet Cong did in Vietnam or the North Koreans with their tunnels deep into the South.

Sudan

Despite the 1978 discovery in Sudan of some of Africa's largest oil reserves, much of the country is devoid of paved roads, hospitals and schools. The ongoing conflict has made many regions off limits to aid workers and doctors who could help stave off unnecessary deaths.

As if things aren't bad enough in Sudan, the violence is now pursuing the victims across the border into Chad as the *Janjaweed* fighters repeat their atrocities there as they try to transform Chad into a fundamentalist Islamic country like Sudan.

Massacres continue in the presence of lightly armed U.N. soldiers who are instructed not to use force. The U.N. investigation into the human rights abuses in Darfur concluded that the violence there was not genocide. The green light for the Darfur genocide trials to begin in the International Criminal Court was finally given by the U.N. when it was agreed that U.S. citizens would be exempted. The initial opposition to punish came from America, worried about its citizens being prosecuted, Arab countries that are sympathetic to Khartoum, and from Security Council members such as Pakistan, Russia and China, which are heavily invested in Sudan's emerging oil industry.

Sudan is Africa's biggest country by land area and produces 250,000 barrels of oil a day and the government announced in 2003 that significant discoveries had been made in Darfur. Oil is what triggered the current genocide. African tribes had been demanding for decades that the Arab-dominated government's policies of neglect and discrimination end. The government retaliated by sending in the *janjaweed* after the discovery of oil.

Sudan's oil is the glue that solidifies the close relationship it has with China. China is Sudan's biggest export market. China sliced $80 million off Sudan's debt mountain and built a new railway line to Red Sea ports and a presidential palace in early 2007 during Hu Jintao's visit to the country. Arms sales naturally follow. Something the U.S. used to do so well. Let's not forget who got the North Koreans to sign the de-nuclearization agreement, offered millions of dollars in aid to Sudan in early 2007 for Sudan to start searching in earnest for a peaceful resolution to the Darfur tragedy and allow U.N. peacekeepers in Darfur. China has U.N. peacekeepers in the south of Sudan. The criticism of China for its failure to utilize its relationship to end the carnage in Darfur is unfair.

The Security Council voted unanimously in August 2007 to send 26,000 peacekeepers by the end of the year, to end four years of rape and slaughter. Reality is they will not be in place until the end of 2008 at the earliest. To put together that large a force consisting of troops, police, logistics and sophisticated military hardware from different countries, most of them from Africa, will take time.

China persuaded Sudan to accept the peacekeepers, the world's largest peace-keeping operation. Hollywood succeeded to get China to do what career politicians in Washington, D.C. failed to. It scripted, directed and acted out the political fallout if China failed to act, something *We the Apathetic Maids* can also do to bring about change. Steven Spielberg quit his position as artistic advisor to the Beijing Games. George Clooney publicized the plight of the Darfur refugees. Mia Farrow and Hollywood friends demanded the U. S. boycott the Beijing Olympics.

The groundswell for a boycott of the Beijing 2008 Olympics was a potential embarrassment for China, which wants to use the games to showcase its rise in the world. The 2008 Beijing Olympics is an opportunity for China and America to address and remove many of the thorny issues that repeatedly prick the Sino-U.S. partnership necessary to lead a peaceful and harmonious world through the 21st century.

Beijing did, and continues to put pressure on Khartoum. In a move to pressure Sudan into accepting peacekeepers there, China removed Sudan from its list of countries for which it will provide financial incentives to Chinese companies seeking to invest. That was just the first squeeze. China has used "very direct language" to persuade the Sudanese government to end the conflict in Darfur.

Gender Justice

The U.N. Security Council referred to the International Criminal Court in The Hague for prosecution a case of mass rape and other war crimes against two senior Sudanese officials, former state minister for the interior Ahmed Harun and *Janjaweed* militia commander Alui Muhammad Ali Abd al Rahman, also known as Ali Kushayb. Sexual violence has been traditionally under-reported and under-prosecuted. Women as the victims or pawns of belligerents could demand no recourse. All sorts of crimes against humanity do not get prosecuted because the victims are often reluctant to come forward, largely because they have little confidence that justice will be done.

Both the U.S., a strident opponent of the ICC, and China abstained on the vote. The Sudanese government protested violently and threatened to "cut the throat of any international official ... who tries to jail a Sudanese official in order to present him to international justice." If Khartoum remains defiant, the Security Council will hopefully enforce its ICC resolution. The Security Council is the ultimate guarantor of the ICC's credibility. Failure to ensure compliance would encourage not only Sudan, but other governments whose officials are targeted by the ICC, to defy it.

Nevertheless, there is room for maneuver if legitimate reasons for progress or compromise exist. The Rome Statute, which established the ICC, permits the Security Council to put prosecutions on hold for a 12-month period, renewable annually. How the Security Council responds to Sudan's defiance will go a long way to determining whether the ICC will meet its founders' expectations that it "put an end to impunity for the perpetrators of [atrocity crimes] and thus to contribute to the prevention of such crimes." It will also determine whether anyone will be held accountable for the shocking atrocities in Darfur.

China Rising

China's single-largest source of foreign crude oil is Sudan. Oil from Sudan comprises 5 percent of China's total oil imports and almost 60 percent of Sudan's exports. China also has a 41 percent stake in Petrodar, a group that runs a pipeline that carries about 200,000 barrels of oil a day out of southern Sudan.

China today is a net importer of oil. It is the No. 2 petroleum user after the U.S. With 1.3 billion people and an economy growing at 8 percent to 10 percent per year, its appetite for oil will only increase. Since the early 1990s until 2001, China's oil consumption has grown 7.5% a year, seven times America's growth rate, forcing the country to go looking overseas for new supplies. From 2001 to 2004, China's energy consumption rose yearly by an average of almost 10 percent, hitting 15 percent in 2004. China's average annual growth in energy consumption is outpacing both its gross domestic product and industrial development. By 2030, China is expected to have more cars than the U.S. and import as much oil as the U.S. does today. China will need more than 14 billion barrels of foreign oil a day, according to projections. China is willfully heading towards the auto-oil mess that America got itself into, and by 2030 will be right there. Hopefully, by then, America may have come up with some alternatives to the binge of fossil fuels.

It is therefore no surprise that Warren Buffett's Berkshire Hathaway was invested to the tune of 2.3 billion shares in PetroChina, which has indefinte and indirect ties to Sudan, through its parent China National Petroleum Corp., which is state owned, and many shareholders and media outlets are outraged. An executive order issued by President Bill Clinton in 1997, which President George W. Bush expanded, limits U.S. investments in Sudan. Berkshire maintained that it saw no proof PetroChina did business in Sudan. "We think our position is correct," Buffett said.

It should therefore come as no surprise that China National Offshore Oil Corporation tried to buy Unocal. Twenty seven percent of Unocal's proven oil reserves and 73 percent of its proven natural gas reserves are in Asia. When CNOOC's attempt to buy Unocal was thwarted, it moved on and paid $2.3 billion to acquire a 45 percent stake in offshore oil and gas fields in Nigeria that have estimated recoverable reserves of 1.1 billion barrels of oil. It also considered a bid for Nations Energy, a privately owned Kazakhstan oil producer that pumps more than 50,000 barrels of oil per day from a field that contains nearly a half-billion barrels of reserves.

China National Petroleum Corporation has multi-billion-dollar joint ventures in 10 foreign countries including Iran, Kazakhstan, Venezuela, Algeria, Peru, Oman, Azerbaijan, Ecuador, Niger, Chad and Canada. The Alberta oil sand deposits in Canada, roughly the size of Florida, are believed to contain the richest reserves after Saudi Arabia. Three of China's state-owned oil firms have significant investments in the oil sands, including a 40% stake in a $3.6-billion project that will be able to send oil via a new pipeline to Canada's west coast for shipment to China.

The China-Kazakhstan Cooperation Strategy for the 21st century forges the cross-border construction of oil and gas pipelines and works closely on oil and gas processing, building new power facilities and providing electricity to third countries. China's Citic group acquired the oil assets of Canada-based Nations Energy in Kazakhstan for $1.9 billion. Nations Energy's 94.6 percent subsidiary, Karazhanbasmunai, holds 100 percent of the mineral rights to develop the Karazhanbas oil and gas field in Mangistau Oblast, until 2020. The oilfield has proven reserves of more than 340 million barrels and current production of over 50,000 barrels per day.

China's top offshore oil and gas producer, CNOOC, made its biggest-ever overseas oil mining acquisition in Nigeria in 2006. It bought a 45 percent stake in Nigeria's OML 130 oil area – also known as the Akpo deposit – which will be able to pump 225,000 barrels a day of oil after it comes on stream in 2008, or 9 percent of Nigeria's current production. Crime and militancy flourish in Nigeria's Niger Delta region, which provides all of Nigeria's crude oil exports, and residents complain of neglect and marginalization. Chinese workers are repeatedly kidnapped and released for undisclosed ransoms.

Chinese crews are building roads, bridges, railroads and installing modern electricity pylons throughout Africa in exchange for the right to extract oil. Beijing has won friends in Africa with such big gestures, including a $1.2-billion continent-wide debt-forgiveness program. China is also drilling for oil in Saudi Arabia, a country that U.S. oil companies once had to themselves. Africa gained little from the U.N. under Kofi Annan's tenure. It has gained more from China. The U.N. failure is most notable in the Sudanese region of Darfur. The Sudanese government is opposed to the deployment of up to 20, 000 U.N. peacekeepers mandated by the Security Council in August 2006. Why ask or wait for approval from a government known to be in breach of every one of the U.N. Charter cornerstones? Zimbabwe is another example.

In 2005, China sealed a $70-billion agreement with Iran giving Chinese companies a 51% stake in the huge Yadavaran oil field, Iran's largest onshore field, along with a promise to help develop the largely untapped area. China already gets 14% of its oil from Iran. China and Russia are discussing a 1,500-mile, $2.5-billion pipeline that would supply 700 million tons of Russian crude over 25 years. And Beijing and Kazakhstan agreed in 2005 to work on a $2.5-billion pipeline to transport 20 million tons of oil a year to western China. China can and must take the lead in developing alternative energy sources to oil. Otherwise it risks America and the West overcoming their own self-imposed obstacles to the success of a non-fossil fuel and seeing all its investments and philanthropy flushed down the drain.

China has agreed with the Philippines and Vietnam to conduct a joint seismic survey of the Spratly Islands. The three-year survey of the disputed archipelago in the South China Sea would provide clues to the potential oil and gas reserves in the area, which is claimed by China, Vietnam, Taiwan, the Philippines, Brunei and Malaysia. The mainland and Vietnam, which both have built permanent structures in the Spratlys, clashed over the islands in 1988 and 1992.

China trades on an asset these countries value: its veto power as a permanent member of the U.N. Security Council.

With 60 percent of its oil imports coming from the Middle East, China has no choice but to become more active in the region. The world oil market can accommodate the needs of both China and the U.S. China's thirst is an opportunity for the U.S. to create a closer working partnership in the Middle East that could help bring about stability in the region.

China's extensive interests in Africa also represent a potential opportunity for the U.S. to prevent failed states from spiraling into the abyss of despair by jointly promoting social, political and economic development. It is to America's advantage to work with China – using its leverage to build stability and security – not only in the Middle East and Africa – but globally. Instead, Africa is again going down the old borrowing binge road that keeps the continent in poverty, disease and dispair as it tries to pay off the crushing debt. Yet there is no international or U.N. way of preventing it, which seems very strange after the implementation of the $50-billion Group of 8-sponsored debt forgiveness plan. The plan made Africa "bankable" and as a result rating agencies and banks are working on new sovereign debt programs.

Is it any wonder China is aggressively moving in on the terrain of traditional aid providers? Isn't it time that all poor countries stop being permanent aid supplicants and become normal market economies?

China has sent 10 teams of peacekeepers to take part in U.N. operations in Africa, Haiti and Lebanon. China sent 1,000 peacekeepers to Lebanon. It also gave Lebanon 40 million yuan in humanitarian aid. China is the perfect partner to work with the U.S. to bring about peace in the Middle East because it has good relations with Israel and its Arab neighbors. China is not perceived by the Arab nations as being pro-Israel, as is the case with America.

China overtook Japan as the second-largest oil importer in 2004. The year before, it surpassed Japan to become the second-biggest oil consumer and now, like America, is building a strategic petroleum reserve. When prices dropped 25 percent from a peak of $80 a barrel to $57.95 a barrel in the fall of 2006, China went on a buying binge. It imported an average 3.29 million barrels of crude a day. Hopefully, America also exploited that window of opportunity.

Instead of building a strategic reserve stocked solely with crude oil as America has done, China has decided to emulate European countries and Japan – which hold a mix of crude and refined products such as petrol, diesel, jet fuel and heating oil. The International Energy Agency, an advisor to 26 oil-consuming nations, recommends members keep a stockpile equal to 90 days of net imports. The first phase of China's reserve tank farms in Zhanhai, Zhousan and Qingdao in the east and in the northern city of Dalian, which will hold reserves totalling 16.2 million cubic meters, is expected to be completed in 2008. China is also planning a massive expansion of its nuclear power industry and aims to build a strategic uranium reserve. China currently produces between 700 and 800 tons of uranium a year but consumes more than 1,600 tons. This is expected to grow to 8,000 tons by 2020.

Since the mid-1970s, the U.S. has built the largest government-owned oil stockpile in the world – around 700 million barrels of crude. It was designed as a buffer against further embargoes or cuts in the supply of foreign oil, especially from the Middle East. After Hurricane Katrina hit the heart of the U.S. domestic petroleum supply in and around the Gulf of Mexico, the crude-oil reserve was of little help.

While the U.S. was trying to crank up the oil wells in Iraq, China discovered an offshore field in Bohai Bay with proven reserves equal to about 10 percent of the country's oil and gas reserves. The find of 405.07 million tons of oil equivalent, believed to be one of the biggest oil discoveries in China in 30 years, is a natural strategic reserve that can be kept right where it is while China continues on its oil and gas buying spree in competition with America, Japan, India and Europe.

The U.S. strategic petroleum reserve strategy was just as short sighted as its strategic reason for going to war in Iraq: for the crude oil there to enhance U.S. energy security. When the White House's economic adviser, Laurence Lindsey, said in September 2002 that the Iraq invasion could cost $100 billion to $200 billion – an estimate the White House quickly disavowed as too high – he indicated that one could expect an additional 3 to 5 million barrels a day of Iraqi oil production following the ouster of Saddam. The fact is, the Pentagon spent $281 billion on the war and occupation through fiscal year 2005, but Iraq's oil production today remains below the level sustained by Saddam even under international sanctions. It goes to prove that even cold, calculating Republican businessmen can miscalculate and screw up royally.

The $281-billion figure, calculated by the Congressional Research Service, does not include all the costs that would continue even if the war had ended at the end of 2005, such as benefits for veterans, contributions to Iraqi reconstruction and interest on the national debt. Nor does it include such economic costs as the impact of higher oil prices induced and sustained, at least in part, by the continuing turmoil in Iraq. Stephen Walt, the academic dean of Harvard's Kennedy School of Government, wrote in the last 2005 issue of *Foreign Policy* that, "Although our armed forces have fought with dedication and courage, this war will ultimately cost us more than $1 trillion, not to mention thousands of lives. And what will the United States have achieved?" Hopefully, a lesson by We *the Apathetic Maids* that expensive mistakes can be made by politicians if they are left to their own devices while we tune out.

Did this price tag improve U.S. energy security and, if so, was the improvement worth the cost? I believe the answer is no on both points. On the contrary, the Iraqi invasion has contributed to the demise of the old U.S. energy security structure in the Middle East. America's promises and willingness to use military might to protect the regimes ruling the oil-producing states – their power and their oilfields – in return for receiving assurances of ample oil supplies at moderate prices, is no longer sustainable or justifiable. I agree with John Gault, an independent energy economist who wrote in an editorial in December 2005: "The Iraqi intervention forever changed the traditional equation. It revealed that even a U.S. military occupation could not protect oil installations from sabotage. It revealed that America, tied down in Afghanistan and Iraq, might not be able to come to the rescue of another regime at the same time. It revealed that the Bush administration would promote 'democratization' in the Middle East at the expense of authoritarian regimes. And it continues to fan anti-American feelings in the region, putting governments friendly to America in an awkward position."

It was anticipated that Iraqi oil production would rise to 3 to 4 million barrels a day within two years after the invasion. Iraqi experts, soon after the invasion, spoke of capacity rising to 6 million barrels a day by 2010, given sufficient investment. In fact, at year end 2005, Iraq's oil output was well below 2 million barrels a day and declining. Major oil companies are sitting on the sidelines waiting for a stable government to emerge and an improvement in physical security. So the $1-trillion investment has hardly paid off in terms of U.S. energy security.

Coincidentally, the International Energy Agency estimates that total oil and gas investment in the Middle East and North Africa is projected to amount to about $1 trillion over the period 2004-2030 – in 2004 dollars. In other words, an investment similar to what America is spending on the war in Iraq could assure ample oil and gas supplies from the region, not just for America but for the entire world, over the coming quarter-century – a globally beneficial campaign America and China could jointly lead.

Whose Oil Is It?
An America that consumes more than 20 million barrels of oil a day is warning a China that consumes 6.5 million barrels a day not to try to do what America has been doing for years – lock up world oil resources.

There is a concern because it is projected that China's energy consumption will increase by about 150 percent by 2020. China's move from bicycles to cars has accelerated its oil consumption. By 2010, China is expected to have

90 times the number of cars it had in 1990, and it will probably have more cars than America by 2030. That leaves two options. We either manage our energy resources better or start looking for another planet. America asking other countries to back off the world's oil supply so America's suburban moms can drive more gas-guzzling SUVs and Hummers just doesn't cut it.

U.S. oil consumption is undercutting its foreign policy and national security. The best example of this is Iran. Its oil revenue was about $55 billion in 2006. From 1998 to 2006, Iran earned $300 billion from oil exports. In 2005 the Islamic republic increased defense spending to $6.2 billion while continuing to provide at least $100 million a year to Hezbollah. How much it is funneling to Shiites in Iraq and Hamas in Palestine is unknown. Another example is Russia. It earns more than $100 billion a year from petroleum exports, in addition to the substantial revenue from supplying about a quarter of Europe's natural gas. Oil money has allowed Russia to rebuild its military strength. If oil prices dropped because of lack of demand, both countries would face economic calamities.

The U.S.-China Economic and Security Review Commission recommended at the end of 2005 that Congress mandate the creation of a Sino-U.S. energy working group that would give top-level government and industry officials from both countries a chance to work together "for mutual benefit on energy issues," including a search for alternative fuel technologies. Why isn't Congress listening?

America and China must align their interests as energy consumers and develop a common energy consumption plan that will diminish their growing geopolitical rivalry. Aligning U.S. and Chinese interests would allow them to coordinate resistance to profiteering on world energy markets and take the edge off their geopolitical rivalry. From an economic perspective, there is no reason why U.S. and Chinese oil interests should not be in harmony. Both have an interest in keeping prices low. Both countries can build on the U.S.-China Renewable Energy Development and Energy Efficiency Protocol to help China develop alternative sources of energy. The continued improvement of Sino-U.S. relations is not only mutually beneficial – but globally, especially in Africa, the Middle East and Asia, where Zimbabwe, Congo, Iran, Syria, Myanmar and North Korea are issues America cannot resolve alone.

Human Rights

The United Nations Commission on Human Rights is another example of Charter language contradicting its mission from actual practice. It is made up of 53 governments. Dictatorships are as free to serve as "democracies" because there are no minimum criteria for membership. Members have included such paragons of human rights as Algeria, Cuba, the Democratic Republic of Congo, Kenya, Libya, Nepal, Saudi Arabia, Sierra Leone, Syria, Uganda, Sudan and Vietnam. Do they join to promote human rights or to protect themselves from criticism? They absolve Algeria, Congo, Sudan and Zimbabwe of human rights abuses while condemning America and Israel and absolving Hamas-Hezbollah and Palestinian terrorism. Is it any wonder the U.S. was voted off the commission it founded as human rights has become a major issue in the 21st century? For the commission to be chaired at the dawn of the 21st century by Libya, while Iraq chaired the Commission on Disarmament, is too ludicrous to believe.

Amnesty International and Human Rights Watch estimate that about half its members are abusers and their political bargaining undermines the commission to the extent that it fails to protect human rights.

The Human Rights Commission undermines the credibility of the entire U.N. Former Secretary General Kofi Annan admitted as much when he urged governments to support his plan to reform it. The commission has a "credibility deficit," he told the commission in 2005 when he proposed that a smaller Human Rights Council replace the 53-member commission. The proposed council would operate year round rather than the current annual six-week session. Unfortunately, but not surprisingly, the proposal was rejected as the stalwarts of human rights abuses continue to focus on their own self-interest and provide only lip service to human rights.

A new Human Rights Council replaced the Commission on June 16, 2006. The only difference: the 53-member commission has been replaced by a 47-member council. The idea that any member state will now be booted off the council for human rights abuses is a faith-based proposition given U.N. history.

Whose and What Rights?

Human rights are being violated every day in U.N. member countries by the leaders of those countries who enjoy mingling with the advocates of human rights in New York at every one of the hollow global get-togethers of leaders to celebrate something or other just as meaningless and hollow as the previous soire. This is nothing new. The Khmer Rouge butchery in Cambodia's killing fields was not stopped by the U.N. No different than the genocide in Darfur.

It took more than 10 years after the Cambodian government first asked for help setting up a court to try leaders of the murderous Khmer Rouge regime, for the first hearing to take place. The tribunal was created in 2003 by an agreement between the government of Prime Minister Hun Sen and the U. N. after six years of negotiations. The court's foreign and Cambodian judges were deadlocked over procedure, and the foreign judges threatened to walk out rather than participate in what they feared could become an exercise in politics over justice. The Cambodia tribunal experiment in a local-international hybrid court can't work as it denies justice to the 2 million victims of one of the 20th century's worst acts of mass slaughter. It requires an interlocal tribunal to succeed, presided over by a foreign judge. The alternative is failure.

Granted, Hun Sen's government is interested in the trial so that it can vindicate its own anti-Khmer Rouge credentials – without dredging up awkward facts, such as current officials' own Khmer Rouge ties or the support that China, now a close ally, gave to the genocidal regime.

The Khmer Rouge leaders escaped being tried for their murderous, politically motivated rampage because the U N. repeatedly delayed establishing a tribunal that could function to try them. Ta Mok, the Khmer Rouge leader who died in 2006, had ousted Pol Pot in 1997 – a year before he died in 1998 – and was the group's final leader. He had been held in a military prison since 1999. Several other senior Khmer cadres live freely in the country.

Pol Pot henchman Kaing Khek Iev, known as Duch, the former Khmer Rouge prison chief who ran the notorious Tuol Sleng S-21 prison in Phnom Penh from 1974 to 1979 – a former high school and current museum – is the only surviving Khmer Rouge leader to go on trial. He oversaw the deaths of as many as 17,000 men, women and children. Most were tortured before being killed. Something I couldn't believe until I visited the prison and saw first hand and heard in vivid detail from people who lived through the horror and saw the eyes of the victims in the pictures on the walls as their lives flashed away.

Nuon Chea, the Khmer Rouge's chief ideologue, Ieng Sary, the former foreign minister, and Khieu Samphan, the former head of state, live freely in Cambodia but are in declining health.

The New-York based Open Society Justice Initiative wants a probe into corruption allegations against judges of the long-awaited and long-overdue Khmer Rouge tribunal. It cites allegations "that Cambodian court personnel, including judges, must kick back a significant percentage of their wages to Cambodian government officials in exchange for their positions on the court."

The U.N.'s policy not to release internal audit results has unleashed allegations that the U.N. is burying the truth about the extent of corruption, impropriety in the use of funds and unexplained disappearance of money provided to the Cambodian tribunal. The funds were administered by the United Nations Development Program. "The corruption is unreal," Luke Hunt, the Agence France Press correspondent based in Phnom Penh told me during my 2003 visit. "A lot of people are questioning and wondering whether anyone will ever be tried," Luke said as I asked him and Michael Hayes, the publisher & editor-in-chief of the *Phnom Penh Post* what the likelihood of any member of the Khmer Rouge leadership being tried and convicted was.

I had joined Luke and Mike at the Cantina, a Phnom Penh riverfront bar popular with expatriates and local journalists, for a beer after my tour of Tuol Sleng prison to discuss how U.N. funds are being squandered on a court and judicial proceedings that may not see the light of day. "There was never any way to safeguard a government-dominated court from political influence or corruption, which are woven into the very fabric of the Cambodian court system," Mike told me as he waived away cute child beggars clutching crying babies. Child beggars and souvenir vendors are a bothersome regular nuisance to foreigners at tourist sites, restaurants, bars and hotels throughout Cambodia.

Up to 2 million people were executed or died of starvation and overwork between 1975 and 1979, when the communist Khmer Rouge forced millions into the countryside in their drive for an agrarian utopia. Religion, property rights, currency and schools were abolished.

Washington's decision to host Cambodian police chief Hok Lundy, who is implicated in numerous crimes, including terrorism, drugs, human trafficking, for counter-terrorist talks, has bred cynicism among Cambodians about America's commitment to human rights and political reform.

Human rights are still being violated on a systemic scale by Cambodia's Hun Sen government, according to Yash Ghai, the U.N. secretary general's special representative for human rights in Cambodia. In the United Nations Special Rapporteur for Human Rights in Cambodia he released on September 26, 2006, he said: "With aid-giving comes the responsibility to ensure that it helps the people. The international community in Cambodia must give far higher priority to human rights and actively advocate for their implementation."

Ghai concluded that the government manipulates the democratic process, undermines legitimate political opposition, uses the state to accumulate private wealth, with no rule of law, no property rights, and no independent judiciary. Illegal land expropriations go unpunished and unpaid for. Thousands of families have been forcibly evicted from land their ancestors lived on for generations. In some cases, entire communities have collapsed as a result, since their whole existence was organized around this land. "I am deeply concerned about the continuing alienation of indigenous land through land grabbing, illegal or coercive sales, and the granting of concessions," said Ghai after being called terrible names and shunned by the Cambodian leadership on his follow-up visit in June 2007.

One of the seven natural lakes around Phnom Penh, which are crucial to city drainage, is being developed by a well-connected private firm without any public hearings or approval. It is the largest single displacement of people in Cambodia since the privatization of land in 1989. Sihanoukville beachfront resort vies for the title.

The discovery of oil by Chevron off the coast of Cambodia in 2007 could pull the country out of poverty if its institutionalised graft is properly managed and the oil wealth is not simply pocketed by the political establishment and their wealthy cronies. The newfound oil wealth is an opportunity for Cambodia to pull itself and the current and future generations of children out of poverty.

The publication of *A History of Democratic Kampuchea*, a newly released textbook in 2007 about the Khmer Rouge's 1975-79 rule by Khamboly Dy, a Cambodian genocide researcher, promises to do what the U.N. tribunal was intended to: Shed light on how the now-defunct Communist group became a killing machine. Khamboly works at the Documentation Center of Cambodia, an independent group collecting evidence of the Khmer Rouge atrocities.

Exiled Cambodians like cartoonist Ung Bun Heang focus their work on what they consider the major issues affecting the country today, including corruption, "fake democracy," deforestation, lawlessness, impunity, land grabbing and what he perceives to be an overreaching influence of Vietnam. His cartoons are highly critical of the ruling Cambodian People's Party. Bun Heang witnessed the purges and executions of the Khmer Rouge cadres and the massacre of more than 30 relatives. He managed to survive and found work with the Vietnamese upon their arrival in 1979 as a cartoonist for animated propaganda films that lauded Vietnam's liberation of Cambodia.

Working with Martin Stuart-Fox, a former Vietnam war correspondent, he published his drawings with the story of his experience under the Khmer Rouge in the book *Murderous Revolution: Life and Death in Pol Pot's Kampuchea.*

While the government steals the people's resources and tries to suppress the truth about the Khmer Rouge, it issued an arrest warrant for royalist leader Prince Norodom Ranariddh, who has left the country and failed twice to appear in court. He has been summoned from his home in France to answer allegations that he sold his former Funcinpec Party's headquarters and pocketed the $3.6 million.

Not much different than the military junta in Myanmar. The junta there took power in 1988 after crushing the democracy movement. In 1990, it refused to hand over power when Aung San Suu Kyi's political party won a landslide election victory and has kept her in detention for over 11 years, despite worldwide condemnation and calls for her freedom along with that of hundreds of other political prisoners. It's a dictatorship I had the great displeasure in meeting on several occasions in the mid-1990s to explore business opportunities. My favorite generals to converse with while trying to keep a straight face were the heads of the various "brainwashing" departments masquerading as television executives. Another example of U.N. sanctions not working. Their house arrest of Suu Kyi, Nobel Peace laureate and democratically elected leader, human rights abuses against the country's 55 million people, beating of monks peacefully demonstrating, and persecution and ongoing war with the Karen, Shan and other ethnic minorities with impunity is another mind-boggling example of how useless the U.N. is. Myanmar, like Sudan, uses rape as a weapon against its own people. Gender-based sexual violence obstructs peace and development.

Systematic sexual violence became visible in Myanmar when the Shan Women's Action Network and the Shan Human Rights Foundation (SHRF) published *License to Rape*, a report that documents 625 cases of rape committed by the military in eastern Myanmar between 1996 and 2001. It noted that no one had been prosecuted for these crimes.

A nation that oppresses women, neglects children, exploits its people and abuses its minorities does not deserve recognition. The U.N. Charter was the first international agreement to proclaim gender equality a fundamental human right. Nearly all nations have signed this charter and thus committed themselves to accept these standards.

The U.N. Security Council is unable to pass a resolution condemning the regime because of China and Russia's veto powers. It is rare for a resolution to be jointly vetoed by Russia and China. Their veto of the resolution to condemn Myanmar for its abuses was the first joint veto in 16 years. It was also the first resolution South Africa vetoed. It was serving as a Security Council member at the time. What a shame.

Myanmar is China's most important ally in Asia. Myanmar has become the cornerstone of China's revised Southeast Asia strategy in the face of what Beijing regards as the growing and unwanted influence of America in the region. More than a million Chinese – farmers, workers and businessmen –

have crossed into Myanmar in the last 10 years and are working and living there. Chinese leaders worry that any upheaval would cause these people to flee back across the border, creating increased industrial and social unrest in the border regions.

Sanctions are not the solution for Myanmar, notwithstanding Suu Kyi's insistence and endorsement. Her personality-driven style isn't working either. Her unbending, uncompromising leadership mindset must be replaced by the emerging, more moderate, younger pro-democracy groups.

The Sri Lankan civil war that started in 1983 between the government and the separatist Tamil Tigers trying to proclaim an independent homeland has claimed the lives of more than 70,000 people in the predominantly Buddhist island nation off the tip of India, formerly known as Ceylon. Yet again, the U.N. is paralyzed and unable to muster the votes necessary to bring about peace.

In the Philippines, a U.N. human rights report released in February 2007 concluded that hundreds of political activists, reporters and communist sympathisers have been killed by the military. The military justifies its extrajudicial killings under its campaign to wipe out the communist New People's Army. A nice bunch of guys I had the pleasure of meeting and chatting with about U.S. and Philippine politics ... and the beat goes on.

Deadbeat Freeloaders
The U.N. is so self-serving that its bureaucratic employees protect each other even when it comes to deadbeat dads. Mothers and grandmothers from Africa, Europe, Asia and the United States, now scattered throughout New York, meet every month in a first-floor conference room across from the United Nations. They call themselves the U.N. Family Rights Committee, but one woman said "the dumped wives club" is more accurate.

They are the estranged or divorced spouses of U.N. employees, women who followed their husbands to postings around the world and are chasing after them once again. The agenda at their meetings rarely changes.
Some cannot collect unpaid support orders from U.S. and foreign courts because the United Nations blocks them from doing so. Most are not entitled to a share of their husbands' pensions because of U.N. policy.

One woman from the Middle East who lives in a Manhattan rooming house said her husband, a U.N. diplomat, left her after 40 years of marriage. She won a support order, but knows she may never collect.

Divorce is rarely simple, and is not always fair, but these women have discovered it can be uniquely devastating for the spouse of a U.N. staff member. Had her former husband not worked at the United Nations, a court could have garnished his wages. But the organization is exempt from legal process and refuses to execute family court orders.

Come on. Why is this? If Pinochet's immunity can be removed, why can't that of U.N. bureaucrats? The U.N. is a failure globally even when it comes to its own wives and children. If the U.N. can't practice what it preaches on an individual basis, why is it allowed to continue its dysfunctional global existence?

The failures in peacekeeping and military operations are repeated by other U.N. agencies that provide housing, feed refugees and bring modern medicine to millions of people. The World Health Organization and U.N. High Commissioner for Refugees operate as separate organizations with their own charter, assemblies and staff. They are tied into a "U.N. system" by agreements negotiated with the central U.N. that are considered treaties.

When one U.N. body has failed to fulfill a crucial mission, the tendency has been to form another outfit. Thus there are four U.N. agencies concerned with food production and seven with industrial development in Third World emergency situations. This sharply highlights the resulting problems of duplication and overlap. Consider a not very hypothetical situation: a sudden flood of refugees. The U.N. High Commissioner for Refugees might build camps to house them. But WHO would want something to say about their health problems. One or more of the food agencies might consider feeding them to be its job. And since some of the refugees would surely be children, UNICEF might also get into the act.

The top UNICEF post has been held by an American since its inception in 1946. The agency has 7,000 staff members in 150 countries and one of its primary responsibilities has been family planning. Yet former U.S. Agriculture Secretary Ann Veneman, the Bush administration nominee to the post in 2005, told a press conference that family planning is irrelevant to the mission of the organization – hypocritical dysfunctionality at its glaring, political worst.

The U.N. member states in 1992 created a Department of Humanitarian Affairs to try to bring some coordination to this chaos. But they did not give it enough money or authority. Predictably, the department has turned into one more layer of bureaucracy. What was the U.N.'s response to the 9/11 attacks? The Security Council set up a Terrorism Task Force to play a more significant role in the Iraq War it failed to lead – until its headquarters in Baghdad was bombed to smithereens and staff killed, because of the U.N.'s failure to recognize how vulnerable to attack it was.

The U.N. World Summit on Sustainable Development held in South Africa in 2002 highlighted the delusional hypocrisy and unreliability of the 20,000 freeloaders and the figures published by the U.N. agencies that employ them. For example, when a child dies in Africa, it is often due to a combination of illnesses, such as diarrhea, pneumonia and AIDS. Agencies and programs fighting each of these diseases include the victim in their statistics to obtain more funding from donors. Consequently, because each agency claims credit for the same dead victims, the actual deaths are grossly inflated. The people who benefit from these inflated numbers are the rip-off artists posing as U.N. bureaucrats caring for the needy.

Bureaucratic Rapists

There are so many layers of bureaucracy that it is easy for deadbeat bureaucrats, even criminals, to hide. Scandal after U.N. criminal scandal gets quietly quashed by sending the accused home.

The U.N. police force's direct involvement in the enslavement of East European women in Bosnian whorehouses is a prime example. David Lamb, a former Philadelphia police officer who served as a U.N. human rights investigator in Bosnia, said that he investigated allegations against Romanian, Fijian and Pakistani U.N. officers who recruited women, purchased false documents and then sold the women to Bosnian brothel owners. However, Lamb said his investigating colleagues faced physical threats and were repeatedly stymied by their superiors at the U.N. The U.N.'s response was that the responsibility for prosecuting U.N. police officers belongs to their home countries, not the U.N. Really now? Why not send them to the International Criminal Court?

Before sending a mission abroad, the U.N. negotiates a Status of Forces Agreement that, in almost all instances. deprives local authorities of criminal jurisdiction over peacekeepers. If there is no host-country government to negotiate with, as in East Timor or Kosovo, the countries providing peacekeepers and the U.N. determine the terms of the SOFA.

A "wall of silence" keeps sexual abuse cases from being investigated. Rapes are usually belittled as simple acts of prostitution. Sarah Martin, the author of the Haiti and Liberia report said: "They'd say, 'Why should we ruin someone's otherwise illustrious career over an act with a prostitute?' "She said Liberians had complained to her about some peacekeepers' conduct with the comment, "This behavior would not be accepted in the home country of these soldiers; why are these soldiers playing around with our children?"

The very public charges of rape, pedophilia and prostitution involving U.N. peacekeepers in Burundi, Bosnia, Cambodia, Haiti, East Timor, Ethiopia, Liberia, Kosovo and Sierra Leone pale in comparison to those made in the Democratic Republic of the Congo that highlight the arrogance of U.N. criminal bureaucrats. The 41-page report detailed 150 allegations of sexual misconduct by peacekeepers against women and girls, some as young as 12. That did not include the Congolese women working for the U.N. who were afraid to report supervisors' demands for sex for fear of losing their jobs. More than a year after the shocking disclosures, nothing was done to end the culture of impunity, exploitation and sexual chauvinism. When U.N. peacekeepers, who are sent to help restore stability, guarantee public security and instill the rule of law in countries ravaged by war instead rape the people they were sent to protect and coerce women and girls to trade sex for food, they defeat the purpose of their mission and exploit some of the world's most vulnerable people.

John Miller, a former U.S. ambassador at large on modern-day slavery who teaches international affairs at George Washington University, has accused the U.N. of being among the major promoters of human trafficking in the world by failing to halt sexual abuses by U.N. peacekeepers. "It's very hard to take the lead when you are one of the major promoters of human trafficking in the world," he said.

It gets worse. The United Nations and the Britain-based Save the Children charity said an investigation uncovered allegations of widespread sexual abuse of children by both agencies' relief workers sent to West Africa to help young people buffeted by years of war. Investigations in refugee camps in Liberia, Guinea and Sierra Leone in 2001 turned up accusations against 67 workers. It gives a whole new meaning to "relief workers."

The top U.N. electoral expert who oversaw elections in Iraq and Afghanistan was fired because of an abusive and sexually offensive environment in the Electoral Assistance Division.

The sex scandals at the U.N. are so numerous that a "kiss and tell" book about the organization's field operations is having difficulty seeing the light of day because senior U.N. officials are trying to block its publication. The authors, three U.N. veterans – Kenneth Cain, Heidi Postlewait and Andrew Thomson – detail alleged corruption and incompetence in U.N. relief operations. The book is entitled *Emergency Sex and Other Desperate Measures: A True Story from Hell on Earth*. It includes numerous stories of wild sex and drug parties involving U.N. officials.

Under U.N. rules governing staff, the world body reserves the right to restrict or prohibit any publication of information pertaining to inside activities gleaned during employment.

Who's Raping Whose Scapegoat?
The rape conviction of U.S. Lance Corporal Daniel Smith on December 4, 2006 triggered an outpouring of sympathetic support from Filipino women who lit candles outside his jail cell in an impromptu shrine, along with an e-mail account to collect messages of support and to protest his harsh 40-year prison sentence. He testified that the sex was consensual, in the back of a van, when both of them were drunk. Anyone who has spent any time in Olangapo and Subic knows that nice, innocent virgins don't get drunk and jump into vans to read the Bible – even in staunchly Catholic Philippines. The case not only raises the question of what are U.S. Marines doing in the Philippines, but why a U.S. Marine is sentenced to a harsh prison term for

having consensual sex while the hundreds, if not thousands of U.N. soldiers who have been accused of rape around the world while on humanitarian peace missions get sent home quietly and are never prosecuted.

Under the Visiting Forces Agreement between the U.S. and the Philippines, American military personnel are to be tried in Philippine courts. Under the agreement, U.S. Marines and other members of the U.S. armed forces are in the Philippines to advise the Filipino army and to conduct joint military exercises to fight terrorism.

For years the Philippines has been a haven for Jemaah Islamiah, a network that covers the arc of a predominantly Muslim region from the southern island of Mindanao, through Indonesia to Malaysia and southern Thailand. The record of Islamic terrorism extends from vicious guerrilla war waged by the extremist Abu Sayyaf on the islands of Basilan and Jolo, off southwestern Mindanao, to plotting against the U.S. by operatives in Manila under the guidance of their Middle Eastern masters. At the same time, the ragtag Philippine army has to wage an entirely separate war against the New People's Army, a guerrilla force that has been staging a comeback from the main island of Luzon, down through Mindanao.

Comparing U.S. Marines' sexual escapades on their R&R in the Philippines, for which they can receive a harsh prison sentence, to the sexual abuse U.N. relief workers inflict daily on their job for which they are excused, makes me wonder who is the real scapegoat in Lance Corporal Smith's case? American taxpayers for picking up the tab that put a U.S. Marine in jail?

Bureaucratic Criminals

In 2004, three U.N. police officers were killed in Kosovo when police turned their weapons on each other in a 10-minute gunfight. Two Americans and a Jordanian were shot dead by Jordanian officers over the merits of the U.S. war in Iraq.

U.N. security personnel are so busy with their personal affairs that they are repeatedly accused by independent investigators of dereliction of duty. An independent investigation into the suicide bombing of the U.N. headquarters in Iraq in 2003 that killed 22 people and injured 150 concluded that the organization ignored warnings that it was a potential target and flouted its own security guidelines, leaving personnel vulnerable to attack. "The main conclusion of the panel is that the current security management system is dysfunctional," the 40-page document said. "The observance and implementation of security regulations and procedures were sloppy, and noncompliance with security rules commonplace." Security officers received warnings of the attack several days before it occurred, and again on the day of the attack, but ignored them all.

Carlos Magarinos, director general of the United Nations Industrial Development Organization, was accused of misappropriating $1 million from a fund appropriated from a mining project to pay Argentina's arrears to the U.N.

The U.N. Tribunal investigating Rwanda's 1994 genocide arrested a former U.N. employee who was accused of four counts of genocide, complicity in genocide, crimes against humanity, extermination and rape. How many more are still running around free? Kofi Annan now admits that he should have done more to prevent the 1994 genocide in Rwanda. The genocide occurred while he was the head of U.N. peacekeeping. "I believed that I was doing my best, but I realized after the genocide happened that there was more that I could and should have done to sound the alarm and rally support," he said.

Warehouses of food are routinely stolen in Afghanistan, Indonesia and elsewhere where corrupt U.N. officials seem to desperately need to supplement their income to sustain their corrupt lifestyles. A corn for poppies program financed by *We the Apathetic Maids?*

U.N. officials illegally sold off the organization's historic stamp collection for a song – more than a ton of stamps and stamp-making material belonging to the U.N. Postal Administration in Geneva in 2003. The collection sold for £1.72 million, but was worth three to four times as much when broken up and resold by the buyer. Under the U.N.'s own rules, the sale of the stamps was barred without the express permission of the chief of the U.N.'s archives and records management section. No sign of any such permission has been discovered.

Fraud is rife in U.N. peacekeeping operations. Peacekeepers, for example, spent $10.4 million to lease a helicopter for use in East Timor that could have been secured for $1.6 million, and paid $2.4 million to buy seven air-craft hangers in Congo that were never used. Another $65 million or more was spent on fuel that was not needed for missions in Sudan and Haiti. Collusion, fraud and the U.N. "culture of impunity" in spending resulted in fraud involving contracts whose value totaled about $193 million – nearly 20 percent of the $1 billion in U.N. business examined by auditors at the end of 2005.

The Malaysian government has accused the U.N. High Commission for Refugees of issuing refugee status to i legal immigrants who have forged passports in exchange for bribes. Volker Turk, the UNHCR head in Malaysia, admitted that some UNHCR documents could have been forged.

Alexander Yakovlev, a senior U.N. purchasing official, resigned in 2005 after being accused of getting about $1 million from a company he awarded contracts worth $79 million.

In 2006, U.N. procurement official San aya Bahel was arrested and indicted on bribery charges. He was accused of steering more than S50 million worth of contracts to bidders in exchange for such considerations as a cheap Man-hattan apartment. His misdeeds compromised peacekeeping missions in places like Liberia, Congo and Kosovo. where a U.N. internal investigation says favored contractors were allowed to skimp on employee salaries and pocket the money for themselves. And the reports of corruption just keep on surfacing year after year.

I dread to think of the corruption that took place with the billions of dollars in cash and goods donated to the tsunami victims in Southeast Asia before the the U.N. refugee agency was asked to leave Indonesia's Aceh region. The U.N. has assured international donors it would do everything to ensure accountability and pledged to investigate all allegations of mishandling of funds. If the Oil-for-Food program and other U.N. relief programs are any indication, the Tsunami Relief Corruption Report will be just another scandal-ridden example of corrupt U.N. bureaucrats. Stuart Wolfendale wrote a column immediately after the tsunami, saying effectively, "Stop, right there! Don't write that check now. It almost certainly won't get there. Particularly if it is going to Indonesia." For a while after, he was regarded as callous for denying the movement for "Compassion Come What May," and "Give No

Matter What." The emotional pressure in wealthy communities in developed countries today at the moment of mass death greatly subsidizes the incompetence and corruption of the aid process.

Reform and Abolition

Many prominent politicians have advocated reform of the U.N. Charter and organization. In fact in the closing days of the millennium, the U.N. restructured its dues structure to encourage the U.S. to pay its delinquent dues. Too little, too late. It was the first serious financial overhaul since 1972. It could only be achieved after entrepreneur Ted Turner agreed to donate $34 million to cover the American government's shortfall. Let's get real. Is this any way to run a global institution?

Member nations use the U.N. as a political-patronage funnel and employment agency for second-class bureaucrats – not to mention sons, in-laws and mistresses. Jobs are filled by nepotism and favoritism, not merit. No amount of agency reshuffling and consolidation is likely to bring about fundamental change. It is the idealistic and lowly worker bees that keep the U. N. functioning.

It was perhaps the wars in Kosovo and Iraq that proved beyond a shadow of a doubt that the U.N. is irrelevant in the New World Order. Just like Iraq, the insurgency and violence between Albanians and Serbs in Kosovo continues unabated. Fourteen Orthodox churches and monasteries, many of them considered medieval architectural gems, were destroyed there in 2004.

In the case of Kosovo, Russian and Chinese political leaders were infuriated by NATO's willingness to bypass the U.N. Security Council. In Moscow and Beijing, warnings of a new American hegemony have replaced earlier paeans to a strategic partnership. Wounded pride and big-power jockeying can be seen in everything from the Russian Army's mad dash to beat NATO troops to Kosovo's Pristina airport, to the floundering negotiations over China's eventual entry into the World Trade Organization. The Russian and Chinese profanities heard when America decided to attack Iraq without U.N. approval make for a diplomatically incorrect volume of U.N. speak. Why perpetuate this Cold War hypocritical friction in the 21st century?

America really has chutzpah. While it is delinquent in paying its U.N. dues, it sends Ambassador Richard Holbrooke to Beijing to persuade China to pay more than .97 percent of the U.N. budget – an amount he claimed is paltry compared to the 25 percent and 19.9 percent paid by the U.S. and Japan respectively. Why should China pay? Why should anyone? Congress voted on Sept. 24, 2001, two weeks after the attacks of 9/11, to release to the U.N. $582 million in back dues because America needed the U.N.'s cooperation to fight terrorism. In more ways than one, America should be glad China doesn't want to pay more dues. The more China pays, the more virtuous clout that will give it globally – even though the U.N. is ineffective. It's an insurance policy for which she will have paid her premium, which entitles her to make a claim. That would suit China fine.

The U.N., like Liberia, was a politically expedient and convenient U.S. creation when formed. The U.N., like Liberia, has become a juvenile delinquent, thanks to parental neglect. The U.N. should be placed in receivership, its name and membership changed, and its headquarters relocated.

Just as the League of Nations became obsolete, so has the U.N. The U.N. was established to ensure peace globally, primarily in Europe. Today, the biggest threats to peace and world security are in Asia and Africa. Sudan, Congo, Somalia, Rwanda, Sierra Leone, Cambodia, Korea, Sri Lanka, Bosnia, Kosovo, Afghanistan, Indonesia and Iraq are reminders that the end of the Cold War does not mean the end of local and regional conflicts. Even nuclear conflicts between India and Pakistan, Israel and its Muslim neighbors are possible. Major threats to global peace involve China and its rebellious province of Taiwan, as well as Vietnam and the other claimants to the oil under the Spratly Islands.

North Korea is itching itself raw and giving hives to China, Russia, Japan, South Korea, the Asia-Pacific region and the world. Aceh's, and other oil-rich fundamentalist Muslim regional drives for independence from Indonesia, because of the experienced fundamentalist volunteers from Afghanistan, Chechnya and Iraq that would converge in Indonesia, are further potential flashpoints. Any of these possible conflicts has a far greater global impact than any possible regional conflict in Europe or the Americas, which should be handled by regional organizations such as NATO and OAS.

The need to reform or replace the U.N. with a new body is periodically debated at the Hong Kong Foreign Correspondent's Club Main Bar. "In Asia, the U.N. is primarily engaged in social and economic work," Michael Vatikiotis, former editor of the *Far Eastern Economic Review,* said during one such debate. "The Economic and Social Commission for Asia and the Pacific has 52 members and a staff of almost 600. Based in Bangkok, the commission is appropriately tasked with reducing poverty in the region where more than 800 million people live on less than a dollar a day. Yet no one can expect human security without peace, and it is the danger of conflict in Asia that the U.N. should increasingly be focused on. The world body would have a better chance of navigating Asia's politically treacherous waters, and help maintain peace, if it acquired more Asian expertise."

The campaign for a world parliament is periodically brought up during such deliberations. The Campaign for the Establishment of a U.N. Parliamentary Assembly was again launched in the spring of 2007. It has the signatures of more than 377 members of national parliaments from 70 countries, six foreign ministers and secretaries, prime ministers, and not surprising, former U.N. secretary-general Boutros Boutros-Ghali. Another 21st century do-nothing debating chamber.

"Forget about the U.N. It is obsolete and has to be replaced," I declared rather loudly as a stunned silence befell the bar.

The U.N. is repeatedly ignored, bypassed and is beyond reform. Its structure makes reform impossible. Reform only promises "more out-of-work politicians around the world the chance to live the good life in New York," George Mellon of *The Wall Street Journal* said.

The U.N. is perceived as a tool for the U.S. government to use when it is convenient to serve its geopolitical agenda. The U.S. and China – the global power couple – should attach the highest priority to global security needs in Asia. The future well-being and survival of mankind rests in the hands of all founding civilizations – in Asia.

Interlocal Security Council

The new successor to the U.N. should be named the Interlocal Security Council, or some other suitable and acceptable name. The U.N. Security Council should be replaced by representatives from all major civilizations that have made it to the 21st century. Assyrians need not apply. Its members should be limited to the core states of each such civilization, with rotating membership for the civilizations that do not have a core state. The members of this body would be America, China, India, Russia, with representatives from Europe, to be determined by the European Union, a representative from Africa to be determined by the African Union, a representative from Asia to to be determined by ASEAN, a representative from Latin America to be determined by the Organization of American States, and a representative from the Muslim world by a new Islamic Organization of major Muslim Civilizations that works alongside the Organization of the Islamic Conference. Each major civilization would have an equal say and an equal vote in the ISC. Otherwise, if Muslims want the seat based on religion – music to fundamentalist ears, if indeed fundamentalists allowed music – then the same offer must be extended to Buddhists, Christians, Hindus and Jews. The numbers don't add up for Muslims.

In view of the current ongoing threat of nuclear war between India and Pakistan, the Muslim world should consider nominating Pakistan as its first representative. This would, hopefully, eliminate Pakistan's opposition to India playing a major role in such an organization. Granted, Pakistan has already lived its life as a disasterous single-issue, artificial state, which many argue should not be given any more breath or breadth.

Former President Jacques Chirac of France and former President Nelson Mandela of South Africa have proposed that the Security Council reflect "global diversity." Chirac went on to say in support of the United Nations that "the heads of state and government of the entire world have come here to reaffirm it is irreplaceable." He must have been joking. I just don't get French humor. But then again, what else can we expect from a country that allows 11,000 of its citizens to die during a sweltering summer heat wave.

The one thing Chirac said that I do agree with is that "War is the worst response man can imagine; everything has to be done to avoid it."

The U.N.'s failure to avoid war and reach a consensus on Iraq was its final death rattle. The rebuilding of post-Saddam Iraq could be the seed to germinate the ISC. A body representative of the geopolitical reality of the 21st century's reawakened civilizations contributing the best they have to offer in the rebuilding of our Garden of Eden – a cradle of fused 21st-century civilizations brought together in Hong Kong.

The ISC should be headquartered in Hong Kong. Hong Kong is the crossroads of civilization. Hong Kong was founded as a commercial trading center and has deliberately kept politics and religion out of its daily life. "Thank you" in the local Cantonese dialect mnn goy sounds like UN Goy. Can you get any more all-inclusive in international relations? "English is now an Asian cultural language," said Shirley Geoklin Lim, a Chinese-Malaysian poet and novelist who came to Hong Kong from California to head the English Department at the University of Hong Kong.

Hong Kong people's awareness of the United Nations is among the highest in the world, according to a poll conducted by Gallup International and released on U.N. Awareness Day in 2004. Some 50,000 people in more than 60 countries were asked whether they were aware of the U.N. and their views of the body. In Hong Kong, 96 percent of respondents said they had heard of the U.N. Probably because Hong Kong is owed more than $150 million by the U.N. for the upkeep of Vietnamese boat people. The only way the debt will be repaid is if the U.N. assigns its successor to Hong Kong. By contrast, Japan fared worst in the Asia region, with only 50 percent of respondents saying they had heard of the world body.

It makes sense to rename, restructure and relocate the new global coordinating body in Asia. Europe and the U.S. East Coast have had their fling as power centers. In the New World Order, Asia and the Pacific, which was long ignored in the 20th century, must have their place in the sun.

With the General Secretary from South Korea, Under Secretary General for Economic and Social Affairs Sha Zukang and from China and the WHO head from Hong Kong, and most of the 21st-century conflicts and hot spots in Asia, why not?

We the Apathetic Maids must accept the fact that the wars in the Middle East are in fact in Asia. What's more disturbing is that Asia has shot past the Middle East as the developing world's largest arms market. This happened after India contracted $5.4 billion worth of deals in 2005. This was also the year that broke records by concluding $44.2 billion in global arms deals.

The next highest was $29.3 billion in 2003. A U.S. congressional report entitled Conventional Arms Transfers to Developing Nations, 1998-2005, concluded that since 2002, developing nations in Asia accounted for 48.4 percent – and gowing – of the value of all arms transfer agreements.

Just as the U.N. building was erected on the rubble brought over from the London blitz, the Interlocal Security Council building must be built from the rubble of the World Trade Center. Unfortunately, that may not be possible because 24 tons of steel taken from the collapsed World Trade Center was used to build the warship USS New York. The girders from Ground Zero were melted down and poured into a cast to make the bow section of the ship's hull. The $1-billion vessel is one of a new generation of amphibious assault ships capable of carrying 360 soldiers and landing a 700-strong Marine assault force on a coastline anywhere without the need for a port.

A monument to the victims of the 9/11 disaster was built in New Orleans by survivors of another disaster – Hurricane Katrina. And you thought irony was dead in America? The over-reliance on warships by America was the cause and downfall of the victims to which it is dedicated. One day the ship will be engaged in the failed U.S. foreign policy that continues the recycled violence. Instead of turning 9/11 rubble into a killing machine, why not make it the foundation of a truly global peace body?

If the ISC were located in Hong Kong and restructured to be globally representative, it would greet the new century with a fresh outlook, the requisite diversity, and prevent politicians and bureaucrats from running into so many controversial political stonewalls. The removal of political leaders who are a threat to the world could be openly and honestly debated. Enforceable sanctions could be imposed. The Kim Jong-ils and the Robert Mugabes of our world could be isolated and removed by a global military force that would be established to enforce the council's resolutions. The military base would be located in a strategically suitable country in the region.

The collapse of the Soviet Union and its communist empire was a forerunner to the collapse of the unrepresentative governments We the Maids swept out in Bulgaria, Czechoslovakia, Estonia, Hungary, Latvia, Romania, Yugoslavia, Afghanistan and Iraq.

Now that the communist empire the U.N. was established to contain during the Cold War has imploded and restructured, isn't it time the 60-year-old plus aging American institution created by Presidents Franklin D. Roosevelt and Harry Truman also was restructured?

Isn't it time America and China finally come together as partners at the dawn of the 21st century to spearhead the ISC? China's foreign policy has operated under the principle of economic advancement through conflict avoidance set by Deng Xioping after he witnessed the collapse of the Soviet Union. Deng borrowed Sun Tzu's philosophy to "hide one's views until opportunity turns in one's favor."

Lone Ranger

The 21st-century wars in Somalia, Afghanistan and Iraq show that a determined effort led by America can bring about regime change with impunity. Somalia is a case study. The U.S. failed to do in 1992, with forces on the ground, what it succeeded doing in 2006, by sending a joint force of Ethiopian and Somali government troops into combat on the front lines, while America provided logistical and intelligence support, that ousted the Islamic fundamentalist state imposed by the Islamic Courts Council. It did carry out its first overt military action in Somalia since 1994 with a targeted air strike on suspected al-Qaeda hideouts sheltering the masterminds of the U.S. embassy bombings in Kenya and Tanzania in 1998, using an AC-130 gunship. The Pentagon secretly used an airstrip in Ethiopia to take out its targets in the Horn of Africa. The fact is America did lead a quiet military campaign from Ethiopia to capture or kill al-Qaeda leaders.

The close clandestine U.S.-Ethiopia relationship included significant sharing of intelligence information on the Islamic militant positions. Members of a secret American special operations unit, Task Force 88, were deployed in Ethiopia and Kenya, and ventured into Somalia.

Shouldn't all other rogue regimes like Robert Mugabe's and Kim Jong-il's be changed with a coordinated plan led by the ISC and implemented by its member states – America, China, Russia, India and the regional groupings of Africa, Arabia, Asia, Europe and Latin America?

It won't violate any international law. In fact, there is no such thing as international law. That is why the U.N. can't enforce its sanctions. It has no enforcement powers because it is not a sovereign state. Take it from someone who joined the International Law Society in the early '70s. There are international treaties and conventions and the constant desire and pursuit by countries and people to improve their national self-interest as they violate them in the geopolitical process. This coming together is what is needed to launch the ISC.

The first step to minimize conflicts in the 21st century is to disassemble the General Assembly, and all countries currently represented in the General Assembly should concentrate their energy and resources on their respective local-regional geographic groupings, which they fund. Maybe regional funding will reduce waste and mismanagement. It is easy to mismanage and waste other people's money. Each regional and sub-regional grouping would be represented in the ISC.

Government Support & Cooperation

UNICEF offices in Afghanistan were looted and destroyed by Taliban troops. U.N. vehicles were stolen by the Taliban to enhance their war machine. The U.N. was helpless and useless. Why do career politicians insist on perpetuating such a useless body? It is a body that was symbolically buried in Afghanistan alongside the fallen Taliban fighters that highlighted its failed effort. Sending a peacekeeping force to Afghanistan without the right infrastructure will also fail.

Afghanistan and the war there highlighted the dysfunctionality of the U.N. and the current New World Disorder. The Taliban, which took power in 1996, were not recognized as the legitimate government of Afghanistan by the U.N., even though they controlled and governed most of the country. The Northern Alliance, which the Taliban ousted, continued to hold Afghanistan's seat in the United Nations, even though it did not govern the country anymore.

Afghanistan grew and distributed 80 percent of the heroin sold in Europe to harbor and finance terrorist training. Meanwhile, the U.N. was providing Afghanistan humanitarian aid and other services paid for by American taxpayers. The U.S. government even gave the Taliban government millions of dollars to stop growing heroin. Who was the U.S. financing with this money? Wasn't it the very terrorists who attacked it on 9/11? Is this the type of international body *We the Apathetic People* need to provide nation- building in the new millennium?

The U.N. New Agenda for the Development of Africa campaign in the 1990s was also a dismal failure, according to a U.N.-appointed panel. The continent's economic crisis was aggravated by "despotism and corruption," according to the independent evaluation. What is being done about it other than producing reports that repeatedly identify the same problems?

In the 21st century, nation-building should be the primary goal of the ISC. Preserving peace and ending terrorism are an inherent part of the nation-building agenda because every country is affected by a terrorist attack, as the world witnessed on 9/11. There has to be a collective will represented by the ISC constitution to protect all people's rights everywhere, regardless of borders. Former U.N. Secretary General Kofi Anan was courageous in making this point during his Nobel Peace Prize acceptance speech on the 100th anniversary of the prize. There are inherent rights that are superior to a state's rights of sovereignty, as the war on terrorism after 9/11 clearly demonstrated. That one terrorist act killed people from more than 80 countries and shattered the lives of families all over the world. Osama bin Laden's al-Qaeda cells operate in 60 countries. They work with governments, fellow terrorists, drug lords, money launderers and organized criminals.

Terrorism and human injustices that nourish global uncertainty or instability have to be suppressed by all governments collectively. This includes Saudi Arabia, which has frustrated U.S. law enforcement by not cooperating with the FBI in its investigation of terrorist acts that killed 19 Marines in Dhahran's Khobar Towers and the four Americans who were training the Saudi National Guard. Countries that do not participate in the global peace process should automatically be ostracized by the new global body.

To properly prepare to combat terrorism and protect individual rights, it is not enough to just adopt resolutions for a coalition peacekeeping force made up of armies of every country volunteering to participate without any prior joint training. The different national contingents that show up in the field have never trained together. The equipment they arrive with varies enormously in quality and quantity, and is typically incompatible. To make matters worse, the soldiers sent from the predominantly poor developing nations to enforce international law under the U.N. flag are military thugs looking to make an easy buck.

The ISC of the 21st century must have a rapidly deployable military force from a mission headquarters in Asia spearheaded by America and China. It must be a multinational force modeled after NATO, made up of military units from the countries and core civilizations represented at the council level. It should be much like the force made up of U.S. Marines that brought stability in Haiti during the 2004 civil rebellion. Another example is the U.S. Marines and West African peacekeepers who brought about peace and stability in Liberia.

The ISC must establish bases around the world near potential flashpoints, similar to what NATO does in Europe and America does around the globe, most notably in Kyrgyzstan, Turkey and Uzbekistan. It must consist of forces from more countries than just America. America has to have the right posse, especially in light of what happened to U.S. forces in Somalia. Right now it has no posse. Just a few hangers-on with movable-fire power who hope to get the reconstruction crumbs America leaves on the table. The neocons positively want to ride alone in their American crusade for American values. The ISC force must interface and work with each of the regional organizations that replace the General Assembly.

If countries are reluctant to send members of their armed forces to be part of the ISC rapid deployment force, they should have the option of sending experienced retired military personnel, much as they do in Afghanistan and Iraq today. Outsource the job to mercenaries. Mercenaries used to dominate warfare. The "Hessians" who served Britain in America's War of Independence – many were actually from other German states – became notorious among the colonists for their brutality. Foreigners formed a major part of every army in the world until the French Revolution. Their outlook was pithily expressed by a 17th-century soldier who said: "We serve our master honestly; it is no matter what master we serve."
There are at least 20,000 private "cowboys" employed in Iraq alone, plus thousands more in Afghanistan. There is one private security employee for every four U.S. soldiers in Iraq. Among foreign troop contingents they are second in number – and in casualties – only to the U.S. military. Peter Singer,

a fellow at the Brookings Institution and author of *Corporate Warrior*, quips: "President George W. Bush's 'coalition of the willing' might thus be more aptly described as the 'coalition of the billing.'"

Many of the recruits stem from former police and military forces in the Philippines, Peru and Equador. They are given crash courses that don't prepare them for armed conflicts. Maybe that's why they call them crash courses? They violate human rights because they are armed. While U.S. and European mercenaries working in war zones make as much as $10,000 a month, a Peruvian doing the same job seldom makes more than $1,000 – with the privilege of having his working rights violated.

It was thanks largely to "free lancers" (the origin of that now common term) that absolute monarchs managed to consolidate their power in Europe and carve out vast overseas empires. Private entities like the Dutch and English East India Companies even marshaled their own armies and navies to defend their domains. No different than Halliburton and many other corporations doing business in dangerous places today.

Mercenaries have been effective in stopping human-rights abuses. In 1995-96, Executive Outcomes, a South African firm working for the government of Sierra Leone, made mincemeat of a savage rebel movement known as the Revolutionary United Front that was notorious for chopping off the limbs of its victims. As a result, Sierra Leone was able to hold its first free election in decades. The now-defunct Executive Outcomes also helped the Angolan government quell a long-running insurgency by Jonas Savimbi's Unita, leading to the signing of a peace accord in 1994. Another private firm, MPRI, helped bring peace to the former Yugoslavia in 1995 by organizing the Croatian military offensive that stopped Serbian aggression.

Hired gunslingers, with state-of-the-art equipment like aircraft carriers, could be equally effective in stopping the campaign of rape, murder and ethnic cleansing carried out by the Sudanese government and the *Janjaweed* militia in Darfur. They can end starvation and human rights abuses in places like Cambodia, Myanmar, Mozambique and North Korea. I agree with Max Boot, a senior fellow at the Council on Foreign Relations and author of *War Made New: Technology, Warfare, and the Course of History, 1500 to Today*, who suggests mercenary firms could be employed by a global organization like the ISC, by an ad hoc group of concerned nations, or even by philanthropists like Bill Gates or George Soros.

Sending mercenaries to Africa isn't politically correct. But it would be a lot more useful than sending more aid money that will be wasted or passing ineffectual resolutions that will be ignored.

The "peace force" headed by America and China should also be made up of a significant number of Muslim troops from Bangladesh, Indonesia, Pakistan and Turkey. The Bangladeshi and Pakistani forces are predominantly Sunni Muslims who could be deployed in places like the Sunni Triangle, where insurgents now have a free reign.

It would be a "peace force" interventionist army that would prevent starvation and persecution based on race, religion or gender. An army that would also enlist and train exiles from target countries, like the U.S. did with Iraqi exiles. The peace force must not be limited to soldiers. It should also include doctors, teachers and retired professionals willing to help a country rebuild and modernize. Global Teaches Without Borders, a Global Teachers Corp that will replace the missionary teachers that instill religion instead of education and knowledge that is essential to grow and enter the 21st century with a functional purpose. Doctors and teachers without religious strings attached from member countries. Participating volunteers would be exempted from compulsory military service in their home countries and university students who participate would receive academic credit for their time and service. A global high tech contemporary Peace Corps.

The Club of Madrid, created in 2001 to further "democratic transition and consolidation," is one of the cornerstones for interdependence and cooperation between countries in the 21st century.

The club was established in Spain by current and former government heads of 33 countries. Spain was selected as the host country because it is universally admired for making an effective transition from dictatorship to democracy. Mikhail Gorbachev, who became the president of the club, said: "We know the outcome of the communist utopia. Don't make that mistake again. Democracy is the key. People ask me, 'Why did you give away Poland, Hungary, the Baltic countries, Germany?' I say, 'Did I give them away?'

No, they belong to their people, and it is theirs to decide what happens. It is a great gain for the world."

In addition to its reports and a basic statement of purpose, the Club of Madrid unanimously issued a strong condemnation of terrorism and a pledge to "pursue the guilty."

Another cornerstone is the Global Leadership Foundation of former national leaders and high-ranking officials to improve the world by making their experience and wisdom available to governments in need. The patrons include its founder, former South African President F.W. de Klerk, and his successor, Nelson Mandela, and 20 other founders that include former President George H.W. Bush, former Philippine President Fidel Ramos, onetime French Prime Minister Michel Rocard and ex-Indian Premier I.K. Gujral. Hong Kong's former chief secretary, and Legco member Anson Chan Fang On-sang, is also one of them.

De Klerk, who is the only state leader ever to have renounced the nuclear weapons that South Africa already possessed, hit on the idea that former world leaders could help their in-office counterparts while working with his own pro-peace foundation set up after he retired. It has advised nine nations since its inception in 2000. He is a natural politician. No notes – instinctive and natural. Yet, when he speaks, no one seems to listen.

When he spoke in Hong Kong at the Foreign Correspondent's Club, after arriving from Taiwan in February 2007, the turnout was dismal because again *We the Apathetic Maids* tuned out. Former FCC President Philip Bowring said it best. "It is not clear whether the apathy shown by Tsang and Co. was due to pique at the fact that De Klerk was in town with a power-bunch that included Anson Chan ... or that he was a has-been white guy from a now black majority-ruled nation."

These are initiatives in which America did not take the lead. It is the work of true 21st-century allies – those that have established the foundation cornerstones to the proposed ISC. There is room for many more.

Lebanon & Hezbollah
The Lebanon crisis is the poker hand that will determine how long the U.N.

will remain relevant in the 21st century. Its survival is on the line. How it uses the life jacket it has been given in Lebanon will determine its fate. Resolution 1559 adopted by the U.N. in September 2004 called for the disbanding of the Hezbollah fighting force and all other militas in Lebanon and the extension of the Lebanese government's control over the territory controlled by Hezbollah and other militias. Because the resolution had no enforcement mechanism, it was ignored.

Israel's 34-day effort to remove Hezbollah from southern Lebanon was a futile attempt to enforce Resolution 1559. The exercise was a millennium history lesson of the geopolitical realities in the Middle East that *We the Apathetic People* have to recognize and address in the 21st century to avoid Armageddon. Lebanon is an example of the explosiveness of unfettered regional fusion, one that embraces and melds the various local religions with traditional and contemporary economic and political theories and practices – with deadly consequences if left to their own self-destructive devices by the U.N. The Cedar Revolution that expelled Syria from Lebanon after former Lebanese Prime Minister Rafiq Hariri was assassinated has stalled. Syria has not been punished by the U.N. as promised for its role in the assassination and is again flexing its political muscle to thwart the U.N. Iran, meanwhile, continues to develop its nuclear program while thumbing its nose at threatened U.N. sanctions as it funds, arms and directs Hezbollah in a way that ensures the U.N. is again de-fanged.

The Israeli government's Winograd Commission, headed up by retired judge Eliyahu Winograd, held Prime Minister Ehud Olmert, Defense Minister Amir Peretz and former army chief Dan Halutz principally responsible for Israel's failure in the 34-day war. "The prime minister made up his mind hastily, despite the fact that no detailed military plan was submitted to him and without asking for one despite his lack of experience in foreign policy and military affairs." The report went on to say that "All of these add up to a serious failure in exercising judgment, responsibility and prudence." The Winograd commission was set up after the war after army reservists blasted a lack of preparation that left some units without adequate food supplies. Sounds like the U.S. in Iraq. Shouldn't *We the Apathetic Maids* be doing what Israel did after it lost its war with Hezbollah with the Bush, Cheney, Rumsfeld team that got the U.S. into Iraq? Another bipartisan committee acceptable to both the White House and Congress. "It is worth respect when an inquiry commission is appointed by the prime minister and it condemns Olmert," Hezbollah chief Sheikh Hasan Nasrallah said. He added that he respected Israel for issuing the damning report on the war. Respect leads to peace. A lesson America has to learn before it is too late.

Resolution 1701 that created the ceasefire between Israel and Hezbollah repeats the goals of 1559, and provides more – but not enough – enforcement substance, including an armed U.N. force of up to 15,000 soldiers to support the 15,000 Lebanese soldiers repositioned there. The resolution's failure to allow soldiers to disarm Hezbollah will prevent a negotiated long-term peace settlement. It was the first resolution on a Middle East peace-keeping issue ever to get the backing of all five permanent members of the Security Council. This happened because of America's declining influence and engagement. All the more reason for the mission and objectives of the resolution to be achieved. The stronger hand the U.S. had at the U.N. and in the Middle East has been squandered, just like any bad call in a poker game. Calling terrorists "Islamic fascists" does not endear America to the protagonists in the Middle East.

Ali Fayyad, Hezbollah's top policy strategist, told *Newsweek's* Daniel Kurtz-Phelan: "Hezbollah is part of the reality-based school of politics, unlike the Bush administration. Our problem with America is not with its existence, as it is with Israel. Our problem with America is specifically with the American imperialist project. It gives Israel weapons and then Israel uses those weapons to kill our people." It does so in self defense.

Lebanon's 1.2 million Shiites make up the country's largest religious group and they support Hezbollah. That is why Hezbollah has also become one of Lebanon's strongest political forces, with two cabinet ministers and 12 law-makers in parliament. Is it any wonder the government is helpless? Any attempt by the government's 70,000 soldiers to disarm Hezbollah, the best guerrilla force in the world, would lead to civil war – all the more reason to give the U.N. soldiers fighting power. To leave the securing of the border with Syria and disarming the Hezbollah to the government of Lebanon "at its request, to secure its border and entry points, to prevent entry of arms and related material," is a nonstarter, even though the parliamentary majority is Sunni and Christian.

Hezbollah emerged from the war emboldened, with greater influence over government, and accuses anyone who wants it to disarm of treason and siding with Israel. "We have no problem with UNIFIL (the U.N. Interim Force in Lebanon) as long as its mission is not aimed at disarming Hezbollah," Hezbollah's Nasrallah said during Kofi Annan's first visit to Lebanon to assess the situation first-hand. Hezbollah does have the option of integrating its forces into the Lebanese army if it is serious about disarming itself as a militia. Instead, it decided to bring down the government by having its cabinet ministers resign and organize mass rallies calling for the resignation of the Lebanese government because it is 'a United States puppet." Hezbollah staged a coup Hezbollah-style that failed. A coup that would instate Syrian and Iranian tutelage over the country. But did it? Isn't that democracy?

Such tutelage would prevent the vigorous international legal process that would bring to trial the Syrian perpetrators of the more than 16 high-profile political assassinations in Lebanon. They include the former Prime Minister Rafik Hariri, a Sunni, cabinet minister Pierre Gemaye, a Maronite Christian, and Member of Parliament Walid Ido, chairman of parliament's defense committee and his eldest son Khalid.

The muted responses of Sunni Egypt, Jordan, Saudi Arabia and Libya to the Israeli attack make clear their fear of Hezbollah developing into a local Shiite proxy for Iran. It is a greater threat to their political existence and survival than Israel. Saudi Arabia broke ranks from Arab orthodoxy after Israel set out to destroy Hezbollah and condemned the Hezbollah attack. There is an emerging consensus in the Arab world that Iran and Syria have to be stopped from using their surrogates in Lebanon and Gaza to perpetuate their radical agendas.

Israel, like its Sunni Arab neighbors, has been there before. International peacekeepers and Israel's eventual withdrawal of troops from south Lebanon in 2000 did little to stem Hezbollah and its rocket attacks.

Sunni Arab governments and Israel do agree that the U.N. is ineffective. The U.N is viewed with suspicion and anger by the Arabs because of its inability to pressure Israel into complying with many resolutions. Israel, on the other hand, believes the U.N. is incapable of enforcing its will in a crisis. Foremost in Israeli minds is the U.N.'s role in the prelude to the 1967 Six-Day War. The U.N. deployed an emergency force in Egypt's Sinai Peninsula as part of the 1956 Sinai conflict ceasefire agreement, to serve as a buffer between Egyptian and Israeli forces. But in May 1967, then-Egyptian President Gamal Abdel Nasser, amid growing regional tensions, demanded that the force leave – and they did so without even consulting the Security Council. Within days, the Six-Day War erupted.

UNIFIL is perceived by Israel as pro-Arab and in kahoots with Hezbollah. Hence the bombing of U.N. posts that were used as cover by Hezbollah, resulting in the deaths of four U.N. observers. The U.N.'s failure to remove Hezbollah as mandated by Resolution 1559 is widely expected to be perpetuated and repeated by the new expanded force. It is therefore no surprise that Israel reluctantly accepts soldiers from Muslim countries that do not recgnize Israel.

To hear Kofi Annan beg for peacekeepers to supplement the "worse than useless" 2,000-strong UNIFIL force that has been there for 20 years is a concern and dire warning. To supplement the force with soldiers that cannot engage or "wage war" to enforce the resolution and on condition that Israel not violate the ceasefire, even if Hezbollah does, is a one-way nonstarter, especially when Syria won't support or recognize the U.N. resolution if U.N. forces are stationed along Lebanon's border with Syria. The fact that Syrian President Bashar al-Assad promised to enforce an arms embargo on Hezbollah is just one more in a long string of broken Syrian promises. Hezbollah has received most of its weaponry across the Syrian border. The U.N. is unable to document a single instance of a seizure of arms at or near the border. The same applies to Iran's promise of "full support" for the U.N. ceasefire resolution. If Iran and Syria are serious about stopping arm shipments to Hezbollah and disarming the militant group, they can do so by supporting the U.N. resolution with their deeds.

To adopt rules of engagement that allow soldiers to fire only to protect civilians, or in self-defense, and not to disarm is a mere stopgap measure before the war resumes and reconfirms the U.N.'s uselessness. "There is no flexibility on arms smuggling," Lebanese Defense Minister Elias al-Murr said. However, Lebanese troops are reluctant to disarm Hezbollah or patrol its border with Syria for fear of antagonizing Syria, which has threatened to close the border. It is Lebanon's sole access to the outside world. Its only other border is with Israel, which it refuses to recognize.

Syria sees Hezbollah as its ace in the hole, something to be exploited to make Syria a factor in the region or to be traded in the right circumstances. "We should create a one-two punch with the French to make clear Syria has something significant to lose by not cutting off Hezbollah, and has something to gain from changing course," said Dennis Ross, counselor of the Washington Institute for Near East Policy. I agree. How else do you stop wars? Getting the facilitators to sit down and negotiate is a pre-condition.

Besides, Syria can also help the U.S. in Iraq as it did as one of the facilitators involved in the release of the 15 Royal Navy crew members. The only way the U.S. can draw a wedge between Damascus and Tehran and slow down their political and military alliance and the Iranian-dominated "Shiite crescent" stretching from Iran to Lebanon. Syria is controlled by members of its Allawite minority, a form of Shiism that is rejected as heretical by some Sunnis. Is it any wonder President Assad and his party make sure he runs for re-election in an uncontested referendum to be reannointed as president until 2014? For an election to be legitimate there has to be an opposition. An inconceivable concept since Syria has been under emergency law since the Baath party came to power in 1963.

Syria's alliance with Iran is "a marriage of convenience." Syria is a secular country with a Sunni majority. It is merely an advance base for Iran to funnel munitions to Hezbollah. The two countries concluded a formal alliance on June 16, 2006, which created a new Iranian-Syrian intelligence center that tracks Israeli military movements and relays that information to Hezbollah and Hamas. Syria is also the sanctuary of Hamas leader Khaled Meshaal. It is not comfortable with Iran's Shiite ayatollahs and could be approached with tempting offers such as the return of the Golan Heights. The alternative is another war front for Israel.

History suggests that only force, or the threat of force, can win substantial concessions from Syria. In 1998, Turkey threatened military action unless Syria stopped supporting Kurdish terrorists. Damascus promptly complied. Israel may have no choice but to follow the Turkish example. Shlomo Avineri, a former director-general of Israel's Foreign Ministry, argues that Israel fought the wrong war: Instead of Lebanon, it should have targeted Syria. I agree. Max Boot, a senior fellow at the Council on Foreign Relations, summed it up best: "The choice Israelis face isn't between war and peace. It is between war sooner and on their terms, or war later and on the enemy's terms. Ignoring the threat isn't a serious option."

The U.N.'s unrealistic expectations have to be acknowledged and challenged. It should therefore not be a surprise that the French refused to lead the U.N. force because they would have had to disarm Hezbollah, and the Italians took hold of the reins, which in and of itself should have set off alarm bells. The European Union member states were wary of making firm commitments until the mandate for the new force was clarified, fearing their peace-keepers could be dragged into a conflict with Hezbollah or with Israel if the ceasefire collapsed. "Nobody wants to be saddled with the task that the Israeli military failed to achieve in a month of intense combat," said a European diplomat.

The Europeans do not want to risk the lives of their soldiers or their relationship with the Muslim world. The 3,500 vanguard troops that the U.N. wanted on the ground by August 28 with additional reinforcements of 3,500 joining by October 5 and an additional 3,000 by early November leaves the ceasefire a leaky seive that allows Hezbollah to easily rearm. "It's not going to go in there and attempt large-scale disarmament," said U.N. Deputy Secretary-General Mark Malloch Brown. Why not? So what is it going to do? Why send troops to again just stand idly by as Hezbollah rearms? Is it any wonder Israel is doing what the U.N. repeatedly promises to? To be effective, the U.N. force has to be backed by political will to strike back at either Hezbollah or Israeli forces if they violate ceasefire terms. How else can it help the Lebanese army restore government control of the Hezbollah strongholds?

European troops are needed to give the force the appearance of legitimacy. The fact is, it is not legitimate and won't be unless the force is proactive and can disarm Hezbollah. Otherwise it is just another stopgap delay of another war and reconfirmation of the U.N.'s ineffective, costly and unnecessary waste of lives and money. It will reconfirm that the U.N. has outlived its usefulness.

The U.N. force is supposed to patrol a specific southern demilitarized zone and help the Lebanese government monitor its borders, ensuring that Iran and Syria do not resupply Hezbollah with rockets, missiles and ammunition. If it fails to do so, how long will Israel stand by this time and watch the rearmament of Hezbollah in violation of the resolution? After all, Hezbollah managed to fire off 200 missiles on the last day before the ceasefire, and its leader, Hassan Nasrallah, is still standing, proud and tall. Israel's much-hyped military invincibility proved to be hollow. It didn't even get back the two soldiers it went to war over.

Hezbollah does not believe Israel has a right to exist as a sovereign state. Hezbollah's ultimate objective – destruction of the Israeli state – can only mean renewed conflict sooner or later. Hezbollah leaders, like those of Iran, Syria and the armed wing of Hamas, are dedicated to eliminating Israel. The Middle East will not have durable stability as long as Hezbollah continues its campaign to destroy Israel and refuses to disarm and channel its energies through Lebanon's democratic political structure.

Israel had respected the Blue Line, the demarcation of Israel's withdrawal from Lebanon in 2000, as verified by the U.N., which Hezbollah violated. Shebaa Farms, the small area that Hezbollah accuses Israel of continuing to occupy, was part of Syria, not Lebanon, before Israel captured it in the Six-Day War of 1967. The integrity of the Blue Line must be protected by the U.N. this time around. The alternative is the end to peace in the region and the end of the U.N. The question many Israelis are asking is, "If international borders mean nothing to Hezbollah, why should it mean anything to Hamas and the Palestinians if Israel agrees to a new Palestinian state?" Israel's policy of unilateral withdrawal from Gaza resulted in the resumption of Hamas missiles being fired at Israeli communities, only now, from a closer range and deadlier, which makes a unilateral withdrawal from the West Bank impossible. Israel is not going to put any more Israeli towns within the range of Palestinian missiles unless there is a comprehensive regional peace treaty. Not after Palestinian fundamentalists based in Lebanon fired two rockets at Israel in June 2007, trying to spark an Israeli reaction and replay of the 2006 invasion of Lebanon.

Palestinians have been a part of the Lebanese socio-political-military tapestry since 1948 when thousands moved there during the Arab-Israel war. Lebanon has been a military base for Palestinians war with Israel, now stoked and egged on by Hezbollah and Syria as their fighting proxy, not just against

Israel, but the western backed Lebanese government and military in their attempt to destabilize the country and restart the civil war of 1975-90.

The fact is, Hezbollah won't disarm or leave the territory between the Latani River and Israel border in southern Lebanon. Just like the Russians could not defeat the Taliban in Afghanistan and like the Americans can't defeat the insurgencies in Afghanistan and Iraq, Israel cannot defeat Hezbollah. Both Hezbollah and Israel lost. Both sides have admitted their miscalculations. Israel appointed a commission to probe the failures of the war in Lebanon. Shouldn't the U.N. be doing the same about its failures in Lebanon and elsewhere?

So what is the political solution? Not just for Lebanon but for Palestine? The most important lesson of Israel's incursion is that solutions to conflict must be political, not military – political dialogue between neighbors. The current military respite offers the ideal opportunity to find a political solution before another unnecessary military conflict erupts in Lebanon or Gaza. Hamas won military and political control of Gaza while this paragraph was being edited. Military force is counterproductive and drives the political solution further off into the distant horizon.

How many more Middle East roadmaps with one-way delusional wrong way streets, wrong turns, with a total disrespect and disregard for "the right side of the road" do *We the Apathetic Maids* have to be led down before we wake up? There must be an all encompassing political settlement of the Palestinian, Lebanese and Syrian outstanding issues that is endorsed by Iran.

Iran

Iran's $100-million annual Hezbollah proxy has created a state within a state in Lebanon and built a military infrastructure that even Israel's military might could not dislodge. Iran helped create Hezbollah in the early 1980s. But does that make Hezbollah Iran's puppet? Hezbollah, to a great extent, makes decisions independently of Iran. It is an indigenous Lebanese armed resistance group that owes its popularity to resistance to Israel, biased American policies and corrupt Lebanese politicians. Does anyone seriously believe that unarmed U.N. soldiers, or armed U.N. soldiers reluctant to challenge Hezbollah, can restore a permanent ceasefire? A determined Hezbollah backed by Iran has created a new political reality that must be acknowledged and addressed.

Iran has re-emerged as a regional power and will continue down the bloody path it has embarked with Hezbollah if it is not recognized and treated with the respect it deserves. The West has to acknowledge that Iran is a power. It won't back down, just like it hasn't over the centuries, dating back to biblical times. Iran has always stood tall. That is why it has issued new 50,000-rial notes bearing an emblazoned nuclear symbol and a portrait of the late Ayatollah Ruhollah Khomeini, the father of the 1979 Islamic Revolution. Under the Ayatollah, in 1979, Iran kidnapped and held hostage U.S. Embassy workers and got instant world recognition. It is therefore only natural they would replay this political masterstroke of a tool at the height of their war of words with America and its coalition partners in Iraq over its nuclear program.

The target this time around was a 15-member British Royal Navy crew inspecting an Iranian vessel in the Shatt a -Arab waterway on March 23, 2007, under the authority of the U.N. The same U.N. that imposed the sanctions on Iran for not stopping its nuclear program. Score one for Iran in the propaganda spin skirmish. To most people in the Middle East, Britain has become the distrusted, brown-nosing "Little Satan" puppy to Uncle Sam. The prisoners were released after being held captive for 13-days – to celebrate the Prophet Muhammad's birthday in a dramatic way played up by the global media.

President Mahmoud Ahmedinejad had milked the crisis to the max, showing the Iranian people that former colonial power Britain was not militarily omnipotent, while also boosting his credentials with his Arab neighbors. Britain's former Prime Minister Tony Blair ended the crisis with a flair, when he said London was commited to resolving disputes peacefully with Tehran. "To the Iranian people I would simply say this: We bear you no ill will. On the contrary, we respect Iran as an ancient civilization, as a nation with a proud and dignified history." Something America must acknowledge sooner than later.

Iran is saying and doing what a majority of Iranians believe. Stand firm and proud, yet open to peaceful dialogue and diplomatic relations. America's dismissive, cavalier attitude only further endangers its geopolitical credibility in the region. The Islamic Republic knows it is long overdue for a new definition for itself that redefines its relationship with America and the West. America should assist in the spelling of the definition. China can help America and Iran craft a new cooperative arrangement. Iran and the U.S. did sit down and talk to each other in Baghdad in March 2007, after a 28-year diplomatic freeze. What next, and why not restore diplomatic relations after settling the few minor contentious issues?

Iran is a regional power and has to be recognized and treated as such. It won't be bullied or relegated to secondary status. Trying to repress Iran, much like trying to repress China, is not only futile, but geopolitically counterproductive. Iran is a military, economic and political regional power that has proven its ability and capability through its proxies in Lebanon, Iraq and Palestine. Nevertheless, Iran knows both the propaganda and military costs are becoming rather annoying to the educated and knowledgable Iranians, who are nowhere near as apathetic as *We the Maids* in America. Iran's foreign military adventures are not popular. The money could be better spent at home. Especially after Hezbollah leader Nasrallah said, "We did not think, even 1%, that the capture (of the two Israeli soldiers) would lead to a war at this time and of this magnitude. You ask me, if I had known on July 11 ... that the operation would lead to such a war, would I do it? I say no, absolutely not."

Hezbollah is weakened, and the numerous other angry Lebanese factions are starting to squeeze them out in the footsteps of the Syrian soldiers. Even Nazrallah's major Christian ally, Michael Aoun, has called for Hezbollah to disarm. The March 14th democratic alliance movement is named for the date of their huge protest rally after the assassination in 2005 of former Prime Minister Rafik Hariri. The rally helped force Syria to end 15 years of domination of Lebanese politics. The movement is dominated by figures from U.S.-backed groups who are back in the driver's seat, which has marginalized Hezbollah. This is an opportunity America should not again squander.

The Bridge

It is a diplomatic high-stakes poker game for America to try and engage while accusing Iran of bankrolling terrorism and building a nuclear bomb. With a president from Texas, America should be sitting at the poker table until all the cards are played. The groundbreaking May 2007 meeting between U.S. and Iranian ambassadors in Baghdad, the first since the U.S. severed ties in 1980, 14 months after Iran's Islamic Revolution and five months after Americans were seized and held hostage in the U.S. embassy in Tehran, is a good first hand. The meeting lasted four hours. Whose call is it now?

Negotiating with enemies is necessary to end the hostile relationship and develop a mutually constructive one. Iran recognizes the importance of negotiating and tried to do so as far back as May 2003. The Iran overture, approved by Iran's supreme leader Ayatollah Ali Khamenei and then-president Mohammad Khatami, was rejected outright by the U.S. The proposal was transmitted by the Swiss ambassador to Tehran, who also represented U.S. interests there. The proposal included an end to Iran's support of anti-Israel militants and acceptance of Israel's right to exist. It was an opportunity akin to the 1972 U.S. opening to China – another U.S. foreign policy missed opportunity.

As recently as early 2007, Khameini through his chief foreign policy advisor, Ali Akbar Velayati, declared that suspending uranium enrichment is not a red line for the regime – in lay terms, the mullahs are ready to agree to some kind of suspension. This was confirmed by Ali Akbar Hashemi Rafsanjani, while a third high-ranking official acknowledged that Iran is considering a proposal by President Vladimir Putin of Russia to suspend uranium enrichment at least long enough to start serious negotiations with the U.N.

Velayati also conceded that the Nazi Holocaust is a fact of history and chastised those who question its reality. Ali Larijani, Iran's chief nuclear negotiator, also declared the Holocaust a "historical matter" to be discussed by scholars and not by self-serving ignorant politicians. Iranians are ready to negotiate, and have been for a while. Maybe gunboat diplomacy still works after all? America sent the aircraft carrier Dwight D. Eisenhower, backed by a second Nimitz-class nuclear-powered carrier, the John C. Stennis, a handful of destroyers and a shoal of support ships – ostensibly assisting U.S. operations in Afghanistan and Iraq. Not since the Iraq war in early 2003 has America amassed so much sea power around the Persian Gulf.

Many claim that plans for a U.S. invasion of Iran, again like Iraq, were made long ago and that the armada is there to make possible either another Gulf of Tonkin resolution or an Iranian act of provocation against American forces, which could then serve as the excuse for an attack on Iran. Iran's successful firing of its first rocket only increased the tension. The rocket reached an altitude of 150 kilometers, which is above the internationally accepted boundary between the Earth's atmosphere and space, which is agreed at 100 kilometers above the surface and is known as the Karman Line.

Iran has started making nuclear fuel, according to the International Atomic Energy Agency. It has more than 3,000 centrifuges running, which is enough to refine uranium for a bomb by the end of 2007 if the machines run for long periods of time without breaking down.

"Iran has obtained the technology to produce nuclear fuel and Iran's move is like a train ... which has no brake and no reverse gear," Ahmadinejad said. The U.S. response, so eloquently phrased by Secretary of State Condoleezza Rice, was: "They don't need a reverse gear. They need a stop button." A diplomatic device known as a "nonpaper" – obviously so its existence can be denied – has been circulating since October 1, 2006.

Iran reluctantly agreed in July 2007 to grant U.N. inspectors access to its nuclear reactors in order to prevent a third round of sanctions being imposed. Let's not forget that the U.S. government funded covert operations supporting opposition militias among the numerous ethnic minority groups clustered in Iran's border regions. Just in the year, ending February 2007, there has been a wave of unrest in minority border areas of Iran, with bombings and assassination campaigns against soldiers and government officials. These "incidents" have been carried out by the Kurds in the west, the Azeris in the northwest, the Ahwazi Arabs in the southwest, and the Baluchis in the southeast.

Non-Persians make up nearly 40 percent of Iran's 69 million population, with around 16 million Azeris, 7 million Kurds, 5 million Ahwazis and 1 million Baluchis. Most Baluchis live over the border in Pakistan. Tit-for-tat, America is doing in Iran what it is receiving from Iran in Iraq. Iran did a better job. The damage they can do after an attack by America or Israel is a multi-frontal insurgency we don't want to experience, unless, of course, one is a Christian Evangelical who believes in Armageddon.

Objective intelligence reports claim that the U.S. data on Iran, like Iraq, is flawed. America's evidence on Iran's nuclear plans and programs remains ambiguous, fragmented and difficult to prove. It is belived Iran halted its nuclear weapons program in 2003. One thing certain is that the U.S. has been trying to undermine the Islamic Revolution since 1979. The Iranian regime's fragile sense of legitimacy necessitates dealing with it respectfully.

Negotiating with Iran is essential if there is to be a rapproachment between the two global powers. The arguments made against negotiating with Iran and Syria were also made against negotiating with the Soviet Union during the Cold War. Soviet misconduct easily matches that of Iran and Syria in aggression, oppression, murder, support of terrorist groups and mendacity.

President Reagan challenged Soviet behavior by supporting groups fighting communist intervention, building the military, strengthening NATO, condemning human-rights violations, and conveying the message of freedom in every way possible. Nevertheless, negotiations took place with four specific policies in place, including: Regime Acceptance – which required the U.S. to refrain from activities aimed at destroying the Soviet regime it was trying to influence, while vigorously denouncing its political and moral legitimacy; Limited Linkage – Negotiations on human rights, arms control, regional issues and bilateral relations were pursued without linkage to Soviet conduct, enabling negotiations to proceed while the U.S. responded firmly through deeds; Rhetorical Restraint – Reagan vigorously criticized the Soviet system and its behavior, but promised not to "crow" when the Soviets agreed to U.S. proposals, enabling Soviet leaders to avoid being seen as capitulating to U.S. demands; and Self-Interest – U.S. negotiating policy was based on convincing the Soviets to act in their own best interests.

Why can't these same principles be applied to Iran and Syria? China could be the facilitator and together with the U.S. could bring about a peaceful resolution to the regional conflicts. China has very close political and economic ties to all the protagonists in the region – especially Iran and Israel. The Iraq Study Group recommended that the U.S. do just that. So what are *We the Apathetic People* doing about it?

During a 12-day visit to the United States in 2006, former Iranian President Mohammad Khatami urged Americans to participate in a "dialogue among civilizations." Speaking at an Islamic center in suburban Chicago, Khatami also called on his fellow Muslims to work for peace. "There is a great opportunity for dialogue and cooperation by people of faith," he said. Later, during a lively question-and-answer session at the Massachusetts Institute of Technology, he reminded his audience that "Bush and Ahmadinejad are cut from the same cloth" – all the more reason the two leaders should start a direct dialogue.

Khatami also visited New York to attend a U.N. conference on ways to bridge the gap between the Islamic world and the West. He declared that the 9/11 attacks were an atrocity and that the suicide bombers did Islam an injustice and would not make it to heaven. He said that two crimes were committed in that attack: civilians were killed and it was done in the name of Islam. "Those who do it in the name of Islam are lying," he told the Council on American-Islamic Relations, a human rights group.

President Bush personally approved the granting of a visa to Khatami for the visit because he was "interested in learning more" about Iran. How come Bush needed such a lesson? What are *We the Apathetic Maids* paying taxes for?

Khatami was the most prominent Iranian to visit the U.S. since Washington and Tehran broke off diplomatic relations in 1980, after the seizure of 52 hostages at the American Embassy in the Iranian capital and the 444-day crisis that spoiled President Jimmy Carter's bid for re-election and brought the crusty Ronald Reagan into the White House. Reagan would go on to suffer his own Iran scandal – the Iran-Contra affair.

Iran is indebted to America for getting rid of its two main political and military threats – Saddam Hussein and the Taliban. Iran hoped that the fall of Saddam and the Taliban would be the seeds for detente between the two countries. Iran was then run by reform-leaning President Khatami. Instead, Iran was included in Bush's "axis of evil."
Khatami was the liberal reform-minded president for eight years until 2005, pushing for reforms to no avail. Nevertheless, America failed to grasp or understand that there were two power centers in Iran competing for influence. Contrary to the perception that Iran is firmly in the control of its fiery president, Mahmoud Ahmadinejad, it in fact is torn by competing power

centers that Khatami has been trying to bridge on the road to peaceful relations with America.

Ahmadinejad represents the youthful group of fundamentalist hard-liners who are determined to keep the revolutionary spirit alive. On the other hand is Iran's elite class of conservative clerics, aging former revolutionaries and businessmen wary of reform and less interested in confronting America and the world and risking Iran's isolation. Former Iranian President Ali Akbar Hashemi Rafsanjani, who was defeated by Ahmadinejad in the 2005 election, is a member of this conservative elite and a candidate for the Assembly of Experts, a panel that has a big say in who becomes the next supreme leader after Ali Khamenei, who succeeded the Ayatollah Khomenei and who gets the last word over everyone in the system, including Ahmadinejad and Rafsanjani. He is the ultimate power broker in Iran.

While Khatami was traveling in the U.S., Rafsanjani released a secret letter that the late Ayatollah Khomeini wrote explaining why he was willing to end Iran's eight-year war with Saddam Hussein in July 1988, short of victory. Ayatollah Khomeini said military officers had told him that to continue, they would need more firepower, perhaps even nuclear weapons. The letter was editorialized with the conclusion that Ayatollah Khomeini was wise not to let his revolutionary ideology get in the way of "a realistic understanding of the international situation."

The message for Rafsanjani's conservative supporters is clear: Today's Iran, too, should proceed with caution and pragmatism, a message and opportunity America missed. America did have an offer on the table to discuss with Iran how they could work together to bring about a peaceful resolution to the sectarian violence in Iraq. By the time Iran was ready to sit down, after the conservative and pragmatic side prevailed after several months of internal political wrangling between the two factions – America lost interest. The U.S. unwittingly opened the door for Ahmadinejad to step on center stage and bombast America. America missed another opportunity for peace.
Rafsanjani is now back in a position of power as the head of the Expediency Discernment Council, which is scrutinizing President Ahmadinejad's performance and reportedly even considering his impeachment and removal from office for economic mismanagement.

Seventy percent of Iran's 69 million people are under age 30, and so have no memory of the shah, or the taking of the U.S. hostages, and even less interest in the past. Most Iranians are concerned about what effects U.S. economic sanctions might have on the economy, already badly managed by the mullahs, and are perplexed and hurt by America's anti-Iran political rhetoric and "axis of evil" label.

Islam came late to Persia, a land which boasted a rich and full civilization long before the Arab invaders swept in from the west. While most younger Iranians do admire Islam's sense of discipline, art and architecture, they have little interest in its rigid dogma and social intolerance. Women in Iran, unlike other Arab Muslim nations such as Saudi Arabia, can work, drive and vote, own property or businesses, run for political office and seek divorce. The majority of Iran's university graduates are women. "It is the women of Iran who give me hope that this once-noble nation will one day return to its gracious roots," wrote U.S. journalist Steve Knipp on a visit to Iran during the nuclear standoff. "Most of the young people I spoke with insist that change is coming," Knipp added. "But I was advised that the world must be patient, as the mullahs are not keen to give up power, and it will take time to wrest it from them." Not that long. There is a civil uprising well under way behind closed doors and under chadors (head-to-toe robes). Iran's teen-agers are rebelling in the best traditions of *We the Apathetic Maids* – by embracing, sex, drugs and rock 'n' roll – even with the threat of persecution and whipping – whooping it up to the beat of underground defiant rappers.

They drink *arak*, an Iranian liquor made by fermenting raisins, and swap recipes for disguising the sharp taste of alcohol in homemade drinks. Alcohol is banned in Iran, even for the Christian and Jewish communities, although the authorities ignore its consumption. Fueled with alcohol, they take to the streets and riot when they disagree with a government policy. The riots of late June 2007, when the Iranian government pushed ahead with plans for fuel rationing, is an example. Satellite television and the Internet, both of which are easily accessible throughout the country, are also being consumed without interference – and they are addicted to an official miniseries sympathetic to Jews. An Iranian diplomat in Paris who helps Jews escape the Holocant.

Societal change was triggered by eight years of reformist rule under Khatami,

beginning in 1997. The rebellious behavior of the younger Iranian generation highlights the disgust and disrespect they have for the Ahmadinejad
regime and its policies. Despite its huge energy reserves, Iran lacks refining
capacity and must import about 40 percent of its petrol, a sensitive political
issue if financial sanctions are imposed on Iran.

Trying to shove Iran into a nuclear diplomatic corner with sanctions has
brought together in Iran a coalition of theocratic mullahs and vested interests from the 1979 Islamist revolution, within the region – and beyond. This
at the expense of the reform movement headed by Khatami before misguided
U.S. foreign policy got him replaced by Ahmadinejad, and America and
Israel cornered. Why try and keep anyone in a corner? Iran is entitled to a
deal that will give it security guarantees and recognition as a legitimate regional power.

The U.N. Security Council resolution requiring Iran to suspend all activities
related to uranium enrichment by August 31, 2006, or risk possible sanctions was the direct cause of North Korea launching missiles on July 4 and
the 34-day war between Hezbollah and Israel.

Is it any wonder Iran launched a rocket in February 2007, on the eve of the
U.N. deadline to freeze its nuclear program or face more severe sanctions?
Iran has the largest ballistic missile arsenal in the Middle East and success-
fully tested its missiles in Lebanon when Hezbollah fired one and hit an
Israeli Navy vessel patrolling the Mediterranean during the 2006 Israel-
Hezbollah confrontation. With nuclear power plants ready to go on line with
enriched uranium and plutonium produced by heavy water reactors, Iran has
the ability to produce the fissile material used in nuclear warheads.

Communicative Defiance

President Mahmoud Ahmadinejad formally inaugurated a heavy-water reactor to be used for peaceful purposes in defiance of the U.N. deadline imposed for Iran to comply or else while declaring it is not a threat to any
country, even the "Zionist regime that is the enemy of the countries in the
region." Ahmadinejad was elected in 2005 on a populist economic message,
promising a redistribution of the nation's vast oil revenues and economic
and infrastructure improvements. Instead, while the economy remains
gridlocked and inflation and unemployment run high, Ahmadinejad has con-

verted the nuclear issue to his beliefs. With China and Russia, two of the Security Council members, opposed to sanctions and supporting Iran's call for negotiations with America, as it gets bogged down deeper in Iraq and Afghanistan, is it any wonder that on the heels of the perceived Hezbollah victory over Israel, Iran does not feel threatened by America? Can America afford another war front in the region?

To read about how Bush hardliners are trying to portray Iran's nuclear program as more advanced than it is and exaggerate Tehran's role in Hezbollah's attack on Israel is a bad rerun of what they did months before the March 2003 invasion of Iraq. Officials at the CIA, the Defense Intelligence Agency and the State Department are right in being concerned about questionable information that originated with Iranian exiles. Iraqi exiles said the same and were believed, even though at the time, International Atomic Energy Agency Director General Mohamed El Baradei questioned and challenged their allegations. His assessment proved correct then and now regarding Iran. For America to flex its military power in the region with an aircraft carrier armada while Vice President Dick Cheney pushes for military strikes against Iranian nuclear facilities, was a futile hand played in the poker game. Although it may have contributed to the release of the 15 Royal Navy sailors and marines Iran seized in the Shatt al-Arab waterway. It's a good thing Secretary of State Condoleezza Rice, who is pushing the diplomatic front at the poker table, is being heard above the raucus voices of the neoconservative movement. The carrot approach is always more productive than the stick – and a lot easier and cheaper.

Iran is the most important regional power in the Middle East. This was confirmed by the visit to Tehran of Iraqi Prime Minister Nouri al-Maliki, who went there in September 2006 to seek Iran's support to quell the sectarian violence that America can't. "Iran will give its assistance to establish complete security in Iraq, because Iraq's security is Iran's security," Iran's Ahmadinejad said during Maliki's visit. There is no doubt that some elements in Iran were stoking the violence in Iraq in retaliation for the U.S. occupation of Iraq and the Israeli assault in Lebanon.

The emergence of the Shiite crescent that stretches from Iran through Iraq and Syria to Lebanon – all nations with significant Shiite populations – has been growing stronger and wider because of U.S. geopolitical miscalculations.

Maliki's visit to Iran, like that of his predecessor Ibrahim al-Jaafari in July 2005, was a kind of homecoming. They both spent part of their exile from Saddam's rule living in Iran. Many Iraqi Shiites fled to Iran to escape Saddam's security forces.

The best channels of communication between America and Iran are in the Shiite crescent, namely Iraq. Iran recognizes America is in decline as a regional superpower and is taking advantage of the situation – for a change. Iran can help America for a change in Afghanistan and Shiite Iraq. It is creating chaos in Afghanistan, not only by arming and training the Taliban, but by deporting more than 100,000 Afghan immigrants, legal and illegal, over a two-month period in the summer of 2007.

Iran is a dominant historical economic, political and cultural player, one America should embrace. The Shiite crescent wave being ridden by Ahmadinejad is one America better catch. That is what Ahmadinejad is hoping he can achieve sooner than later. Hence his letter to Bush, to "propose new ways" to end 26 years of acrimony on the eve of the U.S. calling for sanctions, was a political bombshell, followed by an invitation to a political debate to bring people together, rather than reinforce polarized positions.

That does not excuse Iran's behavior of financing, supplying, training and having prior knowledge of an attack on the U.S. and its coalition forces – especially the Iraqis.

Now that America allegedly has proof that U.S. soldiers in Iraq and Afghanistan are being killed by Iranian-trained killers and suicide bombers, what is America waiting for? Since when does America passively ignore an enemy killing its finest?

Nuclear Standoff

Iran has made clear that no one can prevent it from pursuing a peaceful nuclear program. The Iran nuclear issue can be comprehensively addressed only through face-to-face negotiations between Iran, America and Europe. America and Iran have to come out of the diplomatic and economic wilderness they have been in for the last 26 years, establish diplomatic relations and start a direct dialogue on how to resolve the nuclear dispute with a solution that allows Iran to develop nuclear power for peaceful means. Burying the past is the key to better future U.S.-Iran relations. To expect the world's fourth-largest oil exporter to abandon its right to nuclear technology is delusional.

Iran was one of the first countries to sign the Nuclear Non-Proliferation Treaty concluded in 1968, and cooperated with the International Atomic Energy Agency (IAEA) for more than 30 years. America's aim to force Iran to give up uranium enrichment is in breach of the NPT, which clearly states that any signatory country that gives up nuclear weapons and accepts the IAEA's absolute and unconditional control is entitled to produce electric energy from civil nuclear sources, and to receive from the international community, if necessary, technical and financial support. Iran's oil resources are finite and it must develop and control nuclear power to generate energy – a basic right as an NPT signatory.

Iran has said it has enriched uranium to 4.8 percent as of the late summer of 2006, far below the more than 90 percent level needed for a bomb. Iran hopes to reach a level of 20 per cent to fuel a light water reactor it plans to build. Iran is adamant that it is enriching uranium solely to generate electricity. America and Israel are convinced Iran's nuclear program is a front for building atom bombs. Iran did pursue a clandestine nuclear program for 18 years until it was uncovered by the IAEA in 2003. All the more reason America and Iran must sit down and talk to each other directly.

President Bush's boastful remark to "Bring it on!" with a Pentagon response group in place to do just that if Iran becomes unmanageable within 24 hours of a presidential order, is a prudent but dangerous negotiating tactic. Especially if Iran believes America won't fire the first shot because it is too bogged down in Afghanistan and Iraq.

France's tough-talking mama Therese Delpech, the French Atomic Energy Commission's director of strategic studies, tells it like it is. "The meeting of apocalyptic Shiism and the bomb make me very uncomfortable," she says. "Look at the Cuban missile crisis. Had there been a catastrophe, we know now that Castro would have been the cause. The current player resembles Castro, without a Khrushchev" – who reined him in – "and without a Kennedy." She believes, and I agree, that the most effective sanction is a total ban on investments by any U.N. member in the oil and gas industries and the sale or export of refined petroleum products that represent about 40 percent of Iranian needs. Withdrawing government support for either would force the parties to stay at the poker table, unless, of course it goes to the brink as it did in Cuba.

Russia sees Iran as the handle to its front door back to the Middle East. After all, Iran is a convenient counterweight to U.S. dominance in the region, which Russia will exploit to the max. Hopefully it won't go over the precipe and remove all peaceful options.

To block Bank Saderat, one of Iran's largest state-owned banks, from being able to use the U.S. financial system, because it had helped transfer hundreds of millions of dollars to terrorist organizations, including Hezbollah and Hamas, something America has known for years was long overdue.

Iranian financial institutions have not been able to deal directly with U.S. financial institutions since diplomatic relations were discontinued. They nevertheless continued to do business and have access to the U.S. financial system indirectly by working through foreign banks. These so-called U-turn transactions allow U.S. banks to process payments involving Iran if the money transfer begins and ends with a non-Iranian foreign bank. A sanction that is meaningful politically, but totally inpractical. The all inclusive sanctions against all banks and Revolutionary Guards was long overdue.

Iran is entitled to a realistic political, nuclear and economic deal that is as rewarding to Iran as it is to America and the West. Iranians do have the right to technology and deterrence. What sovereign state doesn't? Of course, that doesn't count the countries that gave up those rights voluntarily, Libya,being one example. Let's not forget the damage Libya did before it gave up its pursuit of nuclear technology. We do not want to encourage Iran down the path that America sent Libya.

America and Iran do not need a showdown with each other. New U.N. Secretary General Ban Ki-moon had every reason to be "deeply concerned." The resulting war, especially if prolonged, would create a global economic meltdown. Even worse, a pre-emptive U.S. military strike on Iran could accelerate rather than hinder Tehran's production of atomic weapons, according to the Oxford Research Group, a British global security think-tank. Its warning is backed by the former chief U.N. weapons inspector in Iraq, Hans Blix.

Iran would respond with its "crash program" to develop a nuclear device within a few months. And by the way, what intelligence does America really have than Iran isn't already a clandestine nuclear power, just like Israel was, other than that provided by former Iranian Deputy Defense Minister General Ali-Reza Asghari, who mysteriously disappeared in Turkey in March 2007, or December 2006, depending on who one believes, and is believed to have either been kidnapped or defected to America. The general played a major role in Lebanon for many years as a Revolutionary Guards commander of Hezbollah.

With American troops stretched thin and tied down in Iraq and Afghanistan, the U.S. military is hardly in a position to start another war front in Iran – especially if the Joint Chiefs of Staff are opposed and threaten to resign. Something that is not unprobable with a Democratic-controlled Congress that is opposed to the Iraq war and the thought of moving against Iran. There is a civil-military confrontation brewing in America more serious than anything that has been seen since President Harry Truman fired General Douglas MacArthur during the Korean War.

America better have irrefutable proof of Iran's nuclear capability going live before it attacks, or authorizes Israel to do so on its behalf. Otherwise, what little international standing America has left, if any, will evaporate. A lasting agreement on the Iran nuclear standoff is imperative to a lasting peace in the Middle East – starting with Lebanon. The alternative is ugly. China is Iran's largest buyer of crude oil. China knows how to squeeze concessions out of dangerous clients, as North Korea can confirm.

World War

The confrontation between America and Iran in the summer of 2006 and early 2007 was reminiscent of the summer of 1914. Then, the assassination of the Austrian archduke by a Serbian nationalist terrorist provided the senescent Austro-Hungarian Empire the excuse it had been looking for to wipe out the Serbian nationalists, which provoked the pan-Slavic nationalists at work for the Russian czar to threaten the Austro-Hungarians with destruction. That led Germany's Kaiser to pledge retaliatory war against Russia, which prompted the French, who had an anti-German alliance with Russia, to begin mobilization. "Nobody, wanted a global conflagration, yet nobody knew how to stop it, and American President Woodrow Wilson did nothing to help avert the impending war. Within a month, the war came and took the remainder of the 20th century for the world to fully recover," wrote Harold Meyerson, the editor-at-large of *American Prospect* and the former political editor of *L.A. Weekly.*

The killing of eight Israeli soldiers and kidnapping of three more by Hezbollah, which escalated in less than a week into a bloody 34-day war with ghoulish regional and global implications, felt eerily similar to what happened in 1914 and what happened to the Austro-Hungarian Empire. Iran's Supreme Leader Khamenei has warned America and the world that it would attack U.S. interests around the world if it comes under attack over its nuclear program.

The chief effect of the U.S. invasion and occupation of Iraq is the further destabilization of an already nuclear armed region with a nuclear umbrella. To make matters worse, within Iraq, the Shiite-Sunni conflict that many scholars, diplomats and intelligence experts warned of before the U.S. invasion has depopulated Baghdad – and ignited the Middle East. The battle for the restoration of the Caliphate and the elimination of Israel has pulverized Lebanon, destroyed its democracy, and antagonized the populace of the least anti-American country in the Arab world.

Real security, starting with border security in Lebanon, requires the kind of Interlocal Security Force that can spare the world from another global conflagration, because this time it will be nuclear – with ugly Armageddon consequences. Remember the bitter Iran-Iraq war of 1980-88? More than a million people were killed or wounded. With a nuclear repeat, you do the math – especially if Egypt, the largest Sunni Arab country, and Saudi Arabia decide to join the nuclear club to prevent Shiite Iran from dominating the region. Throw Turkey into the equation and imagine a Middle East with five or six nuclear powers.

Wrong Axis Leg Taken Out

The tragic irony of the Iraq war is that America took out the wrong leg in the "axis of evil" – the only one that was not developing weapons of mass destruction. With 20/20 hindsight, it seems to be precisely the reason it was Iraq that was targeted, because it was not the real threat the other two – Iran and North Korea – pose. Furthermore, it also clarifies why Saddam Hussein bluffed, believing that he could deter a U.S. attack by trying to convince the world that he in fact had weapons of mass destruction.

The U.S. invasion of Iraq accelerated the development of the nuclear weapons programs of Iran and North Korea because it became abundantly clear to both regimes that the only way to deter a U.S.-led attack was to have weapons of mass destruction. "The tragedy of growing up is that human beings acquire the means of killing themselves and others. The human race now collectively has that power," wrote Boris Johnson, a Conservative member of Parliament in Britain in an editorial opinion published in *The Daily Telegraph*. He went on to say, "The Iranians will join in soon enough. It might be sensible if they did so in an atmosphere of cooperation and understanding, and not amid intensifying threats and hysteria, especially when those threats are known to be bogus."

Direct dialogue between America and the other two legs of the "axis of evil" is imperative. Both nations leaders' taunt America with bombastic rhetoric out of frustration that America will not sit down and talk because it prefers the use of miltary threats and sanctions. How can a dispute be resolved without dialogue? "Talking is not appeasement or being a wimp. It is sensible," former President Jimmy Carter said of America's reluctance to sit down and talk with North Korea directly – something China and South Korea repeatedly encourage America to do. How can you resolve a dispute without talking and negotiating?

North Korea's October Surprise

Republicans stood to profit in the 2006 midterm elections from North Korea's nuclear test because of the "fear factor" and their successful push for sanctions in the U.N. – which were unanimously passed by the 15-member Security Council. Pyongyang's unpredictable defiance deserved harsh sanctions. It has a string of terrorist attacks, kidnappings of South Koreans and foreigners, provocations and broken international agreements behind it to prove its defiant untrustworthiness. However, sanctions alone will not resolve the crisis because they are not enough to pressure a government that is economically and diplomatically isolated. The luxury goods banned by the

U.N. resolution imposing sanctions against North Korea are not within the reach of anyone except Kim Jong-il and his inner circle that keeps him in power. U.N. Resolution 1718 condemns North Korea's nuclear test and bans all luxury goods to the country that the Dear Leader craves. Denying Kim what he craves, the theory goes, might prompt better behaviour from a dictator who reportedly spends $1 million a year on rare cognac. So no more cognac, caviar, jet-skis or iPods for bad boy Kim, or his friends.

The only other people that suffered with the North Korean masses were *We the Apathetic Maids,* because the price of oil climbed back above $60 a barrel after North Korea's nuclear test.

On September 19, 2005, North Korea signed a denuclearization agreement with America, China, Russia, Japan and South Korea to "abandon all nuclear weapons and existing nuclear programs." In return, Washington agreed that the United States and North Korea would "respect each other's sovereignty, exist peacefully together and take steps to normalize their relations."

Four days later, the U.S. Treasury Department imposed sweeping financial sanctions against North Korea designed to cut off the country's access to the international banking system, branding it a "criminal state" guilty of counterfeiting, money laundering and trafficking in weapons of mass destruction. The U.S. froze $24 million of Pyongyang's money in Macau banks and brought the regime of Kim Jong-il to its knees. To the point that North Korea was ready to settle for $12 million it earned from legitimate sources to sit down at the Six Party Talks table. Why not? It's their money? Let them in on the same rules of the game that Libya joined, keeping in mind Reagan's four negotiating principles. Reagan also bombed Libya and tried to kill its leader, Moammar Kaddafi, managing to kill only his daughter. But long term, the strategy worked.

When the Bank of China also agreed to impose the U.S. and U.N. sanctions, Kim was brought down from his knees to the floor. I saw the results in Hong Kong. The lack of money prevented repairs on North Korean ships in Hong Kong harbor, and forced Hong Kong-owned North Korean financial institutions with legitimate funds frozen in Macau, together with North Korea's illicit earnings, to challenge the U.S. freeze.

Not only is Kim counterfeiting U.S. dollars, he is counterfeiting Chinese yuan notes. With America and China cooperating in putting financial pressure on Kim where it hurts, he will be begging to not only talk but come to terms. The joint U.S.-China action against Kim's piggy banks has made large and small financial institutions across Asia turn away North Korean business. With traditionally few outlets outside Macau for its cash-based foreign exchange needs, Dear Leader and his elite group of disciples are feeling the pinch. More importantly, Kim has too much to lose if the U.S. and China actions affect his bank accounts in Singapore, Austria, Germany, Switzerland and Russia. They should. Sovereignty can no longer be used as an excuse to do nothing. The fact is, the financial crackdown by the U.S. Treasury Department was one of the most successful sanctions imposed to date.

Criminalizing money laundering and terrorist financing is a more effective tool to bring rogue regimes to the diplomatic poker table. U.S. Treasury Secretary Henry Paulson is right in calling for effective multilateral action and political will by governments still dealing with North Korea and Iran. "I was surprised to learn the extent to which Iran was exploiting global financial ties to pursue and finance its dangerous behavior and the extent to which reputable financial institutions were being drawn into these schemes," Paulsen told the Council on Foreign Relations in New York in June 2007.

While Kim is stashing his loot in foreign banks, his people are dying of starvation, forced labor or attempting to escape the country. The humanitarian disaster in North Korea unleashes periodic torrents of refugees into China in search of food.

Hunger and starvation remain a persistent problem in North Korea, long after the mid-1990s famine in which up to 2 million people are estimated to have died. More than 37 percent of North Korean children are chronically malnourished. A 2006 report commissioned by former President Vaclav Havel of the Czech Republic, Nobel Prize laureate Elie Wiesel and former Prime Minister Kjell Magne Bondevik of Norway concluded that North Korea should be indicted for crimes against humanity for its treatment of its own people. I spoke to Mike Tracy, one of the authors of the report, after he spoke about it at the Foreign Correspondents Club in Hong Kong. He concluded that the U.N. system has failed the North Korean people and that the

Security Council must act now if it is to have any credibility. North Korea is the world's largest prison with over 150,000 people incarcerated who can't leave, are ill treated, starved and abused.

North Korean refugees in China, labeled defectors by their government, have bounties placed on their heads and when captured are repatriated to labor camps or worse – executed. It is estimated there are more than 100,000 North Korean defectors hiding out in China. Many have been sold into slavery and prostitution.

The full economic embargo and naval blockade backed by the Chapter VII provisions of the U.N. Charter that carry the threat of military action that the U.S. wanted to impose after Pyonyang's nuclear test on October 9, 2006, something only Japan supported, is a short-sighted fix that merely delays the inevitable – North Korea going nuclear and ballistic.

Tougher enforcement should be focused on Japan, South Korea, and other countries, against their criminal syndicates that deal in North Korean-sourced drugs, counterfeit currency and cigarettes. Those activities are a bigger threat to world order than whatever North Korea detonated, which had the explosive force of a 10-yard cube of explosive fertilizer, a force equivalent to that caused by 500-1,000 tons of TNT. The Dear Leader's half-kiloton debut was a hundred thousand times less powerful than the world's largest-ever nuclear test – the 50-megaton "Tsar Bomba" set off by Russia in 1961.

The Comprehensive Nuclear Test Ban Treaty Organization, which has some 200 stations worldwide that can monitor nuclear tests, was unable to provide any radiological data that could help determine the type of device tested by North Korea. Whatever the device was, it clearly was a failure, thus mitigating any real nuclear threat. The eight-year "sunshine policy," adopted in 1997 by South Korea to engage Pyongyang, got obscured by severe gloomy storm clouds that have to be acknowledged until such time as North Korea wants to get a real suntan – not an artificially nuked one.

Koreans know they can't trust each other. Sibling family rivalries, business and political mistrust, are a national pastime. It is a foundation stone of Korean culture and politics for reasons I still don't fully comprehend, but which I accept after years of dealings with Korean clients and their fellow adversaries.

The North Korean fascist monarchy is no different. It is rumored that Kim's sons have fought over succession, much like the heirs in a Korean chaebol – the family-run conglomerates that dominate the economy in the South.

Back to the Future – The Proliferation Security Initiative

U.N. sanctions are a tough sell. U.S. supporters of the U.N. sanctions imposed on North Korea, with the exception of Australia and Japan, are reluctant to enforce them. The 2003 Proliferation Security Initiative, an informal U.S.-led coalition to monitor and interdict North Korean ships for missile and nuclear technology, has resulted in a number of prominent catches around the world. However, the two countries that can do the most to stop North Korea's proliferation – China and South Korea – are reluctant to participate. As North Korea's biggest trading partner, the source of 80% to 90% of its fuel and provider of significant food aid, China is the country with potentially the most influence over North Korea's Dear Leader. South Korea has decided to dust off its old war plan, code named OPLAN 5027, which is being revised to include a nuclear option.

Nuclear Proliferation

Today up to 49 nations have the capability to build a nuclear bomb. In addition to the nine nuclear powers, 40 more countries have the technical skill, and in some cases, the material, to build a bomb. When the first test ban treaty was signed in 1963, America, Russia, England, France and China were the only acknowledged nuclear powers. Today they have been joined by India, Israel and Pakistan, with North Korea and Iran chomping at the bit. North Korea's nuclear diplomacy – and blackmail – has merely increased the risk that Japan, South Korea and Taiwan will now want to go nuclear. It is understandable when they are confronted with a neighbor whose slogan and philosophy is *songeun* – or "military first."

When the Dear Leader's economy began to disintegrate in the early 1990s following the collapse of its biggest benefactor, the Soviet Union, Pyongyang maintained 2 million troops in a nation of 23 million people. Today it is still a formidable military juggernaut, now the world's fifth-largest, with 1 million soldiers. The military received preferential rations during the famines of the 1990s that reportedly killed as many as 2 million people. Missile exports became a major foreign currency earner.

Iran, Libya and Syria were provided missile technology and at least 18 countries in Africa, the Middle East and Asia bought military hardware from Pyongyang. North Korea has shown itself to be a virtual bazaar for spreading missiles, conventional weapons and nuclear technology around the globe. It has sold components that could be used in biological or chemical munitions.

Military experts say Japan could build its own nuclear device in a matter of weeks – yes, weeks, because of its huge stockpile of plutonium from the spent fuel of its nuclear power plants. The Pyongyang test has given unintended ammunition to Japan to justify its continued nationalism and abolition of its pacifist constitution. Foreign Minister Taro Aso told a parliamentary committee that Japan should begin debating the issue: "The reality is that it is only Japan that has not discussed possessing nuclear weapons, and all other countries have been discussing it." Abhorrence of nuclear weapons runs deep in Japan, where memories of the U.S. atomic bombing of Hiroshima and Nagasaki are burned into the collective consciousness. But a few weeks before Kim's test, a think-tank run by former Prime Minister Yasuhiro Nakasone proposed in a policy paper that Japan "consider the nuclear option." Tokyo seriously considered the nuclear option in 1995 to counter the threat of a nuclear-armed North Korea. It ultimately rejected the idea because it was concerned it might deprive Japan of the protection of America's nuclear umbrella and alarm its neighbors.

Conventional wisdom is that a constitutional change is two to three years away, given the requirement for any change to win a two-thirds majority in the two Japanese houses of parliament before being put to the people in a national referendum. However, as Prime Minister Shinzo Abe suggested in 2001, there are cabinet legal opinions holding that any move by Japan to obtain small nuclear weapons for defensive purposes need not be covered by the constitution. On a more positive note, North Korea's test also enabled Abe to forge stronger ties with China and South Korea.

North Korea is a country with a gross domestic product the size of Togo's, and yet it acts as if it should be treated as if it were an equal to America, China, Russia, Japan and Iran just because it is a nuclear state. China is Pyongyang's biggest trading partner. It supplies 70 percent of North Korea's food and fuel across its northern border. That is why it has the most leverage on Pyongyang to bring about a peaceful long-term solution – and will – now that North Korea embarrassed and humiliated China with the nuclear test in the middle of the four-day plenary session of the Communist Party's Central Committee. The subject made the blood of many senior Chinese officials and army generals boil.

With the death of the Dear Leader's door man, Paek Nam-sun, North Korea's foreign minister and public face of Pyongyang, Kim is faced with a barrier that only China can open. North Korea is accessible by air only from Beijing. There are three weekly flights from Beijing to Pyongyang – the only air link into North Korea – Kim's only link to the outside world.

Beijing is using its considerable power and leverage to not only try to end Pyongyang's nuclear ambitions, but bring about constructive and orderly regime change. It is in China's long-term strategic and economic interest to see a change to ensure peace and prosperity not only along the 1,400- kilometer border it shares with the Hermit Kingdom, but the Korean Peninsula and the entire Asia Pacific region.

Effective Mediator – Stalled Agreement
China has proven that it is capable of mediation in thorny international disputes. China is a power broker that did strongarm a recalcitrant North Korea to the negotiating table in February 2007, to sign off on an agreement that was hailed as another "breakthrough." John Bolton, the former U.S. ambassador to the U.N. summed up the terms of the agreement best as a "charade" and a "hollow agreement." Let's also keep in mind that North Korea has reneged on many agreements in the past.

The point not to be missed as people debate the merits of the agreement is that China can muscle regimes that ignore U.S. threats and are reluctant to accept America's overtures. What China did to North Korea is something it could do with Iran as well. Especially now that Kim has agreed to stop nuclear proliferation and is known to be helping Iran prepare for its first nuclear underground test. Iranian military advisors regularly visit North Korea to participate in missile tests. North Korean technical knowledge could expedite the Iranian nuclear program and put it on a fast track no one is prepared for. Only China can help the U.S. derail the test and Iranian nuclear program.

The agreement is even worse than the one negotiated by the Clinton administration in 1994 that the Bush administration scrapped in 2002. All North Korea agreed to do was shut down its main nuclear reactor and "eventually" dismantle its atomic weapons program. North Korean media hailed the agreement as a "temporary suspension" of its nuclear facilities. There is no mention of uranium or plutonium in the agreement, nor did the agreement address the half-dozen-p us nuclear warheads Kim is believed to possess. Warheads that could probably strike Japan aboard North Korean missiles. There are too many questions left to be addressed. An invisible road map left to the parties' sincerity and good faith. No wonder U.S. conservatives see the deal as rewarding North Korea for years of bad behavior.

Not surprising, really, considering the nonexistent verifiable evidence. The quality of U.S. intelligence on Dear Leader and his regime is disappointing, considering the billions of dollars America spends gathering intelligence. There is no doubt today that North Korea does have the bomb. The questions are how many, where were they assembled and where are they now? "To declare certain countries are part of an 'axis of evil,' and then to find out that our intelligence on Iraq was fatally flawed – and now our intelligence on another member of the axis may be flawed as well – is not a confidence builder," said Senator Richard Durbin, the second-ranking Democrat in the U.S. Senate.

Kim certainly came out the winner and proved how weak and desperate America is for some geopolitical progress on any international front to shore up its disasterous policies in Afghanistan, Cuba, Iran, Iraq, Lebanon, Palestine, Syria, Venezuela ... where does one stop?

The fact is that although North Korea has tried to formally end the Korean War and normalize relations with America since 1991, it will not give up the nuclear weapons it has worked so hard to develop without regime change. To get the necessary regime change, the six-party talks must be jettisoned and new five-party talks without North Korea started before a new U.S. administration with an eight-year window is in place. Kim is smart and recognizes that the Bush administration will sign off on any deal today to claim a victorious success, and no more. After all, why should Dear Leader trust the Bush administration any more than the Clinton administration it succeeded – and which promptly disavowed and dishonored the 1994 agreement?

The Dear Leader is stuck in the '60s Cold War mentality and is waiting for America's political meltdown, because he believes that he can then get everything he is demanding of America. China will not allow him to continue on his delusional path and will continue to reign in its recalcitrant, overdependent neighbor.

Done Deal?

The political spin of the "deal" reached by North Korea and America is both a "temporary" and "permanent" solution, depending on which party one is listening to or believing. North Korea is supposed to disable its main nuclear plant and account for all its nuclear programs. Five working groups to come up with answers to help seal the deal within 60 days? Three of the working groups are multilateral, involving all parties. The denuclearization, chaired by the Chinese, economic and energy cooperation, chaired by the South Koreans, and the northeastern Asia peace and security mechanism, chaired by the Russians.

What is really worrisome is Japan's decision to do a 180 on what it signed up for in the 1994 Agreed Framework. Under that deal, Japan and South Korea were the largest financial contributors, agreeing together to pay more than 90 percent of the estimated $5-billion construction costs for two light water nuclear reactors, which North Korea was promised for giving up its weapons. This time Japan is the only country refusing to pay anything until it gets an accounting of its abductees. Abe was one of the first Japanese politicians to raise public awareness of the issue and came to office swearing to make it his "top priority" and "never" to compromise. Not much wiggle room.

A nuclear-armed North Korea is Japan's worst nightmare. One that China knows how to masterfully inflame. The Japanese want a detailed accounting and update on the status and release of kidnapped Japanese citizens, on which Abe staked his election platform. Japan's neocons have emerged from the shadows of Japanese politics since Abe came to power. This while their counterparts in America are in a kamikaze crash-and-burn mode. America's offer to discuss delisting North Korea as a state sponsor of terror enraged Japanese nationalists and neocons. If the agreement collapses, Japan could bear most of the blame for not supporting it. If Japan continues to hold its energy assistance hostage to the abduction issue, it may also invite suspicion from neighboring countries, especially China and South Korea, that Tokyo secretly hopes to ensure Pyongyang keeps its nukes as an excuse for Japan to explore its own nuclear option. Japan's domestic politics have always been parochial. Like ostriches with their heads buried in the sand. It is just one of the many thorny issues that Japan will pay a high price for in the future. The first meeting between the parties in Hanoi collapsed.

Under terms of the February 13 agreement, North Korea agreed to close and seal its key Yongbyon facility – long suspected to be at the heart of its nuclear program – within 60 days and admit U.N. nuclear inspectors in return for 50,000 tons of heavy fuel oil. In return, the U.S. agreed to hold talks to forge bilateral diplomatic relations with Pyongyang.

The talks stalled before they really started over the $24 million frozen in Macau, that grew to $25 million during the freeze, and which America agreed to release for humanitarian and charitable purposes. The blatant appeasement by America to keep the talks on track only delayed the next train wreck. The U.S. has advised all financial institutions, including the Bank of China trying to process the funds, to cease all financial dealings and transactions with Pyongyang – public and private The first meeting after the funds were supposedly released was derailed and the North Korean delegation went home because they had not received the funds because no country or bank would touch the money out of fear of U.S. government repercussions.

The end result was that the U.S. Government through the U.S. Federal Reserve Bank of New York accepted the funds and transferred them to Russia's central bank, which had agreed to transmit the funds to North Korean accounts in Russian commercial banks. More importantly, North Korea wants to ensure it regains and retains access to the international financial system, because of the sanctions imposed by the U.S. America ignored its own sanctions on doing business with North Korea. U.S. double standards again on global display and exploited by its adversaries.

While the U.S. was holding up the transfer of the North Korean funds through a U.S. Federal Reserve Bank, it was also using the frozen funds as a bargaining chip and cover for recovering the remains of U.S. servicemen killed during the Korean War and North Korean arm shipments to Ethiopia, despite a U.N. ban on purchases of North Korean arms. Again, another example of U.S. double standards. The exemption was granted because Ethiopian troops were fighting Islamist militias inside Somalia, a campaign that aided the U.S. foreign policy of combating religious extremists in the Horn of Africa.

Funding of the groups and the other key and critical ingredient, political will on the part of the main protagonists, is sorely lacking. A recipe for disaster? No, even though Korean envoys met with each other and their other counterparts to the six-party talks in New York, it will be a while before North Korea and the U.S. establish diplomatic relations with each other and sign a peace-agreement to finally end the Korean War. The talks will falter the way North Korea's top nuclear negotiator staggered, even though propped up by two aides, from the unprecedented four-hour dinner party hosted by party boy Christopher Hill at the Waldorf Astoria Hotel. But then again, it is the U. N. with a new secretary from the South, also staying in the hotel – a sweet-talking Southerner at the right time and place as the U.S does a geopolitical U-turn with China being the conductor of the bilateral talks necessary to get a done deal really well done.

North Korea reciprocated Hill's kindness by inviting him to Pyongyang in June 2007, while the unfrozen $25 million in North Korean funds were navigating their way through cyberspace trying to find their rightful owners bank accounts. The rapport between the key men in the disarmament talks is key to their success. The historical lack of trust between America and North Korea has been a key obstacle that hopefully has been removed.

North Koreans firing off machine-gun rounds at their South Korean counterparts as the six-party talks were to resume in August 2007, is just the first round of surprises that don't just happen in October. Cross-border shooting incidents have been rare since a landmark inter-Korean summit in 2000.

The United Nations Command Military Armistice Commission is investigating the case. Good luck. U.N. officials from neutral nations have monitored the armistice that ended the Korean War.

North Korea will want the U.S. to take North Korea of the list of state sponsors of terrorism. Dropping North Korea from the list, along with freeing Pyongyang from Washington's Trading With The Enemy Act, would make it easier for sanctions to be lifted and help ease international suspicions over dealing with North Korea.

The Dear Leader is going to demand that America come clean of listing North Korea on any of its lists of unsavory characters, before he scraps the nuclear program.

The Koreas have been separated by a 243 kilometer-long and four-kilometre-wide demilitarized zone since the end of the 1950-53 war. Minefields and barbed-wire fences guard the approaches to the zone. One does have to wonder how effective they are considering the zone has more wild life species flourishing and growing on the same trails that the four U.S. military defectors took off from their U.S. bases in South Korea, for their own personal rebellious reasons, against America – not necessarily because they believed, knew or were prepared for what they defected to.

The North refuses to recognize the line drawn unilaterally by the United Nations Command at the armistice. A big issue is the disputed sea border, brought up repeatedly by North Korea, in the course of the denuclearization talks. There will be a lot more misfires between the six parties at the talks.

Fuhgetaboutit

Forget about the stalled six-party talks or the five working groups to end North Korea's nuclear program. Forget about sanctions. Forget about bipartisan recriminations during the 2008 U.S. presidential election. Forget about the blame game – especially picking on China and Russia. Forget about a nuclear East Asia.

The universal opposition and condemnation of the October 9 North Korean detonation necessitates an urgent alternative solution to conclude a peace treaty to the rehashed and recycled proposals that have been tossed around since the 1953 Korean ceasefire went into effect – one that delays, or preferably avoids, a nuclear-armed East Asia – and Armageddon.

China and Russia, which like America opposed the test, have been humiliated and desperately want a solution they can jointly embrace with America. The Dear Leader's nuclear bluff must be called.

America, China, Japan, Russia and South Korea must initiate five-party talks without pre-conditions or sanctions, which only hurt and subject the majority of North Koreans to more misery and suffering because of their self-centered sycophant authoritarian military leadership.

The five-party talks should explore how best to find an honorable face-saving exit for Kim Jong-il and Co. – a la the numerous Haitian dictators who are living in the exiled lifestyle the self-styled Dear Leader enjoys at the expense of his people and the world. This is a negotiating tactic America has perfected with several Haitian dictators over the years. A policy that China, Russia, Japan and South Korea can piggyback on and benefit from, along with the rest of the region and the world.

North Korea borders economic powers China, Russia, South Korea and Japan across the Sea of Japan. These four economic super-powers can set up cooperative cross-border economic zones on their mutual borders, the kind Kim Jong-il visited and admired in China, and is hopelessly and helplessly trying to emulate.

These economic zones would transform the central planned Stalinist communist economy into neutral economic buffer zones in the potentially explosive area and stop the accelerating destabilization effect throughout the region and beyond. It is the only feasible way to bring stability to East Asia. The progress and direction of the five-party talks will be amplified to the Dear Leader at bilateral talks between America and North Korea – the face-saving concession that Kim has been trying to extract from America since the six-party talks collapsed – and U.S. troops come home as a result.

It is in the world's long-term strategic interest to neutralize North Korea's nuclear capability, create a North-South confederation and eventually a unified Korea with prosperous cooperative economic zones with its neighbors.

Economic prosperity will prevent the refugee exodus and crisis that China and Russia are concerned about, especially if American and European corporate citizens embrace the economic zones the same way they did in China. This will allow North Korea to finally sign a peace agreement that allows it to be gradually reunited with the South and the cost of reunification, unlike the case in postwar Germany, is shared by the five parties looking out for what's best for all humanity. The proposed five-party talks will transform the opaque and isolated Hermit State and its crippled economy into a transparent, vital, sunlit renaissance model for basket cases like Zimbabwe and other failed states.

Everyone wins. Granted the perks to be given Kim, his family and military supporters will be the most difficult negotiating points. But no one is more experienced in this type of negotiation than America after its experiences in Haiti, the Philippines and elsewhere.

What is the alternative? More sanctions, tests and political rhetoric that can only lead to Armageddon? Restoring the Korean monarchy? Prince Yi Seok, a singer turned teacher, is on a nationwide drive to restore Korea's ancient monarchy, forced from power a century ago. The dynasty came to an end with Japanese colonial rule in 1910. The prince is in line to succeed as head of the Yi family, which ruled all of Korea during the 500 years of the Chosun dynasty, when the country was known to the outside world as the Hermit Kingdom. And what is it today? Fuhgezaboutit.

Dear Leader's Successor

With no succession plan in place, Kim can reluctantly be forced to accept the terms of the five-party talks. After all, what other choice does he have? He has three sons whose ability to succeed is suspect. In-laws, military cliques and other potential rumored successors only confirm the fact that the future of the only hereditary personality cult communist regime is a short-lived political aberration.

Kim officially took over the leadership in 1997 from his father, founding President Kim Il-Sung, who died in 1994 but who remains eternal president inside his mausoleum. North Korea is the communist world's first dynastic succession and hopefully its last.

Kim Jong-il was formally appointed by his father in 1974 – 20 years before he eventually took power upon his father's death. Since he hasn't appointed anyone yet, even though he is 65 years old, it is a sure sign of his uncertainty about his successor.

His oldest son, Kim Jong-nam, just returned home to vie for his dad's throne, after living a carefree, low-profile high life high in Macau, a place he calls home – much to the embarassment of the Chinese government, which is trying to broker the six-party talks. He travels on Portuguese and Dominican passports. He is known to hang out at bars and dining and drinking establishments in Macau's Outer Harbour and the Mandarin Oriental Hotel, where he usually stays when away from his large family villa in a secluded section of Coloane Island. I've had him pointed out to me on more than one occasion at late-night watering holes in Macau over the years. Seems like a nice, regular kind of guy. No bodyguards, a mixed bag of friends and acquaintances. Chinese, Portuguese, Australians and others.

Before settling in Macau, the Swiss-educated Kim Jr. had held senior posts in Pyongyang, working in domestic intelligence and leading a technology drive. A computer enthusiast, he played a key role in development of the Korean Computer Centre in Pyongyang, to ensure the country keeps up with international technological advances, with special emphasis on cyber-warfare research.

Kim Jong-chul, the No. 2 son, was given a post in the ruling Workers Party in the propaganda division, the same post Kim Jong-il held before he succeeded his father. Kim Jong-un, the youngest of the three sons, is considered the smartest and most capable. Unfortunately for him, the military is smarter.

Multilateral Preemptive Intervention

Article 2 (4) of the U.N. Charter forbids the international threat or use of force unless authorized by the Security Council under Chapter VII of the Charter. Article 51 also expressly preserves "the inherent right of individual and collective self-defense." These seemingly contradictory provisions created the debate about whether the U.S. needed the support of the U.N. to defend itself against terrorism and bring about regime change in Iraq. Israel tried to do the same with Hezbollah. The U.N. Charter simply does not work in the New World Disorder. It is slow to adapt to rapidly changing circumstances. "It is important that international lawyers seek to catch up and ensure that the world's legal framework is relevant to its security challenges," said Robert Hill, Australia's defense minister in 2002.

Every country has the duty to intervene in cases of extreme human rights violations. It is a duty that overrides and supercedes respect for national sovereignty. Failed abusive regimes are bad news for their citizens, country, region and the world as a whole. Millennium examples of what can and must be done are the Australian-led multinational intervention force that stopped the lawlessness in the Solomon Islands and East Timor, and the U.N. deployment of troops to restore law and order in Liberia. Oppressive failed states, monarchies and dictators who lack popular support and jeopardize regional or global security should be removed by the ISC.

How much longer can the world look on at the death and despair in Myanmar, North Korea, Mozambique, Sudan and its numerous neighbors? Watching the 10-minute video of the July 2006 multimillion-dollar wedding of Myanmar's Supreme Divine Leader Than Shwe's daughter Thandar Shwe – in early November of the same year during the Sino-Africa summit in Beijing, where Robert Mugabe and other African despots cruised the highways of the city – banned and cordoned off to its citizens, and caused people I know who live there to flee the city to the civility of Hong Kong.

EU troops should be sent to their former colonies in Africa to work with the Africa Union force. After all, it was the European colonizers who created the ethnic conflicts by drawing borders that forced different ethnic and religious groups together – knowing full well that conflicts would inevitably erupt.

The Arab League's example of bringing peace and an end to the civil war in Lebanon in 1989 should be replicated and copied in Africa and other regions with repeated or continuing conflicts. Where there is political will, there is always a way.

The regimes in Congo, Liberia, Sudan and Zimbabwe cannot be allowed to perpetuate mass slaughter through starvation or forced labor while the world community's impotence magnifies annually. Ethnic minorities in these countries are subjected to humanitarian catastrophes that are merely acknowledged and allowed to self-perpetuate until millions die before a regime change takes place. Regimes that embark on national plunders at the expense and lives of their people must be removed by preemptive intervention.

Military interventions that turn into long-term occupations rarely succeed. To succeed, the intervening force must be well prepared. It must have people trained in military administration, language and cultural knowledge of the countries in which the force will work to restore order. During World War II, the U.S. established civil affairs schools that provided the necessary training, hence the success in Germany and Japan – and the failures in Afghanistan, Iran and Iraq.

Preemptive interventions to bring about regime changes must be multilateral missions carried out by a well-trained and well-prepared ISC peace force. Why limit regime change to abusive dictators who have oil, develop weapons of mass destruction and support terrorists? What about the fundamental premise of universal human rights and fundamental freedoms for all people? Shouldn't regime change be encouraged against any state leader in the 21st century who abuses people's basic human rights and fundamental freedoms? Shouldn't all leaders who decimate their own people be removed by the global community? What about the monarchies in Saudi Arabia and every other abusive sheikhdom? Global missions in the 21st century cannot be limited to military defensive missions if the world is to get rid of terrorism and its breeding grounds.

Terrorists Are New-Age Pirates

The community of nations under the umbrella of the ISC could oversee the implementation of a governing infrastructure to accommodate and implement the will of the majority of indigenous peoples with the "peace and order force." Such a force would make all governments work together as a cohesive, effective coalition that could fluctuate to meet the threat of the day – especially terrorism.

This would supplant colonialism and imperialism because of the collective cooperation of nations to rid a country of a faction or group that rules by brute force or terror against the will of the people. What happened to the Taliban and al-Qaeda in Afghanistan is a 21st-century model for the New World Order.

The threat of piracy, armed robbery and terrorism on the high seas – especially in the Malacca Straits – is a real 21st-century possibility. Today, 30 percent of liquified petroleum gas, 40 percent of commodities and 50 percent of the world's oil production are shipped through this vital waterway between the Indian and Pacific oceans. The 805-kilometer-long Strait of Malacca is practically the maritime lifeline of the entire world, especially

America, China and Japan. Coastal states flanking the straits have taken more effective measures to guard against piracy and terrorism. The armed forces of Indonesia, Malaysia, Singapore and nearby Thailand have agreed to allow their patrol ships to cross into each others waters to pursue pirates, terrorists and other maritime criminals. The 10 ministers of defense met for the first time to discuss territorial and religious conflicts that have simmered for years and have become self-destructive. They met in May 2006 in Malaysia's capital of Kuala Lumpur under the umbrella of the Association of Southeast Asian Nations, 39 years after the group's founding – to make the region a safer place.

This is especially important after an extremist group linked to al-Qaeda called for attacks against U.S. oil suppliers in early 2007. The aim was to cut all U.S. imports of oil "or reduce them by all means," it said. "The targets among oil interests should include oil wells, export pipelines, loading platforms and tankers and all that could reduce U.S. access to oil," it said as it continued and informed that "The instructions from Osama bin Laden concerning the targeting of oil interests are clear, so ... the mujahadeen ... should gather information and choose the target carefully." The straits must be protected after such a pronouncement and call to arms.

More importantly, the agreement to allow the pursuit of terrorists or pirates provides reassurance to China that the U.S. military will not be directly involved in securing the key Malacca Straits, which carry about three-quarters of Chinese oil imports. Consequently, for the first time, Beijing has offered to provide aid to regional countries that want to improve their maritime safety and security. It wants countries close to the Southeast Asian waterway to provide protection, thus keeping America at bay. In 2007, the Chinese Navy for the first time took part in a multilateral military exercise under the framework of the Western Pacifiuc Naval Symposium.

The efforts to secure the Malacca Straits are bearing fruit. The number of pirate attacks in Asia plunged to 17 in the first quarter of 2007, from 68 in the same quarter in 2006. The pirates have moved to Somali waters.

The pirate attack on the MV Seabourn Spirit in November 2005 off the coast of Somalia was the 31st serious attack by pirates since March of that year. The International Maritime Organization has warned ships to stay away from the area because of pirate attacks, which surged to 35 in 2005, up from just two in 2004.

On March 15, 2006, the U.N. Security Council encouraged naval forces operating off Somalia to take action against suspected piracy. Somalia has had no effective government since 1991, when warlords ousted a dictatorship and then turned on each other.

Pirates today are indistinguishable from terrorists. A terrorist attack in the economically strategic Malacca Straits has the potential to cause large-scale economic hardship, not just regionally but globally. The waterway is used by about 60,000 ships each year. A terrorist attack in the straits may have a low probability of occurring but the impact of such an attack could be devastating. Pirates regularly hijack tankers in order to steal the cargo or kidnap the crew. If terrorists were able to take over a tanker carrying highly hazardous chemical cargo, the implications could be disastrous.

U.S. intelligence reports issued in September 2004 said that activists from Jemaah Islamiyah had plans to seize a vessel with the assistance of local pirates.

The 21st-century war on terrorism is very similar to the 19th-century war against piracy that resulted in colonialism. Again, it was America that initiated the first campaign against pirates in the 19th century.

In the 18th century, most civilized states accepted the Roman law definition of pirates as "enemies of the human race." By the end of the century, the rulers of Algiers, Tunis and Tripoli had become notorious for harboring pirates, and engaging in piracy and the slave trade in whites, chiefly captured seamen. European countries found it easier to ransom these unfortunates rather than go to war. Admiral Horatio Nelson, commanding the British Mediterranean fleet, was forbidden to carry out reprisals. "My blood boils," he wrote, "that I cannot chastise these pirates."

By contrast, America was determined to do so. Pirates were the main reason Congress established a navy in 1794. In 1805, U.S. Marines marched across the desert from Egypt, forcing the Pasha of Tripoli to sue for peace and surrender all American captives – an exploit recalled by lyrics from the U.S.

Marine Corps Hymn: "From the halls of Montezuma to the shores of Tripoli."

Paul Johnson, British-born historian and author, wrote a historical piece for *The Wall Street Journal* that summarized how piracy brought about colonialism. He wrote that America followed up on its bold initiatives in Tripoli in 1815 when Commodores Stephen Decatur and William Bainbridge led successful operations against all three of the Barbary states, as they were called. This shamed the British into taking action themselves, and the following year Admiral Lord Exmouth subjected Algiers to what was then the fiercest naval bombardment in history. However, these victories were ephemeral. The beys repudiated the treaties they were obliged to sign as soon as American and British ships disappeared over the horizon. Something America and Britain forgot when they forced Saddam Hussein to surrender after the first Gulf War.

It was the French who took the logical step, in 1830, of not only storming Algiers but of conquering the whole country. France eventually annexed Algeria and settled 1 million colonists there. It solved the Tunis piracy problem by turning Tunisia into a protectorate, a model it later followed in Morocco. Spain also digested bits of the Barbary Coast, followed by Italy, which overthrew the Pasha of Tripoli and created Libya. Tangiers, another nuisance, was ruled by a four-power European commission.

In the 19th century, as today, civilized countries tried to put down piracy by organizing coalitions of local rulers who had been victimized. Arabia and the Persian Gulf were a patchwork of small states, some of which were controlled by criminal tribes that practiced caravan robbing on land and piracy at sea. Pirate sheiks were protected by the Wahhabis, forebearers of the present rulers of Saudi Arabia. Sound familiar?

In 1815, Britain had to take action because ships of its East India Company were being attacked in international waters. But it did so only in conjunction with two powerful allies, the ruler of Muscat and Oman, still Britain's firm friend, and Mohamed Ali of Egypt.

British naval operations produced a general treaty against piracy signed by all the rulers, great and small, of the Arabian Coast and Persian Gulf. But Britain had learned from experience that "covenants without swords" were useless, and that the sheikhs would stick to their treaty obligations only if "enforcement bases" were set up. Hence Britain found itself becoming a major power in the Middle East, with a colony and base in Aden, other bases up and down the gulf, and a network of treaties and protectorates with local rulers, whose heirs were educated at the British School of Princes in India.

The situation in Southeast and East Asia was similar. Amid the countless islands of these vast territories were entire communities of *orang laut,* sea nomads who lived by piracy. Local rulers were too weak to extirpate them. Only the Royal Navy was strong enough. But that meant creating modern bases – hence the founding of Singapore. That in turn led to colonies, not only Singapore, but Malaya, Sarawak and British North Borneo. The Dutch had been doing the same. It was a matter of complaint by the British that the Americans, while trading hugely in the area, rarely sent warships on anti-piracy missions. President Andrew Jackson's dispatch of the frigate Potomac to bombard the pirate base of Kuala Batu in 1832 changed forever America's role in the region.

The war against piracy in Asia was directly linked to colonization – British, French, Dutch, Portuguese and Spanish – a fact finally recognized by the U.S. when it annexed the Philippines after the Spanish-American War. It established a large naval base at Subic Bay, where one of the main duties was pirate hunting. The lesson learned was that suppression of well-organized criminal communities, networks and states was impossible without government coalitions and cooperation to ensure political control. Then, as now, civilized powers preferred to act in concert. It is therefore no surprise that China, like America, is today expanding its naval capability to protect its oil tankers and cargo ships sailing through the Malacca Straits where terrorist attacks and piracy are rife.

No More NAM

The Non-Aligned Movement, founded by the Bandung Conference of 1955, when 29 Asian and African leaders became concerned about their fate in a Cold War world dominated by America and the Soviet Union, has become obsolete, like the U.N. Countries can no longer be nonaligned.

The movement was officially launched in Belgrade, Yugoslavia, in 1961. The leaders of the movement were Jawaharlal Nehru of India, Gamal Abdel Nasser of Egypt, Sukarno of Indonesia, Josip Broz Tito of Yugoslavia and

Archibishop Makarios of Cyprus. At the dawn of the 21st century, it had 116 members, two-thirds of the U.N. membership.

The name of NAM, like the U.N., is a misnomer as the organization – whose members included Cuba and North Korea – was more aligned with the Soviet Union than America. With the demise of the Soviet Union and the U.N., isn't it time for NAM to be added to the funeral procession?

Global Economic Reality

Geo-economics are inseparable from geopolitics, as the global financial crisis of 1997-1998 highlighted and brought home. The Bush administration recognizes this and has restructured the U.S. National Security Council to include economists. Globalization and borderless financial frontiers allow trillions of dollars to circumnavigate the globe through fiber-optic cables in search of better returns, including funds that support terrorism.

The International Monetary Fund, World Bank and other global financial institutions should also be relocated. They should be based in the financial capital of the world rather than the Western political capital if they want to restore their global credibility. Now really, how do the IMF and World Bank think they are perceived in the developing world when they have their own private golf course at Bretton Woods, Maryland, where they decide the economic fate of millions by a putt, and cut and raise interest rates while slicing golf balls? Mortal American taxpayers cannot even join the club or play unless they are invited by someone who works at the IMF or World Bank. People were rioting and hungry in Indonesia because they could not come to terms with the IMF, and the bankers were playing golf. Maybe President George W. Bush had it right, despite the unintentional spoonerism, when he said, "If the terriers and bariffs are torn down, this economy will grow."

Of the billions of dollars the World Bank and IMF lend, the corrupt officials always get their fair share as they distribute the funds and award contracts. The 184-nation World Bank was established in 1946 to lend to developing nations at discounted interest rates in support of projects that deal with health, education, nutrition, environmental protection and HIV/AIDS. "In its starkest terms, corruption has cost the lives of uncounted individuals contending with poverty and disease," U.S. Sen. Richard Lugar told a congressional hearing on May 13, 2004. "Not only are the impoverished cheated out of development benefits, they are left to repay the resulting debt to the banks." Corruption is estimated to have drained anywhere from 5 percent to 30 percent of the roughly $525 billion that the bank has loaned. Some argue that the abuse may have topped $100 billion.

Is it any wonder the IMF corruption reforms proposed by former World Bank President Paul Wolfowitz were resisted by a group of emerging countries? Corruption comes in many forms. The most overt corruption is campaign contributions that oblige the recipient politicians to repay major donors with favors. Corruption of the political process is much more damaging than the backhand kickback to a bureacrat. Single source non-competitive biddings, or rigged competitive bidding is standard practice in many IMF and World Bank beneficiary countries. Hundreds of millions of dollars in loans and contracts have been suspended because of corruption in countries including India, Chad, Kenya, Congo, Ethiopia and Bangladesh. Transparency is essential, especially in a poor country with corruption when funds are being allocated to fight poverty, to ensure it reaches the projects and people that need it and for whom it is meant. After all, corruption is the biggest threat to the efforts to alleviate poverty.

Instead of blaming bribe givers and their bribes for the endemic corruption in some countries, as Wolfowitz did in Singapore, the IMF should just adopt the rules and procedures in common practice in the private sector. Why can't the bank fund like any commercial bank does on a commercial project with advances and installment payments being made after inspections by quantity surveyors – quality control engineers – who sign off that the work on a particular project meets the bid specifications and payment requirements? Why should loans be made for nonexistent equipment and materials?

Because, *We the Apathetic People* allow and encourage it to happen. Is it any wonder that many governments questioned whether they should be again subjugated to Wolfowitz's Pentagonian approach? Bullying to impose his leader's opinions and constituents' beliefs of their mandated force-fed ideas and ideology was a sure recipe for him to sink himself and the bank the way he did Iraq. He's managed to anger as many senior bank managers as he did generals. Without their support, his policies won't have any institutions to enforce them and, worse for him personally, they forced him to practice what he preached and made him resign because of his malfeasance and conflict of interest in awarding his girlfriend Shaha Riza a pricey pay rise in his pay-and-promotion scandal. The World Bank is unravelling and falling apart. Like the U.N., it is not a question of "if," but "when." It has outlived its honest intellectual purpose because it is corrupt to the core. A good excuse for member states not to make their fair-share contribution to the bank.

A closer look at the devastating testimony in the Wolfowitz case and the dysfunctional manner in which the matter was handled by the bank, bears volumes of testimony of the bank's irrelevance today. Wolfowitz begged the board to stay and promised to change his style. This, after his earlier tactics failed. Sounding more like a cast member of The Sopranos than an international leader, in testimony by one key witness, Wolfowitz declared: "If they fuck with me or Shaha, I have enough on them to fuck them too." Now that he has been found guilty of having a conflict of interest, it will be interesting to see how he does get even.

The geopolitical blunders the U.S. committed as it was isolated during its futile attempt to keep Wolfowitz at the bank, and the farcical face-saving exit plans that followed were a global reminder that Wolfowitz and the Bush administration neocons don't practice what they preach. They did what they thought was best for themselves and their disciples and America be damned.

Many people have forgotten that the IMF was originally conceived as a cooperative – it bailed out Britain and almost had to do the same for France. People forget these episodes because the IMF's resources have not kept up with the explosion of global capital markets, so that today it lacks the capacity to bail out an Italy or a Japan. It can only afford to bail out the likes of South Korea, Mexico and Russia. If the IMF's founding noble principles are no longer sustainable in a global environment in which the rich countries alone control policy decisions, then the center of gravity has to shift down the economic prosperity scale if the IMF is to function as a cooperative. That means all who want to participate in the policy decisions have to pony up the cash, not just the rich countries

It is little wonder that it sometimes appears to those outside the U.S. that Washington uses the World Bank and IMF as piggy banks that are an extension of U.S. foreign policy. William Blum, the author of *Rogue State*, calls the IMF the International Financial Mafia. "Like the mafia in Italy, they can put a threat upon any small country and have them do what they want; it's extortion," he said.

The IMF interferes too much in the domestic politics of the countries it seeks to assist. What's more, IMF policies don't generate prosperity or alleviate poverty. That's what a bipartisan congressional commission concluded.

Joseph E. Stiglitz was on the periphery of Bill Clinton's bright financial circle that polished and funded globalization. In his book *Globalization and Its Discontents,* he pointed out how America's brightest financial minds from Wall Street and academia, a group dominated by Wall Streeter Robert Rubin, Lawrence Summers and Stanley Fischer from Harvard and M.I.T., respectfully, committed hundreds of billions of U.S. taxpayer dollars to defend capitalism and spread globalization. He paints a picture of how rampant arrogance, simplistic nostrums and disdain for foreign political realities doomed globalization. He states that this financial brain trust turned globalization into a neoimperialistic force that left hundreds of millions of people worse off in 2000 than they were in 1990.

Sensing a historic opportunity to secure capitalism's victory after the fall of the Berlin Wall, the Clinton team demanded wrenching reforms from Russia, Eastern Europe, Latin America, Asia and Africa. The Treasury Department headed by Rubin, and the IMF, which follows the preferences of Washington, its largest shareholder, used huge loans to compel governments to sell off companies they controlled. Even some of the least-developed nations were instructed to allow competition in their stock, bond and banking businesses immediately. Aid was withheld from governments that did what America does: Spend too much money on protected key industries.

This formula – predictably, in Stiglitz's view – led to financial bubbles and collapses in Mexico in 1994 and in Asia, Russia and Latin America from 1997 to 1999. The Clinton experts compounded the error by linking billions of dollars in emergency aid to even deeper concessions in managing trade, monetary policy, banking and privatization. Nearly everywhere this was tried, Stiglitz says, the changes deepened rather than alleviated recessions. The prescriptions had all the science of a medieval bleeding. "Not for 60 years have respectable economists believed that an economy going into recession should have a balanced budget," Stiglitz wrote.

Vitriolic attacks on Stiglitz and his book by the IMF's economic counselor and director of research makes one wonder. The IMF's chief spokesman, Thomas Dawson, admitted that the IMF erred in its judgments and was caught off guard. "The experience revealed that the IMF had not kept up with the rapid developments in international capital markets, a deficiency it has tried to rectify through a number of steps taken over the last couple of years," Dawson said. To busy playing golf.

To put things in perspective, China has never accepted aid from the IMF, and its economic performance has been miraculous compared with that of Russia, one of the biggest IMF clients. Russia produced two-thirds more than China did in 1990; China produced two-thirds more than Russia did in 2000. China and many other nations want the IMF and World Bank to meet the changing roles for international financial institutions. Is it any wonder China is calling for reform – and getting it?

While the Wolfowitz scandal unfolded in Washington, China hosted the Africa Development Bank board meeting in Shanghai. This is a vivid metaphor: While the World Bank is mired in controversy, China raises its profile in the developing world. Chinese officials stressed the crucial role of public investments as the basis for private-sector-led growth. In a hungry and poor rural economy, as China was in the 1970s and as most of Africa is today, a key starting point is to raise farm productivity. The World Bank has wrongly seen public investment as an enemy of private development.

A neglected and overlooked reponsibility of the World Bank is education. The bank spends $2 billion a year in grants and loans to fast track students into high schools and universities worldwide. The fast track was set up in 2002 to encourage and help leaders of poor countries to devise credible national plans to provide universal primary education and to persuade leaders of rich countries to provide the additional funds needed to implement them. Globally, the fast track has contributed to the sharp drop in the numbers of children not attending primary school from 105 million in 2000 to 77 million in 2007, against a tide of rising populations. But this is still short of and way off the U.N. target of all children completing four years' primary schooling by 2015.

At the bank's last meeting in Singapore at the Suntec City convention center in September 2006, the first to take place in Asia since the Hong Kong meetings nearly a decade ago, the voting power of China, South Korea, Mexico and Turkey increased, while the influence of poorer countries decreased. The basic rights the World Bank and IMF uphold – freedom-of-speech, public assembly, political activity, human rights – were violated by the host country, which barred many accredited representatives of nongovernmental organizations that wanted to be in Singapore to let the bankers know how they felt. Activists have a right to air the grievances of those they represent. As a result, the credibility of the IMF was suspect from the get-go. Nongovernmental organizations held their own meeting on Batam, a nearby Indonesian island 45 minutes by boat from Singapore. Discussing the IMF meeting and the banned protestors a few days later in Singapore, where I had gone with my partner, Mark Sharp, to address the Adidas regional convention, I was pleasantly surprised at the candor and admission by many current and former Singaporean government officials that they disagreed with the government's policies that severely restrict the most basic human rights. "The control of dissent and the blind devotion to the retention of power is unsustainable," said one official, who asked to remain anonymous.

Singapore's list of "troublemakers" included the South Korean farmers groups that stole the headlines at the World Trade Organization conference in Hong Kong in December 2005. The general perception from the sensationalized media reports from Hong Kong was of South Korean farmers running amok, engaging in pitched battles with police. But, in fact, the protests were disciplined and focused – even their protest dive into Victoria Harbor and their daily clashes with police. The police were praised for their response. Many protest groups won the public's heart, and generally each side learned from – and respected – the other. While not perfect, Hong Kong was an example of civil society working as it should.

Asia demands more say at the IMF, especially after the "Asian" financial crisis. They got it, too, because the borrowing in the region from the IMF has declined from a peak of $17.8 billion in 1997 to just $300 million in 2005. Despite being a global powerhouse, China – with 2.94 per cent of IMF voting rights which got upped to 3.72 percent – still has less say than Belgium. Yet it was the biggest change to the IMF since it was established in 1940.

The IMF must better reflect the relative weight of the world's economies. If the IMF can't balance the vote fairly, how is it expected to do what it is really tasked to – balance the world's checkbook? After all, it is the cop tasked to impose austerity measures on countries when they consume more than they produce and run trade deficits. Back then when the rules were adopted, America was the dominant surplus country, and it could insist that deficit countries make any necessary adjustments. How come the same rules don't apply to America? Reducing America's deficits and Asia's surpluses – before there's a financial crisis that hits everyone from Beijing to Boston. America's nearly trillion-dollar deficit and its opposite, the huge trade surpluses in Asia, have to be addressed. This is a conversation America and China must have as the two main protagonists in this global bankruptcy court.

The old financial architecture of the IMF collapsed during America's last big unfunded war – Vietnam. When America abandoned the gold standard in 1971, the rigid backbone of the system disappeared. It was replaced by flexible exchange rates, which allowed gradual adjustments of imbalances.

Ideally, the IMF should be abolished, or at the very least restructured. A radical shake-up of the IMF was even urged in early 2006 by Mervyn King, Bank of England governor, in a speech he gave in India. He warned that the IMF could "slip into obscurity" without radical reforms. He suggested removing the day-to-day duties of the IMF's executives to truly independent managers. He also proposed replacing the existing board of directors, which has a permanent delegation in Washington, with a nonresident board that would meet six or eight times a year in a supervisory capacity. This, he said, would stop the "expensive micro-management" of existing arrangements. The Argentinean financial crisis and default was a 21st-century wake-up call. A new "international financial architecture" is clearly needed and has been discussed since the crises in Asia, Russia and Brazil. How many more crises have to befall taxpayers paying for IMF mistakes before a new structure is in place? The board game, *Deuda Eterna* or Eternal Debt, is about who can defeat the IMF.

Turkey is another example. Since 1999, at the behest of America, Turkey has received funds from the IMF and World Bank – "more cheap money than any other country on the planet," Wall Street columnist Claudia Rosett wrote. It has received $30 billion in below-market funding, making it the top

IMF client. That is in addition to the $10 billion it received from the World Bank. The IMF's failures that started in Mexico in 1994, then spread to Asia in 1997, moved on to the Russian devaluation and default in 1998, ripped through Brazil and Argentina at the dawn of the 21st century and then confronted Turkey as the U.S. was preparing to invade Iraq.

Millions of Turks are unemployed, the Turkish economy is shrinking and the Turkish lira crashed after the government decided to float its currency against the dollar at the urging of the IMF, wiping out the savings and income of the country's poor and middle class. Is it any wonder the traditional career politicians got booted out in the 2002 election and U.S. troops were denied access to Turkish bases? "Next time a valued partner is deemed too strategic to fail, maybe we should note that turning it into an IMF-World Bank welfare queen is a strategy too dumb to repeat," Rosett wrote. Now the Turks don't qualify for the European Union.

At the dawn of 2007, Hong Kong, unlike most countries that have deficits, had fiscal reserves of close to HK$100 billion, and was told by the IMF that it didn't need reserves that large. Needless to say, Hong Kong will ignore the IMF recommendation.

Even the IMF's own Independent Evaluation Office concluded that the fund failed to give proper warning that a crisis was looming and that its remedies were too painfully drastic for the financial crises that afflicted Indonesia, South Korea and Brazil.

Jeffrey Sacks, a Harvard University economist, said, "It's the wrong framework. It hasn't worked in years. Not in Thailand, Indonesia, Korea, Russia or Brazil." I concur. Their strategies and rationale are indefensible and make no sense. Their new proposal for a global bankruptcy court to allow the IMF to control and restructure their original bad idea is unworkable. One can understand why many people in developing countries feel the IMF is deliberately trying to destroy their economy as part of America's conspiracy to take over industries and companies in developing countries. By moving the World Bank and related international funding institutions to New York, any political association with America's capitalist capital and its political machinations will be mitigated.

World Bank economist William Easterly wrote in his book *The Elusive Quest for Growth* that the bank should encourage countries to adopt traditional free-market policies and stop lending to corrupt and incompetent governments. In other words, why not just look at America's experience when it gained independence from Britain and apply that experience globally in the same prudent manner adopted by the Founding Fathers?

It was Alexander Hamilton who came up with a simple solution on how an emerging country can pay its debts. He calculated the debt George Washington and his revolutionaries had incurred and put the numbers in his Report on the Public Credit on January 14, 1790. Foreigners were owed $12 million. The state's debts could be estimated at $25 million. The federal debt amounted to $42,414,085.56. And there lay Hamilton's opportunity. "It is a well-known fact that, in countries where the national debt is properly funded, and an object of established confidence, it answers most of the purposes of money," Hamilton explained to Congress. The debt would make money. The government would pay regular interest on the national debt, dollar for dollar, in hard coin that would come from import duties and the selling of land. Anything left over would go to pay the principal. Investors who knew the interest would be regularly paid in gold and silver would confidently buy debt certificates from one another, and their value, at the time bumping along at a shilling to the pound, would promptly rise. As soon as debt became a desirable commodity, like land and tobacco, it could form the basis of a circulating currency, Jason Goodwin wrote in his well-researched and enjoyable book, *Greenback*.

Today, America's greenback IOUs are still in high demand. Especially by drug dealers, terrorists and anyone else who doesn't want their money traced by governments through the wired banking system. U.S. greenbacks do have a secret life of their own. U.S. Customs researchers recently analyzed dollar bills from suburban Chicago, Houston and Miami. They found that 78 percent were contaminated with cocaine. They were generally older bills, and the bills from Houston and Miami in particular yielded a heavier dose of the drug than bills from Chicago. George Washington is still fighting to defeat corrupt and abusive career politicians and their financiers.

America traditionally gets to choose the president of the World Bank as part of an informal arrangement in which the Europeans select the managing director of the International Monetary Fund. But such nominations must be approved by the boards that represent the two institutions, each of which has 184 member nations. The IMF has become a warehouse for retired French politicians and bureaucrats. The appointment of Strauss-Kahn, a former French finance minister in July 2007, as the new head of the IMF is the latest example. Frenchmen have held the job of IMF managing director for 30 of the 61 years of the institution's existence. France is merely one of 185 shareholders of the IMF, with a miniscule, overvalued 4.86 percent of its voting power.

The World Bank, with a staff of nearly 10,000, lends about $20 billion annually to developing countries for projects aimed at raising living standards.

The bank, set up in the wake of World War II to eradicate poverty, began to lend money to the developing world in the late 1950s. The problems set in when it began to offer ever-larger loans – and began to demand ever-more-extensive conditions. By the 1980s, the bank was – along with its twin, the International Monetary Fund – demanding that countries undergo "structural adjustment" in return for loans. So if poor countries wanted help – or even wanted simply to be able to maintain the huge debts they had already racked up to the bank – they faced a lachrymose choice. They had to sell off their public sector, slash spending on schools and hospitals to the bone, and prioritize debt repayments to the bank – or be declared an international pariah and receive no loans.

The bank has repeatedly shown that it is more interested in debt repayment, neo-liberal ideology and opportunities for transnational corporations than in ending poverty. The World Bank has been force-feeding its market fundamentalism to the developing world for three decades, and ignoring the wreckage that so often follows in its wake.

More than 34 percent of the bank's energy lending in 2004-2005 was for oil and coal extraction – the fuels that are causing global warming – and just 6 percent for renewable energy sources. In 2000, after prolonged pressure, the World Bank was finally forced to undertake a review of its energy policies. It did its best to rig it, putting Emil Salim in charge. Salim was the former energy minister of the corporation-loving Indonesian dictator Suharto, and he was even serving on the board of a coal company at the time he was appointed. To everyone's astonishment, Salim concluded that supporting oil and gas projects doesn't help poverty, devastates the environment and should be stopped by 2008. The bank's response? It ignored its own report. Nadia Martinez – an expert on the bank with the Institute for Policy Studies – believes this reveals the bank's true nature. "The World Bank has repeatedly proved itself to be more concerned with the needs of the oil companies than with the impoverished people it officially serves," she said. "It will not distinguish its goals and standards from the likes of Halliburton, ExxonMobil, Shell and other profit-driven institutions."

The former head of the bank is the petrol-scented Paul Wolfowitz. Because he was a key architect of the Iraq invasion, his nomination has understandably been denounced in many quarters as a move by America to continue using the bank more aggressively as an instrument of U.S. foreign policy. His delusional policies in Iraq failed. It is therefore no surprise that in the great U.S. capitalist tradition, he got promoted to screw up the world. Unfortunately for Wolfowitz, he treated the bank and developing nations the way he did the Pentagon and Iraq, and discovered the weapons of mass destruction he invented and eluded America in Iraq, were in Washington. Any wonder he imploded?

He started down that road even before he started at the bank by getting his girlfriend working at the bank a promotion, and a tax-free raise in contrast to the good governance rules and practices he preaches. "Maybe Wolfowitz wouldn't have so many holes in his socks if he stopped shooting himself in the foot," an anonymous bank staffer wrote in an e-mail, referring to a well-publicised incident in January 2007 when Wolfowitz removed his shoes and was photographed entering a Turkish mosque with his toes poking through. Shaha Ali Riza, his Libyan-born British divorcee girlfriend, enjoyed a meteoric rise from communications officer in one of the bank's offices in the Middle East to a nearly $200,000 tax-free salary at the U.S. State Department, where she earned more even than Concoleezza Rice, the secretary of state. The terms and conditions of her package had not been "commented on, reviewed, or approved" by the ethics committee or the bank board. It is hypocritically scandalous "double standards" behaviour that America is supposed to be opposed to. It was two e-mails sent by an anonymous whistleblower that brought these ethical lapses to light. Is this the kind of guy, and his cronies, we want overseeing an institution that spends $25 billion annually to fight poverty in poor countries?

Wolfowitz shifted his role in the battle of Iraq from the Pentagon to the bank. He has pumped up both its physical and financial presence in Iraq. It should come as no surprise that the bank's higher profile in Iraq is a departure from longstanding World Bank practice of steering clear of countries engulfed in heavy violence. His Iraq policy is prompting criticism that he is turning the bank into a vehicle for Bush-style nation-building while slighting other deserving countries. Democracy a la Iraq style is not very appealing to the neighbors it was supposed to convert and reform. "If democracy brings such chaos in the region, and especially the destruction of society, as it did in Iraq and in Lebabnon, it's absolutely normal, and I think it's absolutely a wise position for the people to be afraid to imagine how it would be in Syria," said Omar Amiralay, a Syrian filmmaker.

America did come to Iraq with the idea of making it a democratic model for the region. The opposite happened. It has become an example of why democracy delivered from a bomb bay, American-style, does not work.

Neo-Colonialism

On August 5, 2004, the White House created in the State Department the Office of the Coordinator for Reconstruction and Stabilization – to balance the U.S. policy of deconstruction. Its mandate is to draw up elaborate "post conflict" plans for up to 25 countries that are not, as yet, in conflict. There will be "pre-completed" contracts to rebuild countries that are not yet broken. Doing this paperwork in advance could "cut off three to six months in your response time," said Carlos Pascual, the head of the new agency, in a speech at the Center for Strategic and International Studies. Sounds just like the Halliburton contracts in Iraq.

His office is about changing "the very social fabric of a nation," he said. The office's mandate is not to rebuild any old states, but to create "democratic and market-oriented" ones. The fast-acting reconstructors will help sell off "state-owned enterprises that created a nonviable economy." Sometimes rebuilding, Pascual explained, means "tearing apart the old." I experienced it first hand in Palau and its over financed power plant.

"We used to have vulgar colonialism," said Shalmali Guttal, a Bangalore-based researcher with Focus on the Global South. "Now we have sophisticated colonialism, and they call it 'reconstruction.'"

I experienced it again while celebrating New Year's Eve 2003 in Phnom Penh, Cambodia. There I was on a five-day bar and party hopping year end celebration that blended the best of all cultures and religions with hundreds of NGO directors, officers, U.N. aid agency employees, consulting engineers and bankers. All foreigners, as very few locals are employed. Expert "democracy builders" lecture governments on the importance of transparency and "good governance," yet most contractors and NGOs refuse to open their books to those same governments, let alone give them control over how their aid money is spent. I also saw the same happen in Mongolia when it established diplomatic relations with the U.S. in the early '90s. There I partied with ladies who were second-generation employees of the U.N. Nepotism at its finest.

The story repeats itself in every country being rebuilt. It could also have come from Afghanistan, where President Hamid Karzai blasted "corrupt, wasteful and unaccountable foreign contractors" for "squandering the precious resources that Afghanistan received in aid." Or from Sri Lanka, where 600,000 people who lost their homes in the tsunami languished in temporary camps for several months. "The funds received for the victims are directed to the benefit of the privileged few, not to the real victims," wrote Herman Kumara, head of the National Fisheries Solidarity Movement in Negombo, Sri Lanka. "Our voices are not heard and not allowed to be voiced."

But if the reconstruction industry is stunningly inept at rebuilding, that may be because rebuilding is not its primary purpose. According to Guttal, "It's not reconstruction at all – it's about reshaping everything." The stories of corruption and incompetence serve to mask this deeper scandal: the rise of a predatory form of disaster capitalism that uses the desperation and fear created by catastrophe to engage in radical social and economic engineering. On this front, the reconstruction industry works so quickly and efficiently that the privatizations and land grabs are usually locked in before the local population knows what hit them. Kumara warned that Sri Lanka was now facing "a second tsunami of corporate globalization and militarization," potentially even more devastating than the first. "We see this as a plan of action amidst the tsunami crisis to hand over the sea and the coast to foreign corporations and tourism, with military assistance from the U.S. Marines." The same holds true on the coasts of Thailand and Indonesia, where the tsunami wiped those areas clean of the communities that had stood in the way of hotels, resorts, casinos and shrimp farms.

Paul Wolfowitz, as deputy U.S. defense secretary, designed and oversaw a strikingly similar project in Iraq: The fires were still burning in Baghdad when U.S. occupation officials rewrote the investment laws and announced that the country's state-owned companies would be privatized. He did in Iraq what the World Bank is already doing in virtually every war-torn and disaster-struck country in the world.

Neo-colonial disaster capitalism has been practiced by the World Bank and International Monetary Fund for at least three decades. It crested with Hurricane Mitch in October 1998. Mitch swallowed whole villages in Central America, killing more than 9,000 people. Already impoverished countries were desperate for reconstruction aid – and it came, but with strings attached. In the two months after Mitch struck, with the country still knee-deep in rubble, corpses and mud, the Honduran congress initiated what the *Financial Times* called "speed sell-offs after the storm." It passed laws allowing the privatization of airports, seaports and highways and fast-tracked plans to privatize the state telephone company, the national electric company and parts of the water sector. Naomi Klein, in her article *The Rise of Disaster Capitalism,* goes into great detail as to how America, in the words of Secretary of State Condolezza Rice, views disasters as "a wonderful opportunity."

John Perkins, in his book *Confessions of an Economic Hit Man*, details how he personally experienced America execute its policy of neo-colonialism and the extremes to which it will go, including the assassination of leaders who refuse to comply with U.S. demands.

Wolfowitz's successor, Robert Zoellick, will hopefully re-engineer the World Bank the way he did the U.S.-China relationship, German reunification in 1990 as lead negotiator at the "Two Plus Four" discussions that brought about the reunification, and the regional peace plan he helped broker in Central America that brought an end to decades of fighting in Nicaragua, El

Salvador and Guatemala. He has a passion for animals and is a former advisory board member of the World Wildlife Fund, a well rounded, experienced caring diplomat. A shrew.

Relocation

New York is the financial capital of the world. Derivatives in world markets pose a "mega-catastrophic risk," according to Warren Buffett, and are "financial weapons of mass destruction." Global hedge funds, which contribute to global financial instability, are based in the "Hedge Fund Hilton," at 237 Park Avenue, a few blocks from the United Nations – and the Bear Stearns global headquarters, representing the first big-time global banking victim of the hedge fund bubble – subprime loans.

Hong Kong, where the ISC should be located, is Asia's asset management center. Foreign leaders who embezzle state funds and drug dealers seem to prefer depositing or laundering their money in New York banks, as the Bank of New York and Citibank investigations have shown.

Why shouldn't they? After all, that is where America's leading corporate fraudsters and their bankers are. JP Morgan, Merrill Lynch, Citibank, Tyco, Arthur Anderson all got exposed for the financial and corporate shenanigans they practiced and got away with because of *We the Apathetic People*. The career bureaucrats at the Securities and Exchange Commission, like their counterparts at the FBI and CIA, were asleep at the bureaucratic wheel. The cozy relationship they all had with each other was shattered and brought down to earth by the collapse of Enron and WorldCom.

New York Mayor Michael Bloomberg said his city risks losing its status as the world's primary financial center to Hong Kong. More money was raised through IPOs in Hong Kong in 2006 than in either London or New York. Another good reason to relocate the ISC to Hong Kong.

All the international financial institutions should be relocated to New York, next door to the financial weapons of mass destruction and global financial fraudsters. The World Bank, IMF and all other global financial institutions should be relocated to the current U.N. headquarters. The Asian meltdown, the crises dogging the Mexican peso, the Russian ruble, Brazil's real, Turkey's lira, Argentina's peso – which are pegged to the U.S. dollar devaluation –

and other financial crises that surely will follow, demonstrate interconnection. Business and international organizations must have a more open dialogue with each other. Where better than in the financial capital of the world? Especially if the financial architects of the New World Order live together under U.S. financial building codes.

The new International Accounting Standards Board that was formed to co-ordinate accounting standards should also be based in the current U.N. building.

A United Global Financial System to ensure future financial stability should be formed to oversee the World Bank, IMF and other global lenders and be located in and take over the current U.N. headquarters.

Globalization of the financial markets, the financial networks of terrorists, the financial crises of Russia, Indonesia, Malaysia, South Korea, Mexico, Brazil, Turkey and Argentina and the financial isolation of North Korea, Myanmar and Zimbabwe dictate that global financial security take on the importance and stature that the U.N. had after World War II.

Hong Kong Monetary Authority Chief Joseph Yam Chi-kwong, in a letter to Alan Greenspan, who was critical of the Hong Kong government's intervention in the equity markets, challenged the central bank to take decisive action to halt market instability. "The free market does not mean that it can be freely manipulated. It needs to be a fair market as well," the letter read.

"Is it possible there is something seriously wrong with the international financial system that needs to be urgently addressed?" Yam asked.

Capitalism and its free markets must be revisited in the wake of the collapse of communism, the reunification of Germany, the eventual reunification of Korea, the emergence of China and India as a major power and today's borderless cyberworld.

Reevaluation Time
These issues will be more efficiently addressed by business, central bankers and the Group of 8 at the proposed United Global Financial System than the current structure and inter-workings of the global financial community. Fin-

ancier George Soros is also calling for a reevaluation of the current international financial system. "The prevailing system of international lending is fundamentally flawed.... The private sector is ill-suited to allocate international credit. It provides either too little or too much," he said.

Proposals for overhauling the IMF have received relatively little attention from the career politicians in Washington, and broad support has yet to emerge. That shouldn't stop governments and think tanks from drawing up reform plans. In a detailed proposal, the American Enterprise Institute, a Washington-based think tank, envisages the IMF as a members-only club that acts like a global central bank. Countries that join would have to enforce Herculean standards on their banks, including keeping 20 percent of their deposits in cash and issuing bonds worth 2 percent of their capital to specified holders, such as other banks. Member countries facing liquidity problems could borrow from the IMF after posting 125 percent bond collateral.

The proposal is designed to protect depositors and strengthen market discipline. But it risks dividing the world into open and closed economies: Those that can't meet the strict membership requirements must fend for themselves. Charles Calomiris, a professor at Columbia Business School who conceived the plan, has no apologies. "It's against the one-world syndrome where everyone should be protected no matter," he said. "If a country can't have the basic institutions of capitalism, it probably shouldn't try capitalism." I tend to agree that the basic institutions must be in place. However, if they are not, those countries must have a way to borrow money if they are prepared to allow those basic institutions to be installed under the guidance and supervision of the bank. In a way, it is neo-fiscal-colonialism limited to installing and building the basic capital markets, the way the British did in Hong Kong.

We could explore the possibility of having a private bank associate membership category that permits private banks to contribute a nominal amount of their capital base as their fee. After all, it is their misleading mantras of "synergy" and "mergers" that have created many of the financial crises. Meanwhile, they earn fees of $25 billion to $50 billion a year promoting these synergistic mergers that require global financial bailouts and then walk away unscarred because their loans are guaranteed. Why not also make member countries contribute an annual nominal membership fee consisting of a percentage of the annual gross taxes they collect? This would ensure a basic global fund is in place for emergency financial relief, which could be supplemented by international or private member banks of the fund.

No more Central Asian American Enterprise Funds. No more appointments by Washington of politicians, lawyers and academics to make investment decisions with taxpayer money that disappears because of ridiculous overheads, poor business judgment, corruption and fraud.

Investors from the private and public sector should also share the pain. They can't just make fees on their "round trips" without sharing in the pain of the mess they sometimes create because of their haste to collect fees and failure to do proper due diligence. They should not be allowed to walk away after being made whole at taxpayers' expense. The IMF Ukraine model is a good example of how things should be in the New World Order. The majority of foreign holders of Ukrainian T-bills agreed to voluntarily convert them into longer-term bonds, even though they lost up to 50 percent of the bond's face value. Russia, Indonesia, Thailand, South Korea and Malaysia should have implemented similar measures. This model should be more widely adopted in the 21st century.

When the IMF was founded in 1944, the U.S. and Britain could easily bend other war-weakened governments to their will. The world has grown more complicated since then, and there is an array of wealthy powers more willing to block proposals they don't like than to take responsibility and lead the way. Even George Marshall might have a hard time figuring this one out.

Debt and Poverty Relief
Watching the "odd couple," U.S. Treasury Secretary Paul O'Neill and U2 frontman Bono, tour Africa together at the dawn of the 21st century to promote debt forgiveness and poverty relief on the continent from which most people were enslaved was an encouraging sign. Debt forgiveness for poor countries while feeding them is no great burden for the rich nations and should be a priority in the New World Order if we are to have peace and prosperity in the 21st century. While millions starve in Africa, rich nations store in silos $100 billion worth of surplus food from subsidized farmers. A "stockpile of misery" was how the *Washington Post* described the behavior

of Europe and Japan, which refuse to dispose of their surpluses through aid programs while they complain of dumping when America makes food donations. "Just one percent of this stockpile, which mostly goes to waste, will fill the yawning hunger gap this year in southern Africa, Afghanistan and everywhere else," the *Post* correctly concluded.

To put matters in perspective, consider the cost of the 2001 "Anti-Poverty" G-8 Genoa Summit. At 100 million pounds sterling, the cost of the summit was equivalent to the combined annual debt-service payments of Malawi, Mali, Mozambique and Burkina Faso. While the G-8 leaders deliberated on the wording of their debt and poverty relief communique, they stayed on a ship, the European Vision, where they had the chance to taste 170 different kinds of cheese, 54 kinds of bread and 7,000 bottles of wine. This while more than 150 million children around the globe suffer from malnutrition.

Some 2.6 billion people in the world, mainly in Africa and Asia, lack access to basic sanitation, increasing the risk of diarrhea and diseases fatal to children, said UNICEF's Progress for Children report released in 2006.

The war on poverty is more important than any one of the many military confrontations taking place in the world today. "Poverty is a threat to peace," said Muhammad Yunus, the Bangladeshi economist who won the Nobel Peace Prize for his work to lift millions out of poverty by granting them tiny loans, especially women in rural areas.

A U.N. review in 2006 found that member states adopt hundreds of mandates each year – confirming "additional responsibilities" with neither corresponding funds nor guidance on how resources should be used. It's political theatre: big headlines, small results. The mandate gap reflects the way the world has done business with the U.N. for decades: big promises, small pay-outs, and much scapegoating," wrote Anne-Marie Slaughter, dean of the Woodrow Wilson School of Public and International Affairs at Princeton University.

Three billion people live on two dollars or less a day. "Something is wrong when the richest 20 percent of the global population receive more than 80 percent of the global income," said James D. Wolfensohn, former president of the World Bank. "Our challenge is to make globalization an instrument of opportunity and inclusion, not fear."

Tanzania, half of whose population is illiterate, spends one-third of its budget on debt payment, and it spends four times as much clearing its debt as it does on primary education.

Niger, where life expectancy is only 47 years, spends more on debt payment than it does on health and education combined.

Consider the 700 million people living in the 40 poorest and most indebted countries. They live on an average of about four dollars a day; in Africa 340 million survive on less than one dollar a day. Yet these countries are expected to repay about $130 billion in loans from the IMF, World Bank and Western countries. Jeffrey Sachs, director of the Harvard Institute for International Development, argues that much more – complete debt forgiveness – is desperately needed for perhaps 25 of those 40 countries.

He starts with the IMF. The 40 countries owe it about $8 billion. Sachs notes that the fund owns gold worth, at market prices, more than $30 billion, but it carries the gold on its books at only about $5 billion. By recognizing the true value of its gold reserves and selling modest amounts over time, Sachs suggests, the fund could write off loans to poor countries while leaving its balance sheet looking better than under current accounting rules. He points out that the World Bank could also easily afford to write off unsubsidized loans.

Beyond the numbers hovers the issue of justice. "Any attempt to collect debt payments from these countries," Representative Tom Campbell, Republican of California, said, "starts from the false premise that they owe the money. But why should a fisherman off the coast of Ghana set aside two extra fish to pay for lavish spending by former tyrants?" How about current ones?

Even the late Pope John Paul II encouraged debt forgiveness. Maybe the Catholic Church should open up its coffers to acquire the debt. At a discount, of course. There is even an American legislative vehicle for it all: The Heavily Indebted Poor Countries initiative, or HIPC. On the day that Uganda qualified for debt forgiveness under HIPC, the president of that struggling African nation signed a $32-million lease-purchase agreement for a brand-new Gulf Stream jet. While more than half of Zimbabwe's population was facing starvation because of Robert Mugabe's farm expropriation policies, his wife Grace would borrow an airliner from the country's national fleet to fly to Europe to shop for a pair of shoes. Why do global taxpayers have to continue funding corrupt, self-indulgent political leaders at the expense of their downtrodden, hungry people?

Ian Vasquez, director of the Project on Global Economic Liberty at the Cato Institute, says 97.5% of all long-term HIPC debt is public or publicly guaranteed. That means *We the Taxpayers* cover it when it is forgiven. It is also an implicit acknowledgement of the failure of the IMF and government planning and development. In other words, a continued waste and mismanagement on the part of career politicians and their bureaucrats, lobbyists and lawyers that *We the Apathetic People* continue to pay for.

In many cases, Rep. Campbell said, "these loans were not loans at all. They were grants for political purposes, like winning the Cold War."

Funds that poor countries would have used to pay off their debts have to be earmarked and monitored for agriculture, education and health in the New World Order. At the 2002 G-8 Summit in Canada, the New Partnership for African Development topped the agenda. *We the Maids* have to sweep in regulations and legislation, modern-day Marshall Plans, not just for Africa, but for Afghanistan, Latin America and the Middle East, that encourage such partnerships but prohibit corrupt career politicians from buying baubles and planes at the expense of their people's health, education and agricultural progress.

A great vehicle already in place to facilitate and expedite such plans is Youth Business International, a joint venture between Britain's The Prince's Trust and the International Business Leaders Forum that helps young entrepreneurs in developing countries get established. Research shows one in five 18-30 year-olds have entrepreneurial potential, though few are able to realize it. Access to bank finance is virtually impossible for many, even with a viable business plan.

The decision by the G-20 nations in November 2004, just before the January

2005 Iraqi elections, to forgive up to 80 percent of the debt and interest owed by Iraq to the Paris Club creditor nations was an indication that the creditor nations were coming to terms with the reality of the misery caused by trying to force a nation to repay the debts of a fallen dictator.

The G-8 decision in 2005 to forgive $40 billion of debts of 23 heavily in-debted countries with the World Bank, the International Monetary Fund and the African Development Bank, at a cost of $1.2 billion a year for three years to rich countries, was a logical extension of the G-20 decision to for-give the Iraq debt and is to be applauded. A good way to begin addressing the alleviation of poverty in the 21st century. The next step is to give China the seat it deserves at the G-8 table. In the Middle East, including Israel and Iran, Beijing has unrivaled leverage that would be helpful in brokering dip-lomatic solutions for regional peace.

Debt relief is an integral part of global reality today. Barriers that impede exports from developing countries to industrialized markets continue to se-verely disadvantage poor countries. Debt relief without increased market access is futile. There is a widely held, managed misperception that masses of money is poured into aid. In fact, industrialized countries spend roughly one-quarter of one percent of their gross domestic product for assistance to the world's poorest countries. A lot more can be done.

The donor community should tighten its requirements concerning corrosive issues such as bribery and graft. Corruption has increased exponentially in urban areas of developing countries, where foreign investment tends to concentrate. Corruption is epidemic. More than two-thirds of the world's countries are rife with corruption, according to the Berlin-based anticorrup-tion group Transparency International. The World Bank and the IMF could appoint nonpartisan international monitors to supervise the disbursal of for-eign aid and investment to ensure equity.

International monetary flow monitoring bureaus also must be created to su-pervise the ever-increasing flow of borderless capital. There are so many money-transfer businesses that operate without a license and avoid the cur-rency-reporting laws, it is a joke. They make Swiss cheese look like a gold brick. *Hawala* is one such informal money-remittance system that operates on the fringes of the global financial system. The word *hawala* is Arabic and can mean "trust" or "exchange." The system is marked by trust and informality. Operators are as sketchy with their records as any bookie. The system is hard to detect because it dates back hundreds of years to South Asia, where traders and merchants on the Indian subcontinent devised the system to avoid being robbed as they traveled.

In South Asia the system is known as *aundi;* South America has the black market peso exchange or *casa de cambio* ("stash house"); a Thai variant is *phoe kuan* ("message house"); "Chit banking" was used by the British in China, while the Chinese themselves, initially rice and tea traders, created their own "flying money," a.k.a. *fei chie'ien*. It is faster and cheaper than traditional banks or companies like Western Union, and reaches desolate parts of the world that most conventional institutions cannot. These systems are the lifeline for the millions of immigrants and guest workers living in rich countries who send money back home. It is estimated that 35 percent of the $150 billion in global transfers to developing countries flows through such channels. Such agencies are also used by terrorists to transfer funds and by criminals to launder funds from traffic in immigrants, illegal drugs, sex slaves, weapons and even body parts. It is estimated there are at least 20,000 informal remittance businesses working out of 24-hour convenience stores, restaurants and small shops in America. To complicate matters, these outfits work from within tight-knit ethnic communities, rebuff outsiders and speak languages unfamiliar to Western ears, like Urdu, Arabic and Hindi.

Agencies similar to customs bureaus monitoring and supervising the flow of goods need to be established, not just to monitor the flow of capital, but to ensure that its intended use is properly and honestly implemented.

Reading Kofi Annan's op-ed piece in *The New York Times* on why billions of taxpayer dollars were justifiably wasted and stolen in the past, as the leaders of a United Nations Conference on aid and economic development opened in Monterrey, Mexico, was pathetic. Particularly as Annan was begging for $50 billion a year more for the Millennium Development Goals - more money for his bureaucrats to steal and waste.

"Until recently," Annan wrote, "most developed countries have reacted with skepticism to this request, feeling that too much aid has been wasted in previous decades by corrupt or inefficient governments. During the Cold

War, the Soviet Union and the wealthier nations of the West used aid primarily to reward loyalty. Corruption and waste – indeed, results of any kind – were secondary to what donor countries wanted most, namely political allegiance."

I guess that somehow justifies corruption and inefficiency. I wonder how Annan rationalized the stupidity and inefficiency of his translation crew that showed up in Monterey, California, instead of Monterrey, Mexico. More importantly, wasn't it just more taxpayer money being wasted?

Capitalize on Members' Experience
Many developing nations have gained formidable experience in such fields as family planning. Why not encourage such nations – India, Mexico, Tunisia, among others – to send more of their local technical experts to other developing nations? Such exchanges would be less expensive than dispatching pricey American and Japanese developmentalists and could foster culturally sensitive programs at the grass roots.

"Today's development mandarins can learn from the ways of yesterday's colonialists," Pranay Gupte, an economist, points out. "How was it that only a handful of Britons governed the billions of the Indian subcontinent for nearly two centuries? Colonial administration turned on two key concepts: co-opting local organizations and formulating policies perceived to be of direct benefit to local citizens. Those policies resulted in establishing educational institutions and creating a civil service for nationwide administration; such perceived benevolence often diverted attention from the fact that the colonialists were simultaneously plundering the treasures of their colonial territories. Colonialism was an early form of globalization; today's globalization needs to promote a fresh concept: empowerment of grass-roots institutions in the cause of social development. In the final analysis, all development is local."

The lofty rhetoric and volumes of global goals advocated at the U.N.'s 2005 World Summit and the 2000 Millennium Summit are hypocritical empty promises when it comes to helping the world's poor. Expensive self-serving bureaucrats with their corrupt consultants preparing reports and proposals that benefit only a closed clique that knows how to milk the system.

Bunker Roy, the founder of the Barefoot College and chairman of the Global Rain Water Harvesting Collective, said of the Millennium Development Goals: "Only intellectual activists who have no idea how to reach the very poor need the virtual reality in which its authors live, full of action plans, road maps and fact sheets." I agree. So long as governments in developing nations are powerless to break the hold of corrupt private contractors and larcenous village-level politicians, the poor will never be free from fear, whatever the U.N. report envisions.

Roy points out that few teachers sleep in the villages where they work. They are not part of the community. So why not train literate but unemployed rural youth as "barefoot" teachers by the thousands, all over the world, to run the night schools, as Roy has proposed? It is clear that the development report's authors are not aware of the tremendous work that community-based groups are doing in primary education. Their work is not recognized or reflected in the official statistics of either UNESCO or of governments because it is still not valued or recognized and never will be. That is because they are a threat to village officials who represent government and who do not believe in changing the status quo. Importing expensive, unworkable ideas, equipment and consultants from the developed world simply destroys the capacity of those communities to help themselves while perpetuating corrupt, self-serving career politicians and bureaucrats.

The Economist wrote that "Inspiring as it may be to talk of redesigning the global financial architecture, the need is for a competent carpenter, not a great artist. Much needs to be done to make capital markets safer. The detailed, workmanlike reports on transparency, strengthening financial systems and managing crisis that the G-22 (an informal group of rich and emerging-market countries, convened by the Americans) ... point in the right direction."

Giorgio Armani, Harry Belafonte, Gerry Halliwell, Angelina Jolie and all the other creative talent wasted in the name of "Goodwill Ambassadors," please take note as we enter the 21st century. Your experience and talent is being wasted at the U.N. It could be put to much better use working as part of a team of hands-on carpenters who can actually get something built and accomplished with the money now being wasted.

Did Nothing Wrong?

The role of bankers in the sham financing of Enron was brought to our attention during the Senate investigation into the collapse of the company. Citigroup and JP Morgan disguised debts as energy trades and claimed they did nothing wrong because they did so on advice of independent counsel and accountants. The mighty banks have been exposed for their "creative financing" and are fighting the hit and fall they have to take now that their "creativity" has been exposed as illegal. The fact is they actively helped Enron conceal hundreds of millions of dollars in financing before the company collapsed under the mountain of debt.

Citigroup's problems are compounded by its security firm Salomon Smith Barney and the inherent conflict of interest it had in financing and giving bullish views on the stocks of bankrupt WorldCom, Global Crossing, Winstar Communications and Qwest. To make matters worse, the bankers tried to spread some of Citigroup's financial risks through bond sales and loan syndications to other banks and the public. Is it any wonder investors are suing and the bankers want to shift the public's attention to the role of lawyers and accountants? Banks seem to have forgotten that they are the ones who pushed the legal and accounting standards to the limit to accommodate their corrupt corporate and government clients.

World Trade Series

The World Trade Organization, the World Series and other "world championships," like the Super Bowl, are uniquely controlled and dominated by America. Today, one day's trade equals a whole year's commerce in 1949, and the U.S. is the trading champ. That is why the WTO is controlled by America. Indeed, it has been suggested that the WTO is a major instrument for maintaining American "neo-imperialism." Not surprisingly, "A United Nations-appointed study team has labeled the WTO a 'nightmare' for developing countries," said the *Financial Times*. Its activities "reflect an agenda that serves only to promote dominant corporatist interests that already monopolize the area of international trade." America must take the lead to truly liberalize trade and enable developing nations to become real trading partners in the New World Order. It is up to *We the Maids* to sweep in such enabling legislation. The alternative is to have the rest of the world continue to despise the WTO, and its trade champion America, throughout the 21st century.

The WTO officially came into existence on January 1, 1995, after the 1986-1994 Uruguay Round of GATT negotiations ended with the Marrakesh Agreement to establish the WTO. The first ministerial conference was held in Singapore in December 1996. The developed countries pushed for investment, competition policy, transparency in government procurement and trade facilitation to be at the top of the agenda, irking developing countries, which saw that agenda as primarily serving the interests of advanced economies. Developing nations have been unhappy ever since. This anger erupted into violence in Seattle during the third ministerial conference in December 1999, which ended in failure.

The fourth ministerial conference, held in Doha, Qatar, in November 2001, proposed the opening of agricultural and manufacturing markets and making trade rules fairer for developing countries. China, after 15 years of negotiations, was admitted to the WTO on November 11, 2001.

The fifth ministerial talks, held in Cancun, Mexico in September 2003, were again marred by violence and collapse after members failed to reach agreement because rich countries were unwilling to give up farm subsidies. Progress was made on that issue in August 2004 in Geneva when developed countries agreed to lower farming subsidies while developing economies agreed to lower tariffs on manufactured goods and open their services sectors. However, in November 2005, expectations for the sixth ministerial conference held in Hong Kong the following month dropped after the European Union, led by France, refused to agree to cuts in farm subsidies without reciprocal market access concessions for industrial goods and services. Agricultural exporters, including the U.S., criticized the EU's "bottom line" farm tariff offer as inadequate and counter-productive.

I was in Hong Kong during the six-day conference while politicians from 149 countries, along with almost 6,000 bureaucratic freeloaders, argued with each other and the more than 1,000 representatives from non-governmental organizations. At the same time, more than 10,000 protestors – watched by nearly 3,000 journalists – took to the streets to protest globalization. It confirmed my concerns about the fragility of the global trading mechanisms in place to deal with 21st-century realities. The widening gap between rich and poor and the definition of "fair trade" between the G-8 industrial nations and the G-20, led by Brazil, India, China and South Africa, will surely rupture if not bridged within the fragile remains of the WTO framework .

The meeting's most noteworthy accomplishments were that it did not collapse in complete chaos and mayhem, as it had in Seattle in 1999 and again in Cancun in 2003, and that rich nations agreed to eliminate their farm export subsidies by 2013, while the world's poorest countries will get duty-free and quota-free access to markets in the developed world for 97 percent of their goods by 2008. That last provision needs further work, as it allows rich nations to exclude 3 percent of tariff lines.

"You could drive a horse and truck through it," Andrew Hewett, chief executive of Oxfam Australia, said of that loophole. "Rich nations might allow DVDs and CDs in, but they could exclude rice, sugar and bananas, the things developing countries have to export."

However, on the issues at the heart of the Doha round of trade talks – cutting farm tariffs, freeing trade in in industrial goods and opening service markets – almost no progress was made.

Under the terms of the agreement, the world's 50 least-developed countries will get duty and quota-free access for their farm products into the rich nations.

The EU, which already gives duty-free and quota-free access to the poorest countries and produces little cotton, saw an opportunity to embarrass America and divert attention from Europe's own refusal to make deeper cuts in farm tariffs. America, in turn, offered just enough on cotton and on duty-free access to avoid being painted an enemy of the poor.

The WTO has provided more than a decade of noisy theater. It has achieved little and, now that they're letting in everybody, it will cease to count for anything.

Saudi Arabia is the newest member of WTO, with Russia and Iran aspiring to join. Their governments have radically different political values than the developed world. With their inclusion, it is difficult to see how the WTO will be able to reach consensus on anything. The agenda of the WTO is dictated by unrepresentative agro-business lobbyists at a cost of $280 billion a year to *We the Apathetic* taxpayers and consumers.

Russian President Vladimir Putin has assailed the WTO as "archaic, undemocratic and inflexible," and proposed the creation of "regional Eurasian free trade organizations" that would draw on the experience and failures of the WTO learned at the failed Doha round.

The lack of political will and the failure of corporate business interests in America and Europe to push their governments to reach a comprehensive agreement acceptable to all parties in Hong Kong on farm subsidies and tariffs – and the failure of the Doha round – does not bode well for the world's poor, hungry or humanity as a whole in the 21st century.

Money Cops

The U.N. headquarters building should also be shared with the International Criminal Police Organization (Interpol) and the charity Transparency International to reflect the growing role of monitoring money-laundering and related enforcement laws in the 21st century.

Interpol helped identify and blacklist individuals who tried to attend the sixth WTO Ministerial Conference in Hong Kong.

Money-laundering, corporate bribes to foreign governments, the funding of civil wars and terrorism have all given corruption and its role in money-laundering a much higher profile. Peter Eigen, chairman of Transparency International, said that the 9/11 attacks made clear how high the stakes are in areas such as money-laundering. "Without corruption, the terror attacks would not have been possible," he said. "To fight corruption means to fight terrorism."

Companies such as FIMACO, owned and controlled by bankers at Russia's Central Bank, who launder and illegally move around billions of We the People's money, should be thoroughly investigated and brought to justice. Would Americans allow the Federal Reserve to secretly run money through offshore Cayman Island accounts? That's what other government bankers do with U.S. and other countries' taxpayers' money loaned by international banks for local development. For example, how about the factory that U.S. taxpayers funded to the tune of $26 million in Siberia to dispose of rocket fuel from ballistic missiles? Once the factory was built, there was no fuel to dispose of. The Russians forgot to tell the U.S. that they were using the fuel to launch commercial satellites. Where were the career bureaucrats looking out for U.S. taxpayers?

Let's not forget that Russia has been given more than $6.4 billion from U.S. taxpayers over a 10-year period to dismantle its stockpiles of poorly guarded weapons of mass destruction, which include 40,000 tons of chemical weapons and 600 tons of weapons-grade nuclear material. Despite that, Russia and America still have the world's largest arsenals of weapons of mass destruction.

Crony capitalism must be investigated much closer in the New World Order. Not just in America, but globally, especially at international organizations. The same holds true for bribe money, especially drug protection money paid to politicians and their relatives. The seizure of hundreds of millions of dollars in Swiss bank accounts held by Raul Salinas de Gortari, brother of the former president of Mexico; the arrest of Francisco Lopes, the former president of Brazil's central bank for income tax evasion; the detention of Pavlo Lazarenko, the former Ukrainian prime minister, for embezzling state funds; and the arrest, trial and conviction of Vladimiro Montesinos, the former spy chief under ousted Peruvian President Alberto Fujimori and once the most-feared man in Peru, are steps in the right direction. The warrant issued for the arrest of Fujimori – who lived in exile in Japan – by Interpol for the murder of 15 people by his military death squads in 1991 confirms the new moral order of the 21st century. They are examples of how illegal gains and criminal activities should be traced and confiscated. The arrest and trial of Indonesia's Suharto and the Philippines' President Joseph Estrada is a New World Order cornerstone. The fact that they went home to retire and die in luxury is another matter.

Interpol today is the most sophisticated international law enforcement agency. It has a vast, state-of-the-art global computer network that links seemingly unrelated suspects from airline flight records, telephone numbers, criminal records and code names. More than 150 of Interpol's 177 member nations are now linked by computer in the world's most extensive law enforcement communications network. Indeed, with international crime increasing sharply in line with the global economy, many experts regard Interpol as vital in bringing not only drug smugglers but also such criminals as fraud artists, money-launderers, pedophiles and other sexual criminals and computer crooks to justice.

Interpol should work not only with its member countries but with regional crime-busting organizations. The Association of Southeast Asian Nations has agreed to set up a regional center in the Philippines to battle transnational crimes. All regional associations might consider direct cooperation with Interpol.

Mobsters cross borders as if they were chalk lines in a hopscotch game, trafficking in sex, slavery, drugs, money-laundering and terrorism. U.S. agencies as diverse as the Citizenship and Immigration Services, the Drug Enforcement Agency, the Treasury Department and the various counter-intelligence groups in the government agencies are cooperating with each other and Interpol to crack down on international gangs. "Globalization has created a new kind of national security threat that is not fully recognized by the administration or Congress," said Richard Clarke, the former counterterrorism coordinator on the National Security Council. "American citizens are being threatened on a daily basis by criminal organizations here and overseas." The National Security Council report describes how Russian, Chinese, Nigerian, Middle Eastern and Italian gangs have enthusiastically embarrassed globalization and their fellow criminals in America. According to the report, more than 50,000 women and children are sold into slavery in the United States each year, compared to 700,000 globally.

The proposed ISC and the relocation of Interpol and the world international financial institutions have a more realistic chance of dealing with slavery, racism and the numerous other New World Disorder geopolitical messes – including global warming – than the U.N.

Climate Terror
The last decade of the first millennium was the warmest in 1,000 years. Greenhouse gases are warming up our oceans, changing their chemistry and becoming a greater threat to the world than terrorism. The oceans are humanity's canary in the coal mine. Greenhouse gases such as carbon dioxide emitted from power plants and automobiles are trapping heat in the atmosphere. The result is a warmer planet, with melting glaciers and arctic ice sheets sending an unprecedented flow of fresh water into fragile saltwater habitats.

Global warming is expected to create at least 1 billion refugees by 2050 as water shortages and crop failures force people to leave their homes, sparking local wars over access to resources.

Scientists predict that average temperatures will rise by between 1.8-3 degrees Celsius this century because of greenhouse gas emissions, mainly from burning fossil fuels, causing floods in some areas, droughts in others, and putting millions of lives at risk. The Intergovernmental Panel on Climate Change, an international group of scientists, says that by 2080 as many as 3.2 billion people – one-third of the planet's population – will be short of water, up to 600 million will be short of food and as many as 7 million will face coastal flooding.

Security experts fear that the tidal wave of forced migration will not only fuel existing conflicts but create new ones in some of the poorest and most deprived areas of the world. "A world of many more Darfurs is the increasingly likely nightmare scenario," claims the report.

Since 1965, a volume of water equivalent to the Great Lakes has melted in polar regions and flowed into the world's oceans, making them less salty. The Intergovernmental Panel on Climate Change has projected that sea levels will rise up about 0.91 meters by 2100.

The U.N. estimates that by 2025, two-thirds of the world's people will be living with water stress, with North Africa, the Middle East and West Asia hit the worst. Regions that get more rainfall may get it in the form of fierce rainstorms that cause flash floods rather than a useful drizzle that soaks into the ground.

"The culprit responsible for warming has been identified. As far as I am concerned, the debate's over. What we need to be debating is what we're going to do about it," said Tim Barnett, an oceanographer at the Scripps Oceanographic Institution in San Diego. The Pentagon agrees.

A study commissioned and suppressed in 2005 by the Pentagon warns that major European cities will sink beneath rising seas and Britain will be plunged into a "Siberian" climate by 2020. Nuclear conflict, mega-droughts, famine and widespread rioting will erupt across the world. This threat to global stability vastly eclipses that of terrorism, say the few experts privy to the report. "Disruption and conflict will be endemic features of life," concludes the Pentagon analysis. "Once again, warfare would define human life."

The major threat of mayhem comes from large populations simply upping the stakes and moving into other people's territories. I don't know which way global warming will run, but won't it be interesting if the zones that suffer most are Europe and North America and the ones that remain or indeed become more habitable are in Africa and the southerly Asian lands. Colonialist imperialists on the move again – firing as they go.

Global warming should be elevated beyond a scientific debate to a U.S. national security concern, say the study's authors, Peter Schwartz, a CIA consultant and former head of planning at Royal Dutch/Shell group, and Doug Randall of the California-based Global Business Network. According to Randall and Schwartz, the planet is already carrying a higher population than it can sustain. By 2020, "catastrophic" shortages of water and energy will become harder to overcome, plunging the planet into war. They warn that 8,200 years ago, changing climate conditions brought widespread crop failure, famine, disease and mass migration of populations that could soon be repeated.

Randall told *The Observer*, which first reported the leaked Pentagon report in 2005, that the potential ramifications of rapid climate change could create global chaos. "It is a national security threat that is unique because there is no enemy to point your guns at and we have no control over the threat."

"You've got a president who says global warming is a hoax, and across the Potomac River you've got a Pentagon preparing for climate wars. It's pretty scary when Bush starts to ignore his own government on this issue," said Rob Gueterbock of Greenpeace.

Jeremy Symons, a former whistleblower at the Environmental Protection Agency, said that suppression of the report was a further example of the White House trying to bury the threat of climate change. Symons, who left the EPA in protest of political interference, said the Bush administration's close links to high-powered energy and oil companies was vital in understanding why climate change has been received skeptically in the Oval Office.

"This administration is ignoring the evidence in order to placate a handful of large energy and oil companies," he said.

The Pentagon study is confirmed by numerous other reports, including one entitled "Meeting the Climate Challenge," prepared by a task force of senior politicians, business leaders and academics from around the world to coincide with former British Prime Minister Tony Blair's promise to advance climate change policy as the chair of both the G-8 group of rich nations and the European Union.

With this ecological time bomb ticking away, how much longer can *We the Apathetic People* afford to ignore the global warming threat? The threat must be immediately addressed by a climate control agency headquartered alongside the global financial and law enforcement agencies to ensure that alternative energy sources are properly and timely funded – and environmental polluters punished. The U.N. is the wrong place to address the global climate challenge.

International Fund-Raising

Whatever space is left over at the U.N. after the global financial, law enforcement and climate control agencies move in can be used for income generation, including charitable foundations. Significant donors, such as Ted Turner, who give $1 billion or more should have the ability to easily interface with global financial institutions and their protectors.

A Museum of Peace Dreams with a display of all the modern-day conflicts and wars, with special emphasis on those in which the U.N. has played a role, should also be established. The U.N. blue berets have had a few successes, as well as their numerous failures. The U.N. does have a colorful history that should be memorialized in a museum that reminds our children of our dream for peace and the human folly that prevents it. The proposed Museum of Freedom and Remembrance as the centerpiece of the World Trade Center memorial, which envisions including Ellis Island, the Statue of Liberty and the New York Stock Exchange as key elements of a Freedom Park, should explore how the Museum of Peace Dreams can also be incorporated.

When the U.N. celebrated its 50th anniversary on October 24, 1995, it attracted the largest gathering of world leaders in history – more than 170 heads of state came together for the three-day celebration. In 2005, the three-day 60th anniversary summit in New York was again the "biggest gathering of world leaders in history." The U.N issued 4,915 delegate passes and allowed 2,167 journalists to cover the failed proceedings. More than 150 presidents, prime ministers, monarchs and dictators celebrated the U.N.'s 60th anniversary. While having a jolly old time and getting great press back home, they all knew that the U.N. was bankrupt. Much of what was said to commemorate the U.N. is more realistically achievable with a new ISC. Otherwise, many of the great ideals pronounced will wind up alongside the other grand dreams and hopes, expounded upon by every world leader that has been to the U.N. over the last 60 years. I think it would be illuminating to look back on that tableau of leaders at the 60th anniversary event and reflect on it as a wake.

Interlocalism

To view, through the calm sedate Medium of Reason, the influence which the establishments now proposed may have upon the Happiness or Misery of Millions yet unborn, is an Object of such Magnitude, as absorbs, and in a Manner suspends, the Operations of human Understanding.

–George Mason of Virginia, in a letter written to his son while attending the Constitutional Convention in Philadelphia in 1787

Localism

Secession and devolution are hot buttons that arouse people's emotions regardless of their religion, civilization, country of origin or county of residence. America, Canada, China, Great Britain, Spain, the former USSR, Africa, Iraq and the entire Middle East are the most controversial and emotional. Whenever the topic comes up at the Foreign Correspondents Club Main Bar in Hong Kong, the verbal combatants become more vocal as each round is consumed. Especially between the Canadians, who don't like to be called North Americans, and the Americans who do not want to be associated with Canada or Mexico.

In Hong Kong's Victoria Park, or any local "candidate forum" in America, the concerns are universal. What has the government done for me lately? Who does the government represent? What is the government doing for me? Central, federal, provincial, state and local.

Over the decades I have observed that while people get close to the local issues, they tend to lose interest in the divisive national issues and candidates. Nowhere is this truer than in America. The 2004, 2006 and 2008 elections refueled the acrimonious debate over who the federal government represents? Citizens in the blue states feel alienated from the federal government and their fellow citizens in the red states. Especially when told to move to Canada or go back to Mexico.

People have become more sensitized and localized in their focus and attention to bread-and-butter issues. As a result, America is a divided nation. Republicans entered the 21st century with an advantage over the Democrats because of their ruthless and smarter tactics – and the Republican-dominated Supreme Court. The Founding Fathers did not see the presidential election as a straight national head count. Far too radical for 1778 America. The popular vote was to be refined and filtered through a state by state device – controlled by the party in power in that state. Having run for elector in California, I can attest to the bipartisan battles to control the Electoral College. Few people understand what the Electoral College is. They think it is some quaint procedure that came into play after the president is elected. In 2000, they found out the college is alive and kicking and the Bush-Cheney neocons are on the battlements with knives in their teeth to prevent any change to the system they control. Amendment now? Fuhgeddaboudit, unless *We the Apathetic Maids* wake up. Florida could happen again any day, as Ohio almost did.

The Senate was split fifty-fifty. America hasn't been so divided since the 1880s – also the last time the winner of the popular vote lost in the electoral vote. Is America condemned to more Floridas and Ohios in the 21st century? The electoral stasis of the 1880s was rooted in deep divisions over a non-economic issue – the Civil War. The country was then divided along the Mason-Dixon Line. Yankees versus Confederates. Today it is divided urban versus rural. Liberal versus conservative. Red versus blue. The 2004 and 2008 presidential elections and 2006 congressional elections further magnified the division.

People have become so localized and alienated from the central government that the issue of civil war, secession, separatism or independence as witnessed in Quebec, Scotland, Taiwan, Indonesia, Africa, Czechoslavakia, Iraq, Yugoslavia and the former USSR surfaced to the top of many political agendas in the closing decades of the last century and the opening decade of the 21st century. Militias and extremists in such countries as Israel, Iran, Ireland,

China, Spain, France or the U.S. who refuse to recognize central governments may be appeased and brought back into the political process if the overture is couched in terms of localization and interlocalism rather than abolition of constitution, secession or separatism.

City States
American cities are not stopping at the city limits. The New World Order economy gives urban centers a global role. "You can't be mayor today without having your own foreign policy," said Marc Morial, the former mayor of New Orleans. If in the past all politics was local, "in the 21st century, perhaps all politics will be global," Morial added.

Federal and state governments get the prestige, but cities are where trade, education and culture develop and are at a "tipping point" to create new international alliances. As cities grow and expand because of cultural, economic and political maturity, they create regions that include clumps of cities, like Raleigh-Durham, Silicon Valley, Southern California, South Florida, the Pearl River Delta in southern China and every other region. "Suburbs and the countryside are cities that never made it," Bruce Grill, a friend and client from New York who lives in Hong Kong – a real city slicker – told me when I told him I liked living in the country. I love city life but sometimes like to wake up to the sound of silence and birds rather than honking horns, sirens and early-morning garbage trucks.

Wellington Webb, the former mayor of Denver, said that mayors are like soldiers on the ground, state governors are like sailors and Congress is like the Air Force, "which drops things on us from high which we had not asked for and on which we were not consulted." He adds that "I believe that the 21st century is the century of cities in both America and Europe. Globalization gives us new opportunities for partnership."

Global Urban Slumization
By 2008, more than half the world's population, about 3.3 billion people, will live in towns and cities, a number expected to swell to almost 5 billion by 2030, according to a U.N. Population Fund report released in June 2007. The onrush of change will be particularly extraordinary in Africa and Asia, where between 2000 and 2030, "the accumulated urban growth during the whole span of history will be duplicated in a single generation," the report

says.

This surge in urban populations, fueled more by natural increase than the migration of people from the countryside, is unstoppable. Cities will edge out rural areas in more than sheer numbers of people. Poverty is now increasing more rapidly in urban areas as well, and governments need to plan for where the poor will live rather than leaving them to settle illegally in shanties without plumbing and other basic services.

With millions of people settling into cities in the coming decades, it is critical for interlocal urban planners to design cities that can absorb the human influx and seamlessly integrate the different communities into multicultural education systems in order to avoid the plight of today's slums – while addressing their needs.

In Latin America, where urbanization came earlier than in other developing regions, many countries and cities ignored or fruitlessly tried to retard urban growth. People were left to fend for themselves in slums. There are a billion people, one-sixth of the world's population, who already live in slums, 90 percent of them in developing countries.

In sub-Saharan Africa, more than 7 out of 10 urban dwellers live in a slum. The region's slum population has almost doubled in just 15 years, reaching 200 million in 2005. Its urban population is already as large as North America's.

The first great wave of urbanization unfurled over two centuries, from 1750 to 1950, in Europe and North America, with urban populations rising to 423 million from 15 million.

That was then and interlocalism is now. Globalism died in the last decade of the 20th century. It was a 19th-century model of economics based on scarcity, but the whole world was in surplus. The debates on globalization, secession or separatism have to therefore be replaced with an all-encompassing discussion on interlocalism. Interlocalism will accelerate as the economic benefits and natural growth become evident in the 21st century.

Interlocalism is adaptation and expansion of the industrial concept of "clusters." Compatible communities competing and collaborating in a network of mutually supportive, global-wired urban hubs that recognize and accept that economics – fueled by the natural resources that empires, countries, communites, tribes and villages have gone to war over – are, and always have been, the underlying driving engine of the loccmotive of politics and senseless wars that get innocent, uneducated children killed because of their parent's ignorance.

China has rejected the globalization economic model just as it did rural communism, and is forming Confucian humanist city clusters as the essential national cornerstone and integral part of its future interlocal cluster economic model. Most of the megacities such as Beijing, Shanghai and Wuhan – already home to millions of people – have room to grow. Smaller cities around the megacities – especially those with populations of around 1 million – will become an integral part of city clusters.

China, the world's most populous nation, is now at the peak of its urban transformation. Urbanits will outnumber peasants within a decade. China will then have 83 cities with more than 750,000 residents, but only five with a population of more than five million.

City clusters have already formed on the Yangtze River Delta and the Pearl River Delta, with Hong Kong, Shanghai and Guangzhou as their respective cores. With plans to turn Kowloon Bay and Kwun Tong into Hong Kong's third-largest commercial district by 2010, the market is decentralizing to compensate for the lack of large commercial property in Hong Kong's central business district. No different than New York or Los Angeles, which just keep spreading, whether it's from Manhattan to Brooklyn, Queens, Bronx, Statten Island, the Hamptons or Fire Island. L.A.? Beverly Hills, Bel-Air, Santa Monica, Culver City, Malibu all the way to the Ventura County line. Let's not forget the coastal cities from Manhattan Beach all the way to the Laguna Beach-Capistrano county line – actually all the way down to La Jolla to Acapulco with a lot of interlocal communities in between. All had two great things in common. Great interlocal people and seafood restaurants, actually, just like Hong Kong – all kinds of phenomenal international, local, and interlocal cuisines, because all their respective best chefs seem to want go and interlocalize ingredients and cuisines.

Imagine setting up restaurants for people and their pets in a cafe inside pet superstores with a veterinary clinic and free space for local animal welfare organizations in China to make sure that the senseless killing of abandoned pets is better understood because of irresponsible *We the Apathetic Maids*. That's exactly what I did. The key to succesful growth is good management.

Hong Kong is the best-managed city in China, probably the world. It has the population density of most cities in China but with full employment, yet is the most efficient and functional. A great place to raise children and enjoy pets – not by eating them – but loving, bonding, teaching and learning. A concept that is definitely already proven and working in many major U.S. cities like New York and Los Angeles. It's about making cities a more livable environment for our children and granchildren. What is wrong with the picture of our grandchildren enjoying what we enjoyed the way we did instead of experiencing it through their favorite interlocal, inter-connected totally wired network. Is it any wonder Blackberry is doing so well for now? Think of its recent predecessors. Telex, fixed line phones, fax, cheap internet phone calls, broadband.

Federalism was, and still is, a noble concept – when conceived and born. Today the way it is practiced by career politicians and their bureaucrats, lobbyists and lawyers is bogus and a total fraud being perpetrated on our Founding Fathers and *We the Apathetic People*.

Interlocal Attachments

Interlocalism is the proposed interaction between different local communities promoting their collective well-being with minimum government participation. The concentric circles start with the local village, town or city and expand over the county, country, and compatible global communities. It is the fusion of local strengths spread widely over similar-minded and compatible people. From the San Fernando Valley, Los Angeles, California, Mexico, the Americas, Quebec, Hawaii, Scotland, Wales, Ireland, Italy, Indonesia, Cyprus, Germany, Korea, China and every other country in the world that has a history and an expatriate community.

The city of Milwaukee and its engine maker Briggs & Stratton are a glowing American-made interlocal model. Home to a cluster of global businesses, including temporary staffing firm Manpower, auto parts maker Johnson Controls and Harley Davidson motorcycles. Briggs & Stratton is the world's largest maker of small petrol engines for lawnmowers, power generators and outboard motors.

Instead of moving to China in 1985 as so many other U.S. manufacturers did, it abandoned virtually all manufacturing in Milwaukee and set up a network of plants further south in non-unionized locations such as Alabama, Georgia, Missouri and Kentucky. Each new plant employs a maximum of 1, 000 people, making it easier to manage fluctuations in demand for engines from big "box store" retailers such as Sears, whose in-store Craftsman brand of mowers accounts for much of the Briggs & Stratton's business.

The debates on globalization, secession or separatism have to be replaced with an all-encompassing discussion on interlocalism. Interlocalism will accelerate as the economic benefits and natural growth become evident in the 21st century.

The muted celebrations in Great Britain on the 200th anniversary of the Act of Union, which on January 1, 1801, brought Ireland into the United Kingdom along with England, Scotland and Wales, brought home that devolution and interlocalism are the order of the day in the New World Order of the 21st century.

Interlocalism allows communities to live and practice their beliefs as they please on a local level and interact with like-minded communities anywhere on our planet.

Interlocalism creates modern-day empires based on common religion, culture, language and desires. This global interlocal connection is witnessed every year in America, and every other country I have lived in, every Chinese New Year when the lion dancers take to the streets and firecrackers are ignited. Cinco de Mayo, Bobby Burns Nights, Saint Patrick's day, and national Independence Day celebrations are just as global.

China, Scotland, Ireland, India, Israel and many other countries have long recognized and capitalized on this interdependence and constantly reach out to their fellow globally dispersed peoples through a variety of overseas clubs and cultural organizations. Isn't it time America did so as well, instead of exploiting and oppressing people who have the natural resources America craves?

Interlocal Racism

Watching the replays on the TV monitors of South Korean farmers trying to break through the police lines at the World Trade Organization meeting in Hong Kong on December 14, 2005, the discussion at the Main Bar of the Foreign Correspondents Club, naturally turned to America's continued exploitation of poor nations – especially Muslim nations – with oil and other natural resources. Having just returned from the U.S. a couple of days earlier after my November 3, 2005, horseback ride to protest U.S. government energy policies, and having done more than 50 radio interviews about short sighted U.S. policies, I was in no jet lag mood to engage in another prolonged U.S- bashing debate.

Leaving the next day for Sydney, Australia, where the country's worst race-related violence since 1860 (when Chinese miners were killed,) had just taken place in Cronulla on December 11, involving more than 5,000 people, and the subsequent revenge attacks that had shaken the nation to its core – with more violence expected during my visit – I decided to change the subject and move down the bar and join Australian photojournalists Bob Davis and Terry Duckam and Aussie correspondent Paul Bayfield, who were discussing the matter. "Surf, lifesaving clubs and lifesavers are as Australian as vegemite, cricket and rugby," Bob Davis said in response to my question of why the riots started. "Once those Leb gang members attacked lifesavers, they attacked the very soul of Australia and ignited a spark that Christian Anglo-Europeans who feel Muslim Arabs don't respect Australian traditions exploited," Bob continued as I probed deeper. "But aren't most Australians of Lebanese descent Maronite Christians who were born there?" I asked.

The race riots of the 1860s resulted in the Australian government adopting a White Australia policy that prevented non-European immigrants from entering the country until 1966. The policy wasn't officially scrapped until 1973.

The next morning, while waiting for the plane to Australia, I telephoned

Tony Manton, an Australian friend from Sydney who lives in Singapore with his Hong Kong Chinese wife Jane. I've known Tony, a white Australian who can trace his heritage back to one of the first convict ships to arrive from England to Australia in 1788, for more than 15 years. Tony is a television executive who over the years has represented Viacom, Turner, Intelsat and various other U.S. media companies in Asia. I wanted to hear his thoughts about the Cronulla riots.

"It's not a race issue, he said. "Not that Aussies aren't racist, mind you. They are the most racist people I know. Having said that, it's strictly a law enforcement issue that has been exploited by racists. Politicians have given in to political correctness and taken away all effective police powers. The police can't do anything to enforce the law or stop gangs for fear of being disciplined. Law enforcement is out of control, nonexistent. I'll e-mail you an eye witness report from a local as well as a letter written by a policeman to the local papers explaining why police are helpless to prevent what happened. It's a political issue and politicians are again blaming anyone they can – except themselves – while the Lebanese gangs and white neo-Nazis exploit the situation." I thanked Tony and headed for my flight.

Global Mutt

Living as I have as a member of a minority community my whole life, with a grandfather and father who lived and died in Australia, I decided to explore the underlying racial, cultural, religious and law enforcement issues further once I got to Australia, since racism is a global issue – especially in the wake of the destructive race riots across France by French-born disillusioned North African Muslims the previous month – which was still being analyzed and debated in France and the media worldwide.

My white Russian paternal grandfather migrated to Australia sometime in the early part of the 20th century after the Russian revolution and worked as an engineer building the Sydney Bridge. My father, who was also born in Russia but raised in England, immigrated to Australia in the 1950s after he divorced my mother in Cyprus and decided to get as far away from her as possible. Both men died in Australia as proud Australians. Since the 1970s, I have visited Australia on several occasions. Although I am a white male, I can totally relate to the cultural and ethnic isolation – even racist exclusion – of minorities.

In Switzerland, as a Russian-speaking 2-to-4-year old, I got into scraps with Swiss-German toddlers because they would tease me over my "different" Bern-Deutche accent. Not that I remember, but my mother would remind me when I got into fights in Cyprus with Greek or Turkish children because I was a Jewish Anglo, or with British children at the Army Childrens School because I was being raised by a single Jewish mother and living off the military base in a mixed Greek-Turkish neighborhood.

Going to Israel as a teenager who did not speak Hebrew and had a Christian father didn't make matters easier. Moving to America in the '60s to attend university with the Scottish-English Cockney accent I acquired in Cyprus with a touch of Hebrew gravel, I was again easily identified as an immigrant –and occasionally mocked. Living in Hong Kong, China and the Philippines, there is no question about my minority status. "Gracious me! We are all going to have to be a lot more rude to you than we have been," yelped columnist Stuart Wolfendale as we shared our English roots over a good ale that he, a Lancashire lad, found so unbelievable. "Problem is, its very confusing over what to be rude about to a Russo-Anglo-Jewish-Australian-American who spoke Kraut and has consorted with Cypriots!" Wolfendale gasped as I gave him a glaring smile and we both burst into laughter.

Australia

Arriving in Australia on December 15, 2005, during a furious national debate about the causes of the Cronulla race riots the previous weekend and possible cures, I decided to take a deeper look because I believe there is a global millennium lesson to be learned from the ugly incident which has also been experienced in many multicultural communities around the world. The race riots across France the previous month – the Watts race riots of 1965 in America along with the more recent race riots of the '90s there that followed the acquittal of the police officers that beat Rodney King, race riots across Britain at the dawn of the new millennium and the assassination of a prominent Dutch politician by a Muslim extremist – all are race riot footnote reminders of how little career politicians have done to socially address an ongoing global problem.

Australia was established as a prison colony by the British in 1788. Australia's British roots run deep. It's political, legal and social development parallels that of Britain, where "homegrown bombers" who lack a sense of belonging to their country of birth has taken hold among a significant minority of British Muslims.

Australia is a country where one in every four people was born in another country. Cronulla, a Sydney suburb, is an Aboriginal word meaning "small pink sea shell." Cronulla is about as old-style "white bread" casual, middle-income surf town Australia as it gets. Nine out of 10 people who live there are of Anglo-Saxon heritage. It is an area at odds with the multicultural brew that makes up the sprawling western suburbs just a short train ride away. For decades resident "surfies" have clashed with successive generations of migrant Italians, Vietnamese and Lebanese who headed for the cool of Cronulla on hot summer days – beach, barbeque. alcohol, Christmas celebrations and enjoying the summer holidays – which in Australia are in December. With summer fast approaching, the beating of two lifeguards, one of them unconscious, by a Muslim gang who were asked to stop playing football on the beach, caused the long suppressed multicultural racial male turf wars on Cronulla and nearby beaches to erupt.

According to the last Australian census of 2001, the Lebanese community in Sydney numbered 114,491, so would be 120,000 in 2005, or three percent of Sydney's population. About a third of them are Muslims. Ninety percent were born overseas or have at least one foreign-born parent. The community is almost as diverse as Lebanon itself – Maronite, Orthodox, Shiite, Sunni, Druze and secular. The majority are Maronite, who dominated the first 80 years of Lebanese migration to Australia and whose children blended into the Catholic school system.

Though the Lebanese Muslim community is about 40,000 – just one percent of Sydney's 4 million population – the social gulf, like other European countries with large Muslim populations, has drifted to the point of danger.

Lebanese families migrated to Australia in the mid 1970s and early 1980s as they fled the civil war in their country. Many were uneducated and transplanted their traditional life styles to Australia. Girls were kept under strict control while the boys ran free. Parental guidance in the new environment was nonexistent. Young boys looked elsewhere for the strong connections they crave. A subculture of gangs evolved – and finally exploded in 2002 when members of a Lebanese gang hurled racial abuse at their rape victims, all of whom were white. The ring leader was sentenced to 55 years.

Men of Middle Eastern descent must follow traditional beach etiquette, such as not beating up lifeguards, walking around the beach in jeans and sneakers and deliberately kicking sand on other beach-goers, and not disrespecting women in bikinis, spitting on them and making racial or vulgar slurs, threats of gang rape and intimidation. Telling non-Muslim women in bathing suits to cover up and calling them sluts while trying to force exclusionary zones on the beach for their women to swim fully dressed and wearing head scarfs is not acceptable behavior in Australia.

Women of any culture or religious belief can no longer be perceived by Muslim men as merely a life-support system for a vagina.

Sydney University lecturer in gender, Clifton Evers, says Cronulla's violence and intimidation are consistent with the battle out on the water, where surfers negotiate spaces and pecking orders in the understanding that the best surfer takes the best waves, and locals act together to ensure "mates rule."

"Localism and respect and worship for the male body and its ability to put itself in, and out, of dangerous situations, are the driving forces of surf culture," Evers said. "Mateship's the thing among bloke societies, but especially in sports. You go in with your mates, no matter the consequences – look at the guys on Cronulla beach or Maroubra. For that matter, the Lebanese guys are just Australian, too, fighting alongside their mates, just like the surf guys."

Surfing allows the confrontation of shame and pride. "If you pull back paddling onto a wave, everybody in the water knows you've squibbed it. You know it too. The only way to overcome the shame is to build your body up and make it conquer your fear. I'ts instant self-knowledge and a constant proving ground for masculinity."

The surf culture of Australia started in surf lifesaving clubs after California lifeguards visited in 1956 to compete in Olympic surf carnivals. They brought small, solid balsa boards with strange skegs at the rear that – unlike the long, hollow, wooden Australian boards – allowed surfers to cut across wave faces and stay in the slippery unbroken curls.

Young Australian men eschewed the surf lifesaving club movement, with its military discipline and marching and team ethos, and searched for uncrowded peaks and self-indulgence. Early surf heroes, such as Freshwater's Bernard "Midget" Farrelly, reflected Californian cool values: going with the flow and blending with the wave. Some thought it almost feminine. In 1966, Auzzie surfer Nat Young became world champion with a new and masculine surfing technique based on super-short boards, where he "ripped." Young's nickname was "The Animal" and his victory asserted Australia's dominance of a sport evolving into a lifestyle fueled by drugs, alcohol, travel and ultranationalism.

Extremists

It is therefore not surprising that the disrespectful un-Australian behavior of Lebanese thugs on Cronulla beach that culminated in the beating of the lifeguards on December 4 – in a neighborhood that hated Muslim extremists because it had lost several local surfers in the Bali bombings of 2002 that killed more than 200 Australians and left hundreds more injured – would bring about a violent response by the Australians to retake the beaches. The text messages and calls by Neo-Nazi groups and other white racists asking people to converge on Cronulla from all parts of Sydney was pure racist thuggery to capitalize on a local beach turf war between local surfers, beachgoers and Lebanese thugs. The scenes of white Australians draped in the county's flag with a bottle of beer in one hand and chasing and beating anyone who looked Middle Eastern on Sunday, December 11, 2005, were horrifically racist.

The text messages by both sides the following week calling on their followers and community to show up armed and in force on the weekend to attack their "enemy" and retake the beach forced the police to declare six popular local beaches unsafe for public use and close all access roads. The lockdown decision was made after police received "credible threats" that the beaches would become race-riot zones and that some groups had been stockpiling guns and other lethal weapons for use that weekend. You can take a boy out of Beirut ....

The volatile situation was made worse by popular aging male Anglo-Saxon shock jocks. Sydney's highest-rated breakfast show host, Alan Jones, called for a "community show of force." Brian Wilshire called Lebanese-Australians "inbreds" and questioned their intelligence on air. Discussing Middle Eastern boys involved in violence he said: "Many of them have parents who are first cousins whose parents were first cousins, whose parents were first cousins .... The result of this is inbreeding." Not much different than Don Imus on his CBS radio show in America making racist remarks about the Rutgers University women's basketball team, or the Chinese racist remarks made on the same station by vocal and active supporters of Imus being reinstated, Vandergrift and Dan Lay, the hosts of The Dog House With JV and Elvis. The show's prank call format resulted in a call to a Chinese restaurant, in which the take-away food order was interspersed with lewd and racial slurs.

The pretrial hearing that same week in an Australian court of would- be suicide-bombers Abduua Merhi and Hany Taha, who were part of a group of 10 men charged with being members of a Melbourne terrorist cell – competing with a Sydney cell to commit the first act of terror on Australian soil – whose chilling taped conversation about plans to kill Prime Minister John Howard and little Australian kids at a football game or railway station made headline news and further fueled the already volatile environment. The spiritual guiding light for both terror cells was Abu Bakr, who preaches strict adherence to Islamic law and the strict interpretation of the Koran. He was arrested and charged with the other cell members. The fact that he had overstayed his visa and was declared an unlawful citizen but was able to stay in Australia after marrying a Lebanese-born woman with Australian citizenship was not overlooked – in fact played up – in the media. In an interview with Australian Broadcasting Corporation a month earlier, replayed and quoted during the pretrial hearing, Abu Bakr pledged his commitment to holy war and martyrdom. "My religion doesn't tolerate other religion," he said. "Jihad is a part of my religion. The only law which needs to spread, it can be here or anywhere else, has to be Islam."

Freedom of Speech
We must remember that the reason the extreme Jihadists have sought out open and democratic societies where they can openly express their views, like Australia, America and Britain, is that they fled from the persecution and lack of tolerance of free speech at home – from Muslim governments

that will jail or kill them because they will not tolerate their views.

For a government to allow preachers to preach and run websites that advocate the violent death of Australian, British or U.S. soldiers is unacceptable behavior in a civilized country. The laws drawn up in America after 9/11 and in Britain after the London train bombings of July 2005. designed to end such provocations by extreme Muslim fundamentalists that lead disgruntled young men and women towards violence, must be backed by the judiciary and enforced. Anyone who advocates that Muslims, in any country, kill their embracing hosts in the name of Islam should be jailed or deported.

The Bush administration, under laws toughened after 9/11, has prosecuted a number of individuals for encouraging terrorism, but not enough. In one high-profile case, a Muslim scholar in Northern Virginia, Ali al-Timimi, was sentenced to life in prison in 2005 for urging his young Muslim followers to wage war against America. At a dinner meeting on September 16, 2001, Timini told some of the men in the group that it was their Muslim duty to fight for their religion overseas and to defend the Taliban in Afghanistan against U.S. forces, according to testimony at his trial. In an Internet message in 2003, he described the destruction of the space shuttle Columbia as a "good omen" for Muslims in an apocalyptic conflict with the West.

We the Apathetic Maids are in the midst of an apocalyptic conflict that is fueled by unbridled freedom of speech. Responsible governments have a duty to curtail such destructive self-fulfilling prophesies without curtailing or violating the basic civil rights of law-abiding citizens.

Racist Misfits
To make matters worse, on the West coast in Perth, Damon Blaxall, a member of the ultra right-wing Australian Nationalist movement who had sprayed slogans and swatstikas on a synagogue the previous year, was being sentenced to one year in jail.

One common theme emerges in Blaxall's racial vilification trial, like that of all racists trials, be they the trials of Klu Klux Klan members in America, Lebanese or Anglos in Cronulla, or the Muslim North Africans in France. The racists are disaffected, angry men who are socially isolated and feel marginalized. Often, good jobs, cars and success elude them – and immigrants or the establishment white devils are to blame. The Internet and modern telecommunications makes their recruitment and organization easy.

It was groups of neo-Nazis and white supremacists who stirred up the drunken crowd at Cronulla.

People with guns, Molotov cocktails – even a car equipped to function as a bomb factory – and other weapons on their way to Cronulla and other nearby beaches were arrested during my visit. There were 289 arrests, 15 vehicles seized and 42 mobile phones confiscated. Less than 200 people converged on beaches that are usually enjoyed by more than 10,000 people. The heavy police presence in patrol cars, inflatable dinghies, planes, helicopters and on bicycles and horseback along with sniffer dogs kept a close eye on potential trouble spots.

It was the biggest police operation in New South Wales since the 2000 Olympics. Legislation was rushed through Parliament to allow police to lock down trouble spots, search people and cars and confiscate vehicles and mobile phones for seven days. The draconian police powers were necessary as political correctness had gradually stripped police powers over the previous two decades. Reading the letters to the editors of local papers from former police officers and the anonymous letters from current police officers made clear how their powers to stop, question or arrest hooligans, gang members and known drug traffickers had been stripped by career politicians and the courts in an act of pure criminal political delinquency. The Cronulla riots, like the race riots across America, Britain and France, are directly attributable to the failure of political leadership.

Police must have basic search and arrest powers without fear of censure because of a possible charge of discrimination. Most importantly, the public and politicians need to ensure that police work is supported with a serious legal system that provides genuine and fair punishment to those who don't respect the law continuously, not periodically and sporadically in response to a racist riot that should not have been allowed to brew and spill out onto a public beach in the first place.

I decided to spend a couple of days in Sydney to learn more about the riots before going on to Brisbane where I had business meetings. I had not planned to get directly involved with angry drunk Australian young men. I got on a train at Circular Quay to get back to my hotel near the airport. Unfortunately, I got on the wrong train and had to change trains several stops later at Sydenham and take another train for one stop then change again for the right train. As I boarded, I noticed several loud and rowdy drunks, one of whom tried to either hit or grab my vital parts as I walked by him to get to an empty seat. I jumped sideways and blocked his attempt and continued to proceed to the seat. "Why did you jump" the loud drunk Aborigine man repeatedly asked me. I ignored the question and slowly took off my glasses and put them in my shirt pocket as I stared at him and cautiously eyed the movements of his three younger drunk teenage buddies. An Anglo man was sitting across from me clutching his briefcase and trembling with fear, obviously having been harassed before I arrived.

"Do you have a cell phone? I need to make a call," the aggressive drunk asked when he realized I was not going to answer his first question. I continued to ignore him and tried to think how to respond while eyeing the menacing movements of his friends. "I do but I am getting off at the next station," I finally replied. "So are we. We are on our way to Cronulla," he said to a chorus of laughter from his friends. "Come on mate, give me the phone" he persisted as he approached me. I refused to do so and positioned my legs and body for a quick evasive response should he try to again make bodily contact. Fortunately, he stopped several feet away as one of his friends jumped up in front of him and yelled, "We are the only real Australians. All of you stole our land and aren't fucking Aussies," to the rapturous applause of the others. I smiled and nodded my head in agreement as they turned and headed for the opening doors. I followed as I tried to figure out which track I had to be on to catch the right train – knowing it was not the one they were on to Cronulla.

Rape
Nothing has changed since Egyptian-born Sunni cleric Sheikh Taj Aldin al-Hilaly, Australia's top Muslim cleric, sparked an outrage in October 2006 in a sermon he gave at his Sydney mosque in which he likened scantily dressed women to "uncovered meat" inviting sexual attack as he praised militants in Iraq, Afghanistan and the Palestinian territories in violation of Australia's counter-terrorism laws.

Australia's Islamic leaders cannot ignore the "vile acts" committed in the name of their faith and must do more to denounce extremism, Andrew Robb, parliamentary secretary for immigration and multicultural affairs, urged more than 100 imams in Sydney. "Because it is your faith that is being invoked, it is your problem. You cannot wish it away or ignore it just because it has been caused by others," he said. Robb told them to preach in English, the first language of most of Australia's Muslims – and denounce terrorism. Australia has done a better job than Catholic France in integrating Muslims into the Australian multi-faceted Christian community, dominated by Protestant WASPs.

Pauline Hanson, who founded the anti-immigration One Nation party in the 1990s, announced in 2007 she was returning to politics as the head of the newly formed United Australia Party and ran for a senate seat because she believed ordinary Australians were being ignored by the major parties. Prime Minister John Howard "has sold us out by not halting further Muslim immigration and dumping hapless refugees from Africa on us without any consultation," she said. "Australia must withdraw immediately from the 1951 U.N. Convention on refugees."

At the same time, an Australian who had been held and tortured at Guantanamo, Mamdououh Habib, ran for a New South Wales state parliament seat. Habib, a father of four, was an early case of "rendition." He was seized in Pakistan in October 2001. He was released from Guantanamo and returned to Australia in February 2005, without charge, because the Bush administration did not want the torture allegations aired in court.

Indian doctor Mohammad Haneef, who was arrested in Australia after the attempted terror attacks in London and Glasgow in late June 2007, was charged with "reckless support" of terrorism because it was alleged that his SIM card had been found in the Jeep that crashed into Glasgow Airport, and that Dr Haneef had lived with his terror suspect cousins in Britain.

The politically charged legal soap opera Dr Haneef was subjected to before he was released and allowed to fly back to India, confirmed Muslims racist beliefs about Christian Anglo-Celts. The case is being exploited by radical elements in Australia to sow discontent. The Haneef legal scandal is a salient warning to all.

This while Chinese and Vietnamese shops were being forced to display and advertise their wares and services in English because there are too many shopfront signs in their native language to reflect "Australian values."

Meanwhile, surf livesaving clubs now recruit Asians and Muslims, including women – who wear a *"burqini,"* a full-length lycra suit which is loose enough to enable them to swim and rescue bathers in trouble. They even have a built in *hijab* (headscarf) in the distinctive color of the lifesaving movement. With over 100,000 unpaid lifesavers patrolling Australia's beaches and more than 300 clubs, Surf Life Saving Australia is the nation's largest volunteer organization that is no longer just white Anglo-Saxon.

Almost one in four Australians was born overseas, the highest proportion in more than 100 years. Yet multiculturalism is being seen in an increasingly negative light. Aussies have gotten terrorism and multiculturalism mixed up. "Australia is like Catholicism. The company is sometimes questionable and the landscape is grotesque. But you always come back," said Thomas Keneally, Aussie musician.

Australian citizens are routinely detained as illegal immigrants under a long-standing government clampdown on asylum seekers and its tough border protection policies. Australia is unsure of itself and how it fits into Asia because it grew to become a free nation surrounded by what its colonial overlords considered the "backside" of the world. More than two centuries later, the tables have turned. China's economy is now bigger than that of Britain.

If Australia truly wants to be part of Asia, it has to start to do so ethnically. Open its door wide open to immigrants from Asia. Australia's 20 million inhabitants live on an island the size of the continental U.S. About 74 percent of its population is Anglo-Celtic and 19 percent is classified as "other European." Only 4.5 percent is Asian. Maybe Kevin Rudd, who speaks putonghua and cut his politial teeth in foreign policy issues will change that.

The country can easily absorb 20 million monied and educated immigrants from China, Japan, Korea, Vietnam, India and Indonesia. The Northern Territory capital Darwin is closer to Jakarta than it is to Sydney. As a result all students in Northern Territory schools must learn the Indonesian language.

A 40-million strong Australia, with strong ethnic and cultural ties with Asia, would be better equipped to become part of Asia and be better equipped to be part of the economic growth engine of the century. This does not mean losing its distinct, easy-going culture. On the contrary, a bigger and more influential Australia will have the opportunity to spread its values.

Rap

Rap was the music of choice of the Lebanese gangs and was played loudly in their hoods in preparation for the Cronulla fights. Every introspective adolescent on the planet – including Chinese – listen to it. Pride and shame are powerful forces – in rap and in the hearts of African-Americans, South Asian British, African French and Lebanese Australians. Gangsta rap is full of gun violence, cops and bad-ass bitches, a culture of rejection and victimhood and an intense claim to the unfettered right of revenge. It dove-tails perfectly in the lives of those who feel oppressed and want to instill fear. Oppressed Muslim youth around the world can easily identify with a black minority in America that sees itself as still oppressed and victimized by the white man.

The race riots at Cronulla beach, like the ocean itself, is a symbol for the subconscious. What lurks beneath it is unseen, unknown, mysterious and often frightening. For most of us, somewhere deep in our subconscious, there lies the potential for racism, simply because we fear the unknown. The obligation of an educated civilization is to ensure that this potential fear of the other, of what is different, is eradicated and never surfaces again. Social mobility for all people is essential in a civilized society.

In Brisbane, during a Peking duck dinner with a Hong Kong Chinese friend, Selwyn Mar, and his daughter Sandrea, her riding teacher Chantal Wigan and her mother Lorette, the owner of the riding school, I brought up the subject of racism and asked Selwyn, who had attended school in Australia and has a brother, uncle and a home in the Brisbane area, whether he had personally experienced racism or discrimination. He hadn't. On the contrary, he found Australians very welcoming, kind and courteous. He shared several touching personal stories of their graciousness and kindness. "A kind elderly neighbor who voluntarily helped guide me to a parking spot at the local supermarket the other day said a profound thing as we walked to the market after I parked. He said people only have a right to hate a person, not their race," Selwyn said. We all shook our head in agreement.

More than 200 languages are spoken in Australia and multiculturism has generally been a success. Unlike America, Britain and France, Australia does not have a large number of immigrants from any one country or ethnic group. That is not to say each group didn't experience racism. They did and assimilitated. There is racism towards Chinese, Asians and other immigrant groups in Australia. Pauline Hansen and her supporters are the most obvious offenders. Unemployment among Muslims of Lebanese background is at about 20 percent, four times the national average. That is because they are among the least educated and least integrated – which is often because of their own choices in life.

Lorette, a fifth-generation Anglo-Australian, was married to a Lebanese-Australian and divorced him because of the pressure and culture clash of Lebanese family practices and traditions with those of her Australian upbringing. "Family dinners were an all-inclusive compulsory family affair. Every member of the family, even cousins several times removed, had to attend. The dinner table was half the size of this huge dining room and everyone, and I mean everyone, had to obey and do whatever they were told by my in-laws. What to wear, what to say, political opinions, religion, education, you name it, there was only one opinion. There was no room for discussion, debate and certainly not for disagreement – which was interpreted as disrespectful." I was pleasantly surprised by her unsolicited comment because Selwyn had told me she was a widow who was married to a Frenchman. I could see he was also surprised to find out she had been married before, as he had known her late second husband – the Frenchman.

"The Lebanese, like many immigrant communities in Australia, stick to their own in their own neighborhoods and many never learn to speak English. Their children can't wait to leave and many in fact move far away when they finish their schooling and only come back for occasional family or religious celebrations," Lorette continued as we all listened intensely.

"The only way to break the ignorant racist cycle is to expose immigrant children to other cultures and traditions, especially Australian culture, in the schools and the eduction system," Chantal responded to my question as to how the old ways of an old country can be changed or broken in a multicultural society.

"Being exposed to other children of other cultures and native Australians of all backgrounds is the only way immigrant children can be integrated into society," Lorette added. "What I found offensive, and still do, is how so many Muslim Lebanese only allow their children to go to Muslim schools and give them no exposure to the culture or people of Australia," she said as Selwyn, who attended a local high school concurred.

Multiracialism is a politically correct notion to be distinguished from integration. It doesn't work. The British have found this out the hard way with their Muslims. Literally, scores of second and third-generation young British born Pakistanis have shown themselves willing to blow away their fellow citizens in suicide bombings.

Apartheid

A couple of days later I met up with my partner Pauline Taylor's South African doctor friends, Abel and Elna Stoltz, who had immigrated to Australia via New Zealand in 1995. Pauline, a Scottish lass, Abel and Elna had all lived and worked together in Turangi, a Maori community in New Zealand. In 1974, South Africa would not play rugby against New Zealand if it had a Maori on the team. "When I left South Africa I was a racist," said Abel. "Arriving in New Zealand I couldn't differentiate a Maori from other Kiwis. Living and working in a Maori community, after working in black ghettos in South Africa, to me they were all Kiwis," Abel said as he reflected back on his New Zealand days.

Abel's brother Ben and his wife Betsy, who had immigrated to Australia from South Africa 25 years earlier, joined us for dinner at the Stoltz's Brisbane home. South Africans were immigrating to Australia by the thousands. "I remember when I'd open a phone book to look up Afrikaans names like Botha, and I was lucky to find a couple," Ben said. "Today there are pages. Their children, like ours, are fully integrated, most don't speak Afrikaans and they consider themselves pure Aussies."

The Stoltzs were eighth or ninth generation South Africans. Elna's family are French Hugenot; Abel, Ben and Betsy are German-Dutch. Leaving South Africa and assimilating and integrating their children into Australian society was a conscious, deliberate parental effort. Elna shared a story about a school show and tell assignment her 15- year old son Pieter did when he was 12 on the South African Boer Wars of the 1300s. In addition to doing the basic research on the war, he did an in depth presentation of the role his great grandparents played in the war. He talked to his grandparents and parents and was even able to secure family heirlooms from the war.

His great-great grandfather had made a rare blackwood dining table set with 12 chairs and given it to his great-great grandmother as a wedding present. During the war, the dining set and other valuables had been buried to avoid the British "scorch and burn" campaign that destroyed everything that could be burned. Two chairs from that dining set survived and were brought by Pieter to show his classmates. Having children of different backgrounds and culture share personal family stories and cultural history is an important part of assimilation, education and understanding of others. After-school activities also play an important multicultural socialization role.

Apartheid in South Africa, racism in Australia, Africa, New Zealand, America and the world was discussed over several bottles of wine and champagne until the wee hours of the morning. There was a cricket match taking place in Australia between South Africa and Australia during my visit. The penultimate test, I decided, was to see which team the Stoltzs supported. "When there is a rugby game between Australia and South Africa, or a cricket game for that matter, like the current Test Series, which team do you support and root for?" I asked. "Australia," Abel said without hesitation. The unanimous consensus was that parental guidance, school integration and the objective, unbiased education of children about the different world cultures and religions contribution to world history and today's civilizations are the key to ending racism.

Affirmative Action

I decided to stay in Australia after my Brisbane business meetings and celebrate the Christmas and Hannukah holidays in Byron Bay with friends I'd met in Hong Kong in 1999. Malcolm, a proper English gentleman is married to Monique, a Hong Kong-born Chinese-Australian. The festivities included their four children, Monique's mother and two sisters. Monique's mother Helen was born to Cantonese parents in Papau New Guinea, where she married Bruce, a white English-Danish Australian. They migrated to Australia where Moniques's two sisters were born.

Malcolm and Monique are veterinarians living and practicing in Dubai. Discussing racism towards Muslims in Australia with a mixed-race family living in a Muslim country gave the conversation another perspective. "Muslims have one set of laws for themselves and another for everyone else. They probably think that's the way it should be here in Australaia as well," said Monique, who is rather outspoken and direct. "Why can't they assimilate and integrate with others at home or here in Australia? That question has to be directly addressed by their political leaders and ours here in Australia. They have to be forced by our political leaders to integrate and assimilate their children in our schools so they can learn from others and teach others about themselves. Disrimination and racism starts at home with parents. It is up to parents to teach their children to accept others regardless of ethnic background, culture or religious belief," Monique continued as I toasted her brutal honesty. Their daughter Maisy does not recognize racial or ethnic differences in Dubai, where 90 percent of the children are expatriates of all cultures and ethnic groups. To her they are all classmates regardless of their ethnic background or religion.

Osam bin Laden's niece, Wafah Dufour – like Maisy – is another millennium example of interlocal multiculturism in the 21st century. She was born in Santa Monica, California, while her parents studied there. Her mother, Carmen bin Laden, was married to Yeslama bin Laden, Osama's half-brother. She has a U.S. passport and does not speak Arabic. "I want people to know I am American," she said.

I can relate. Growing up in Cyprus in a mixed Greek and Turkish neighborhood, I played with Muslim and Greek Orthodox children and never gave a second thought to their ethnicity. They were neighborhood playmates. I see the same attitude today on the street where I live in Hong Kong. Chinese children playing with Danish, Filipino, French, Scottish-English, Chinese-Japanese, South African and Rhodesian kids without regard to ethnicity or color. Children are born and grow up unaware of their playmates ethnic or religious background. Racists are created by parents and teachers who consciously, sometimes unconsciously, raise children to be intolerant of others.

Before returning to Hong Kong I stopped off in Surfers Paradise to visit Earl Klein and Catherine Newman, North American friends from Hong Kong, who moved to Surfers three years earlier. Earl was born and raised in Los Angeles and Catherine is from Toronto, Canada. Earl and Catherine are refreshingly rare, honest and outspoken North Americans, not only in Australia, but in North America. I brought up the subject of the Cronulla race riot knowing the discussion would be lively. Earl was in Los Angeles during the 1965 Watts riots and I wanted to hear his perspective of how the two events compared. Earl, a retired banker, was driving on the San Diego Freeway in his Austin Healey convertible on a hot L.A. summer day on his way to Gardena, a Los Angeles suburb, the day the Watts riots started. He noticed a huge plume of dark smoke rise from the Compton-Southeast area of Los Angeles and decided to get off the freeway at the off-ramp closest to the smoke to see what was burning. "I couldn't believe my eyes when I got off the freeway. There were blacks running in all directions. There was nothing on the radio yet and I had no idea what was going on. When I stopped at a red light, a big black guy with his shirt off approached me and looked down at me and said, 'If you want to continue to live, you better turn around and get the fuck out of here.' I did just that." Earl said. "I didn't need to be told twice." Earl had experienced racism and fights with angry African-Americans in the Navy.

Listening to Earl's stories of race based fights in the Navy, I couldn't help flash back and reflect on all the U.S. Navy men and women that get disgorged in Hong Kong every time a U.S. carrier group arrives. Blacks, Latinos and white Americans all drinking, partying and getting down together as fellow Americans. The military is America's best affirmative action program. That doesn't mean it is perfect. Asians, Blacks, Latinos and whites still prefer to hang out with each other and their different clusters of three to a dozen or so are regularly seen walking, drinking and just hanging out with each other.

Earl went to Dorsey High, an inner city school in Los Angeles – class of 1960 – where 60 percent of the student body was black, and remembers when schools were forced to integrate in Little Rock, Arkansas, in 1957. "Television camera crews came to our school to film an integrated student body and show how integration can work. We were supposedly a model of integration," said Earl. "The fact was we were not. We may have all been going to the same school and been in the same class, but each race stuck to their own.

There were three separate triangle lawn areas behind the administration building and between the four classroom buildings that protruded from the main administration building. Whites had the C lawn, blacks the D lawn and the others were mixed lawns with Latinos, Japanese and other minorities. The majority of the students were in either the C or D lawns. When Little Rock happened, the black students decided to converge onto our lawn. I'll never forget what a fellow club member said when the first blacks came onto the C lawn: 'Gee, its getting dark here,' and fights between blacks and whites started that day and continued until I left school," Earl said as he continued to argue his case for why forced integration does not work.

"Things haven't changed that much since then," I said. "The only difference is that instead of whites saying it's getting darker these days in L.A. and all over California, it's the Latinos. Look at what happened at Jefferson High earlier this year," I said, referring to the race riots at the school between Latinos and blacks Americans in Los Angeles. "Latinos are afraid to go to the school store because that's where the blacks are and they are afraid they are going to be jumped." More violent melees followed with dozens arrested, others hospitalized and dozens of students suspended or transferred. Hundreds more stayed away from classes, and those that did show up did so with fear.

Catherine and I disagreed with Earl. She believed in busing and integration. As our discussion heated up, I decided to cool things down with a toast. "To our continued honest search for an education system for our grandchildren and their fellow classmates around the world growing up in a multicultural civilization," I said as we hoisted our glasses.

Catherine, a fifth or sixth-generation English-French-Scottish Protestant, grew up in white-bread Toronto and moved to Chapaqua, New York, in 1978-82 when her father, who worked for IBM, was transferred to the company headquarters in America. Catherine went to private schools her whole life. She attended Byron Hills High in Armonk, New York. There were roughly 10 African-American students in her school of roughly 600. Catherine and Earl's upbringing, education and opinions on how to integrate immigrant children and minorities differed dramatically and made for an intellectually stimulating debate.

While we ate the pasta and shrimp dish Catherine prepared, "Over 50 percent of Italian-Australian children don': speak Italian because of integration in the Australian school system," she said as we continued to discuss the merits of integrating immigrant and minority children.

Catherine, a fluent Italian speaker, was also a columnist for *Gold Coast Dante,* the local Italian-Australian Alighieri Society's newsletter. "They take up Italian when they go to university," she said. "They, like other immigrant communities here, become true Australians by being integrated early on. Do you realize that Japanese is the number one language taught here in Queensland, Chinese is number two, a European language number three and that the fastest-emerging language is Russian?" Catherine asked. I didn't. It makes perfect sense, with Japanese and Chinese being the highest number of non-English speaking tourists to Australia – with the Russians fast catching up – not just in Australia, but all over the world.

Catherine's father had received numerous awards during his tenure at IBM for championing the rights of handicapped and minorities. "Dad is compassionate and believes in supporting minorities, education, integration and progress. He doesn't believe in throwing good money after bad – he supported the Inuit and other indigenous people who he felt had been oppressed and abused by the white man – but not in the Pierre Trudeau welfare policies as the means. He believed people should be taught to take care of themselves, regardless of color or background," Catherine said as she paused and took another sip of her wine. "Yet when I dated an Irish Catholic, he'd say 'don't let him Jew you out of everything....'" Before she could continue, Earl interrupted and asked, "But isn't that a racist expression that contradicts everything you just said?"

Before Catherine could answer, Pauline, my Scottish Presbetyrian partner who was traveling with me during my Australian trip and was party to all the earlier discussions of racism and religious prejudice, jumped right in. "When I was growing up in Scotland, because of my upbringing, I wouldn't even think of going out with a Catholic. There was a local Catholic community, including Italian and Polish families after World War II. We were polite and respectful in public towards each other, but I would never consider going out with a Catholic, yet alone a Jew." Earl and I, two Jew boys from LA, just looked at each other and shrugged as we toasted our tolerant "shiksas."

Earl's experience at high school was not that different than the experiences of many high school students in America today. At Lafayette High in Brooklyn, New York, like many high schools across America, Chinese and other Asian students are repeatedly harassed and beaten by schoolmates because of their ethnicity and the fact that they get the better grades. The abuse is so pervasive that school officials agreed to a Department of Justice consent decree to curb alleged "severe and pervasive harassment directed at Asian-American students by their classmates."

The high-achieving Asian students rarely fight back because of their stature. Those who do fight back do so as members of a gang. A 2003 California survey by the Services and Advocacy for Asian Youth Consortium found that 14 percent of young Asians said they joined gangs for protection. Schools and ghettos in America, France, Australia and every other country with a multicultural society are a microcosm of the country. A society that fails to integrate its minority students and communities peacefully and harmoniously is breeding future malcontents and isolated criminal ethnic ghettos that can become the backbone of a failed state – no matter how strong the national boundaries. Ignorance and violence is self-perpetuating.

African-Americans, unlike the Lebanese immigrants in Australia, are descendants of slaves who were brought to America against their will. When freed, they were segregated and denied the educational and econonomic opportunities available to whites. The riots in Los Angeles, like the race riots across France, were brought on by economic deprivation caused by racism. The Cronulla riots, in contrast to the riots in the U.S. and France, were caused by the children of volunteer immigrants who chose to perpetuate and impose by force their cultural and religious practices in their host country in defiance of the local culture, we concluded after several bottles of great Aussie wine.

Interlocalism recognizes and respects the maintenance of a person's cultural background and heritage while respecting and accepting both his country of cultural origin or birth and country of residence. In all important aspects, it should be eroding. All ethnic groups, regardless of whether they are Anglo Celtics, African, Arab, Asian, European, Latino or Scandinavian – Atheist, Christian, Hindu, Jew, Muslim or any other religion – have the right and obligation to live in peace and harmony with their neighbors from different cultures and beliefs in the country they call home.

Listening to the Spirit and Sounds of Oz Summer on my nine hour flight back to Hong Kong on New Year's Eve 2006, I reflected on my conversations about Cronulla, surfing and education. While listening to Paul Kelly's Roll On Summer, Kid Confucius' Sunshine, Maxjudo's Sun Days, and the songs of Beautiful Girls, who take their surfboards when they go on tour, I dozed off thinking back to the days I went to L.A. in 1966, a year after the Watts riots, and got a job as a photographer for surf-movie producer Dale Davis, listened to Jan & Dean and the Beach Boys – deja vu. I respected America for what it is and was, a country that embraced me with open arms as an immigrant – in Detroit and New York the previous two years after I arrived in 1964 from Cyprus. What I heard in Australia confirmed and validated what I had experienced in America.

Back in Hong Kong, I decided to go to Zahra, my favorite Middle Eastern restaurant, owned and operated by Tarek El-Mahmoud, a Muslim Lebanese immigrant-chef extraordinaire, and his wife Vivienne. I hadn't been there in months, and after my trip to Australia talking and reading about Lebanese immigrants, I felt like having Middle Easten soul food and a conversation about racism with a Lebanese immigrant.

Tarek was born in Lebanon and most of his classmates from the elementary school class of 1965 immigrated to Australia. Tarek's family immigrated to Ghana. The Lebanese, much like the Chinese, and Indians, do business in the most implausbile places. "Darling, marry me and we'll escape to wealth and riches in Accra."

Tarek grew up in Ghana and both his parents are buried there. He met his wife at university in London where he studied computer science. Vivienne was born and raised in Hong Kong. Her parents were Christian Lebanese. Their three children were born in Ghana and immigrated to Hong Kong with their parents in the early '90s. Tarek and Vivienne opened Zhara in 1993 and told me when I walked in that they were going to retire and close the restaurant after they serve the last meal on January 31, 2006. I made a point of going back for a last memorable supper there.

"My daughter is a lawyer, my other son and daughter are grown up and doing well," Tarek said as he pointed them out at a nearby table. The El-Mahmoud family and friends had come to celebrate the closing. "Vivienne and I just want to take a break, rest, enjoy life and then decide if we want to reopen," Tarek told me. "Are you going to move back to Lebanon or Ghana?" I asked? "Absolutely not," Tarek responded without hesitation. "Hong Kong is our home. We have an expression in Arabic, which when translated into English roughly means, 'When you find the right place, you stick to it like glue.' Of course we'll travel and visit Lebanon and Ghana, but we will return. Our children are here, our home is here," he said as we toasted our children and home.

I told Tarek about my visit to Australia and asked what he thought of the Cronulla race riots. "Racist and stupid. Lebanese have been immigrating to Australia since the country was founded. There are Lebanese immigrant descendants there today that are more Australian than many European Australians. Look at my children. Their mother is Christian. I told them to believe in the God of their choice. It is about being good citizens and contributing to society, not picking or fighting over religion and ethnic background. Look at me. I am going back to visit my family and pay respect to my parents buried in Ghana," said Tarek and added, "I'm African," as we both laughed and clinked our glasses as he moved on to greet other guests.

Immigrants to any country must learn, understand and respect the local host culture, no matter how strange and different it is, and, believe me, every new country and culture is. Raising children today is no different than it was in the '70s and '80s when I raised Alexandra and Jonas in California. We were just as interlocal then as we are today. We just have to get back to basics.

It is time for parents of all cultural and religious backgrounds to take responsibility for the upbringing of their children in any society – especially in a country that is their adopted home. In addition, schools must integrate immigrant children of all cultural backgrounds and teach them, especially Muslim children, that the oppressive sexist treatment of women – one of the underlying causes of the race riots in Australia – is wrong and unacceptable.

Only parents and a functional multicultural education system and integrated communities can end racism in the 21st century. Parents must be responsible for the upbringing of their children, making families strong, children safe and eager to learn and to work and become responsible citizens.

The burn, baby, burn race riots in America, Britain, and more recently in France, are the result of irresponsible citizenship. Ten thousand cars were destroyed in France, along with more than 200 public buildings set ablaze in 2005. Property damage estimates are up to $330 million. There were more than 3,200 arrests and more than 400 rioters sent to prison.

We must distinguish true racism from criminal behavior by gangs and thugs. Criminal behavior cannot and must not be tolerated. It must be severely punished. Law enforcement and education are not mutually exclusive. They can and must go hand in hand in the 21st century.

One of the most remarkable features of unintegrated immigration in which lower-class Muslim economic migrants seem to specialize is that they flee a home country which is an economic failure for a foreign one which has more successful social and cultural systems, yet they insist on bringing with them, standing by and even propagating the habits and practices of their failing homeland and publicly pronouncing their moral superiority over that of their host state. It's not surprising that their mosques are burned from time to time.

The race riots in America, Australia, Britain and France brought into focus the global and interlocal scale of 21st-century religious and ethnic racism and growing divide and the violence it breeds. Yet racism continues rolling on into the 21st century. Whether it's in America, where popular radio talk show host Don Imus referred to Rutgers womens basketball team, the national champions, as "nappy-headed hos." That was not his first on-air racist or sexist remark, and probably not his last, if he remains unemployed.

The dismissal of the case against three Duke University lacrosse players for allegedly raping an African-American stripper on the heels of Imus' disparaging comments magnified and highlighted the highly combustable subject of race in America, especially on the eve of the 60th anniversary of baseball great Jackie Robinson breaking the color barrier in America's national pastime.

In France during their 2007 presidential election, farmers got more political attention – and subsidies – than the burning of North African Muslims ghettoes in its major cities. The embers of the last race riots a couple of years earlier were warming up and ready to reignite. Police are being ambushed in the Paris outskirts by young *banlieusards* alienated by racial discrimination, poor housing and a jobless rate that hits 40 percent in some hoods. "With Sarko winning the presidential election...people will be killed," they warned. An urban guerrilla war is continuing in the run-down neighborhoods that ring many of the nation's major cities, much like the U.S. ghettoes of the '60s. French government officials are forbidden to collect information about a citizen's ethnic or racial origins when conducting a census or other efforts to gather stastistical information on the population. One of the main reasons being that the painful and still vivid memories of the Vichy regime of World War II, when citizens' "racial" and religious origin was stamped on identification documents and used in rounding up French Jews for delivery to the death camps. Is it any wonder North African French Muslims are concerned and upset? Hey, they could wind up in concentration camps in a Catholic-dominated Christian Europe.

Things aren't much better in Great Britain, where the Asian community, which also lives in run-down ghettos, is reluctant to desegregate as it creates new divisions – not much different than Australia. Living parallel lives in any community by any two or more groups, be they ethnic, religious, cultural, sexual or political in any village, town, city, county or country, makes no sense in the 21st century. *We the Apathetic People* have to interact and communicate with each other at all levels. Schools have to be integrated and our children must be exposed to the real geopolitical world and taught to respect all cultures, races and religions.

The first step is to admit that racism is a reality. Assimilation and integration are the next step. To narrow the gap, parents, religious leaders and teachers of all colors, religious beliefs and cultures have to join hands and educate and show future generations by example the benefits of multiculturism. All people are equals. With love, patience, respect for others, education, rule of law and order, our children will grow up in a kinder, safer, more tolerant and harmonious multicultural world. How many more generations must *We the*

Apathetic People lose to gangs, prison or extreme religious and political ideologies before we wake up?

Interlocal Western City

New York, like Hong Kong has a diverse populace and is a model of harmonious interlocalism. Cities of bastards – in the nicest possible way. The residents of both cities are people from every country, past, present and future. They are hybrids who have been cross-pollinated culturally, religiously, sexually, morally and politically. Who to best represent the political extremes than two political lawyers: Rudy Giuliani and Hillary Rodham Clinton.

September 11 reminded the world how diverse yet united and collectively resilient New Yorkers were at the dawn of the 21st century. Thousands donated blood and clothes. They walked the streets, gathered in homes and public areas to share stories of resourcefulness, courage and generosity.

I first came to New York in October 1964, riding the wave of the British music invasion from Palestine, via Cyprus and Israel. I was on my way to Detroit, where I had a job in a machine shop waiting for me. I returned to New York in the spring of 1965 after a blizzard the likes of which Detroit had not seen since the previous century. Unfortunately, the circumstances of my return to New York were not of my choice. I was riding my motorcycle back from work on a cold, snowy and icy Michigan windswept day when a drunk new draftee on his way to Vietnam ran a red light and smashed into my bike, catapulting me over a few cars. Had it not been for the helmet I was wearing, I probably wouldn't be here today.

I lived in New York from the spring of 1965 until the summer of 1966. I first moved in with my half-sister on 83rd Street and Riverside Drive, where her new born twins delighted in throwing their milk bottles at the interlopper sleeping in their room. I was in a thigh-high cast as a result of the motorcycle accident. There was also a steel plate and a number of screws in my leg, trying to pull the whole thing together, which made for constant excruciating pain. The experts thought I should have skipped the procedure and opted to have the leg amputated but was an unacceptable option to me. Finally the leg had healed enough so that I could walk on my own with the aid of a cane, although I still wore a full-length leg brace. I then moved into a rooming house on 137th Street, between Riverside Drive and Broadway. The place also housed a couple of veterans, one having served in Vietnam and the other in Okinawa. We were a 10-minute walk to City College of New York, and that's where I began my university education.

Walking through Spanish-Harlem on the way to and from school, I sometimes stopped in at a pizza joint run by a Greek on the corner of 138th and Broadway, where we would converse about the home country, in this case, Greek-Cypriot Cyprus. It was a real interlocal eye-opener, especially when I would walk in with a friendly black or Latina classmate.

During that time, I also worked as a picture caption editor and photographer to support my pre-veterinary academic pursuits. But my academic path would change dramatically once I took the required political science and philosophy classes.

I have been returning to New York as often as possible ever since to see family, friends, attend political conventions and to take care of business - not to mention the pleasure of the theatre and watching holiday parades with my children.

New York has more students enrolled in every grade from kindergarden through graduate school, more who have not graduated from high school, and more with doctoral degrees than any other city in America. More New Yorkers live in jails, nursing homes, college dorms, mental wards and religious quarters – like convents – than in any other American city, according to the Census Bureau.

Whenever I can, I stay with family or friends – preferably girlfriends – rather than hotels. Because I am on the road that I love, most of the time staying in hotels is a resort of last choice.

Staying with friends Michael and Michal Yudin during the '90s at the United Nations cooperative at 49th and 1st Avenue, a place that once turned down Richard Nixon as an owner – and occasionally hanging out and rapping with Walter Cronkite, who lived there was a refreshing reminder of what America was and and can be again.

When I met a cosmetic company executive who lived in New York's legendary Ansonia building, at 74th and Broadway, I enjoyed spending as much time with her as I did in the building. The building occupies the entire city block between 73rd and 74th streets. Built as a residential hotel between 1899 and 1904, the Ansonia is one of the Upper West Side's oldest and most famous buildings. And like New York itself, it has gone through scores of incarnations.

The Ansonia looms like a palace, with towers on either side of alternating chimneys and water towers on the roof. Aging metal balconies, iron fretwork and dark-domed apartments poke out on all sides. The inside is no less impressive. The ornate black and white marble lobby has chandeliers and intricately molded high ceilings. A marble staircase curls up the full 17 stories with dizzying grandeur. When it was built, the area around it was little more than shantytowns and farmland. There was only one rival to it – the famed Dakota building on West 72nd and Central Park West, where John Lennon would live and die decades later. But the Dakota was a mere seven stories tall.

The Ansonia had the world's largest swimming pool in the basement. On the roof it had a "farm in the sky," complete with 500 chickens, six goats, ducks and "a small bear." It was once the height of glamour: socialites sipped champagne in its huge ballroom, seals frolicked in a lobby fountain and paparazzi staked out the entrance.

Boxer Jack Dempsey trained for the world heavyweight championship of 1919 there. Babe Ruth moved in after the Red Sox traded him to New York in 1919. And the deal that immortalized "Shoeless" Joe Jackson, the Chicago White Sox player who agreed to throw the 1919 World Series, was sealed in an Ansonia suite. Florenz Ziegfeld lived on the ninth floor in a 13-room suite. In the years leading up to the Roaring '20s, the building became a hotbed of intrigue. Gangsters died within its spacious suites. Spies mingled with deposed dictators planning comebacks – much like the opera stars, voice coaches and all kinds of classical and contemporary musicians trying to make it or hold onto what they had.

Later in the 1960s and '70s, the Ansonia's fortunes mirrored those of the city as a whole; the middle classes fled to the suburbs and left behind a falling tax base and a rising crime rate, which brought the city to the brink of financial ruin. The grand building fell into disrepair and the owner rented the basement out as a gay bathhouse, where Bette Midler and Barry Manilow kickstarted their careers, crooning to young men in towels. In the 1970s, the gays moved out and gold-chain wearing swingers moved in. They frolicked naked at a club called Plato's Retreat, which boasted a 50-person Jacuzzi and a mattress-lined orgy room.

Through it all, the building's connection to the opera world made it a beacon for creative types, enduring even through New York's most tumultuous years. Indeed, the ramshackle chaos of the bankrupt, crime-ridden metropolis fueled creative energy and nourished a certain bohemian pride within the "Palace of the Muses," as local wags christened it.

New York then, as now and always, is the most progressive mecca of interlocalism in the world. It is best represented in the post 9/11 world at the corner of 1st Avenue and 11th Street, where Veniero Pasticeria, which has been run by the same Italian-Catholic family since 1894, sits catty-corner across from the Madina Magid Islamic Council of America.

The East Village, which I remember as Bedford Stuyvesant, the crime-infested ghetto no photographer wanted to go into in the '60s, gave me my photographic break after I volunteered to cover an assignment there. Thank God it was knives and chains in those days and not the weapons of choice available today.

New York subway passengers are the most interlocal in the world. Bankers and lawyers in their pinstripe suits and tassled loafers standing next to gang-bangers in their gang colors and baseball caps worn sideways as homeless singers and panhandlers seek a handout. Watching rats scurry across the subway rails, listening to Chinese violinists playing classical European tunes, or African-Americans beating their rhythmic drums to the driving rhythm of the trains, I read the advertisements on the trains promoting English language classes between the ads promoting bankruptcy and immigration services. All I can say is this is interloclaism and America at its finest.

Interlocal Asian City
Hong Kong was created from scratch. Globalization and commercial

interaction fused the best of all civilizations in Hong Kong. The British historian Paul Johnson in his analysis of the past 1,000 years said that: "Human beings are fantastically ingenious creatures, and usually industrious too. Given reasonably stable and just government there is no limit to what they can achieve in time." Johnson goes on to cite Hong Kong as an example of how small places with virtually no resources have created stability and the good life for most of their citizens, by using their brains, and, not least, by devising minimalist systems of government that work. Hong Kong is a free port that encourages the free flow of money, information and talented people from all corners of the planet.

Since its reversion to Chinese rule on July 1, 1997, Hong Kong has developed the potential to become a model society for America to emulate. It blends the best of Anglo-American and Sino-Latino cultures that already are the cornerstones and foundations of today's Eastern and Western civilizations. It did not look likely, but Hong Kong has become the millennium's World Model.

America and Hong Kong have a common heritage. America, like Hong Kong, was fertilized and created by the same British colonial parent. Both are capitalist democracies with a solid foundation rooted in the Anglo-Saxon rule of law and religious freedom. Hong Kong journalists and democratic activists, like their counterparts in America, have been subtly and insidiously muffled by Beijing and Washington, D.C. Like America, Hong Kong faces serious economic and political challenges at the dawn of the 21st century. However, unlike America, Hong Kongers are questioning and challenging the government's economic policies, remedies and political proposals, something *We the Apathetic Maids* have forgotten.

Interlocal Fusion

I've used every opportunity I can to go back to New York from Hong Kong. Business, pleasure and just plain old staying in touch with what America and interlocalism is all about – especially in a post-9/11 globalized world. It's a city where the region's largest American Indian gathering in Brooklyn is not as incongruous as it might seem. The annual Gateway to Nations Powwow is celebrated there in the original homeland of the Canarsie Indians at Gateway National Recreation Area, in a metropolis that census takers estimate is home to more American Indians than any other city with a population of more than 100,000 in America. New York also has more Yiddish speakers and more who speak Spanish, Urdu, Arabic, Chinese, Japanese and English and more people that identify their heritage as Italian, German, Scottish, Nigerian or Swiss than any big U.S. city. It has more who claim Irish ancestry than any city in the world except Dublin. More people born in Pakistan, France, Greece, Israel, Lebanon, Ghana, New Zealand, the Dominican Republic and almost every other country except Cuba and Mexico, live in New York than in any other city in the America. There are 173 nationalities represented in New York.

Theodore Roosevelt, the U.S. president who made a name for himself fighting in Cuba, was born in a Victorian brownstone at 28 East 20th Street, between Broadway and Park Avenue South, in Gramercy Park. The National Historical Site is next door to a FedEx office and across the street from Italian, Japanese and Thai restaurants.

New York's interlocalism greets visitors the minute they land at one of the city's airports. They are the taxi drivers who arrive from Central Taxi Hold. There, Haitian drivers play dominos, Russians crowd around backgammon boards on trash bins, while Hispanics crouch between vehicles throwing dice. Religious Muslims kneel and pray towards Mecca. Card games and soccer are open to everyone.

The pen, as the taxi hold is called, is no different than many of the interlocal pubs, bars and restaurants in the city. Nevada Smiths, on 3rd Avenue between 11th and 12th is a typical interlocal hangout. Postal Service workers from nearby Cooper Station – Asian, African, Irish, Latino and other ethnic groupings – Americans betting, watching and cheering on the horses in each race at Belmont Park on the TV screen in the corner they dominate. The loser of each race buys the next round. Others prefer to watch Venus Williams play Sharapova at Wimbledon, while those of us at the bar watch Brazil play Argentina soccer while discussing third world debt relief. Many of the patrons, especially during Happy Hour, are students from nearby NYU and Cooper Union. Meanwhile, the Washington-Chicago baseball game on another TV screen was ignored.

Sharing interlocal travel experiences with Alex Berman, who lives in the East Village, after he returned from a European music tour in the fall of

2005 was a millennium reminder of how important cross-cultural interlocal travel is. Alex had been in Europe for a little more than 30 days and had traversed from Scandinavia, Slovenia, Germany, Italy and France, playing different cities just about every night. Playing at night, traveling by day. The stories and experiences were a refreshing millennium reminder of how dumb Europeans think Americans are.

"You know, it never ceased to amaze me how Italians don't think we know Italian food or the ingredients that go into the most basic foods," Alex said. He couldn't wait to share his experiences after I picked him up at JFK after his return. "Man, Europeans think we are stupid. The Italians weren't that bad. My God, the French are the worst," Alex screamed as he rolled down the car window and yelled out to the astonished looks of other drivers. "America is the best. Great to be back home," Alex said as he settled back into his seat. "Actually it's not America, it's New York City. I'm glad to be back home in New York, not America. Americans are just as dumb as the Europeans," Alex rambled. I realized he hadn't slept in 36 hours and was glad to be home. "Without a doubt, New York is the most progressive, together, avande garde, renaissance city in the world," he repeated for the umpteenth time as we pulled up to his apartment.

Hanging out in Alex's apartment in the East Village for a couple of days while he was on tour in Europe was a another reminder of how New York is indeed the world – Western and Asian – interlocal model. Breakfast coffee with a Muslim doctor, lunch with a homeless person in Tomlinson Park where we laugh about politics, dog owners and dogs. Congresswoman Nydia Velazquez's office is across from the park at the corner of 11th and Avenue B. It triggered the political discussion. Dinner with bankers at one of the many great ethnic restaurants in the neighborhood is always a delicious surprise. Regardless of the type of cuisine. I'm always amazed at how many of the chefs and kitchen staff are Cartonese speakers from Hong Kong. Cantonese and Mandarin, Spanish, Indian and many other foreign tongues – it all makes for good and interesting geopolitical conversation over a great meal.

Listening to country music in the Living Room, near the corner of Stanton and Ludlow in Soho, during the Honky Tonk Happy Hour, while New York's Gay Pride Parade was in full swing and the Reverend Billy Graham was giving his last sermon on his last Evangelical Tour in the summer of 2005, was just another 21st-century example of New York interlocal fusion the world can emulate.

The panhandlers in the village are younger than their more mature and experienced elders on 5th Avenue and other posh New York neighborhoods, but nonetheless, they are daily reminders of the poverty settling over America at the dawn of the 21st-century. Looking into the nail salons and spas that seem to have become a fixture on every other block, and are run by Vietnamese and Koreans catering to every ethnic interlocal group in New York, are snapshots of this progressive mecca of interlocalism.

City Cab Ride

What a contrast between most New York City cabbies and their Hong Kong brethren. New York cabbies who speak English with an accent that betrays their immigrant status and country of origin are more lost in New York than I am in Hong Kong, even when I'm in a cab being driven by a clueless illegal immigrant relative of the real cabbie license holder who only speaks Cantonese. No problem. Piece of cake in Hong Kong. Just call the trilingual dispatcher who gets on and becomes an instant interpreter and gets me there without a hassler. Unlike New York, where the cabbie, usually Muslim, gets in touch with his brother on the other end of the line and starts speaking in a foreign tongue, even arguing and disagreeing with the passengers, who actually know their way around New York better than the cabbie.

Devastating Earthquake and Bird Flu

While America was coming to terms with the devastation of Hurricane Katrina, an earthquake measuring 7.6 magnitude hit Kashmir, Pakistan and India in early October 2005. According to official estimates, it killed more than 50,000 people and left over a million people homeless." Don't believe what the news is saying. It is pure propaganda," said Mahmoud, a Pakistani cabbie in New York City in response to my question if he had lost any relatives in the quake. "I have family in Kashmir and no one has heard from them. My family and friends in Islamabad tell me more than a million people have died, but the government is afraid to say so because they were so ill prepared for what happened," Mahmoud said as he wiped a tears from his eyes. "No one will ever know the truth. Politicians are always lying. That is why I left. I am lucky to be here and not there. My family is from

Muzaffarabad, the capital of Pakistani Kashmir."

The quake victims were going without aid because the global emergency relief system is overstretched, needs better coordination and has less than half the funds needed, a U.N. official admitted. "I really admit ... that the system is overstretched and is not working as it should do," said U.N. emergency relief coordinator Jan Egeland. Why not? America sent generous aid to Pakistan, much to the chagrin of many Katrina victims – only to attack Pakistan with missiles fired from a Predator drone on a suspected gathering of al-Qaeda leaders a few months later, killing 18 people, including women and children.

Relief supply convoys were attacked and drivers beaten by cold and hungry survivors before they could reach remote villages high in the Himalayan mountain region. Frenzied crowds of men battled one another to clamber into relief trucks to grab boxes of bottled water, blankets and biscuits. "We only see things coming and going – we need food, we need water," said one man taking part in the melee on the main road from Muzaffarabad to the Indian sector of the disputed Himalayan region. The response to the disaster was slow and ineffective. "Officially there is aid but on the ground there is nothing," said Syed Abdul Wadood Shah, a Kashmiri villager.

The best early warning systems for an earthquake that has to be further developed are animals. In New Zealand, Maoris listen to the birds for an early warning of an earthquake. If birds don't chirp in the mornings for three days in a row, Maoris know an earthquake is on the way. A number of studies have shown that animals, dogs in particular, pick up on something that humans don't that warn them of an impending earthquake. It could be electromagnetic signal or perhaps even a sixth sense. Scientists have concluded it is more likely the high-frequency sounds that many dogs can hear that are emitted before an earthquake, perhaps from rocks scraping or breaking underground.

The idea is not so far-fetched. While America and Western society have been reluctant to use animals as earthquake predictors, China has embraced the idea. At the Nanning earthquake bureau in Guangxi autonomous region, experts use a video link to keep a 24-hour watch on snakes in farms across the country. If reptiles in any of the farms begin making desperate and concerted attempts to escape from their enclosure, the observers raise a warning. Animal quake prediction early warning systems are a cost-effective way of saving millions of lives and should be put in place in all earthquake prone zones.

Mahmoud dropped me off at the WOR radio station at 111 Broadway, near Trinity Church off Wall Street – a few blocks from Ground Zero. I was on a radio tour promoting my books and decided to ask my host, Bill Bertenshaw, why most of my interviews during the tour, including his, were being taped for broadcast at the end of the year or early 2006. "Bird flu," he replied without a moments hesitation.

"When the pandemic hits, later this year or next, America will be quarantined and we won't be able to have guests like you from overseas – especially from Hong Kong or Asia ." How absurd and impractical, I thought to myself. The virus is not transmittable from human to human. "Sounds like SARS all over again," I said as I reflected on the absurdity of how authorities had handled the SAR crisis and treated people such as myself from the epicenter – Hong Kong. It is right for governments to join forces and present a united front against a common enemy. But human quarantines? By mid January 2007, bird flu had killed more than half of the 200 affected in Asia and Turkey since late 2003.

Hong Kong is the safest place to be and be from when a global pandemic hits. It is the global nerve-center in identifying pandemic viruses. Hong Kong microbiologist Malik Peiris and his team first identified the deadly bird flu strain as H5N1 after the 1997 outbreak in Hong Kong and have been working ever since to identify its genetic make-up and find ways to fight the disease. In 2003 he led the team that first identified the virus behind SARS, which emerged in Guangdong province in late 2002 and went on to infect 800 people in more than two dozen countries.

Everyone, I met in America – including my ex-wife Gail, wanted me to get them Tamiflu. "It is easy right?" was not an uncommon question I had to address at least several times a week. "No, it is not easy to get in Hong Kong because the Tamiflu there is probably a pirated knock-off. There are some generics though. I'll check into it," was my usual response. The fact is, both Tamiflu and Relenza, the front line drugs, are only marginally effective, according to experts. Anyway, it was not available in any form in Hong Kong, even pirated. Generics were also hard to find. When I returned to Hong Kong, I shared the story and experience with Philip Bowring, a Hong Kong-based journalist and commentator, at the Foreign Correspondents Main Bar. "This dilemma is not new. Indeed, one of the first written discussions of it was penned by none other than one of Hong Kong's early colonial governors, John Bowring – a distant forebear," Philip said as we toasted the Year of the Dog.

John Bowring was no medical expert, but was a widely traveled man of great learning who had a keen understanding both of statistics and the process of government. In 1883, he delivered a paper to the British Association of Science, entitled Observations on the Oriental Plague and on Quarantines as a Means of Arresting it," Philip continued. 'It was the result of a lengthy visit to Turkey and Egypt. Plague epidemics occurred sporadically throughout the southern and eastern Mediterranean, and quarantines of whole cities – such as Alexandria in 1834 – were the usual official response. The 1834 epidemic killed some 200,000 people – or five percent of the population – in Egypt.

"Bowring quoted a Scottish doctor resident in Alexandria that quarantines were due to 'superstition and ignorance,'" Philip said."He concluded that plague was endemic, and epidemics were localized and closely associated with weather patterns. The disease could be spread by birds and animals, so quarantining humans was pointless," Philip concluded. Closing borders and quarantining people is definitely a quick political spin – not a fix – at least until H5N1 kills thousands globally.

A few weeks later, a dead oriental magpie robin with the H5N1 virus was found in Hong Kong. According to experts, the bird was infected by domestic poultry or migratory birds.

The January 2006 International Pledging Conference on Avian and Human Influenza, held in Beijing, pledged $1.9 billion to contain the virus. The money was spent to assist the nations affected with the virus to develop the capacity and infrastructure to fight bird flu. The conference was cosponsored by the Chinese government, the World Bank and the European Commission.

The fact is that avian flu is not being transmitted across borders by humans. It is carried by migrating birds and chickens. "Globalization has turned the chicken into the world's number one migratory bird species. Movements of chickens around the world take place 365 days a year, unlike the seasonal migration of birds," said Leon Bennum science director of Birdlife International, a wild bird conservation group.

Hong Kong's Mai Po Nature Reserve in the northwestern New Territories bordering Shenzhen, China, is a natural early-warning system for bird flu. It is probably one of the most beautiful natural bird reserves surrounded by polluting factories on earth. The best time to visit is early morning, as I have done, when all the migrating birds are fed with truckloads of fish that are dumped into abandoned fish farm ponds as the birds swoop in to scarf them up.

For the whole of 2006, 17 out of 10,000 birds collected and tested were infected with H5N1. That is a long way from being a major threat to humans

The ominous predictions by the World Health Organization about bird flu wiping out millions of people around the world was simply political spin to aid planning and preparedness. It was not an accurate forecast of the virus' threat, Imperial College London Department of Infectuous Diseases epidemiology professor Geoffrey Garnett said. "I think it's not necessarily going to be the H5N1 strain that will cause the next influenza pandemic," Garnett said. "There are other influenza strains out there causing infection in birds that could start to spread from human to human." His remarks were an attempt to calm down the looming fear and hysteria over the possibility of a bird flu pandemic.

Governments are ill-prepared for a global killer that could wipe out millions of people. "Only about 30 countries, mainly wealthy ones, have stockpiled or ordered antiviral medicines for treating bird flu victims. However, some of the drugs are being sent to epicenter countries like Indonesia, which cannot afford large stocks.

There are no vaccines that are effective against bird flu, although laboratories in the United States and other nations are racing to develop them," said Michael Richardson, a visiting senior research fellow at the Institute of South

East Asian Studies in Singapore.

Sounds like Katrina all over again – worldwide. Why? Is it the Year of the Rooster? Is this any way for *We the Apathetic Maids* to live in the 21st century?

America's Response

Wha: was the U.S. government response and advice to its citizens living in Hong Kong at the height of the bird flu scare? Think Katrina, but dumber. U.S. citizens like myself living in Hong Kong were warned to build an emergency three-month stockpile of food, water and medicine as part of a survival plan in case of a bird flu pandemic.

Do they have any idea the amount of space needed for such a cache of supplies? Twelve weeks of water, food, toilet paper, batteries and cooking fuel would take up around 40 cubic meters, a third of a normal-sized Hong Kong flat. Which means that any citizen deciding to follow the advice will need a larger apartment according to this official U.S. government notice. However, since the former Republican-dominated Congress drastically cut the tax break for overseas housing costs, that means U.S. citizens would have to pay for the move out of their own pocket.

The U.S. State Department sent advisory warning notices to its embassies and consulates warning about the impending flu season.

The loud and clear message was, don't count on us or you'll be like the victims of Katrina. In other words, Americans were on their own if they didn't comply. One thing Americans thought they could count on was the U.S. Navy to come to the rescue. Fuhgeddaboudit. The Israel-Lebanon War was a reminder. America was not a country its citizens could count on. While other countries sent ships and aircraft to rescue their citizens. America sent notices that its citizens had to find their own way out.

Let's Play Ball

The perfect visual metaphor of interlocalism was the parade New York threw for the Yankees when they won the 1999 World Series. There was Orlando "El Duque" Hernandez, who defected from Cuba, with his reunited family, sharing in the triumph and the joy expressed by the American Hispanic community with their white and black fellow New Yorkers. And this a game that only in the last half of the closing century of the millennium allowed African-Americans to play in the previously all-white major leagues. It was the Brooklyn Dodgers that broke the color barrier when they brought first baseman Jackie Robinson onto Ebbets Field in 1947.

A million people showed up in miserable weather to celebrate the Yankees winning of the last World Series of the millennium. Alex Thomas, a participant from Jamaica, Queens, said the parade represented a lot more than baseball. "When you have 50 different cultures in the city and everyone's thinking the same thing, it's very exciting."

New York City brings it all together. It has lived it since its birth. It has seen and experienced every nationality, culture, religion and color. You name an ethnic group and they've passed by the Statue of Liberty. The Big Apple is interlocal and interglobal to the core.

New York's interlocalism is representative of America. Texas, San Antonio Spurs, the National Basketball Association champions of 2007, are another example, with their mercurial French point guard, backed by a Slovenian point guard; their sometimes dazzling Argentine shooting guard and their MVP center from the Virgin Islands.

It should therefore have come as no surprise when New York Yankee Alex "A-Rod" Rodriguez decided to play for the United States team instead of the Dominican Republic in the 2006 World Baseball Classic. A-Rod was eligible to play for the U.S. team and the Dominican Republic because he was raised in the U.S but his parents are Dominican. "Following dialogue with caring friends and players, both Dominican and American, I reached the conclusion that if I played in the Classic, I would play for the United States and honor my American citizenship," Rodriguez said.

New York is a city of interlocal renewal. Its residents are being encouraged by students to get back to their cultural roots, the stoop. Sit on them, talk to the neighbors, watch children play on them. Stoop ball and the cultural and social interaction on the stoop is what made New York the interlocal city it is. Immigrants becoming millionaires and real estate tycoons, as the naked cowboy plays his guitar in Times Square with nothing on but his underpants, boots and hat even in the freezing temperatures – the city's third-most revered tourist attraction.

New Yorkers have a way of coming together, as 9/11 showed the world. How they can stay together, regardless of their ethnic or religious background, is represented by Colors, a restauarant put together and opened by some of the surviving immigrant staff of New York's Windows on the World restaurant that was perched on the top two floors of the north tower of the World Trade Center, to honor the memory of their co-workers who died that fateful day. Any wonder the New York Giants won the superbowl against the New England Patriots – at the last minute at the dawn of the lunar year of the Rat?

Inter-Cubano

Cuba's baseball team, the defending Olympic champions, are another millennium reminder of interlocalism. They are the world champions of a game from America – a country that does not recognize Cuba because of U.S. politics. Interlocalism is driven by human nature and cannot be suppressed forever by any politician or political philosophy. Time keeps getting shorter in the information age as people gain knowledge.

Oddly, the late Pope John Paul II was a strong advocate of interlocalism. So is Fidel Castro. The Pope's visit to Cuba in 1999 was a living testament. He was trying to unite his Catholic flock in Cuba, the only Catholic Latin American country where abortion is legal, with their brothers and sisters worldwide, while Castro tried to unite his Cuba with the overseas Cubans and Latinos, notably in Miami and the rest of the United States and former Roman Catholic Spanish Empire. Getting the U.S. to drop its trade embargo against Cuba would help bring Castro's dream of an interlocal Cuba closer to reality. American cities are pairing with Cuban cities – despite 40 years of hostility and the embargo. The clamor to join the U.S.-Cuba Sister Cities Association is an indication of how interlocalism is already in play – even between America and Cuba. "The plain fact, painful though it may be to face, is that after years of Castro's rule, the hard line against him has failed to get rid of him. It is time to shift the central focus of our policies from hurting Cuba's government to helping its people." Those are the words of President Richard Nixon, a staunch anti-communist who helped engineer and enforce the embargo.

One Country, Multiple Systems

The concept of one country, two systems, proposed by Deng Xiao Ping for China and Hong Kong, can be expanded to one country with three or more systems, depending on the country – it's political, ethnic, religious and linguistic makeup. In the case of China, it may be expanded to one country with four systems in order for it to fully integrate Taiwan and Tibet back into the arms of the motherland. Tibet is being integrated Chinese-style. There'll be no need for "integration" when it's finished.

China's new railway line from Beijing to Lhasa, Tibet, was inaugurated in the summer of 2006. It is the highest railway line in the world with parts above 5,000 meters in elevation. It has linked the remote plateau to the mainland and become the iron horse bringing Hun Chinese settlers from the mainland to the Tibetan plateau, as well as tourists. The Dalai Lama, Tibet's exiled spiritual leader, has recently argued that remaining part of the mainland is in the economic interest of Tibetans. He was just concerned that the integration of Chinese culture and capitalist values would erode Tibetan traditions.

The fact is the Chinese are the one's embracing everything Tibetan and absorbing it in the mainland. Not just its mysticism and religion, but everything from Lhasa beer, yak butter tea, barley wine and dried yak meat, as well as music and culture. Hopefully, Tibet and China can resolve the remaining few outstanding issues during the lifetime of the Dalai Lama.

The concept might even work in Nepal, where Maoist rebels are now part of the national government, and India, where Maoist rebels have gone on a raging insurrection. They pose a greater threat to India than the allegedly Pakistani-backed Kashmiri separatists. The rebels all swear by Mao Zedong, but are not backed by China. Initially, the Chinese government fanned the revolt to settle a score with India after the 1962 war, but quietly cut off support when relations with New Delhi were normalized in the 1980s. The Maoists promise land and social dignity, essential political ingredients in an agriculture-based economy. Farmers are also angry over the seizure of their land and paddy fields for the creation of factories and special economic zones.

Maoists are active in more than half of India's 29 states, with a "red corridor" from the country"s border with Nepal in the north to the deep south. Intelligence officials believe there are between 7,000 and 10,000 armed Maoist guerrillas. Their activities are funded to the tune of $10 million annually by their financial backers. Therefore it is no surprise that India is also a fertile recruiting ground for al-Qaeda. The failed 2007 terrorist attacks in London and Glasgow are being blamed on a group of Bangalore-bred doctors and aeronautical engineers. Political commentators and security experts in India blame Saudi Arabia's brand of Wahabi hardline Islam for leading Indian Muslims towards violence. They also attribute their apparent radicalization to domestic discrimination and virulent anti-Muslim campaigns by Hindu nationalist groups.

In 1994, Israeli police arrested a Palestinian student in Bangalore and recovered explosive devices. Israel cautioned New Delhi that southern India, particularly Bangalore, was attracting students who had the potential of becoming terrorists. Cairo also alerted the Indian authorities in the mid '90s that radical students denied admission to Arab universities were managing to get into Indian institutions without the government being aware of their extremist background. Indian Muslims are tempting assets for recruitment by al-Qaeda because they are not subjected to the intense surveillance members of the Pakistani diaspora are.

India has no grudge against China, but it is worried about the impact on India of Nepalese Maoists sharing power in an interim government in the Himalayan nation. After years of guerrilla warfare to replace the monarchy with a socialist republic, Maoists joined the cabinet in early 2007. Doubts remain about their commitment to democracy and human rights. Nepalese Maoists resent New Delhi's support for the monarchy and army so much so that they have branded India a "colonizer" and "imperial" power, along with the U.S.

The one-county, two-systems concept could also be applied to other countries. It is the ideal model for the two Koreas, which like China are one people and one nation divided by self-serving career politicians. Korea is a daily painful reminder of how personal politics that benefit the few in power is a destructive force that divides families, communities, resources and people. The tearful reunions of families separated by the Korean War are a bitter legacy.

In September 2002, North Korea decided to emulate China's prosperous economic zones, like Shenzen on the Hong Kong border. Here you have a form of terrorized, hermetically sealed insanity quite beyond focusing as we understand it. It is a regime that cannot be "brought to its knees" because it is already on them and quite enjoying it. North Korea tried to create a special administrative region at Sinuiju, on the China border, to be administered by a mainland Chinese businessman with Dutch citizenship. Unfortunately, Pyongyang was preoccupied with its nuclear program and failed to consult with China, which promptly had the new administrator arrested for tax evasion.

The Friendship Bridge connecting China and North Korea over the Yalu River does offer businessmen and government intermediary deal-makers opportunities. Instead of looking north to China, North Korea should focus its efforts and energy on the south and adopt the one country, two-systems model. Hopefully, the appointment of Julie Sa, former Fullerton, California mayor, to run the huge free trade zone will revive the interlocal dialogue.

Sa was born of Chinese parents in Pusan, South Korea, where she studied international politics before moving to California. She was first invited to North Korea in 1993 and is well qualified to interlocalize the diverse Sino-Korean communities. Kim Jong-il's January 2006 visit to Shenzen, to see first-hand the benefits of special economic regions, bodes well for North Korea's interlocalization – notwithstanding America's bellicose empty threats.

U.S. Ambassador Alexander Vershbow and other ambassadors to South Korea, based in Seoul, who visited the Kaesong joint North-South Korean free zone project, see it as a flagship for inter-Korean interlocalism. "Cooperation" was the actual word used by the diplomat.

Taiwan

Taiwan's polemic dialogue advocating independence or a confederation between China and Taiwan is a nonstarter. The 1992 Hong Kong Consensus – the tacit agreement reached by the mainland and Taiwan in Hong Kong – got both parties to agree that there is only one China. Taiwan's Kuomintang party now has an office in Beijing to service the needs of Taiwanese investors on the mainland. Direct flights between China and Taiwan – via Hong

Kong airspace – is again a reality starting in the Year of the Rooster, 2005, after being suspended in 1949. Direct shipping started in early 2008.

Taiwanese military ships and aircraft were allowed into Chinese waters and airspace in 2002 to search for victims of the Taiwanese China Airlines plane that crashed as it headed for Hong Kong. Two mainland vessels helped in the search for bodies carried into their territorial waters by strong currents. As the two former rivals get closer and interlocalize, there is a story that Mao Zedong once admitted that he made a mistake in proclaiming the establishment of the People's Republic of China in 1949. "If I had only kept the name Republic of China," he is said to have lamented, "the Taiwan problem would not have existed." It certainly would be easier to invade under the theory of "renegade province."

In July 2005, China exempted from tariffs 15 types of fruit from Taiwan to encourage Taiwanese farmers to export their produce to China. The top official in charge of the 2008 Olympics has expressed a wish for Taiwan, along with Hong Kong and Macau, to be included in the torch relay – and it is.

The election of Taipei Mayor Ma Ying-jeou as chairman of the Kuomintang party in 2005 ensured his party's 2008 presidential candidacy and likely winner of the election, notwithstanding his trial for misappropriating party funds. He was embraced by the Beltway and Congress on his 10-day visit in March 2006, where he secured his unchallenged status as the U.S.'s preferred choice as the island's next leader. Ma has touched on three themes that will define his China policy: accommodating the mainland; ending self-imposed isolation from China, and waiting for conditions that would make unification palatable to the Taiwanese. Ma has vowed that if his party comes to power in 2008, he will seek a peace deal with the mainland. He has repeatedly come out against military arms purchases from the U.S. He believes the purchases are unnecessary in principle but recognizes that China does not pose a military threat unless provoked by Taiwan declaring independence.

Ma, like his counterparts in China, knows that Hong Kong is proof that the one-country, two-systems works. With the passing of the 10-year anniversary of the July 1, 1997 handover, Hong Kong has proven the implementation of one-country, two-systems has been a major success. Today Hong

Kong is economically stronger and politically more open and vocal with free, uncensored press that covers all political views, regardless of whether they support Beijing or not. Capitalism and socialism have fused harmoniously and the principle of "high autonomy of Hong Kong people governing Hong Kong" has been successfully implemented. Hongkongers do enjoy wider democracy today than during the colonial period. Hong Kong's economy on the 10-year anniversary of the handover was its best in 20 years, enjoying high growth and low inflation for three consecutive years leading up to that anniversary.

Hong Kong has witnessed an average year-on-year growth of 4 percent for the 10 years since the handover, and also 7.6 percent for the past three years, following the recession after the Asian financial crisis. It also remained the freest economy for the 13 years leading up to the handover anniversary celebrations, and the unemployment rate has remained at a low 3 percent.

During the past 20 years, Hong Kong has been the largest source of overseas investment in the Chinese mainland. Capital from Hong Kong or from foreign countries via Hong Kong accounted for 41 percent of the mainland's total. It is the safest business center in the world with world class universities that share their research worldwide. Hong Kong is the world class standard of a harmonious, functional city.

That is why the "referendum" periodically promoted by Taiwan leader Chen Shui-bian over whether the island should join the U.N. under the name "Taiwan" is a non-starter. The Taiwanese won't vote for de jure independence and the U.N. won't accept Taiwan as a sovereign nation. Is it any wonder China treats Taiwan as hazardous waste?

What does the U.S. do in this situation? It turns up the heat on Taipei by allowing high government contacts that push Taiwan to buy the $10-billion arms package the U.S wants to sell it. Naturally, activists protest, China objects and says trying to lift the ban on high-level U.S. contacts with Taiwan is a "serious violation" of the basis of Sino-American relations, and America looks dumb – but yet again in a place it shouldn't be in the first place. The meeting between Ma's predecessor Lien Chan and Chinese president Hu Jintao in Beijing in 2005 ended the Chinese civil war.

The reality that *We the Apathetic Maids* must come to terms with is that Taiwan is a convenient U.S. military base in China's backyard. The U.S. military-industrial complex's insistence on continued arms sales to Taiwan is nothing short of installing U.S. military hardware on the base – and have someone else pay for it.

The mass resignation in January 2006 of 34 Taiwan cabinet members led by premier Frank Hsieh, over President Chen Shui-bian's hardline New Year's speech about his future policy toward China. was a clear signal that Taiwan does not want to provoke China. Chen's decision to scrap the island's National Unification Council on February 27, 2006 resulted in a mass rally in opposition to his decision and a motion in the legislature to unseat Chen.

Chen's decision was a brazen breach and betrayal of his own so-called "five nos." He delivered his famous five nos after his presidential election wins in 2000 and 2004, committing himself not to declare independence, not change Taiwan's national title, not hold a referendum or institute a new constitution specifying Taiwan's statehood, and not to scrap the Unification Council. Although Chen may want to go down in history as the leader of Taiwan's independence movement, he has certainly caused America to question his credibility and the wisdom of its continued military support.

He has defiantly refused to step down amid a scandal that finds his wife, Wu Shu-chen, being prosecuted for alleged financial corruption. Chen himself is suspected of involvement in the scheme, but he enjoys immunity from prosecution as the sitting president. He could well face prosecution when he leaves office. Adding to the scandal, his son-in-law, Chao Chien-ming, has been charged with insider trading in a high-profile case involving the Taiwan Development Corp. Meanwhile, his daughter and son-in-law were also accussed of using government funds to pay their household maids. And in an embarrassing turn of events, his son Chen Chih-chung and his pregnant wife Huang Jui-ching were forced to scrap plans to have their baby born in the United States because it conflicted with a vow made by President Chen that he would never be the grandfather of an American. The political fallout forced the couple to return home and have their interlocal child born in Taiwan.

The political fallout stands as an astounding testimonial to the vagaracies of democracy. A truly independent prosecutor's office, backed by legislators like the KMT's Chiu Yi, who is determined to expose and prosecute corrupt elected officials and civil servants if he can dig up enough dirt to stand up in court. That includes the president and members of his family. Hundreds of thousands of people have taken to the streets around the presidential palace in Taipei to demand that Chen resign. But he has refused, knowing that the split makeup of Taiwan's 221-seat legislature makes it impossible for the opposition to muster the votes necessary to remove him through a recall or impeachment.

While the political circus raged over the pros and cons of removing Chen from office, the president took off in September 2006 on a tour of South Pacific Island allies to shore up diplomatic support for Taiwan from switching their loyalties to mainland China. He used three different airplanes for his visits to Palau, Nauru and Guam. He attended a summit in Palau with the leaders of six South Pacific allies, including Palau, Nauru, the Solomon Islands, Marshall Islands, Tuvalu and Kiribati – all great diving and fishing areas where Taiwanese and Indonesian fishermen are repeatedly arrested for poaching.

When Chen returned to Taiwan, he arrived in fighting mode. On the eve of the 60th anniversary of the so-called 228 Incident, he assailed Chiang Kai-shek and his Kuomintang Party for violating the human rights of native Taiwanese. That massacre took place on February 28, 1947, when Taiwanese police pistol-whipped an elderly Taiwanese woman for selling contraband cigarettes outside the Taipei train station. The episode set off rioting throughout Taiwan, which Kuomintang security forces brutally suppressed, at the cost of thousands of civilian lives. Chen went on national television to accuse the Kuomintang Party of failing to accept responsibility for the incident. His vicious attacks on Chinag Kai-shek resulted in people removing statues of the late Nationalist leader from public parks and buildings. The ones that remained were defaced. Tourists from the mainland now appear to be the only ones interested in visiting the discarded busts and statutues of Chiang in a quiet hillside park in northern Taiwan.

Chen's brazen and arrogant decisions, and his stone-walling in the face of corruption allegations against members of his family, are in the tradition of Chinag Kai-shek, who he now vilifies as he fights for his political survival.

It's a lesson in political brinkmanship. And, as if he didn't have enough on his plate at home, he decides to goad China again by calling for Taiwan independence and holding military exercises to practice against a large-scale invasion. Chen's ruling Democratic Progressive Party, in the midst of all this scandal, fared better in the local elections than expected. It proved that Chen is better at scamming the vote and the public than he is at scamming his fellow politicians in the legislature.

During my stay in Shanghai in the early '90s, I had the privilege of sharing several quiet dinners with Wang Daohan, the former mayor of Shanghai and the head of the Association for Relations Across the Taiwan Strait, who negotiated the 1992 Hong Kong Consensus. "The promotion of peaceful economic development and stability between us and our brothers and sisters in Taiwan is how we will become reunited," Wang said in response to my question about the possibility of China invading Taiwan. "There is no need for a military conflict, unless of course Taiwan declares independence," he continued as we toasted the peaceful reunification of Taiwan.

Unification is only a matter of time. In the meantime, as the mainland and Taiwan interlocalize, U.S. concerns that China will attack Taiwan are pure political spin to justify U.S. arms sales to Taiwan while stopping the Europeans from selling arms to China. All America is doing is marginalizing itself in the region. The U.S. should reverse course and promote and expedite unity by withdrawing military sales and support from Taiwan. By promoting unification, America can maintain its presence in the region and be a major participant in the multilateral regional cooperation to maintain peace, stability and prosperity.

Only a handful of countries in the world recognize Taiwan, and the number decreases annually. They are a handful of small and poor countries in Africa, the Pacific and Latin America. Taiwan buys this recognition. The Vatican is Taiwan's only European ally. To make matters even more dysfunctional, Taiwan dropped Mongolia from its map even though its constitution still claims Mongolia as part of the Republic of China. Unlike Beijing, which recognizes Mongolia's independence, Taiwan claims to be the government of all China and continues to claim Mongolia as part of the Republic of China. Beijing is recognized by more than 160 countries.

Throughout most of its history, Taiwan, which means "terraced bay" in Chinese, was inhabited by different ethnic aborigines and was not considered Chinese. Some Chinese settled there about the year 500. In 1517, the Portuguese christened the island "Ilha Formosa" – beautiful island. It was only in the 1600s that Taiwan attracted interest as a settlement by the Chinese and Europeans. The Portuguese were followed by the Dutch, Spanish and then again the Dutch. In 1623, Dutch traders asked China for a trading post on the coast, similar to the Portugese post in Macau.

The Chinese gave them Taiwan. Forty years later, during the civil war in China, a half-Japanese general named Koxinga, like Chiang Kai-shek later, fled there and he ridded the island of the Dutch. His family ruled until 1683, when mainland armies invaded and took over. It was treated as a distant Chinese colony for the next 200 years. Only in 1887 did China upgrade Taiwan into a full province. Eight years later, in 1895, it was taken over by the Japanese. After World War II, the Allies decided Taiwan belonged to China.

Few people expect reunification in the near future. But as Foreign Correspondent Club regular Frank Ching, a columnist for the *South China Morning Post,* points out: "By talking to each other, they are leaving the door open. The only alternative to a dialogue is the virtual certainty of war some time in the future." Taiwan's idea that its ties with the mainland should be "state to state" is a bad joke. It is a province of the mainland. They are not Siamese twins. China ceded Taiwan to Japan in the 1895 Treaty of Shimonoseki and the island was returned to Chinese sovereignty under terms of the 1945 Cairo Declaration. The fact that America helped create democracy in Taiwan does not entitle Taiwan to become an independent country – or America going to its defense if it does and China were to attack. America has been put on notice by Chinese Army Maj. Gen. Zhu Chenghou that China "would not hesitate to use nuclear weapons against the United States" if it came to the defense of Taiwan.

If Mao and Chiang Kai-shek could shake hands and toast Japan's defeat in the Chung King Foreign Correspondents Club in 1946 – and after the treachery they exchanged during the battle against the Japanese, – so can today's mainland and Taiwan leaders. They can toast their reunification and unified political, economic and military dominance over Japan in the New World

Order as they share a Nobel Peace Prize.

The first Taiwanese planes to land on the mainland since 1949 did so in 2003 with stopovers in Hong Kong and Macau to bring home for the lunar New Year holiday some of the 500,000 Taiwanese working on the mainland. Taiwanese firms are believed to have invested more than $100 billion in China since the late 1980s. Taiwanese citizens now make about 3 million trips a year to the mainland. Nonstop flights were started during the 2006 lunar New Year. The planes had to fly over Hong Kong or Macau airspace. Regular direct nonstop air links will become a reality as a prelude to reunification. Again, it is just a matter of time since cruise ships already have.

The one-country, two-system model China has effectively implemented in Hong Kong could, with some modifications, work in Korea, Cyprus, Sri Lanka, Indonesia, Saudi Arabia and many other countries – as well as disputed territories like Kashmir – in need of political harmony in the 21st century.

Kashmir is the highest and best political laboratory to test interlocalism. It borders China-India-Pakistan, countries with different religions and cultures, clashing with each other on the high mountain ridges around the Himalayas, yet ready for an end to political and military hostilities. Indian and Pakistani troops have faced off across the cease-fire line in Kashmir since it was created in 1948. Kashmiris deeply distrust Indians, who have been battling a separatist insurgency in the territory since 1989. More than 68,000 people have been killed in the conflict. The removal of the Line of Control, with a demilitarized zone, under the joint management of India and Pakistan, would help develop a roadmap to sovereignty. Peace in Kashmir will facilitate an interlocal economic merger that will deter future violence.

A peculiarly painful example of interlocalism is Northern Ireland, because it is a textbook example of what can go right and wrong. Two communities split over religion and national loyalties sit side by side in a small territory. For decades the news has been bad. Even now there is little love lost, but in the last year of the 20th century, interlocalism – albeit in a stop-start fashion – became the overpowering common sense model behind a shared community that edged the two groups together under the 1998 Good Friday Agreement that largely ended 30 years of violence between majority Protestants committed to ties with Britain and a Catholic minority in favor of a united Ireland.

Recent visitors to Northern Ireland say the reduction in violence doesn't seem to come from any lessening of hate, but rather from pure exhaustion, which is a legitimate cause for cessation. It's a tribute to former British Prime Minister Tony Blair, who recognized the exhaustion and seized the opportunity to add to his legacy.

Sinn Fein's vote to endorse and support the policing and justice system in Northern Ireland forced the Protestant Unionist's hand, which Ian Paisley graciously extended to Gerry Adams, his Catholic counterpart. Paisley honed his skills as a preacher and orator, denouncing Catholism as "popery" and "superstition."

The Good Friday accord's underlying premise is that the corruptive forces of power can be used for the common good. The lust for political office has pushed the two arch-enemies to overcome or at least ignore their sectarian divide and work together in a power-sharing deal that is in the best interests of the people of Northern Ireland. A political truism that Spanish Prime Minister Jose Luis Rodriguez Zapatero fails to grasp in his dealings with the Basque separatist group ETA.

The ETA is Western Europe's most active separatist group, seeking independence for territory in both northern Spain and southwest France. It declared a permanent cease-fire and gave up for a while its desire to create a Basque country, and will settle for an interlocal self-governed province. The three provinces that form the Basque Autonomous Community along the Bay of Biscay are already the most prosperous region in Spain.

ETA declared in June 2007 that it is returning to "war on all fronts" after it failed to reach a peace agreement with Spain. The rhetoric between both sides is widening the divide instead of attempting to narrow it. "It's over, and that's it," Spain's defense minister, Jose Antonio Alonso, declared. As soon as ETA made its announcement, the Spanish courts moved to enforce highly controversial prison sentences against Arnaldo Otegi, the leader of the group's banned political front, *Batasuna,* and against a veteran ETA killer.

When Prime Minister Zapatero made the offer of peace talks to ETA in May 2005, he insisted that the group must permanently abandon its violent strategy in pursuit of Basque independence. ETA agreed, but unfortunately for the Spaniards and Basques, Zapatero did not have bipartisan support in parliament for his peace offer. It was renounced by the opposition as a "betrayal of the dead."

Unlike Sinn Fein *Batasuna* lacks any authority over its armed military wings. But if ETA returns to violence, its voters are likely to continue migrating to legal and nonviolent pro-independence interlocal groups. The divide can be narrowed and bridged if ETA immediately abandons violence, and if Zapatero brings ETA prisoners closer to home to make it easy for relatives to visit. Bold but necessary first steps.

Interlocalism can definitely work in Indonesia. Separatist sentiments are strong in East Timor, which became independent, as well as the provinces of Aceh, in Sumatra's northern tip where rebel leaders were elected to govern in the flowering democracy in a fiercely Muslim province in the country with the largest Muslim population in the world. In Iriana Jaya, the talk of secession that was so widely reported has also spread to Riau, Kalimantan, Ambon and even Bali. The Indonesian archipelago of 18,000 islands has more than 200 million people, the world's fourth-most-populous country. The world's largest Muslim population, 200 languages and 300 ethnic groups. No wonder many an Indonesian asks, "What does it mean to be Indonesian?"

After three centuries of Dutch colonial rule and three years of Japanese occupation, the world's largest archipelago had been declared one nation on August 17, 1945, although it was another four years before the Dutch abandoned their attempts to retake their former possession and recognized Indonesian independence. Sukarno, Indonesia's first president, who ruled the country for 20 years, had a vision of a united and secular country speaking one language, an ideal first adopted at a meeting of young nationalists in 1928 during Dutch rule.

The very viability of Indonesia as an economic and political entity is now being challenged across the vast country. The country has unravelled, socially, as well as economically and politically. Maybe it never was a country, just old-fashioned empire building that resulted in a Javanese colonial structure. Interlocalism is the only way the country can stay together as a viable political entity.

A joke about Indonesia applies to America and the New World Disorder. Indonesia's first president, Sukarno, represented the old order; the next president, Suharto, named his government the new order; post-crisis President Jusuf Habibie's government had no order; and President Abdurrahman Wahid's government was out of order. Americans can substitute their own presidents in any order in the dysfunctional disorder of 21st -century America.

Interaction

Tibetans, Mongolians, Taiwanese and Shanghainese have as much in common in interlocalizing China as the Scots, Irish, Welsh and English do in Britain and the Native Americans, African-Americans, Southerners, Yankees, Latinos and Californians do in the U.S. They are their own distinct indigenous, cultural and religious groupings within today's definitions of "state" and "country."

The overseas Americans, Chinese, Israelis, Arabs, Scots, Indians, Latinos, Italians, Irish, Albanians, Jews, Christians and Muslims exemplify interlocalism today and how it will expand in the 21st century. They interact with each other no matter what corner of the world they are in. The most graphic recent example was the 1998 front page picture of Albanian-American volunteers gathered in a parking lot in Yonkers, New York dressed in fatigues with the insignia of the Kosovo Liberation Army, ready to go fight the Serbs in Kosovo. It was followed by a picture of three brothers killed there and returned home to America for burial. At the same time, American Serbs were protesting in support of their brethren in Yugoslavia and against NATO bombing. Cambodian-Americans registered the Cambodian Freedom Fighters in California and Thailand in the '90s to overthrow the Cambodian government. They attacked the Cambodian Ministry of Defense with rocket launchers, grenades and assault rifles, killing eight and wounding many others.

It is an American tradition that dates back to the English Civil War of 1640-1650 when New Englanders from Massachusetts, New York and Connecticut went back to England to fight on the side of the Parliamentarians. The

English Civil War started after King Charles Stuart dissolved parliament and was determined – together with the Orthodox Anglican Church – to do away with the parliamentary system of government. The bloody Puritan Revolution of the English Civil War accelerated the growth of the American colonies when Puritans fled the conflict by the shiploads.

The victorious Parliamentarians executed Charles Stuart in 1649, determined to get rid of the monarchy. The English Civil War became the model for the American breakaway from Britain and the Founding Fathers' determination to form a republic without a king or a church.

Interlocalism acknowledges that the national unit, the country, like the family unit, shall be true to its origins, heritage and evolution and retain its cultural identity. Whether American, Chinese, Christian, Jewish or Muslim. Smiths, McGregors, O'Malleys, Chens Cohens and Mohammads have their own ethnic and religious identity, but each retains their individuality and local grouping identity. One family can have several members living throughout the world. The same holds true for a country It can have many communities that identify with it, no matter where they are located in the world. How Israel, Scotland and China interact with the global Jewish, Scottish and Chinese diaspora are good examples.

The best is Americans throughout the world who aspire to live the ideals advocated by the Founding Fathers. Then there are the Turks throughout central Asia, the Kurds in Turkey, northern Iraq and Iran. Shiites in Iran and Iraq. Azerbaijanis in Iran with their cousins to the north. Mexicans and their cousins to the north. The 21st-century possibilities of interlocalism are so numerous that they can be the glue that connects communities that have been fighting each other for historical or religious reasons.

Britain and Ireland are a good example. They have agreed to restructure, localize and interact at the dawn of the new millennium. Their agreement would provide for an "intergovernmental council" of representatives from the two governments. Seeing pictures of Northern Ireland's Protestant and Catholic leaders, arch-foes during decades of bloodshed, launching an interlocal power-sharing government in the British province aimed at putting a final end to violence is an example for the world.

Hardline Protestant cleric Ian Paisley and Sinn Fein's Martin McGuiness took a pledge of office as first minister and deputy first minister in the government that will have authority over local issues. Paisley's Democratic Unionists took five cabinet positions and Sinn Fein four, while the moderate Protestants of the Ulster Unionists received two and the moderate Catholics of the Social Democratic and Labour Party one.

The exceptionally concilliatory speeches by Paisley and McGuiness, as well as the British and Irish prime ministers, Tony Blair and Bertie Ahern, whose close cooperation since 1997 has underpinned the entire process – is something to be emulated by other religious combatants around the world today. Paisley, who leads his own fire-and-brimstone church, quoted King Solomon's teachings that all societies "face a time to kill and a time to heal, a time for war and a time for peace," words the fighting mullahs around the world should integrate into Muhammads peaceful teachings.

"I believe Northern Ireland has come to a time of peace, a time when hate will no longer rule," Paisley said. "How good it will be to be part of a wonderful healing in the province."

McGuiness said they had "astounded the sceptics" and gestured to his new government partner, Paisley. "I want to wish you the best as we step forward into the greatest and most exciting challenge of our lives," he said. Isn't this the ideal model for Palestine's Hamas and Fatah, Iraq's Shiites, Sunnis and Kurds, Kashmir's Muslims and Hindus and Africa and Asia's tribal rivals?

The Northern Ireland Assembly's construction has symbolized the pain in bringing Protestants and Catholics together in a chamber. The plan is to take back local government functions that the London government took over in 1974 at the height of "The Troubles." Since 1921, Ulster had always had its own parliament. The trouble was that only one segment of the community participated. The resounding 1999 71 percent "yes" vote for peace in Ireland brought home local rule by a vote of the people. That did not please the Protestant minority, which had been running things until the votes were cast. They then resorted to violence because "the only way to be heard is the way the Catholics do it – with violence," said David Hamilton, whose neighborhood in East Belfast was trashed by Protestant rioters in 2005.

The Protestants, Catholics nationalists and unionists of Northern Ireland joined forces in sorrow – and weeping together – united in grief at the end of 2005, when they said goodbye to soccer legend George Best. His coffin was taken from the family home in east Belfast, where he grew up, through the city's streets for the tens of thousands of mourners of all faiths to say farewell to Britain's greatest footballer. In a way, Best is a neat if discouraging summary of Northern Ireland's persistence in self-destruction. An alcoholic incapable of recovery, he developed sclerosis of the liver, received a liver transplant and then resumed drinking and died, wasting a perfectly good liver transplant. He was both lamented and excoriated.

The Islamist London train station terror bombings of July 2005 also united all peace-loving Britons – of all religions – against fundamentalist extremists. The Jewish mothers, Muslim men, West Indian teenagers, South Asian businessmen all interlocalize harmoniously in a multicultural British society. I was in Santa Fe, New Mexico, at the time visiting my friend Joe Hempfling, a born and bred New Yorker, and his partner Leslie Wolfman, an English lady. They had just visited London the previous month. "The English, all Britons for that matter, are a very tolerant and accepting bunch," Joe told me. "We were staying in a hotel where a lot of Brazilians who live and work in England live and congregate," Joe continued after I questioned him about the possible racist bias involved in the killing of Jean Charles de Menezes, the Brazilian illegal immigrant mistakenly killed by British police who believed he was involved with the bombings.

"No way, Jose. The Brazilians we met were the loveliest, gentlest and friendliest people I ever met. They always had a smile, a hello, or a joke. Everyone loved them, all the English people," said Joe as we concluded that the killing was a tragic case of mistaken identity.

The March 11, 2004, Madrid train bombing – carried out by Moroccans – had an unexpected benefit. It brought Spain and Morocco, which are separated by a 14.5km strip of water but centuries of political and military confrontations, closer together. There are two dusty, centuries-old Spanish enclaves perched on Morocco's coast. In the summer of 2002, the ill-will nearly boiled into a military clash over a rocky inlet inhabited only by goats. But with six Moroccans charged with the mass killings in the Madrid attacks, both countries have been working closely to investigate the alleged Islamic terror cells based in Tangiers. Interlocalism is sweeping across many isles and continents. Shouldn't it be examined in America?

Integration

People who want to integrate, regardless of their historic religious differences, have the power to do so. In America, and every country for that matter, people have the power to belong to different groups while allowing them to interlocalize with their respective communities elsewhere. No different than the Chinese, Scots, Turks, Kurds, Kiwis, Shiites and Sunnis.

Frederick Douglass objected to black Americans forming a nationality distinct from the larger American community. "A nation within a nation is an anomaly. There can be but one American nation under the American government, and we are Americans.... Our policy should be to unite with the great mass of the American people in all their activities, and resolve to fall or flourish with our common country." That does not preclude African-Americans from interlocalizing with other Africans, wherever or whatever they may be. Louis Farrakhan, the leader of the Nation of Islam does so. He is calling for a "Muslim superpower," although he is hardly a model of restraint, integration or interrelationship.

El Pueblo de Nuestra Senora la Reina de Los Angeles del Rio de Porciucula, better known as Los Angeles, and the questions raised and debated on the question of the secession of the San Fernando valley brought all the benefits of interlocalism, one-country, two-systems, to the forefront. Anglo versus Anglo and Latino versus Latino replaced the traditional conflict of Anglos versus Latinos.

The new Our Lady of the Angeles cathedral in Los Angeles is a representative visual metaphor. The area's 4.5 million Catholics, long-time Angelinos, new immigrants – legal and illegal – are representative of all corners of our interlocal world. A courtyard fountain is engraved with the words for "living water" in the 38 languages in which Mass is said in the L.A. archdiocese each Sunday. One country, two systems can be replaced with "one county, two or more cities," or "one city, two or more systems." Israeli-American Haim Saban leads a group that buys Univision Communications Inc., the largest U.S. Spanish-language broadcaster for about $12 billion.

The 2005 election of Antonio Villaraigosa to the mayor's office in Los Angeles, the first Hispanic mayor since 1872 when the city was merely a dusty outpost of about 5,000 people, confirmed the rising political power of Latinos in the second-largest U.S. city.

To paraphrase Hector Tobar's *Translation Nation: Defining a New American Identity in the Spanish-Speaking United States,* America has become a black-bean nation. "All across this country," Tobar writes, "people without a radical thought in their bodies are beginning to embrace ... that idea Che Guevara staked his life on in the last century: they believe they have a transnational identity, that their bodies and souls can live between two countries, that the physical border need not exist in the mind." I can totally relate. When in Los Angeles, I am reminded of this truism every morning when I take my stroll to get the morning newspapers and coffee fix. Anglos having burritos and coffee with Latinos off a "roach coach" – a food truck – and Latinos having bagels and cream cheese with Anglos in the coffee shop. No different than Hong Kong, where Chinese eat English breakfasts and Expats eat congee.

Meanwhile, nearby Beverly Hills swears in Jimmy Delshad, an Iranian-born mayor, in March 2007.

L.A's old and new Chinatowns are also representative of the old and new interlocal worlds of the different generations. The old one, established as an entry point for Chinese immigrants, made up of century-old family associations, is giving way to the modern hip art galleries trendy boutiques and lofts that have taken over the traditional storefronts. It's a community more about style than tradition, created by a mix of white artists and second-and-third-generation Chinese-Americans who came from the suburbs to form their own vision of Chinatown.

The new Chinese Garden, the largest outside China, being added to the Huntington Library in suburban San Marino to honor the many contributions of Chinese-Americans is another example. The money to build the Huntington originated from the vast fortune of Collis Huntington, one of the founders of the Central Pacific Railroad. His nephew and heir, Henry Huntington, founded the library in 1919, supplementing the bequest with his own wealth from the Pacific Electric Railway, utilities and real estate deals around Southern

California.

Much of the Huntington wealth was made off the sweat and blood of more than 10,000 Chinese laborers who worked on the Central Pacific Railroad to connect it from Sacramento, California to Promontory, Utah. They laid the tracks along the most treacherous part of the transcontinental railroad through the Sierra Nevada in the 1860s.

The money to build the $80-million Chinese Garden is being donated by Chinese-American descendants of these railroad workers, to showcase their reversal of fortune. When completed in 2008, the first phase of the Chinese Garden will include a small lake, an ornate teahouse, a zigzag granite bridge, and lush landscaping with native Chinese plants such as bamboo, camellias and tree peonies. The 650 tons of rocks, granite and limestone was mined at Lake Tai west of Shanghai. Getting U.S. visas for the 13 artisans associated with the Suzhou Institute of Landscape Architectural Design, to supervise the placement of the rocks and granite, was another Homeland Security bureaucratic nightmare. It was not as easy as it was for Collis Huntington, who could easily import boatloads of Chinese laborers.

The old deeds of trust in San Marino stated clearly that land within the city limits could not be sold to Jews, blacks or Chinese. By the 1980s, San Marino, like the rest of the San Gabriel Valley, saw a huge wave of immigration from Hong Kong, Taiwan and later China, which has transformed once-white-majority San Marino to another Chinese enclave. They still have tight city rules about how to behave with your property. There is even a homeowners handbook and the white Republican residents have passed on their values to the Chinese Republican residents.

Los Angeles in many ways is like New York – a sprawling inaccessible city. It is a city where more than 200 languages are spoken by ethnic groups whose ties to their home countries can interlocalize trade and culture. The city can become "the Venice of the 21st century," as Villaraigosa hopes. That will only happen if the troubled Los Angeles Unified School District is taken over by the city, following the lead of mayors in New York and Chicago. Los Angeles will not be able to compete in an interlocal world if its public education system is rife with dropouts and graduates who "can barely fill out a job application."

Bushfires

The Oxford Dictionary defines bush as "wild uncultivated land, especially in Africa and Australia." Two places where bushfires are common. Unfortunately, they are also common in the Middle East, the Far East and the rest of Asia, where the Bush Doctrine is burning itself indelibly into the minds of future arsonists – terrorists. The only difference is that these bushfires are started because of George W. Bush and oil. Not the traditional dry brush and high winds. Granted, there are a lot of high-winded career politicians and their bureaucrats stoking the fires to make sure they keep burning.

America's political bushfire doctrine is nothing new. It is just finally being openly admitted to because America is the world's sole arrogant superpower and unrestrained arsonist with the most incendiary firepower ever known to humanity. The problem is the firepower is creating bushfires that our firefighter children have to put out. As the father of a former U.S. firefighter, I'm not convinced it is a good idea. Especially if the fires are biological or nuclear.

Bushfires and the empire-building firefights they create are nothing new in American history. The Mexican, Spanish and other firefights in America's young history were an earth-scorching foundation for today's bushfires.

My personal favorite bushfire is the one America set in Hawaii, America's recreational playground and Missile Defense Shield frontier. In 1873, Gen. John Schofield visited Hawaii as a tourist and while there identified Pearl Harbor as "the key to the Central Pacific Ocean." Thus, Hawaii was invaded by thin-lipped, morally oppressive Calvinist missionaries who kicked out the queen of the indigenous population, decimated the people with disease and consigned the population to virtual slavery on sugar plantations. Hawaiians found themselves caught up in the U.S. 19th-century bushfire of empire-building that made them "American citizens by force, not by choice."

The Hawaiian Kingdom, being rebuilt by "Bumpy" Kanahele, is a place where "Haole, go home!" and variations of whites-aren't-welcome are shouted from the front porches. Locals rule there – a government of Hawaiians for Hawaiians. It is a place where Hawaiian is taught as a first language in some schools and spoken among neighbors. People openly accuse America of stealing Hawaii and believe that someday their lands will return to the Kanaka Maoli, the ancient Polynesians who settled the islands.

Noam Chomsky, a renowned professor of linguistics at MIT, and author of books ranging from mathematics to politics, wrote that the bushfires in the Middle East were first started when Franklin D. Roosevelt and the House of Saud signed their treaty on a U.S. aircraft carrier. "The State Department recognized in 1945 that the Middle East was the main energy resource of the world and that Saudi Arabia alone was a stupendous source of strategic power and one of the greatest material prizes in world history," wrote Chomsky. "They immediately moved to kick out France and to reduce Britain to a kind of junior partner. Controlling Middle East energy reserves has been a centerpiece of U.S. policy since the 1940s."

America has won significant military advantage elsewhere by starting bushfires to further its economic and political gains. Following the bushfires of Iraq in 1991, the U.S. had military bases in Kuwait, Saudi Arabia, Oman and the United Arab Emirates. The bushfires of Serbia eight years later netted U.S. bases throughout Europe and the Balkan region, most notably in Hungary, Macedonia, Kosovo and Bulgaria. From the bushfire in Afghanistan came military installations in 10 locations, including Uzbekistan, Turkmenistan and Pakistan.

The first millennium bushfire in Afghanistan was a rehearsal for the second one started in Iraq. Hopefully, it won't burn out of control as bushfires often do.

Fusion

The British encountered hundreds, make that thousands, of "Custer's last stands" in New Zealand against the native Maoris. This allowed the Maoris to retain their dignity and be true to their heritage more than the rest of the colonized world. What repeatedly amazed me in New Zealand was how European white Kiwis with no Maori blood consider their heritage Maori. "We're Maori even though they call us 'Pake Ha' – white pigs." The New Zealand Maori values are very strong. That is why they all do the hakka war chant at any All Blacks rugby game or rowdy drinking session anywhere. The European and Maori values and mutual respect are totally fused. From the road signs and other fundamental documents that are written in both

English and Maori, to the all-inclusive history classes taught in the schools. The same holds true for Iraqis and Kurds in a modified, fused kind of way because of their longer history together. Iraq's multiethnic mosaic includes not only Arabs and Kurds, but Turkmen and biblical Assyrians. More than 60 percent are Shia Muslims who resented Saddam Hussein's Sunni domination. The Maoris and Shia Muslims do share this mutual bone of contention: both have experienced ethnic cleansing and a common vision. Both insist on truth and reconciliation to spotlight abuses and promote national healing.

The Kurds, like the Maoris, have a long and proud history of integrating and dominating the new kids on the block. The Kurds did it with Saladin, who recaptured Jerusalem from the Crusaders, and the Maoris did it by holding off the British Empire's expansion plans and recapturing their cultural heritage by having it fully acknowledged by their European and Asian career politicians.

Diffusion

Watching the news about the Iraq election from Australia, while Australians who are active and vocal partners of the U.S. in Iraq were reeling from the Cronulla race riots against Muslims, was another reminder of how interlocal and media-spun the world is.

The December 15, 2005 election to choose Iraq's first full-term parliament was hailed universally as a "historic day," with a "great turnout." More than 12,000 Iraqi-Australians cast their absentee ballots in Australia.

The Iraqis were not voting for a united Iraq. They were voting for sectarian separation and the restoration of water and power and other basic necessities. The jubilant Iraqi voters were not excited about a democratic Iraq. They were excited about the prospects of a diffused Iraq. There were over 150,000 Iraqi soldiers and police on the streets with a backup of nearly 160,000 U.S. soldiers to prevent insurgent attacks. All automobile traffic and flights in and out of the country, except for the U.S. helicopters patrolling the air above, were banned.

That's democracy? There were also masked Sunni insurgents protecting polling stations in Sunni neighborhoods to ensure maximum voter turnout, especially in Saddam Hussein's home town of Tikrit. Why, for a representative government to hold Iraq together? Highly unlikely. The appearance of unity to hasten the removal of U.S. and coalition troops as Republican and Democratic leaders promise in America in the face of the looming 2006 congressional and 2008 presidential elections, is more likely. Iraqis traded dictatorship for chaos and bloodshed in the short term in the interest of sectarian separation.

The fundamentalist sectarians took nearly 90 percent of the nationwide vote. The U.S. and British backed secular and nationalist parties and candidates lost big time, even though they ran well-financed campaigns with slick television ads. Dr. Ayad Allawi's ticket, which included prominent Sunnis and Shiites, won only 25 of the 275 seats – that represented a 38 percent loss from the number of seats won in the January election. Ahmad Chalabi, the former Washington darling did not even win a seat. Their dream of establishing a pro-Western secular democracy in a united Iraq failed miserably.

Trying to build a coalition government of historic enemies – who distrust and are reluctant to work with each other – is doomed. The Shiite United Iraqi Alliance won 128 of parliament's 275 seats. The Kurdish Alliance won 53 seats, leaving the Shiites and the Kurds three seats short of the two-thirds majority needed to elect a president and push through constitutional reforms.

The Sunni Iraqi Accordance Front won 44 seats and another Sunni coalition won 11 seats while a few more Sunnis won seats on other tickets. There were still complaints of election irregularities and promises to challenge the results in the Iraqi courts, something no one could do under Saddam's Sunni dictatorship. The political combatants had 48 hours to appeal the results of the December 15 election to a judicial commission after the electoral commission released final but uncertified figures.

The commission had two weeks to rule on the appeals before the final results were certified and the parliament could meet. "These big Sunni political groups will have limited influence on former Baathists who support Saddam, and no influence over Islamic militants," said Hazim al-Naimi, a political science professor at Iraq's Mustansiriya University.

The mixed results left the door open for militia groups and guerrillas to continue their insurgency. Sunni Arab rebels claim they are digging in for a long fight with the next Iraqi government. "We'll spread snipers in all of Iraq's cities," said Abu Huda al-Aslam, a senior member of the Iraqi militant group Mujahedeen Army Brigades, who served in Saddam's army. A report released in early 2006 by the U.S. Agency for International Development said the security situation in Iraq was dire, amounting to "social breakdown" in which criminals have "almost free rein."

America gerrymandered the election in the hope of getting a working coalition together to keep Iraq united. What it got instead is gerrymandered borders for three separate states at war with each other. The Iraqi columnist Nibras Kazimi summed it up best: "Iraq did not hold an election ... it held a census." No different than what happened in Britain between the English, Scots, Irish and Welsh before they united – and now have again separated.

Much like America after independence from Britain – resulted in a civil war along sectarian and ethnic lines – 19th-century style – and today again divided into religious red and secular blue. The most recent Middle Eastern bloodletting example is the Lebanon 1975-90 civil war. The Americas, like Europe, Asia, Africa and other continents and regional groupings, will also be engaged in similar interlocal civil war in the 21st century unless traditional soft borders are redrawn and reinstated.

The dissolution of Iraq – a bogus colonial state – could well be of benefit to the occupants. Objections mostly come from non-Iraqis. There is no doubt that the absence of a strong client Baghdad government will jeopardize Western control of the oilfields. U.S. dignity and future geopolitical credibility is more important than oil.

The U.S. "surge" in troops in early 2007 aimed at ending sectarian violence and restoring order in Baghdad has failed to create the island of stability in which Sunnis, Shiites and Kurds can work together in a united Iraq. This message was brought home loud and clear when Vice President Dick Cheney's secret unannounced trip to the U.S. Embassy in Baghdad on May 10, 2007, was jolted by a nearby explosion that rattled the windows. Reporters covering the vice president were briefly moved to a more secure area. Cheney told the reporters after the incident that based on conversations he had with Iraqi leaders, sectarian violence was "down fairly dramatically."

Right. Sounds like they are trying to bring Cheney and America down in a dramatic fashion. U.S. soldiers were kidnapped and murdered in Baghdad as a Cheney send off reminder. The insurgents have home court advantage in urban warfare at the expense of increased U.S. casualties. Four years after Saddam Hussein's giant statute came tumbling down, Iraqis burn the American flags that greeted U.S. troops as liberators as they march through the streets of major cities chanting "Death to America."

The only thing regime change brought to Iraq is chaos and the lynching of Saddam Hussein. Even President Bush admits his Iraq policy has failed. Iraq's Vice President Adel Abdel Mahdi called the U.S-led occupation "idiotic." The U.S. has tried everything from direct talks with revolutionary Iraqi Shiite leader Abdul Aziz al-Hakim, who has links to sectarian militias and Iran, to installing and openly supporting "a government of thieves and their cousins" led by Prime Minister Nouri al-Maliki, who is beholden to the Shiite militias and death squads and describes American policy as an "ugly picture" as he feebly supports the U.S. crackdown on militias and boycotts a meeting with President Bush.

The U.S. struggle to keep Iraq unified is a self-delusional catastrophic fiasco. Even the U.S. could do nothing as radical Shiite cleric Moqtada al-Sadr ran for cover during the crackdown, ordered his six cabinet ministers to quit the already shaky government, and fans the flames of war in some other city where he has the home court advantage. As America blames Iraqis for their predicament, it threatens to cut and run. Iraq finds itself looking at Turkish threats of a cross-border strike against Kurds and Saudi promises to finance Sunnis in an Iraq civil war that will send thousands more Iraqis fleeing the country, joining the 4 million of their countrymen who already have sought safety in Iran and elsewhere.

The deadly bombing of the Iraqi Parliament building in the heart of Baghdad as the U.S. tried to convince itself it had control of the city was a reminder that the civil war to partition Iraq continues to rage despite the troop surge.

Until 1920, there was no country known as Iraq. It was created by the carving up of the Ottoman Empire by the victorious forces of World War I. Iraq was literally cobbled together by the British, who merged the three provinces of Shiite Basra, Sunni Baghdad and Kurdish Mosul into a single state and decided to empower the Sunni minority because they believed that the majority Shiites' religious devotion made them unsuitable to govern a modern state. The succession of oppressive Sunni autocrats since Iraq achieved independence in 1932 culminated with the brutal regime of Saddam Hussein.

The civil sectarian war to split the artificial country created by Britain started at the end of the 1991 Gulf War to retake Kuwait from Saddam Hussein – the only remaining issue is the revenue sharing formula for the oil revenues – which are in the Shiite south and Kurdish north. The majority of the people went to the polls in 2005 as Shia, Sunni or Kurds, not as Iraqis. The forces pulling it apart are greater than those trying to glue it together. The British are well entrenched and in coalition control of the south, as is America in the north to oversee and supervise the funeral of the new democratic state they thought they gave birth to – unless they reverse course and create three independent states and fulfill the democratic aspirations of those liberated by America, Britain and their coalition allies.

The alternative is new Taliban-type insurgencies throughout the country. The Saudis in the center with their fellow Sunnis, control the biblical antiquities and the Sunni communities. They are in an uncomfortable alliance with secular Baathists and number one enemy Osama bin Laden and his al-Qaeda led insurgency. Not really a dilemma since the number one representative of al-Qaeda in Iraq was, until he was killed, Abu Musah al-Zarkqwi, a Jordanian Sunni determined to take out whatever and whoever he can in Jordan, where he had been imprisoned by the Hashimite royal family, who are in Jordan after being displaced from Saudi Arabia after World War I, while maintaining a legitimate claim to their throne there in Mecca – the holiest of Muslim cities.

Tough to beat the intrigue of an Arabian night, especially when one looks up at the moon-reflected Middle East clouds that include Israel, Turkey and Iran. Let's not forget that Shiite Arian Iran was at war with Shiite Arab Iraq run by secular Sunnis with American support then – just as now. Is it any wonder America and Iran are at it again?

Former U.S. ambassador to Iraq Zalmay Khalilzad put it despairingly blunt: "It looks as if people have preferred to vote for their ethnic or sectarian identities.... But for Iraq to succeed, there has to be cross-ethnic and cross-sectarian cooperation." Unfortunately for Bush's fundamentalist Christian coalition, the fundamentalist Muslim Shiites and Sunnis control two of the three future democratic divisions in what is Iraq today.

When the autonomy-minded Kurds and a Norwegian company announced their joint oil exploration deal was under way in November 2005, followed by deals with Turkish and Canadian oil companies, the Shiite and Sunni Iraqi political leaders, not to mention U.S. career politicians and Iraq's neighbors, were shocked. Why? Because they all fear the possibility of Iraqi Kurds using revenue generated by the oil to fund an independent state that might lead the roughly 20 million Kurds living in Turkey, Iran and Syria to revolt. Now, what is wrong with this picture?

The minority Sunnis were stunned at the results of the election and the persecution they are being subjected to at the hands of the Shiites and Kurds. Most of the military and police forces being trained by the U.S led coalition forces are Shiite.

If there is any doubt about what the Kurds are thinking, think about this. The Kurdistan regional government is investing $325 million in a new futuristic airport at the Irbil International Airport to handle millions of passengers a year and a runway that will be big enough to handle the new double-decker AirbusA380. Irbil is one of the oldest continuously inhabited towns in the world. The government is building U.S. style mega-malls with office towers and developing the overloaded infrastructure. The Kurdistan regional government has placed special emphasis on attracting investors from the U.S. and Britain, unleashing a slick advertising campaign in English dubbed "The Other Iraq."

On the military front, the Kurds have inserted more than 10,000 of their *peshmerga* militia members into the Iraqi army divisions in northern Iraq to lay the groundwork to swarm south, seize the oil-rich city of Kirkuk, the seat of a province and possibly half of Mosul, Iraq's third-largest city, and secure the borders of an independent Kurdistan. Kirkuk's Kurdish population was driven out by Saddam Hussein, whose "Arabization" program paid thousands of Arab families to move there and replace recently deported or murdered Kurds. The Iraqi army's 2nd Division which oversees the Arbil-Mosul area, has about 12,000 soldiers, and at least 90 percent are Kurds.

Like all Kurds, they believe "Kirkuk is Kurdistan." No central government in Baghdad can stop them without America there.

The more the U.S. military hands over prematurely, the more it will be handing over to these milita members who are focused more on advancing ethnic and religious interests than on defeating the insurgency and preserving national unity. The soldiers admit that while they wear Iraqi army uniforms they still consider themselves members of the *peshmerga* and are awaiting orders from Kurdish leaders to break ranks. Many admit they won't hesitate to kill their Arab Iraqi army comrades if a fight for an independent Kurdistan erupts.

The Kurds believe the Shiites in the South are doing the same. The Shiites have stocked Iraqi army and police units with members of their own militias and have maintained a separate presence throughout Iraq's central and southern provinces. The Shiites plan to create their own independent religious fundamentalist state. Is it any wonder there are so many Shiite-dominated Iraqi forces carrying out death-squad-style executions in Sunni neighborhoods – before and after the highly publicized historical vote in response to the Sunni insurgent attacks on the Shiite government forces?

It should therefore have been no surprise when tortured Sunni prisoners were discovered in an Interior Ministry building in Baghdad. American and Iraqi officials acknowledged that Sunni inmates had been tortured. Corpses bearing signs of torture are discovered by the score every day around Bagdhad.

The story of Sheik Fassal al-Guood, a Sunni Muslim tribal leader and former provincial governor, mirrors the war itself – a series of shifting alliances, missed opportunities and lives ended in murky circumstances. When he first approached the U.S. military in 2004 with an offer to help rout insurgents linked to al-Qaeda from Al Anbar province, he was rebuffed. The Americans eventually came around and accepted his offer. Guood and 11 other Iraqis were killed in 2007 in a bombing at a Baghdad hotel where tribal sheiks who had joined forces with the U.S. were due to meet. When does the definition of civil war begin?

No wonder the Sunnis questioned the outcome of the election. With a truck full of forged ballots seized coming in from Iran and the driver acknowledging there were other trucks with forged ballots favoring Shiite Iraqi candidates, one can understand why the Sunnis wanted a recount. The large Sunni voter turnout was not reflected in the vote count.

The Pentagon wasted hard-earned taxpayer dollars trying to bribe Iraqi clerics to get their followers to vote for America's hand-picked puppets, and to believe the stories planted in Iraqi newspapers preaching the American message. America still has not learned the lesson of "take the loot and scoot," practiced in the Muslim world, especially when it comes to infidel loot for a fellow Muslim – a lesson America was last taught in the Bora Bora mountains of Afghanistan when it tried to capture Osama bin Laden by bribing local Muslim allies.

Billions of dollars earmarked for rebuilding Iraq have been diverted from reconstruction projects to fight the insurgency because of under-estimated security needs. This is the assessment made by Stuart Bowen, the special U.S. inspector-general for Iraq reconstruction. He said the funds had to be diverted from much needed water, sewage and electrical projects to help cover the costs of providing security, and combating a consistent and aggressive insurgency.

The sectarian civil war is already in full swing. While Iraqi politicians and U.S. bureaucrats haggled over the formula of a national unity government two months after national elections, the February 22, 2006, bomb attack that destroyed the golden dome of the 1,000-year-old Shiite mausoleum of Iman Ali al-Hadi in Samarra was the most graphic visual of the political rubble the U.S. has created in Iraq, and also a sneak preview of the expanding civil war. Iraq is clearly sliding into anarchy as the sectarian bloodbath in the wake of the Golden Mosque bombing made clear again in 2007 when its minarets were destroyed by suicide bombers.

The Sunnis boycotted the unity government talks as the sectarian violence spread and 168 Sunni mosques were attacked, 10 imams killed and 15 abducted. It took Bush's personal intervention to bring the parties back to the negotiating table. "I think the danger of civil war as a result of this attack has diminished, although I do not believe we are completely out of danger yet," forme U.S. Ambassador Zalmay Khalizad said after the talks resumed.

He went on to warn Iraqi politicians that they risk a loss of America's support if they do not form a genuine national unity government, saying America will not invest its resources in institutions run by secterians. Why not? That is exactly what it should be doing in a civil war. Why should Iraqis have to be subjected to several more years of sectarian carnage and wait another five to seven years for a reliable electricity supply?

The sectarian violence gets worse after every election that America stage-manages. Is it any wonder the U.S. cannot train an Iraqi military capable of replacing U.S. military personnel? It is impossible to do so. Iraq is already torn apart by sectarian religious and cultural centrifugal forces that America can only manage constructively if it acknowledges the country cannot be kept together, unless America makes a long-term commitment, similar to what it did in Japan, Germany, Korea and other mishandled war trophies. To pull troops out of Iraq prematurely because of the political spin needed to benefit Republicans and Democrats during the 2006 congressional elections and 2008 presidential election is short-sighted and self-defeating. It will give al-Qaeda the victory it has been promising.

The new constitution Iraq overwhelmingly approved in a referendum on October 15, 2005 created three defacto states: Shiite in the south, Kurdish in the north, and Sunni in the center. Local laws are superior to national law. The Shiites in the south and the Kurds in the north will own newly discovered oil reserves. It should therefore not come as a surprise that the Shiites and Kurds do not want to allow substantive amendments to the constitution, especially to the provision that keeps the central government weak. The Sunnis participated in the election believing they would be able to amend the constitution. It's another reason for the ongoing violence that will only get worse if America leaves prematurely or tries to keep a united Iraq.

U.S. military deaths have exceeded 4,000 and can easily reach 5,000 or more. Over 35,000 Iraqis have been killed as a direct result of insurgency attacks and U.S. military actions. That is an average of more than 1,000 per month since the war started. Some estimates are much higher, claiming that anywhere from 50,000 to 100,000 Iraqis have died from all manner of war-related violence, including criminal activities. The Iraqi crime rate is now the highest in the Middle East, with around 10,000 homicides a year that would not have happened before the invasion. During 2002, Saddam

Hussein's last full year in power, their were 1,800 violent deaths – not count-ing those executed by Saddam's regime. These numbers show graphically that America has not been able to bring security and stability to Iraq.

America was and continues to be ill-suited to handle counter-insurgency operations. America's sense of technical and intellectual superiority is in-culcated from the schoolroom. Inside the U.S., "American this or that is the finest/greatest in the world" are regular and unremarkable statements made as fact everywhere everyday. This is especially true when applied to the military. So when abroad or dealing with foreigners, Americans come from the position that everything American is bound to be better and foreigners must be reminded of this. In fact the U.S. "cultural insensitivity, almost certainly inadvertent, arguably amounted to institutional racism," Brigadier Nigel Aylwin-Foster, who was the second-most-senior officer responsible for training Iraqi security forces, wrote in the U.S. Army magazine *Military Review.*

The global nation building that occurred right after World War I, when the Allied victors dismembered the Habsburg and Ottoman empires, left us with Yugoslavia and Iraq. The new lines that defined borders left us with the Balkans, Africa and the Middle East. The result, Saddam's and Tito's dicta-torships held Iraq and Yugoslavia together, as other dictatorships hold other peoples together within boundaries drawn by outsiders and in some cases – Nigeria, for example – even gave them their national name.

Let's not get into flags and colors. Is it any wonder the Iraq Study Group recommendations were ignored because it was made up of "political has-beens?" Political hacks who are still indebted to their patrons and political godfathers. Meanwhile, Iraq and Syria restored diplomatic ties after 25 years. Iraq ordered Syrian diplomats out after raiding their embassy in 1980. The two countries, then ruled by rival wings of the Arab nationalist Baath party, severed all ties in 1982, when Syria sided with Iran in the 1980-88 Iraq-Iran war.

The Kurds' historic reluctance to be part of an Arab-dominated Iraq, and their U.S. protectorate after the 1992 Gulf War, is going to make it impos-sible in the long term to form one central government in Iraq for several reasons. They are afraid of losing their cultural identity and a majority want full independence. More than 1.75 million Kurds – half the population in north Iraq – have signed a petition demanding a referendum on Kurdish independence.

Under the Iraqi constitution, a binding referendum was supposed to be held in Kirkurk before year end 2007, giving the residents the option of choosing whether to become part of autonomous Iraqi Kurdistan. The Kurds, who hold a majority in the multiethnic city, are widely expected to win any such vote, which would give them control of Kirkuk's extensive oil resources.

The Kurds and Shiites have abided by a largely unspoken quid pro quo. The Kurds allowed Shiites to solidify their control over Arab Iraq, while the Shiites stood aside as the Kurdish Regional Government in the north took on more and more of the trappings of an independent state. But with neither side willing to budge over Kirkuk, the impasse is threatening to unravel that delicate compromise.

Article 140 of Iraq's constitution says "normalization, a census, and a referendum in Kirkuk" must be held before Dec. 31, 2007. Shiite officials agreed to the "normalization" – pushing out the Arabs brought to Kirkuk by Saddam Hussein and replacing them with displaced Kurds, the census and the vote on the referendum. The government has failed to honor any of the agreements or deadlines. Nevertheless, the Kurds insisted that the referendum be held before the end of 2007, infuriating prominent Shiite political leaders.

The Shiites in Iraq are opposed to the referendum. Prime Minister Nouri al-Maliki, a hard-line Shiite, as of the publication of this book, had not set a date for the referendum or allocated any money to carry it out. The Kurds have responded by threatening to pull out of Malik's government if the vote isn't held on time, which would trigger new elections and months of sectarian instability.

There is the possibility that the Kurds might try to seize the city by force and declare independence, a move that could trigger armed clashes between Kurdish and Shiite forces and possibly an invasion by Turkey. U.S. officials have been pressing Kurdish leaders to delay the referendum until next year as a way of lowering tensions. A wave of attacks in June 2007 destroyed two of Kirkuk's main bridges and left dozens dead. Kirkuk is the issue that will ignite the partition of Iraq.

The Kurds, who speak their own two mutually intelligible languages, are one of the world's largest groups without a state, counting 25 million people whose mountainous homeland is split among Iraq, Turkey, Iran, Syria, Armenia and Azerbajian. They are an ancient people whose ancestors were mentioned by Greek historian Xenophon. Most Kurds are Sunni and secular.

The Kurds were promised self-determination during World War I if they helped the Allies defeat the Germans and the Ottoman Turks. The victorious powers reneged on that promise at the 1923 Treaty of Lausanne. Then both President Richard M. Nixon and George H.W. Bush double-crossed the Kurds, encouraging them to revolt, then withholding the support they needed. Is it any wonder Kurds have taken matters into their own hands? Kurdish rebels repeatedly fire rockets and grenades at Turkish military outposts killing soldiers and heightening tensions with Turkey that threatens an incursion into northern Iraq to root out Kurdish rebel bases.

The first major clue that America's attempt to force the Kurds to live in a united Iraq would fail came on July 15, 2004 – in Albuquerque, New Mexico. A film crew from Kurdistan TV (KTV) in Iraq arrived to film a panel discussion of Native American tribal leaders hosted by the New Mexico Indian Affairs Department at the Indian Pueblo Cultural Center. The tribal leaders were interviewed by KTV because the Kurds want to learn more about Native American tribes and American federalism. The key questions? What is sovereignty? What does sovereignty mean to your community? How does your tribal court function? The lessons they learned from the interview are surely ones they do not want to repeat.

Article 6 of the U.S. Constitution honors and preserves the treaties America has signed. America signed 371 treaties with Native Americans – most of which have been breached and egregiously violated. Native American activist Russell Means justifiably says that "America is the biggest reservation in the world," dependent on Washington, D.C. because *We the Apathetic People* are not living life according to the ideals of America's Founding Fathers, but just surviving on the reservation off the government's handouts. Native Americans didn't become U.S. citizens until 1924. America has become, in the words of Means, a perfect one-party system of

"Demopublicans," something the Kurds, Shiites and Sunnis do not want to replicate.

Meantime, Iraq's government has endorsed plans to relocate thousands of Arabs who were moved to Kirkuk as part of Saddam's campaign to force ethnic Kurds out of the oil-rich city, in an effort to undo one of the late dictator's most enduring and hated policies. Population exchanges have been going on for years as Sunni and Shiite families flee mixed communities for the safety of areas where their own sects are dominant. Even Baghdad can be split between Sunni and Shiite, which would break up a lot of multi-religious and cultural marriages that took place in Saddam's secular Iraq. Kurdistan is quickly becoming the most autonomous commercial gateway to Mesopotamia.

The cultural sentiment of the Kurds is shared by the Shiite Arabs who, like the Kurds, were persecuted for more than 1,500 years by their Sunni bretheren. The sect was born of defeat in 661, when the Prophet Muhammad's son-in-law, Ali, was killed and Sunnism became the dominant political and religious force in Islam. To think that the Kurds and Shiites in Iraq can forget their history and embrace the Sunnis in one central government is delusional and defies logic and reality.

The Bush administration apparently paid little or no attention to pre-war assessments by the CIA that warned of major cultural and political obstacles to stability in post-war Iraq. Two classified reports prepared for President Bush in January 2003 had predicted that a U.S.-led invasion of Iraq would increase support for political Islam and would result in a deeply divided Iraq society prone to violent internal conflict.

It is time for America to come to terms with the reality that a united democratic Iraq is unsustainable. How much longer must We the Apathetic People pursue the belief that the Iraq war was a good idea? The ongoing civil war in Iraq will lead to a broader Middle East conflict, pitting Sunnis against Shiites, as the Saudis, Turks and Iranians have already made perfectly clear.

America cannot abandon Iraq, but it must leave the right way and time. John Bolton, former U.S. ambassador to the U.N., said it best. The U.S. has "no strategic interest" in a united Iraq. U.S. National Intelligence director and former U.S. ambassador to Iraq, John Negroponte, admitted as much in a frank assessment in early 2006 after the bombing of the Golden Mosque. "If chaos were to descend upon Iraq, or the forces of democracy were to be defeated in that country ... this would have implications for the rest of the Middle East region, and indeed, the world," he told the Senate Armed Services Committee. Saudi Arabia and Jordan would support Iraq's Sunnis with Iran coming to the support of the Shiites.

Amid the sectarian bloodbaths, the Bush administration is in denial that there is a "civil war" in Iraq and rejects the idea that the only peaceful democratic solution and honorable U.S. legacy is to divide Iraq into three separate independent countries. Not federal states held together in any manner shape or political form, only economic. In April 2007, that most comprehensive independent study of Iraqi oil since the U.S. invasion of 2003 concluded that Iraq has an additional 100 billion barrels of oil in the Western desert. That makes Iraq the world's second-largest source of oil reserves – something to fight for and go to war over – an additional incentive for peace, partition and revenue sharing with Sunnis who will govern the antiquities and earn tourist dollars, to ensure a peaceful, harmonious and prosperous tri-state economic union.

Truly independent sovereign states that fulfill America's moral responsibility to the Iraqis who want a better Iraq – partition. Mission accomplished. The futility of the U.S. policy of a united democratic Iraq is best expressed by the story of Khamael Muhsen and her husband, Mohammed Sadiq Falhee. Khamael was a reporter with Radio Free Europe, the U.S. government-funded broadcaster who was killed for being a reporter and a Shiite in the middle of the Baghdad crackdown that the Bush administration claimed was making the city safer. She had been a TV personality in Saddam Hussein's era. The 54-year-old Khamael became one of those statistical bodies dumped on the side of the road like garbage – one of at least 158 journalists, most of them Iraqis, who've been killed since the U.S.-led invasion of Iraq in 2003.

In Iraq, if a mobile phone is switched off for an hour or more, that usually means the phone owner is dead. That is how Mohammed knew his wife had been murdered. "If you say you'll be home at 5 and it is 6, you are dead," he said. They had met and fallen in love during the first Gulf War after Saddam invaded Kuwait in 1991. He'd helped her with her broken-down car during an air raid. He saw her again in a flower shop. This time, her mobile phone wasn't working. He helped her fix it, and she asked him why he wasn't married. He jokingly asked her if she'd marry him. She said yes.

Khamael and Mohammed were Shiite Muslims and targets for Sunni extremists in their al-Qaeda controlled neighborhood. She said it would just be a matter of time before the Sunni extremists would take her life. They sent their two teenage daughters to live in Syria. At school in Baghdad, the girls were called separationists and Safawis, the Arabic word for the Persian Safavid Empire, and now a common label for Shiites that implies they are part of an Iranian conspiracy to take over Arab Iraq. But Khamael was determined. She would not be forced out of her home and her neighborhood just because she was a Shiite.

Khamael's body was found with a drill hole and bullet wounds on each side of her head and a cracked skull. She'd duck out after curfews for a story when only insurgents, militias and security forces roamed the streets. She hated those that killed in the name of Islam.

Damascus and Tehran's ties to the extremists at both ends of the Sunni and Shiite political spectrum are responsible for the destructive collision course they are on not just in Iraq, but Palestine. Let's not forget who Palestinian President Mahmoud Abbas spoke to by phone, to explore ways of ending the Palestinian conflict because of the Gaza "madness." Exiled Hamas political supremo Khaled Meshaal, who is living in Damascus. Iran and Syria are key players to the elusive peaceful puzzle – partition. America has to stop paying tribute to American soldiers in Iraq as their death tolls hit 3,000 and most recently 4,000 and the next milestones of death. It is time for Congress to come up with a realistic timeline and plan – partition. All other plans, military and political, have failed. What other option is there? The solution to peace in the Middle East, starting in Iraq and Palestine, is partition.

The five-year plan for Iraq adopted by the leaders of the 50 countries that gathered in Egypt in May 2007, aimed at rescuing the war-ravaged country from chaos and bankrupcy will, like the rest of the plans, fail because the main aim of the so-called "International Compact" is to rebuild a unified federal Iraq. The only part of the plan that has any hope of survival is the oil revenue-sharing plan – but in a partitioned Iraq. Setting withdrawal plans without a partition plan is another mistake future generations will pay for – emotionally, politically and financially.

Islamistan

Hamas' refusal to renounce violence and acknowledge the sovereignty of Israel has resulted in the de-facto partition of what was to be the state of Palestine – Gaza and the West Bank, territories long troubled by complex clan rivalries. Gaza is now embracing its 1.4 million lost true Palestinian wandering tribes people, albeit a lot more religious and extremist than its founders in pre-Roman times. Today, the impoverished coastal strip is Islamic and extremist to the core. It is an Iranian-backed terrorist state, not much different than North Korea, but thankfully without nuclear weapons. There is no way in the foreseeable future that Hamas and Fatah will see eye to eye. So let's cut to the chase – partition. Hamas is supported financially and militarily by Iran and Syria. Gaza can be Islamistan, Palestine or some combination thereof. America and its allies should stop trying to isolate Hamas while they support Fatah. It can and should support both.

The West Bank on the other hand, is a lot more secular and politically moderate. A quarter of the more than 2 million Palestinians living there are refugees from the 1948 Arab-Israel war. In Gaza two-thirds of the residents are refugees of the war. The West Bank could easily interlocalize with either Jordan or Israel as a partner in a federated state. Israel and Jordan can both use its 50,000 armed forces to combat the 6,000-member force that Hamas fields.

The failure of the Saudi initiated Mecca accord, signed by Hamas and Fatah in February 2007, to last more than 90 days is a good hint that their power-sharing idea is a non-starter. The power-sharing idea agreed in Mecca was in order to avert a looming civil war and ease an international blockade on the previous all-Hamas government. Neither ambition has been achieved.

The Widening Interlocal Conflict

Just as a united Iraq is delusional, so is a Palestinian state in Gaza and the West Bank, a united Lebanon and a regional alliance with Afghanistan and Pakistan. Believing America can avoid a conflict with Iran is delusional, unless they sit down and have a serious chat.

The missiles fired at the village of Damadola in Bajaur, Pakistan by a U.S. Predator drone launched from Afghanistan, which targeted al-Qaeda No. 2 Ayman al-Zawahiri and killed 18 people, including women and children in January 2006, while the Iraqi ballots were being counted, was a grim reminder of how America's widening war on terror has failed – and how interlocalized it is. The militants retaliated three days later in the Afghan town of Spin Boldak, with a suicide bomber from Pakistan who drove his motorbike into a crowd watching a wrestling match. The Taliban and al-Qaeda leadership are alive and well, even though America has been determined to get them "dead or alive" since 9/11. In fact, not only are they alive but active in Afghanistan and Pakistan, where they still control significant territory and call the shots in both countries. Pakistan is the meat in the sandwich.

The Taliban and al-Qaeda leadership, including bin Laden and his top deputies and new militants from Arab countries, Central Asia and the Caucuses, are believed to be living somewhere in the 500-mile-long rugged Afghan Pashtun controlled border tribal areas in Pakistan. Taliban militants dispense their own justice, run their own private jails, rob banks, traffic heroin, shell military and civilian government compounds and attack convoys at will. In 2005, 108 pro-government tribal elders and four or five government officials were assassinated. The presence of 19,000 U.S. troops on the Afghan side of the border, and their hammer-and-anvil strategy of pressing from the Afghan side of the border, has done nothing to slow them down. There has been a sharp rise in attacks on Western troops in Afghanistan beginning in 2006. The Taliban and al-Qaeda militants moved to Pakistan where the U.S. troops are forbidden from pursuing them. "We run a government on paper, but not on the ground," said a Pakistani official.

"We were using Pakistan as a base during the resistance times," said Hakim Taniwal, governor of Paktia province, referring to the war against Soviet occupation in the 1980s. "Now al-Qaeda and the Taliban are using Pakistan to attack in Afghanistan." Pakistan today is not so different from 19th-century Pakistan under the British Raj. Now, as then, Islamabad's influence ends where the tribal border areas begin.

The mountainous region has been beyond the control of any government for centuries. Both sides of the border are populated by Pashtuns, who traffic in money, drugs and weapons. Pakistan has stationed 70,000 troops in the area to help America hunt down bin Laden and other al-Qaeda fugitives. Pakistan, an old and derisive axiom goes, can only be governed with the help of the 3As – Allah, Army and America. Juggling between the mullahs, the military and the U.S., Pakistan's President Pervez Musharraf's hold on power is tenuous. Musharraf's decision to dump Chief Justic Ifikhar Mohammad Chaudrhry in early 2007 galvanized lawyers and the opposition that took to the streets and clashed with police. Pakistan's military intelligence is notoriously pro-fundamentalist.

The Taliban regrouped in Pakistan while the U.S. was distracted in Iraq and is now back again fighting a full-scale multipronged offensive, taking over village after village, province by province, as it did during the Soviet occupation. America has failed to deliver in Afghanistan.

The resurgence of the Taliban in Afghanistan is due primarily to poverty and prejudice. Afghans hate Americans more than they ever did the Russians in the 1980s. The "collateral damage" from the military operations conducted by the U.S. and NATO forces is one of the main reasons. With a safe base in Pakistan that the U.S. cannot attack, the Taliban have it made in the shade. A U.S. embassy convoy was attacked by a suicide bomber on a major highway. Afghan intelligence officers are being taken out like flies by suicide bombers, and a bomb went off near the new National Assembly.

In 2006, 4,000 people, a quarter of them civilians, were killed as a result of the new fighting and a string of 140 suicide attacks. By the end of the first quarter of 2007, the numbers had already hit 1,000. In June of the same year, Taliban militants fired rockets at Afghan President Hamid Karzi in an apparent assassination attempt. The interlocal and intra-tribal conflicts caused by prejudice are on the rise because of ignorance. With knowledge, people will reject the Taliban's harsh enforcement of Sharia with beheadings, summary executions, and amputations. An opportunity for America to exploit.

To make matters worse, border skirmishes between Iran and Iraq along the Shatt al-Arab shifting tidal shoals periodically erupt. In June 2004, three British naval patrol boats were briefly seized by Iran. In early 2006, Iran kidnapped an Iraqi coast guard boat after it stopped and boarded an Iranian-skippered ship suspected of smuggling oil in Iraqi waters. The Iraqi boat was overpowered by an Iranian patrol. In 2007, 15 British marines were kidnapped while inspecting a ship in Iraqi waters after allegedly doing so in Iranian waters.

The Iranian mullahs' handpicked mouthpiece, President Mahmoud Ahmadinejad, who has said the Holocaust is a myth and that Israel should be wiped off the map, further accelerated the widening conflict with America by reactivating his nuclear program when he brazenly removed the International Atomic Energy Agency seals from a uranium-enrichment facility at Natanz, in central Iran. Does anyone doubt that Israel, with America's support, will destroy Iran's nuclear capability before it is capable of wiping out Israel if a peaceful solution is not reached?

It's no wonder Iran's neighbors in the gulf worry that Tehran's military support of the Taliban in Afghanistan, Shi te militias in Iraq and nuclear ambitions could destabilize the whole region.

Iran's nuclear challenge is a classic case that justifies pre-emptive military action under the Bush-promulgated policy of 2002 and the U.N. Charter. Iran will strike back with Hezbollah militants and an embargo of oil shipments. Iran believes it has America over a barrel, literally. The resulting global oil price increase could cripple America and oil-dependent economies. Although America already bans oil imports from Iran, if Iran withheld some of the 2.7 million barrels of oil it exports daily, the U.S. would suffer from the rise in international crude prices. It is a political bluff America can call. Withholding oil would be more painful for Iran.

Oil accounts for more than 80 percent of its exports and about half of its government revenues. What happens inside Iran is not important and Muslim extremists rejoice in struggle and deprivation anyway. It is the mayhem that will be caused in Western society that will be crucial to the mullahs, and they are prepared to put up with any degree of domestic discomfort to enjoy that.

The best hope for diffusing the crisis is Russia's offer – which has U.S. and EU support – to form a joint venture with Iran to enrich uranium in Russia, or China for that matter.

Why do *We the Apathetic Maids* allow ourselves to repeatedly be at the mercy of oil companies and their political expeditors in Washington? Since the oil shocks of the 1970s, when I rode my Arabian horse in Los Angeles to protest U.S. government dependency on Middle East oil, America has inexcusably allowed its dependence on oil imports to grow, from about one-third in the '70s to nearly three-fifths at the beginning of 2006. The U.S. Energy Information Administration projects that by 2030, the U.S. will import 62 percent of its oil, up from 58 percent at the beginning of 2006. That is why I again rode an Arabian horse in November 2005 to protest America's continued dependence on oil and its reluctance to pursue alternatives such as renewable energy and biofuels. The world has become too interlocally dependent on oil.

Iran's threat of oil blackmail is just the latest wake-up call for America to actively pursue the development of alternatives to oil. I agree with Ronald Brownstein, columnist for the *Los Angeles Times,* who said, "Increasing energy efficiency and reducing dependence on foreign oil should be as much a cause for neo-conservatives concerned about preserving U.S. autonomy in the world as it is for environmentalists worried about global warming." The fallout from global warming is far greater than any fallout from destroying Iran's nuclear facilities.

Baluchistan
Baluchistan is the biggest province in Pakistan and where most of the country's oil and gas is located. It borders Afghanistan and is a smugglers paradise where guns, missile launchers, drugs and child slaves are easily available at a price from Taliban and al-Qaeda fugitives. The U.S. has two bases in the province from which U.S. forces fight the war on terrorism. There were also many Chinese there building a huge commercial and military port in Gwadar, at the mouth of the Persian Gulf. Their presence was made public worldwide with the killing by militants of three Chinese engineers and their Pakistani driver in February 2006.

The province is under siege and constant attack by Pakistani forces because it has never been fully integrated into Pakistan. Baluchistan's rough tribal leaders feel like exploited colonials and have embarked on their fourth insurgency against the government in 67 years. They demand a fairer share of royalties generated by the production of natural gas in their province. Pakistan argues that the gas is a national asset. The manipulation of the 2002 election gave control of the provincial government to a coalition of Pakistani conservatives and Islamists, depriving the Baluch nationalists of any say in the allocation of natural resources.

Baluchistan is yet another trouble spot for America to address. The looming civil war there, like that in Iraq, will destabilize the region and further weaken America in its war on terror.

United Front

Politics and war make strange bedfellows. France supported the American colonies in their quest for independence from Britain because of their hatred and ongoing conflicts with Britain. This is nothing new.

When America colonized the Philippines, the Chinese revolutionaries trying to shed the "Tartar yoke" supported the Filipino revolutionaries. A brief review of this episode of history is very enlightening in that it exemplifies how people of different political persuasions and religious beliefs, like the French Catholics and American Protestant revolutionaries, can join forces to defeat a common enemy. It all started at a dinner in Tokyo in the winter of 1899 when Ponce de Leon, a Filipino revolutionary, met the Chinese revolutionary, Dr. Sun Yat Sen. Ponce had read about Sun and his work for the liberation of China as early as 1896, when Sun made headlines after being detained at the Chinese Embassy in London.

In 1899 Ponce and Sun were residents of Yokohama and became friends. Ponce tried to get Japanese support for the fight against the Americans, but the Japanese government did not want to rupture diplomatic relations with the United States at the turn of the century.

So Ponce turned to Sun for help. Sun agreed, hoping that when Filipino revolutionary Aguinaldo succeeded in attaining Philippine independence, the Chinese revolutionaries could then launch an attack on China from a friendly nation.

Ponce gave 100,000 yen to Sun as a token of Filipino sincerity and Sun started to purchase arms for the Filipino Independence Army.

On July 19, 1899, Sun dispatched a miserable secondhand ship, the Nurlobiki Maru, from Japan via Taiwan under the guise of taking railroad ties to China. The ship carried 6 million rounds of ammunition, 10,000 rifles, one artillery piece, 10 machine guns, seven field telescopes, one ammunition loader and other supplies bought cheaply from the Japanese army as scrap. All of this sank halfway to the Philippines when the overloaded vessel met a typhoon.

Undaunted, Sun and Ponce arranged for a second shipment of arms in 1900. A hitch came when a Japanese sympathizer to the Philippine cause was arrested in Manila, prompting the United States to request the Japanese government to keep watch over Ponce and the Filipino revolutionaries in Japan.

With agents constantly following Ponce, it was difficult for him to send arms to the Philippines. Yet Ponce still managed to hand over 65,000 yen to Nakamura, a Japanese sympathizer, for the purchase of arms.

With the pressure from Japanese authorities, it was decided that the arms shipment be postponed and Sun requested that the Chinese borrow the Philippine arms and use them in a planned uprising in Huichow, in southern China. Ponce agreed.

When Sun followed up the arms shipment, he was surprised to discover that the weapons turned out to be nothing but scrap iron. Ponce was dismayed to learn that Nakamura had swindled them out of 65,000 yen.

Who knows how the Filipino-American War would have turned out if the Filipinos had received the 1899 arms shipment that sank at sea?

The alliance of Saddam's secular Sunnis with the fundamentalist al-Qaeda fighters from Saudi Arabia and al-Qaeda-like groups from all over the Middle East to fight the U.S.-led coalition forces that invaded Iraq on March 21, 2003 to liberate the country, is similar to the alliance of convenience formed between Ponce and Sun.

Revolutionaries and terrorists have always joined forces with their brothers and sisters to create a united front against a common enemy.

The 21st century of terror has brought them together again in their common fight against the infidels America and Israel. Al-Qaeda, Hezbollah, Hamas and numerous other groups and individuals have formed a united front, as has America and its allies and coalition. The 21st century dawned on a modern-day interlocal rip-roaring-clapping crusade.

It is up to *We the Maids* to form an interlocal united front to sweep out all religious extremists and sweep in peace and global interlocal interaction.

New World Conquistadors

Today, a half a millennium after Cortez landed in Mexico, a new wave of Spanish conquistadors is descending on Latin America. They are armed not with the cross and the sword but with briefcases, cellular phones and laptop computers. Markets not territories are their prize. Instead of building colonies, they are buying up banks, phone companies, electric utilities and investment companies. Since 1990, Spanish companies have sunk more than $35 billion into Latin America, making the country of nearly 40 million people the biggest investor in the region after the United States.

Spain's rediscovery of its former colonies, however, is not simply a matter of economics. For all the conflicted feelings left by 500 years of shared history, the two sides have a cultural affinity that touches everything from language to the law, from courtship to Roman Catholicism, from a passion for soccer to a studied indifference to punctuality. Even their recent histories follow parallel paths from dictatorships to democracy, from state-run economies toward the free market. And as the United States slowly retreats from Latin America in the wake of the Cold War, Spain is eagerly filling the void culturally, politically and economically. This is not neocolonial intervention – it is interlocalism.

Spain's decision to go ahead with the sale of military aircraft to Venezuela, despite America's request that it not do so because of a U.S. ban on the export of military technology to Venezuela, is a 21st-century example of interlocalism – and waning U.S. power. Spain's $12 billion deal to supply 12 transport and maritime surveillance aircraft and eight patrol boats to Venezuela went ahead with substitute European technology.

It will not do for America to get into juvenile spats every time a regime it doesn't approve of appears in "Monroe Country." Yet it repeatedly does so to the point where its historical behavior practically everywhere south of the Rio Grande has been reprehensible.

Tribes & Clans – Good Riddance to Imperial Powers

The patriotic discussions of these monumental global and local historical changes took on a distinctly local flavor at the Foreign Correspondent's Club Main Bar in Hong Kong in 1998. "We got rid of you over 200 years ago" said John Rittger, an American, to Arthur Hacker, a Brit, and Mitch Davidson, an incomprehensible Scot, as Joan Howley, a very Irish lady, looked over at me in disbelief at John's comment. With raised eyebrows arching over her glasses, Joan uttered, "Can you believe what he is saying? I think he had one too many." To which John shot back: "You Brits complained when you had to leave Hong Kong last year after 156 years and now you're bitching about giving Northern Ireland back." Joan, in her distinct Irish broque interrupted to add: "We Irish have been trying to get rid of you for over 800 years!" Mitch and I walked safely away.

We are all descendants of tribes and clans. Humanity and the world started with tribes and clans. Many people today are still primarily loyal to their tribe or clan and its traditions and beliefs. America's Founding Fathers believed in principles higher than clan and tribal traditions. Unfortunately, many Americans, starting with the Pilgrims, fiercely held onto their tribal and clan loyalties above those of flag and country. America's Civil War and the graves at Gettysburg are living testimonials.

The fierce religiosity of Anglo-Celtic Texans can be traced back via Tennessee and West Virginia to Ulster and Scotland, Michael Lind writes in *Made in Texas*. The 18th-century Scots who moved to the American colonies from Northern Ireland combined frontier ferocity with simple and fervent Calvinist Protestantism. (Each man in the fabled Scottish Cameronian regiment in the British Army was equipped with a Bible and a dagger). Like the Protestant Dutch Afrikaaners of South Africa, the Protestant Scots-Irish Southerners compared themselves to the ancient Hebrews.

So, of course, did African-Americans. But whereas black Americans dwelled on the Exodus of the Hebrews from slavery in Egypt, the Southerners much preferred the chapters in "the Bobble" about the conquest of the Promised Land and the slaughter of the Canaanites. "For all their nominal Christianity, white Southerners have never been comfortable with meek and mild Jesus, who turned himself over for execution without a fight and counseled his followers to turn the other cheek when struck and to forgive their enemies. "Deep down, all true Southerners prefer Hebrew generals like Moses, Joshua, Gideon and David," Lind wrote.

In addition to being legalistic, Old Testament Protestant morality is communal. A single moral code traditionally has been enforced by the community, employers, schools, the state and – until a few decades ago – the Klu Klux Klan and lynch mobs. Among clannish, tight-knit, old-fashioned Anglo-Celtic Protestant Southerners, as among Orthodox Jews and the Wahabi clans of the Saudi desert, there is little toleration for individual deviance from tribal norms.

People forced together as a country by conquering powers cannot stay united forever. The fact that imperial powers capitalized on traditional tribal rivalries – hatred and animosity – and imposed their unworkable European model to exploit tribal natural resources must be acknowledged and redressed. Too many countries in 21st-century Africa, Latin America, the Middle East, and some in Europe will reconfigure themselves to their natural cultural and religious components, just like the Roman Empire, India, the Soviet Union, Yugoslavia, Czechoslavakia and Hong Kong did.

The same can be said about America as a result of the Civil War. The current divide in the U.S. today can be traced to that union imposed by war. The South reluctantly joined the Union because, like many defeated populations throughout the world, it had no choice. The cultural divide between red and blue Americans is wide.

The secular blue's tax dollars finance the religious reds who want to convert the blues to their religious fervor. The reds preach "freedom" and tolerance while pursuing their divisive national and global crusade. Is this any way for a country to grow and remain prosperous in the 21st century? Differences have to be either cast aside and hands joined in a harmonious embrace or there must be a parting handshake. Granted that secession today – blues from reds – would be geographically much harder. In 1860 "the South" was a contiguous geographical entity. Today the Southern mentality of sectarian intolerance over a ton of issues beyond race runs through the country, including the Midwest and some Mountain states. The Blues appear stranded on both coasts.

The Afghan and Iraq wars brought home the dominance of tribes and clans in the 21st century. The tribes of Israel, Native Americans, Bedouin clans, Scottish clans, and the tribes and clans of Africa must be acknowledged and welcomed back from the cultural and religious graveyards they were buried in by their colonizing oppressors. They can make significant contributions to the stability of our New World Disorder as I am awakened and reminded every noon on Chinese New Year day by the clanging cymbols of local clansmen.

This was made abundantly clear in Iraq after the ouster of Hussein. The Iraq Governing Council installed by the coalition forces was not acceptable to the Iraqis, who are a nation of tribes knitted together by tribal kinship, because the Governing Council was made up largely of former exiles and urban Iraqis. The resistance and attacks against the occupying coalition forces were carried out by members of the different tribes that have historically always resisted the leadership in Baghdad. Their loyalty and peace has always been negotiated and bought.

It should therefore come as no surprise that the violence in Iraq has not abated since America handed "sovereignty" back to Iraqis in June 2004, or after the elections in 2005.

The Hawaiians, Californians, Native Americans, Mayans and countless native tribes in Latin America and Africa will rise again and play a role in their governments in the New World Order of the 21st century. Just as the Anglo-American tribes and the tribes of Israel, China and India interact with their fellow tribe members, so will the members of all native tribes that have been able to hold onto their heritage and not allow it to become diluted and polluted by their colonizing conquerors. It has already happened in Bolivia and Nigeria and will continue throughout Central and South America, Africa and the Middle East.

President Clinton signed a resolution in 1998 that not only apologized but also acknowledged that Hawaiians "never directly relinquished their claims to their inherent sovereignty as a people over their national lands."

Speaking of Clinton and Hawaii, I am reminded of an interlocal woodpecker story I heard in Hawaii a few years ago. A Hawaiian woodpecker and a Canadian woodpecker were arguing about which place had the toughest trees. The Hawaiian woodpecker said that the islands had a tree that no woodpecker could peck. The Canadian woodpecker challenged him and promptly pecked a hole in the tree with no problem. The Hawaiian woodpecker was in awe.

The Canadian woodpecker then challenged the Hawaiian woodpecker to peck a Canadian tree that was absolutely unpeckable. The Hawaiian woodpecker accepted the challenge. After flying to Canada, the Hawaiian woodpecker successfully pecked the tree with no problem.

The two woodpeckers were now confused. How is it that the Canadian woodpecker was able to peck the Hawaiian tree and the Hawaiian woodpecker was able to peck the Canadian tree when neither one was able to peck the tree in their own country? After much woodpeckering, they both came to the same conclusion: Your pecker is always harder when you're away from home.

I experienced firsthand how frustrated and angry tribal chiefs of the Micronesian Republic of Palau are at America for what it did to their people and traditions at the end of World War II after it defeated the Japanese and made Palau a U.N. Trust Territory. "We used to fish, enjoy nature and the environment and teach our children how to live and survive harmoniously with the world around us" Chief Ibedul Gibbons lamented during an outdoor cookout on his rocky island. "Now we are a welfare state dependent on U.S. handouts, while our children get drunk and drugged and can't interact with each other without usually getting into a drunken brawl. Look what happens every payday. They go spend their money on booze and drugs, fight, and our jails get filled with confused and lost children."

Tribal chiefs and traditional tribes do have a role to play in the New World Order. Granted it is difficult to reconcile democracy with chieftainships. That is something I also experienced firsthand in Palau.

In Iraq, Saddam Hussein's Bu Nasir tribe from his hometown of Tikrit helped him maintain his grip on power and continue to fight U.S. coalition forces.

Just like in Afghanistan, the tribal loyalties run deep. Clansmen can be rented, but never bought.

The same holds true in Lebanon and Syria. The two countries, which at first were one after World War II, are another example of countries created by force. Traditional tribal and religious enemies were forced to live together despite their desire to live apart. Lebanon is struggling to become a country again after 29 years of Syrian occupation and domination. The overriding question of identity – do people belong to a country or to their tribe – is being played out. The traditional clan rules were agreed to when the Palestinian refugee camps were established. Arab countries had agreed, after their miscalculation of their military prowess during their first organized war against the newly formed state of Israel, that no Arab country or host country can enter the Palestinian refugee camps, which are also located in Syria and Jordan. The fighting between the Palestinian fundamentalists and the Lebanese army in the summer of 2007 helped conjure and reinforce fears of Iraq-style sectarian violence.

Lebanon is a complex and sophisticated country with 17 different sects, long a meeting place between East and West, Islam and Christianity. Sunni Muslims and Greek Orthodox Christians make up the majority of city dwellers, while Druze tribesmen and Shiite Muslims dominate the countryside. It is the most urbane and Westernized of Arab countries, but also a place where power has long been held by near-feudal strongmen known as *zaims*, and where the primordial loyalties lie with one's sect. There has been no census in Lebanon since 1932, because of the potentially unsettling political ramifications.

"At one time or another, each one of the dozen or so major armed groups fought against each other, at least for a short while," a British military expert, Edgar O'Balance, wrote in *Civil War in Lebanon, 1972-92*. "Machiavelli would have been out of his depth in this web of intrigue and violence." The March 14 Cedar Revolution that took place after the assassination of former Prime Minister Rafik Hariri, the Hezbollah tactics to bring down the democratically elected government, and the post-Syrian military withdrawal political machinations of the competing Christian and Muslim clans and tribes, before and after the Israeli-Lebanon war, would stump Machiavelli – as they have everyone else.

While their role in a democracy may be hard to figure out, there can be little doubt that the tribal chiefs continue to hold enormous sway, particularly in the rural areas, where they function much as they did before democracy, doling out land, settling disputes and punishing those who break traditional law. We saw it in Fiji and Africa. Tribal chiefs and locals reverting to their traditional practices because tribes are having a hard time digesting the colonial models imposed by brutal colonizers – going as far back as the Assyrian invasion of Israel in 722 BC.

Jewish tradition says 10 tribes from Israel were enslaved after the Assyrian invasion. They later fled Assyria and wandered through Afghanistan, Tibet and China. Around AD 100, one group moved southward from China and settled around northeastern India and Myanmar. These "wandering Jews," the Chin-Mizo-Kuki people, who speak Tibeto-Burman dialects and resemble Mongols, are believed to be the Bnei Menashe, one of the lost tribes of Israel. After a decade of DNA tests, Israeli authorities are convinced that there are up to 2 million Bnei Menashes in the hilly regions of Myanmar and northeast India who are now being allowed to immigrate to Israel. "This recognition clearly means we have got into the process to return to our homeland, ending our 2,726-year Exocus," said K. Elisha Singson, a tailor and community leader.

Now that African-Americans and pretty much everyone on Earth can trace their roots to their tribal grasslands in Africa through DNA testing, why don't more do so and interlocalize with their long lost bloods, like Israel has done with the lost tribe of Israel? Slaves and their descendants are the lost tribe of Africa. Their lost children have a right to know their roots and reconnect with their lost family.

The Kalmyks are doing just that. The Kalmyks, a semi-nomadic branch of the Oirat Mongols, migrated from Chinese Turkistan in the 17th century, leaving their native lands in western China in search of better pastures and settling near the mouth of the Volga River in southwestern Russia close to the Caspian Sea. They became allies of the Russians and were charged by Peter I with guarding the eastern frontier of the Russian empire. But in 1771, Catherine the Great abolished their autonomy and ordered them to accept Christianity. Two hundred thousand Kalmyks, followers of Tibetan Buddhism, responded by going on a seven-month march back to Xinjiang,

China. Thousands were killed on the way by Russians, Kazakhs and Kyrgyz. Now they want 10,000 of their brothers and sisters from Xinjiang and Inner Mongolia to join them to save their language and culture from extinction.

It's a tempting and attractive proposition for those in Xinjiang who want to get away from the war on terror there between the pro-independence East Turkistan Islamic Movement and government PLA forces. The Uygur Muslim separatists want an independent East Turkestan. Uygurs make up 9 million of Xinjiang's 19 million population, many of whom want autonomy or independence. No different than what is going on in southern Thailand or the Philippines. In both countries' southern provinces, Muslim separatists have stepped up their bloody campaigns. Beheadings of Buddhist monks inside temples and taking the fight inside schools. In the Philippines, Christians get beheaded by local al-Qaeda affiliate Abu Sayaf, just because they are Christian in retaliation for earlier successful military assaults.

The new borderless Silk Road from China to Europe and the Middle East to secure long-term oil supplies, and a free-trade agreement between China and the Gulf Cooperation Council, whose members include, Saudi Arabia, Bahrain, Kuwait, Oman, Qatar and the United Arab Emirates is fraught with peril. Especially since Gulf Arab leaders are considering a joint civilian nuclear program that will only increase nuclear proliferation. A delicate dance for China to stay balanced as it invites high-tech Israeli firms to China to help farmers deal with advancing deserts and turning desert sands into fertile arable land.

Drip irrigation was invented in Israel in the '60s when I was attending Agricultural High School there. China is looking at Israel, a water-technology powerhouse, for solutions. Israel is a world leader in desalination and recycling technologies, and China is negotiating a series of agreements in the field. China-Israel trade has soared since official relations were established, rising from $50 million in 1992 to $3.3 billion in 2006. It is expected to reach $4.5 billion in 2007, reaching $10 billion by 2010. China ranks as one of Israel's leading trading partners in Asia, with at least 800 Israeli companies doing business there.

The growing ties between China and the rest of Asia with the Middle East wiill have dramatic reprecussions as the oil-rich Middle East states start to play China off against the U.S.– another good reason for the two to work together as Siamese twins. The new Silk Road is reaching its potential as Middle East firms keep signing bilateral trade agreements and investing in Asian telecoms, as Egypt's Orascom did when it bought 19 percent of Hong Kong's Hutchison Telecom for $1.3. billion.

With so many people traveling with two or more passports, resident cards and multiple entry business or visitor visas to anywhere they want to go, especially in and out of America, what does citizenship really mean these days? The place called home, where money is being earned, not to mention family and friends? Add up all the people moving across borders legally with their illegal relatives and one does have to question what the point is. As borders are erased paradoxically, cultural identity becomes more important. As we yield a little of our identity by becoming so economically interdependent, we seek a stronger cultural identity. Our roots, our tribal nationality, become more important.

This reality crystalized one balmy spring evening in April 2007 in Beijing's Ritan Park, where I started the evening having cocktails in the Stone Boat Pavilion with Chris Lanzit, an American businessman living in Beijing with his partner Linda Jacobson, a professor from Finland teaching and research-ing in Beijing. They had arrived on their bicycles. I walked there from my hotel. Catching up on the revolutionary changes taking place in Beijing in preparation for the 2008 Olympics was breathtaking. Moving on to a de-lightful fusion dinner at Xiao Wang's Home Restaurant at the northeast cor-ner of the park emphasized the rapidity with which fine dining has become a fine art again, like the good old imperial days, with the exception that now the masses can enjoy such pleasures.

We left the park through the West Gate, past the U.S. ambassador's home across the street from the Russian Moscow Restaurant, and turned onto Guang Hua Lu, past the South Gate to Schindler's Filling Station, a restaurant-bar run by Stefan Schindler, the former East German military attache to Beijing, who, like many East German diplomats in foreign embassies around the world, was stranded there without a country after the fall of the Berlin Wall.

He started the German Food Center, importing German food and beer and opened Schindlers Tankstelle, or Filling Station, a German-style brauhaus with an active bar that serves generous portions of cholesterol.

After Chris, Linda and I said our goodbyes, I decided to walk back past the Vietnamese Embassy to the hotel, 10 minutes away. Walking past Maggies, a favorite haunt known for its delightful Mongolian takeout dishes – not food, but women, that had just relocated to the area, but decided to just get to bed on my own because of an early start the next morning. Past the Mexican Wave, a nice tequila bar that has been there forever, where staff from the local embassies, especially Latino, hang out. The multi-lingual propositions from the streetwalkers strutting their wares on the main boulevard on which my hotel was situated was a real millennium reminder of how interlocal the world has become with China at the center of the interlocal-post global world.

Tradition

Former South African President Nelson Mandela remarried Graca Machel, the former first lady of Mozambique in 1999. They went through a traditional ceremony in his own Eastern Cape village, Qunu. Machel, who is a lawyer and active in children's rights, wore a traditional Xhosa outfit with face paint and underwent rituals to make her a full member of Mandela's Tembu clan.

Well-wishers included at least a dozen cabinet members. "Any great man who is not in touch with his culture is like a thin piece of paper dangling in the air," said the sports minister, Steve Tshwete.

Pieter Delport is an eighth-generation Afrikaaner, who immigrated to Australia in the early part of the 21st century. A lawyer and the city clerk of Pretoria during apartheid and the post-apartheid era in South Africa, Pieter shared a few traditional African beliefs and practices by educated Christian Africans, who, notwithstanding their conversions and high educational achievements and postgraduate degrees, still believe and practice traditional tribal beliefs. Tokolosh, or Thakulosi, and Shaka Zulu are two revered deities worshipped by Africans.

Tokolosh is a two-foot divine supernatural and very powerful god that can only operate and function in corners of a room or other space. He cannot function in a circular space. "Educated people who I worked or studied with would put their beds on three or four bricks to make sure there was room for Tokolosh to get under without banging his head," Pieter said as I listened in awe. "Devout Christians teachers, lawyers and politicians. They all believe in Tokolosh and Shaka Zulu," he continued as we hoisted our glasses of South African wine to his toast, *"Foute en ervaringe van die ver lede is n riglyn vir die toekoms –* The mistakes and experiences of the past are a good guide for the future."

South Africa needs a vigorous opposition to keep the ruling African National Congress (ANC) on its toes, call it to account, pick holes in some of its policies, and offer people alternative ideas if not the likelihood of an alternative party in power.

The ANC took power in the first multiracial elections in 1994. Riots, marches on parliament, a local ANC councilor in the central Free State hacked to death by rioters, have marked growing unrest at the government's failure to improve the lives of South Africans who bore the brunt of apartheid. The residents of Soweto, the township on the outskirts of Johannesburg which was a hotbed of opposition to the former whites-only regime, remain as neglected as ever by the ANC authorities. "We have nothing," said Sowetan Ngethembi Myaka, 24. The mother of two had been hit in the back by a rubber-coated bullet during protests against apartheid. "Better life and freedom is something we only read about in the newspapers."

The Democratic Alliance (DA) is emerging as a vigorous opposition. Headed by Helen Zille, the mayor of Capetown, a survivor of the Holocaust. Her parents were refugees from Nazi Germany. She was a notable anti-apartheid journalist and campaigner.

The number of white women in top management positions has, as a percentage of their share of the population, increased more than any other grouping since 2001. White women make up 5.5 percent of the economically active population, but hold 14.7 percent of executive positions in the 4,380 companies surveyed and 22.2 percent of middle management jobs.

The DA has evolved through several changes and alliances. At its core is the old Progressive Party, whose leonine survivor, Helen Suzman, was the sole liberal opponent of government in the all-white apartheid-era Parliament. Competing in 1994 as the Democratic Party it got a paltry 1.7 percent of the vote. In the last general election in 2004, as the Democratic Alliance, it got 12.4 percent. In local elections in 2006, it got nearly 15 percent, and now it heads a coalition that runs Cape Town.

The DA votes come from whites and coloreds, South Africans of mixed race, who each represent about 9 percent of the population. To become a force to be reckoned with, it has to attract black voters. The deep divisions in the ruling alliance of the ANC between president Thabo Mbeki and Deputy President Jacob Zuma, who is backed by the communist party and trade unions, may just be the break DA needs to attract blacks.

In her acceptance speech, Zille signaled her desire to appeal to all by speaking in English, Afrikaans, spoken by whites of mainly Dutch descent and by many coloreds, and in Xhosa, one of the country's most widely spoken African languages.

The warrior chief of the Zulus, Shaka Zulu won many a battle against the British and gave the colonials a real run for their money. He is honored every year in South Africa by the Zulus. The week-long festivities honoring his power and achievements are attended by natives who believe he is still all empowering.

"I'll never forget my law professor, an educated Zulu Christian who got his law degree in England and taught there before returning to South Africa," Pieter said as he was about to share another story and cultural experience. "The festivities honoring Shaka Zulu were coming up the following week. The class asked him if he would be going to participate in his village because we wanted to know if we should come to school or not. 'Absolutely not,' he said. 'That is a superstitious tribal belief and celebration that I as a devout, learned Christian do not believe in,' he told us. The next week when we came to school he was absent and neither the school or class had any idea where he was. He showed up the following week. When we asked him where he had been and inquired about his health, he told us he went to celebrate the Shaka Zulu festivities because 'What if Shaka noticed I wasn't there and cursed me?' he asked us."

Tribalism overrides any sense of nationalism. Political parties form along tribal, not ideological lines, and opportunities often stem from blood ties.

Before colonialism, tribal structures served as the equivalents of the modern state, and people turned to their leaders for loans, health care, and mediation in domestic disputes. The European colonial powers, arriving in the late 1880s, carved up Africa into new nations that often ignored and sometimes exploited longstanding tribal alliances. As a result, tribalism has caused many of Africa's existing conflicts and problems. An often-quoted Swahili phrase heard throughout the continent is, "If you leave your culture, then you are like a slave." The nation states created by the colonials in Africa – and the Middle East and Latin America – are unsustainable if there is to be peace and prosperity in the 21st century.

Nigeria is a prime example. It is the size of Egypt with a population about half that of America. Militants from the dominant Ijaw tribe in the oil-rich Niger delta in the south repeatedly attack pipelines, kidnap oil workers and extort money from the oil companies. They are frustrated that they have been ruled for most of their history, since independence, by corrupt Muslim generals from the north who exploit and steal the oil revenues from the south. They want local control of their oil wealth.

The 2007 presidential election that former state governor Umaru Yar' Adua won was fraught with irregularities and was "not credible" due to vote-rigging and violence, international observers said. The handover of power was billed as a democratic landmark in Nigeria because it is the first transfer from one civilian leader to another in a nation scarred by decades of army misrule. But the flawed election wiped the gloss off the occasion. President Yar' Adua's biggest challenge will be how to handle his predecessor, Olusegun Obasanjo, who picked Yar' Adua from obscurity. Many suspect Obasanjo intends to use him as a puppet.

"Nigerian unity is only a British invention," northern politician Abubakar Tafawa Balewa said in 1948, 12 years before independence made him Nigeria's first federal prime minister. Well, it was a nice idea but obviously not one Nigerians can easily sustain.

A report on the future of sub-Saharan Africa published in 2005 by the National Intelligence Council, a government think tank for U.S. intelligence services, identified the collapse of Nigeria as the most important risk facing the continent today.

Tribalism is also at the root of the anarchy and civil wars in Somalia. Somalia is one of the most homogeneous countries in Africa, with one language, Somali, and one religion, Sunni Islam, yet it is one of the most violently divided. Clan allegiances rule.

A sad story coming out of Africa is the removal of the oldest known tribe in the world, the Kalahari bushmen, from their homeland to make room for a game reserve and diamond mining. Naturally, the bushmen will not share in the benefits, not that they have asked. All they want is to continue to live by their traditional ways in the arid landscape, as they have done for eons. Genetic evidence suggests the bushmen are the direct descendants of the first evolved members of the modern human family – homo sapiens – who appeared more than 100,000 years ago.

Thankfully, the High Court of Botswana ruled that the Bushmen had been wrongfully evicted from ancestral hunting grounds and ordered they be allowed to return.

Africans, Fijians and all Pacific Islanders feel that their paradise and cultures were compromised by the colonizers who opened them up and awarded them to global barbarians. Shouldn't Americans feel the same way about the "federal barbarians" who have compromised the Constitution and usurped state rights by awarding them to themselves? Even worse, they have imposed Washington's ways on states and cities in direct contravention to America's Constitution.

For the federal government to use its authority to preempt state laws that are tougher, more progressive and protective of their citizens is unconstitutional and must be swept out by *We the Maids* in the 21st century. Hurricane Katrina was a millennium reminder of what happens to a city and state when they give up their state rights to the federal government. Alcatraz Island, the former federal prison in San Francisco Bay, like New Orleans, is a symbol of the prison Americans have allowed themselves to be incarcerated in.

The occupation of "The Rock" by Native Americans in 1969, when they claimed the "abandoned" federal property under the terms of treaties between tribal and government leaders – and where they celebrate "Unthanksgiving Day" every year since – is another example of what Americans can do to reclaim their constitutional rights.

Interlocalism – Afghan Style

The ideal interlocal workshop at the dawn of the 21st century is Afghanistan. Local clans and tribes form the backbone of the new government and only hope for future peace and prosperity.

Modern Afghanistan was stitched together as a buffer state in the late 19th century by British India and czarist Russia, with its first modern ruler, Amir Abdur Rahman Khan, picked from among the princelings of a warring Pashtun clan. In return for giving up control of the country's foreign affairs to Britain, he received arms and money to conquer various ethnic and linguistic groups: other Pashtuns, Tajik, Farsiwan, Uzbek, Turkmen, Baluch, Hazara, Aimaq and others.

He established a firm foundation for an oppressive and corrupt centralized system. A brief experiment with a constitutional monarchy from 1965 to 1973, under Zahir Shah, was aborted by a palace coup, followed in 1978 by the Soviet-inspired communist regime that plunged the country into a quarter of a century of proxy wars that culminated in the rise of the Taliban. Most people in Afghanistan have no memory of an effective, functioning national government.

Another important historical footnote to the fierce independence to this day of the tribes along the Afghan-Pakistan border is that Pakistan – at the time the British were drawing up the Afghan border to create the buffer zone between Russia and India – was part of India.

Today under Pakistani law, the tribal lands, which stretch for 1,000 miles along the border of Pakistan and Afghanistan and hold some 6 million people, are roughly equivalent to American Indian reservations, where federal intervention is legally permissable but only under certain circumstances. America's desire to capture Osama bin Laden is not one of those justifiable circumstances. The implacable tribal law of *melmastia,* the rule of hospitality, which forbids harming or dishonoring a guest, only makes capturing Bin Laden the challenge it is.

The old monarchy and Taliban regimes share the common myth, first fabricated by British India spin doctors, that the Pashtun have the exclusive right to rule Afghanistan. This myth is echoed approvingly by Pakistan and other powers who want to dominate the country. The international community should dispel this myth and encourage the creation of a government that recognizes the crucial role of the local clans and tribes and regional communities in self-governance, as existed in earlier, peaceful times.

Local autonomy and the political integrity of every ethnic and sectarian segment of Afghan society should be guaranteed by a national constitution and decentralized federal governance structure adopted by the grand council of tribal and religious elders – the Loya Jirga. The task is daunting, but the rewards are liberation from terror for the people of Afghanistan and a new precedent for combating the conditions that give rise to terrorism elsewhere. The main task of any international body is to bring law and order to all the provinces and cities, not just Kabul. The main task is to inculcate a secular ethos, enlightened management of the bigotry, in a society steeped in bigotry. Democracy will follow.

The New Way

Jiang Zemin, Bill Clinton and Tony Blair led the charge to change their governments and lead them and their allies in a new direction as we entered the 21st century. Their goal was to give formal direction to the general trend in which liberal, labor and socialist parties are abandoning government ownership of major industries and tax-and-spend programs that aggressively seek to redistribute income and interlocalize with each other. China, India, Japan and America all jockeying with each other and Brazil, Russia and all regional neighbors and interlocal communities for economic superiority. Africa, Latin America and the Middle East are all seeing dramatic geopolitical transformations in bilateral and multilateral relationships.

Even sworn enemies Israel and Saudi Arabia have come together to contain their common enemy, Iran. With its growing influence in Iraq, Lebanon and Syria, Israel sees its security less dependent on the U.S. in the future and more reliant on Egypt, Jordan, Saudi Arabia and Turkey. Israel is riding the "Sunni Solidarity" wave that is becoming the decisive factor in the war for the soul of Islam – and the mastery of the Middle East.

During the debate on the future of Quebec as an independent state, Jean Marc Leger, president of Canada's largest Francophone polling organization, said, "Instead of two overlapping governments, federal and provincial, there would be only one; instead of two health ministries, there would be one; instead of two transportation ministries, there would be one. There is redundance in everything now." This also holds true in America today and most other countries.

Like America, every country has duplication and in some cases triplication. The tentacles of federal functions control must be cut where they overlap with local and interlocal functions.

Former Minnesota Gov. Jesse Ventura believes that states should do away with the bicarmel system of two governing bodies and replace it with a unicarmel system. "Switching state governments from bicarmel to unicarmel legislation not only trims an entire redundant layer away from government, it also fixes half a dozen other problems," Ventura said when asked how he would like to change government.

Belgium is a good example of excessive multiple layers of government bureaucracy. It has 58 ministers, secretaries of state and special commissions – an extraordinary high number for a nation of 10 million. The French-speaking Wallonia region in the south has three separate ministers of education for primary schools, secondary schools and universities, when one is sufficient in its neighbor France. Wallonia has two separate governments – one for administration and one for cultural affairs, and it has 17 ministers. All this for only 3 million people. That's just for Belgium. It doesn't count the legions of bureaucracy that the European Union and other European bodies have headquartered there.

We the Maids everywhere should sweep aside historical, religious and political dogma and replace it with economic prudence and political expediency. We must focus our attention and concentrate on how to eliminate unnecessary layers of career politicians and their self-serving bureaucrats. Only then will we be able to build a better future.

Local Focus – America
In the New World Order, America and other crusader nations should start to

focus on themselves first and foremost. Locally on their city, state, and national realignments to minimize duplication. Their time, dedication and resources spent on regional organizations should also be carefully reassessed from a national perspective to see if they have the will to comply with the majority will of the global and regional organizations they belong to. Even the U.S., the "global bully," does not live up to the international covenants it signs because of state governments that have chosen to adopt laws that suit their local needs, and not the federal government's international obligations. The U.S. is in breach of the International Covenant on Civil and Political Rights, as its own report to the United Nations Human Rights Commission points out. The committee favors the abolition of the death penalty, but the U.S. told the U.N. it cannot comply because "the majority of citizens through their freely elected officials have chosen to retain the death penalty." Have they?

The U.S. refusal to recognize and respect its economic, political and military limitations will sideline it in the 21st century as it is eclipsed by China. The U.S. preoccupation with Iraq, Taiwan and providing freedom to all people living under repressive totalitarian regimes not only highlights U.S. duplicity – because of the number of repressive totalitarian regimes it supports – but underscores the debilitating cost it is saddling *We the Apathetic People* and future generations of our children with. Former Prime Minister Mahathir bin Mohamad of Malaysia once said that the U.S. economy is standing on "feet of clay" and that "if people do not keep giving money to the U.S., it will go bankrupt."

As if the political divide between the red and blue states isn't enough, America is bankrupt politically more than most people realize. That is because more than 50 million, or 44 percent, of the 115 million people who voted for either George W. Bush or John F. Kerry in the 2004 election, live in states that voted for the other guy. In red states, one can find three churches on every block, whereas in the blue states there are three Asian restaurants on every block.

America clearly has become a country with two separate and distinct populations that not only dislike each other – they despise each other.

Is it any wonder so many political writers and pundits suggested the Blue states join Canada and form the United States of Canada? Canada is now North Mexico, while Mexico is South Canada and America is the meat in the sandwich. North America is interlocalizing. Canada is a country where most people can't name their first prime minister, who was a Scot named after an American hamburger chain: Sir John A. MacDonald. Becoming part of America has started dumbing down Canadians to culturally interlocalize with their neighbors to the south.

In the northwest corner of North America, British Columbia, Washington and Oregon have a lot more in common with each other than they do with their federal government or national identity. "They should just name the province with people from both countries Cascadia. Its flag should be a coffee mug with two marijuana leaves," suggested columnist Jake van der Kamp during one of our discussions about how America and Canada are fusing into one nation.

A nation with another nation within after Quebec is recognized as a nation within a united Canada. Interlocalism as separatism loses its appeal, as the Bloc Quebecois which is seeking separation found out. In Vermont, Americans cross over the border into Canada to buy their prescription drugs. One can even argue that Canada has more in common with Hong Kong and China because of the large number of Chinese there. The 2003 SARS outbreak confirmed just how close the two are. Canada had the third-highest number of SARS cases after China and Hong Kong.

Just how interlocal China and Canada are was made clear during Chinese President Hu Jintao's visit there in September 2005. China is Canada's second-biggest trading partner, after the U.S. A long term and stable "strategic partnership" based on the large Chinese immigrant population and grounded in energy and resources is the foundation of the growing interlocal relationship.

Chinese is the third-most-spoken language in Canada, after English and French. Annual trade in 2005 reached $24 billion and is projected to reach $30 billion by 2010. Chinese companies have invested billions of dollars in Canada's energy sector, including a 40 percent stake in a $3.6-billion pipeline project. Many Canadians view the China card as a way of reminding their U.S. neighbor not to take them for granted.

There are numerous similar regional groupings that make sense in North America. The Southwest, the South and Northeast.

Let's not forget that at one time all of California, and much of America's Southwest, was Mexican territory. And let's not forget the Alamo. Mexican-Americans haven't. America has through military intervention, starting in 1846 and the war against Mexico, which is the first moment the idea of empire took center stage in American affairs. As President James Polk said, "We've just got to have California!" Well, America got California and the Mexicans are now quietly reclaiming it. The U.S.-Mexican border is blurrier than ever, especially for those with dual citizenship who travel freely from their home on one side of the border to their work on the other side.

Is it any wonder both Democrats and Republicans try to woo legal and illegal future citizens from Mexico by welcoming them to America? In the 1960s John F. Kennedy's political machine registered them in droves, hoping to win their Catholic votes. Later that decade, Caesar Chavez helped millions more gain their rights by battling California farmers. Today every politician in both parties is running in their footsteps – except California Gov. Arnold Schwarzenegger, even though Mexico is California's largest trading partner. Is he afraid of being called a senorita-hombre?

Some pundits have gone further and said that Enron executives in Texas must have thought they were in Mexico where they could keep their employees, regulators and shareholders in the dark because of their strong political connections. With the right education standards and systems, interlocalism can only enrich and enlighten the larger interlocalized community.

Virtually every family in Poland is interlocalized with America through relatives and friends in the Midwest. America, and Chicago in particular, became the promised land for several generations of Poles, who joined forces with their Solidarity movement brothers and sisters in Poland to bring an end to communism.

Global cartography changes constantly and will continue to do so in the New World Order. History is no guide. Nations are not some natural phenomenon. They are complex accumulations of strength, alliances and enmities. And the passion for nationhood has swung between eras of consolidation and fragmentation: the single-state world of the Roman Empire; the 500-odd nations of the Renaissance. In the post-Cold War age, people impatient with the map they've inherited appear to be caught in between. A globalized economy is melting down the relevance of nationhood at the same time that the dispossessed, unrealized yearnings to be a state are gaining legitimacy. Interlocalism can accommodate these conflicting desires.

Regional Dreams

NATO has redefined itself after the collapse of the Soviet Union. Its first war in its 50-year history was against Serbian Yugoslavs for their ethnic cleansing of Muslim Kosovars. NATO interfered in the domestic affairs of Yugoslavia because of its outrage at the genocide and ethnic cleansing taking place. NATO, a regional force, dealt with a regional issue because of the impact millions of refugees fleeing Yugoslavia would have on Europe.

After the attacks of 9/11, NATO invoked for the first time the NATO charter's mutual defense clause, thus giving the U.S. the full military support of its NATO allies. Now that Russia is also a member of the New World Order of the 21st century, it has indeed changed the European alliance dramatically. Russia is interlocalizing itself back to Europe while keeping its interlocal options in Central Asia and Europe open. Independed Ukraine and Kosovo are test tubes to watch.

When America and Britain tried to get NATO to defend Turkey in the event of a war in Iraq, NATO refused. It voted 16-3 in favor of the U.S. request to defend Turkey after intense U.S. lobbying efforts. Germany, France and Belgium voted against such assistance. No wonder France and Germany were defeated in World War II and their other 20th-century military adventures. They are out of touch with geopolitical realities. Then and now. They deserve each other and the Belgium chocolates they enjoy so much. As we enter the 21st century, NATO is a glaring example of how regional alignments must be restructured to work cohesively.

The November 2002 NATO summit in Prague transformed the alliance to meet the challenges of the 21st century. It welcomed Russia and agreed to take over peacekeeping responsibilities from America in Afghanistan. The summit also agreed to establish a response force to ensure all NATO allies can contribute to the most demanding military operations, including Iraq.

NATO, a U.S. - European military alliance, is now on the ground outside of Europe in Muslim Afghanistan with a platoon of Russian soldiers.

Existing regional organizations have to rethink and redefine their purpose. NATO was founded to protect Western Europe from a Soviet Bloc invasion. Now that some of the former Soviet Bloc countries are members, NATO had to go out of region or out of business. Richard Nixon was right when he admonished people to study NATO. "Those who yearn for an international body to serve as a framework for key elements of American strategic planning need look no further than NATO, whose credibility, dependability and formidability far outstrip the United Nations," the late president said.

NATO celebrated its 50th birthday in the closing years of the last millennium, at the dawn of the New World Order. NATO was the brainchild of a rough-hewn former trade union leader with a grade-school education, the illegitimate son of a housemaid.

His name was Ernest Bevin, and he was Britain's foreign secretary. In the anxious days of 1948, with Czechoslavakia slipping under communist sway and Berlin blockaded, he feared that the Soviet Union would pick off the nations of Western Europe one by one.

Bevin proposed that his government should seek to form with the backing of the Americas and the dominions a Western democratic system comprising Scandinavia, the Low Countries, France, Italy, Greece and possibly Portugal. "As soon as circumstances permit, we should, of course, wish to include Spain and Germany, without whom no Western system can be complete."

Sen. Joseph R. Biden Jr. told the Senate Foreign Relations Committee that "if we do not achieve our goals in Kosovo, NATO is finished as an alliance." Thus the war that eventually ousted Slobodan Milosevic was a good example of NATO acting as a regional policeman rather than a body of collective defense.

The war in Yugoslavia was a test that NATO met surprisingly well. Bill Clinton, England's Tony Blair and Gerhard Schroeder of Germany, all former peaceniks, marched shoulder to shoulder. Massimo d'Alema of Italy, a former communist, pledged to help bring down one of Europe's last remaining communist dictators. Even Prime Minister Costas Simitis of Greece was quietly on board despite his country's religious links to Serbia. Central European countries, such as Bulgaria and Romania, quietly did what they could.

NATO's expanding role in Afghanistan and Iraq has reaffirmed why the 21st century geopolitical challenges dictate the reassessment of regional alliances to meet the new global reality.

Talk Turkey, Not Crusades

Looming over the whole EU process is the question of what to do about NATO stalwart Turkey. Turkey is in many ways a schizophrenic country. The Turkish republic was founded in 1923 in the rubble of the Ottoman Empire and defined itself in stark contrast to it. The early republicans associated the empire with everything that was archaic, religious and backward. They modeled the new republic on modern, secular and progressive lines, similar to those they saw in Europe. It became the first secular Islamic state.

It remains a secular Muslim democracy with powerful military generals who ensure that Muslim fundamentalism is held in check. This was self-evident again in May 2007, after the military backed by secularists derailed former Islamist Foreign Minister Abdullah Gul's parliamentary campaign for president. More than three million pro-secular demonstrators took to the streets of Ankara, Istanbul, Izmir, Canakkale, Manisa and many other cities.

A key element of the opposition's position was that it would be a disgrace for a headscarf-clad first lady to live in the mansion once occupied by Turkey's founder, Mustafa Kemal Attaturk – who established the modern secular state.

The military establishment had issued a public reminder that it was the ultimate defender of the secular Turkish state. The army has removed four civilian governments in 50 years in a country that hopes for European Union membership.

That all changed after the July 2007 election in which Prime Minister Tayyip Erdogan's ruling Justice and Development Party (AKP), won a decisive parliamentary election, garnering 47 percent of the votes. The turnout was estimated at around 80 percent in a country of 74 million people where voting is compulsory. Erdogan has presided over strong economic growth and falling inflation since his party swept to power in 2002 on the back of a financial crisis. That got Gur the presidency.

The party will be able to form a government by itself, but will lack the two-thirds majority needed to bring about institutional changes. The only check on the AKP is its own conscience and a crackdown by the secular-oriented armed forces. But, as part of its effort to get into the European Union, Turkey implemented reforms that undercut the military's political role.

The AKP chose the president, who in turn names the head of the armed forces, a power that could potentially turn the military into a servant of the government.

Turkey is the political fulcrum of the Middle East. As Turkey goes so goes the Middle East. Turkey is the key to peace in the Middle East. It is a Muslim democracy that borders Iran and Iraq and is on good terms with all countries in the Middle East, including Israel.

Turkey has been trying to get into the European trade bloc since 1959, and has achieved a comprehensive association agreement with it.

Many European governments have never considered Turkey to be part of Europe. Why not? From the prospective of geopolitical location, Turkey occupies a central stage in the southern belt of Eurasia, at the intersection of Asia and Europe, the Black Sea and the Mediterranean Sea, and the Balkans, the Middle East and the Caucasus.

This is the southern passage between West Asia and Eastern Europe. As a result, Turkey is an East and South European and West Asian country all at the same time. Turks have fought and died with American and European soldiers in the Korean conflict and have been prepared to do so again if called upon. Turkey offered to send 10,000 troops for peacekeeping duty in Iraq but were turned down when the Kurds objected. It let the U.S. use its air bases for NATO-and U.N.-approved military campaigns. In Afghanistan, it took over the command of the international peacekeeping force in 2004.

Turkey scares Europeans because with 70 million people in 2006 – and a population that will reach 80 million in 2025 – Turkey is bound to become the most populous of all European nations. Europeans overlook the fact that Turkey is the only Muslim nation that separates church and state and has made a concerted effort to be part of the peaceful transition into the New World Order. It has amended its constitution to comply with EU requirements and has given the 12 million Kurds living in Turkey the freedoms mandated by the EU.

By pushing Turkey away from Europe and ignoring interlocalism, Turkey has been given no choice but to interlocalize with all the other Turkic states in Central Asia that used to be part of the Ottoman Empire before they became part of the Soviet Union. The Turkish-speaking people of Western China and the nearby Muslim states, including Iran and Syria. As always, it is the bridge between Christian Europe and the Muslim Near and Far East. This geographic and geopolitical fact is brought home to me every time I visit Istanbul and take the ferry from the European side of the city to the Asian side.

Turkey is the only Muslim free-market democracy in the world. A modern country with 70 million people and the world's 19th largest economy, Turkey can encourage and more easily communicate with its fellow Muslims in Central Asia, Indonesia and Malaysia. Indonesia and Malaysia, although imperfect in their ways, are officially democratic and secular. Turkey can show these two more progressive Muslim states and others the way to becoming stable secular democratic states.

When the street outside one of the two synagogues that were suicide-bombed in Istanbul in 2004 was reopened, the chief rabbi appeared at the ceremony hand in hand with the top Muslim cleric of the city and the local mayor. The Turkish prime minister, Recep Tayyip Erdogan, also paid a visit to the chief rabbi. When a judge was killed and several injured in May 2006 by a fundamentalist lawyer who shot them after they ruled in favor of a lower court ruling against the promotion of a teacher because she wore a head scarf to and from school, Turkish politicians, including the prime minister, joined the hundreds of thousands of people who joined the funeral cortege in a show of solidarity for secularism.

Turkish politicians are not intimidated by religious fundamentalists because they have the legitimacy that comes from being democratically elected. They are setting the example for all other Muslim countries. Denying Turkey a place at the European table will be a huge strategic defeat for Europe in its war on Islamic fundamentalism. By rejecting Turkey, Europe will pour more fuel onto the fires of anger that are burning throughout the Islamic world. Not a good thing for Europeans.

The European Union must carefully review why it has rejected Turkey from full membership and why it fast-tracked former Soviet satellites Poland, the Czech Republic, Hungary and Slovenia along with Cyprus, while Latvia, Lithuania, Slovakia, Romania and Bulgaria are on a slower track and Ukraine is stuck back in the station.

Coincidentally, all the candidate nations, with the exception of Bulgaria and the eastern half of Romania, lie west of the historic line between Roman Catholic or Protestant Christianity on one side and Orthodox Christianity and Islam on the other. The European Commission says it makes no cultural or religious judgments in assessing potential candidates for membership. What counts is their ability to compete economically and their commitment to democracy.

It sure doesn't look or sound that way when you have the late Pope John Paul II urging European countries to remember the "religious, cultural and spiritual" heritage of the continent on the eve of the EU meeting to consider Turkey's membership. The pope went on to say it was important to ensure the "common European house" was built with "the cement of that extraordinary religious, cultural and civic heritage that has made Europe great down the centuries, and not adopt a constitution that fails to mention Christianity." The pope lamented what he called "the loss of Christian memory."

Ironically, he made his divisive pronouncements to the members of Italy's two legislative chambers in 2002 in the Chamber of Deputies in Rome where he brought 142 years of tense relations between the Vatican and the Italian state to a close by making the first ever papal speech to Italy's parliament.

Former French President Valery Giscard D'Estaing, chairman of the European Union's constitutional convention, joined the pope's chorus and said that Turkey's EU membership would represent "the end of the European

Union," and added: "Those who are pushing hardest for enlargement in the direction of Turkey are adversaries of the EU."

When Silvio Berlusconi, the former Italian prime minister, asked Prime Minister Recep Tayyip if Turkey was seeking a marriage of convenience or of love with the EU, the Turk riposted that he was after "a Catholic marriage – one that lasts forever." The undeniable fact is that Turkey, Islam and democracy bound by EU marriage vows would prosper and Europe would show that it is not a Christian club.

The first Christian evangelization trips of Saint Peter and Saint Paul were to Turkey. For more than a thousand years, Constantinople was the center of the Christian world. Later, Ottoman Turkey was for centuries considered part of the "concert of Europe," proving indispensable in defining and securing the strategic balance among the European continent's great powers.

The devastating earthquakes that struck Greece and Turkey in 1999 moved both countries closer than any politician could and pushed Turkey about four feet closer to Europe. More significant, though, has been the fact that since the quake, Turkey and Europe have moved closer politically and psychologically. Almost every European country rushed to send relief to Turkey. Hopefully, this wave of sympathy can be converted into a permanent policy change that could help heal the breach between Turkey and Europe.

European hypocrisy and double standards for Muslim countries was again highlighted during the extradition hearing in Italy of Kurdish separatist leader Abdullah Ocalan who had been arrested in Italy. He was the founder of the Kurdistan Workers Party. He had led a 14 year separatist war in Turkey. In the process, he and his party had killed many innocent victims. Nevertheless, although Chile's Augusto Pinochet was extradited earlier from Europe by one Christian country to accommodate the wishes of another, the same legal standards were not applied when a Muslim country made a similar request. The double standard was highlighted by the fact that Italy and Turkey, unlike Chile, were NATO allies.

If Turkey is good enough to be a member of NATO and in the quarter-finals of the first World Cup of the 21st century in 2002, it is good enough to be a member of the European Community. Only one European Union country, Germany, made it to the 2002 World Cup quarter finals. The New World Order of the 21st century mandates that *We The Maids* sweep out historical religious and cultural prejudices and gamble for practical long-term realistic political change without the shortsightedness of current career politicians. An EU without Turkey is an illusory oxymoron.

Moderate Islamist groups, in particular, are watching events in Turkey as a test of the merits of engagement in democratic politics. The showdown in Turkey, and the EU, will have far-reaching implications for the evolution of Islamist movements in the region. Muslims remember the Algerian army's intervention in 1991 to stop an Islamist victory in legislative elections. Everyone knows the Turkish Army's moves were supported by Washington and the EU. After all, the army is the constitutional guardian of secularism in Turkey. Any reason the U.S. military establishment in the U.S. is not?

Muslim Brotherhoods that have solid constituencies and political bases, have every legitimate right to demand recognition of the public support they have at the polls. Their frustration does not justify the brutal violence they periodically put on spectacular display.Why the U.S. is backing the wrong horse again in the Arabian deserts is unfathomable to me. They should be backing them.

Autocratic Arab states that confront Islamist parties, but seek legitimacy from Islam and base their constitution on Islamic principles are doomed to fail. Turkey's constitutional model is what they should be adopting. That is why success in Turkey will lend support to Islamist parties stepped up in their political participation in the aftermath of 9/11, even though some of them have moderated their language to distance themselves from jihadi groups. Why America is again backing authoritarian regimes is something *We the Apathetic Maids* have to question.

The Turkish political and geopolitical issues have to be determined at the ballot box. Otherwise it will merely confirm to the Islamists of how "intolerant" America is if Islamisists win. America should embrace democratic Islamisists. Failure in Turkey and its EU accession negotiations, will be a tsunami scale Katrina political disaster for the western dream of encouraging secular Islam.

European Wake

The Iraq war confirmed that Europe is not just antagonistic towards Turkey, but no longer a true U.S. ally now that the Cold War is over. Europe is more of a refueling point. The U.S. should consider withdrawing its active membership in the NATO alliance and change its status to observer. Notwithstanding the NATO alliance and the billions the U.S. spent there under the Marshall Plan, Europe is still not a genuine partner. By the time the Marshall Plan ended in 1952, the U.S. had disbursed in foreign aid more than all previous administrations put together.

As an equivalent share of America's gross domestic product today, the Marshall Plan would cost around $200 billion. A cheap price to keep the Russians and their communist parties out of power. Britain and France got the largest amounts in absolute terms, though the relative impact on smaller countries, including Italy, was greater. Europe knows the end of the Cold War liberated it from the "struggle for mastery in Europe," but hesitates to put aside the U.S. crutches and subsidy. Europe is suffering "Walheimer's disease" – the inability to remember what you did during the war, named after Kurt Waldheim, the Austrian secretary general of the United Nations who became Austria's president in 1986.

It is no great loss because the EU was a non-starter from the outset. A club that was founded in 1957 with six members that has grown to 27 members speaking 20 different languages "Did you just say this was a budget for a mean Europe?" a Danish journalist asked Jose Manuel Barroso, the Portugese president of the European Commission during the 2005 budgetary debates. "No, I said it was a budget for a mini Europe," he replied. In fact, Barroso meant both.

Europe's mean history and identity is rooted in religion – Christianity. Austria, which was in the forefront of opposition to Turkey's membership, is encumbered with the historical baggage of conflict with the Ottoman Empire. Dismembering the Ottoman Empire may have been the most damaging and dangerous thing Europe ever did for itself. Nation states then, like now, tried to maintain religious monopolies. At best, a concordat could be struck with other Christians, although often only after generations of civil war. "Ultimately, antagonistic religions mean antagonistic cultures," T.S. Eliot warned, "and ultimately, religions cannot be reconciled." He was writing in the aftermath of World War II and probably had in mind Catholics and Protestants, and perhaps Jews. Europeans today might think of Muslims and perhaps agree with Eliot.

The French certainly do. According to Article 4 of a law passed on February 23, 2005, it is now compulsory in France to emphasize the positive dimension of the French colonial era in high school history courses and textbooks. It is clear that France's Muslim and African minorities do not appreciate this compulsory interpretation of history.

Representatives of the black community chose the 200th anniversary of the battle of Austerlitz, which fell on December 2, 2005 – Napoleon's greatest military feat – to denounce Napoleon's racist attitudes. Napoleon reinstated slavery, which had been abolished during the French Revolution. As a result, the French government commemorated its naval defeat by the British at Trafalgar more lavishly, including the participation of a French vessel, than its land victory at Austerlitz. The symbol is powerful. France and Britain – within the framework of the EU – are more reconciled with each other today than the French are with their own past.

Austerlitz was the greatest victory of Napoleon Bonaparte's career. By defeating the combined armies of Austria and France, Napoleon was able to redraw the map of Europe, conjuring up a new Confederation of the Rhine from the Baltic to the Alps. Moreover, by forcing the Austrian Emperor Francis to renounce the title of Holy Roman Emperor, Napoleon snuffed out an institution that had been at the heart of Europe for more than a millennium. Voltaire famously said of the Holy Roman Empire that it was neither holy, Roman, nor an empire.

By imposing political correctness on the teachings of the past, the French National Assembly has committed more than an educational crime. It has made a national mistake. If one of the big challenges confronting France is that of integrating its minorities, then the imposition of a unilateral reading of history on all French people, whatever their origins, is not only anachronistic but offensive.

The 450-page European Constitution as drafted is disconnected from Europe's history. To make matters worse, its language, like the EU, has been dictated

by bureaucrats – unelected "experts." The text, which has as many excep-
tions as rules, isn't written for the ordinary citizen, but for the bureaucrat.
For example, Article III-139, which declares: "This sub-section shall not
apply, so far as any member state is concerned, to activities which in that
state are connected, even occasionally, with the exercise of public authority.

European laws or framework laws may exclude certain activities from
application of this sub-section." As a lawyer, I can't figure out what that
means. Any wonder French and Dutch voters turned it down? I don't know
of any European, yet alone a French or Dutch person, who will vote in favor
of a document that begins with the words "His Majesty the King of the
Belgians...." Just because the proposed EU will be headquartered in
Belgium does not make all Europeans Belgian.

The fact is the European Constitution is dead – dead and cold – unless it gets
back to its historical competitive roots. Europe is the product of intense
competition of numerous states on a small continent. The competition has to
get a lot stiffer for Europe to survive as a union.

The 27 EU leaders acknowledged as much at their June 2007 summit in
Brussels with the modified constitution rebranded a "treaty," making it easy
for governments to avoid putting the issue to a vote. Only 18 of Europe's 27
countries have ratified the constitution.

The leaders squabbled like third world leaders at their regional summits.
The EU summit was supposed to be the event in which the new generation
of leaders shed the protectionist ways of Europe, turning the awkward pachy-
derm into a nimble feline capable of outrunning the U.S. and Asia. Right.
The exact opposite happened. It confirmed Europe is divided into at least
two distinct political and economic groupings. Some in favor of the treaty in
its current form and others demanding a reduction of the role of the EU as a
national political objective. It is understandable why. With 23 official languages and 15 currencies, even after creation of the euro, it is difficult to see
how Europe can ever be one cohesive unit.
French President Nicolas Sarkozy's "feat" was to persuade his colleagues to
drop "free and undistorted competition" as one of the aims of the treaty. He

believes in promoting "national champions" – the corporate welfare recipients the government wants to boost and support. Instead of free markets, the new treaty upheld interventionist policies responsible for the fact that Europe's unemployment rate is nearly double that of the U.S.

The treaty will now be picked apart by the 27 legislative bodies in an attempt to reach further compromises. Poland's former ruling Kaczynski twins led the charge for a change in the voting rules because of their deep suspicion of Germany, rooted in Poland's suffering under Nazi occupation. The treaty must be ratified by all 27 members.

The treaty agreed to at the summit means that from 2009, the EU will have a long-term president of the European Council instead of a rotating presidency, under which each country chairs the union for six months every 13½ years. Now there will be a European president chosen by 27 countries for 2½ years. It will no longer have a foreign minister, but a foreign policy and security "high commissioner," and a convoluted voting system, in which the 27 commissioners from each member state will be replaced in 2014, with the number of commissioners equal to two-thirds of member states; the countries represented will be changed every five years and won't be fully implemented for 10 years before the simpler system goes into effect. With a high commission dealing with international diplomacy, it is understandable why the system is so convoluted.

Starting in 2014, decisions will be taken by double majority, and will need the support of 55 percent of member states representing 65 percent of the EU's population. The national veto, however, is retained by each country in sensitive areas such as foreign affairs, defense and taxation.

The deep freeze that parts of Europe were subjected to after Russia cut off natural gas supplies to Ukraine in the height of winter 2005, when they failed to reach a new agreement, causing Ukraine to siphon off gas supplies to Central and Western Europe from the primary conduit – the pipeline from Russia going through the country – was a metaphor for how illusory warm European unity and functionality really is. The fact is that we must contemplate and address a dire European future in which France, Germany and Italy, which contribute just over two-thirds of the gross domestic product of the euro zone and just under half that of the 25-member European Union, become paralyzed.

They were the three dominant members of the original EU of six and its most influential promoters, without whose continued active participation would make it impossible for the EU to function. The European continent must contemplate a future in which its most important countries with fragile governments preside over a disgruntled population questioning the merits of a united Europe. The Russian-Ukraine gas dispute that caused the shivers in Austria, France, Germany, Italy, Poland and Slovakia, happened on the day Russia's Vladimir Putin took over the chair of the Group of 8 leading industrialized nations.

Why Europe is represented by four countries at the G8, while China and India have none, makes no sense and is unsustainable in today's interlocal world.

Fickle Europe
Europe is an unpredictable and unreliable U.S. partner. More than 20 European states helped the CIA establish a global web of human rights abuses by setting up clandestine prisons and secret flights to hold and transfer terror suspects after 9/11 to countries where they faced torture in breach of the continent's human rights treaties. First, Europe is a willing partner and then it reneges on the deal. Europe is a continental basket case. The description that French "national psychiatrist" Gerard Mermet gave France applies to the union it founded. They both suffer from a collective form of three mental illnesses: paranoia, schizophrenia and hypochondria. Europe is terminally ill.

The European Union's hypocrisy has hit a 21st-century cyber Berlin Wall and imploded. As a result, Western Europe experienced a prolonged economic stagnation at the dawn of the 21st century. The International Monetary Fund estimated the GDP growth for 2005 at 1.6 percent, down from 2.5 percent in 2004, while growth in the 12-member euro zone fell 0.8 percent year on year to 1.2 percent – a stagnation that could turn into a depression. Should that happen, the pluralist democracy there may be at serious risk.

The EU is much like the Byzantine Empire before it disappeared – a weak center with limited means to pursue its interests and stabilize its periphery.

The EU is rudderless and directionless since its draft constitution was defeated in the French and Dutch referendums in 2005. The defeat of the "European Dream" at the ballot box continued to perpetuate European inertia in the face of globalization, protectionism and a rise in national self-interest. European solidarity is an illusory dream. Of the 15 "old" EU members, 12 have refused free access to their labor markets to eastern Europeans. The images of the cheap Polish plumbers invading France that helped defeat the constitutional referendum, loom larger than life. An EU without the free flow of laborers across national boundaries – as France advocates – is a non-starter.

The carrots held out by the EU to aspiring future members are not juicy enough to motivate political elites to undertake the painful reforms required to grow or survive. Europe has to go back to the drawing board and be refounded. "One must unfortunately note that Europe seems to be going down a road which could lead it to take its leave from history," Pope Benedict XVI warned calling Europeans who want less children "dangerous" individuals. Europe is searching for a new identity that is relevant to the 21st century.

The failure of the EU to agree on a 2007-2014 budget was the latest ominous sign in Europe's long history of shortsightedness. Germany, the perennial European wild card, can no longer afford to be the EU's sugar daddy because of the high cost of integrating what was East Germany into the nation's economy.

Germany, like Eastern and Western Europe, was split in two after World War II because of the 1945 Yalta treaty signed by President Franklin D. Roosevelt, Soviet leader Josef Stalin and British Prime Minister Winston Churchill. The pact defined zones of control among the wartime allies and followed in the "unjust tradition" of the 1939 Ribbentrop-Molotov Pact signed by Stalin and Hitler to partition Central Europe. The Yalta accord opened the door to Soviet occupation of Eastern and Central Europe – and the Cold War.

When the Yalta agreement was signed, the priority after World War II was to bring conflict to an end – without starting a new one. The Soviet Union had paid the highest human price to defeat Hitler. It had lost 26.6 million people in a brutal four-year struggle to drive the German forces out of Russia – and extracted a handsome territorial reward for its huge human sacrifice.

A new and genuine trans-Atlantic partnership is long overdue, but for now, career politicians on both sides of the ocean confirm Lord Keynes dictum, "The difficulty lies not in the new ideas but in escaping from the old ones." The merger of the New York Stock Exchange with the Paris-based Euronext that is transforming into the first transatlantic stock market is just such an escape.

American-British Alliance

The British no vote to joining the EU was the final nail in the EU coffin. The Europeans have Napoleonic law and economics, and the British, whom Napoleon did not conquer – like America – have common law and the free market. A new globalized Maginot Line has been drawn between Napoleonic Europe and the U.S.-British alliance.

The U.S.-Britain coalition in Iraq represents an alliance that has a long history, going back to the founding of America. When Tony Blair addressed a joint session of Congress in 2003, he reminded America how special that relationship is. Winston Churchill summed up the relationship best after America stopped the 1956 Anglo-French operation to seize control of the Suez Canal. "We must never again allow our foreign policy to be decided in Washington – never." The Iraq war has put the special relationship under strain because Blair failed to heed Churchill's caveat. British soldiers killed by U.S. friendly fire only adds to the strain. The troubled cross-Atlantic U.S.-Britain relationship is a "special relationship" underpinned by much more than strategic interests. It is based on ties of culture, ideas, language and history.

This was highlighted by Queen Elizabeth and President George W. Bush when they toasted their countries' tight bonds in the grandest White House dinner of Bush's administration in 2007. "Our's is a partnership always to be reckoned with in the defense of freedom and the spread of prosperity," the queen said in a toast at the white-tie state dinner. Bush paid tribute to the queen's commitment to the transatlantic alliance during her long reign. "We're confident that the Anglo-American friendship will endure for centuries to come," he said. "Our alliance is rooted in the beliefs that we share," he added. Those beliefs date back to the first pilgrims who landed on America's shores.

The queen toured Jamestown in Virginia to mark the 400th anniversary of the New World's first permanent English settlement. "I would also like to take this opportunity, on the day that has seen the formal transfer of power to the devolved Northern Ireland government, to thank you and your predecessors for your contribution to bringing peace in Northern Ireland," she said, noting the U.S. role in bringing about the historic Good Friday peace agreement in 1998. It's a role America can play again constructively in other regional conflicts, starting in the Middle East to fix the mess it contributed to so mightily.

Ties That Bind

Churchill and Roosevelt highlighted the bond and relationship between their two countries during World War II. Abraham Lincoln and Prime Minister William Gladstone had a very high regard and respect for each other as America was convulsing to rid itself of slavery.

This respect has survived more than a century and a half to the recent and current U.S. and British political leaders. Is it any wonder that Bush pushed for Blair to take on the role of Middle East envoy? His primary task will be to work with the Palestinians to help them strengthen their political and economic systems.

The idea that no monarch should be able to rule arbitrarily and that there had to be accountability, was actually British, and the American Revolution was built around that idea. Both sides in the American War of Independence claimed to be basing their case on the idea of liberty. "So the values that Britain and America hold in common are essentially part of the same intellectual tradition," said British Prime Minister Gordon Brown shortly after taking office in 2007.

What a sight watching Gordon Brown and George Bush smiling together at their press conference at Camp David in 2007 – two GBs united in a sense of shared duty. Karma, coincidence or synchronicity? The differences are discussed in *Custom Maid Spin for New World Disorder.*

America, like Britain, has numerous political and economic differences with

Europe. Britain has more historical differences with Europe, especially France. In fact, it is not sure it wants to adopt the new European Treaty, or even be part of the European Union. America looks down on the "old Europe" while embracing the "new Europe." Many in America resent Europe for not supporting the U.S. in Iraq. Newspaper editorials and stories have lamented how America can't depend on Europe even though America rebuilt Europe after World War II and defended it against Soviet aggression for 50 years. The feeling is mutual. Most "old Europeans" look down on America and Britain with disdain and contempt.

Since America and Britain have so many differences with Europe at the dawn of the 21st century, doesn't it make sense that they establish a more comprehensive bilateral transatlantic alliance? Isn't a more robust bilateral transatlantic alliance preferable to trying to sustain and salvage the frazzled hostile multilateral transatlantic alliance? In fact, why not throw Australia and New Zealand into the mix, since they are not really part of Europe or Asia. Both countries have more in common with America and Britain than they do with Asia or Europe. Australia, like Britain, has stood by America through all its conflicts – Korea, Vietnam and Iraq. Australia and New Zealand are America's most logical alliance in Asia – after China.

China's New Silk Road
The Shanghai Cooperation Organization, originally five – now six countries, which takes in China, Russia, Kazakhstan, Tajikistan Kyrgyzstan, and Uzbekistan – can serve several important functions. A regional bloc that can act as a counterpoise to the U.S.-dominated alliances in the region and Muslim religious extremism. In Urumqi, China, through which the Silk Road runs, Islam has been the dominant religion for more than 1,000 years. The organization may eventually incorporate other countries in the region, including Turkmenistan, and even Mongolia, Iran and other members of the former Soviet Union – conceivably, even Turkey if it is shunned by Europe.

China is taking over the role once held by Russia in Central Asia and is now the region's rich and powerful benign leader. China's authoritarian politics and central planning have a strong appeal for many of the former Soviet republics of the region. Kazakhstan, Uzbekistan and Turkmenistan all prefer dealing with China rather than the West. The Chinese are concerned about the U.S. military base in Uzbekistan and the Indian base in Tajikistan because all three countries are competing to secure access to the region's oil. China is perceived in the region as a new superpower lacking aggressive intent.

With the EU determined to break Russia's grip on the bloc's gas imports, all roads lead to Kazakhstan – the same country that Borat, Sacha Baron Cohen, portrayed as racist, sexist and anti-Semitic in the film. Borat is a cultural and national – interlocal – representative connector of cross-border homophobic dots, especially in Muslim Central Asia.

Kazakhstan is a vast country that stretches from the Caspian Sea to China. It is closer to Europe. Kazakhstan not only has oil and gas, but it has one of the world's largest uranium reserves. Aside from natural resources, China could well use the considerable talents produced by the universal education system of the former Soviet Union, which trained many of its space engineers and scientists in Kazakhstan and Uzbekistan. Computer programmers are making the 21-hour trip from the Kazhak city of Almaty into China's westerly metropolis of Urumqi.

Bates Gill, a China specialist at the Center for Strategic and International Studies in Washington, said: "The Chinese are sending people all the time to meet prime ministers and presidents and generals and all the way down the diplomatic ladder. This is all about soft power, and strategic and diplomatic relationships. Central Asia is a fantastic lens, or model, for what China is trying to do all over its periphery: reaching out and settling old scores, and trying to establish a benign kind of hegemony."

China is updating its old Silk Road relationships and catapulting them into the 21st century. In 2004 it established the China-Arab Cooperation Forum, marking a new milestone in the history of close ties between China and Arab states.

The China-Kyrgyzstan joint military exercises in 2002 was the first time two countries held cross-border military exercises within the framework of the Shanghai Cooperation Organization. It was also the first time the Chinese army conducted a live ammunition war game with a foreign army. It soon followed up with a joint naval exercise with France in the Yellow Sea. China and Russia held their first ever joint military exercise in August 2005.

The eight-day military maneuvers, code-named Peace Mission 2005, was designed to protect their security and energy interests from external threats and to counter U.S. influence in the region. It was also an opportunity for Russia to showcase its high-tech military hardware to China, which spends heavily on such equipment. It included 8,000 Chinese troops and 1,800 Russians and their anti-submarine vessel, the Marshal Shaposhnikov, a large landing ship and a destroyer as well as Tu-95 strategic bombers, Tu-22M long-range bombers and Su-27SM fighter jets. The guests included the defense ministers of the two countries as well as observers from India, Iran, Mongolia and Pakistan. Iranian President Mahmoud Ahmadinejad was invited as a guest to the 2006 summit, together with representatives of the U.N., the Association of Southeast Asian Nations and the Commonwealth of Independent States.

China and Russia are united in their opposition to a U.S.-dominated security order that involved the revolutions in Georgia, Ukraine and Kyrgyzstan. The strategic realities of Asia are being realigned – to America's detriment.

Together, the Shanghai Cooperation Organization countries have a population of 1.5 billion, thousands of strategic and tactical nuclear weapons and a combined conventional military force of 3.6 million.

Jiang Zemin and Vladimir Putin see a strong Shanghai Cooperation Organization as a check against the eastward expansion of NATO and related efforts to spread U.S. standards under the guise of globalization. However, like Russia, China has also started a strategic dialogue with NATO on common strategic threats in Central Asia.

Beijing also wants to counterbalance the United States in Asia by forming a strategic triangle between Russia, China and India. Former U.S. Secretary of Defense Donald Rumsfeld presided over a commission in 2005 that concluded that Russia, China, India and North Korea were potentially dangerous countries whose "growing missile and weapons of mass destruction capabilities have direct effects on U.S. policies, both regional and global, and could significantly affect U.S. capability to play a stabilizing role in Asia." Public relations at its finest. In other words, limit America's political and economic expansion in the region.

China and India can be the bulwark of regional security. Both Buddhist countries face a common enemy – seccessionist rebellious Muslim groups that pose national and regional threats.

The first China-India joint army drill in late 2007 on the extensive border both countries share is a practical interlocal military exercise that is a lot more practical than naval drills. "Life is a great big canvas, and you should throw all the paint on it you can," said the late comedian Danny Kaye. The Chinese are doing just that – interlocally.

Is an Asian defense force modeled after NATO far behind – a force including America and China? Robert Sutter, a professor of Asian Studies at Georgetown University's School of Foreign Service, sees the possibilities. "Just as China's leaders appear to recognize that directly competing with the U.S. for influence in Asia is counterproductive for Chinese interests, so should U.S. leaders recognize that direct competition with China in Asia is counterproductive for the U.S."

Now that America is redeploying its troops in the Asia-Pacific region, it should consider forming an Asian NATO-like alliance. In 1954, the U.S., Australia, Britain, France, New Zealand, Pakistan, the Philippines and Thailand created a regional defense alliance called the Southeast Asia Treaty Organization (SEATO). Pakistan withdrew in 1968, France suspended financial support in 1975 and the organization held its final exercise on February 20, 1976, and came to an end on June 30, 1977. Australia has become the regional policeman. Australia took on the active military leadership in East Timor and the Solomon Islands.

With all the new millennium conflicts centering in Asia, it is logical for America to consider forming a new regional alliance with China, Japan, Australia, Korea, Thailand, Philippines and other countries that meet the entrance qualifications. But then again, a basic question is why does the U.S. need to maintain such a large military presence in Asia?

China-Russia Economic Alliance

The Sino-Soviet communist alliance of old has been transformed into a 21st century economic alliance now that they have resolved all their border disputes in 2005 – for the first time in 40 years. The Chinese and Russian economies are complimentary. Many of the products they generate do not compete directly. That is why Russia is not as concerned about China's rising economic might as the U.S., Europe and Japan. Nevertheless, there is an inherent built in historical lack of trust that undermines the relationship.

Little Russia in Beijing makes Chinatowns in America look like one-horse towns. Hundreds of square blocks with stores of Russian made merchandise, restaurants, residential towers and direct factory outlets. Russian is spoken everywhere by Russians and Chinese alike.

Russia's Primorsky Territory, with Vladivostok as its capital, borders three provinces in northeast China that have century-old trade ties with each other. Heliongjiang and Jilin provinces are in the forefront of the cross-border trade. Suifenhe, a mountain city in China's northeast Heliongjiang, is a booming border town because 5,000 Russians cross the border each day to shop. Not just for personal goods but for substantial trade deals involving textiles, shoes, fur coats, watches, appliances, electronics and food. They spent $1 billion in 2006. It is not one-way trade. China buys Russian timber, fertilizer, cement, steel and frozen fish. Heliongjiang spent $135.6 million in 2005 promoting its business ties with Russia with the aim of boosting the bilateral trade volume between the two countries to between $60 billion and $80 billion by the end of 2010. The provinces' trade volume with Russia jumped from $1.79 billion in 2001 to $20 billion in 2004.

Russia's Jewish Autonomous Region on China's border, is a territory for Jews created by Josef Stalin. Stalin carved the oblast, or region, out of the marshy fringes of Russia's Far East as a homeland for Soviet Jews, part of a policy in which each national group in the Soviet Union had its own territory. It received autonomous status in 1934.

Today, 185,000 people live there and only a minority is Jewish, but more are returning after an exodus following the break-up of the Soviet Union. Today it is playing a major role in Russia's drive to boost exports to China. Located in the far southeast of Russia and closer to Beijing than Moscow, the region is gearing up for the completion of a bridge across the Amur River in 2010, the first to link Russia and China.

A 540-kilometer stretch of the Amur River defines the border between the region and China's Heilongjiang province, where 40 million people live. The bridge will carry iron from largely untapped deposits in Russia's Far East to steel mills in China, a new front in Russia's push to develop the region and sell raw materials, including timber and water, to China.

Vladimir Putin launched the "Year of Russia" in China in 2006, with more than 200 political, economic, military and cultural programs planned to highlight the warming ties. When Russia took on the presidency of the G-8 summit, Putin invited China's Hu Jintao to attend as Russia's guest. China reciprocated with Hu launching the "Year of China" in Moscow in 2007 with its largest ever overseas exhibition of 200 events, including a cultural festival, business forum and investment conference. Both countries have agreed to cooperate in the exploration of Mars. The relationship is purely strategic. It is a marriage of convenience without any passion.

Russia is not only China's main defense partner, but is fast becoming China's primary source of energy. A 2,300km multi-billion dollar oil pipeline from eastern Siberia to China was started in late 2005 and will become operational in November 2008. It will carry 30 million tons of oil, over three times the current volume of Russian oil being exported to China by rail. Russia has pledged to expand the flow to 50 million tons a year, roughly 1.2 million barrels a day. The alliance is a natural one. They share a peaceful common border and both want to extend their influence in central Asia and reduce U.S. influence there. They are succeeding – America is becoming isolated.

Given the huge gap between the populations and the very distant interest of Moscow compared to the close involvement of China, the Russian Far East risks being transferred, in all but name, to a form of Chinese control. There are several hundred thousand Chinese, if not millions, living and doing business in the country. Russia is acutely aware of this and has started cracking down on Chinese migrant communities in its retail and farming sectors.

China-ASEAN
China is Southeast Asia's leading trade partner. In Asia, China is viewed as an opportunity – not a threat. China recognizes that a stable regional environment allows it to devote its energies to its economic development. To this end, China has agreed on a declaration of a code of conduct for the

South China Sea and joined the Association of Southeast Asian Nation's Treaty of Amity and Cooperation. Unlike America, which is making terrorism its mantra in Asia, China is focused on economic and regional cooperation. U.S. absent-mindedness, missteps and negligence in the region have enabled China to embrace its southern neighbors.

A recent example of a U.S. setback is President George Bush's cancellation of his scheduled first summit with ASEAN leaders on September 5, 2007, and that Secretary of State Condoleezza Rice's annual visit to the region was also uncertain. The landmark summit was aimed at highlighting 30 years of official ties between America and ASEAN. The 27-member ASEAN is the only high-level official security group in the Asia-Pacific region and includes China, Russia, India and the EU.

Trade between China and ASEAN is growing at nearly 40 percent a year and appears likely to exceed $20 billion a year by the end of 2008. China and ASEAN will create the world's biggest free trade area by 2010, one that will comprise almost 2 billion people with a total gross domestic product of almost $3 trillion. In 2004, China and ASEAN signed a landmark agreement to cut tariffs which will be abolished in 2007 between the group's more developed nations: Brunei, Malaysia, Indonesia, the Philippines, Singapore and Thailand. All tariffs between the countries will be abolished in 2012. The ASEAN group includes Brunei, Cambodia, Indonesia, Laos, Malaysia, Myanmar, Singapore, Thailand, the Philippines and Vietnam. With China's active participation, the group is now known as 10+1 and was the forerunner to the East Asia Summit.

The largest global economic interlocal attachments are the World Economic Forum, which meets annually in Davos and the World Social Forum which meets at the same time in a different developing country. Two interlocal groupings at the dawn of the 21st century that are on a disasterous collision course if accommodation is not reached.

East Asia Summit

America was not invited to the first East Asia Summit held in Malaysia in December 2005. The highlight of the three-day agenda of the 16-member summit was that it actually took place at all in light of the strong opposition from America, which had once acidly dubbed it the "caucus without

Caucasians," because as originally envisaged its core membership would be the 10 nations of ASEAN along with China, Japan and South Korea and be known as 10+3. Australia, New Zealand and India joined China, Japan and South Korea at the invitation of Japan, Indonesia and Singapore, which see them as a balance to China.

Northeast Asia – comprising China, North and South Korea, Japan, Mongolia and Russia – is the only vast geographic region in the world with no free-trade agreement. The Tumen River ties together this vast region and is at the crossroads of trade and vital transport routes of this last regional frontier. It is only a matter of time before China and Russia create the greater Tumen free-trade region.

The existing U.S. arrangements in Asia are bilateral alliances that are hold-overs from the Cold War. China on the other hand, is developing multilateral security and economic frameworks based on "mutual trust, mutual benefit, quality and coordination." It is even trying to convince America to use the six-party talks on North Korea as the core for a regional security forum. This competition of ideas in Asia is the defining battle of the 21st century – one in which America should change course and embrace before it loses more ground.

Interlocal Role Reversal

The irony of ironies – karma going full circle – is contagious America being blamed for Asia's looming economic meltdown. The 2007 Asia-Pacific Economic Cooperation forum unfolded amidst increasing volatility in global markets. The U.S. subprime-mortgage-market contagion was blamed for the volatility. The meeting illustrated how interlocal and interconnected global economies are.

The U.S. decided to blow-off the event. U.S. Treasury Secretary Henry Paulson decided not to join his fellow finance ministers at the APEC meeting in Australia.

It was illuminating to listen to Paulson's underlings blame Asia for saving too much and holding down currencies, while Asians blamed the U.S. for saving too little and relying too much on Asia's money.

What goes round comes round full circle as America found out at the APEC meeting. It had to be one of the biggest ironies in global finance. Ten years earlier, it was contagion from Asia that imperiled the global economy after Thailand devalued its currency in July 1997. At the time, U.S. officials reassured markets that Asia's woes were containable. Once the Dow-Jones Industrial Average began plunging several hundred points in a day, investors knew better.

America's confidence in an economy facing the worst housing recession in 16 years and massive current account and budget deficits sounded again like deepening denial and political spin. America was vocally blamed for the looming economic downturn on Asia's horizon. Asia can handle the downturn. Asia's rapid growth and booming economies in China and India, mean Asia is less reliant on America.

China-India

After decades of mistrust an rivalry, China and India, are eager to set aside political differences to focus on strengthening economic and political ties now that they have also resolved their border differences. The border dispute led to a month-long bloody war in 1962, which ended in a stalemate. China formally recognized Indian sovereignty over the tiny Himalayan territory of Sikkim for the first time, even producing a new map to prove it. In return, India reaffirmed its position that Tibet is part of China.

The two governments also agreed on a three-phase process for resolving other territorial claims along their 3,500km border. Each claims large swaths of land held by the other. The compatible low costs and high skill sets that China and India have allows both countries to join forces to compete more effectively with America and the West, particularly in information-technology services, where both countries have an abundance of engineers. Indian companies find Chinese software producers to be competitive in cost, quality and scale, while Chinese companies want to tap the expertise of Indian engineers.

Business lobbying groups in India are no longer urging the government to shut out Chinese imports. Conversely, Indian manufacturers are slowly setting up operations in China, while software companies from India are using the Chinese market as a springboard to new markets in East Asia, notably

Japan. Bilateral trade that was nonexistent 20 years ago topped $20 billion in 2006.

"Chindia" is a handy semantic shortcut that refers to 21st-century China and India together, their surging economies and related synergies dovetailing and complimenting each other. China's manufacturing and infrastructure combined with India's service and information technology. Chinese hardware with Indian software.

The biggest employers of Chindian engineers are a who's who of America's top technology firms, which have outsourced their research and development to both countries because of the high cost of doing business in America. IBM, GE, Intel and Microsoft all outsource research and development to both countries.

Both countries signed wide-ranging agreements in April 2005 and early 2006 that confirmed their emergence as "strategic partners." The opening of Nathu Pass, part of the legendary Silk Road trade route between India and China in July 2006, which used to account for 80 percent of the trade between the two countries early in the 20th century, will only enhance and increase the volume of trade.

The most dramatic development between the two countries is in the energy sector. Policy-makers on both sides realize that they need to work together more to fulfill their energy needs. The two are already collaborating in countries like Sudan, Russia and Iran. China National Petroleum Corporation and India's Oil and Natural Gas Corporation joined forces and successfully purchased a 38 percent stake in Al Furat Production Company, Syria's largest oil producer, sold by Petro-Canada.

In January 2006, China and India signed the Memorandum for Enhancing Cooperation in the Field of Oil and Natural Gas, a landmark agreement to cooperate in securing crude oil resources overseas to avoid bidding against each other and raising the price. Nevertheless, there is an underlying distrust between the world's most populous and rapidly growing economies.

Mistrust is fueled by China's close relationship with India's arch-rival Pakistan, and its burgeoning ties with India's other subcontinental neighbors,

Bangladesh, Sri Lanka and Myanmar. When China fired a ground-based ballistic missile that destroyed one of its own aging satellites 865km above earth, India's military establishment bristled with anger and further fueled the legacy of distrust and suspicion between the two Asian giants, who fought a full-fledged war in 1962 and have yet to demarcate their border.

It is no surprise therefore that the Bush White House rolls out the red carpet for a glitzy White House dinner for India's first couple in 2005, only the fifth such dinner the Bush administration has ever given. America wants to draw India into a military alliance and is trying to help India become a major regional power that will contain China. The fact that it plays well to the millions of American Indian immigrants is a side benefit.

Sounds a lot like what happened in the period before 1914, when Britain and France, the traditional great powers who were facing a future of relative decline, sought to contain the rapid growth of German industrial might by making an alliance with the other rising power, Russia. That led to the first world war. America is playing the role of Britain and France, with China cast in the role of Germany, and India gets to play Russia.

The policymakers in Washington are trapped in an old paradigm that didn't work for the great powers a century ago and won't work today, especially with Russia catching up and offering lucrative nuclear deals that do not need U.S. congressional approval. The fact is, Russia is arming the world's two largest re-emerging empires of the 21st century because of shortsighted U.S. foreign policy blunders.

The good news is that India is not buying into America's interlocal strategy that can lead to war. The Sino-Indian relationship is more important to India and is unlikely to become a pawn in any strategy designed to contain China. India, the largest democracy in the world, stoutly adhered to a socialist-influenced planned economy until the Soviet Union collapsed. It began to economically liberalize only when China's reforms clearly demonstrated the economic superiority of opening up. India's traditional economic models were Western – American and European – which have now been replaced by the Chinese model for development. India wants to become like China – not America.

India and China are both starting to outsource computer services jobs to

Mexico. Jobs are coming back from Asia to the Americas. America can get these jobs back from Mexico and many other parts of the world. It just has to stay true to the ideals of the Founding Fathers and their political will. The lack of political will is America's biggest political liability today.

China-Philippines

China and the former U.S. colony the Philippines signed a landmark deal in 2004 to explore for oil near the disputed Spratly Islands, claimed by China, the Philippines, Vietnam, Brunei and Vietnam, and also agreed in principle to start building defense cooperation between the two countries. China also granted the Philippines nearly $1 billion worth of investments and soft loans in the trade, energy and agri-fisheries sectors.

China is today the biggest lender to the Philippines. Philippine state-owned agribusiness firms have signed deals worth more than $5 billion. China has also extended loans of $500 million in official development assistance, in addition to the $900 million that China has lent the Philippines for railway modernization. These fresh loans are part of a $6-billion package the China Export-Import Bank has committed to Manila through 2010.

The two countries declared that their goal is to expand trade to $20 billion by 2009. Yet the Philippines is one country where the U.S. is welcomed with open arms but has abandoned the country by default to China.

China-Australia

The rapidly growing economic cooperation between China and Australia is breathtaking. The state visits of former Australian Prime Minister John Howard to China, and Premier Wen Jiabao's visit to Australia in 2006 cemented the relationship They are partners in a $25-billion natural liquified gas project in Guangdong, China. Beijing is also set to become a key buyer of Australian uranium. Australia has the world's largest uranium deposits.

Sino-Australian relations hold promising prospects for mutual prosperity. China's soft approach is not limited to Asia or Australasia. It is reaching out of the region to Europe, Africa and Latin America as well.

China-Europe

China and the European Union are embracing each other in a panda hug.

The flirting dates back to 1985 when the European Community-China Trade and Economic Cooperation Agreement was signed. The EU's policy to "engage rather than to isolate" has yielded more benefits to both sides than America cares to admit. China's middle class today has more disposable income than the entire population of America. The fact is that the EU has become China's main trading partner because of America's shortsighted foreign policies.

China is the EU's second-biggest trading partner and the EU is China's biggest trading partner. What is more significant is that today there are close to 200,000 Chinese students studying in Europe. An ironic twist of history considering that ancient Europeans lived in caves while Asian civilizations flourished. China, India, Egypt and the Levant, modern-day Turkey, were reading and writing while illiterate Europeans living in caves were killing each other for basic necessities.

China sees the EU as the ideal market for its fast-expanding industries. The introduction of the euro has simplified currency transactions and expedited the process. "There is more to the EU-Sino love affair than goods, investments and trade. China and the EU believe that besides love, peace and prosperity, the world needs more than one superpower. And who could better contribute to the realization of a multipolar world system than a reformed China and a more self-confident EU?" said Fabio Scarpello, a researcher based in Jakarta and an expert in EU foreign policy and orientalism. It should come as no surprise that China and the EU are continuously engaged in talks to update the Sino-EU agreement on trade and economic cooperation inked in 1985.

China-Africa

China is also challenging the U.S. in Africa, according to an independent study released by the Council on Foreign Relations at the end of 2005. It has become a key U.S. competitor for oil there as other world supplies have dwindled. China issued its first ever African Policy Paper in January 2006, to promote long-term growth of China-Africa relations. The New Partnership for Africa Development (NEPAD) has drawn up an aggressive and encouraging plan of rejuvenation and development. Among the total of 53 countries in Africa, 48 have established diplomatic relations with China. The rest are being wooed away from Taiwan.

The weekend Forum on China-African Cooperation that China hosted in November 2006 for the heads of state of the 48 African nations was the biggest red-carpet event that China ever hosted. The routes along which the heads of state traveled were blocked off for the likes of Zimbabwe's Robert Mugabe to drive unimpeded. The summit was held on the occasion of the 50th anniversary of the inauguration of diplomatic relations between China and Africa, and celebrated more than 1,000 years of ties dating back to Ming Dynasty explorer Zheng He, who took his fleet to the east coast of Africa.

After China established diplomatic relations with Egypt in 1956, it spread its influence across the continent, following Mao's famous advice to "teach how to fish instead of giving developing countries the fish," with aid, public health, education and infrastructure projects. One of its most ambitious projects was the 1,848km TanZam railway linking Zambia's copper belt to the Indian Ocean port of Dar es Salaam in Tanzania, which took about 16, 000 Chinese workers five years to construct and opened in 1976.

Beijing sent the first medical teams to Algeria in 1964 and has sent more than 15,000 doctors to about 47 countries and treated more than 180 million patients. Isolated jungle villagers, like Gabon's pygmies are benefiting from China's insatiable appetite for raw materials and are thrilled that someone cares. They are getting medical attention, roads, public buildings, schools and libraries. At the other extreme, in countries like Zambia, China's policy of importing Chinese workers is breeding resentment, hostility and accusations of "new colonialism."

China is focused on the development of transportation, communication, water conservation, electricity and education. It is also committed to go all out with its African Human Resources Development Foundation to train Africans. The aggressive student exchange programs between China and Africa will continue in the 21st century. China will increase the number of government scholarships for African students, continue to send teachers to Africa to teach Africans the Chinese language – and carry out educational assistance programs in every technical and vocational field – through the teachers it sends and by distance learning while encouraging more student and teacher exchanges and cooperation between Chinese and African educational and academic institutions.

When most countries in Africa became independent in the '50s and 60s, their economies were based on the export of natural resources, oil and agricultural products and the import of manufactured goods and services. Africa's primary trading partners were their former colonial masters. The system worked relatively well until the late 1970s, when prices for export commodities from Africa tumbled on the world markets while the cost of imported manufactured goods and services increased. As a result, despite the increase in export-volume, revenues decreased, making it difficult for Africa to buy the equipment needed to build a modern infrastructure and manufacturing sector.

Today, China's emergence as a major trading power has given Africa an unprecedented opportunity to sell its natural resources at higher prices than it received from its former European colonial powers. This powers China's economy and also allows Africa to buy cheaper manufactured goods from China – a win-win for all. In 2004, Sino-African trade volume reached $29.5 billion compared with $19 billion in 2003; that is a 58.9 percent growth rate year-on-year. In 2005, trade volume reached $40 billion, then $50 billion in 2006 – and is growing fast. It is estimated it will reach $100 billion by 2010.

China imports a third of its foreign oil from Africa. Angola passed Saudi Arabia in 2006 to become China's top oil supplier.

African countries need investment to exploit their resources for economic development and China is willing to cooperate. It has more than 800 infrastructure projects in Africa. How many does America have? Zippo.

China describes its relationship with Africa as "all-weather friends and partners." In Zimbabwe, Chinese farmers are settling on tobacco farms abandoned by white owners who were driven off by Mugabe's government to make room for landless Africans. In Nigeria, China has struck a deal to export 30,000 barrels of crude a day to China. China is willing to pick up where the colonial forerunners left off. "The Chinese are willing to work the dregs," said Lyal White, Asia specialist at the South African Institute for International Affairs. Mineral concessions worked to exhaustion and abandoned as unprofitable are all game for the Chinese. "They are prepared to go in and start operations in places that the French, British and Americans have long given up on," said White.

But many are also paying with their lives. Today, China is paying the discounted human price that colonial powers did in the 19th and 20th centuries. One of the worst incidents took place in Ethiopia, where a Chinese-run oilfield was attacked in 2007, and 77 people were killed, including nine Chinese nationals. Seven Chinese nationals in the remote and barren southeast Ogaden region were kidnapped by the Ogaden National Liberation Front, ethnic Somalis fighting for independence for the Somali-majority province since 1984. The killings and kidnappings occurred nine months after nine Chinese workers were abducted and released in Nigeria.

China is Ethiopia's largest trading partner with bilateral trade exceeding $600 million. Between 1949 and 1979, only 280,000 Chinese traveled or went to study or work abroad, while in 2006 alone, 32 million did so, according to Foreign Ministry figures. That figure is expected to reach 100 million by 2020.

China doesn't lecture on human rights, degradation of the environment or corruption. It doesn't make improvement a condition of building roads or factories. It only wants to do business – and African countries like that. During my December 2005 visit to Brisbane, I asked Abel Stoltz what will happen to Africa and how it can lift itself out of poverty. "China will take over and make it part of China. They are everywhere. That's the only way," Abel replied. My South African and Rhodesian neighbors in Hong Kong agree.

China-Saudi Arabia

It is estimated that by the year 2025, China will consume as much oil as the U.S. – 21 million barrels a day. It should therefore come as no surprise that China and Saudi Arabia are signing oil, natural gas and mineral deposit agreements. The agreements were signed in the Great Hall of the People during a visit by Saudi King Abdullah bin Abdul Aziz in January 2006, on his first overseas trip. The king chose China as his first overseas stop because it represents "the great emphasis our country has attached to the relationship with China," said Saleh al-Hujeilan, the Saudi ambassador to China. It was a warning shot to America that the kingdom is no longer solely dependent on America. Abdullah's visit was the first tour of a Saudi king to

China since the two countries established diplomatic relations in 1990. President Hu Jintao reciprocated by visiting Saudi Arabia three months later to further cement the relationship.

Saudi Arabia is China's largest trading partner in the region comprising the Middle East and North Africa. Two-way trade exceeded $57 million in 2005. Saudi Arabia is the number one supplier of crude oil to China. It supplied 14 percent of China's oil needs when the agreements were signed, or 450,000 barrels a day. Sinopec of China is already drilling for oil in the Saudi desert and building a refinery with Saudi Aramco in Fujian Province, in southern China. ExxonMobil has a 25 percent interest in the venture. The partners will also establish a joint venture to operate 600 gas stations in the province and market the products produced by the Fujian Integrated Project. Aramco and Sinopec are also exploring the feasibility of developing a grass-roots refinery in Qinqdao, Shandong province.

China is also in discussions to establish a free trade area with the Gulf Cooperation Council, a regional economic organization with the six member states of Saudi Arabia, Kuwait, Qatar, Oman, Bahrain and the United Arab Emirates. The two sides, which in 2005 saw trade volume rise over a third to $33.8 billion, signed a free trade agreement at the end of 2006.

Peaceful Interlocal Islam

China can also be the expediter and facilitator of getting Asian Islam, as practiced in China, India, Indonesia and Malaysia, to the Muslim Arab Middle East. Asia's Muslims can influence the Middle East. Instead of sending Christian missionaries to convert the heathens to Christianity, we should be supporting and sending mellow Malaysian and Indonesian Muslim missionaries who support themselves with local greasy spoons and finer dining establishments. The Asian hospitality business spreading peace and tolerance is long overdue.

Malaysian cleric Sheikh Ashaari Muhammad's preach-and-fry restaurant and gift shop has franchises as far west as Syria, Egypt and Iraq. Asian Islam is pluralistic, tolerant and anti-extremist. "Arabs are tired of militant ideologies and hungry for an alternative. If the largest Islamic movements of Malaysia and Indonesia started sharing their teachings with Arabs the way Sheikh Ashaari does, they would find many followers and friends here," said Jordanian cleric Mustafa Abu Rumman, who preaches at a government-controlled mosque.

Even a turbaned champion of the Iraqi insurgency, former Saddam Hussein confidante Sheikh Abd al-Latif al-Huayyim, told Joseph Braude, a columnist for the *New Republic* and author of *The New Iraq,* in November 2006, that he has his eye on the Muslim East. "After the Americans depart," he said confidently, "Iraqis will look to models in Malaysia, Indonesia and India to try and resolve our problems. These exemplars are crucial to the future of Iraq."

Until now, it's been Saudi and Iranian coffers pouring money and manpower into madrassas, the Islamic religious schools, fostering a hardline Islamist bent. But the beginnings of a more moderate trend are forming – and a nudge from China and America may just be what the doctor ordered. Neither country has done much to promote progressive Islam or advance the liberal Islamic tendencies manifest in Indonesia and Malaysia. The U.S. Congress has finally started addressing the issue.

There is a reason Indonesian Islamic pluralism and tolerance doesn't get exported as the Saudi and Iranian extreme preachings do. The Indonesian government doesn't finance such programs because Indonesia is not an Islamic state. Language and culture are also realistic formidable barriers separating much of Asia from the Arab world. Shouldn't bringing down these barriers be something *We the Apathetic People* get behind?

China-Latin America

China's overall investment in Latin America is relatively small when compared to the U.S. – but it is growing. China's investment in Latin America and the Caribbean at the end of 2005 was $8.3 billion compared to America's more than $300 billion. But China has become Brazil's No. 3 export destination after the U.S. and Argentina. These include iron ore, airplanes, soya beans and pulp. China also plans to invest more than $3 billion in Brazilian infrastructure – ports, roads and railways – while Brazil's Foreign Ministry has hinted at some $5 billion in direct investment in China.

The link between Brazil and China connects the biggest emerging markets of the Western and Eastern hemispheres. In the words of Celso Amorim,

Brazil's foreign minister, it could be part of a "certain reconfiguration of the world's commercial and diplomatic geography."

Venezuela is the third-largest foreign supplier of oil to the U.S., and owns Citgo, one of the largest refinery complexes and gas distribution networks in America. Venezuela's President Hugo Chavez, did threaten to replace the U.S. oil market with China on more than one occasion – and emphatically so after Christian commentator Pat Robertson called for Chavez's assassination and the White House's deafeningly silent rebuke. Condemning the incendiary remarks would have been the decent thing to do and in the U.S. national interest.

The alternative? Exactly what happened. When Chavez, in mid-May 2007, continued to aggressively nationalize Western energy companies, including BP, Chevron, Conoco, Exxon, Total and Statoil, forcing Exxon Mobil, the largest U.S. oil company, and Conoco Phillips, the third largest to end their participation in exploration ventures. In the past the global oil companies paid only 1 percent in royalties for the crude they extracted in the country's oil-rich Orinoco Belt. After Chavez was elected in 1998, royalties increased to 33.2 percent, while taxes went up from 34 percent to 50 percent. Chavez also re-nationalized American-owned telecoms and electricity companies.

With the extra revenue, it was only a matter of time before "The oil boss of the Americas" would propose his plan for a Banco del Sur – Bank of the South – a development bank funded and run by Latin American countries. He periodically threatens to leave the Organization of American States and pull out of the IMF. It would be nice if he spent the people's money developing their education and health systems, infrastructure and lives in general, instead of just glorifying and enriching himself.

China has increased its investment in Venezuela along with the number of barrels of oil it is buying from the country. Chavez threatened to give China and Cuba 22 U.S.-made F-16 jets after the U.S. refused to sell Venezuela spare parts for the planes. A deal Venezuela made with Israel to buy the parts was cancelled after America intervened. Chavez brought up the possibility of giving the planes to China and Cuba at the presidential palace in 2005 to mark the signing of a satellite production agreement with China.

Venezuela bought the F-16s in the early 1980s and for a long time was the only Latin American country to possess the sophisticated warplanes, a reflection of how bad the relationship between Venezuela and the U.S. has become. The tit-for-tat expulsions of diplomats and name-calling by both countries is not the way to bridge the widening political rift.

The "eternal friendship" expressed by China's Defense Minister General Cao Gangchuan at the start of his 2007 visit to Cuba was aimed at bolstering strategic ties. The long-standing friendship between China and Cuba heated up when China's Hu Jin-tau and Cuba's Fidel Castro announced after the 2004 APEC meeting in Chile that China would mine Cuba's nickel as Castro cut off the use of U.S. dollars. Today Cuba sells China nickel, sugar, medicines and crude oil.

Initially, Cuba was a stepping stone for Chinese business and trade with Latin America. In the long term it is already serving as a lever on Washington in more ways than one. Watching Castro on TV step down from one of the 12 diesel locomotives that arrived from China in 2005, as I puffed a Cuban cigar and sipped Director's Reserve whiskey from Venezuela. I took a healthy swig when I heard that China had become Cuba's second-largest trading partner after Venezuela in 2005. Exports grew more than 95 percent in 2005 to more than $500 million and $1.8 billion in 2007, due mostly to China's exports of machinery, vehicles and consumer goods, financed with Chinese credit. Relations between Beijing and Havana first took off after the collapse of the Soviet Union in 1991. How much more self-destructive do U.S. embargo policies have to become before *We the Apathetic Maids* sweep in the foreign policy changes needed for America to again be embraced by its Cuban and Latino neighbors?

President Evo Morales, Bolivia's newly inaugurated president on January 22, 2006, embarked on a 10-day victory tour of Spain, France and China before his swearing-in ceremony. China pledged to strengthen bilateral ties with Bolivia by developing partnerships in investment and trade. Morales said the Bolivian people regard China as a trustworthy friend and partner. "Expanding relations with China will be a priority among the policy goals of my presidency," Morales promised. "I made a priority of answering the invitation of China because I consider it to be a political, ideological and programmatic ally of the Bolivian people," Morales told Hu Jintao after the two leaders shook hands.

Morales invited China to help Bolivia develop its vast gas reserves. Bolivia has the second-largest natural gas reserves in Latin America and is also rich in silver, tin and other minerals.

In 2005 China joined the Inter-American Development Bank, giving its construction companies access to the bank's infrastructure projects.

China is able to develop its relationships in Latin America because of U.S. neglect and alienation of goodwill in the region. America's relations with Argentina, Brazil, Cuba and Venezuela are anything but cordial – which some Latin American countries have decided to exploit.

America's failure to get a free-trade agreement at the 2005 Americas 34-nation summit in Argentina was the latest indication of how little goodwill America has even in the Americas. America tried to revive negotiations on a free-trade area of the Americas stretching from Canada to Chile and failed. Venezuela's Chavez led the attack against America and the agreement. Chavez also managed to block a U.S. push to set a date to resume negotiations.

Things didn't go much better for America in its efforts to push through the Central American Free Trade Agreement, which would eliminate most trade barriers and open up trade valued at $32 billion between the U.S. and Costa Rica, El Salvador, Honduras, Guatemala, Nicaragua and the Dominican Republic.

The twin defeats, coming on the heels of America's earlier defeat in its choice of secretary general of the Organization of American States, is unprecedented. It was the first time in the organization's history that a candidate initially opposed by the U.S. will lead the 34-member regional grouping.

The OAS was founded in 1948, part of the same post-World War II American effort to construct a multilateral foreign policy that also led to the creation of entities like NATO. The U.S. contributes about 60 percent of the organization's $76-million annual budget and has traditionally played the dominant role in the group, whose missions include monitoring elections and mediating political disputes in member countries. America struck out three times in the Americas in 2005. With left-leaning parties winning elections in Nicaragua and Ecuador and their leaders joining the Castro-Chavez bandwagon, America is spending millions of dollars to finance its political foes instead of mending its political fences there.

While America has been squandering millions of dollars and its goodwill alienating its neighbors, China has moved into its hemispheric backyard.

Poli Sci 101
It is political science 101 that regional geopolitical alliances, especially in America's own backyard, are critical to support and preserve. This fundamental axiom goes back to America's Monroe Doctrine – enunciated in 1823 by President James Monroe – America's fifth president. The Monroe Doctrine was adopted to deter European imperialism in the Western Hemisphere and ensure U.S. hegemony in the region.

Hegemony cannot be sustained in the 21st century without the backing and support of the countries in the Western Hemisphere that feel they are being used and abused by America. The heavy-handed regional alliances America has created in the hemisphere favor America, which leaves Latin countries no option but to look elsewhere for fair and balanced economic and political arrangements. Argentina, Bolivia, Brazil, Cuba, Ecuador, Nicaragua and Venezuela are just the tip of the Latino political iceberg.

Singapore's Tommy Koh, former ambassador to the U.S. and the U.N. and executive director of the Asia Europe Foundation, asked some direct questions at a Foreign Correspondents Club lunch in 1995. "Who could have foreseen in 1945, that two generations later, Western Europe would be united, peaceful and prosperous? No one would have believed that 50 years later, the historic enemies, England, France and Germany, would be reconciled and that never again would they take up arms against one another. The European Union is nothing short of miracle. It is for this reason that I wish to ask what lessons can East Asia learn from the European Union.

"The first lesson which East Asia can learn from the European Union is that history need not repeat itself. It is possible to put aside deep divides of language, culture, religion and centuries of conflict and war. It is possible for visionary leaders to win the hearts and minds of their peoples in order to persuade them to discard the bitter legacy of the past and to embrace the sweet promise of a better future.

"The second lesson which East Asia can learn from the European Union is the importance of the capacity, and the willingness of the members of the union, to engage in a free and candid exchange of views, no matter how controversial the issue.

"The third lesson which East Asia can learn from the European Union is that institutions matter. As Jean Monnet once wrote, nothing lasting can be built without institutions. The European Union has established a number of key institutions, for example, the Council of Ministers, the European Commission, the European Parliament, the Court of Justice, the Commission on Human Rights, the European Central Bank, etc. At every critical juncture of its history, the European Union has been able to move forward towards its goal of an ever closer union by creating or re-engineering institutions." China learned these lessons well. Why doesn't America?

Europe is studying even harder to improve its model of regional cooperation. For the first time in their history, the 25 countries of the European Union agreed to make Europe a military power with independent command, control and troops. Independent, that is, of the United States. It is a prime example of military interlocalism.

When Britain accepted a long-standing French proposal calling for the European Union to be able to conduct military actions on its own where the United States and other NATO allies choose not to, it was historical, timely and inevitable. These are two countries that were on opposite sides in the American War of Independence and countless other conflicts over the last millennium.

The change was inevitable since European forces were geared to defend against a land attack from the Soviet Union and its Warsaw Pact countries. The collapse of the Soviet Union rendered the traditional European-NATO model obsolete. To build an effective military force, Europeans are going to have to increase their annual military budgets. At the dawn of the new millennium, America spends 3.5 percent of its gross domestic budget on defense, compared to 1.5 percent for Germany, 1.9 percent for Italy, 2.4

percent for France and 2.6 percent for Britain. Whether a European military force ever sees the light of day is another matter.

Since 9/11, America has become more isolated from NATO and is acting more unilaterally and ignoring many of its allies' pleas concerning Iraq, Taiwan and the Middle East. While verbally embracing NATO, America is looking "more like a serial dater – lover of many, husband of none," with a series of coalitions that are useful to it in its war on terrorism and pursuit of oil.

European governments agree that the EU must take in the former communist nations of Eastern and Central Europe, but cannot find a way to handle that potentially turbulent and costly process. Britain, Denmark and Sweden are leading the Euro skeptics while welcoming in new member states from the former communist bloc.

The North American Free Trade Agreement has been similarly useful for America. NAFTA succeeded in what it was designed to do by reducing trade barriers. Today the U.S. exports nearly four times more to Canada and Mexico than to Japan and China and 40 percent more than to the 25-nation European Union. U.S. firms have become more continental and more competitive, more integrated. More interlocal. It has proven interlocalism can work and be expanded globally in the 21st century.

Southeast Asian leaders have taken the cue and endorsed a proposal to create a free trade area with China to be completed by 2015. Imagine the ramifications of a borderless Asian free-trade zone modeled on the EU. It would have 3 billion people – half the world's population, with a combined gross domestic product of more than $6 trillion. The economic and political clout is staggering. African and Caribbean nations also look to interlocalize trade. Meanwhile, India, Sri Lanka and Bangladesh have rekindled relations with Iraq because of its oil and gas.

I concur with Robert Cooper, a British diplomat who was Tony Blair's adviser on Afghanistan and then went to work for the EU's foreign policy chief, Javier Solana. Cooper argues that there are three types of state: "premodern," defined by chaos and feudal loyalties such as existed in Afghanistan under the Taliban; "modern" nation states with clear boundaries; and the "post-modern," in which nation states are interdependent through bigger institutions, such as the EU and NAFTA.

African leaders have reluctantly acknowledged this reality and are also considering a regional dream. The fifth annual "Smart Partnership" of nine African heads of state in the opening year of the millennium debated the benefits of working together as friendly neighbors.

Interlocal Pariahs

Isolated international pariahs Myanmar and North Korea restored diplomatic ties in 2007, 24 years after Yangon broke them off in protest of Pyongyang agents blowing up a South Korean delegation visiting the country. Pyongyang staged a failed assassination attempt during a visit by South Korea's president at the time, Chun Doo-hwan. He was saved because his car had been delayed in traffic, but the blast killed 17 of his entourage, including four cabinet ministers. Four Myanmese officials also died. Three North Korean commandos were detained.

Today Yangon has buried the hatchet because it wants to get its hands on North Korean nuclear and ballistic missile technology.

One Country, Two Systems

China, the country that developed the political concept of "one country two systems" is itself experiencing provinces and municipalities setting their own political agenda and financial goals, like their predecessors who ignored the emperors in faraway places.

The concept of one country with two or more systems is a functional model for the New World Order. Imagine one country and several systems all converging in Hong Kong, the bastion of British colonial democracy, capitalism and Chinese communism, Confucianism and nationalism. Taiwan will probably become the third system, and who knows how many more might develop like Hong Kong and Macau?

The provincial governments in China, never close to the emperors in Beijing, are already transforming their local economic and political institutions to ensure their growth and compliance with the socialist market economy guidelines laid down by the communist party leaders in Beijing to maintain the party's growth and survival. Consequently, interlocalism is rapidly manifesting itself in the oldest and largest civilization in Asia, where its cornerstone "one country, two systems" was laid.

The status of Tibet is inevitably debated at the FCC Main Bar in Hong Kong whenever the Dalai Lama is received by a foreign government. "After all, China has turned to Buddhism in some of the greatest periods of its history, and has adopted Tibetan Buddhism at that," Tony Clifton, an FCC regular and old China hand, volunteered. "Live long enough," he told the Dalai Lama when he interviewed him for *Newsweek,* "and you'll be the Dalai Lama of the whole of China." The European parliament proposal to the Chinese that the Dalai Lama be made the governor of Tibet also has some merit. The visits of the Dalai Lama's brother and envoys to Beijing since 2002 acknowledges that the Dalai Lama has accepted the fact that Tibet is part of China. He confirmed this to FCC member and *South China Morning Post* columnist Laurence Brahm in 2005. "We want modernization. So for our own interest we are willing to be part of the People's Republic of China, to have the PRC govern and guarantee to preserve our Tibetan culture, spirituality and our environment," he said.   China now supports the indigenous culture and the Tibetan language was given equal status with Mandarin Chinese in Tibet.

All Han Chinese there now have to learn Tibetan as well. "This is the message I wish to deliver to China. I am not in favor of separation. Tibet is a part of the People's Republic of China. It is an autonomous region of the People's Republic of China. Tibetan culture and Buddhism are part of Chinese culture," the Dalai Lama stated. His words were confirmed by his actions during Hu Jin-tau's U.S. visit in April 2006. He ordered Tibetan activists not to protest or demonstrate against China. Chinese officials know and acknowledge that the Dalai Lama is not seeking independence. Interlocalism does offer various alternative viable flexible working solutions for the 21st century.

Singapore and Malaysia separated when Singapore became independent in 1965 after their post-independence union was tried and failed. Yet both are interdependent and interlocalize daily. The relationship between the two is uneasy. Singapore is dependent on Malaysia for its drinking water, and both are dependent on each others' tourists and commerce. Despite the mistrust and occasional hiccups, trade and investment have been flourishing. Malaysia and Singapore are forging new and exciting ties that are promising for both countries. The interlocal joint venture they have announced commits Singapore to investing in Malaysia's southern Johor's Iskandar Development Project, a high tech park, logistics and industrial precincts, an educational park, regional hospitals, a marina, waterside villas, theme parks and exclusive gated residential communities. The decade-old discussion of a road-and-rail bridge replacing the causeway that links Singapore to Johor is just a matter of time.

Hong Kong Interlocalism

Hong Kong is a city-state within China that is in the process of being integrated with the mainland. As such it competes with other cities and has emerged as the centerpiece of the Pearl River Delta. Shenzen, Macau, Hong Kong, Zhuhai and Guangdong are interlocalizing to create one of the world's "economic super zones." Hong Kong is the gateway to the Middle Kingdom and the bridge to China's emerging economic empire in Asia and across the Pacific to America.

The Pearl River Delta comprises nine Guangdong cities on both sides of the river – Guangzhou, Shenzhen, Zhuhai, Dongguan, Foshan, Zhongshan, Jinangmen, Zhaoqing and Huizhou. Its 80 million inhabitants interlocalize regularly with Hong Kongers who have as many as 65,000 companies doing business in the delta. There are about a half a million Hong Kongers living in, or spending substantial periods of time on the mainland, much like the American citizens living in Mexico. It is estimated more than another 160,000 Hong Kongers will move their home base across the border.

The Pan-Pearl River Delta, commonly referred to as the "9 plus," consists of nine provinces – Guangdong, Fujian, Jiangxi, Hunan, Guangxi, Guizhou, Sichuan, Yunnan and Hainan along with Hong Kong and Macau. This larger integrated economic region is interlocalizing in the fields of science and technology to take advantage of the implementation of the Closer Economic Partnership Arrangement with Hong Kong and Macau. With Guangxi and Yunnan bordering Vietnam, Laos and Thailand, the Pan River Delta would also directly benefit China's growing free-trade relationship with the rest of Southeast Asia.

The CEPA between the mainland and Hong Kong is probably the only free-trade agreement between two parts of the same country. With Hong Kong now tipped to get the lion's share of the benefits when the Hong Kong-Zhuhai-Macau Bridge is up and running, it is indeed a political model to be emulated. The consensus is that all provinces benefit. The bridge will bring Zhuhai, Zhongshan and Jiangmen closer to Hong Kong – the interlocal financial center that can provide foreign direct investment. Is it any wonder Hong Kong's leading think tank, the Bauhinia Foundation, recommended in August 2007, that Hong Kong and Shenzhen merge and allow two million Chinese citizens from the maonland to migrate to Hong Kong and move freely between the two special administration regions of China? The proposal has gained the support of the Hong Kong government and a number of the territory's political parties.

The cross-border interlocal cluster that will be created between Hong Kong, Shenzen and the rest of the Delta region, will become the model for the rest of the world to emulate.

Within the larger integrated economic region, Hong Kong, Macau, and Guangdong form the Pan-Pearl River Delta region, a complimentary and interdependent interlocal relationship. Hong Kong is the regional logistics, communications and financial hub, Macau the gaming center, while Guangdong is the manufacturing base. In 2005 there were 10,000 kilometers of highways and 9,000 kilometers of main roads. A total of 30,000 kilometers of highways and main roads will crisscross the delta region and connect to the border gateways in Guanxi and Yunnan. This elaborate network will include the proposed bridge linking Hong Kong, Macau and Zhuhai. Bridge or no bridge, Hong Kong and the PRD are interconnected.

The Greater Mekong Subregion Economic Cooperation Program is an obscure group that has existed since 1992. It is made up of the six nations linked by the Mekong River: China, Thailand, Vietnam, Myanmar, Laos and Cambodia. It helped lay the foundation for China's Free Trade Agreement with ASEAN and promises to benefit from the development of the delta region because China's Yunnan Province is the window to the greater Mekong region.

Former Philippine President Fidel Ramos, former Australian Prime Minister Bob Hawke and former Japanese Prime Minister Morihiro Hosakawa joined hands and released a joint statement that said: "It is important to address the need to establish a new regional focal center."

Their Boao Forum was established in Boao on Hainan Island, China. It aims to foster interaction among industrial, political and academic leaders in Asia to tackle economic, social and human resource development as well as environment protection.

The three former leaders said Asia needs a "responsive non-government organization of prominent stature" similar to the World Economic Forum in Davos, Switzerland, and the Aspen Institute in the United States. The organization would be an association of "Asians and friends of Asia, established for Asia, centered on Asia and would aim to promote the interests of the region." The annual Boao Forum for Asia launched in 2002 acknowledged China's emerging regional status.

The economic transformation of China and Hong Kong is being warmly embraced by their Asian neighbors at the expense of America. China has signed a strategic partnership agreement with ASEAN and the annual Boao Forum brings the region's top political and economic leaders together on China's Hainan Island. It is the cornerstone of China's multilateral nongovernmental outreach program for its neighbors.

China's PRD is the largest regional economy in China in terms of GDP, and also the most complex international, environmental and social interlocal system, with Hong Kong as the hub of the experimental spokes of the wheel. More than 500,000 Hong Kongers live in, or spend substantial periods of time visiting China while utilizing Hong Kong's medical and welfare services – much like the hundreds of thousands of Americans living in Mexico and doing the same. The September 25, 2005 "ice-breaking trip" by a delegation of 59 Hong Kong legislators headed by Chief Executive Donald Tsang to the PRD, was the foundation stone laid for Hong Kong to become the business base for Chinese companies going global.

Hong Kong can and should take the next step in the outreach process and host an annual Post Global Interlocal Forum that fuses the best of the World Economic Forum and World Social Forum so that the benefits of China's economic transformation – namely, poverty reduction on a massive, unprecedented scale – can be replicated throughout the developing world in the 21st century.

The world is moving from a collection of nation-states to a collection of networks, and Hong Kong can become the network's economic and political server.

End of the Nation?

The attacks of 9/11 brought back the reality of the nation-state and the need for states to exert their military might to protect themselves. The nation-state was said to be obsolete before the attacks by the New Economy gurus because technology, capital and services were inherently borderless. The apostles of the New Economy declared the irrelevance of everything invented before the Internet. Historian Francis Fukuyama said, "The weightlessness of the New Economy will not protect you from falling concrete; your only hope in this kind of crisis is the heroism of firefighters and policemen. Microsoft or Goldman Sachs will not send aircraft carriers and F-16s to the Gulf to track down Osama bin Laden; only the military will. The 1990s saw the social and economic gulf widen between the Harvard and Stanford-educated investment bankers, lawyers and software engineers who worked in those Twin Towers, and the blue-collar types who went to their rescue."

Growth and stability also depends on people's willingness to remain a part of a nation-state that does not properly feed or educate its children. The nation-state can only keep them if it gives the people what they want and expect of their government. The American Declaration of Independence asserts the basic premise of a democratic union – membership must be voluntary. In other words, any group of people has the right to break the bonds that join it to another unless there is a specific and compelling moral reason to oppose the action.

There is a transracial American nation that would continue to exist even if the American nation-state, the United States of America, were wiped off the map. Americans are more like their neighbors the Mexicans – racially diverse – than their neighbors the Canadians – a collection of two or more nationalities lacking any common Canadian identity that would survive the breakup of Canada into several states.

American bandits and cowboys had a lot in common with their Mexican counterparts. Pancho Villa, like Butch Cassidy, did what was necessary to beat the system. Interlocalism works well between Mexico and the former parts of Mexico like California, Texas, and Arizona, where many legal and illegal immigrants interact with their family and friends back home.

It has often been said that we should re-examine the national borders imposed on local tribes by Western colonial powers. In America, this is best exemplified at the Sturgis County Line, in South Dakota at the "world's biggest biker bar," a 600-acre campground and outdoor concert venue built 2 miles north of Bear Butte and within sight of where Native Americans gather to fast and pray. The Indianss claim that rally-related noise disturbs the sanctity of a spiritual place whose past visitors included Red Cloud, Crazy Horse and Sitting Bull.

Maybe all borders, county, state and national should be redrawn to comply with tribal and historical alliances and not the realignments imposed by the colonial European empires.

Many national boundaries create tension. The colonial powers – namely England, France, Spain and Portugal – are at the root of much of today's political strife. Although it is opportunistic for corrupt politicians like Robert Mugabe of Zimbabwe to blame the colonial past, the powers did demarcate their colonies according to political balances by drawing artificial lines that forced traditional enemies to live under one rule. This had a singular advantage by allowing the colonials – outnumbered, of course – to rule by dividing the locals. This is helpful in understanding what regional associations must remedy in the New World Disorder.

There are two kinds of colonial powers. The most obvious is the colonial power that establishes colonies in overseas lands. The second form of colonialism is when a strong nation expands and extends its frontiers to absorb its weaker neighbors. When, in 1960 Soviet Premier Nikita Khrushchev proposed in the United Nations the liquidation of the colonial system and the granting of independence to colorial countries and peoples, he did not consider the fringe Soviet republics as colonies. Now, through other forces, they do have independence and interact with each other because of interlocalism.

The breakup of the crumbling Ottoman Empire began with Britain annexing Cyprus – a country China established diplomatic relations with in 1971 – at the end of World War I, with an agreement with the French that it could grab Tunis. The British bought Egypt's shares in the Suez Canal and stayed on in Egypt and Sudan while France, Italy and Spain grabbed the other North African territories of the Ottoman Empire. The colonial powers chose to divide their territories mainly astronomical frontiers, ideally, straight lines running along meridians and parallels, like the frontiers between Libya and Egypt, and Egypt and the Sudan. They tended to ignore the ethnic origins of the population.

After the defeat and collapse of the Ottoman Empire in World War I, the carving up of the Gulf states, Lebanon and Palestine into spheres of influence and mandates followed the straight-line frontiers formula. This disastrous policy was compounded by conflicting promises and questionable secret treaties.

Today this is highlighted in Iraq, Lebanon, Syria, Saudi Arabia and Jordan. They are all artificial countries carved out of the Ottoman Empire. Four distinct groups – Shiites, Sunnis, Hijazis and Kurds – who have been in Mesopotamia since before modern history, were carved into three countries by Winston Churchill so that in Iraq the oil in the Kurdish north would be in the same country as the oil in the Shiite south with the hapless Sunnis in the middle. In Saudi Arabia, the Shiites who dominate the oil-rich eastern province were cut off from their fellow Shiites in southern Iraq, and the Hijazis, who belong to the holy cities of Mecca and Medina, still regard the Hashemites – who were sent to Jordan – as the legitimate rulers of the region. It was a sure-fire recipe for the current conflicts, which will continue unless properly addressed and remedied in the 21st century.

An interesting interlocal sidebar about Jordan is that it is home to some 8,000 Chechens, many of whom have supported the rebels in Chechnya by raising money and even fighters. A minority in a sea of Arabs, Jordan's Chechens have retained their language and customs for more than a century. Chechens originally came to Jordan from 1895 to 1905 when they fled op-

pression in czarist Russia. Like Jordan's 80,000 Circassians, who began fleeing Russia's southwest expansion in 1879, the historically Muslim peoples
of the Caucausus found a home among fellow Muslims in what was then
part of the Ottoman Empire. Is it any wonder Chechens cycle to and from
Mecca? Dzhanar-Aliyev Magomed-Ali did just that. He went on his pilgrimage to the *hajj* on his bicycle, which took him through war-torn Iraq,
where he had a run-in with American soldiers who thought he was a Russian,
smashed his bicycle and sent him back to Iran. He then had to go around
Iraq through Armenia and Georgia, down through Turkey, Syria, Jordan and
finally to Mecca in Saudi Arabia.

The tribal interlocalism of Muslims in Mecca is a relatively new phenomenom
when compared to its neighbor Oman. In the Jebel foothills of Oman, in
Jable littin, lies the tomb of Job, Nabi Ayoub, who is mentioned in both the
Koran and the Bible. The Queen of Sheba's palace was at Khor Ruri, near
Samhuran, which was a famous frankincense port located between two creeks.
The Dhofar region is also the final resting place of Nabi Imran, the father of
the Virgin Mary, and the prophet Emran, the father of Moses.

Before Britain granted the Indian Empire independence in 1947, there were
lengthy negotiations and a serious attempt was made to divide the territories
on religious and ethnic grounds. The result was the creation of Pakistan and
Bangladesh. In spite of these efforts, there was a post-independence holocaust and millions were massacred in religious and racial strife that spread
throughout India and Pakistan – which continues today. Kashmir is the one
remaining unresolved territorial dispute between the two dominant countries of the former Indian empire. Kashmir was divided along with the Indian subcontinent by the British in 1947, with India later gaining control.
Pakistani militants invaded what is now Pakistan's zone, splitting the territory.

Manmohan Singh, India's 17th prime minister and the first non-Hindu
premier, has been able to strengthen the county's secular character and bridge
the contentious religious obstacles in Kashmir. Singh and Pakistan's President Pervez Musharraf have agreed to increase the frequency of a new bus
service launched in April 2005 to reunite families on opposite sides of
Kashmir's heavily militarized Line of Control, and to open a new rail link
between their countries.

The same thing happened to the European colonies of West Africa. They were originally trading posts for gold, ivory and slaves. These early settlements developed into bridgeheads, and the first scramble for Africa began in the early 1870s. The imperial powers sorted out their differences peaceably at the first Berlin Congress in 1878. Most of the frontiers of the new African colonies were straight lines and rivers that split tribes and forced traditional enemies to live together. This technique was again used by the British in India and the French in Indochina.

Slavery had played a large part in the establishment of the early trading posts. Ironically, it was the anti-slavery movement that led to the colonization of much of Africa in the second half of the 19th century. Conflict between the missionaries and the Muslim Swahili-Arab slave traders in east and central Africa was used as an excuse by the European powers to grab more territory. The establishing of the British and German East African colonies was not without bloodshed, but it paled beside the atrocities of the Belgians in the Belgium Congo, which King Leopold governed as a private fief.

While the Arabs and Europeans plundered Africa of its natural resources, including human beings sold into slavery, Americans and their leader put their lives on the line to emancipate slaves. President Abraham Lincoln put his life on the line and paid the ultimate price because of his determination to win the Civil War and enact his Slavery Emancipation Act.

The British acquired the Orange Free State and Transvaal, what is today South Africa, as the result of the Second Boer War (1899-1902), which was engineered by arch-imperialist Cecil Rhodes. His ambition was to paint a pink strip on the map from Cape Town to Cairo. This was not achieved until after World War I when Germany's former colonies in Africa became British protectorates. British and Dutch imperialism was trade oriented, whereas German and Italian imperialism had more to do with prestige.

In Africa it was quite impossible to even attempt to divide any of the colonies into tribal states, simply because there are so many nomadic tribes. In East Africa alone there are at least 200 tribes. Some of these are nomads to whom the concept of land ownership or borders is alien. They are like a leopard skin, some of the spots of the leopard have an alarming habit of moving. In 1969, the leaders of the African countries decided to recognize the old colonial frontiers. Article 3 of the Charter of the Organization of African Unity affirms: "Respect of sovereignty and its inalienable right for independent existence." They, like the Europeans and at their urging, decided that to attempt to redefine national frontiers would be like opening Pandora's box and would cause more problems than it solved – a decision they should reconsider in light of what has happened since.

In Nigeria, the killings between Muslim Fulani cattle herders and Christian Tarok farmers that have been ongoing for decades over land and cattle, culminated in 2004 when 500 to 600 Christians were killed in the Muslim city of Kano. In Africa, guns aren't the only killers. Studies by Physicians for Human Righs and by the International Rescue Committee in 2005, concluded separately that the major cause of death is the disruption that a few thousand armed men create in the lives of millions of civilians. The first killer, the studies concluded, is flight

The killing is caused by historical tribal conflicts, greed and the control of natural resources and minerals which in Central Africa particularly are making borders look febrile – and deadly. Liberia's "blood diamonds" supporting the conflict in Sierra Leone is an example.

The borders in the developing world were drawn by the colonial powers for administrative convenience rather than nation-building. This is the primary reason nation-states have failed to develop behind these artificial borders. Iraq is a 21st-century example. The same holds true for Pakistan across two of its unnatural borders in Afghanistan and Kashmir. Of the three land borders Pakistan acquired at the time of its independence in 1947, only one – that with India – was reasonably well-defined. The borders drawn by Sir Mortimer Durand in 1893 – the Durand Line – between Afghanistan and the British Indian Empire was never accepted by Afghanistan. The same is true for the Line of Control that separates the Indian and Pakistani regions of Kashmir.

Shahid Javed Burki, the former finance minister of Pakistan and former vice president of the World Bank, has suggested that the colonial-imposed borders of Pakistan be turned into "soft frontiers" that allow the easy movement of people, goods and commodities across the border. I agree but advocate that the concept be applied to all artificially imposed borders until such time as new natural borders are drawn and accepted by the neighboring states. There should be no visa requirements and trade would take place unhindered by tariffs and customs procedures. Economics would trump ethnic and religious obscurantism.

Borders created by the European colonials have to be redrawn along ethnic and tribal lines if there is to be peace in the 21st century in conflicted countries. The same applies to conflicted communities in America and the rest of the developed world. The alternative is more failed states. This was brought home to me in Scotia, the oldest pub in Glasgow, founded in 1792. There on the wall was the Scottish Declaration of Independence from 1320 with a picture of Nelson Mandela on the left of it and one of Fidel Castro and Che Guevara on the right.

The Glasgow City Council chambers has a Statute of Liberty on the roof under the Scottish flag. The chambers are across the road from George's Square, wher King George's statute, which was supposed to go on the top of a tall pedestal in the square, was replaced with a statute of Walter Scott looking south to the borders, because George lost the American colonies.

Scotland is one of the most interlocal countries in the world. With a population of 5 million, it has over 35 million interlocal Scots around the world who can trace their heritage back to Scotland. All are proud sons and daughters regardless of the circumstances under which they left Scotland, especially those forced out by the English. James Hepburn, the Fourth Earl of Bothwell, who was married to Mary Queen of Scots, is one such example. He died a lonely death in a foreign jail, and is today buried in Denmark. His descendants are campaigning for Denmark to repatriate the remains to Scotland. Hepburn married the queen in 1567 but they were separated just a month later when Mary was imprisoned by Elizabeth 1. He fled to Bergen, now in Norway, but then part of Denmark, and was arrested as a pirate by the Danish authorities who thought he was a useful political pawn.

The center-left Scottish National Party won a one-seat victory over Labor in the 2007 parliamentary elections while pursuing its dream of ending the 300-year old union with England. The SNP has pledged to hold a referendum in 2010 on Scottish independence.

Failed States

Liberia was founded in 1816 by freed slaves from the U.S. who decided to return home during the administration of President James Monroe. The country was founded by an unusual alliance of slaveholders and abolitionists as a means of speeding slavery's demise and demonstrating the capacities of people of African descent. It would also renew the continent with an infusion of evangelical Christianity. To many, the freed slaves who left for Liberia were Dupes of Southern plantation owners who wanted to deport free People of color, thus ridding themselves of free slaves who demonstrated the possibility of black freedom.

The capital of Monrovia was named after the U.S. president, and Liberia became an independent nation in 1847. It is Africa's oldest republic. The only difference between Liberia and South Africa is that the new colonials in Liberia were freed African-Americans who, like their white counterparts in South Africa and Zimbabwe, took the land away from the locals, ran the government and used the local mineral riches to enrich themselves at the expense of the locals. If there is one country in Africa that is an offshoot of America, it is Liberia.

During World War, II Liberia was an important source of rubber for the U.S. During the Cold War, Liberia was the center of the U.S. government communications bases to monitor Soviet activities in the region. Although never a formal U.S. colony, Liberia is the sole country in Africa that is a U.S. progeny. One that can no longer be neglected.

The ongoing civil wars and conflicts in Sudan between Muslims and Christians and Arab and African Muslims are a never-ending saga. It is estimated that the various civil conflicts have killed 2 million people and uprooted 4 million people in a country four times the size of France. The ongoing conflict in Darfur is one of the world's worst humanitarian disasters.

Congo is another example at the dawn of the 21st century. Burundi, Rwanda and Uganda with Congolese allies form one side. Angola, Zimbawe, Nambia, Sudan and Chad and their Congolese allies form the other side. The country is in shambles. It is brutal global capitalism at its ugliest. A Belgian legacy of a culture of brutality which has left more than 4 million people killed in Congo's wars since 1998, making it the most lethal conflict since World War

II. The Grand Hotel in Kinshasa is the epicenter of a global bazaar that rapes the people of their natural resources as they are left in abject poverty by self-serving corrupt politicians.

Muslim Africa

Nearly half of Africa's population is Muslim, making it a fertile recruiting ground for al-Qaeda and other extreme Muslim fundamentalists. America must devote more attention and money in Africa if it wants to avoid the rebirth of more Idi Amins and Charles Taylors. Corruption, brutality and terrorism are on the rise in Africa. Unless America and China join forces and take the lead in Africa with the new Interlocal Security Council recommended in the previous chapter, it will become the new spawning ground for the New World alienated and angry terrorists.

After decades of stagnation and regression, Africa has awakened at the dawn of the New World Order. The majority of its 750 million people live under elected governments for the first time ever. But most are corrupt and directly or indirectly condone violence and terrorist regimes.

To put an end to the ongoing conflict in Africa, African leaders established a joint African Standby Force to act as peacekeepers to intervene in civil wars, cross-border conflicts and coup d'etats across the continent. Although a constructive first step, the force is a toothless tiger with no powers of enforcement – best witnessed in Darfur.

Hope

There are reasons for hope – from within Africa, not from without. Thabo Mbeki's inauguration as South Africa's second democratic president was a milestone for the continent. So was Olusegun Obasanjo's coming to power in Nigeria after decades of dictatorship, notwithstanding the rampant voter fraud in the 2007 presidential elections and the separatist movements in several parts of the country. They are world-class leaders of black Africa's biggest economies. They are expected to lead the continent, creating an axis of stability that will attract international investment – interlocalism.

There are signs of a turnaround in Africa, and plenty of reason for optimism. In the early 1960s, most of Africa was richer than Asia and many economists expected Africa to zoom far ahead of Asia. Back then, the World Bank named a group of African countries that it projected to grow at 7 percent annually. Wrong again. Instead, Africa got stuck in the slow lane, as Asia moved up front into the fast lane.

The five worst-performing economies in the world from 1960 to 2001 were all in Africa because of government mismanagement and war. This is best showcased today in Sudan's Darfur region. The reason for hope is that Botswana was the fastest-growing country in the world from 1960 to 2001. South Korea was second, Singapore and China tied for third place. Mozambique, Benin, Tanzania, Liberia and Mauritius, are other bright African stars that are building their country's future on trade, not aid. Hence the optimism building in the dark continent. One of the best kind of aid that America, and other developed countries can provide would be to expand the African Growth and Opportunity Act program which encourages imports from Africa.

The African Union should, in light of the tribal conflicts in the closing decades of the last millennium, revisit the question of tribal and economic harmony, even if it means redrawing the borders set at the conference in Berlin. The alternative is continued chaos.

The Global Leadership Foundation uses its roster of former national leaders and high-ranking officials to improve the world by making their experience and wisdom available to governments in need. Founder and former South African President F.W. de Klerk and 21 others like former Philippine President Fidel Ramos, one-time French Prime Minister Michel Rocard and ex-Indian Premier I.K. Gujral are the backbone. The patrons include de Klerk's successor, Nelson Mandela, and former U.S. President George H.W. Bush. They offer advice to countries seeking advice on fighting corruption, political, educational and health reform issues and economics.

I had the privalege of meeting de Klerk when he came to make a speech at the Foreign Correspondents Club in Hong Kong in early 2007. He is a man who not only ended apartheid and saved South Africa from a racial war, but is the only state leader to have renounced the nuclear weapons that it already possessed. Asking him if he agreed with the South Africans I met in Australia, who feel that Africa is becoming a province of China, he said: "I speak as an African. My family arrived in Africa over 400 years ago. Africa has much to offer in the way of resources and China is hungry for them. There's nothing wrong with that. What should be avoided is that involvement through aid, imports and exports should not develop into a form of prescriptiveness. When big brother starts to tell small brother what to do, for instance, how to vote at the U.N. This is very dangerous." But isn't that what politics is all about?

With China and South Africa signing a nuclear cooperation pact on the peaceful use of nuclear energy, it is just a matter of time before a free trade agreement follows.

The scramble for resources by the major powers is nothing new. The ongoing race to corner resources led to both world wars. The ongoing race can lead to future conflicts or peace. The fight in the board rooms and government ministeries for natural resources has historically led to war and will lead to more wars unless *We the Apathetic Maids* slam on the brakes.

The Counterweight

China is actually a great counterweight to al-Qaeda and the other extremist Muslim terror cells throughout Africa. America defaulted on its role of protector of rights in Africa when it got booted out of Somalia in 1994 and it is back today supporting Ethiopian troops to oust Muslim extremists. China's investments in Ethiopia help fund the fight. China's citizens kidnapped by Nigerian terrorists and the Ogaden National Liberation Front in Ethiopia are released for a price.

Haiti is an example of a former colony in the Western Hemisphere that has become a chronic failed state. It is the poorest country in the Americas, one of the poorest in the world, and continuously spirals into mayhem and bloodshed. More than 80 percent of the country's 8 million people live in poverty and have suffered repeated coups and civil wars. Haiti has been ravaged by AIDS, with a life expectancy of 53 and 80 percent of the population living on less than $4 a day.

In 1804, Haiti became the world's first independent republic, after a 12-year revolt by slaves to oust their French masters. On independence day in 1904, president Rosalvo Bobo told his countrymen that he was "tired ... of our stupidities" and lamented "a century of slavery of negro by negro." He urged Haitians to mend their ways, so that by January 1st 2004, their descendants might have something to celebrate on their country's bicentenary. They didn't and still don't.

New Map

As we look at the damage done by colonial mapmaking, is global re-drawing either practical or politically feasible? Can the existing sovereign states sit down at some modern "Berlin" with the prospect of trading territory? Absolutely. There is no authority on Earth that can hand down a decision on where to draw a tribal boundary. It is up to the tribal chiefs and heads of state. Local tribes and communities are already doing it entirely by themselves, moving and trading along old lines and habits, from Central Africa to Central Asia. In many deep continental areas, the Congo Basin, Russia, Pakistan, China triangle, the interplay of people is rendering borders less and less relevant, while at the same time central governments' efforts to hold these lines are less and less successful. The only viable solution is peaceful interlocalism.

A good example is Tatarstan, a country of 5.5 million people that provides nearly 10 percent of Russia's oil supply. The Tatar Autonomous Republic was ruled for 4.5 centuries by Moscow. In fact Ivan the Terrible, the first czar of Russia, sacked the area in 1552 and destroyed all mosques and tried to Russianize the region by relocating Russians there and making Russian the local language. Nevertheless, today most of the population is Muslim Tatar. Tatarstan flags fly throughout the land, and the republic has its own constitution. But unlike the breakaway republic of Chechnya, Tatarstan has managed to negotiate autonomy without provoking the wrath of the Russian army, largely because Mintimer Shaimiev, its president since 1991, has never seceded or resorted to terrorism.

Lions of Mesopotamia

The interlocal, Shiite, Sunni and Kurdish Iraqi soccer team, crowned the 2007 Asian Cup champions, for the first time, with their shocking 1-0 win over Saudi Arabia – seven time finalists in the last eight years, and three-time winners of the tournament, was not only a surprising upset in the sport, but a signal that if people of different cultures, religions and races are determined to work together for a common goal, they can prevail, against all odds.

The driven Iraqis showed great resolve and immense inner strength throughout the tournament, crushing Australia 3-1 and beating South Korea on penalties. The Iraqis were determined to win the final after a mother had dedicated her 12-year-old son, one of more than 50 people slain in a car bomb attack in Baghdad while celebrating Iraq's semi-final win over South Korea – as a sacrifice to the Iraqi national team.

Iraqi skipper Younis Mahmoud's thumping headed goal in the fiercely contested all-Arab final in Indonesia, was his fourth goal to finish joint-leading scorer in the tournament with Saudi Arabia's Yasser Al Qahtani and Japan's Naohiro Takahara. Younis is a Sunni Turkman. Teammate Houar Mullah Mohammad, who put the ball in position for the score, is a Kurdish Shiite. Goalkeeper Noar Sabri is an Arab Shiite.

The team could not go home to parade the Asian Cup in Baghdad out of fear for their lives and that of their fans. The victorious lions celebrated their win in Dubai and Amman, Jordan. Younis Mahmoud and other teammates did not go to Iraq with the cup out of fear. The Iraqis do and will continue to turn on each other. Many members of the football team have lost loved ones in the ongoing sectarian violence. The team is tight and determined. Determined to show the world that they can beat anyone, including America. They are united as a team to first get rid of America and other foreigners, before they get down to business with each other.

Iraqi footballers, unlike their Saudi counterparts who only play in the kingdom, are highly prized and play for foreign teams throughout the Middle East and Africa. If no country wants Saudi footballers, why does America continue to play in the Arabian desert and embrace Saudi political leadership?

Interlocal Israel
Two Arab Israeli citizens – there are 1.2 million of them comprising more than one-fifth of Israel's population – are the stars of Israel's national soccer team. Abbas Suan and Walid Badir are cheered by all Israelis during their international competitions – Muslim, Jewish and Christain. In Israel, as elsewhere, sports have been an equalizer. Israel's integrated national squad "isn't just a team" said Suan. "It's a symbol."

Israel's unilateral withdrawal from the Gaza Strip in 2005 reaped a surprise benefit in the Muslim world: diplomatic recognition from Muslim countries from Tunisia to Indonesia. The diplomatic opportunities in Asia and North Africa are allowing Israel for the first time to interlocalize with the Muslim world in the 21st century. The failure of Muslim nations to condemn Iran's President Mahmoud Ahmadinejad's verbal attacks on Israel was disappointing, but understandable – any wonder Iran and Iraq are boosting their economic and military ties?

Interlocalism in the extreme are the five-meter wide anti-Israel and anti-Zionist banners in Iran, a physical reflection of Ahmadinejad's declaration that the Jewish state should be "wiped off the map." They were created with technology made in Israel. Ahmadinejad's predecessor, Mohammad Khatami, was seated close to Israeli President Moshe Katsav at the funeral of Pope John Paul II in April 2005 and the two shook hands and chatted briefly. Katzav was born in the Iranian city of Yazd, which is Khatami's hometown. Khatami had proposed a dialogue among civilizations and pursued a policy of detente – a path Iran will again embark on once the current mullahocracy is replaced with true democracy. Khatami has expressed an interest in visiting Israel. As a side bar, England's Prince Charles was forced to shake hands with Robert Mugabe at the Pope's funeral. Great seating plan.

Football Diplomacy

America and China brought down the bamboo curtain with "ping pong" diplomacy. Mao Tse-tung and Richard Nixon initiated ping pong tournaments between America and China to thaw the Cold War diplomatic isolation between the two countries. The establishment of diplomatic relations has led to the mutual dependence of the two global giants on each other because of their tight economic embrace.

Football diplomacy can do the same for the Middle East. An Israeli team with Jews, Muslims and Christians, playing Shiite, Sunni and Kurdish Iraq, Lebanese, Egyptian and Jordanian Muslims and Christians playing Shiite Iran, Sunni Saudi Arabia and Sunni, Shiite Syria. The secular Gulf states and Turkey host and play in the playoffs.

The tunnels under the fortified borders of the Middle East, like the Sino-U.S. bamboo curtain, have to be kicked away during interlocal football tournaments and replaced with open peacefull borders to allow cross border commerce to grow and the region's people to prosper.

Interlocal Soccer

The last millennium's first-ever get-together of 12 South American presidents and their "Declaration of Brasilia" pledge to unite South America's two main trade blocs into a single free trade zone with 340 million consumers is an example of regional interlocalism that goes beyond the annual America's Cup in soccer that has Latinos debating which country has the best team and players. The proposed 34-nation Free Trade Area of the Americas created an interlocal zone of 800 million people that produced $11.5 trillion in goods in 2005 and is growing annually.

When Mexico beat Brazil 4-3 in the Confederation Cup final in Mexico City in 2000, celebrations turned into riots not only throughout Mexico but also in Los Angeles County's Huntington Park. Jubilant Mexican-Americans were interlocalizing with their brothers and sisters back home. The same happened when South Korea beat Italy in the World Cup 2002. Italian-Australians rioted in Melbourne. In China, popular soccer commentator Huang Jianxiang had to publicly apologize for his personal emotional outburst when Italy beat Australia 1-0 in the World Cup. He shouted "Long Live Italy" and declared, "I don't like the Australian team."

Likewise, Arabs throughout the Arab world and Saudi Arabia openly vented their anger at the favoritism and nepotism at the Saudi Football Federation when Saudi Arabia was knocked out of World Cup 2002. Germany's 8-0 win led to caustic Arab humor. Saudis, who love luxury cars, "banned the import of eight-cylinder German cars" was my favorite joke. Conversely, when South Korea's co-host, Japan, was knocked out of the competition, a crowd gathered in a popular entertainment area in Tokyo and hoisted a Korean flag. Korean drums could be heard along with cheers – in Japanese – for the success of the South Korean team.

David Beckham joining the Los Angeles Galaxy soccer club is a millennium public relations and advertising coup for interlocalism and shows how interlocal soccer has become. English footballers and soccer, the game of the English working class, have found an Asian audience, and take American, Russian Thai and Hong Kong money to build the most popular sports league in our interlocal world.

As a former American Youth Soccer Organization coach, with my son Jonas playing in the league and since I enjoy soccer, football – American and Australian – basketball and baseball, I think there is a parallel between national politics and sports. With soccer's World Cup 2006 hosted in Germany prior to the 2006 World Series and congressional elections, it occurred to me that America's championship games of its national pastimes, the Super Bowl, World Series and others, are inextricably linked to America's history just as German football is in Germany. Adolph Hitler was disgusted when Germany lost 2-0 to Norway at the 1936 Berlin Olympics. Hitler never saw a football match again.

World Cup football still helps define the idea of Germany. Football took off in Germany thanks to the first world war. The troops on the western front played for relaxation and, after the armistice, they took the game home. Germans who like certainty never got used to the game's uncertainty. When Germany was defeated by Switzerland on Hitler's birthday in 1941, that ended Germany's sporting exchanges, unless the results were assured. German football had never been particularly good, and the national team never very significant. That changed one Sunday in July 1954 when West Germany beat Hungary in Bern, Switzerland, to win the World Cup. The Germans won the World Cup again in 1974 and 1990.

The German game remains characterized by kampf – struggle – strength and never giving up. Generations of the country's footballers have been raised in a style of play set under Hitler. The military antecedents of this style are now forgotten and would be considered an embarassment if remembered, but they live on in players' nicknames. The great striker Gerd Muller was "Der Bomber," any decent playmaker is a "feldmarschall," and Franz Bechenbauer, greatest German footballer of all was "Der Kaiser" – monarch and soldier in one. Not much different than what the U.S. military tried to do with U.S. footballer Pat Tillmar, who was killed by friendly fire in Afghanistan. He had given up a lucrative football contract to go to Afghanistan to join his brother in the Rangers.

The Germans, British, Italians, Portugese, French and Spanish brought soccer to their former colonies in Africa, Asia and Latin America. Today the Hispanics are exporting their telenovelas to America, Europe and Asia, including China. Meanwhile, America has also started getting hooked on soccer as well as telenovelas, as more soccer-playing immigrants and soccer fans cross the border.

Inter-Latino

The Andes Mountains, the great rivers, the rain forests and the savannahs did more to establish the frontiers of the post-colonial republics in South America than the *conquistadors*. Argentina is a triangular country, which is contained on the west by the Andes, the east by the Atlantic Ocean and the north by the great Pilcomayo, Parana and Uruguay rivers. This is a much smaller area than the viceroyalty of the Rio de la Plata of the Spanish empire, and today's boundaries are geographical, not ethnic.

Apart from the Inca empire, there was no significant pre-conquest civilized nation in South America. At its largest, the Inca empire stretched from southern Columbia to halfway down Chile. But before the conquests of the ninth Inca ruler, Pachacuti (1438-1471), the heartland of the Inca Empire was in Peru. Most of the original inhabitants of South America had been killed off by European disease and were not considered important by the revolutionary Spanish creole leaders when they established the frontiers of modern South America after the collapse of the Spanish empire. Today's frontiers were finally established by a series of border wars that had more to do with the power struggle of the creole generals than the ethnic origins of the original inhabitants.

The defeat by Chile of Bolivia and Peru in the 1879-84 War of the Pacific, and the redrawing of their borders, is an example. As the victor, Chile took the province of Arica from Peru, and from Bolivia the province of Antofagasta, the mineral-rich central Atacama Desert and all 4000km of its coastline. That is why Bolivia is landlocked today. It has long hoped for a sovereign corridor to the Pacific. The country even still retains a navy, stationed on Lake Titicaca. The issue has resurfaced now that new local indigenous leaders have won elections and taken the helms of the three neighbors in 2006. Chile's Michelle Bachelet has said she is prepared to look at granting sea access to Bolivia.

Socialist Bachelet, an agnostic single mother with three children from two relationships, also benefited from the Latin American shift of colonial ideals to indigenous secular values. A former political prisoner and exile, was be-

lieved by the public to be more trustworthy and representative of their values.
A fact not widely reported is that Latin America, with some of the world's
most stringent abortion laws, has the developing world's highest rate of abortions – higher even than in Western Europe, where abortion is widely and
legally available. Latin American women have mounted campaigns to legalize abortion.

According to the World Bank, Latin America also has the highest level of
inequality in the world today. This entrenched inequality has contributed to
a crisis level of conflict between the indigenous populations and the descendants of European colonizers and the exploiters of natural resources, namely
energy and mining companies.

The Aymars Indians of western Bolivia forced President Gonzalo Sanchez
de Lozada to resign in 2003 after they fought the army with sticks, sling-
shots and muscle. They built barricades, derailed a train and cut off the capital from the rest of the country to protest the inequities between the natives
and politicians of the ruling classes of European descent. It was the most
recent expression of growing militancy and political frustration of the natives of the Americas. Mexico's Zapatistas, Ecuador's Pachakutiks and
Guatemala's Mayas are the most vocal. Indigenous identities are being embraced and reasserted. "There are even people now who are beginning to
question Christianity, who are saying we should return to our original
religions," said German Jimenez, a Peruvian teacher and local tribal leader.

Bolivia's election of Evo Morales, an Aymara Indian llama herder and former
head of the Bolivian coca growers union, to the presidency, marked a significant shift in local and interlocal politics with grave consequences for
America. His election is the most prominent example of recent democratic
revolutions in Latin America. Throughout the region, the indigenous and the
poor, increasingly mobilized by frustration with Washington-backed economic prescriptions, have used the ballot box to put in place leaders more
representative of the majority. "The 500-year indigenous and popular campaign of resistance has not been in vain," Morales said after being sworn
into office.

The day after becoming his nation's first indigenous leader, Morales branded
Bush a terrorist. "The only terrorist in this world that I know of is Bush. His

military intervention, such as the one in Iraq, that is state terrorism. There is a difference between people fighting for a cause and what terrorists do. Today in Bolivia and Latin America, it's no longer people that are lifting their weapons against imperialism, but it is imperialism that is lifting its weapons against people through military intervention and military bases," Morales said.

In Mexico, America's second-largest trading partner, there has long been resentment of the wealth of Americans created at the expense of Mexicans. The annexation by America of Texas, Arizona, New Mexico and California are at the root of the resentment. No matter the original wrong, these states would not benefit by being returned to Mexico. The question is will they benefit by Mexico returning to them. That has been aggravated by disputes over trade and especially the issue of Mexican immigrants, legal and illegal, to the U.S. The 1,100km fence along the U.S.-Mexico border approved by the U.S. House of Representatives in 2005, has been labeled by many Mexicans the "Berlin Wall."

The rampant political corruption ravaging Latin America today is a legacy of Spain and America. The corruption of career politicians has left 43 percent of the 220 million people living in South and Cental America in poverty. The people's disgust is manifested in people power – from Bolivia to Venezuela. Career politicians are being removed from office violently – even killed. In Peru, the mayor of Ilave was dragged through the streets and lynched. His killers are known and have never been brought to justice. It was no surprise therefore that Ollanta Humala, a left-wing opponent of free-trade who condemns globalization, won the presidential election in 2006.

"Latin America is paying the price for centuries of inequality and injustice, and the United States really doesn't have a clue about what is happening in the region," said Riordan Roett, director of Latin American studies at John Hopkins University. Why not? U.S. foreign policy sometimes seems to have only two postures: the heavy-footed democratic missionary stomping virtue all over the place, or the naughty but clever frat house boy who has come up with a high-tech political scheme.

I agree with Keith Black, a senior policy advisor at Oxfam America, when he said: "The tragedy unfolding in Bolivia is clear evidence that the global economic rules made in places like Washington and Geneva have real and often very painful effects in poor countries. It is squarely within the interest of the U.S. and other highly industrialized nations to finally put the basic economic, social and cultural rights of the Southern Hemisphere's poorest above sheer profit alone."

Brazil

One of the most openly Christian countries in Latin America is Brazil. One really experiences that as a visitor being mugged in broad daylight a few feet from the hotel. It is also the only Portuguese-speaking country in Latin America. When the Portuguese arrived, the indigenous people they conquered spoke more than 700 languages The Jesuit priests concocted a mixture of Indian, Portugese and African words they called "lingua geral," or the "general language," and imposed t on their colonial subjects. Today, tribes that have lost their own mother tongue are now taking refuge in lingua geral and making it an element of their identity.

The reason Brazil is different from its Latin neighbors is that not only was it a Portugese colony, unlike the rest of Latin America that was Spanish, but the entire Portuguese royal family fled Fortugal in 1807 and moved to Brazil.

The flight of the Portuguese royal family, the Braganzas. took place at a critical time in Western European history, when the Peninsular War was heating up. Eclipsed by Britain and France, Portugal was in decline. Napoleon's army was advancing from the north. The deposed kings of France and Holland had both gone into exile in England; the British fleet was blockading the Tagus River in an attempt to counter the French advance. As the French army drew closer to Lisbon, the Portuguese prince regent, Dom Joao, under pressure from the British envoy, made a decision that would be fateful not just for the Portuguese crown, but also for Brazil, the New World colony that was Portugal's major source of revenue.

On November 29, 1807, a day before the French army entered the city, Dom Joao and his Spanish Borbon queen, Dona Carlota, fled by the only route available to them: the sea. A convoy of three dozen frigates, brigantines, sloops, corvettes and ships of the line, with the entire Portuguese court on board – 10,000 strong – set sail for Brazil with a British escort.

The Portuguese court stayed in Brazil for 13 years. They returned to Europe after the British defeated Napoleon and wanted to restore royal authority in Europe. It lasted 95 years. However, Dom Pedro, the son of Dom Joao and Dona Carlota, whose paternity was disputed, decided to stay in Brazil and declared himself Emperor Pedro I of Brazil – establishing the first European Catholic monarchy of the New World.

One thing has not changed. Today Brazil continues to be home of exiled Latin American leaders. It grants them political asylum. The latest was Ecuadorian President Lucio Gutierrez in 2006, who was ousted by Congress amid street protests that called for his removal for abuse of power. Brazil is also the country that exports to Europe and America great interlocal footballers and interlocal corporate chameleon extraordinaire Carlos Ghosn, the quadrilingual, French-educated Brazilian of Lebanese descent who was brought in to turn around Japanese automaker Nissan's fortunes, which he did. He forced the Japanese staff of the car maker to learn English in preparation for their overtaking General Motors. America and GM didn't see it coming. Why am I not surprised?

Algarve

I spent a week in May 2006 in Albufeira on the Algarve coast of Portugal. Algarve means the west in Arabic and was named during the Moor occupation. It is home to the oldest slave market in Europe. Political and religious discussions over the merits and demerits of colonialism, and the benefits of interlocalism over a bottle of Portugese wine or firewater, often got heated.

The Portugese I met, although they lamented the loss of Brazil and Macau, prefer their current interlocalism with Europe. "We are civilized Europeans, not barbarian imperialists like America," was a common theme. How ironic, I thought to myself. How the times have changed.

Discussing the results of the Montenegro referendum with Portugese, Spaniards, Brits, Canadians and Russians in Portugal on May 22, 2006, the day after Montenegro decided by a vote of 55.5 percent to devolve and become independent from Serbia, aroused fervent deep-seated devolution sentiments that quickly developed into heated, passionate and emotional outbursts that were easily cooled off with copious jugs of sangria.

At the Versailles peace conference after the First World War, the great powers acquiesced in the forcible incorporation of Montenegro into the new Serbian-dominated kingdom of Serbs, Croats and Slovenes, which later became Yugoslavia. Absorption by the Serbs was fiercely resisted. Montenegro fought fiercely in the Allied cause from 1914, but King Nicholas made the fatal mistake of placing his army under Serbian command, a lesson well learned by the insurgents and combatants in Iraq. The "Christmas Uprising," after the union had been proclaimed on November 13, 1918, began an unsuccessful war of independence which was also a civil war, finally resulting in their independence in 2006. The writing was on the wall at the 2006 Eurovision song competition when the Montenegro boy band was pelted with missiles by Serbs. The history of Montenegro reflects that of many states and people who have been forced over the years for a variety of political reasons to be part of a country they have no desire to be part of.

Serbia, though possessing a navy, is now landlocked. That is one way to defang a navy.

Yugoslavia, which was founded after the First World War, was made up of Slovenia, Croatia, Serbia, Macedonia. Kosovo, Montenegro and Bosnia-Herzegovina. Yugoslavia no longer exists. Heartened by the Montenegrine example, Kosovo's overwhelming Albanian majority declared independence. The U.N. urged and recommended that Kosovo be granted independence from Serbia. U.S. evangelists joined Serbia's Christian Orthodox Church to campaign against independence for the mainly Muslim province of Kosovo.

Kosovo set an unprecedented interlocal breakup because, unlike other bits of Yugoslavia that have broken off so far, Kosovo is not an autonomous republic within the Yugoslav federation, but was merely an Albanian-majority province within Serbia. Now that Kosovo has broken away, other disgruntled minorities will follow, further interlocalizing with their brothers and sisters across today's demarcated borders.

The Brits supported the Montenegro decision, the Russians were opposed, and the Spanish and Portugese had mixed emotions because of the Basque separatist movement and the impact that devolution would have on Spain and Portugal.

Many Spaniards feel the government is appeasing the Basque separatist group ETA. The peace process that was underway was derailed by a December 2006 bombing at Madrid airport, despite the fact that three calls were made by ETA, giving exact details of the location of the explosive device. It killed two people who were sleeping in their car. The Basques aren't the only ones who want to interlocalize with Spain. The Catalans also want greater autonomy to interlocalize.

The Spaniards lead the field in adopting Chinese children. Spain now adopts the highest number of Chinese children in the world. Ninety percent of the adoptees are girls. Spain needs a major immigrant intake to stop its population going into decline. Yet Spain is unable and refuses to face the legacy of the civil war and come to terms with its past. The history and legacy of Spain's pitiless civil war of 1936 to 1939 still arouses passionate reactions.

Some historians contend that the civil war's international dimensions – with Joseph Stalin supporting the Republic with weapons and advisers and Adolf Hitler providing air support for the Nationalists – constituted the opening round of World War II. Today the war still elicits bitter memories and discord. After Franco died in 1975, the world admired Spain's move to constitutional monarchy and democracy. But the process required what became known as el pacto de olvida, the pact of forgetting. No generals or torturers stood trial. No truth commissions chronicled Spain's past. The regime died in its bed along with its founder. And therein lay the problem for the left. It never had a chance to overthrow the regime, or to take part in Spain's transformation. Hence the "Two Spains."

I was actually pleasantly surprised to find Spaniards and Portugese supporting devolution of the Basque provinces and interlocalizing with each other and Europe. Their broad support of devolution in France, Italy and Germany, based on the U.K. model , in addition to Spain, was a political eye-opener.

Decolonization
After World War II, the United States and the Soviet Union were in the forefront of the crusade of decolonialization. They defined colonialism as when a power ruled an overseas or "tropical colony" like Kenya and not as one that controlled a neighboring state, territory or country that had been annexed through expansionism, like the Ukraine or Texas. The Americans

call their colonies "commonwealths," the Portuguese used the word "provinces," and the Chinese use "autonomous region," even though the inhabitants of these territories may belong to a different race, speak a different language and practice a different religion. Most of the obvious overseas colonies have already gained independence, but what is left are those that do not want independence, such as Northern Ireland and the Falkland Islands. The age of massive decolonization is over, but rapid decolonization created the problem of artificial frontiers, a legacy of the colonial age. A legacy of negative scars that must be cosmetically and politically corrected.

When Kuwait gained independence from Britain in 1961, Iraq not only claimed ownership, but also threatened invasion. The threat was carried out 30 years later when Saddam invaded and precipitated America's military involvement to this day. The rivalries: ethnic and religious, political and economic, ideological and personal, compounded by the struggle for primacy in the Gulf, was also the proximate cause of the Iraq-Iran war. That war had been sparked "by the arbitrary way in which nations had been created and borders in the Middle East overlaid on the map of the defunct Ottoman Empire Indeed, geography was decidedly at the heart of the conflict," Daniel Yergin wrote in his Pulitzer Prize-winning book *The Prize*.

For thousands of years border wars have kept many nations in an almost perpetual state of conflict. The European powers agreed at the end of the Helsinki Conference in 1975 "that one another's frontiers as well as the frontiers of all states of Europe are inviolable." With its checkered history, every state in Europe has some legitimate claim to territory which is ruled today by another state. The Helsinki objective was simply to prevent war. Although Germany has been reunited and the Soviet empire has collapsed, with the exception of the Balkan states and Northern Ireland, peace has been largely preserved in Europe as a result of the treaty. The artificial boundaries created in Africa, Asia, Europe and the Middle East are counterbalanced by the natural boundaries of Latin America. Isn't it time all the borders in Africa, Asia and the Middle East be revisited in the 21st century to see how conflicts can be minimized or eliminated?

Border Lines
Going back to visit Cyprus and the neighborhood I grew up in at the dawn of the new millennium is when I came to the realization that it is time to redraw

the artificial border lines in the 21st century. At the time, Cyprus was an island divided between Greeks and Turks. The absurdity of the division was brought home by Savvas Christodoulou and his donkey Shelidonia. To protest the artificial border line, he crossed from the Greek part of the island to the Turkish section equipped only with a "donkey passport." He was allowed to cross and was then promptly arrested along with his donkey. The donkey was heavily pregnant and was identified in her passport as a male. It was unclear whether the arrest occurred because of the false information given in the passport or the fact that they had crossed the border. I suspect it was the latter. The point of the protest was that since donkeys are the only species that are indigenous to Cyprus, not the Greeks or the Turks, why create artificial borders that only create conflicts?

The U.S. coalition efforts in Iraq to create a new governing body that is acceptable to the Sunnis, Kurds and Shiites is a nonstarter. Iraq is an artificial country that has to be divided into three different countries. The Kurds should be allowed to form Kurdistan in the north, and the Sunnis should form their own separate country in the center, and the Shiites should interlocalize with the Shiites in Saudi Arabia. Democratic elections will only propel the Shiites to power, which will be unacceptable to the Sunnis and the Kurds. So what is the point? Perpetuate more conflicts in the future? If politicians in America can gerrymander districts in every state of the union to perpetuate and increase the power of the ruling party, why not borders? It is up to *We the Maids* to sweep away the artificial countries created by colonizers that perpetuate conflicts and create a new harmonious world of countries of like-minded people in the 21st century who interlocalize with their counterparts globally.

Arabia
The Wahhabis of Saudi Arabia are detested by both the Shiites and Hijazis, the two largest groupings in Arabia, because they have been treated as second-class citizens by the Wahhabis ever since the Al Saud family made their pact with the Wahhabi clan that enshrined its extreme fundamentalism as both the religion and law of the land.

Other tribes, especially those from the border region with Yemen, also have little tolerance for the Saudi royals and their extreme Wahhabism. Many in Saudi Arabia, especially the Hijazis, still regard the Hashemites – including the Jordanian royal family – as the legitimate rulers of the region. The Saudi royals forced the Hashemites out of Arabia with the support of Britain, which had enthroned them in Iraq and Jordan.

The borders of Arabia must be redrawn to include the Shiites in southern Iraq, present-day Jordan and the proposed Palestinian state. Interlocalism will allow them to interlocalize as one country of Arabs with different religious beliefs, as they have done going back to biblical times.

Let's not forget that successive U.S. administrations built up Iraq to protect Saudi Arabia from Iran. When that didn't work, America went to war twice with Iraq – both times to protect the Saudi kingdom. The Saudi royals and their Wahhabi hard-line fundamentalism have been described in open congressional hearings as the epicenter of terrorism. The kingdom's biggest export after oil is suicide bombers. Most of the suicide bombers in Iraq are coming from Saudi Arabia. An online magazine named *Jihadweb* claims that 70 percent of the suicide bombers in Iraq are Saudi nationals. Of the 154 foreign fighters killed in Iraq over a six-month period, 61 percent were Saudis. Is this a grouping *We the Apathetic People* want to continue to keep in power in the 21st century so they can continue to foment terror? Isn't it time *We the Maids* sweep them out and sweep in interlocal borders that allow all the tribes in the region to prosper in peace from their oil resources instead of just one family? If the oil wasn't there, nobody would give a damn what they did between themselves.

Devolution

"Britain is an invented nation, not so much older than the United States," historian Peter Scott has written. Historian Linda Colley argues that a distinctive British nationality, encompassing English and Scots, developed between the Act of Union of England and Scotland in 1707 and the accession of Queen Victoria in 1837. Most of the things that are thought of as British do not antedate Queen Victoria: royal ceremony, Dickensian Christmas imagery, the imagery of empire and Burns Night. America, like its British parent, is made up of states that interact as a federal government.

Restoring U.S. state's rights, like those restored to the Scottish, Welsh and Irish governing bodies will allow the United States, through interlocalism, to continue its form of nationhood with few political cosmetic changes. In turn, the locals in America and England can continue to interact with their overseas compatriots in the 21st century as they have for the last several hundred years. The several million Scots in Scotland interlocalize with the 35 million-plus overseas Scots, and the Irish and Welsh do the same with their families, mates and business associates throughout the former colonies, just like global Americans.

The people of Scotland voted 3 to 1 in favor of establishing their own parliament – a 300-year-old dream. The vote for devolution spelled the end of the "era of big centralized government," declared Tony Blair. A 19-page report written in 1975, and suppressed for 30 years, revealed how North Sea oil could have made an independent Scotland as prosperous as Switzerland. In 2005, Chancellor of the Exchequer Gordon Brown underlined the vital revenue stream that North Sea oil still represents in the context of British politics – $88.5 billion over a three-year period. The parliament in Edinburgh is only just up and hardly running and unpopular. In a small country, another layer of bickering second-rate legislators and bureaucrats has been placed over the Scots – and they don't like it.

The Parliament in London retains control over Scotland's defense, foreign and financial affairs and employment and welfare. In the New World Order, interlocalism allows the Scots to have the best of all worlds. Imagine what the oil could have done for a Scotland that chose independence in the mid 1970s and claimed ownership of the reserves. The English haven't had a parliament in which neither Scotland nor Wales was represented since the Middle Ages.

The same holds true for Spain. Catalan, Basque, and all other Spanish provinces can interact with each other while retaining certain local controls in their community and region. Spain's Basque region, from northern Spain and southwestern France, like Britain's Scotland, Ireland and Wales, is itching for self-determination – and winning at the ballot box. The political arm of ETA, the Basque separatist party, which is similar to the political arm of the IRA, is calling for a referendum and a pact with Spain and France. Spain, like Britain, has gone from being a global colonizing empire in the last millennium to disintegrating as a country that can only stay as one with interlocalism.

Separatism is also on the march in Italy. The northern Italians debate the merits of independence. The opponents to independence argue that greater rights for regional government and reform of the bloated Rome bureaucracies are the solution. "Federal reform, not separatism, is the best response to frustration with high taxes, government bureaucracy and inefficiency." There is discontent with Rome but northern Italians, like their global counterparts, rather selfishly want to unburden themselves of the subsidized rural south. Sound familiar?

Local governments, under the concept of interlocalism, become responsible for everything except defense, foreign and financial affairs. Everything else goes back to the states, provinces and other local political units to distribute the responsibilities among themselves on a local basis.

Both Alexander Hamilton and Thomas Jefferson wanted a limited American government. A limited federal government with power vested in the states. Why have *We the Apathetic People* allowed career politicians to hijack local powers to Washington, D.C.? Isn't it time *We the Maids* swept them back home?

U.S. Constitutional Interlocalism

Government in the United States beyond the local level generally is held to be limited in its scope and divided in its structure. These constraints were expressly written into the country's founding document, its Constitution, in response to perceived oppression by the British monarch and Parliament against whom the American colonists rebelled. The new system was to be a "compound republic" in which "the power surrendered by the people is ... divided between two distinct governments:" first, a central national level to act on particular common concerns such as defense, and secondly, a diffused "state" level allowing citizens more immediate control over elected representatives. The details underlying this concept of "dual federalism" and its legal and political implications have been objects of serious contention for more than 200 years.

Author John D. Donahue in his 1997 book *Disunited States*, wrote: "The framers at Philadelphia launched not only a nation, but an appropriately endless argument over the proper balance between federal and state authority – an argument whose intensity ebbs and flows and whose content evolves, but which is never really settled."

The Articles of Confederation adopted in 1781 provided for only a feeble form of union, specifying at the start that "each state retains its sovereignty." The central government's economic authority was tightly constrained – it could not collect taxes, regulate trade or levy tariffs on imports – and was largely mediated through the constituent states. There were several reasons behind this weakness. Officials in the individual states were jealous of their authority and resisted any hint of subordination. The English and Scottish political traditions in which most American intellectuals were steeped celebrated the radical new idea of limited government. Yet *We the Apathetic People* have over time allowed Washington's career politicians to take them away and tax us to boot.

The framers believed that the allocation of responsibility across levels of government would need to change with the times, and the Constitution sets broad parameters around the allowable division of powers between state and national governments. Within those limits, the framers left it to the wisdom of their successors to find the right balance to fit the circumstances of the world to come and the priorities of future generations of Americans.

In our country's early years the states enjoyed far more legitimacy than the distant national government. Washington's rise in public esteem has been a 20th-century phenomenon because of *We the Apathetic People*. The Depression, the New Deal, World War II and the civil rights movement all tended to allow career politicians to detach popular loyalties from the states and move them toward Washington. A 1936 Gallup Poll found that 56 percent of Americans favored concentrating power in the federal government, while 44 percent favored state authority. Forty-one percent of respondents in a 1939 Roper Poll felt the federal government was "most honest and efficient in performing its own special duties." The states came in last in the New Deal-era survey at 12 percent, with 17 percent awarding their confidence to local government. Talk about effective managed misperception of apathetic Americans.

Contemporary opinion surveys, by contrast, show dwindling faith in the federal government. In regular polls commissioned by the Advisory Commission on Intergovernmental Relations, the fraction of respondents identifying the federal government as "the level from which you feel you get the least for your money" rose by 10 points (to 46 percent) between 1989 and 1994. Mid-1990s polls conducted by the Gallup Organization, the *Wall Street Journal* and NBC News, *Business Week* and the Harris Group, Hart and Teeter, and Princeton Survey Research Associates found, with striking consistency, support for enlarging the role of the states. Majorities of respondents – often lopsided majorities – favored state rather than federal leadership in education, crime control, welfare, job training, low-income housing, highway construction and farm policies.

Late 1994 polling on trust in government among Missourians and Kansans found about a 6 to 1 advantage for the states. A bellweather poll conducted by Princeton Survey Research Associates in 1995 for the *Washington Post*, the Kaiser Family Foundation and Harvard University found that by a margin of 61 to 24 percent, respondents trusted their state government over the federal government to "do a better job of running things." Most subgroups also gave the edge to the states, including self-defined liberals (who favored the states by a margin of 49 to 36 percent), Democrats (43 to 35 percent), and voters under age 30 (72 to 21 percent). Today the numbers are even more lopsided in favor of local governments

Not just instinct and tradition, but some powerful logic as well supports the ascendancy of the states. Supreme Court Justice Louis D. Brandeis framed a resonant metaphor when he wrote that "a single courageous state may, if its citizens choose, serve as a laboratory, and try social and economic experiments without risk to the rest of the country." Isn't it time *We the Maids* sweep in such a courageous laboratory to our states?

The richer the diversity of competitors in a private market and the more intense their rivalry, the more likely is the consumer to get the right deal at the right price. So, too, with government. Charles Tiebout, an economist, wrote that the "greater the number of communities and the greater the variance among them, the closer the consumer will come to fully realizing his preference position." People can sort themselves out among communities based on their tastes and their pocketbooks, and public officials must manage adroitly – minimize taxes, weed out waste, keep a keen eye on citizens' priorities – or lose constituents to other locales. Another example of interlocalism.

Thomas Jefferson, in his 1821 autobiography, emphasized the administrative advantage of decentralization: "Were not this country divided into states, that division must be made that each might do for itself ... what it can so much better do than a distant authority." Philip Burgess contends that beyond the bias toward decentralization that prevailed even in Jefferson's day, in our own era modern technology systematically favors small-scale organizations, so that the federal government has been rendered obsolete, a "mainframe government in a PC world." Burgess and many other proponents of stepped-up devolution base their case as much on the states' presumed efficiency advantages as on constitutional claims of state sovereignty. Senator George Voinovich of Ohio, when he was governor, for example, presented as a "simple fact" the proposition that "states often excel when the federal government falters."

In a letter to Madison during the Constitutional Convention, Connecticut's Roger Sherman put it bluntly: "The people are more happy in small than in large states."

Alexis de Toqueville wrote that the local government is to democracy what schools are to science. They nurture, they educate, they train people in what is necessary for democracy to work. These kinds of activities were so necessary to bring community back into the realm of society. Former Massachusetts Gov. William Weld expressed the same sentiments in the political idiom of 1996: "We're closer and more directly answerable to our citizens than the cloud-dwellers in Washington are."

Texas Sen. Kay Bailey Hutchison seemed to speak for many when she declared that the "states can be more efficient and more responsible if Washington just gets out of the way."

Back To Constitutional Basics

Isn't it time America held a new Constitutional Convention in the 21st century? Seizing the momentum of their surge to the forefront of American government, some state leaders at the sunset of the 20th century laid plans for a new Constitutional Convention – the first since 1787. Their hopes for having the century's final word in the argument over federalism's proper balance were undercut, however, by bipartisan nervousness about the consequences of unleashing on the Constitution the passion of the mid-1990s.

Erstwhile advocates of a Constitutional Convention settled instead for a "Federalism Summit" that united nine governors and scores of other state officials in a 1995 convocation on "restoring the balance" in the American system.

Michael O. Leavitt, the former Republican governor of Utah, led the effort to convene the summit, and in a passionate speech at its commencement invoked the ghosts of Thomas Jefferson, James Madison and Alexander Hamilton in support of his call to strengthen the role of the states. "As stewards of their creation, the Constitution of the United States," Leavitt said, "I believe they would tell us we have an obligation to restore the balance." Aren't *We the Apathetic People* long overdue for a new balance of power between the states and the federal government in the New World Order of the new millennium?

The authority of states in the U.S. to reclaim constitutionally surrendered powers is apparently limited to their ability to demand a convention to propose amendments to the Constitution itself. Article V provides that:

"The Congress ... on the application of the legislatures of two-thirds of the several states, shall call a convention for proposing amendments ...."

Ratification by three-fourths of the states must then be obtained for any proposed amendments to become valid. The constitutional impediment to allow states to amend the federal Constitution does not apply to the states' ability to restore their original basic state rights. This can be done by each state and a rational referendum.

The ideal expressed by the Declaration of Independence-all men are created equal, was not fully realized at first because of America's original sin of human slavery. The destruction of slavery by Abraham Lincoln, the saintly martyr of freedom, and the eradication of legal racism in the 1960s, completed the American Revolution.

The Lincoln Memorial opened to the public in 1922. It is, in my humble opinion, America's equivalent of Mecca's Black Rock, bringing grown men and women to their knees, moved without quite comprehending why. Martin Luther King chose the Lincoln Memorial as the place to give his "I have a dream," speech in 1963.

Lincoln is huge and looks so troubled in his armchair gazing down at the Reflecting Pool and beyond at the domed Capitol building. The two miles between the Capitol building and the Lincoln Memorial are referred to as the National Mall and is the heart of Washington, D.C. Lincoln's spirit seems to dominate with both frailty and strength. Even his great weary hands, resting on the sides of the armchair, somehow suggest the hopes and limitations of *We the Apathetic People.*

America is the oldest republic, the oldest democracy and the oldest federal system. It has the oldest written constitution in terms of continuos constitutional experience without revolutionary disruption.

The same can continue to hold true especially if the original state powers are restored to the 50 states. Interlocalism will allow them to continue to interact with each other as Americans and with the federal government on the limited issues of defense, foreign and financial matters. This will ensure the continuation of government in the new millennium in the form intended by the Founding Fathers.

Freedom, Individualism and Egalitarianism

Robert Samuelson, in his 1996 *Newsweek* article *The Vices of Our Virtues,* points out that "The American Creed – our distinct set of values – blends freedom, individualism and egalitarianism. This mix has fired economic advance. But the same emphasis on individual striving, success and liberty can also inhibit social control and loosen people's sense of communal obligation." Interlocalism allows people to regain their sense of communal obligation. Locally at home and interlocally with compatible groups globally – and pro-democracy groups funded by the U.S. government in the Ukraine, Georgia, Iraq, Venezuela and Iran.

Global immigration will increase in the 21st century. People leave home to seek more knowledge and better their lives and that of their family and community. We must always remember people are selfish and take care of themselves and their families first. By doing so they expand the interlocal community already in place. They usually follow or search out their local cultural counterparts.

One of the few domestic policy statements of Richard Nixon that I agreed with wholeheartedly was: "More than any reform plan, limiting government to its proper sphere will enhance the public's faith in government. Reinvigorating the principle of federalism by transferring power from Washington to state and local governments would permit citizens to run more of their own affairs at a manageable level. At the same time, state and local governments provide laboratories for testing new approaches to domestic problems."

Congressmen are repeatedly attacking cities for their "culture of waste for which they want us to send a check." Nothing could be further from the truth. Common sense dictates that. Especially with all the subsidies that agricultural communities get. However, spin doctors have us believing otherwise.

The metropolitan economies of older cities such as Chicago, Boston, Cincinnati and Detroit all send billions of dollars more to Washington in federal taxes than they get back in social programs, military spending or public works.

And the biggest contributor of all to the federal budget is the place Newt Gingrich derided as a dead weight on the rest of the country: New York City, which in 1994, contributed $9 billion more to the federal government than it received in return.

The former House Speaker's home state of Georgia, meanwhile, is one of the large number of Southern, largely Republican states that receive far more from the federal government than they send in taxes.

The idea that cities like Los Angeles and New York provide huge surpluses for Washington is, according to urban experts and economists, one of the best-kept secrets in American politics, an idea that – if it ever gained currency – could force a fundamental transformation in the relationship between the federal government and the states. Managed misperception perfected by spin doctors that *We the Apathetic People* allow to be perpetuated. Isn't it time *We the Maids* sweep away this myth and clean up and recapture our states' rights?

The decline of many Northeastern American cities is not the result of mismanagement, as is popularly imagined, but of the emptying of their coffers by the federal government. How can *We the Apathetic People* allow this practice to continue in the 21st century? Isn't it time *We the Maids* sweep it out?

New York state got $3,948 per person from Washington in 1994 while New Jersey received $3,648. Both were well below the national average of $4,732 and far behind North Dakota at $6,001 or New Mexico at $6,734, both of which receive large federal agricultural and land management subsidies. From 2004 through 2006, the states gave more and got less. Why should blue states continue to subsidize red states? Is this right? Can it be allowed to continue?

Author David Halberstam, in *Century,* noted that "The governors are today, I think quite possibly our best public servants. The better and more experienced ones are well ahead of their counterparts in the Congress in sensing where this country is and where it is headed. One of the ironic outcomes of the Reagan Revolution, with its greatly diminished federal aid to the states, is that it forced state governments, however reluctantly, to become better and more accountable. The senators and members of the House of Representatives live in Washington, where the aura (and the pleasures and the perks) of hegemony still linger; by contrast the governors must live more closely with the realities of posthegemony America." The bipartisan career anarchists in Washington better come to grips with this reality before they find their excessive power involuntarily swept back to the states by *We the Maids.*

The U.S. was founded on July 4, 1776, upon the signing of the Declaration of Independence, which proclaimed freedom from British rule. The Articles of Confederation and Perpetual Union, which was fully adopted in 1781, was the first document that attempted to unite the 13 colonies that had broken free from Britain. These new states were governed by the Articles of Confederation until the Constitution took effect in 1789. The Constitution provided a more structured government and created the executive, legislative and judicial branches of the U.S. government, which are separate to provide checks and balances for each branch.

The Constitution permits the federal government to create regulation and allows for the states to legislate that which the federal government does not.

This division of power, or dual sovereignty, between the states and federal government was designed to ensure checks and balances were present at both levels.

The debate over federal power continued through the Civil War, which was fought over the question of slavery between the North, known as the United States of America, and the South called the Confederate States of America. Not only did the Civil War exemplify a struggle for power, it became a means of employing stronger powers. President Lincoln exercised tremendous presidential powers that some would argue were beyond the scope allowed by the Constitution.

The next president to employ tremendous federal powers was Franklin D. Roosevelt through the New Deal. Roosevelt's programs such as the Works Progress Administration, Federal Emergency Relief Act, and the Social Security Act of 1935 established a new era in the role of the federal government. With the advent of the New Deal, the constitutional power of the national government expanded so dramatically that the doctrine of dual sovereignty virtually lost all meaning. While the New Deal was questionable in terms of constitutionality, it was eventually supported by the courts after Roosevelt proposed adding more justices to the Supreme Court to uphold the New Deal.

After the New Deal, the Commerce Clause, which was designed to regulate interstate and international commerce, was strengthened by a ruling in 1942 that included intrastate commerce that has effects outside of the state. The decision paved the way for even greater federal expansion.

The 1970s also experienced an increase in the role of the federal government because of the oil lobby and oil embargoes. Energy became heavily regulated like never before after the Organization of Petroleum Exporting Countries enacted an oil embargo against the U.S. in 1973 for its support of Israel, which created an energy crisis that required gasoline to be rationed. The price and availability of gasoline was federally controlled, which led to an imbalance in supply and demand when the energy crisis occurred. The government had mandated that gasoline be distributed equally among the states and regions, which created a surplus in rural areas and massive shortages in urban areas due to the difference in population density.

Then in 1974 Congress enacted the national speed limit of 55 miles-per-hour to reduce gasoline consumption. It was introduced as a temporary measure to last one year, but in 1975 it was made permanent. Prior to 1974, states were in charge of determining speed limits. To ensure compliance, the federal government required that states follow and enforce the new limits in order to receive federal funding for highway projects.

In 1987, the Surface Transportation and Uniform Relocation Act allowed states to increase the maximum speed limit to 65 mph. One reason it was possible to increase the speed limit was that there was no federal agency that enforced the 55 mph speed limit, thus the actual implementation and enforcement of it was nonexistent. Very unbureacratic.

States and *We the Apathetic People* have to take advantage of these loopholes in existing legislation that are easiest to overturn due to a lack of funding and commitment from federal agencies. States should focus on the fields of alternative energy, which is not highly regulated by the federal government now that global warming and climate change have become political issues of concern. The federal government and states have tended to focus on alternative energy incentives. However, there is a lot of room for states to assert their dominance to create legislation in other areas such as requiring that a percentage of energy used within the state comes from renewable sources from the state. States can also elect to only use renewable energy in government offices and vehicles.

The No Child Left Behind Act enacted in 2001 strengthened the federal government's ability to intervene in public education from kindergarten through high school at the local and state levels. Several states, including Colorado and Vermont, opted out of NCLB and thus forfeited their federal funding. Fortunately, the federal government is responsible for less than 10 percent of the funding that schools receive.

The National Center for Home Education found that Ohio school districts had to fill out an average of 300 forms, with 173 forms slated for the federal government. Essentially, the Department of Education imposes over 50 percent of the paperwork burden placed on school districts for them to receive less than 10 percent of their funding. This heavy burden of bureacratic paperwork for limited sums of money can be the catalyst for states to reclaim their right to educate their students and abolish the federal Department of Education.

States and *We the Apathetic People* need to stand up and reassert not only our educational rights for our children – but all constitutional rights. That is the first step for all Americans if citizens are to retake control of our government. Each state and its citizens are unique, something the federal government cannot adequately address with its one-policy-fits-all that it repeatedly tries to impose on its citizens.

Fundamental constitutional state rights must be reasserted by the states. These rights elevate states from inferior sovereigns with inferior powers to the proud and respected bearers of the constitutional rights granted them by our Founding Fathers. Once these rights are re-established it will be extremely difficult for the federal government to quash them.

The federal government was created by the states. The states can again redefine its role. It's up to *We the People* of each state to make our will known. What are the Democratic and Republican parties and their career politicians doing about this political conundrum? They must stop, think, observe and plan how America can best interlocalize if the republic is to survive, thrive and continue to guide in the 21st century.

Break on through.
– The Doors

Author's Note
Storyteller.
– *Ray Davies*

The widening economic prosperity gulf between America and China in the 21st century is best highlighted on train rides across both countries. Being a 21st-century cowboy who travels as much as I do, when time permits, I prefer iron horses – trains – to planes because they give me the opportunity to experience and interact with people of all nationalities, cultures and walks of life. The dining car, snack bar and observation car are great moving town hall settings with changing audiences sharing breathtaking landscapes between the heart-wrenching scenes of decay and deprivation and the uplifting sights of progress and prosperity.

Two train rides I took in July 2005, one in America and the other in China, crystalized the depressing disparity between the two countries and the diametrically opposed economic directions they have pursued in the last half of the 20th century and the dawn of the 21st.

I took an Amtrak train from Los Angeles to Santa Fe, New Mexico. The abandoned warehouses, junkyards, junked cars, trailer-trashed neighborhoods, garbage-strewn railroads and graffiti-covered walls and rail cars of America's backyard are a dramatic contrast to the lush green farms, rows of neat and clean public housing, factories and homes under construction and the spotless railroad lines and graffiti-free walls and rail cars between Shanghai and Nanjing.

The bicycle and motor-driven carts on China's divided two-lane roads with the occassional car are a sharp contrast to the convoys of gas-guzzling SUVs and trucks on similar highways running alongside America's railroad. Gas guzzlers driven by aimless apathetic American wage slaves who are clueless about how they are being manipulated by career politicians and their financial backers. The highways of both countries are laden with trucks, buses and cars speeding to their destination. The disparity in the number of vehicles is noticeable. America's highways transport more than 10 times as many trucks and cars. The vast number of neon-lit motels and hotels on America's highways are in sharp contrast to the pristine suburbs and villages that straddle China's transportation arteries.

The quaint, antiquated one-story 19th-century railway stations in America, although architecturally pleasing, are dwarfed by the modern, multistory glass and steel behemoths built or being built in China. Arriving on a Sunday morning in Nanjing, I couldn't help but marvel at the five-story-high steel beam girders and connecting steel suspension wires of the rail station under construction. The sound of drilling and hammering and the flash of welding torches as hundreds of male and female workers labored to complete another 21st-century architectural wonder was awe-inspiring. Avoiding the workers with pushcarts of sand, cement and sheets of marble as I made my way to the exit was a dramatic contrast to the homeless panhandlers visible in railway stations across America.

During a 45-minute stop at the railroad station in Alburquque, New Mexico, on a Sunday morning a few hours before my final stop at Santa Fe, I decided to walk through the station and the nearby neighborhood to stretch my legs, take in the local sights and pick up the local papers. The panhandling homeless drug addicts and alcoholics reminded me of the beggars at Chinese railway stations in the early 1980s but who today are nowhere to be seen.

The local Sunday papers were full of stories, pictures, testimonials and editorials commemorating the 60th anniversary of America's first atomic bomb test at nearby Los Alamos. How advanced and progressive America was at the dawn of the Atomic Age I thought to myself. A country that had not experienced the horrors of a foreign invasion on the homefront while China lay in ruins, devastated by Japan's invasion and brutal occupation as the Bamboo Curtain came down after the ensuing civil war. What a difference at the dawn of the 21st century, when it is China that is advancing and progressive while America languishes in its glorious atomic past.

The voters of New Mexico are practical people. They elected 2008 presidential candidate, Bill Richardson as governor, not because they like him – but because he was connected in Washington and knows how to work the system to get federal dollars for New Mexico. Is it any wonder so many billion federal ethanol research tax dollars wound up in New Mexico?

Amtrak, like America, is bankrupt and operated by morally corrupt career politicians. Travelers bemoan the high prices of the mediocre meals served in the snack bar and dining car, while train personnel apologetically explain Amtrak's depressing financial state of affairs to justify the excessive cost – and the tardy departures and arrivals. This is exactly what *We the Apathetic Maids* – Joe and Jane sixpack – brought on ourselves. We wanted big interstate highways that give us the liberty to travel when and where we like carrying what we like. Then we wanted airplanes to take us very quickly instead, so we gave up our liberty and baggage for greater speed in a sardine can flying out of noisy and rude airports. Then came the terrorists, Homeland Security and strangers feeling up our bodies before we boarded. We asked for this and we got it. The train will not come back unless suicide bombers make the air too dangerous and expensive.

By contrast, the Chinese government-run trains serve a much wider range of delicious snacks and meals at a fraction of the cost. Tickets are cheaper, the trains run on time and operate profitably.

These contrasting train rides were followed by trips to the airport to catch a plane to my next destination. In America, cars or buses are the usual mode of transport. By contrast, in Hong Kong, the clean, fast, time-saving and cost-efficient Airport Express Train is the preferred environmentally progressive choice. In Shanghai, it is the 433kph Maglev train. America, like China, has to get back on the fast track of domestic and geopolitical progress and prosperity if it is to survive and thrive in the 21st century.

Dropping Japan as its Pacific partner and embracing China to lead together is a first constructive step in America's Long March to universal prosperity. China's growth has lifted Japan out of its economic recession and contributed more to global growth than America, the European Union or Japan in the opening years of the 21st century. China has over a trillion dollars in reserves, invested in U.S. treasury notes and other offshore investments.

The biggest investors in the U.S. in 2004 were Switzerland with $878 billion, and Japan with $431 billion. China invested only $8 billion, while America invested $105 billion in China. Shouldn't America be focused on its investment?

On August 6, 2005, the 60th anniversary of the atomic bombing of Hiroshima, I was stranded in Shanghai because my flight back to Hong Kong had been cancelled indefinitely, courtesy of killer typhoon Matsa that left 10 people dead, many injured and millions of dollars in property damage. Watching television replays of the atrocities committed by the Japanese during World War II, and of the bombing of Hiroshima and Nagasaki by America, were stark reminders of who America's enemy and true ally were during the war in the Pacific.

China, like America, was attacked by Japan. On September 18, 1931, Japanese soldiers set off explosives along a railway line near Mukden, now Shenyang, in northeastern China. Japan then used the "Mukden Incident" to mobilize troops to invade China. The Germans used the same ruse to invade Poland at the start of World War II in Europe, and America did the same with the Gulf of Tonkin incident in Vietnam.

From 1942 to September 1945, the legendary U.S. Flying Tigers brought essential supplies such as ammunition and fuel from India to China. To do so, air crews had to traverse the 880km "Hump" route over the Himalayas, dodging Japanese attacks and fierce weather. By 1945, the Flying Tigers, with more than 2,000 Chinese and U.S. planes, ferried 730,000 tons of material over the Hump, destroyed 2,600 Japanese aircraft and 44 warships and killed 66,700 Japanese soldiers. The Flying Tigers were backed by 75 CNAC "humpster" pilots – American and Canadian Mercendries – who flew 33 planes ferrying fuel and military supplies from Calcutta to China. Four of the pilots shared their experiences at a Foreign Correspondents Club dinner in Hong Kong in September 2007. "America won the war but lost the peace" in China said Fletcher Hanks. He shared his disgust at his recent visit to China after seeing all the Japanese businessmen and tourists. "They raped your women. How can you accept them?" was all he could say.

China even built a museum in 1991 in Chongqing dedicated to U.S. General Joseph Stillwell, who served as the Chinese government's chief of staff between 1942 and 1944.

Coming on the heels of my visit to Nanjing and the Memorial Hall of the Nanjing Massacre, the televised pictures of the atrocities committed by the Japanese, and the recently unearthed mass graves filled with the remains of innocent women and children, convinced me, of Imperial Japan's inhumanity to fellow man – including Americans. Why is it so difficult to this day for Japan to admit and acknowledge its wartime atrocities? Japanese war veteran Shiro Azuma, often referred to as the Conscience of Japan, took it upon himself to make public these outrages when he published his wartime diary in 1987. He served in the Imperial Army in 1937 and was witness to the wanton rape and killing in China. Haunted by guilt, he decided to become a role model for his countrymen, one of the few former Japanese soldiers to admit to his participation in the Nanjing massacre.

Confronting and acknowledging history is not just about looking back, but about learning and seeking new ways to achieve lasting peace. It is important to remember the horrors of war so that we do not repeat the same mistake. The 20th century left many people with unforgettable memories of two world wars and many regional conflicts in which millions of people lost their lives. The 20th century offers many important lessons if we truly want to achieve lasting peace. The lessons are all there in the testimony of the Nazi and Japanese war criminals tried in Germany and Japan at the end of the war.

Japanese courts have affirmed the historical record of forced labor in Japan during World War II but refused to compensate the victims or their families. Concealed for decades, official records confirm in meticulous detail that 38, 935 boys and men between the ages of 11 and 78 were violently dragooned from war-torn China and forced into brutal labor in mines, docks and construction sites in Japan between 1943 and 1945. Most of the Japanese firms involved are still in business, including Mitsubishi, Mitsui, Kajima, Sumitomo and Nippon Steel. In 1946, remarkably, Japanese companies became "double winners" by receiving generous payments from state coffers to repay them for costs incurred through their use of Chinese laborers – who were never paid a penny.

In 1950, the Japanese government quietly set up a "special deposit system" for wages that corporations never paid to the Chinese, as well as hundreds of thousands of Koreans conscripted during the war. Tokyo reluctantly admits that the Bank of Japan holds millions of dollars in unpaid wages, unadjusted for over six decades of inflation and interest. Former Prime Minister Shinzo Abe is the grandson of wartime cabinet minister Nobusuke Kishe, who served as the bureaucratic czar of forced labor – before spending three years in prison as a Class-A war-crimes suspect during the Allied occupation. He went on to become Japan's prime minister from 1957 to 1960, and is the founding father of the long-dominant Liberal Democratic Party.

Germany is the leading model for proactively addressing past injustices with reparations. It provides the obvious model for Japan in settling this festering multi-lateral sore. The Rememberance, Responsibility and the Future Foundation was established in 2000, with $6 billion provided by the German government and more than 6,500 industrial enterprises. By late 2005, about 1.6 million forced-labor victims or their heirs had received individual apologies and symbolic compensation of up to $10,000 each. Japan has avoided making any apology or payment because it has the strong backing and support of the U.S. State Department. The fact that there are thousands of former allied prisoners of war who performed forced labor, including Americans, makes the U.S. position all the more unfathonable to many Americans and Chinese.

Japan has to have true closure with America, China, Korea and the other Asian countries it invaded after it initiated war – World War II for America. Americans have forgotten that to end the war Japan started, America conservatively killed 83,793 in Tokyo on March 10, 1945 during its fire-bombing campaign. That was just the beginning of the indiscriminate bombing of 69 Japanese cities that killed more than 500,000 Japanese civilians. The atomic bombs dropped on Hiroshima and Nagasaki killed 140,000 and 70,000 respectively. Is this a former enemy America wants to embrace at the expense of an ally who helped it defeat Japan?

Watching the TV replays of the bombing of Hiroshima brought to mind a bullet train ride I took in 1986 with fellow American Ralph Herman. We were on our way back to Tokyo from Kyoto after visiting the former Imperial Capital to see the temples spared by American bombers during World War II. We were standing at the bar in the dining car, sipping whiskey and watching the countryside flash by, exchanging opinions on Kyoto's temples and geisha houses. We were the only two foreigners at the bar, among about 15 people. Ralph and I were standing towards one end of bar. Most of our fellow travelers were staring blankly out the windows.

I noticed an elderly Japanese man, obviously drunk, approaching and I said to Ralph, "There's trouble and it is heading straight our way." The man approached with an outstretched arm that he placed firmly on my neck and he began to shout at us in Japanese. The only word I could make out, as he tightened his grip and his voice grew louder, was "Hiroshima!"

"How about reminding him of Pearl Harbor" Ralph said. "Do you want me to deck him?" I've got a real clean shot." "Not a good idea Ralph," I replied. "We're heavily outnumbered and will probably wind up on one of the telephone poles speeding by." I asked out loud if anyone spoke English, but no one responded. They pretended not to notice what was happening. No one came to our assistance. Another two dozen or so people ordering food and drink in the car also ignored the situation. I began signaling to the waitresses moving through the dining car, trying to get them to summon a security officer. One finally seemed to understood and went for help. By this time, the Japanese drunk was pounding on the bar and screaming at the top of his lungs. Our glasses bounced with each thud, spilling whiskey of the bar and on my shirt. Still, the only word I could make out was "Hiroshima!"

"You sure you don't want me to whack him?" Ralph offered.

"Be cool, man," I shot back. "If anyone is going to do any whacking here, it's me. I've got a clear shot, too, but I'm not convinced it's the best way out." I said. Just then, two security guards showed up, grabbed the Japanese man by his arms, and pulled him off me, almost ripping my head off in the process. As I massaging a sore neck, Ralph offered to go get us a fresh drink and walked off. The one Japanese who was still at the bar suddenly said in English, "Japan and America friends," and lifted his glass in a toast.

"Where was your English when I needed it, friend?" I shot back. "Fuck you and your culture of deceit."

The stunned man turned on his heels and moved away, leaving his drink on the bar. Just then Ralph showed up with our drinks and suggested we get back to our seats. We walked out the dinning car to bows from the wait staff. I put the memory out of mind in Shanghai, as I heard the reports on Typhoon Matsa, which had lashed the city for three straight days with rain, flooding the streets uprooting trees and causing countless accidents. A few people had been killed and many injured. Rather than try to get to the airport and deal with what would surely be thousands of hysterical people trying to get flights out, I decided to take a train back to Hong Kong.

The 27-hour train ride was an unexpectedly pleasant eye-opener. There were miles of lush green trees in nurseries, unfortunately broken or flattened by the lashing of Matsa, interspersed by stands of proud, older trees, undamaged in the lee of newly built high-rises. It struck me as a testament to China's push to balance development in an environmentally conscious way. New suburban developments of contemporary three-story homes, in Chinese, American and European styles, stood next to thatched-roof farmhouses and weather beaten tile-roof Chinese homes. It was a reminder of how quickly China is embracing the best of East and West.

Mingling and chatting with fellow travelers in the hallway in front of our sleeper cars or the dining car, I eventually got the conversation around to the Hiroshima bombing anniversary. A group of German and Swedish travelers, who had also visited the memorial in Nanjing and the Pingdingshan Massacre Relics Memorial Hall in Fushan in Liaoning province, were just as surprised as I am at Japan's reluctance to admit to its World War II atrocities. They spoke remorsefully of their own countries World War II "mistakes."

"A little-known fact is that so-called neutral Sweden was in fact collaborating with the Nazis," said Jan, an economics student from Stockholm. "We are now discussing it openly and admit it was a terrible mistake. We should have stood up to them like the Danes did," he continued as the Germans shook their heads in agreement and proudly brought the conversation back to the recent 60th anniversary celebration of the liberation of Auschwitz. The young Germans' frank expressions of shame for their parents' and grandparents' attempt to exterminate Jews were just as shocking as they were refreshing. "We live with the older generations' demons and just cannot comprehend how it was allowed to happen," was an often-repeated mantra. Why can't the Japanese be as forthright?

Even more surprising was their knowledge of history, especially the story of John Rabe, a member of the German Nazi Party who used the swastika as a force of good in Nanking – Nanjing as it is known today – during the 1937-38 massacre to save hundreds of Chinese innocents from being sent to the mass graves we had just visited. Rabe was the Siemens representative in China, a Nazi Party member who hid the Chinese in his garden in shacks made of old doors and sheets of tin that were of little protection against the winter's bitter cold, snow and rain.

I wondered out loud how America can align itself in the 21st century with a country that refuses to acknowledge its past. My fellow travelers and I hoisted our glasses of wine to my toast, "Past experience, if not forgotten, is a guide for the future – to truth and peace." The U.S. is largely responsible for Japan's behavior today because it did not force Japan to confront its wartime conduct at the time. The Japanese imperial system was encouraged to continue on its merry way, down to the village policeman and postman. Hiroshima, Nagasaki and the Tokyo firestorms are misleading. Japan as a whole was not raised to the ground. Its rulers were not imprisoned, executed or forced to flee. Its institutions of government were not eradicated, its land was not dissected by occupiers. Its women were not raped by the hundreds of thousands as the Japanese did in China and the Russians did in Germany. Its soldiers did not disappear off the face of the earth as happened to many Germans. The Japanese are not good at collective guilt because, if it was done by the collective what could be wrong? There was a war. Mistakes were made and the war was lost. The victor had to be accomodated at all costs so the system could continue and every opportunity taken for recovery. Not an easy mindset to change. What is Japan's guide for the future?

China's future, by contrast, was made abundantly clear by the extensive economic and infrastructure development of its Eastern Seaboard. The rapidity of the regional interlocalism of Hong Kong and the Pearl River Delta stunned me. The endless construction taking place on new roads – bridges, schools, homes, apartment buildings, factories, office buildings, hotels, railroad tracks, power plants and power lines – something definitely missing on the U.S. rail network and America in general. Why?

Grazing water buffalo in open, lush green fields with white cranes perched on their backs are a dramatic contrast to the fenced-in black and white and brown cattle scattered across America's open prairies. The dry river beds across America are a dire comparison to the overflowing rivers of China.

The primitive dirt roads leading up to the wooden rail crossings at small towns across China, with commuters patiently waiting in every mode of transport, is a distinct contrast to the slick automobiles waiting at the computerized high-tech crossings over America's asphalt roads, built in the wake of America's progressive Atomic Age. My, how the times are changing.

The flatbed rail cars on the sidings along China's rail system laden with precast concrete slabs for bridges and highways under construction, are a sharp contrast to America's rail system where train engines pull hundreds of 40-foot containers filled with consumer goods from China for distribution all across the U.S.

While America's Founding Fathers were waging their struggle for independence in 1776, China was already not only the most populous, but the wealthiest nation on earth. You "snooze, you lose," America. One day soon, Americans will awaken to find themselves threatened on the home front as impoverished debtors at the mercy of creditors in China unless *We the Apathetic People* wake up fast – now.

China was the leading high-tech civilization in the 10th and 13th century in silk, the compass, navigation, book-printing, and porcelain – and the furnaces used to make it. China has a big balance of payments surplus today, as it had in the eighteenth century, when it accumulated gold, silver and credits from the West to pay for its silk, porcelain and other luxury goods. The West, and Britain in particular, was only able to offset this by exporting opium to China.

The smiles and waves of construction workers on the China rail system, sipping their tea, is a refreshing contrast to the dour laid-back attitude of America's beer-drinking railroad workers. A friendly smile makes a difference and is very telling of one's state of mind – including on the national level.

The soccer and basketball games on every visible field from the train was either an indication of China's sport craze mentality leading up to the 2008

Beijing Olympics, or an even more depressing reminder of the couch-potato nation America has become. The countless empty sports fields, with the occasional little league baseball game was another reminder of how America has become a nation of wage slaves who no longer have time to enjoy the simple basic pleasures of life with America's future – our children.

The smiling and waving peasants, to a train incidentally that carries over 90% Chinese and less than 10% foreign tourists, is just another example of how "cool" Americans are towards each other. Why? Is this any way for America to develop and grow as a 21s-century nation against a cohesive Chinese nation that make up a quarter of the world's population?

The entrepreneurial and service sectors of America and China are also on display on trains – and planes for that matter. The only thing worse than bad service, is no service at all. Service in U.S. retail establishments in general is reflected on trains. Customers are all but ignored unless they take the initiative to be served. One has to ask to be served by rude or arrogant staff.

In China, and in Asia in general, it is the exact opposite. Polite staff on trains, as on planes and in retail establishments, go out of their way to assist the customer.

Staff on trains in China, just like the staff on America's trains of glory years past, are very entrepreneurial. Everything from fake name-brand bags, watches to antique coins and stamps are on offer. Capitalism, at its American best.

The entrepreunurial peasant farmers raising and tending their ducks, backyard vegetable gardens, fruit trees, goats, oxen and rice paddies are a constant reminder along the thousands of miles of Chinese rail lines of how the communist nation has transformed itself and re-emerged as a 21st-century capitalist powerhouse. It was peasant farmers who propelled Mao and the Communist Party to power. The same peasant farmers can remove the party from power if not allowed to prosper equitably alongside the party capitalists. No different than *We the Apathetic Maids* could do should we decide to remove the career politicians from our state capitals and Washington, D.C.

Speaking of railroads, take a quick look at what happened to railroads in

Iraq after the U.S. invasion of 2003. Railroad employees are assassinated and major communications and signaling equipment gets looted along its 1,900 kilometers of tracks. Tons of copper wire have been stripped out of the railroad signaling system, and radio and electronic signal equipment has been stolen, rendering safety systems useless. What is the point of spending hundreds of millions of dollars on new equipment that would almost certainly be ripped off as quickly as it was put up. The solution? Develop a system so small, independent of wires, and cheap that it would not tempt thieves – but still work. Wabtec Railway Electronics, based in central Iowa, has come up with such a system at the low cost of $17 million, a small fraction of a similarly sized U.S.-style traffic-control system.

Basically, each locomotive is being fitted with a small computer linked by satellite and VHF radio to the dispatching office in Baghdad. There will be no color-light signals along the tracks to steal. The dispatcher will be able to give only one train clearance to travel between any two stations. Once the train is in the block between the two stations, the dispatcher cannot clear any other train onto the track until after the train arrives in the next station. Any train that tries to enter the block will automatically receive an air brake command and grind to a halt. For trains that do have clearance, the system will enforce speed limits all along the way with automatic brake commands if an engineer is going too fast.

In America, the Federal Railroad Administration will not approve such an "on the cheap" system for use there without an exhaustive and expensive analysis to prove that it is at least as safe as other systems – something smaller U.S. railroads cannot afford.

Fortunately, Iraq is not bound by U.S. bureacratic regulations. Mafeks International, a U.S.-Turkish joint venture, is the prime contractor and is providing logistical support and helping train some Iraqi railroad employees in its use. Railroaders in Iraq are just like railroaders in America and China. They just want to run trains and go home at night. Isn't this the track America should be patiently getting the rest of a partitioned country on? Patience, perserverence – not a premature American withdrawal with chaos left in its wake.

Capitalism in America and China, like in Iraq, relies on railroads as one of the pillars in the development and growth of capitalism – and globalization. To put things in perspective on the growth of capitalism, we just have to flash back to 1848, when John Jacob Astor died as America's richest man. He left a fortune of $20 million, mere chump change when compared to today's wealthiest individuals. How did this transformation happen within 50 years? Big Business. It is big business that developed the Rockefellers, Carnegies and Fords. It was the new technologies of the railroad, telegraph, and the steam engine that favored the creation of massive businesses that needed – and, in turn, gave rise to – superstructures of professional managers, engineers, accountants and supervisors.

It began with railroads. In 1830, getting from New York to Chicago took three weeks. By 1857, the trip was three days. In 1850, there was 14,400km of track. By 1900, that figure increased to 320,000km. Railroads required a vast administrative apparatus to ensure the maintenance of locomotives, rolling stock and track – not to mention scheduling trains, billing and construction, as historian Dr. Alfred Chandler showed in his Pulitzer Prize-winning book – *The Visible Hand: The Managerial Revolution in American Business*. The lesson is an important one because no matter how efficient a factory might be, it would be hugely wasteful if raw materials did not arrive on time or if the output couldn't be quickly distributed and sold.

The lesson for companies and countries is that old established firms, like political parties and dated ideologies – despite ample capital and technical knowhow – often don't dominate new industries or geopolitics. Google, eBay and Yahoo rule the Internet, not General Motors, Sears or Disney.

Today America and China have to develop a new successor model to capitalism and globalism. Globalism is benefiting only a handful of the richest people and impoverishing the rest of the world. A "New Deal for Interlocalism." A new interlocal economic and political system that is in tune with the new global economic world thrust upon us by the worldwide internet is necessary to get the global economy back on track.

China is re-emerging as a global economic and military power. A power America should embrace in a strategic alliance. The alternative is a futile and costly exercise of containment and encirclement that is doomed to fail. America is trying to do to China today what Britain and France tried to do to contain the rapid growth of Germany before World War I. Britain and France formed an alliance with Russia to encircle Germany. The U.S. is trying to form a similar alliance with Japan and India to contain China. But China, unlike Germany, has no desire to conquer the world. This is a historical fact that I address in detail in this book. America's thinking is outdated. It didn't work for Britain and France and it won't work for America. The only outcome, like in 1914, is an avoidable war.

Watching the Japanese election results come in on 9/11, 2005, a brilliant election call, as America commemorated the fourth anniversary of 9/11 in the wake of Hurricane Katrina, with New York's finest men in blue in New Orleans, was just another nightmare reminder of all the police and fire departments that have to repeatedly come to the aid of each other across state lines because of federal government incompetence. How many more disasters do people have to endure before *We the Maids* wake up?

The anemic encore of the 60th anniverary of the U.N. in New York, with a record number of world leaders gathered in one place, who collectively failed to agree on anything other than to disagree, was just another global reminder of the world leaders' continued incompetent failures that led to 9/11 – and Hurricane Katrina – at an expense that *We the Apathetic Maids* bear. The world's Big Daddy – America – turned out to be just a "Girlie Boy."

The cancellation of President Hu Jintao's visit to the White House – Katrina being the convenient excuse – is a worrisome reminder of the continued discord between America and China. After all, the two presidents were only going to spend half a day together, hardly enough time to warrant canceling the visit. Katrina was a convenient excuse, albeit a major crisis of Bush's presidency. An excuse that is not a trivial matter in our complex electronic age of foreign political diplomatic currents – especially Sino-American relations at the dawn of the 21st century.

A state visit includes an arrival ceremony on the White House South Lawn accompanied by a customary 21-gun salute for a head of state, a summit meeting at the Oval Office and a state dinner. The U.S. agreed to welcome Hu with the salute, but drew the line in the salad at a state banquet – no state dinner, just a lunch.

Hu was the first Chinese leader not scheduled to receive a state visit on his maiden trip to the U.S. as head of state. Because the visit was cancelled, they had to settle for a photo-op meeting in New York during the U.N. 60th anniversary's wasteful wake. It is no surprise therefore that China locked the doors on all of the issues America pressed for during Bush's later visit to China in November 2005 – not just the door to his press conference in that hilarious moment when he was trying to escape without success – but the doors to discussions on currency revaluation, human rights and piracy.

When Hu finally did make his landmark visit to the White House's South Lawn in April 2006, his "symbolic" visit was greeted with pomp and pageantry and was riddled with gaffes. It was interrupted by a Falun Gong protestor and the White House announcer called the mainland the "Republic of China" – the official title of Taiwan – and President Bush had to pull Hu back in line as a result of a miscue. To make matters worse, Bush's speech was translated into Chinese in a halting, stuttering fashion that had Chinese officials shaking their heads in disbelief. Apparently, while the Chinese had provided the Americans with an advance copy of Hu's remarks, the Americans had not reciprocated with Bush's speech. Maybe that was one of the reasons Bush did not make it onto *Time Magazine's* 100 most influential people in 2006. Hu made the list along with 6 others of Chinese descent.

When Japan's Prime Minister Junichiro Koizumi visited the White House in June 2006, not only was the red carpet laid out with a gala official state dinner, but America's president accompanied Koizumi and gave him a ride on Air Force One to Memphis, Tennessee for a tour of Graceland because Elvis Presley is a musical hero of the former prime minister. It was the ultimate state reception in the history of U.S. diplomacy, and a slap to the Chinese face – a tremendous loss of face. The presidents of Mexico, Poland, the Philippines and Kenya were honored with White House state dinners while Hu was treated to a mere "social lunch." Is this any way for America to treat China, America's third-largest export market, ahead of fourth-place Japan?

Japan's denial of history is a dark ugly regional shadow that will only be replaced by a bright rising sun when they come clean.

With America getting its sheriff's badge ripped from its shirt and handed back in Afghanistan and Iraq, China is clearly a major beneficiary of America's geopolitical and economic quagmire.

Hu's visit was a sadly lost opportunity because America believes "that the Chinese dragon will prove to be a fire-breather. There is a cauldron of anxiety about China," according to former Deputy Secretary of State Robert Zoellick. On the contrary, it is America that *We the Apathetic Maids* have to worry about as the source of ANXIETY and FEAR. The end result is the victims and families who have lost loved ones and propery in Iraq, Louisiana and Mississippi due to the debacle caused by Hurricane Katrina, Homeland Security and FEMA. The damage done by Plamegate and the jailing of New York Times reporter Judy Miller to justify America's failed foreign policy in Iraq is the ultimate cauldron of anxiety.

The most challenging conundrum facing our interlocal world and *We the Apathetic Maids* is how to balance the growing conflict between free trade and national security concerns. This has already impacted everything from Chinese direct investment in America, the European Union's subsidies of a new European search engine to challenge Google and Yahoo, and for Airbus to challenge Boeing, as well as barriers to trade in the high-tech sector and agricultural policy in developing countries. The use of "essential security" interests has become an excuse for protectionism. How far should *We the Apathetic Maids* allow considerations of national security to interfere with trade and commerce?

America's decision to change its trade policy towards China in early 2007, starting with the filing of the widest-ranging WTO trade case ever put forward by America against Beijing, followed up by imposing countervailing duties on Chinese coated paper – paper which has been treated to give it certain qualities, including weight and surface gloss, smoothness or ink absorbency. They were the first imposed in 23 years by the U.S. of so-called countervailing duties in response to subsidies in a "non-market economy," as China is classified by America. The U.S. Commerce Department's long-standing position had been that it is difficult to determine subsidy levels in a non-market economy, which China is considered under U.S. trade laws. Though China's coated paper exports to the U.S. account for less than 1 percent of the total bilateral trade, the duty could be followed by similar action against Chinese steel, textiles and other products because the U.S. industries claim cheap imports from China have hurt them. America then follows up with another WTO lawsuit against China for piracy and counterfeiting of U.S. goods and blocking access to American movies, music, books and other publications.

Washington is blasting Beijing with both barrels. Hearings are looking into everything from Beijing's test of an anti-satellite weapon, military build-up, policy on forced abortions, support of ruthless regimes, "cheating" on its trade commitments, undervaluing its currency, repatriation of North Korean refugees in violation of international law, and one to even end normal trading relations with China – all leading to the question of Beijing's suitability to host the 2008 Olympics.

Anti-China trade legislation reached fever pitch less than six months after the U.S. 2006 midterm election, with at least 15 bills in Congress seeking to punish Beijing. The early start of the 2008 presidential election in 2007 reignited unprecedented China bashing. Especially when the Chinese yuan reached a post-revaluation high on May Day 2007. It was the highest intraday level since it was revalued and freed from the dollar peg in July 2005. The yuan has risen 9 percent in value since being delinked from the dollar.

The bipartisan bill introduced by Senators Max Baucus, Chuck Grassley, Charles Schumer and Lindsey Graham is designed to tackle the trade deficit with China, by requiring the Treasury Department to identify fundamental misaligned currencies – driven by explicit government policies. However, the senators acknowledge that reducing the U.S. trade deficit will require a lot more than punishing China – at the expense of U.S. consumers.

The bill, if passed into law, will permit companies to seek anti-dumping duties on rival Chinese imports based on the undervaluation of the currency and calls for a new trade case to be brought by the U.S. at the World Trade Organization, alleging that the depressed currency amounts to an illegal subsidy. China again became the scapegoat of U.S. economic and political anxiety. Especially after the Bush administration, in its semi-annual currency report of June 2007, said that China did not fit the technical profile of a country that is manipulating its currency. If the bill becomes law, China "will respond." The reevaluation of the Chinese currency will not help reduce America's trade deficit. It will merely shift the source of imports to other low-cost countries. American consumers will be the victims of the trans-Pacific crossfire.

Americans have to boost national savings, promote U.S. exports and invest in responsible education and healthcare policies if we are to curb the trade deficit with China. It hit a record $233 billion in 2006, estimated to reach $250-300 billion in 2007, and continues to rise. It is important to keep in mind that after China joined the World Trade Organization in 2001, many companies from low-cost manufacturing countries in Asia moved their operations to China and brought with them their long-standing trade surpluses with the U.S. to the mainland.

About 60 percent of China's exports by value are produced or assembled by foreign firms. American, European and Latino. But most are from Hong Kong, Taiwan, South Korea, Japan and Southeast Asia. The actual added value of mainland inputs is no more than 30 percent of the total value of mainland exports. That is why passage of the legislation will penalize mainly foreign firms, including American. Protectionism will have global and interlocal repercussions that will paralyze the international trading system. Protectionism is just so not American. It is totalitarian.

Protectionism flies in the face of international agreements that reduced or eliminated trade tariffs and capital controls, legalized subsidies and lowered transport costs.

As if that wasn't bad enough, the U.S. media, led by Fox News, were quick to blame a Chinese student for the Virginia Tech rampage. Other news outlets picked up the story and ran with it without verifying its authenticity. They were all wrong. The murderer at Virginia Tech was of South Korean origin, not Chinese. Rupert Murdock's Fox News must have had a lot of explaining to do to Murdoch after his Chinese-born wife got through with him that night. Dragon lady Wendy must have been a sheer delight to come home to.

What about the billions of subsidized tax breaks, soft loans and offsets that U.S. industries like agriculture, steel and many others have been living on for decades? For America to say that American farmers suffer because of

China's subsidies on manufactured goods, as U.S. Commerce Secretary Carlos Gutierrez said, especially in light of the billions upon billions of dollars in annual U.S. farm subsidies that flood the global markets with below-cost American foodstuffs to the detriment of struggling farmers in every poor corner of the world, is not only hypocritical but counter-productive. America's first "MBA president" and the Democratic-led Congress are botching things up again. America is picking the wrong fight. The careful analysis of Lawrence Lau and his team at the Stanford Center for International Development is objective and persuasive. They argue that the U.S. actually benefits more from the trade imbalance because there is more value-added to the U.S. economy from America's exports to China, than to the Chinese economy from its exports to the U.S.

Let's keep in perspective the fact that the overall U.S. trade deficit rose 6.5 percent to a record $763.6 billion in 2006, of which China's portion was $233 billion.

China's decision to end its bid for the U.S. oil firm Unocal, because of the rising opposition in Congress on the grounds of national security, highlighted Washington's intolerance of China's economic resurgence. Had the acquisition been concluded, China would not have posed any threat to U.S. energy supplies. What has been created is a precedent for China, and other countries, to keep U.S. firms out of their own energy sectors on similar grounds. China's quest for oil should not lead to a military clash with the U.S., as many pro-Japan analysts predict.

Is it any wonder then that Beijing is becoming protectionist and, like America, concerned about economic nationalism? This became patently obvious in 2006 when U.S. private equity fund Carlyle agreed to buy half, rather than 85 percent of a state-owned construction firm, after Beijing intervened. To date, unlike America, China has not blocked any major deal. Kicking Starbucks out of Beijing's Forbidden City is not of earth-shaking importance.

China and America must weave their geopolitical strategic alliance to match the Chinese goods woven into the fabric of American life and the U.S. treasury bonds woven into the Chinese economy. Hopefully, the Chinese delegation that signed $4.3 billion in deals in the U.S. in May 2007, primarily in the high-tech field, buying knowhow, software, semiconductor and telecommunications equipment for its rapidly expanding economy, is the first of many more such delegations to help shrink the U.S. deficit. The delegation was made up of executives from more than 200 mainland companies who met their U.S. counterparts in 24 cities across 23 U.S. states.

Morgan Stanley estimates that U.S. consumers have saved $600 billion in the past decade by buying goods made in China. A reality U.S. Senators Lindsay Graham, Tom Coburn and Charles Schumer reluctantly acknowledged after their fact-finding trip to Beijing in March 2006. They went to Beijing to pressure China to liberalize its yuan policy and to threaten punitive sanctions if Beijing didn't comply, but came back believers and withdrew their bill after they realized the 27.5 percent tariffs they proposed would ultimately be paid by the U.S. consumer. China's growth is an inevitable historical process that America grudgingly acknowledged during Hu Juntao's April 2006 state visit. China is more than a "stakeholder" in the new economy and global community. It is the dominant player with whom America must form a strategic partnership.

The U.S. political landscape has to stop looking like a political Disneyland.

The world is changing from global to interlocal. When Greece and Turkey announced a joint gas pipeline, with a Greek prime minister visiting Turkey to announce the deal – the first visit by a Greek leader in 40 years – it signaled the irrevocable arrival of interlocalism. The pipeline planned through Pakistan to India, from Bangladesh to India, and from Egypt to Israel, bringing Myanmar and eventually Iran into the global loop, was the interlocalism seal of approval. Russia will soon supply Europe with most of its energy needs. Our interlocalized world is one in which we must live in economic and political harmony with our neighbors.

With America's enemies, North Korea and Iran – China's friends – going nuclear, a major geopolitical alignment is taking place that America must come to terms with. A nuclear Shiite Iran next door to Shiite Iraq, next to nuclear neighbor Israel, will trigger a nuclear arms race among the neighboring Sunni Arab states. The same will happen in Asia with a nuclear North Korea. Japan and South Korea will be compelled to go nuclear.

The only solution to avoid Armageddon is for America and China to interlocalize, cooperate and for America to accept the fact that the center of gravity has moved to Asia in the 21st century with China in the center at the controls. This was made clear during the North Korea de-nuclearization talks. North Korea was the catalyst in getting the U.S. and China to work together for a common goal and get closer to each other. "Not bad for a couple years' work," Secretary of State Condoleezza Rice said, referring to the period of time Washington and Beijing worked together on the North Korean nuclear issue. China acknowledges and accepts its importance and role in working with America to secure a peaceful and harmonious world. China voted twice in three months with the U.S. and its allies on the U.N. Security Council for a resolution denouncing North Korea. Gone forever are the days when Beijing would describe its relationship with North Korea as being as close as that between lips and teeth.

America and China are better off forging a strategic partnership to prevent a bipolar nuclear world instead of backing any regional nuclear grouping on opposite sides. America and China are both better off working together to ensure a nuclear-free Asia and Middle East. The alternative is Armageddon.

America is ready for another "Nixon on China." When President Richard Nixon and Chairman Mao Zedong signed the historic Shanghai Communique in 1972, the rapprochement was not only long overdue but far-sighted. Both countries benefited from the peace and prosperity that followed.

The right-wing Republican rule that has uncomfortably settled over America after the 2004 and 2006 elections is reminiscent of China's Cultural Revolution and the "Red Peril" Nixon embraced. If China is prepared to embrace America even closer, why is America rejecting the gesture? America must again overcome the red scare that career politicians have instilled in the country. President Bush's acceptance of China invitation to the 2008 Beijing Olympics is a step in the right direction.

China is more popular universally today than the U.S., according to a 2005 and 2006 survey of global attitudes conducted by the Washington-based Pew Research Center, because it does not pose a military threat. Paradoxically, the U.S. is more unpopular around the world than it has ever been. Over the last five years, since 2002– post 9/11 sympathy factor – favorable ratings of the U.S. have decreased "in 26 of the 33 countries for which trends are available," Pew said. By embracing China, America can again begin the journey to redeem its popularity and standing in the world.

U.S. foreign policy can no longer afford to ignore or alienate China, either politically or economically. Sino-U.S. cooperation – a strategic alliance – is essential for America to survive the 21st century. America and China can and must be friendly, cooperative competitors pursuing a mutual goal of peace and prosperity. Shanghai Communique IV is long overdue.

The U.S. dollar hit a 15-year low against a basket of currencies in August 2007. It is only a matter of time before the yuan will overtake the U.S. dollar as the most accepted currency among the world's central banks. The People's Bank of China has accumulated over $1 trillion of reserves. Since it has no domestic use for them, it turns around and lends them back to the U.S. and they find their way back into the housing loan market. This means that both Treasury borrowing costs and mortgage interest rates are lower than they otherwise would be. American homeowners and taxpayers are the beneficiaries. If China did comply with U.S. pressure to revalue its currency, American consumers would face a fiscal apocalypse.

China let its currency rise very quickly and quietly – it even broke through 7.9 to the dollar for the first time in September 2006. It appreciated at a daily rate of 0.8 percent, which works out to an annualized rate of 10 percent. That was quite a contrast to the annual pace of 2 percent to 2.5 percent during most months after China's 2.1 percent revaluation on July 21, 2005. The acceleration came at a time when the Chinese economy settled down to sustained but controlled growth, which made Chinese officials more willing to experiment with the value of the yuan. Some China watchers gave the credit to the quieter U.S. policy advocated by Treasury Secretary Henry Paulson Jr., who with decades of China experience, pursued a much more low-key approach to the currency issue.

The fact is that at the dawn of the 21st century, the Chinese yuan is now an internationally recognized currency that is giving the dollar a run for its value. The dollar slid to a 12-year low against a basket of currencies, and a 26-year low against the British pound in July 2007. The yuan is quietly becoming a universal currency at the expense of the dollar. It delivers everyday economic values without devaluation. There is enough of the currency to finance capital anywhere and anytime – and it does.

There is even talk that the yuan may be the next reserve currency. The U.S. dollar has had a relatively short run so far as the global reserve currency. It assumed the position after World War II and the establishment of the Bretton Woods system of global monetary stability. Back then, the dollar was pegged to gold – at $435 an ounce – and was established as the fallback monetary unit that underpinned the postwar era of economic growth around the world until the Iraq war fiasco.

China, the world's third-largest gold producer, is likely to surpass the U.S. to become the second-largest producer of the precious metal. It will produce 260 tons in 2007.

All China has to do today is pass laws that all its exports be purchased in yuan instead of dollars. The currency would then begin a serious push for reserve status. China can bring down the U.S. greenback With $1.33 trillion currency reserves it holds the ultimate bargaining chip.

With inflation on the rise in America, oil prices pushing through $100 a barrel, with a recession on the horizon because of concerns of a major Persian Gulf supply disruption, and America's trade deficit growing, China may just be tempted to make the yuan the global reserve currency.

The U.S. trade deficit and gap in other international transactions was an unprecedented $788 billion in 2005, about 28 percent of that with China, a 24.5 percent increase over 2004. America claims the deficit with China rose to $201.6-billion, while China claims it was only $114.2 billion. The discrepancy is largely because the U.S. counts the cost of shipping and insurance in its figures, which China objects to because most of that business goes to non-Chinese firms. America managed to survive the year economically because of the higher interest rates it paid foreign buyers of treasury notes that have financed the rapidly widening deficits. America needs $2.1 billion of foreign cash a day to plug the deficit gap, which in 2005 reached 6.5 percent of gross domestic product. This is unsustainable as the European Central Bank and Japan raise their interest rates and attract many of the funds now financing America's deficit. For Congress to consider more unpaid-for tax cuts in the 2008 election year – instead of pursuing ways of developing an economic and political partnership with China – is economic suicide.

Over the past 20 years, China's economy has grown by nearly 10 per cent a year, lifting some 377 million people out of poverty. Even the rampant fraud that exists in the Chinese banking system can't slow economic growth. U.S. manufacturers, farmers and service providers have seen exports to China grow an average of 22 per cent a year since China joined the WTO in December 2001. The rise of protectionism in America has triggered a rise in economic nationalism in China that could undercut the mainland's promises to the WTO. China can and will backtrack on free market reforms if America fails to change its tune.

China's economy hit an 11-year high in July 2007. It grew by 11.9 percent in the second quarter. It produced an output of $2.9 trillion in 2006. China's economy could surpass Germany's by the end of 2007, leapfrogging ahead of the 2010 date most economists predicted, exceed Japan's by 2020 and become the world's leading economy by 2040. China's overall economy is larger and healthier than that of five G-8 members – and its people richer – than current government figures show.

By another measure, known as purchasing-power parity, China is already the world's second-biggest economy. If exchange rates are adjusted to equalize the cost of goods in different countries, then the value of China's total output was $10 trillion in 2006, according to estimates by the IMF. That eclipses Japan's $4.2 trillion and Germany's $2.6 trillion, and hot on the heels of America's $13 trillion.

It is not just the Chinese government that has trillions of dollars in reserves. So does the consuming public – who are savers. In fact, China's bank depositors are stuffing more money into banks than they can possibly lend or invest, endangering bank profitability and operations in general. The People's Bank of China, the country's central bank, has more than $3.5-trillion in savings accounts.

It is a bankers nightmare because the bank must pay interest to depositors while unable to put the cash to work to generate income for the bank. Gross national saving in China amounts to more than 40 percent of gross domestic product, suggesting that Chinese households are much more frugal than their U.S. counterparts, who are swamped by debt after chasing the American dream and designer lifestyle. Eight out of 10 mainlanders are satisfied with the way things are going in China, the 2006 Pew Global Attitudes Project concluded. The 81 percent satisfaction rate is an increase from the 72 percent recorded in 2005 – the opposite of dissatisfied Americans.

America is characterized by the opposite imbalance: an excess of gross domestic investment over domestic savings. If, and when, these basically symbiotic imbalances becomes unsustainable, tinkering with the yuan/dollar exchange rate will have little impact. Quite different policy changes have to be made by career politicians in Washington, D.C. to boost U.S. savings rate, while lowering China's. To do so without triggering a recession in America and inflation in China is the challenge.

In the 1970s, a middle-class existence in America didn't include central air conditioning, computers, mobile phones or cable television. Today, new drugs and surgeries raise the cost of health insurance, reducing coverage and take-home pay. From 1991 to 2005, the cost of fringe benefits, mainly health insurance, rose nearly twice as fast as wages. American household budgets have been stretched beyond the breaking-point by huge repayments and the impact of rising interest rates, mortgage payments and inflation that led to a housing bust and recession in 2007. America has seen its heyday in the sun and Americans are desperately trying to spend their way there again.

The subprime mortgage meltdown in America led to a recession in the runup to the 2008 U.S. presidential election. The U.S. housing boom that turned to bust can lead to a hard landing. Higher interest rates and falling home prices do not bode well for America. About 30 percent of the increase in employment and almost two-thirds of the growth in the gross domestic product in recent years stemmed directly or indirectly from property. Homes became ATMs in the "net equity extraction" game, financed and backed by banks and hedge funds to the tune of more than $100 billion that will be wiped out, with Bear Stearns, the Wall Street investment bank, being the first major casualty.

It is not really surprising based on how the risky subprime loans were packaged into attractive investment products with fictitious valuations. These elaborately constructed securities, called collateralized debt obligations, or CDOs, are designed to yield juicy returns while also carrying high credit ratings. They have proved popular with hedge funds as well as long-term investors such as pension funds and insurance companies, many of which have bought billions of dollars of such securities in recent years – thus providing the liquidity that was then funneled into subprime mortgage loans.

The fact is, the 21st-century CDO emperor has no clothes. Unlike stocks listed on an exchange or U.S. Treasury bonds, CDOs are rarely traded. Indeed, a distinct irony of the 21st-century financial world is that while many bankers hail them as the epitome of modern capitalism, many of these new-fangled instruments have never been priced through market trading. Instead, CDOs, which are designed to be held until they mature, have often been valued in investor portfolios or on the books of investment banks according to complex mathematical models and other non-market techniques. In addition, fund managers and bankers often have broad discretion as to what kind of model they use – and thus what value is attached to their assets – and their annual bonus. Not real comforting. It will be interesting to see how the "not-so-educated guess" valuated CDOs will be phased out.

The late July 2007, worst meltdown of the New York Stock Exchange in 5 years, that triggered a worldwide sell-off record one day plunge, was a sneak preview of the pending economic doom. The London FTSE stock market followed suit in early August with its worst performance in four years.

The U.S. Federal Reserve, the U.S. central bank, injected $38 billion into the financial market in August 2007 to sustain liquidity, as the European Central bank poured a record 94.8 euros in the aftermath of France's largest listed bank, BNP Paribas, shutting the door on withdrawals of funds worth 1.6 billion euros tied to subprime securities, and Asian central banks, including those of Australia, Japan, Malaysia, Philippines and Hong Kong poured in billions of dollars into the jittery markests after American Home Mortgage Investment filed for Chapter 11 bankrupcy protection and this book went to print.

The worst is yet to come for the U.S. financial picture and housing market. The national median home price is poised for its first annual decline since the Great Depression, and the supply of unsold homes is at a record of more than 4 million. The combination of over-consumption, repossessed homes that millions of Americans will lose and reduced availability of mortgage financing will lead the fall.

A recession is not all bad for America, although devastating for Asia and Europe. It could help reduce the gigantic U.S. trade deficit. The U.S. economy would be healthier if Americans consumed less, imported less, saved more and exported more. These changes are needed to persuade other countries to stimulate their domestic spending. To hear President Bush lecture Chinese in September 2007 at the APEC conference in Sydney, Australia was amusing. There he was urging mainland Chinese to go on a consumer spending binge. Instead, he and other career politicians in America should be urging Americans to save.

It is commonly believed in Washington that Congress will re-examine the Bush tax cuts after the 2008 presidential election, with the outcome depending on the balance of power after those elections. Now, is this any way to manage and adopt a budget at the expense of *We the Apathetic People?* The first global crisis of the 21st century, like the Great Depression, will originate in America.

The resulting decline in demand in America for consumer goods made in China will not have a significant negative impact on China. The accelerating demand in Europe and Japan for Chinese-made consumer goods will take up some of the slack, with domestic demand in other Asian countries and China itself making up the balance of the shortfall. The composition of Asia's economic growth is shifting away from export-focused towards more consumption at home This combination will mitigate the ill effects of a U.S. slowdown. This time around, when the U.S. economy sneezes, China won't catch the economic flu.

By contrast, in China, the precautionary motive for saving is very strong among Chinese households because of the lack of an adequate pension system and the sharply rising costs of healthcare. Sound familiar? The need to finance education has also bolstered saving. Corporate savings in China have also risen and now account for almost half of national saving. Corporations in China, unlike America, have an incentive to retain their earnings in order to self-finance their investment.

It is impossible for a developing country as large as China with its vast underground economy to report accurate gross domestic product figures. It is estimated that as much as 4.4 trillion yuan of personal income in China is not reflected in the official figure, suggesting that potential growth in consumer spending and the property and stock markets may be stronger than perceived. One thing is certain. China is the world's fastest-growing economy. China's GDP is second only to the U.S. – the world's largest economy. But the gap is shrinking and it won't be long before China's economy surpasses that of the U.S.

Economists at the People's Bank of China are now forcasting gross domestic product to grow 10.8 percent in 2007. That will be the fastest pace of expansion in 12 years and almost 3 percentage points higher than the 8 percent target. Monetary policy in China has fallen so far behind that it may be to late to achieve a soft landing. The collapse, when it comes, will resemble the 19th-century U.S. boom-busts when there was no U.S. Federal Reserve managing the business cycle.

The last time the Chinese economy seriously overheated – from 1993 to 1995 – the annual average inflation rate was 15 percent, 24 percent and 17 percent, respectively.

China is the world's third-largest consumer of luxury goods after Japan and the U.S. Yet China's widening of the urban-rural gap since 1987 has been one of the most worrying accomplishments to China's economic miracle. If the bubble grows for another couple of years, the unsustainable demand and gap may become too large for a soft landing. Chinese stock market investors are going to find out the hard way that what goes up does come down and not everyone gets rich.

China's growth strategy has been different from Japan's. When Japan rose to economic power after World War II, it did so in a predatory fashion, pushing its products and investments in other markets but keeping its own market closed. China has done the opposite, opening itself up to foreign trade and investment. A 2006 reminder of Japanese predatory business ethics was the collapse of Japanese blue chip Internet darling Livedoor. Its executives violated securities laws by deliberately plotting to mislead investors – Enronomics Japanese-style. A raid by prosecutors during an investigation into the company's fraudulent predatory practices triggered the Japanese stock market's biggest loss in nine months. The Nikkei-225 Index fell 2.84 percent. The resulting market chaos created a surge in orders that overloaded the computers and shut Japan's stock market down. The company was accused of spreading false information related to shares in a subsidiary and executives at the company's Livedoor Marketing unit exchanged e-mails in which they agreed to mislead the public about the acquisition of a publishing firm.

If We the People want to survive the 21st century, America and China have to learn how to live together as a family – a pan-Pacific family – with Japan acknowledged as a difficult hostile cousin. America has to chill and mellow out and learn how to accept and live with its richest and very supportive Chinese relative.

The Council on Foreign Relations in New York, issued an excellent report in June 2007 on the state of relations between Washington and Beijing. It says that the growth of U.S.-China economic relations "is occurring against the backdrop of a shift in the structure of U.S. employment from manufacturing to services.

China is by no means the only cause of this transition, nor is it a major source of U.S. job loss." Unfortunately, America's perception is different and wrong. An enlightening paragraph in the 106-page report says: "A growing number of Americans believe that trade with China harms the U.S. economy, and that the U.S. trade deficit with China is mainly the result of unfair Chinese trade practices. Both notions are false." Is it any wonder China is now in the process of buying small and indirect stakes in many U.S. enterprises? Much like it did in Long Beach and San Pedro harbors in California. Its $3-billion investment in U.S. banking firm Blackstone Group, while insignificant relative to Beijing's $1.3 trillion of reserve assets, is a test run.

America's new foreign policy consensus, released in October 2005, encouraged closer U.S.-China ties – a policy Congress must initiate. The U.S.-China Working Group in the House of Representatives, was set up in the middle of 2005 to make the U.S.-China relationship the primary bilateral relationship in the 21st century. The 35-member bipartisan group received bipartisan support and encouragement from their colleagues in the U.S.

Senate, where a similar working group was formed in January 2006. On the other hand, the Quadrennial Defense Review, published by the Pentagon in February 2006, concluded: "Of the major and emerging powers, China has the greatest potential to compete militarily with the United States.... Shaping the choices of major and emerging powers requires a balanced approach, one that seeks cooperation but also creates prudent hedges against the possibility that cooperative approaches by themselves may fail to preclude future conflict."

One of the hardest adjustments that may have to be made over this century is the U.S. accepting at some point that it is no longer the world's sole superpower or that such a status is no longer pertinent to unfolding conditions in various regions. America has come to a position that the British used to occupy with its Royal Navy. Any other state that came close to rivalling it in power and scope was perceived as a threat to peace. The China threat is the current flavor of the military industrial complex.

The world is going through a geopolitical economic and political transformation. The global awakening has caught America off guard. Nevertheless, it does have a second chance to join up with China and lead the transformational charge. It is time America accepts China as its partner and a part of a larger world the two can lead together.

China's strong and stable economic performance drives regional development and has lifted millions out of poverty. Its economic performance has shifted world attention to China. The one thing Asia does not want to experience again is the financial crisis of 1997. Driven by the Beijing 2008 Olympics and the World Expo 2010 Shanghai, the Chinese economy can be expected to continue to grow and attract more international capital. China is like a giant elephant riding a bicycle – it has to maintain its speed at its own pace – otherwise it will crash. What it really needs is a truly independent monetary policy oriented to domestic objectives. That would enable the central bank to manage domestic demand by allowing interest rates to rise in order to rein in credit growth and deter reckless investment. Having an independent monetary policy that could counteract boom-and-bust cycles would be the best way for China to deal with such risks.

Pressuring China to revalue the yuan against the dollar is similar to the pressure America put on Japan in 1976 to make the yen appreciate. Back then, "Japan bashing" came to mean the threat of U.S. sanctions unless Japan softened competitive pressure on American industries. By 1995, the Japanese economy had become so depressed by the overvalued yen that the U.S relented and announced a new "strong dollar" policy. Now "China bashing" has taken over, and the result could be a lot worse.

When China revalued its currency by 2 percent in July 2005, it moved its peg from the dollar to managing its currency against a basket of currencies, potentially allowing the yuan to rise further against the dollar. Economists predict China will allow its currency to rise 10 percent more, which would reduce its need for U.S. government securities.

The reality is that the People's Bank of China is bankrupt, bust. It has a bare 22 billion yuan in capital to support total assets of more than 14 trillion in its balance sheet. If the U.S. dollar falls by 5 percent against the yuan and 80 percent of China's reserves are in U.S. dollar instruments, then the value of those reserves falls by more than $50 billion. "This represents many multiples of the bank's capital. How can the central bank absorb this hit without going bust?" columnist Jake van der Kamp asks? In other words, China's Central Bank, the holder of the world's largest dollar reserves, is bankrupt. It should therefore come as no surprise why China is in no rush to revalue its currency and literally break its own bank.

China announced in January 2006 that it could begin to diversify its massive and rapidly growing foreign currency reserves away from the U.S. dollar and government bonds – a potential shift with significant implications for U.S. and global financial and commodity markets. It is estimated that more than 70 percent of China's reserves are in U.S. dollar assets, which has helped sustain the huge U.S. deficits. If China were to stop acquiring such a large proportion of dollars with its reserves – currently accumulating at about $15 billion a month – it would put heavy downward pressure on the greenback.

When China sold off a record $6 billion of U.S. treasuries in June 2007, the first drop in holdings since October 2005, world markets took notice.

Chinese held over $1.2 trillion worth of U.S. assets, mostly in Treasury debt, at the end of the first quarter of 2007. If China decided to use its reserves to finance infrastructure projects in China and clean up state-owned enterprises, or to invest in higher-yielding assets rather than financing U.S. borrowing, America's downspin economic spiral would go into freefall.

Rich nations need to try to capitalize on the inevitable emergence of what could become the engine of the world's economic activity before it is too late.

"Most people in the rich countries don't really look at what's happening in these large developing countries," said former World Bank President James Wolfensohn, who is now chairman of Citigroup International Advisory Board and his own investment and advisory firm.

Within 25 years, the combined gross domestic products of China and India would exceed those of the Group of 7 wealthy nations, he said.

"This is not a trivial advance, this is a monumental advance."

Wolfensohn said that somewhere between 2030 and 2040, China would become the largest economy in the world, leaving the United States behind.

By 2050, China's current $2 trillion GDP was set to balloon to $48.6 trillion, while that of India, whose economy weighs in at under a trillion dollars, would hit $27 trillion, he said, citing projections by investment bank Goldman Sachs.

In comparison, the $13 trillion U.S. economy would expand to only $37 trillion, more than $10 trillion behind China's .

"You will have in the growth of these countries a 22 times growth between now and the year 2050 and the current rich countries will grow maybe 2.5 times," Wolfensohn said.

In light of these forecasts, it is clear that Western nations and Australia are not investing enough in educating the next generation to be able to take advantage of the coming realignment.

The realignment became blatantly obvious on February 27, 2007, when a one-day drop in the Chinese stock market – an 8.8 percent plunge in the

Shanghai stock market and 8.5 on Shenzen's – had an enduring negative impact on major stock markets around the world. The world realized overnight just how important China's economic might has become. U.S. stocks lost about $900 billion in value that week, almost 5 percent.

Overseas markets used China as an excuse for their corrections in their overheated economies. America's economic vitality and financial stability depends on China's continued purchases of U.S. Treasury and dollar investments. The U.S. cannot afford to have China start selling its Treasury holdings or significantly diversifying its greenback purchases. That would spark a run on the U.S. dollar that would destabilize America's financial stability. It is a real possibility, and something China can afford to do. Can America? Do we want to find out? If America continues to alienate China by refusing to distance itself from Japan and Taiwan, we well may.

The new Sino-U.S. strategic economic dialogue on long-term issues announced in the fall of 2006 was long overdue. Beijing and Washington must better manage their multifaceted political, military and economic relationship in the 21st century. It is vital not only to America and China, but the entire world. A deeper mutual understanding and better cooperative interaction can only enhance global economic stability and security. America and China can and must accommodate each other and work together to transform the current world economic and political disorder – something neither can do alone. America must start listening more and preaching less. Otherwise it will be consumed by China, just like many countries are by the fast-breeding killer Chinese seaweed *Undaria pinnatifida,* which grows up to three meters long, and is described as one of the world's most threatening invasive species. China can be just as invasive economically and militarily, probably more so.

The Pentagon's 2006 Quadrennial Defense Review contains this saber-rattling passage: Of "the major and emerging powers, China has the greatest potential to compete militarily with the United States and field disruptive military technologies that could, over time, offset traditional U.S. military advantages [without] U.S. counter-strategies."

The last thing America and the world needs in the 21st century is a Sino-U.S. war. In the first half of the 20th century – from the outbreak of World

War I to the famine that followed Mao Zedong's Great Leap Forward – about one in every 10 people alive on the planet was shot, gassed, stabbed, burned or starved to death by fellow human beings. The religious and political differences that inflicted so much pain and suffering in the Old World Disorder, many of which have been passed on to our wired 21st century, must be replaced with religious and political tolerance, understanding and respect.

America and China can no longer afford to miscommunicate or have cross-cultural misunderstandings. America has to recalibrate its geopolitical compass to develop a strategy that will forge a partnership with China if it is serious about regaining international legitimacy and being a significant player in the New World Order. America has to accept that it is no longer "a city upon a hill" that the rest of the world will emulate as it did since isolationist, idealistic Puritan John Winthrop first spoke those words in 1630. It has to accept the geopolitical reality that it is no longer the strategic center of global gravity. Pax Americana has been replaced by interlocalism with Sino-U.S. pillars at the center of gravity. China, working together with America, can forge peace deals with North Korea, Iran and the Middle East. America and China have to become the "double engines" driving world peace and prosperity.

The U.S.-Japan military alliance embracing the security of Taiwan does not benefit either America or China. The primary beneficiary is North Korea. America must do militarily what it did economically with China. It must open its door wider to U.S.-China military ties and cooperation. The fond farewell America bid Japan's Junichiro Koizumi during his last visit to the U.S. as prime minister in 2006, is the type of farewell America should bid the U.S.-Japan relationship.

America and China should build military establishments that are complimentary and compatible with each other. Why continue to compete to develop mutually incompatible, destructive and wasteful military hardware and starategies? They can cooperate and share intelligence on Islamic terrorists, tracking and interdict financial transactions that may support terrorism and many other ways to contain common enemies – starting in the Middle East where both countries sell their military hardware and software.

The more than $60 billion worth of arms, ammunition, bombs, missiles and warships America committed to sell to countires in the Middle East, while China tries to compete and keep up, but running a distant third, can only fulfill the Christian evangelical prophesy of the second coming of Christ and Armageddon.

Arm sales to Saudi Arabia and Gulf States will not contain a nuclear Iran. Arms sales and military containment operations bring anything but democracy and security, as is made chrystal clear daily in Iraq and Afghanistan. Selling weapons to a region where hatred can easily ignite a global conflaguration in which American soldiers are killed by American guns, is irresponsible.

America has clearly forgotten its recent geopolitical military blunders. The weapons America gave Saddam Hussein to fight against Shiite Iran, were then turned on his own people and now are being used against U.S. soldiers in Iraq.

The U.S. military industrial complex are ecstatic about the extra income and jobs, which, they claim, would have gone to China, Russia, Britain and France. Isn't it time that the governments of arms producing countries sit down with each other and draw up policies that control what regimes their arms merchants can do business with? Policies that apply to all members and are uniformly enforced.

To allow a U.S. government to pursue a policy that has U.S. made weapons, kill American troops put in harms way based on flawed intelligence, to sell more weapons to unreliable allies that can again be turned on America must be challenged to avoid the abyss of Armageddon.

The Japanese are concerned about a new "Nixon shock" – the surprise 1972 rapprochement between China and the U.S. – this time concerning North Korea. It is long overdue. The long-term military relationship America is pursuing with Japan is unsustainable because it is unlikely that Japan's aging society will be prepared to spend the money needed to maintain a robust military alliance down the road.

America doesn't want to repeat with China the mistake that got it into Iraq.

In the words of former CIA Director George Tenet, Dick Cheney and other administration officials pushed to invade Iraq without a "serious debate" about whether Saddam Hussein was an imminent threat. There was never "a significant discussion" about containing Iraq without an invasion. America definitely does not want to repeat that mistake with China and Japan over Taiwan.

America used to excel as a team player. Today it is a dazzling and shining example of excellence in individual events. Just like Tiger Woods, Andy Roddick and the Williams sisters, *We the Apathetic Maids,* as individuals, have to make America shine again. Fuhgetabout the Democratic and Republican political teams.

The career politicians' continuing spin of China as a threat allows Beijing to thumb its nose at America and the rest of the world. China's desire to work with America and support its geopolitical war on terrorism, is something that Beijing could easily and gladly withdraw, unless America changes direction and turns away from Taiwan and quits beating the human rights drum. Doing so can only bring peace and prosperity and a new dawn on a vibrant, energetic and constructive Sino-U.S. century and beyond.

Stop The Spread of Stupidity

Fear not the path of truth for the lack of people walking on it.
– Senator Robert F. Kennedy

Only in America ...... do drugstoress make the sick walk all the way to the back of the store to get their prescriptions while healthy people can buy cigarettes at the front.

Only in America .... do people order double cheeseburgers, large fries, and diet coke.

Only in America .... do banks leave both doors open and then chain the pens to the counters.

Only in America ...... do we leave cars worth thousands of dollars in the drive way and put our useless junk in the garage.

Only in America .... do we buy hot dogs in packages of ten and buns in packages of eight.

Only in America .... do we use the word 'politics' to describe the process so well; 'Poli' in Latin meaning 'many' and 'tics' meaning ' bloodsucking creatures'.

The world needs a drink.
                    – Terri Clark

Chapter Notes and Bibliography

*An educated person is one who through the
travail of his own life has assimilated the ideas
that make him representative of his culture, that
make him a bearer of his traditions and enable
him to contribute to its improvement.*
– Mortimer J. Adler

Extensive chapter notes and bibliography are available at
http://www.custommaidbook.com

Life is limited, but study is limitless.
– Chinese philosopher Zhuangzi (369-286 B.C.)

Index

Your education begins when what is called your education ends.
– Justice Oliver Wendell Holmes

Imagination is more important than knowledge.
— Albert Einstein